MARKETING
AN INTERACTIVE LEARNING SYSTEM

JOHN H. LINDGREN, JR.
UNIVERSITY OF VIRGINIA

TERENCE A. SHIMP
UNIVERSITY OF SOUTH CAROLINA

THE DRYDEN PRESS
HARCOURT BRACE COLLEGE PUBLISHERS

Fort Worth   Philadelphia   San Diego   New York   Orlando   Austin   San Antonio
Toronto   Montreal   London   Sydney   Tokyo

Acquisitions Editor: Lyn Hastert Maize
Developmental Editor: R. Paul Stewart
Project Editor: Cheryl Hauser
Designer: Linda Wooton Miller
Production Manager: Ann Coburn
Product Manager: Lisé Johnson
Marketing Assistant: Sam Stubblefield
Art & Literary Rights Editors: Cheryl Hauser, Cindy Robinson

Copy Editor: Cheryl Hauser
Proofreader: Dee Salisbury
Indexer: Leslie Leland Frank
Compositor: OffCenter Concept House
Text Type: 10/12 Palatino

Cover: © 1995 Yves Courbet

Copyright © 1996 by Harcourt Brace & Company

Address for orders:
The Dryden Press
6277 Sea Harbor Drive
Orlando, FL 32887-6777
1-800-782-4479 or 1-800-433-0001 (in Florida)

Address for editorial correspondence:
The Dryden Press
301 Commerce Street, Suite 3700
Fort Worth, TX 76102

ISBN: 0-03-017479-1

Library of Congress Catalog Card Number : 95-72013

Printed in the United States of America

5 6 7 8 9 0 1 2 3 4   067   9 8 7 6 5 4 3

The Dryden Press
Harcourt Brace College Publishers

JHL: To my parents who gave me the belief that I could accomplish any goal and to my children, Kirk, Krista, and Jackie, who taught me that there is truly "Hope For the Flowers."

TAS: To the oldest family member, my dear mother, Letha Shimp, and to the youngest, my beautiful grandson, Kirk Aubrey Shimp. To the rest of you, I am unable to express my gratitude.

Preface ◈

This text had its inception nearly a quarter century ago. Its form then was nothing like what it has evolved into. In the early 1970s we were unable in our wildest dreams to imagine the technology now available. Our idea then was vague, unclear, embryonic. We had, at that time, no intent to write a basic marketing text. Rather, we were two young teachers who shared a mutual love for teaching and a desire to do the best job we could to ensure that our students learned marketing principles well, enjoyed the learning process, and acquired an effective working knowledge of marketing and its role in the business enterprise or nonbusiness enterprises.

The idea of writing an introductory marketing text remained dormant for twenty years as we both established our careers as marketing teachers and scholars—Jack at the University of Virginia and Terry at the University of South Carolina. During this period we honed our teaching skills and, in process, earned a few awards in recognition of our commitment to outstanding teaching. One of us, Jack, had been a computer aficionado for many years and had the ability to develop sophisticated computer-based teaching aids that students responded to with great enthusiasm. The other, Terry, had been teaching introductory marketing to mass sections of 400 students using two slide projectors to simultaneously present and illustrate concepts. Students enjoyed this unabashedly show-and-tell presentation format, and learning was greatly enhanced by the visual illustration-upon-illustration format that reinforced concepts and made the abstract more concrete and the learning process more relevant to student's backgrounds and interests. The slide-projector technology was primitive by todays standards. It also required rather unidirectional and noninteractive teaching and learning styles because moving forward and backward from slide to slide was cumbersome and time-consuming.

But along came CD-ROM and with it a technology to accomplish what we were already doing but in a fashion far superior to how we had been doing it. This text, *Marketing: An Interactive Learning System*, was made possible with advances in computer technology. The technology presented us with both the reason and means for accomplishing what we had only vaguely contemplated over 20 years ago. *Interactive learning* is the key to the title and the essence of what this text, or learning system, is all about. We have developed a bundle of materials that will enable you, the student, to expand your knowledge and appreciation of modern marketing.

In the process, we think you will truly enjoy this learning experience. The learning system—consisting of a set of audio and video CDs and a conventional text—enables the following modes of studying and learning:

- For students who own multimedia computers, you will be able to read, study, and *interact* with the text in the comfort of your dorm, apartment, or home. Moreover, in those instances where a CD-ROM player is unavailable, you still have the book to study at your convenience. (Pretesting with students in using this learning system reveals that some like to first peruse the book version to obtain an overview and then interact with the text via CD-ROM.)

- For students who have access to multimedia computers at your college or university, you can interact with the learning materials in the exact fashion as do those who have a personal multimedia PC. Because sometimes it is difficult to get access to a computer at school, you always have the text to study.

- For students who do *not* have access to a multimedia computer, your out-of-class study will be from the conventional text that is part of this learning system. It is important to realize, however, that the CD-ROMs bundled in your learning system need not go to waste. Like most Americans, you undoubtedly in the near future *will* have access to multimedia computer at work or at home. Keep your CDs, and in the future you can peruse them when you require information about some pertinent aspect of marketing.

- The CDs that are part of the students package contain text, photos, audio, and video materials. Specific advantages of this form of studying and learning include the following:

  It is incredibly easy to **navigate** through the material, moving from one section to the next, and, where desired, from chapter to chapter. Interacting with the text, you choose what to read, what to view, what to listen to, and how often to read or view particular material.

  A **notepad** feature makes it easy to highlight key points and concepts and extract materials from the text much like you have done throughout your educational experience but without the effort and time required in taking traditional notes. Notes in your notepad can be printed for test-preparation purposes or later perusal.

A detailed **glossary** of key concepts makes it easy for you to access terms and review definitions. The search and find function provides the ability to access any definition instantaneously and to review the definition in context.

Practice test questions in each chapter allow you to examine your mastery of the material. Incorrect answers automatically take you to the section from which the question was drawn, thereby permitting immediate review of material perhaps not so well understood.

In class, all students will be exposed to a lecture, discussion, and interaction format in which your out-of-class study will be augmented with a CD-ROM presentation format. The professor's teaching aids, like yours, consist of key concepts and principles along with illustrative still pictures (advertisements, photos of marketing events, etc.), videos (such as TV commercials), and audio snippets. The professor can readily *navigate* through the material to demonstrate interrelations, to augment earlier points, to facilitate making connections between related concepts, and to pull from relevant material and examples from other sections of the text. The student is ensured a lively and visually compelling presentation.

Pedagogical Philosophy and Text Content

Psychologists of human learning have for decades studied the process by which people learn new information and apply that information in making decisions. The process is complicated with nuances depending on the particular learning circumstances and characteristics of the learner. There are, however, some rather universal principles about learning. These principles include the fact that learning is enhanced with repetition, when the material is made more relevant to the learner's particular situation, and when the subject content is not purely abstract but made real and concrete. These features—repetition, relevance, and concreteness—are crucial features of *Marketing: An Interactive Learning System. Repetition* is inherent in the interactive learning process. *Relevance* is achieved by drawing examples from everyday life and using brands, companies, and people that students know. *Concreteness* is accomplished by backing up every concept with visual or audio illustrations, of which there are literally hundreds via the CDs provided as part of your learning package.

Marketing: An Interactive Learning System makes no claim of being dramatically different in content from other marketing texts. Our treatment includes the venerable concepts, principles, classification schemes, and frameworks that have served marketing education well for a number of years. Of course, we—like our competitors—have included discussions of more current concepts and issues—market orientation, brand equity, brand-concept management, cross-functional teams, relationship marketing, single-source research systems, integrated marketing communications, and the like. We have presented the standard fare and the new points of emphasis in a straightforward, relevant, and concrete style that students can readily understand and enjoy.

The text is relatively short, only 16 chapters in total. We have attempted to avoid the fallacy that everything known about marketing should be contained in a single, introductory text. We have aimed at simplicity, not complexity. In baseball language, our objective has been to throw 60 mile-per-hour fastballs down the middle of the plate. No curves, sliders, knuckleballs, or screwballs. We want students to make contact with the ball, not to strike out. This learning system will satisfy the needs of nonmarketing majors by introducing them to the basics of marketing, fulfill the requirements of marketing majors in their preparation for more advanced and specialized marketing study, and, we hope, provide an additional nudge toward marketing as a major for those students who are undecided about a major when entering this course.

Supplements

The Dryden Press will provide complimentary supplements or supplement packages to those adopters qualified under our adoption policy. Please contact your sales representative to learn how you qualify. If as an adopter or potential user you receive supplements you do not need, please return them to your sales representative or send them to:

Attn: Returns Department
Troy Warehouse
465 South Lincoln Drive
Troy, MO 63379

Acknowledgments

Much of the work and inspiration for a project of this sort is due to people behind the scenes. Lyn Hastert Maize, Executive Editor, deserves our hearty praise for her efforts to get this project underway, her insight as to the form it might take, and her persuasive ability to convince us to do it. (She will be the first to admit that it was no easy selling job.) But we are delighted, in retrospect, that her persuasive abilities are so adroit. We also are deeply appreciative of the attention to detail and special care devoted to the project by Paul Stewart, Associate Acquisitions Editor, and Jim Lizotte, Acquisitions Editor, and their willingness to work around our rather hectic and divided work schedules. We also appreciate the marketing expertise of Lisé Johnson, Senior Product Manager, who has tirelessly worked on our behalf to create and execute a thorough promotional effort.

Cindy Robinson, that wonderful voice at the other end of the phone, deserves to be praised for her willingness to keep looking for that hard to find picture and to work with last minute deadlines almost every day. We also want to thank Sarah Jones at Dryden for her willingness to help us with media.

Our appreciation is extended to Janet Martin who made sure that this project was on target throughout the first year of development. Kathy Alderson deserves praise for keeping at least one of us organized.

Our colleagues have also played a key role in the development of this product and in our plans for the future. The following people graciously reviewed or class tested all or part of these materials:

Todd Baker, Salt Lake City Community College
Ed Cole, St. Mary's University, San Antonio
Brian England, University of Evansville
Ivan Figeroa, Miami Dade College—North
Lisa Flynn, Florida State University
Greg Gundlach, University of Notre Dame
John Gwin, University of Virginia

Robert Gwinner, Arizona State University
Larry Harris, Quinnipiac College
Dave Jones, LaSalle University
Kirthi Kalyanam, Santa Clara College
David Light, University of San Diego
Walter Miller, Quinnipiac College
Ed Mosher, Laramie County Community College
Robert Robischeaux, University of Alabama
John Ronchetto, University of San Diego
Sharon Tomlin, Angelo State University
Bill Vincent, Santa Barbara Community College
Dave Wasson, Johnson County Community College

Finally, we want to thank each of our schools and deans for their support.

Stuart and Graham Wong played an instrumental role in the development of the CD-ROM materials. Stuart was the senior programmer on this project and programmed the entire student book. His brother, Graham, assisted on the programming of the instructor materials during the first year of development. We want to send a special thank you to Stuart, who worked tirelessly from day one until the last day he was needed—even after he started his new job. Both Stuart and Graham are special, creative people and we appreciate their dedication to this project.

Our families deserve our deepest gratitude for adjusting their schedules around ours and allowing us the time to devote full attention to the project. Their patience with two very goal-oriented people is greatly appreciated.

About the Authors ■

John H. "Jack" Lindgren, Jr., D.B.A. (Kent State University), is the Consumer Banker Association Professor of Retail Banking at the University of Virginia McIntire School of Commerce. Professor Lindgren teaches undergraduate and graduate courses in Principles of Marketing, Marketing Research, Advertising, and Services Marketing. He has published widely in the area of services and retail marketing. His work has been published in the *Journal of Services Marketing, Journal of Retail Banking, Journal of Professional Services Marketing,* and *Journal of the Academy of Marketing Science.*

Professor Lindgren is a former vice-president and board member of the American Marketing Association, current president of his local AMA branch, on the Virginia board for the Multiple Sclerosis Society, and is actively involved in local hospice efforts.

Terence A. Shimp received his doctorate from the University of Maryland in 1974. He is Professor of Marketing and Distinguished Foundation Fellow in the College of Business Administration, University of South Carolina, Columbia. Professor Shimp teaches undergraduate and graduate courses in marketing communications and research philosophy and methods. He is Program Director of the Marketing Department at the University of South Carolina. He has published widely in the areas of marketing, consumer behavior, and advertising. His work has been published in the *Journal of Consumer Research, Journal of Marketing Research, Journal of Marketing, Journal of Advertising Research, Journal of Advertising,* and elsewhere.

Professor Shimp is past president of the Association for Consumer Research and past president of the *Journal of Consumer Research Policy Board.* He is on the editorial policy boards of *Journal of Consumer Research, Journal of Consumer Psychology, Journal of Marketing, Marketing Letters, Journal of Marketing Communications, Journal of Marketing Education,* and *Marketing Education Review.* Professor Shimp represents the Federal Trade Commission and various state agencies as an expert witness in issues concerning advertising regulation.

CONTENTS IN BRIEF

CONTENTS

Chapter 3   The Role of Research in Marketing 73

Chapter 4   Consumer Behavior 103

Chapter 5   Organizational Buying Behavior 139

Chapter 6　Market Segmentation　163

Chapter 7　Planning and Forecasting for Marketing Decisions　191

Chapter 8   Product Concepts and Strategies 223

Chapter 9   Product Development and Management 261

Chapter 16   Personal Selling and Sales Management 559

MARKETING

AN INTERACTIVE LEARNING SYSTEM

CHAPTER ①

Introduction to Marketing

Chapter Objectives

The Nature of Marketing

Marketing: An Exchange-Process Perspective

Marketing: A Separations Perspective

Marketing: A Functional Perspective

Marketing: A Utility-Creation Perspective

The Evolution of Marketing

The Marketing Concept

Marketing Strategy Formulation

■ The Nature of Marketing

How does your day begin? Many Americans rush to their Braun coffee maker to make their Folgers coffee. They then have Carnation Instant Breakfast, a Thomas' English Muffin, or some Nature Valley Granola for breakfast. They might hop into the shower and wash with Dial Soap and shampoo their hair with Head and Shoulders. They brush with Crest and splash on some Old Spice. They slide into their Reeboks as they run for the Toyota. Each day is filled consuming products made available by an extremely sophisticated and efficient marketing infrastructure.

Marketing is a powerful force in our society. Marketing is everywhere. You see it. You hear it. You wear it. Everywhere you go, you are exposed to some marketing message. Even church bulletins carry advertisements for florists and funeral parlors. If a site is a gathering spot for consumers, it is a potential target for a marketer who is looking for a unique means of reaching a target market.

Intensive marketing efforts are not limited to the United States. Marketing is an international activity as well. "Big Mac" means hamburger now in at least nine languages. Even in the country of India, once considered an economic vacuum, placards on the streets read "America's No. 1 engine oil now in India—Pennzoil."

Marketing is responsible for creating demand, products, and jobs in many fields such as research and development, transportation, advertising, and retailing. And marketing satisfies consumers, which in turn increases their standards of living. Marketing has been a major contributor to making the U.S. economy a world leader.

Each and every person in the world is a target for some marketer. After all, everyone eats, shops, and dreams of owning something of particular value to them. In their everyday lives people continuously interact with marketers and even perform the role of marketer at times. You are marketing jeans for Guess? whenever you wear their product with their name on the hind pocket. You are marketing clothing and shoes for Nike whenever you wear their products flashing the company name. You are marketing yourself when you send out your résumé to a potential employer. And you are marketing the goods or services of TaylorMade, Ping, or Taipai Bank whenever you wear the golf hat sporting the company's name.

Marketing is an exciting, dynamic field, a subject worth studying for several reasons. Everyday we are affected by marketing in the stores where we shop, listening to the radio in our car, and in handling and buying the products we use daily. Each of us also pays for marketing—when we buy a product, part of the money we spend covers the advertising, promotional, packaging, and research costs for the item. And finally, marketing is a major force in our society responsible for the quality of life we enjoy and the satisfaction we receive.

Most people, if asked, would say that marketing is selling or advertising. Marketing *includes* selling and advertising activities, but it is much more. The American Marketing Association defines marketing as "the process of planning and executing the conception, pricing, promotion, and distribution of ideas, goods, and services to create exchanges that will satisfy individual and organization objectives."[1] In simpler terms, marketing is the process of identifying and satisfying customer needs with want-satisfying goods and services.

Marketing is not just a practice of major consumer products organizations like Procter & Gamble, Nabisco, Nestlé, and Coca-Cola. Rather, marketing is undertaken with varying degrees of sophistication by organizations who direct their efforts at other businesses (so-called business-to-business firms), by large and small retailers, by physicians, dentists, certified public accounting firms, and lawyers, and by numerous nonprofit organizations that exist for altruistic reasons and to enhance the quality of life via cultural programming and other offerings. The American Red Cross uses marketing to bring in donations and volunteers. The state of Arkansas uses marketing to attract businesses who wish to relocate. The United States Armed Forces uses marketing to recruit inductees. And the Centers for Disease Control use marketing to educate people on a number of issues including AIDS and safe sex. Marketing is a powerful tool used by a multitude of organizations for a variety of purposes.

Because of marketing's complexity and diversity, scholars employ a variety of conceptualizations to understand the practice of marketing. The following sections provide perspectives that are intended to provide an understanding of what marketing is and why marketing is a critical activity to the success of all organizations. The chapter begins by describing marketing from four different, albeit related perspectives: (1) marketing as an exchange process; (2) marketing as the activity that actualizes separations between potential exchange parties; (3) marketing as a practice that performs important business and nonbusiness functions; and (4) marketing as a utility-creating endeavor.

◆ Marketing: An Exchange-Process Perspective

The basis for any marketing activity is exchange. **Exchange** is the process by which two or more parties give something of value to each other to satisfy each party's perceived needs.[2] This "something of value" can be a product, service, or idea. The exchange process takes many forms. Consider the following examples:

1. An exchange process occurs when a fan attends a concert of a popular performer. The fan exchanges money for entertainment. The performer provides the entertainment in exchange for the price of the tickets.

2. An exchange process occurs between a petition writer and potential supporters. The potential supporters exchange their signatures and support for improved conditions as promised by the petitioner. The petitioner tries to provide the promised action in exchange for the signatures.

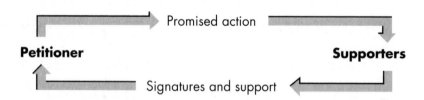

3. An exchange process occurs between a business client and its advertising agency. The client exchanges money for the agency's expertise. The agency provides its talent and experience in exchange for money.

4. An exchange process occurs between a company and its customers. The company exchanges a product or service for the customer's money. The customer provides money in exchange for the desired product.

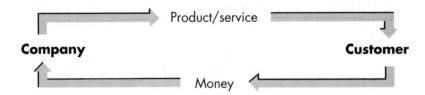

5. And, finally, an exchange process occurs between manufacturers, wholesalers, and retailers, or channel intermediaries. A manufacturer provides products to a wholesaler, who in turn provides the products to the retailer for final sale to the consumer. The consumer seeks out the retailer who will acquire the desired product from a wholesaler that has been supplied by the manufacturer.

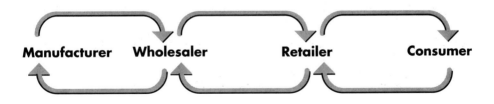

Whatever form it takes, the process of exchange should be satisfying to both the seller and the buyer. If the seller does not receive a price that covers his or her costs and provides a profit, the seller will not be satisfied with the exchange. On the other hand, if the buyer does not receive the perceived benefits from buying the product, the buyer will not be satisfied with the exchange. The objective for both parties is to achieve satisfaction by receiving something more than what they are giving up. Sometimes, though, certain conditions—or separations—exist, which keep the buyers and sellers apart and prevent exchange. The following discussion describes these potential separations and how marketing serves to remove them and encourage exchange.

■ Marketing: A Separations Perspective

Exchanges are necessary because of the "separations" that naturally exist between producers and consumers, buyers and sellers, and any other parties who enter into exchanges. **Separations** are gaps that divide potential parties and create marketing opportunities. The purpose of marketing is to close, or actualize, these gaps. There are five different forms of separation between potential exchange parties (see Exhibit 1.1).

Spatial Separations

Consumers and producers are usually separated by space and geography. Producers operate in areas that are advantageous to them (i.e., close to suppliers of parts or ingredients, in areas where labor is less expensive). Consumers, however, live everywhere. Marketing attempts to close this gap. For example, Florida oranges have little value for a consumer in Maine, until the oranges are transported to stores in Maine or are made into orange juice and shipped to retail outlets in the area. Marketing bridges spatial separations by transporting and storing products.

Temporal Separations

Consumers and producers want to consume and produce at different times. Producers need to allow adequate time to produce a product and transport it to a retail outlet in time for the consumer's purchase. Producers of candy, such as Brach's, are producing Valentine heart boxes six months or more prior to the holiday. This long lead time allows the company to produce an ample supply, transport the

Exhibit 1.1   Separations Existing between Exchange Parties

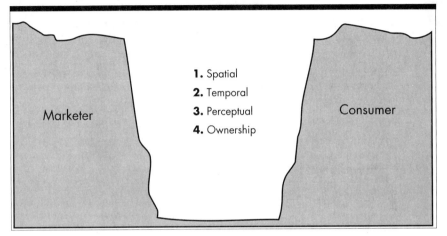

product to distribution centers, and make the product available in retail outlets in January. The consumer, however, is not interested in buying the heart boxes until just days before the February 14 holiday.

Perceptual Separations

Producers may lack information about consumers, such as who they are, where they are, what they need, and at what price are they willing to buy. Consumers may also lack information, such as what products are available, where, and at what price. Marketing closes this gap. For example, consumers with the common cold suffer for days gingerly wiping sore noses with tissues. Kleenex recognized the need for a softer, easier-on-the-nose product and developed Kleenex Ultras. Consumers were unaware of this product, though, until Kimberly-Clark advertised the product, sent product samples to consumers' homes, and distributed coupons to make consumers aware of the new product.

Ownership Separations

Producers or retailers own the product, and hold the title to it, until the consumer buys it from them. In buying a new car, for instance, the dealer gives the title and the automobile to the consumer when the consumer pays for the product. If the consumer borrows the funds from a bank, the distributor gives the title to the lending institution who will hold the title until the consumer pays off the loan. A sophisticated credit system in North America, Western Europe, and other areas enables consumers to take possession of products before consumers have fully paid for them. Credit terms, installment purchasing, and the use of credit cards are the major mechanisms for bridging the ownership separation.

Value Separations

Producers value their products and services based on their costs and competitive prices. Consumers, however, value the products and services based on how much they have to pay and what utilities are provided. For example, a consumer who needs a new watch buys a Timex product since the product is durable, functional, and inexpensive. He may have wanted a Rolex watch but found that the product was too expensive and, therefore, did not satisfy his needs. It is the job of marketing—via personal selling efforts, advertising, or other forms of persuasive communications—to convince customers that the marketer's offering is worth the price that is charged.

◆ Marketing: A Functional Perspective

A variety of functions must be performed to close the divide between buyers and sellers or between other exchange partners (e.g., lawyer and client). These functions are performed by many different parties such as manufacturers, wholesalers, retailers, lending institutions, transportation companies, advertising agencies, marketing research firms, and so on. The marketing functions shown in Exhibit 1.2 are the exchange functions—buying and selling, the logistic functions—transporting and storing, and the facilitating functions—financing, risk-taking, providing information, and standardizing/grading.

Exchange, or Transactional, Functions

The exchange process involves buying and selling. The **buying function** seeks, evaluates, and pays for a desired good or service. As

Exhibit 1.2   Functions Required to Bridge Separations

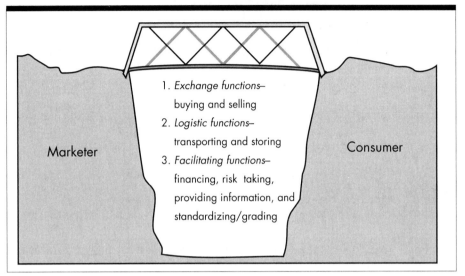

1. *Exchange functions–* buying and selling
2. *Logistic functions–* transporting and storing
3. *Facilitating functions–* financing, risk taking, providing information, and standardizing/grading

Marketer

Consumer

consumers, we perform multiple buying functions almost everyday of our adult lives. Professional buyers (purchasing agents, stock investors, or talent scouts) buy products and services on a less frequent basis but typically in a more formal and objective manner.

The other side of a marketing transaction, selling, involves convincing another party that the seller's product or service is worthy of its offering price. The **selling function** involves the promotion of products through personal selling, by telephone, via computer interactive network, and by other means. The exchange process applies to a neighbor selling another neighbor a used lawn mower as well as a consumer purchasing a pair of Armani eyeglass frames from an optical store. Selling the lawn mower requires personal, face-to-face interaction between the neighbors. The Armani eyeglasses must be advertised through media, promoted at the point of sale with displays, and personally sold by an optician or trained sales representative. In either case, an exchange does not take place unless selling is performed.

Logistical, or Physical, Distribution Functions

In all exchanges, except the simplest ones such as the neighbors lawn mower sale, certain logistical functions must be performed to ensure

MARKETING HIGHLIGHTS

Reduced Fat Food Claims . . ." Reduced-Fat Foods Claim a Larger Portion of Market Share"

The pursuit of a healthier lifestyle for millions of Americans in the last decade or so has meant altering the way people eat. Gone are the days of fried chicken and cream gravy served over buttermilk biscuits or bacon and eggs as the standard fare for breakfast. Medical studies linking high fat diets to heart disease and cancer have forced consumers to evaluate their eating habits and make some changes.

Food companies have sought to profit from this change in eating habits by producing healthier foods. Some emphasize "low cholesterol" or "low fat" on their labels to attract consumers. The main challenge for food manufacturers has been to come up with products that are truly lower in fat than traditional offerings, but that taste as good as the real thing and approximate the texture of the food.

Obviously some have been successful, judging from the sales figures. Sales of low-fat processed foods have climbed from $29 billion in 1990 to $32 billion in 1991 and are expected to reach $55.5 billion in 1996. A record 519 new low-fat or low-cholesterol products were launched in 1992, representing a 39% gain from the previous year. Dairy products topped the list in 1992 with 172 new entries, followed by baked goods, prepared foods, condiments, and meats. In addition, 48 new items in the low-fat snacks category were introduced that same year.[a]

A study released by the Calorie Control Council in 1993 showed that 81% of adult Americans consume low-calorie and reduced-fat foods and beverages, encompassing a 170 million member market. Women over the age of 55 accounted for the most purchases in this category, but men aged 35 to 49 had a strong showing. What are people seeking who purchase these products? Less than half of the consumers in the survey purchased them as a means to lose weight but rather as a way to stay healthy. Dieters remain a large segment of the reduced-fat food product purchasers, however.[b]

The main question posed by the Calorie Control Council survey was do consumers really like current reduced-fat products? Of the respondents, 69% claimed to be satisfied with existing products, leaving 31% who think there is room for improvement. The challenge for food manufacturers seems to point to the main reason consumers purchase a product more than once: taste. Does it taste as good as its full-fat, full-calories competitor?

Salad dressings are the category of low-fat foods most frequently purchased by adult Americans, and the reason for that is probably due to the fact that good reduced-fat versions can be made with polydextrose or hydrocolloids. Low-fat cheese and other dairy products like imitation sour cream are the second most frequently purchased category. Since these foods are often mixed with other foods before consumption, consumers seem to be less sensitive to the product's texture or flavor. Dairy manufacturers continue to work to develop better enzyme-modified dairy flavors and starter cultures for products like low-fat cheese.

Although low fat represented only about 5% of the total baked goods segment in 1992, manufacturers are

Products Bearing Health Claims

	1988	1989	1990	1991	1992
Reduced/low calorie	475	962	1165	1214	1130
Reduced/low fat	275	626	1024	1198	1257
All natural	215	274	754	561	996
Reduced/low salt	202	378	517	572	630
No additives/preservatives	153	186	371	526	631
Low/no cholesterol	126	390	694	711	677
Added/high fiber	56	73	84	146	137
Reduced/low sugar	52	188	331	458	692
Added/high calcium	4	27	20	15	41
Organic	98	140	324	370	510

working to come up with new products to add to this growing category. Nabisco developed a brand of low-fat products called SnackWell's, which has been very successful initially. After its introduction, the line earned a 2.5% share in less than six months, ranking it as one of the top 10 cookies and cracker brands—regular or low-fat in 1993. The company made a number of smart decisions in getting the product from the factory to the store shelf. First green packaging was used to position the products as healthy. Second, by listing a small serving size of the relatively small cookies and crackers on the label, they could list impressive nutritional statistics. Third, the products are very crispy because they are easier to machine and have a longer shelf life, thus satisfying the important component of texture. Product shelf life is further extended by tightly packing the product in lift-and-lock packaging.

Witness the phenomenal success of SnackWell's Devil's Food Cookies to prove that low-fat products that taste good can compete directly with traditional products. When these cookies appeared on grocery store shelves, consumers bought them so quickly that Nabisco was unable to keep up with the demand. The company even produced a television commercial for SnackWell's featuring three angry women confronting a Nabisco baker about their supply problem. A sign posted in a Giant Food store in Charlottesville, Virginia, in March 1994 stated that Giant was not responsible for the unavailability of the product. It seems that the manufacturing process necessary to make these cookies is much more complicated than simple cookies like shortbread or chocolate chip, and the company has lost sales because of shortage of the product.

Continued on next page

MARKETING HIGHLIGHTS, continued

Consumers were hungry for a low-fat cookie that had some taste, and these made of cocoa, which is low in fat naturally, with a layer of marshmallow inside, satisfied their cravings for something chocolate, something sweet that wasn't so high in fat. An article in *The Wall Street Journal* dealing with the making of these cookies described consumers as viewing the fat-free cookies as the perfect food: healthy sweets.[c]

ConAgra came up with a winning entry in the low-fat frozen food category with its Healthy Choice frozen foods line. Healthy Choice stayed away from fat replacers wherever possible, using a combination of spices, natural flavors, and reaction flavors to enhance naturally lean starting materials. The company also came out with entrees packaged in more expensive but consumer friendly trays rather than plastic bags in 1994 to appeal to the consumer who wants to be able to microwave the meal and eat it in the same container, thus reducing clean-up time. Sales for Healthy Choice rose 6% to $422.3 million for the 52-week period ending October 3, 1993.[d]

Statistics listed in *New Product News*, April 9, 1993, show the steady increase in the number of new products featuring health claims since 1988.

NOTE: Health claims categories are not additive, as new products may carry more than one claim.[e]

The successful products in the low-fat food market, as evidenced by Nabisco SnackWell's and ConAgra Healthy Choice frozen foods, are not substitutes for traditional foods but offer consumers a healthier way of eating. As Americans continue to live longer, living healthier becomes more important, and low-fat or reduced-fat foods that taste good may contribute to a healthier lifestyle.

[a] Leticia Mancini, "Low Fat Comes of Age; Now More Mainstream than Niche, Low-Fat Products Struggle to Improve their Quality Head to Head," *Chilton's Food Engineering*, June 1993, 149.

[b] Ibid. Chilton Food Engineering, June 1993, 149.

[c] Kathleen Deveny, "Man Walked on the Moon but Man Can't Make Enough Devil's Food Cookie Cakes," *The Wall Street Journal*, September 28, 1993, B1.

[d] Julie Liesse, "ConAgra's New Ethic Brings Return to Ads; Marketing Efforts Rise with Smith's Leadership," *Advertising Age*, January 10, 1994, 4.

[e] Lynn Dornblaser, "'Health' Claims Make Healthy Gains," *New Product News*, April 9, 1993, 8.

that the buyer receives the product or service as ordered. The two logistical functions are transporting and storing. The **transporting function** is the movement of goods and services from the seller to the buyer. The **storing function** is the holding of goods and services until the customer needs them. BMW cannot sell a car manufactured in Germany to a consumer in Oklahoma unless the car reaches Oklahoma. BMW must transport the car via boat and train and then deliver the car to the dealership and ultimately the consumer in Oklahoma, if it wants to make the sale.

Facilitating Functions

Other functions involved in an exchange facilitate, or ease, the process for both parties. If these functions are not performed, the exchange function may not occur. These **facilitating functions,** which assist both the marketer and the buyer, include the following:

1. *Financing* is the extension of credit from the seller to the buyer. Financing enables a buyer who does not have adequate cash to purchase the product or service. The buyer would be unable to purchase the product or service if the seller did not extend the credit. Most sellers of big ticket products like homes and automobiles rely on financing to attract buyers.

2. *Risk-taking* involves assuming the risk of not being able to sell a product that has been taken into inventory. Taking title to the merchandise enables a wholesaler, retailer, or other marketing intermediary to earn a profit from selling the merchandise, but the act of holding title involves taking the risk that the merchandise will not sell at all or will not sell at the desired profit margin. In the record industry, many small producers cannot obtain distribution for their records, tapes, and CDs because retailers are not willing to take the risk of buying the products and holding them in inventory. These producers overcome the problem by eliminating the risk entirely for the retailer. Products are offered on consignment whereby the retailer carries the product in inventory but does not pay for the product until it is actually sold.

3. *Providing information* is a critical function in the exchange process. Exchanges would typically not occur unless the seller or title holder actively advertised a product or otherwise communicated its availability and virtues to potential buyers. These activities involve providing information to potential buyers. Examples of providing information include direct mail, telephone sales, or advertising on bus stop benches or via television.

4. *Standardizing and grading* involves sorting goods by their size and quality. Many products are graded and standardized as much as possible prior to making them available for purchase. Prices vary depending on the quality, or grade, of product. Baseball cards that have a newer appearance

command a higher price than do worn or handled cards. Diamonds are graded based on the clarity and number of imperfections in the stones. The higher the clarity and fewer the imperfections, the more expensive the stone will be. Thus, a man buying an engagement ring could purchase a poor quality, low-grade one carat diamond for $750 or a better quality carat for $2,000. Both are diamonds, but the level or grades of quality are extremely different.

Each of these functions must be performed in any exchange process: *Who* performs these functions and *how* they are performed will differ depending on the exchange and the parties—either individuals or companies—involved.

◼ Marketing: A Utility-Creation Perspective

Each of the functions of marketing serve to bridge the separations between buyers and sellers. Performing these functions also provides utility—or values—to a marketer's customers. Marketing is responsible for creating and providing time, place, and possession utilities. It also plays a role in creating form utility. Exhibit 1.3 identifies the various utilities created, or in the case of form utility, influenced by marketing: form, place, time, and ownership. Let's briefly consider each utility.

Form utility involves the transformation of raw materials and/or labor into a finished good and/or service that the consumer desires. The actual creation of form utility is accomplished through the production process and, hence, is not a utility directly attributable to marketing. However, marketing plays a vital role in *directing* the ultimate shape, size, quality, and design of products. For example, although consumers need bleach for cleaning and laundry, many dislike the strong odor associated with the product. Through research Clorox's marketing department found that consumers would be happier and use more bleach if the smell were more pleasant. Clorox introduced a fresh lemon-scented product to overcome the consumer objection. The marketing department was responsible for directing this form utility, and the operations unit of the company produced the actual product.

Place utility involves making the goods and services available where the consumer wants or needs them. The creation of place utility overcomes, or actualizes, the spatial separation that exists

Exhibit 1.3   Utilities Influenced or Created by Marketing

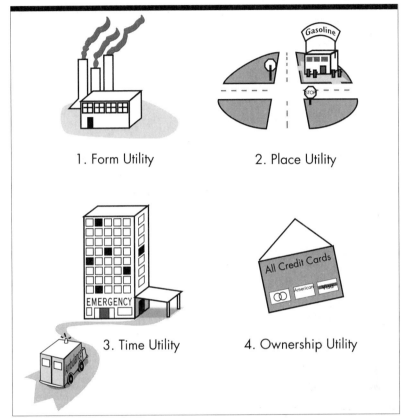

1. Form Utility

2. Place Utility

3. Time Utility

4. Ownership Utility

between buyers and sellers. United Airlines, for example, creates place utility by transporting a consumer from one place to another. Lands' End also provides place utility by sending a catalog to a consumer, so he or she can shop from home when the need arises.

Time utility involves making the goods and services available when the consumer wants or needs them. The creation of time utility overcomes, or actualizes, the temporal separation that exists between buyers and sellers. If a consumer in Idaho needs to get a package to Georgia by tomorrow, Federal Express provides this service and creates time utility for the consumer. Burger King's drive-thru windows save consumers the time of parking, walking in and out, and standing in line. And Bank of America's ATMs have made some banking services, such as withdrawing and depositing funds, available at any time the consumer needs them.

Ownership utility involves the transferring of title for a good or service from the producer to the consumer. Visa or the American Express card gives the consumer the means to exchange money for product ownership.

◆ The Evolution of Marketing

Marketing efforts we see today are considerably different from those used in the past. Marketing is now a more sophisticated process. That is not to say that all of today's marketers are in the same class as those who work for Campbell's Soup, Ford Motors, or Southwestern Airlines. Many firms today are not any more sophisticated in conducting their marketing activities than were firms who were perhaps ahead of their time and were sophisticated marketers decades ago. But overall, there has been a gradual increase in the appreciation of marketing's importance to increasing profits and the quality of marketing practice. This evolution of marketing can be delineated, albeit somewhat simplistically, into three distinct eras: production, sales, and marketing (see Exhibit 1.4).[3]

The **production era** coincided with the Industrial Revolution in the United States, a period extending roughly from 1870 to 1930. Businesses emphasized manufacturing efficiency; relatively little consideration was given to consumers and their needs. New technology such as electricity and assembly lines allowed companies to mass produce products and saturate the marketplace. The production philosophy succeeded at the time because it was a *seller's market*—demand exceeded supply. Competition was less intense than it is today, and consumers were enthusiastically buying up existing inventories. Firms focused on increasing production, reducing costs, and offering low prices. Some firms in the United States today are still production-oriented. And many, if not most, firms in other countries still operate under a production philosophy. In countries such as Russia, Cuba, Vietnam, and, to a lesser extent, China, consumers stand in long lines just to purchase the basic necessities, because the supply for goods is outpaced by the demand.

By the 1930s, technology had improved and goods were readily available in the marketplace. Conditions gradually changed from a seller's market to a *buyer's market*—supply exceeded demand. Firms realized that aggressive selling of products resulted in increased profits. In the **sales era**, firms focused on selling existing products. Their philosophy was to sell what the firm produced,

Exhibit 1.4   The Evolution of Marketing

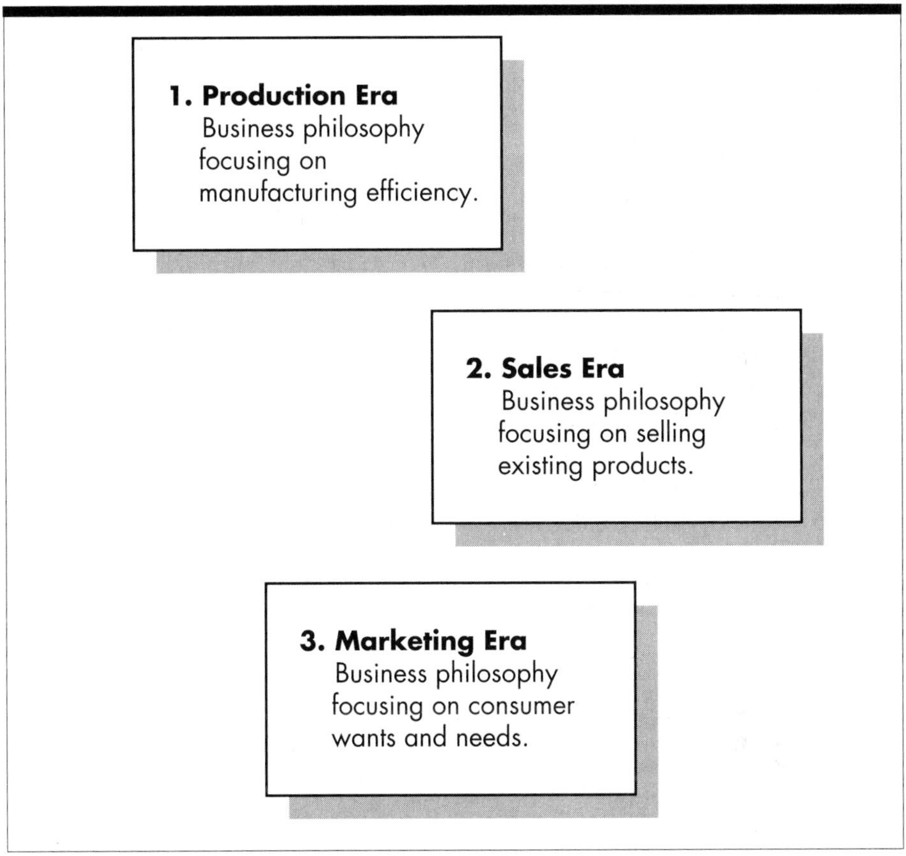

1. Production Era
Business philosophy
focusing on
manufacturing efficiency.

2. Sales Era
Business philosophy
focusing on selling
existing products.

3. Marketing Era
Business philosophy
focusing on consumer
wants and needs.

which was still not necessarily exactly what the consumer needed. Moreover, excessive emphasis on selling led to aggressive tactics that often offended potential customers and backfired.

The sales era continued until at least the 1950s when many firms began realizing that efficient production and the "hard sell" did not mean that consumers would always buy the products or be satisfied with their purchases. Consumers could be more selective in what they bought because their purchasing power was greater than ever, and their choices were unparalleled with many companies competing for their brand loyalties. In the **marketing era,** which characterizes modern marketing in the United States as well as in other advanced economies, firms must emphasize customer need

CAPTAINS OF INDUSTRY

Edwin L. Artzt

Procter & Gamble Chairman of the Board and Chief Executive

Date of Birth: April 15, 1930, New York City

Education: B.A., Journalism, University of Oregon, 1951

Career Path: After graduating from college, juggled several jobs: a newspaper, a TV station, a public relations firms, and ad agency in Los Angeles. Hired by Procter & Gamble in 1953 in a sales training position. Has remained with the company and worked his way to the top, now serving as Chairman of the Board and Chief Executive.

Profile: When he saw how dull the promotional materials for detergents were, he designed his own posters featuring Ivory Soap babies holding miniature boxes of Oxydol, Tide, and other P&G detergents when he was given the assignment to get more stores in Los Angeles to buy more full-page ads to feature P&G brands. He paid for the posters himself and remembers that his sales group sold more full-page ads than anyone else.[a]

Personal: Son of classical musicians, Artzt attended college on a basketball scholarship.

Procter & Gamble's CEO, Edwin Artzt, is a tough manager. Some employees have described his management style as one of "fear and intimidation,"[b] but his ability to carry out tough decisions has brought about a big change at P&G. In 1991, the company adopted a "value pricing" strategy to lower list prices and slash discounts across most of its U.S. product line, in order to even out the swings in P&G's demand that such promotions cause. Artzt eliminated one brand, Citrus Hill orange juice, because it was so unprofitable, and is cutting 25% of its many shapes and sizes of products. In addition, P&G is closing 20% of its factories and cutting 13,000 jobs, 12% of the total.[c] P&G's Solo liquid detergent became Ultra Bold and White Cloud bathroom tissue adopted the Charmin name, Charmin Ultra. The Mr. Clean name was extended to include a glass and surface cleaner, replacing its own Cinch brand, which had lagged behind the leading cleaners in sales. The strategy is to rely on brand extension based on the strength of a key brand rather than trying to build a weaker product into a stronger-selling one. "Procter is putting their money behind their leading key brands and letting the other ones drift—or eliminating them," states Lynne Hyman, analyst at First Boston Corp. "They are really concentrating their resources. It makes sense to use an umbrella brand name for niche cleaners."[d]

Brands themselves have come under fire in the past few years as sales of private brands have taken off. Consumers have begun choosing private labels in lieu of premium brands, because of their lower price. Between 1988 and 1992 store brands experienced tremendous growth, causing companies like P&G to take notice. The move to lower pricing was motivated by the need to become more competitive. P&G's strategy toward this end is to restructure the company, reducing layers of management worldwide, lowering prices on their products, eliminating weaker brands, and continually coming out with new product innovations to compete against private-label and low-price brands. P&G believes value pricing will generate greater brand loyalty.[e] Artzt told shareholders at the company's annual meeting in October 1993, "What is working best for the company worldwide is a flood of value-added product innovations in virtually all product lines. We have also focused on the value benefit of these innovations in our advertising."[f] Since 1989, P&G has accelerated its new product introductions by 30%, producing over 2,300 brand varieties in 1993. Global expansion is also very important to the company's overall strategy, as evidenced in Europe, which accounts for 29% of worldwide sales.

Ed Artzt has worked his way up the corporate ladder at Procter & Gamble, beginning in 1953 as a sales trainee. His first assignment in Cincinnati was as assistant brand manager for Dash. After a series of marketing and management promotions, Artzt was named group executive for the European Common Market in 1975 and took over all of P&G's European operations in 1977. In 1981 he headed all foreign operations, and in 1984 was named vice-chairman and president of the international unit. Foreign operations grew to account for 40% of sales and 35% of profits by 1989, as P&G expanded into new foreign markets. When he was named as the successor to John Smale as chairman and CEO, effective January 1990, many were surprised, however. John Pepper, then President of P&G, had been the heir-apparent, but it was Artzt who had the international experience, who had led P&G from the status of typical U.S. multinational, viewing its foreign operations as subsidiary to its domestic business, to a global company focusing heavily on overseas business.[g] Artzt also brought with him a reputation for toughness—earning him various nicknames, such as "Prince of Darkness." But he is a company man, having spent all but two of his working years at P&G. He learned one of his first lessons—about the importance of timing—at age 25 while a manager in the soap division. He launched a new cleanser called Comet during the Christmas season, sending out product samples that ended up being thrown away by overloaded postal carriers. Artzt had to start over in January, but his persistence paid off. Comet soon became the top-selling cleanser.[h] And it is just that—his persistent drive to make P&G more competitive and profitable—that earned him the position of CEO of P&G.

Has the value pricing move been effective? So far, it has paid off for P&G. The company posted a 6% improvement in U.S. unit volume for the first two quarters of 1993 and is improving its market share in 66% of its 44 U.S. categories, from deodorant to dishwashing detergent. P&G's net margins were at 6.8% in 1993, their highest in nearly a decade.[i] The company continues to introduce product innovations, such as Crest toothpaste with baking soda, while eliminating brands that have been continually unprofitable. In January 1994, P&G announced that it would discontinue the manufacture of its Clarion line of cosmetics because of weak sales. It has come out with a new reformulated liquid and powder Tide detergent and Tide refill in hopes of further dominating the category and putting pressure on its chief competitor in the category, Lever Brothers. P&G

Continued on next page

CAPTAINS OF INDUSTRY, continued

was named eighth on *Fortune's* list of the most admired companies in 1993, slipping from its sixth position in 1992. It was listed as second in the attribute category of "Quality of Products or Services." So, in an age when brands themselves are under scrutiny, P&G stakes its reputation on the brands that it produces, continuing to innovate, cut costs, and stage aggressive campaigns in the categories in which its products compete. And Edwin Artzt has been a dominant force in its success.

ED ARTZT'S CAREER AT P&G

1953 Sales Training
1954 Assistant Brand Manager
1955 Brand Manager
1958 Associate Brand Promotion Manager
1960 Brand Promotion Manager
1960 Manager of Copy
1962 Brand Promotion Manager
1965 Manager, Advertising Department, Paper Products Division
1968 Manager, Food Products Division
1969 VP, Food Products Division
1970 VP (Acting Manager, Coffee Division)
1972 Member, Board of Directors (1972–1975)
1975 Group VP (European Operations)
1980 Executive VP (International Operations)

1980 Member, Board of Directors
1984 Vice Chairman and President, Procter & Gamble International
1990 Chairman of Board and Chief Executive

[a] "The Prince of Darkness," excerpt from Alecia Swasy, *Soap Opera, the Inside Story of Procter & Gamble,* appearing in *Advertising Age,* September 27, 1993, 16–19.
[b] Ibid. *Advertising Age,* September 27, 1993, 17.
[c] Patricia Sellers, "Brands: It's Thrive or Die," *Fortune,* August 23, 1993, 52.
[d] Jennifer Lawrence, "P&G Strategy: Build on Brands," *Advertising Age,* August 23, 1993, 3.
[e] Jennifer Lawrence, "P&G Hikes Ad Spending, Slashes Work Force; World's Top Advertiser Could Trigger Competitive Reaction," *Advertising Age,* July 19, 1993, 3.
[f] Jennifer Lawrence, "P&G's Barrage of New Items Pays Off, and Will Continue," *Advertising Age,* October 18, 1993, 8.
[g] Zachary Schiller, "P&G's Worldly New Boss Wants a More Worldly Company," *Business Week,* October 30, 1989, 40.
[h] Patricia Gallagher, "Changing of Guard at P&G; Artzt to Give Giant a Broader World View," *USA Today,* November 9, 1989, 1B.
[i] "'Value Pricing' Pays off," *Business Week,* November 1, 1993, 32–33.

fulfillment and customer satisfaction. Marketing departments determine consumer needs, via formal marketing research and other market intelligence activities, and then produce products designed to fulfill these needs. But marketing in the marketing era involves much

Exhibit 1.5   Elements of the Marketing Concept

1. Customer orientation
2. Coordinated effort by all departments
3. Emphasis on long-term profit

more than merely providing need-fulfilling products. It requires that companies satisfy customers' needs, indeed demands, for convenient purchasing, fair prices, environmentally safe products, and so on. In short, the emphasis in the marketing era is on doing a better job than competitors in meeting customer needs, and doing this in a way that is profitable in the long run for the company.

The Marketing Concept ◆

The foundation of the modern marketing era is the marketing concept. When an organization focuses all of its efforts on making products or providing services that satisfy its customers at a profit, it is employing the **marketing concept.**[4] This concept is so important to marketing that it is referred to as *the* marketing concept.

There are three fundamental features of the marketing concept (see Exhibit 1.5): customer orientation; coordinated effort by all departments within the organization (marketing, production, finance, accounting) in an effort to provide customer satisfaction; and emphasis on accomplishing long-run profit goals.

Years ago, the various departments in an organization (finance, production, engineering, and sales) worked somewhat autonomously. Rarely were efforts carefully coordinated across all departments. Each department had its own objectives and preferences, which were not always shared by other departments. Now in many organizations the customer is the focal point for how each unit is run. Products are created with the goal of satisfying customers' needs and wants. All departments within the organization must work together toward the same goal. It is critical for departments to closely coordinate their efforts both to satisfy customer needs and achieve long-run profit goals. For example, a production department may realize its greatest efficiencies and profits when producing large sizes of products. However, if the marketing department determines that a single-use package is needed to stimulate trial of the product, the production department must forego a greater degree of efficiency to produce the smaller package. After all, the larger size will not sell if the consumer has not even tried the product.

Organizations employing the marketing concept, though, must realize that every need of every consumer cannot possibly be met. If an organization attempted this philosophy, it would not be in business very long. For example, a marketing department's research determined that the flavor of a new beverage product should be orange. Out of a study of 250 respondents, 242 voted for this flavor while 4 opted for cherry and 4 chose strawberry. It would be unprofitable and unrealistic to produce a cherry and strawberry product for so few consumers. An organization must satisfy consumer needs while achieving its own goals—the most important being profitability.

The marketing concept is an ideal state of affairs. Most companies can only aspire to use this philosophy in its purest form. When a firm attempts to implement the marketing concept, it has a market orientation. **Market orientation** is the organization-wide *generation* of market intelligence pertaining to current and future customer needs, *dissemination* of the intelligence across departments, and organization-wide *responsiveness* to it.[5] The meaning of the concept of market orientation is that the marketing department of a firm develops an understanding of customer needs and the factors that influence and determine these needs. This understanding is shared across various departments within the organization. The various departments then respond by attempting to meet select customer needs.

A firm's success usually depends on the firm's having a marketing orientation. In some cases, though, a market orientation is not critical. When competition is not that intense, when market preferences are stable, during periods of booming economies, and when industries are characterized as technologically turbulent (e.g., the computer industry), market orientation is less important than during situations not characterized by these conditions.[6]

Many companies employing the marketing concept have taken the philosophy one step further. The concept has been extended to transcend the profit focus of business organizations and to consider the needs of society as a whole. According to this broadened, or societal, marketing concept, firms must also factor environmental, health, and safety considerations into their decision making. For example, automobile manufacturers must adapt a societal marketing concept when producing cars. Fewer companies are manufacturing leaded-gas-guzzling models because of societal environmental issues. Most car manufacturers are including safety air bags as a standard feature, even though they add to the overall cost of the product. This is in deference to societal safety issues.

Marketing Myopia

In applying the marketing concept to form its own company philosophy, a company needs to define its business. What business does the firm see itself in? Does MCI view itself as a telephone company? Do the Garden in New York, the Stadium in Chicago, or the Forum in Los Angeles consider themselves ticket sellers to events? Does McCann-Erickson consider itself a writer of advertising copy? Although each of these functions may be part of these companies' businesses, the definitions are far too narrow. MCI is in the communication business. The arenas are in the entertainment business. And the advertising agency is in the creative service business. However it views and defines itself, an organization must avoid defining the organization's purpose too narrowly. This short-sightedness in company definition is called **marketing myopia.**[7] Rather, companies must focus on satisfying its customers. For example, if a director of a zoo defined the organization as a place that houses and exhibits animals, she would be suffering from marketing myopia. A better characterization of a zoo would be that it provides entertainment and education by introducing people to wildlife they rarely see in everyday life. An organization's survival can be threatened by marketing myopia.

Marketing Strategy Formulation

Discussion to this point has provided a broad overview of what marketing entails. We turn now to a description of the more nitty-gritty aspect of marketing, or the actual decision-making nature of marketing. This aspect is called **marketing strategy formulation.** Marketing strategy entails (1) identifying target markets and (2) developing marketing mixes directed at fulfilling the needs of specific market segments.

Marketing efforts generally are not aimed at the entire population, or market, but instead, are directed at specific **target markets,** or those groups identified as potential users of the product. New age beverages such as Snapple and Sundance Sparklers, for instance, are not designed to appeal to the entire market, but rather are targeted at weight- and health-conscious consumers who avoid highly caloric, highly sugared soft drinks. Organizations divide the whole market for their products into groups of consumers who have similar needs or similar purchasing behavior. Upscale, educated consumers aged 18 to 35 represent a potential target market, or market segment, for Snapple and Sundance. Consider also the case of Bayer Aspirin, which dominated the pain relief market for years by marketing their aspirin to the entire population. The introduction of ibuprofen-based products like Motrin and non-aspirin products like Tylenol eroded Bayer's share of the market. In response, Bayer introduced the Bayer Select line of non-aspirin products designed to relieve specific problems, such as arthritis, sinus pain, or headaches. Each product is targeted to narrow market segments, or those consumer groups who suffer from specific pains. A detailed discussion of target markets and market segments will be the focus of Chapter 6.

After a target market is identified, a marketing mix is developed to reach, appeal to, and convert these targets into customers. A **marketing mix** is a specific combination of four sets of variables—products, distribution elements, prices, and marketing communications, or promotions—designed to appeal to and satisfy the needs of market segments. These variables can be combined in unlimited ways. For example, a product can be packaged in a pint, quart, half-gallon, or gallon size. The product can retail for as little as $1.09 up to $1.99. The company can hire a direct sales force or a broker network to sell the product. And finally, the company can promote its offering through television, radio, or print. It is the challenge of marketers to develop the appropriate marketing mix that best matches the needs of the target market. Exhibit 1.6 graphically portrays both elements of marketing strategy. Let's briefly examine each variable in the marketing mix.

Product Strategy

The objective of product strategy is to develop the right product for the target market. This process includes identifying consumer wants and needs and designing products to satisfy these wants and needs. Product strategy also includes brand naming, package design, the determination of the size of the product line, level of quality, and so forth. New product development is another important aspect of product strategy.

Exhibit 1.6   A Marketing Strategy Framework

Distribution Strategy

The objective of the distribution strategy is to get the right product or service to the right place—where the customer is. A product is no good to a customer if it is not available where and when the customer wants it.

The distribution strategy involves both the physical movement of products (i.e., the logistical aspect of distribution) and the selection of channels of distribution. Channels represent the network of organizations that play a role in performing the various exchange and facilitating functions: manufacturers, wholesalers, agents and brokers, and retailers. Some manufacturers distribute products directly to retail outlets, whereas other companies reach consumers through channels of distribution where another company is involved in the distribution process such as a wholesaler or broker.

Price Strategy

Once a company has the right product, developing the right price is critical. If a product is priced too high, consumers won't buy it. If a product is priced too low, the consumer may be skeptical of product quality or the company may not make a profit. Organizations set overall pricing objectives and policies to ensure that the price is one that is acceptable to the customer, competitive within the marketplace, and profitable for the company.

Promotion Strategy

The promotion strategy involves communicating with customers. A company uses such promotion variables as advertising, personal selling, direct marketing efforts, sales promotions, point-of-purchase materials, sponsorships, and public relations as means of informing target markets about the company and its products. The objective of promotion strategy is to stimulate interest in the product and encourage trial use and purchase by the consumer.

◼ Chapter Summary

Marketing serves an important function in today's society for all types of businesses—both for-profit and not-for-profit organizations. The basis for marketing is exchange, whereby two or more parties give something of value to each other to satisfy each party's perceived needs. A service, product, or idea can be exchanged.

Natural separations such as geographical location, lack of information, and timing in production versus demand exist between exchange parties. Marketing is the process that bridges these separations. Several functions such as exchange, logistical, and facilitating functions must be performed by a variety of parties to enable potential exchange parties to complete any exchange.

Marketing creates time, place, and possession utilities for exchange parties. Products are available when and where a consumer wants them thanks to marketing. And services such as credit extension or financing make exchange possible for many parties.

Marketing has not always existed to the degree of sophistication we know today. The practice developed over many decades as companies evolved from focusing their efforts on production to realizing greater sales and profits by focusing efforts on satisfying customer needs. Today, most companies have tried to adopt the marketing concept to some degree. The three fundamental features of the marketing concept are customer orientation, a coordinated effort by all departments to satisfy customers, and achievement of long-run profits through customer satisfaction.

Marketing efforts are not generally directed at an entire population but rather at specific target markets. Marketers develop a coordinated marketing mix consisting of product, pricing, distribution, and promotional strategies to appeal to and convert target consumers into product users. These features can be combined in an unlimited number of ways. The ultimate challenge for the marketer is to develop the appropriate marketing mix that best matches the needs of the target market.

Notes

1. Peter D. Bennett, *Dictionary of Marketing Terms* (Chicago: American Marketing Association, 1988), 115.

2. For further discussion of the theory of exchange, see Franklin S. Houston and Jule B. Gassenheimer, "Marketing and Exchange," *Journal of Marketing,* 51 (October 1987), 3–18.

3. The notion of three distinct eras of marketing practice has not gone uncontested. For an interesting discussion, see Ronald A. Fullerton, "How Modern Is Modern Marketing? Marketing's Evolution and the Myth of the 'Production Era'," *Journal of Marketing,* 52 (January 1988), 108–125.

4. For further discussion, see Franklin S. Houston, "The Marketing Concept: What It Is and What It Is Not," *Journal of Marketing,* 50 (April 1986), 81–87.

5. Ajay K. Kohli and Bernard J. Jaworski, "Market Orientation: The Construct, Research Propositions, and Managerial Implications," *Journal of Marketing,* 54 (April 1990), 1–18.

6. Ibid.

7. Theodore Levitt, "Marketing Myopia," *Harvard Business Review,* July–August 1960, 45–56.

Study Questions

1. Marketing is practiced by
   a. only profit-oriented firms.
   b. only public firms.
   c. all organizations to some degree.
   d. only sales firms.

2. An exchange
    a. needs at least two parties to take place.
    b. gives something of value to both parties.
    c. satisfies both parties' needs.
    d. all of the above.

3. Which of the following is *not* one of the separations that divide buyers and sellers?
    a. form utility
    b. geography
    c. lack of information
    d. value

4. Marketing acts to close separations between exchange parties by performing three general categories of functions? Which is *not* one of these categories?
    a. exchange functions
    b. facilitating functions
    c. perceptual functions
    d. logistical functions

5. Standardizing and grading represent
    a. a facilitating function performed by marketing.
    b. a form of utility created by marketing.
    c. a separation between buyers and sellers.
    d. all of the above.

6. Which department in an organization creates form utility?
    a. marketing
    b. finance
    c. production
    d. accounting

7. In the evolution of marketing, which era prevailed until around 1930 in the United States?
    a. production
    b. financial
    c. marketing
    d. sales

8. What is *not* one of the three fundamental features of the marketing concept?
   a. customer focus
   b. coordinated effort by all departments
   c. profits through customer satisfaction
   d. efficiency of production

9. The organization-wide generation of market intelligence, dissemination of intelligence across departments, and organization-wide responsiveness to it is called
   a. marketing myopia.
   b. market orientation.
   c. ownership utility.
   d. facilitating function.

10. Which of the following activities is part of the product strategy component of the marketing mix?
    a. brand naming
    b. financing
    c. storing
    d. sales promotion

11. Which of the following is true?
    a. Form-utility creation is the role of marketing.
    b. Spatial separations are actualized via advertising.
    c. Ownership separations are actualized via advertising.
    d. None of the above is true.

12. The promotional strategy component of a firm's marketing mix is
    a. its means of rewarding employees.
    b. synonymous with advertising.
    c. its means of creating time utility.
    d. its means of communicating with customers.

CHAPTER (2)

Marketing and
Its Environment

Chapter Objectives

Analyzing the External Environment

Internal Environment: An Organization's Own Objectives
and Resources

Competitive Forces

Economic Conditions

Technological Developments

Political and Legal Considerations

Social Forces

Chapter Summary

The previous chapter introduced the concept of marketing strategy. Marketing managers are responsible for creating a marketing strategy for a product by addressing each element of the marketing mix (product, price, promotion, and distribution decisions) and directing these at a target market. The marketing mix elements are *controllable* factors for the marketer, which is to say that marketing managers determine prices, formulate creative advertising strategies, and make other marketing-mix decisions based on their discretion and aided by marketing research information. Unfortunately for the marketer, though, external pressures, or relatively *uncontrollable* factors, play a major role in determining the effectiveness of marketing programs. Changes in the environment necessitate adjustments in marketing strategy. Successful marketers remain ever vigilant of environmental developments. For example, technological innovations and competitive developments may force a company to alter its product offerings and lower its prices.

◼ Analyzing the External Environment

As used in the context of marketing, the term **environment** should be understood to mean all forces outside marketing management's direct control that influence marketing programs and their potential success. To keep abreast of changes in the marketing environment, marketers must be able to effectively track all developments that might affect the business. Changes in consumer values and lifestyles, the economy, technology, and competition all could directly cause a company's marketing programs to either succeed or fail. Many companies use environmental scanning to analyze these developments. **Environmental scanning** is the collection and analysis of pertinent information about the company's marketing environment. The information obtained through environmental scanning comes from many sources: marketing research, business and trade publications, and government data to name a few.

By identifying current changes and trends in the environment, a marketer can attempt to predict future changes and how these changes may affect the profitability of the company's marketing programs. New opportunities for the company may be identified in the process. And potential threats may be identified, averted, and turned into opportunities.

Most of the time, marketers who analyze their marketing environment choose to adapt to the current situation—changing it seems like a monumental and impossible task. U.S. clothing manufacturers, for instance, may be resigned to the fact that clothing produced overseas will always undercut their prices; it may be an accepted fact of life for them.

This does not mean, however, that a firm needs to roll over and play dead. Sometimes a firm is able to influence uncontrollable forces. For example, clothing manufacturers can lobby state and federal legislative bodies to limit the imports from overseas or perhaps increase the tariff rates in an effort to reduce the amount of competition. When a firm attempts to influence the external environment in which it operates through the implementation of strategies, it is engaging in **environmental management.** [1]

Now let's take a closer look at the environmental forces affecting today's marketers. In general, there are six sets of environmental factors that marketers must contend with: (1) the organization's own objectives and resources; (2) competitive forces; (3) economic conditions; (4) technological developments; (5) political/legal considerations; and (6) social forces.

Exhibit 2.1 provides a framework that incorporates these six environmental forces. The model illustrates that these forces impinge on and influence all elements of the marketing mix.

Internal Environment: An Organization's Own Objectives and Resources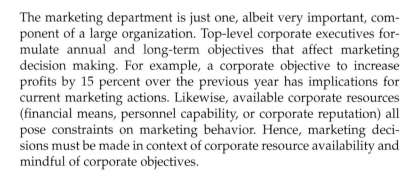

The marketing department is just one, albeit very important, component of a large organization. Top-level corporate executives formulate annual and long-term objectives that affect marketing decision making. For example, a corporate objective to increase profits by 15 percent over the previous year has implications for current marketing actions. Likewise, available corporate resources (financial means, personnel capability, or corporate reputation) all pose constraints on marketing behavior. Hence, marketing decisions must be made in context of corporate resource availability and mindful of corporate objectives.

Exhibit 2.1   Environmental Forces in Marketing

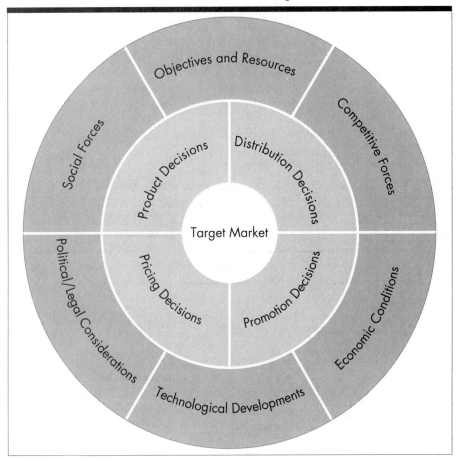

Objectives

Objectives are critical to any company's success. Without objectives, a company has no direction. If no objectives are set, a company will waste a great amount of time, money, and effort in pursuing what may prove to be unprofitable or unrealistic strategies. A company must know where it is going, if it is to be successful. A firm needs an overall set of objectives to guide its efforts. Every functional area in a company (operations, finance, marketing) also has its own objectives, but these individual objectives must fit into or be guided by the company's overall objectives. It is imperative that the entire company work together towards the same goals. Hence, marketing decision making is influenced by and even constrained, to some extent, by overall corporate objectives.

Resources

Marketing decisions also are constrained by available resources. A firm's resources include finances, technological and production capabilities, managerial talent, and so on. Resource constraints prevent marketing managers from pursuing every available opportunity. For example, financial restrictions can prevent a firm from running a prime-time television campaign for a new product introduction. But it may be able to afford a national radio campaign instead. Or a firm's current production line may not be equipped to package a trial size of an existing product. New equipment may be needed, but perhaps the finances won't allow it at this time. If a firm is fully aware of its limitations, strategies can be developed and opportunities pursued that *are* within its limits.

Competitive Forces

Competition has never been more intense than it is today. The increase in competition is attributable to several factors. First, competition is no longer limited to local, regional, or national marketers; international competitors now contend for consumer dollars in almost every product category. Second, marketers today are more sophisticated than those in previous decades. New technologies and the accessibility of pertinent data contribute to the increased knowledge. For example, 20 years ago, before the introduction of UPC codes and scanning equipment, a buyer for a grocery chain relied on manual inventories and the depletion of backroom stock to determine how well a product sold. Because of UPC codes and scanning, a buyer today knows how many units of a product sell on a daily or weekly basis, how many sell at discounted prices versus everyday retail, and so on. This kind of development has proven to be a powerful source of information for all buyers whose main goals are high turnover and profitability.

And third, competition is more intense because today's consumers are also better informed. Years ago, consumers purchased products based largely on brand loyalty or price. Some consumers

Exhibit 2.2   Types of Competitive Market Structures

- ■ Pure competition
- ■ Oligopoly
- ■ Monopolistic competition
- ■ Monopoly

today still do. But more and more consumers are reading labels, analyzing fat and salt content, and doing their homework *before* going to the store. This diligence is forcing marketers to produce better products and provide more information to consumers.

Competitive Market Structures

A firm's competitive environment—the number and type of competitors as well as the shares of market each controls—greatly affects the type of marketing strategies the firm employs. A firm will price its product differently, for example, if it has no strong competitors versus having several intensely competitive challengers. A marketing manager will operate in one of four types of competitive market structures: pure competition, oligopoly, monopolistic competition, and monopoly (see Exhibit 2.2).

Pure Competition.   Pure competition exists when many firms are selling the same basic product. No one competitor has the power to affect supply or price. All buyers and sellers have full knowledge of the market. And competitors can freely enter or exit the market at their own discretion.

   Few markets can be classified as pure competition. Agricultural commodities represent the closest any market comes to pure competition. Thousands of farmers or agribusinesses produce corn in this country. All grow virtually the same product. Price is dictated by the amount in supply and demand. And if one farmer in Nebraska decides to raise wheat instead of corn, it does not affect the market as a whole. A pure competitive situation obviously is a situation that a marketer would hope to avoid insofar as terms of sale (e.g., price level) are dictated by the market rather than the marketer. This example explains why many agricultural items are branded and promoted as unique and superior to their unbranded counterparts.

Chiquita bananas or Sunkist oranges may not be physically much different than other bananas or oranges, but some consumers evidently think otherwise and choose to purchase these well-known brand names. Branding is just one effort by marketers to extricate themselves from the commodity, or undifferentiated, status that they otherwise would face.

Oligopoly.   An oligopoly exists when a few firms control the majority of an industry's sales. Each firm has a powerful influence on the market price. Oligopolies are difficult market structures for potential new competitors to enter—usually because of the enormous capital investment, a *barrier to entry*, required to establish a market position. Many automobile companies and financial authorities were stunned in 1994 when Samsung, a large conglomerate in Korea, announced its intent to become a household name in the automobile business by the year 2000. It is estimated that Samsung will spend at least $5 billion to make a ripple in the automobile market.

Oil companies operate in an oligopoly market structure, as do automobile manufacturers and cereal makers. If, say, one oil company increases its price and its competitors do not match the higher price, the company's sales will decrease. If the same company drops its price, its sales will not increase dramatically because its competitors will probably match the lower price. Since lower prices equate to lower revenues, the competitors are best off leaving their prices at the market price.

Monopolistic Competition.   Monopolistic competition is the most typical market structure in the United States and other advanced economies. Monopolistic competition exists when a large number of sellers produce and sell similar products that are differentiated by minor characteristics such as formula variations, packaging innovations, and brand image. Competition is intense because of the large number of companies making similar products. Pricing is based on the consumer's image of the product: the consumer may be willing to pay a higher price than the market average if she sees the product as having a distinct advantage, perhaps based on image, over the competition. And new competitors can enter the market because the technology is readily available and the required capital investment is relatively low. Manufacturers of apparel are monopolistic competitors in the consumer arena, and the many producers of tools characterize monopolistic competition in the business-to-business segment.

Monopoly. A monopoly exists when only one firm produces and sells a product to an entire market. There are no substitutes for the product. And the barriers to enter the market are tremendous in the areas of capital investment and product knowledge. Electric companies and other public utilities illustrate monopolistic market structures. The United States has strict antitrust laws controlling monopolies, as will be discussed at a later point in the chapter.

Anticipating and Analyzing Competition

Whether operating in an oligopolistic, monopolistic competitive, or pure competitive market structure, it is essential that a firm know as much about its major competitors as possible. It is critical for marketers to identify opportunities and points of product differentiation.

The first step in analyzing the competition is to research the market thoroughly. How long has it been in existence? What technological developments have changed the market over the years? What is the history of the retail pricing? And why did the early market leaders fail? With a thorough understanding of how the market got where it is, a marketer has an idea of what has worked and what has not worked and why. This knowledge will be beneficial to a marketer formulating his or her own strategies.

The second step in analyzing the competition is to identify the current competition within the market. Who are the competitors? What share of the market does each control? Have the market shares changed dramatically in recent years? If so, why? What are the competition's strengths and weaknesses? A firm must know as well as possible its competition in order to compete effectively.

Third, a successful marketer must anticipate competitive actions. If, for example, a marketer plans to drop a brand's price and offer high-value coupons to cut into the market leader's share, how will the competition respond? If the market leader has a history of matching competitor's promotional efforts, chances are they will continue to do so. If they match the program, how will that affect sales? This process is very similar to a chess match: good anticipation can often prevent a marketer from making wrong moves.

Global Competition and Strategic Alliances

Global competition is intense and is manifest when organizations manufacture products, in whole or part, and market these products or services in other countries. Companies participate in the global arena in various ways: importing and exporting products, producing products in other countries, and engaging in strategic alliances. **Strategic alliances** are agreements between organizations who work together toward a common goal. The Probe GT, for example, is a collaborative effort between Ford and Mazda Motor Corporation. Robert Mondavi of California and the Rothschild family of France formed a joint venture to produce a line of highest quality wines. MCI and British Telecommunications joined forces to form Concert, in an effort to improve worldwide communications. Samsung will work with Japan's Nissan Motor Company, which will supply the technology to Samsung for producing a midsize passenger car. A marketer must be aware of its competition wherever it exists and be prepared to act in a manner that will be most beneficial and profitable even if it means joining forces with a major competitor.

Economic Conditions

The economic environment greatly affects both a firm's marketing activities and consumers' purchasing decisions. Because economic conditions are dynamic, especially now that markets are interconnected worldwide, it is critical that marketing managers stay abreast of economic developments and business cycles. **Business cycles** are recurring fluctuations in the economy that run from *prosperity* (a period of low unemployment and high income and consumer spending), to *recessions* (a period of increasing unemployment and reduced consumer spending and business productivity), to eventual *recovery,* (a period when unemployment declines and business and consumer spending intensify).

Marketing activities differ considerably during the various periods of a business cycle. During a recession, consumers are mostly concerned with value and price due to limited resources. In the early 1990s, organizations witnessed a huge increase in sales of store brands (also called private brands), because recessionary pressures during this period forced many households to pinch pennies. Marketers must keep in mind the economic conditions when promoting products. Promotional efforts geared towards value—coupons, heavy trade allowances for price discounts, value packages (e.g. "25% more")—are attractive to consumers. However, during prosperity when consumers are willing to buy, activities promoting value are not as important.

MARKETING HIGHLIGHTS

Customer Rapport

Modern database marketing is old hat for Bloomingdale's department store.

As one of today's most progressive retailers, Bloomingdale's has achieved considerable success with mailings to its carefully managed database of credit card holders and other prospects. Targeted mailings not only promote store traffic on special occasions, they maintain a special relationship with the company's loyal, affluent clientele.

Bloomingdale's customers are in general affluent (making in excess of $50,000 a year) and extremely loyal. They are the kind of busy people who build a relationship with the store name and even its sales associates. And while their mailboxes are often cluttered, they are extremely receptive to Bloomingdale's mailings.

According to Susan Harvey, the consultant whose firm, Susan Harvey Marketing, manages Bloomingdale's customer information, mailings (some 500,000 at a time) go to customers in specific lifecycles. In the case of semi-annual furniture promotions, for example, new movers who relocate into a store's trading area are selected. Because Bloomingdale's customers tend to be upwardly mobile (from an apartment to a house or from a small house to a larger house) they often purchase better and better furniture as they move along in life.

Unlike sales in other categories like cosmetics, there is very little impulse sales in the furniture department, said Harvey. Purchasing decisions for furniture are made over the course of months, the data shows, and direct mail is an effective way to bring the customer through the door to take a look.

For this kind of promotion, Bloomingdale's taps the database to find new movers—consumers most likely to purchase big-ticket items such as cabinets, dressers, armoires, and upholstered chairs and sofas, and sends them a handsome 24-page, full-color catalog of the newest offerings. Although the book does include smaller items, such as decorative lamps and pillows, the thrust of the semi-annual campaign is the large items, or case goods, which require shipping.

Furniture sales become a built-in database builder, since each large item must be shipped to the customer's residence. New movers even identify themselves by writing or phoning the company to change a billing address. In addition to the customer-driven moving information, Bloomingdale's incorporates other list sources, including credit bureau files. All mailings are run through the USPS' National Change-of-Address program to increase deliverability.

In the furniture promotion, Bloomingdale's tapped Denver-based National Demographics & Lifestyles

Marketers must closely monitor the economic environment. This task is critical since the environment can change quickly. Marketers must be prepared to alter strategies depending on the current economic conditions. A marketer unwilling or unprepared

Inc. (NDL) and MBS Multimode. MBS first identified known purchasers of high-end furniture by modeling the customer file with transactional data such as recency, frequency and monetary information, along with product/department point-of-sale data and promotional history information.

NDL then enhanced the modeled file with its detailed demographic and lifestyle data to find existing customers who looked like the known furniture purchasers. Taking the new customer model one step further, NDL identified prospect lookalikes from its 30 million+ name database. The end result was a much stronger customer file and a prospect list with profit potential.

Response rates—calculated by orders placed and then matched back to the mailing address—for the furniture promotion usually add up to 1 percent or 2 percent, Harvey said. That may sound low, but not for big-ticket items and average order size of $1,000. Tracking prospect lists has also become easier because of the nature of the merchandise.

Harvey disagrees with some retail analysts who say department stores have conditioned their consumers to shop only during sales.

"Consumers in the '90s are trained to know and look for value, and value is a relative term," she said. "It's not always the lowest price."

Bloomingdale's often has sales promotions with a window of one to several days. But the relationship marketing

really proves itself when mailings pull responses for promotions like the furniture promotion, which runs several weeks.

"People tend to have a personal relationship with retail stores," said Harvey, "especially with department stores. With other media our voice is not heard as loudly. Newspapers carry three or four other affluent department store ads."

Harvey credits direct mail for maintaining customer loyalty in Miami, where the Bloomingdale's was destroyed in 1992 by Hurricane Andrew. During the entire rebuilding period, Bloomingdale's kept up its dialogue with consumers through phone calls and its Bloomingdale's By Mail catalog. By the time the Miami store reopened, the company found great enthusiasm. The loyalty efforts had paid off. The company hopes to build similar enthusiasm for a handful of new store openings including Huntington, New York, and possibly Chicago.

"Bloomingdale's is a laboratory for direct marketing techniques in a retail environment," said Harvey. "A lot of retailers have been using direct response advertising for years, but they didn't know to call it such."

Source: Greg Gattuso, "Customer Rapport," *Direct Marketing Magazine,* January 1994, 46. Reprinted with permission.

to shift strategies may quickly experience plummeting sales and a declining market share.

Inflation is another important economic development that attracts the careful attention of marketing managers as well as financial analysts. **Inflation** is a rise in price levels. The United States, which on average experiences an inflation rate of approximately 3–4 percent per year, has enjoyed lower inflation rates than other countries in the world, some of which experience triple-digit rates. Inflation results in decreased purchasing power for the consumer. When their purchasing power decreases, consumers tend to buy based on price rather than on brand name, and they tend to buy more when a value is found.

Marketers need to consider inflation in formulating strategies. Just because the seller's cost of goods increases as a result of inflation, a price increase to the consumer may not be a wise strategy to employ. The consumer may determine that the product is not worth the higher price and buy a competing brand instead or forego the product entirely.

Resource availability is another fact of economic life that has important implications for consumer behavior and marketing action. When a resource is readily available, prices are lowered and demand increases. When the supply of the same resource dries up, prices increase. The decreased supply and higher prices discourage most consumers from buying the product. And, unfortunately, businesses who use the resource as a component in a product must either absorb the higher price in its costs or pass the higher price on to the consumer. This practice will also discourage consumers from buying the product.

Consider the case of tomatoes. California's draught in the late 1980s and early 1990s reduced the supply of tomatoes. Those available sold for up to $3.99 per pound and the quality was poor. Most consumers were unwilling to pay this price and stopped buying the product. McDonald's, however, had just introduced a new offering, the McDLT, one of the main ingredients being tomatoes. The company was forced to buy up the overpriced supply to keep the new product on the menu at an affordable price. McDonald's was forced to absorb the higher cost to support the new product's introduction.

Marketers must be flexible and aware of changes in the availability of resources. It may prove profitable to stock up on resources when they are readily available and lower priced. On the other hand, marketers must have alternate suppliers of substitute products ready in case of a shortage.

A final economic factor that has substantial implications for marketing activities is the level of income and its growth rate. Approximately two-thirds of all households in the United States earn between $18,000 and $75,000, which is considered a middle-class

CAPTAINS OF INDUSTRY

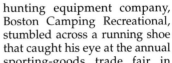

Paul B. Fireman

Chairman, President, and Chief Executive Officer

Reebok International Ltd.

Date of Birth: February 14, 1944

Education: Attended Boston University

Career Path: Worked in the sales operation of his family's sports equipment distribution company, Boston Camping Recreational. Formed his own company in 1979 in order to buy the North American rights to the Reebok name from Reebok International, Bolton, England. Purchased worldwide right to the Reebok brand in 1984 .

Profile: Boston native, married, three children.

Personal: Described as handsome, stocky, aggressive; a perfectionist and stimulating to work for, comes across as a nice guy who enjoys what he's doing—a people person. "When I got into Reebok, I had no idea it would be this big," he says. "I just wanted to make a living doing something I liked."[a]

The phenomenal growth of Reebok International Ltd. from 1979 through the 1980s is truly a Cinderella story or, as Fireman put it, due at least partly to Tinkerbell's dust rather than his own genius. "The difference between good products and great products, between good marketing and great marketing, is Tinkerbell's magic dust."[b] But the real story of Reebok's success revolves around its protagonist, Paul Fireman.

Back in 1979, young Fireman, having taken over his family's fishing and hunting equipment company, Boston Camping Recreational, stumbled across a running shoe that caught his eye at the annual sporting-goods trade fair in Chicago. The shoe was made by an English company called Reebok, named after the speedy African antelope. The company dates back to 1895 when J. W. Foster & Sons Inc. started making running shoes by hand for runners around the world. Fireman obtained the rights to sell the shoes in the United States but wasn't very successful selling them, because of their high price in an already saturated market. In 1981, down on his luck and out of money, Fireman considered selling his company. His friend, David Epstein, now president of Taymor Shoe Company, suggested he contact a friend of his, Stephen Rubin. Rubin was chairman of Pentland Industries, a London-based conglomerate, and he agreed to invest in the venture. Later the group bought worldwide rights to the Reebok brand. Tinkerbell sprinkled her magic dust on the deal just as the aerobic exercise fad was beginning to take off in the United States. James Barclay, Fireman's friend and partner, was on a business trip to California when he picked up on the aerobics trend. He learned that women were searching shoe stores for an aerobics shoe, and he and Fireman thought it sounded like a possible market to enter. Despite the reservations of Pentland Industries, they decided to produce a shoe ". . . . that combined a comfortable, colorful, stylish ballet slipper top with a durable rubber sole. They called it the Freestyle."[c] But the shoe didn't fly out of the stores at first.

Continued on next page

CAPTAINS OF INDUSTRY, continued

So Fireman and Barclay tried using discounts and giveaways to entice aerobics instructors to wear the shoes during their classes. All of a sudden, the shoe caught on—not only for wearing to aerobics class but for everyday wear. These guys had hit upon the successful combination of style and comfort at a time when people were dressing more casually, walking more, and desiring a comfortable shoe to wear for many occasions. The Freestyle became the largest-selling athletic shoe of all time and is still a staple of Reebok's business.

Reebok grew at a remarkable rate, and in 1984 the U.S. company bought out its British parent, Reebok, but retained the Union Jack logo. "The company sustained growth by refining its products for the aerobics market while maintaining the trademark Reebok chic. And it branched out successfully into new categories: running, tennis, basketball, cycling, walking, even children's shoes."[d] Reebok was also able to push up the price for its

shoes by concentrating both on style and performance. As one analyst pointed out, more fashion-oriented items often have fewer technical features and consequently yield higher margins. Reebok's margins soared to a peak 28% in 1986 and settled to 23% in 1988.[e] In 1985 Reebok earned $39 million on revenues of $307 million, and in 1989 earned $175 million on revenues of $1.8 billion.[f] But such phenomenal growth couldn't be sustained indefinitely. "The industry had its first overall revenue drop in 1992. Athletic-shoe revenue fell to $11.8 billion after exploding 230% between 1982 and 1990."[g]

Fireman left the daily operation of the company between 1986 and 1989, bringing in outside management. But when it became obvious that the company wasn't thriving under this arrangement, Fireman energetically reentered the day-to-day running of business. The challenge facing Reebok in the 1990s comes not only from its archrival—Nike—but from niche marketers, companies like Doc Martens, Teva, Converse, and

income.[2] The median income adjusted for inflation increased by 3% between 1980 and 1990.[3] This increase is partially attributable to the rising number of dual-income households that often have a large amount of **disposable income,** or after-tax income. Disposable income is used for savings and spending. After the consumer has purchased the basic necessities—food, clothing, housing—the disposable income that is left is considered **discretionary income.** Purchases such as vacations, hobbies, furniture, appliances, and electronic equipment are made with discretionary income. Larger discretionary income represents an opportunity for marketers. Marketing efforts can be focused on higher priced goods and services to attract those dollars. Rising levels of income and discretionary income represent sales and profit opportunities for marketers.

Timberland, who are wooing that fickle customer who is more interested in fashion than in performance.

Reebok is keeping up with the competition. Its Boks casual shoe line is designed to appeal to the Generation X customer, and Fireman is betting on Reebok's relationship with NBA star Shaquille O'Neal and its Shaq Attack basketball shoes to energize sales. And he remains optimistic that the fashion shift is short-term while the athletic shoe business, taking a much-needed breather, will remain strong.[h] Fireman remains focused on what he perceives to be his major competition: Nike. He has set a goal of replacing Nike as the largest U.S. athletic footwear manufacturer by the end of 1995, just in time for Reebok's 100th anniversary.[i] "We have the resources, we have the right strategy, we have the strongest management team ever assembled and our advertising has shifted significantly." Fireman's words reflect the soul of a true competitor. "I want to win. I'm not going to gear up my whole life to come in second."

And he quips, "I'm not doing this for the money."[j] It's a good thing he's got his running shoes ready.

[a] Aimee L. Stern, "Reebok: In for the Distance," *Business Month,* August 1987, 24.

[b] John Sedgwick, "Treading On Air," *Business Month,* January 1989, 30.

[c] Ibid.

[d] Ibid.

[e] Ellen Benoit, "Lost Youth," *Financial World,* September 20, 1988, 30.

[f] Fleming Meeks, "The Sneaker Game," *Forbes 400,* October 22, 1990, 114.

[g] Gary Strauss and Martha T Moore, "Nike, Reebok Out of Step. New Fashions Slam-Dunk Sneakers," *USA Today,* June 24, 1993, 1B.

[h] Ibid.

[i] Reebok International Ltd. 1992 Annual Report, 4.

[j] Mark Tedeschi and Rich Wilner,"Fireman's World War III; Paul Fireman, Reebok International Ltd. CEO," *Footwear News,* February 1, 1993, vol. 49; no. 5; S18.

Technological Developments

*Another environmental force marketers must closely monitor is technological advances. Technological advances that affect marketing decisions come in many forms, including the following:

- adjustments or new parts for existing equipment or completely new equipment, which lowers production costs
- an ingredient change, which improves a product or lowers its price
- a new, more efficient method of distributing products

- a new advertising medium (e.g., cyberspace, the information superhighway, and interactive media), which lowers advertising costs or increases effectiveness

Any of these advances directly affects the marketing mix and the firm's bottom line. Advances in technology can contribute to an increased market share or, if preemptively introduced by a competitor, seriously jeopardize a firm's future. New technology comes from various sources: workers on the firm's production line, from outside sources such as equipment manufacturers, from a company's research and development department, and from private inventors. Therefore, it is vital that marketers are aware of new advances in technology that may affect their business and profits.

Of all the environmental forces a marketer faces, technology is the most manageable. If a new technology becomes available—a new manufacturing process, a new ingredient, a new distribution technology—a firm can usually buy it, if it has the necessary resources, or hire an individual who specializes in the field. The firm has the choice of using or bypassing the new technology. Other environmental forces such as legal constraints and economic conditions, however, are not as manageable.

If a new technology becomes available, a firm can adapt its marketing operations to accommodate it and turn the advance into an opportunity for the company. Other environmental forces—lack of resources, local environmental laws—may, however, affect the firm's ability to use the technology. But if the technology is readily available, a marketer must be aware of it and act on it or risk falling behind the competition.

For example, laundry detergents were traditionally 1 to $1\frac{1}{4}$ cup formulas sold in sizes ranging from 1 up to 20 pound packages. Consumers found these products to be cumbersome and difficult to transport either to laundromats or up and down stairs. In the late 1980s, Procter & Gamble realized that concentrated formulas would have positive effect on consumers, grocers, and the firm itself. Consumers got more washloads in a smaller, easily stored and transportable package. Grocers were able to fit more packages and products on their shelves, which meant increased profits. And the concentrated detergents required less packaging materials and resources and less storage space in distribution centers, which reduced costs and increased profits for P&G. Soon, the majority of detergent manufacturers were offering concentrated formulas. This technological advance, which revolutionized the industry, proved to be a win-win situation for all—including the environment because fewer trees needed to be harvested to produce packaging materials, and landfills were less encumbered with bulky detergent boxes.

Political and Legal Considerations

The political and legal environment poses another uncontrollable force for the marketer. It is the job of the government to establish the rules and regulations to which businesses must conform. These rules and regulations affect each element in the market mix—product, price, promotion, and distribution. Marketers must therefore be fully aware of and conform to all laws affecting their business.

The Political Environment

On some occasions, marketers take a passive approach to the political and legal environment: legislation is passed, regulatory agencies are established and headed by political officials, and firms attempt to operate within the created conditions. At other times, however, firms take a proactive approach by trying to influence political and legal events. This proactive approach is usually accomplished through contributions to political campaigns for officials who may favor the firm or lobbying efforts.

Whether passive or proactive within the political environment, a firm must take into account the attitudes and reactions of citizens that will directly affect its business. One movement that reflects the attitudes of citizens is **consumerism,** which seeks to protect and increase the rights of consumers. Consumerism had its heyday in the 1960s as a social movement, but it has grown to be a powerful political force. The basic rights of consumers are outlined in the Consumer Bill of Rights, which were promulgated by the Kennedy Administration. These four consumer rights are the right to safety, the right to be informed, the right to choose, and the right to be heard. Consumer groups work today to provide information and encourage the enactment of safety standards. Consumer groups often are behind the recall of unsafe products, like car seats or baby toys. Marketers must be aware of these groups and their concerns. After all, these groups are made up of the same consumers who buy the marketer's products.

A second movement that reflects the attitudes of citizens is **nationalism** where a country's interests become the top priority.

Firms such as Wal-Mart have responded to this movement by featuring a "Buy American" theme in their stores and advertising efforts. This theme appeals to those consumers who feel it is important to support their country's businesses and the jobs they represent.

Nationalism can dictate which markets a firm may enter, because businesses usually must obtain permission and licenses to operate. Some countries encourage new business and make the permission process an easy one. In other markets, red tape discourages businesses from entering. Japan, for example, does not make it easy for foreign competitors to compete freely with Japanese companies. By comparison, the North American Free Trade Agreement (**NAFTA**) passed in 1993 creates a free flow of products among Canada, Mexico, and the United States. This agreement promises to enhance the economies of all three countries, although only time will tell.

Vietnam is an example of a new market for many businesses. The United States recently relaxed an imposed economic embargo on Vietnam because of their cooperation in the POW/MIA issue. American products are in great demand in Vietnam and the government is trying to streamline the investment process to encourage foreign investment in its economy. This political environment represents an opportunity for American marketers. Those marketers who kept abreast of this situation and possibly lobbied in its support had the advantage of moving quickly when the time was right.

The Legal Environment

The free-enterprise system promotes healthy competition. Any business that tries to limit or control competition is viewed as not acting on behalf of the public good. After the U.S. Civil War, which ended in 1865, many industries enjoyed tremendous growth. At that time, businesses operated how they wished without government controls or regulation. The American free enterprise system operated under the economic philosophy of the late-eighteenth century economist, Adam Smith, who had proposed that economic marketplaces were self-correcting and that the "invisible hand" of competition would prevent untoward practices and excessive powers falling into the hands of any single competitor. Some industries, however, quickly turned into monopolies headed by wealthy industrialists. Businessmen such as Andrew Carnegie and John D. Rockefeller aggressively accumulated land and other resources.

This period is referred to as *robber-baron capitalism*. Smaller manufacturers and producers found it difficult to compete. Congress stepped in by the late nineteenth century and enacted laws to prevent such activities and regulate business practices in general.

During the next century, a number of laws were enacted, which fall into two general categories: those that regulate competition, or procompetitive laws, and those that are designed to protect consumers.

Procompetitive Laws.   Many laws have been enacted over the years aimed at ending unsavory business practices and preserving competition. Some of the most important procompetitive laws include
1. **The Sherman Antitrust Act**   Passed in 1890, this act prevents businesses from restraining trade and monopolizing markets. The act prohibits any contract, combination, or conspiracy which restrains trade. The act also prohibits any attempt by businesses to monopolize either a specific market or industry. The act pertains to all firms operating in interstate commerce. The act covers any activities conducted by American firms in foreign commerce as well. The antitrust division of the Department of Justice is responsible for enforcing the Sherman Antitrust Act. For example, in July of 1994, a four-year case undertaken by the Justice Department against Microsoft culminated in a decision that prevents the giant software developer from continuing to engage in unfair practices that are harmful to competitors.
2. **The Clayton Act**   The Clayton Act of 1914 was passed to strengthen the vaguely written Sherman Antitrust Act, which was being widely interpreted and inconsistently applied. The Clayton Act specifically prohibits price discrimination, exclusive dealer arrangements, tying contracts, and the acquisition of stock in another corporation where the effect of such practices is to "substantially lessen competition or tend to create a monopoly." Members of one company's board of directors are also prohibited from holding a seat on a board of a competitive company according to the act.
3. **Federal Trade Commission Act**   The Federal Trade Commission Act of 1914 created the Federal Trade Commission to regulate untoward business practices. Note that the FTC Act was passed the same year as the Clayton Act. Both were efforts to strengthen the original, procompetitive Sherman Antitrust Act. The FTC Act specifically was designed to prevent unfair methods of

competition that had the effect of injuring competitors. The language was intentionally vague so that judges could use their discretion in interpreting what was fair or unfair in view of the particulars of a business situation. Shortly, we will discuss the Wheeler-Lea Amendment of 1938, which substantially expanded the Federal Trade Commission's original statutory mandate.

4. **The Robinson-Patman Act**   The Robinson-Patman Act is an important piece of legislation passed in 1936 to prohibit the practice of *price discrimination,* whereby sellers offer different prices or price-related deals to different customers. The practice of price discrimination was rampant at this time and was seen by Congress as reducing competition by giving an unfair competitive edge to some purchasers.

   The Robinson-Patman Act deals with price discrimination that takes place between businesses; it does *not* apply to prices charged at the retail level to consumers. A retailer can charge different prices to different consumers and not be guilty of any price-discrimination violation. Of course, if the discrimination is systematic, say, if for some odd reason a merchant charges higher prices to men than women, then such a practice would be subject to equal rights violations and civil penalties.

   The Robinson-Patman Act was passed to prevent business sellers (manufacturers and wholesalers) from charging different prices to different customers in a discriminatory fashion. The act does *not* prevent sellers from charging different prices to competing customers. Such a law would be economically unsound if the cost of serving different customers was nonequivalent. Sellers can justify charging differential prices to competing customers if the price differences (1) are occasioned by *cost savings* to the seller, (2) are needed to *meet a competitor's lower prices,* or (3) reflect *changing market conditions.* Let us briefly examine each condition.

   Consider a simple situation where a producer of an all-purpose lubricant (Manufacturer X) sells its product to a very large grocery chain and also to a small independent grocery store, both competing in the same market. Suppose the manufacturer charges a price that is five percent lower to the large grocery chain than the price charged to the small grocery store. Although there is a price differential, Manufacturer X is perfectly justified in charging a lower price if, say, due to selling in larger quantities it is five percent less costly to sell to the large chain than to the small store. Hence, a price difference in this case is not tantamount to price discrimination.

Also, Manufacturer X would be justified in charging the lower price to the large grocery chain than to the small store if it was forced by a competitor, Manufacturer Y, into lowering its price in order to compete against Manufacturer Y for the grocery chain's business. Any law that prevents any price differential would be rigid and out of tune with the economics of many competitive marketplace situations.

Finally, a firm can charge a lower price to one customer than is charged to another customer if changing economic conditions justify a price differential. For example, if Manufacturer X had just negotiated a new, higher wage labor contract with its employees, it could economically justify charging a higher price next week to one customer than the price charged for the exact same product last week to a different customer.

The important point to appreciate is that the Robinson-Patman Act does not prevent businesses from ever charging different prices to different customers. Rather, the act is designed to prevent price discrimination that cannot be justified on the basis of the economic conditions that surround the pricing decision.

It is further noteworthy that price discrimination is based not just on the list price charged to different customers, but also includes any form of special deals or discounts a seller offers to a customer. That is, a seller cannot avoid Robinson-Patman action by charging two customers the identical list price but then offering one, but not the other, a special discount or other price-related concession. The act requires that all such offers be made available to competing customers on proportionately equal terms.

5. **Wheeler-Lea Act**   This act passed in 1938 strengthened the Federal Trade Commission Act. The powers of the FTC were expanded with the Wheeler-Lea amendment to prohibit any practices that might injure the public without necessarily affecting competition. Wheeler-Lea has been used by the FTC in regulating false, deceptive, and unfair advertising practices.

Consumer Protection.   Antimonopoly laws protect competition, but additional laws were needed to protect consumers. Consumer protection laws date back to 1906 when Congress enacted the Pure Food and Drug Act as a result of unsanitary meat-packing practices in Chicago stockyards. This law controlled the quality and labeling of food and drugs in interstate commerce. For the first time, consumers had protection.

Exhibit 2.3   Major Laws Affecting Consumers

Act	Prohibitions
Child Protection Act of 1966	Prohibits the sales of hazardous toys.
Fair Packaging and Labeling Act of 1967	Requires certain information be listed on all labels and packages, including product identification, manufacturer or distributor mailing address, and the quantity of contents.
Consumer Credit Protection Act of 1968	Requires the full disclosure of annual interest rates on loans and credit purchases.
National Environmental Policy Act of 1970	Established the Environmental Protection Agency to deal with organizations that create pollution.
Consumer Product Safety Act of 1972	Created the Consumer Product Safety Commission and empowered it to specify safety standards for consumer products.
Nutritional Labeling and Education Act of 1990	Prohibits exaggerated health claims and requires all processed foods to provide nutritional information.

Another major victory for consumers came with the Consumer Product Safety Act of 1972. The act created the Consumer Product Safety Commission to monitor and control product safety. The commission has the power to force products off retail shelves. Marketers must be aware of the laws and ensure that their products conform to established standards early in the development stage. Exhibit 2.3 lists other major federal laws that affect consumers.

Besides federal laws, marketers must also be aware of state and local laws that affect their business. These laws vary from state to state. For example, the state of California has strict pollution laws. Any company with a manufacturing facility within the state must be aware of these laws and obtain the necessary equipment for their facility or be subject to closure.

It is one thing for Congress or a state legislature to enact laws. It is another matter to enforce them. Enforcing statutes is the task of regulatory agencies. Some regulatory agencies are created and run by the federal government; others are administered by nongovernmental bodies.

Federal Regulatory Agencies.   Federal regulatory agencies are directly involved in marketing activities such as pricing, advertising, and product safety. The activities of federal regulatory agencies often reflect the current political environment and the administration's philosophy and political agenda. Federal regulatory agencies perform the following functions:

- enforce specific laws
- protect the best interest of competitors and consumers
- create operational rules guiding industry practices
- determine penalties when laws are not followed

The federal agencies that are active in regulating marketing activities include the Food and Drug Administration (FDA), the Environmental Protection Agency (EPA), the Consumer Product Safety Commission (CPSC), and the Federal Trade Commission (FTC). We will consider only the latter two agencies.

The Consumer Product Safety Commission (CPSC) consists of five members, each appointed by the president of the United States to a seven-year term. The CPSC protects the safety and health of consumers in their homes. The commission is responsible for ordering mandatory safety standards for the majority of consumer products and imposing penalties on those who fail to meet the prescribed standards.

The Federal Trade Commission (FTC) has the most power to influence and control marketing activities. The commission consists of five commissioners, each appointed by the president to a seven-year term. The terms of the commissioners are staggered. The main objective of the commission is to prevent businesspeople and businesses from using unfair methods of competition in commerce, including misleading pricing, false advertising, and deceptive packaging.

The FTC is responsible for enforcing laws and regulatory guidelines falling under its jurisdiction. Both consumers and businesses can register a complaint with the FTC against a company if they feel the company is breaking a law. The FTC is empowered to investigate the questionable business practices. The FTC can either conduct hearings on matters pertaining to the laws involved or issue a complaint to the company in violation. The company is expected to stop the questionable activity. The FTC can take the company to court if it chooses to seek a monetary penalty.

Another responsibility of the FTC is to provide businesses with information on how to comply with the laws. Marketing guidelines are reviewed every year. The FTC looks to individual firms within a particular industry to help in establishing these guidelines.

Marketers must be aware that policies may change when administrations change.

Nongovernmental Regulatory Forces. Many industries attempt to regulate themselves when federal agencies are not involved. Trade associations often develop a code of ethics for their members as a means of preventing the creation of laws and regulatory agencies to oversee their marketing activities. Although associations lack the power to enforce guidelines, self-regulatory programs are less expensive and more operational for its members.

The **National Advertising Review Board (NARB)** personifies the role and value of self-regulation. Created by the Council of Better Business Bureaus and three advertising trade organizations, the NARB monitors truth in advertising cases. The NARB, a court of appeals consisting of 50 representatives in 5-member panels, hears appeals of cases from the National Advertising Division (NAD). The NAD is the investigative arm of the NARB. Cases are brought to the NAD by competing advertisers, local Better Business Bureaus, and consumer groups. The NAD screens the complaint, contacts and begins discussions with the advertiser in question, obtains the advertiser's substantiation to claims, and takes action. If the advertiser chooses to appeal, the case is then reviewed by the NARB.

Deregulation. Discussion of business regulation would be incomplete without at least brief mention of deregulation. In the 1980s during the Reagan Administration, the federal government deregulated some industries in an effort to cut costs, administrative paperwork, and regulatory agencies. Some industries that were deregulated were airlines, banking, and trucking. On the positive side, competition has increased as a result of deregulation. But on the negative side, some industries and consumers have suffered as a result. For example, since deregulation many savings and loan companies have failed, often due to illegal or unethical activities, and taxpayers have paid millions of dollars to bail out the S&Ls.

◆ Social Forces

Social forces play a major role in determining how consumers live and act. It is necessary that marketers attempt to forecast any significant social changes or trends that will affect the performance of

Exhibit 2.4   Major Demographic Developments

- Population growth and movement
- Changing age structure
- Changing U.S. household
- Income dynamics
- Minority population developments

their products and services. This task is difficult in that social developments often are dynamic and rather subtle, though important nonetheless. As part of their environmental scanning efforts, it is critical that firms stay abreast of demographic developments, changes in consumer values, and social trends. The following sections discuss each of these major topics.

Demographic Developments

Demographic variables are measurable characteristics of populations. Demographic variables include age and income distribution, household living patterns, regional population statistics, and minority population patterns. By monitoring demographic shifts, marketers are better able to (1) identify and select market segments, (2) forecast product sales, and (3) select media for reaching target customers.[4]

Following sections will highlight five major demographic developments that are important to today's marketers (See Exhibit 2.4).

Population Growth and Movement.
The world population is growing at a staggering rate. In 1960, 3 billion people inhabited the planet; in 1984 this number increased to 5 billion; by 2025, the world population is expected to exceed 8 billion.[5]

Unlike the rest of the world, the United States is experiencing a slow population growth. The U.S. population increased by nearly 10 percent from 1980 to 1989, whereas it is expected to increase by only 7 percent during the 1990s.[6]

Where the population resides is also an important factor. The geographical distribution of the population has shifted. In the past, the population was concentrated in the Midwest and Northeast. By the year 2000, however, a majority of the population will reside in the South or West.

Changing Age Structure.   The population of the United States
is aging. The median age of Americans is increasing: in 1970, the
median age was 28, in 1980, it was 30, and in 1990, 33. It is expected
to rise to 36 by the year 2000.[7] This shift in age structure is due to
the aging of the **baby boom generation**—the more than 75 million
Americans born between 1946 and 1964. This generation proved to
be a boon to marketers who targeted their products to the teen and
young-adult markets in the 1970s and 1980s. But these marketers'
sales have declined as the baby boomers aged and changed preferences. Levi Strauss appealed to baby boomers with its line of blue
jeans. As the baby boomers aged, however, sales of blue jeans
declined. Levi responded to the decline by introducing Dockers, a
line of dressier casual pants targeted to aging baby boomers. As a
result, Levi's sales have rebounded. The aging baby boomer market
represents an excellent opportunity for many firms.

Another opportunity exists in marketing products to mature
consumers. Nearly 55 million United States citizens are over age 55,
representing approximately 21 percent of the total population. In the
past, only marketers of stereotypical geriatric products—laxatives or
denture cleaners—focused on this group. But today's marketers are
realizing that since this group controls about $7 trillion of the coun-
try's wealth, the over-55 market is definitely worth pursuing.

Some major advertisers who have recognized the importance
of marketing to this segment have begun using seniors in cross-gen-
erational ads. The Coca-Cola ad featuring Art Carney sharing a
Coke with his grandson, and Anheuser-Busch's ad of seniors swim-
ming in an ice pond sharing drinks with a group of young ice sports
players both appealed to all age groups.

The Changing U.S. Household.   In the 1950s, 90 percent of all
households consisted of families—2 parents and their children; in
1985, this percentage dropped to 72.3 percent; in the year 2000, it is
expected to reach a low of 68.2 percent.[8] Nonfamily households—
persons living alone or with one or more unrelated persons—have
increased dramatically from 24 million in 1985 to almost 34 million
by the year 2000.[9] Households are growing in number, shrinking in
size, and changing in character because of increased divorce rates,
increased housing costs, and the influx of women in the workplace.

The changing U.S. household has tremendous implications for
marketers. In the past, a marketer usually developed one advertisement intended to be used in network TV advertising. Today, advertisers are forced to develop separate ads to appeal to the various

household groups within its target market. And to reach these groups, network television advertising is no longer as effective as it used to be.

Women in the work force is another major development with great implications for marketers. Consider these statistics about today's women:

- 70% of women between the ages of 25 and 54 are in the labor force.[10]
- Women head nearly 1 in 3 of all households compared with 1 in 7 in 1950.[11]
- A larger share of women are remaining single into their 30s because of disenchantment with marriage and more educational and employment opportunities.[12]

Marketers must consider the changing roles of women both in marketing their products and in reaching target markets. A traditional medium like daytime television is no longer an effective medium for reaching the working woman. Direct mail, magazines, and radio are proving to be more effective in reaching this group.

The dual-income family has had great impact on marketing. These families have larger disposable incomes, but they also have less time in which to spend it. Longer times spent commuting and working have left less time for family and leisure activities. Roles within the family are changing also. More men are doing the shopping, cooking, housework, and childcare than ever before. These families seek out products that will save them time and provide a valuable service.

One such product is the VCR+. Many homes in the United States have a VCR. However, an unofficial estimate within the industry is that almost 80% of all VCR owners are unable to set their machines to record a program. The VCR+ simplifies the process by using special code numbers which appear in the TV Guide to automatically program the VCR. Apparently the need was real: over 6 million VCR+ units have been sold around the world.[13]

Income Dynamics.   The gap between the rich and poor is growing. More than 30 million Americans are living below the poverty level.[14] At the other end of the spectrum, 10 percent of U.S. households are defined as affluent with disposable incomes of $62,000 or more.[15] Many U.S. households enjoy continually rising incomes due in part to the increase in dual-income earners. Marketing communications and media vehicles need to be customized to reach the affluent market. Appeals to elegance, quality, and durability are very effective with the affluent market. And media selection is also extremely important because research shows that media-behavior patterns change with increases in income—television viewing and radio listening decrease while magazine readership increases.

Minority Population Developments.   The United States has always been known as a melting pot, accepting immigrants from all countries. The largest minority groups in this country are Hispanics and African Americans, both of whom are growing rapidly. By the year 2010, minorities will represent one-third of the U.S. population.[16]

African Americans will account for approximately 13.4% of the country's population by the year 2000.[17] Blacks tend to be younger urban dwellers, who are more brand conscious on average than other Americans. Although some African Americans have similar values, beliefs, and distinguishable behaviors, it would be simplistic, however, to think they represent a single market or culture.

Considering the number of African Americans in the United States, it is surprising how relatively little effort many firms have made to target that segment of the market. However, marketing efforts have increased. The retail chain JCPenney has changed its merchandise lines in urban areas to appeal to blacks and Hispanics. Greater numbers of blacks are being used in advertisements, both as celebrity endorsers and in regular roles. Some firms use African-American athletes and entertainers in their commercials as a way to appeal to a variety of audiences. For example, it is estimated that 20% of white teens identify with black pop culture. Pepsi features basketball star Shaquille O'Neal in its television ads targeted to the teen audience.[18]

Hispanic Americans currently represent about 10% of the country's population.[19] The largest percentage of Hispanics are Mexican Americans (63%), followed by Puerto Rican Americans (12%), Latin Americans (11%), Cuban Americans (5%), and other Hispanic Americans (9%).[20] Approximately 75% of Hispanics live in California, Texas, New York, Florida, and Illinois.[21]

Hispanics tend to be younger, have larger families, live in urban clusters, and are becoming more mobile.[22] The Hispanic market also represents an excellent opportunity for marketers. But special efforts must be taken to communicate with Spanish-speaking Hispanics. The most effective ads are those utilizing Spanish run in Hispanic media vehicles.

Walt Disney Company used an ambitious marketing program targeting Hispanics to promote their *Aladdin* home video. Tie-ins were created with major marketers such as AT&T, Quaker Oats, and Burger King. Disney felt that the film had built-in appeal to Hispanic consumers who tend to be young, with larger families, and strong family ties.[23]

Asian Americans now number 7 million in the United States. This segment of the population is expected to reach 15 million or more by early next century.[24] Asian Americans are better educated, have higher incomes, and occupy more prestigious job positions than any other Americans.[25] Asian Americans include people of Chinese, Japanese, Korean, Vietnamese, Filipino, and East Indian descent. These cultures vary widely on product and brand preferences. Asian Americans are considered the newest "hot ethnic market."[26]

Advertisers must be careful in planning their marketing efforts to the Asian community. What is acceptable and has meaning to one group, say Chinese Americans, may not hold true for the Japanese, Korean, and Filipino Americans. For example, a Thai translation of "Come alive, you're in the Pepsi generation" read "Pepsi brings your ancestors back from the dead." New York Life Insurance recognized the potential problems and hired an advertising agency specializing in Asian American advertising. One campaign was developed emphasizing financial security for the family. But each ad was slightly modified for the different markets such as the Chinese ad which featured different props, models, and copy.[27]

Changing Consumer Values

Values are the principles and standards that society considers important. Some of the cultural traits, or values, that were characteristic of our country in its early years have changed considerably. Early Americans were hard-working individuals who valued their independence. They supported themselves and were dedicated to their families. The government and authority figures were highly respected. These Americans valued success and were not wasteful individuals but rather frugal in their spending habits. Although these values still hold true for a good portion of today's society, some do not. Many individuals make no attempt to work and be self-sufficient and feel that the government and society have an obligation to support them. Respect is lacking now, too, as violence in our society is on the rise. And dedication to family seems less important to many as is reflected in the high divorce rate and lack of child support payments.

A study conducted in the late 1980s found the following values to be the most important to today's consumer: (1) self-respect, (2) security, (3) warm relationships with family and friends, (4) sense of accomplishment, (5) self-fulfillment, (6) respect from others, (7) sense of belonging, and (8) importance of having fun and excitement.[28]

These values had even changed somewhat from the late 1970s. Then, women emphasized self-respect and security. But as more and more women entered the workforce and achieved success, less emphasis was placed on these values. Today, self-fulfillment and a sense of accomplishment are more important to women. One value did not change, however, in the ten years: people still place heavy emphasis on having fun!

Values of Young Americans.

Americans between the ages of 18 and 29, referred to as Generation X, are socially liberal but politically and economically conservative. They are skeptical of the efficiency of most government programs. These young Americans are concerned about social issues facing the nation such as the poor and homeless, but they also favor cuts in government spending. The world to them is in bad shape and they feel they can do little to change it. But most still want the good life—including nice clothes, cars, high-quality entertainment equipment, and a vacation home.[29] Much of the media portrayal of Generation X is simplistic, however. It would be misleading to think that "Xers" represent a single market just because they share a common age range.

Values of Baby Boomers.

The values of baby boomers have changed over the years. What was once important to them—possessions, success, and big bucks—no longer holds the same appeal. Baby boomers discovered that the attitude of "work hard–play hard" may have gotten them a houseful of possessions, but one important factor was missing—a quality of life. Baby boomers are finding more satisfaction and joy in marriage, family, and home life. A quiet evening at home with take-out food and a rented video is now preferred by many over an expensive dinner and dancing at a trendy restaurant.

Holiday Inn recognized this shift and recently spent $8 million in television, radio, and print ads attracting families. The chain, which claims to be the "official hotel for family fun," offers free food to children accompanied by parents.[30]

Social Trends. Many researchers track various social trends and developments for marketers. One such study is the Yankelovich MONITOR, a well-known national study of social developments based on annual surveys of 2,500 Americans aged 16 and older. The 1993 study identified five major social trends that have implications for retailers and other marketers.[31]

1. **Erosion of Trust.** Most customers today are distrustful of just about every institution in this country including the government, businesses, and educational facilities. Consumers feel that integrity, credibility, and competence are lacking in general.

   Consumers are wary of misrepresentation and are determined to rid their lives of deception. This trend, however bleak, offers an opportunity for retailers and other businesses to develop a bond of trust with the consumer. Those that are successful in obtaining the bond will win in the long run with increased customer loyalty.

2. **A Victim Ethic.** Discrimination has always made some demographic groups feel as though they are victims. But today, those who feel victimized are increasing to include many mainstream Americans. The feelings of frustration of gridlock, perceived purposeful incompetency, mismanaged expectations, and lack of accountability make many consumers feel they are being mistreated by businesses. The consumer is angry and wants to "make someone pay," reminiscent of the 1993 movie, *Falling Down*, in which Michael Douglas portrayed the victim ethic to the extreme.

   Retailers and other businesses can respond to consumers' sense of victimization by offering fair prices and honest marketing communications. Every attempt should be made to fully satisfy the customer by backing up products with realistic policies and guarantees. Wal-Mart advertises that it is reducing the prices of many of its products every day. The company is offering honest pricing and promoting it.

3. **Stress.** Stress is a fact of our everyday lives. Whether you are the family breadwinner, a stay-at-home mom, or a school-age child, a majority of Americans are faced with high levels of stress. At one time, women wanted to have it all—a career, marriage, children. Today, women are the most stressed group in this country. Juggling career and family proved too exhausting. Women are now setting priorities and delegating more of their workload.

   The implications for today's marketers are simple: women want honest pricing, value for their money, and accountability. They want a minimum of stress in their shopping with no hassles. This trend has contributed to the increases in catalog sales and shop-at-home services.

4. **The Ascendancy of Value.**   The 1980s witnessed an increased demand for expensive and prestigious products. In the 1990s, however, consumers have reevaluated their priorities and are now more interested in quality and value. Happiness no longer equates to a BMW, a Rolex watch, or dinner at an elegant restaurant. Value is now at the center of consumer purchase patterns. Although the concept of value differs somewhat from consumer to consumer, usually consumers determine value by equating price to product and assessing whether the quality received is worth the price paid.

   This trend offers numerous opportunities for the middle markets in business. Car manufacturers, for instance, are no longer dependent on only the cheapest and most expensive models. The market for mid-range cars—$15,000 to $22,000—is growing. Consumers who were once mesmerized by BMWs and Mercedes are realizing that Saturns and Pontiacs are good values for the money. Businesses that stress value will win customer loyalty.

5. **Personal Satisfaction.**   The 1970s and 1980s were decades of self-absorption and narcissism. The 1990s is witnessing the resurgence of personal satisfaction that is achieved not by spending but rather by pleasures, either large or small. Consumers are looking for any little means of reducing stress—an occasional glass of good wine, a big piece of macadamia nut cheesecake, or a weekend away. Many of these indulgences are bought as impulse purchases by the consumer.

   Businesses who associate pleasure with their products will be winners. In this case, pleasure means making the purchase process pleasurable for the consumer. Consumers derive pleasure if they get what they want, when they want it, and how they want it. Nordstrom's is an example of a retailer that makes every attempt to make the shopping experience a pleasurable one for consumers.

◈ Chapter Summary

Marketers make controllable decisions when determining product, price, promotion, and distribution strategies. These decisions are not, however, unconstrained. Rather, a variety of environmental forces, or relatively uncontrollable factors, have a major impact on both the determination of and eventual success of marketing strategies.

The first such uncontrollable factor is an organization's own objectives and resources. Objectives must be clear and obtainable. Each department can have its own set of objectives. But the individual objectives must be guided by the firm's overall objectives so that the entire company is working together towards the same goals. A firm's resources must also be taken into account when developing strategies and objectives.

Competitive forces is another uncontrollable factor for the marketer. Competition is more intense today because competition comes from local, regional, national, and international marketers. Marketers are also more sophisticated and consumers are better informed. A firm's competitive environment also affects the types of strategies a firm employs.

A third uncontrollable factor is economic conditions. Factors such as business cycles, inflation, unemployment, and income exert the most influence in the economic environment and, therefore, on marketing strategies.

Technological developments are the most manageable uncontrollable force a marketer faces. Firms must be aware of new technologies in the marketplace and turn these advances into opportunities and a competitive edge.

Political and legal considerations are a fifth uncontrollable force for the marketer. Many laws affect each element of the marketing mix. Marketers must be aware of and conform to all laws affecting their business.

The sixth and most difficult uncontrollable force to predict is social forces. Changes in the social and cultural environment affect customer behavior and therefore sales of products. Social forces important to today's marketers include demographic developments, changing age structure, changing American households, income dynamics, and minority population developments.

Notes

1. Carl Zeithaml and Valerie Zeithaml, "Environmental Management: Revising the Marketing Perspective," *Journal of Marketing*, 48 (Spring 1984), 46–53.

2. Louis Richman, "Why the Middle Class Is Anxious," *Fortune*, May 21, 1990, 106–109.

3. "Snapshots of the Nation," *Wall Street Journal*, March 9, 1990, R12.

4. Thomas S. Robertson, Joan Zielinski, and Scott Ward, *Consumer Behavior* (Glenview, IL: Scott, Foresman and Company, 1984), 340.

5. "People, People, People," *Time*, August 6, 1984, 24, 25.

6. Alecia Swasy, "Changing Times: Marketers Scramble to Keep Pace with Demographic Shifts," *Wall Street Journal*, March 22, 1991, B6.

7. "The Year 2000: A Demographic Profile of the Consumer Market," *Marketing News*, May 25, 1984, 8.

8. Richard Kern, "USA 2000," *Sales and Marketing Management*, October 27, 1986, 8–30.

9. Ibid.

10. Susan E. Shank, "Women and the Labor Market: The Link Grows Stronger," *Monthly Labor Review*, 111 (March 1988), 3–8.

11. Daphne Spain and Suzanne M. Bianchi, "How Women Have Changed," *American Demographics*, May 1983, 18–25.

12. Ibid.

13. Richard Zognlin, "Can Anybody Work This Thing?" *Time*, November 23, 1992, 67; "Simpler Programming of VCRs Is Possible with 2 New Gadgets," *Wall Street Journal*, September 24, 1992, B1.

14. "A Portrait of America," *Newsweek*, January 17, 1983, 31.

15. "They're in the Money: A Look at America's Affluent Market," *Sales & Marketing Management*, June 1990, 34.

16. Christy Fisher, "Ethnics Gain Market Clout," *Advertising Age*, August 5, 1991, 3,12.

17. William Lazer, *Handbook of Demographics for Marketing and Advertising* (Lexington, MA: Lexington, 1987), 92.

18. Bernice Kenner, "On Madison Avenue," *New York*, April 11, 1994, 12.

19. Jon Berry, "The New 'Multilingual' Pitch," *Adweek's Marketing Week*, April 22, 1991, 35; Christy Fisher, "Ethnics Gain Market Clout," 3.

20. Lazer, *Handbook of Demographics for Marketing and Advertising*, 92; Christy Fisher, "Hispanic Explosion," *Advertising Age*, August 26, 1991, 30.

21. Ibid.

22. Craig Endicott, "Marketing to Hispanics: Making the Most of Media," *Advertising Age,* March 19, 1984, M10.

23. Marcy Magiera, "Disney's 'Aladdin' Eyes Hispanics," *Advertising Age,* November 16, 1992, 12.

24. Cyndee Miller, "'Hot'" Asian-American Market Not Starting Much of a Fire Yet," *Advertising Age,* January 21, 1991, 12.

25. Richard Kern, "The Asian Market: Too Good To Be True?" *Sales and Marketing Management,* May 1988, 39–42.

26. John Schwartz, Dorothy Wang, and Nancy Matsumoto, "Tapping into a Blossoming Asian Market," *Newsweek,* September 7, 1987, 47–48.

27. Betsy Wiesendanger, "Asian-Americans: The Three Biggest Myths," *Sales and Marketing Management,* September, 1993, 1.

28. Lynn Kahle, Basil Porilos, and Ajay Sukdial, "Changes in Social Values in the United States During the Past Decade," *Journal of Advertising Research,* February/March 1988, 35–41.

29. "The '80s Materialism Marks American Youth," *Wall Street Journal,* May 16, 1990, B1.

30. Ira Teinowitz, "Holiday Inn Tie-ins Stress Family Vacation Positioning," *Advertising Age,* March 30, 1992, 12.

31. Barbara R. Caplan, "The Consumer Speaks—Who's Listening?" *Retailing Issues Letter,* Texas A&M Center for Retailing Studies, 5 (July 1993), 1–6.

Study Questions

1. Which of the following is *not* an uncontrollable factor for the marketer?
   a. competitive forces
   b. pricing decisions
   c. economic conditions
   d. social forces

2. Environmental scanning
   a. is the collection of pertinent information about the marketing environment.
   b. can be obtained from marketing research studies.
   c. can be obtained from government data.
   d. All of the above are correct.

3. Company-wide objectives
   a. are not needed if each department has set its own objectives.
   b. should be as general as possible so as not to be too restrictive.
   c. are necessary so the whole company is working towards the same goals.
   d. should be idealistic.

4. Which of the following best captures the meaning of "environment" as used in the context of marketing?
   a. Environment refers to the weather conditions that influence many marketing decisions, such as retail sales performance on a rainy day.
   b. Environment refers specifically to competitive activity.
   c. Environment refers to the various social forces that influence marketing decisions.
   d. None of the above adequately capture the meaning of environment.

5. When a firm attempts to influence the external environment in which it operates through the implementation of strategies, it is engaging in
   a. environmental scanning.
   b. environmental management.
   c. corporate espionage.
   d. data snooping.

6. Which market structure is the most common structure in advanced economies such as the United States?
   a. pure competition
   b. oligopoly
   c. monopoly
   d. monopolistic competition

7. A certain market structure is characterized as one where many firms sell the same basic product, no one competitor has the power to affect supply or price, all buyers and sellers are assumed to have full knowledge of the market. The described market structure is a(n) _____ structure.
   a. pure competitive
   b. oligopolistic
   c. monopolistic competitive
   d. monopolistic

8. A certain market structure is characterized as one where a large number of sellers produce and sell similar products that are differentiated by minor characteristics. Competition is intense, and consumers' images of product are a major determinant of prices. This is a(n) _____ structure.
   a. pure competitive
   b. oligopolistic
   c. monopolistic competitive
   d. monopolistic

9. When organizations work together toward a common goal, such as the collaboration between Ford and Mazda in the case of the Probe GT, this is termed a
   a. cooperative effort.
   b. strategic alliance.
   c. dualistic endeavor.
   d. None of the above are correct.

10. Which is *not* a business cycle?
   a. market maturity
   b. prosperity
   c. recession
   d. recovery

11. A household's after-tax income also is called
   a. disposable income.
   b. discretionary income.
   c. nondiscretionary income.
   d. indisposable income.

12. A household's income that remains after the basic necessities are purchased is called
   a. disposable income.
   b. discretionary income.
   c. nondiscretionary income.
   d. indisposable income.

13. The so-called Consumer Bill of Rights includes all of the following except
   a. the right to safety.
   b. the right to be informed.
   c. the right to choose.
   d. the right to be satisfied.

14. Which of the following is *not* a procompetitive law?
    a. The Sherman Antitrust Act
    b. The Clayton Act
    c. The Consumer Product Safety Act
    d. The Robinson-Patman Act

15. The act that is explicitly designed to prevent price discrimination is the
    a. Robinson-Patman Act.
    b. Sherman Antitrust Act.
    c. The Wheeler-Lea Act.
    d. The Federal Trade Commission Act.

16. The Robinson-Patman Act deals with price discrimination for all transactions except between
    a. manufacturers and retailers.
    b. manufacturers and wholesalers.
    c. wholesalers and retailers.
    d. retailers and consumers.

17. Under the Robinson-Patman Act, a manufacturer is justified in charging nonequivalent prices to different customers except in which of the following situations?
    a. When the price differential can be justified in terms of cost savings to the manufacturer.
    b. When competition forces a manufacturer to charge a lower price to one of its customers than to another.
    c. When it is the manufacturer's best interest to charges different prices to different customers, because doing so is more profitable.
    d. All of the above are justifiable instances for charging nonequivalent prices.

18. Which of the following acts expanded the powers of the Federal Trade Commission to prohibit practices that might injure the public without necessarily affecting competition?
    a. Clayton Act
    b. Robinson-Patman Act
    c. The Truth in Advertising Act
    d. The Wheeler-Lea Act

19. The National Advertising Review Board is
    a. under the jurisdiction of the Federal Trade Commission.
    b. a federal agency parallel in status and power to the Federal Trade Commission and the Food and Drug Administration.

c. the most recent federal agency.

d. a self-regulatory body.

20. During the 1990s the U.S. population is expected to increase by approximately _____ percent.

  a. 1

  b. 3

  c. 7

  d. 20

21. By the year 2000, the median age of the U.S. population is expected to be

  a. 23.

  b. 28.

  c. 36.

  d. 44.

22. Baby boomers were born between the years 1946 and

  a. 1952.

  b. 1958.

  c. 1964.

  d. 1977.

23. By the year 2000, African Americans will account for approximately _____ percent of the U.S. population.

  a. 5

  b. 13

  c. 20

  d. 25

24. Which ethnic group in the U.S. is the best educated and highest income earning?

  a. African Americans

  b. White Americans

  c. Hispanic Americans

  d. Asian Americans

25. Which of the following is *not* an accurate statement about Generation X Americans?

  a. They are aged 18–29.

  b. They are socially liberal but politically and economically conservative.

  c. They represent a single market by virtue of their homogeneity in buying preferences.

  d. All of the above are equally correct.

CHAPTER 3

The Role of Research in Marketing

Chapter Objectives

Marketing Information Systems and Decision Support Systems

Traditional Marketing Research

The Marketing Research Process

Chapter Summary

Movie studios use *it* to predict the box office success of new movies before release. Television networks use *it* to predict the popularity, and thus, advertising revenues, for new tv shows. The success of new products is based on *it*. *It* can provide useful and valuable information upon which many marketing decisions are based. However, *it* can also provide information that if used incorrectly can do serious harm to a company or product. Coca-Cola used *it* in developing its New Coke product, one of the worst marketing fiascos of the century, which cost the company millions of dollars. What is this thing, this "it," that can be so useful for businesses today? This it is *marketing research.*

A good working definition of marketing research is provided by the American Marketing Association, which defines **marketing research** as follows:

> Marketing research is the function which links the consumer, customer, and public to the marketer through information—information used to identify and define marketing opportunities and problems; generate, refine, and evaluate marketing actions; monitor marketing performance; and improve understanding of marketing as a process. Marketing research specifies the information required to address these issues; designs the method for collecting information; manages and implements the data collection process; analyzes the results; and communicates the findings and their implications.[1]

Marketing research is an essential ingredient in any organization. A well-designed study can provide answers to almost any marketing question. Is the formula right? Is the packaging right? Is the product priced appropriately? Do consumers even know about it? Marketing research can shed some light on these questions.

Some managers may feel that the cost of conducting research is too high and not worth the investment. But in the long run, most marketers will agree that the information obtained in a well-executed study will save the company more money than it will cost them. After all, if a small change in the product, packaging, or advertising can potentially turn a marginal product into a winner, the investment in marketing research is well-justified.

Information is the key. A marketer needs good, reliable information to formulate successful marketing strategies. This information includes sales, the competition, individual markets, and so on.

Without reliable information, a marketing decision maker must rely on past experience and intuition in making marketing decisions. Surely, experience and intuition enter to some degree in most marketing decisions, but in today's competitive marketplace it is insufficient to rely exclusively on hunches when making extremely important decisions. As noted in Chapter 1, a true *marketing orientation* demands marketing intelligence activities and the useful information produced.[2]

Many marketers complain that they are overwhelmed with information. A wealth of internal and external data is available. **Internal data** is information that comes from within the company itself. Internal data typically is in the form of company reports. An abundance of reports are usually available to managers showing sales, spending, pricing, profitability, inventory levels, and distribution by key accounts. Reports of this nature are usually made available to managers on a weekly, monthly, quarterly, and annual basis.

External data is information that has been generated from outside the company. Reports are published by the government, trade associations, advertising agencies, and research firms on a variety of topics that may prove useful to a company. If information is not readily available, a marketer may choose to obtain specific information by commissioning a study by its own marketing research department or by an independent research firm.

Information is crucial to effective marketing decision making, but the fact that the information exists does not guarantee a marketing success. Information must be collected, organized, and made available in a usable form.

In the past, marketing managers at various levels of the organization kept their own files containing information they felt relevant or valuable to their business. Many times, research studies would be conducted and copies of the findings would end up in someone's files. Often, when that person left the company, so too did the information. It was only a matter of time before a more organized system would take hold in sophisticated marketing organizations. Indeed, starting in the 1970s and accelerating through the 1980s and 1990s, many companies have implemented data collection, storing, and retrieval systems to facilitate efficient and effective marketing decision making. These are called *marketing information systems* and *decision support systems* and are discussed in the following section.

Marketing Information Systems and Decision Support Systems

Companies have instituted marketing information systems (MIS) and marketing decision support systems (MDSS) to enable managers to readily access information and make decisions. These systems are designed to synthesize and store data from internal and external sources and to enable managers to access the data, convert it into useful information, and from this make important marketing decisions. The objective of these systems is to maintain an accurate, timely, and complete bank of information for marketing decisions.

In actuality, the problem confronting many marketing managers is that they have too much, not too little, information at their disposal. For example, the voluminous data acquired from optical scanning of UPC bar codes ("scanner data") can be overwhelming. Marketing managers need this wealth of information to be organized and in a form that is readily usable. Advances in computer technology have made this possible. The role of MIS and MDSS is to link the power and promise of the computer with marketing managers' day-to-day and strategic information needs. The personal computer is an essential tool for most marketing managers.

The Marketing Information System (MIS)

Most major corporations—as well as many smaller businesses and even not-for-profit organizations—require a systematic way to organize, store, and retrieve the vast amount of information produced. A management information system provides the technology and know-how for accomplishing these purposes. A marketing information system is just one facet of an organization's overall management information system. A **marketing information system (MIS)** deals specifically with the information needs of marketing managers. Information regarding sales volume, product movement, customer reactions to marketing programs, and a host of other types of information are generated, stored in computer memory, and produced as output in the form of valuable reports that address managers' information needs.

Internal data from product sales, customer responses to frequency programs (e.g., airlines' frequent-flyer programs), and analyses of competitive marketing activities are combined with a myriad of *external data* (e.g., scanner data, economic forecasts, government reports, and documents produced by trade associations) to form a **marketing database.** It is from this database that data can be accessed and transformed into reports for marketing managers' decision-making purposes. A marketing decision support system exists for the purpose of enabling marketing managers to access computerized data and to use the data to address pressing questions.

The Marketing Decision Support System (MDSS)

Whereas a marketing information system stores tons of information and enables its quick retrieval, a **marketing decision support system (MDSS)** provides the mechanisms (e.g., spreadsheet programs, graphics, statistical tools, and analytic models) that make it possible for a manager to obtain answers to key questions. For example, a spreadsheet program (such as Lotus 1-2-3 or Excel) enables a brand manager to summarize tons of data and to engage in "what-if" exercises such as the following: "What level of sales volume might be obtained in Region 3 if we lowered Brand X's price by five percent and increased television advertising by 20 percent?" "What would be the impact on costs and profits of reducing the sales force by 10 percent?"

Marketing managers at various levels in the organization (from brand and sales managers all the way to the VP of Marketing) can sit at their desks and use personal computers networked to the MIS to obtain key reports and make decisions. Useful decision support systems do not require their users to be computer experts. Rather, the typical user simply wants to have his or her information needs satisfied quickly and with as little aggravation as possible. Management information system experts and analytic specialists (called management scientists) work with marketing managers to identify the managers' decision-making needs and requirements for specific types of reports. Programs and systems then are developed that are easy for managers to learn and use. A truly useful MDSS is not rigid and restricted to generating only a limited number of reports, but rather allows managers to structrure reports that match the manager's precise information needs.

◆ Traditional Marketing Research

Marketing research is an essential component of the overall marketing decision support system. Marketing research is usually conducted on a project-by-project basis to serve specialized information needs and to answer specific questions that cannot be answered by merely querying an organization's extant information database.

Marketing research is intended to be a *support system* to decision making. Many marketers make the mistake, however, of using the research findings as the cure-all to their marketing problems. Marketing research is not meant to provide a decision; it can only increase the probability that the most informed decision will be made. The research findings should be considered along with other pertinent information, such as management insight and sales force experience and knowledge.

Conducting marketing research encompasses several activities. The first and, perhaps, most important activity is to **specify the information needed.** The data provided by a research study will be of little, if any, value unless the issue is accurately defined upfront. For example, if a company's snack food sales are declining, a marketer may turn to marketing research to discover some answers. If the marketer feels the problem is the taste of the product, a comparative taste test study would be commissioned. This study may provide good information, but many other factors such as price, shelf positioning, packaging, and availability also may be affecting sales. Declining sales is probably only an indication of a much deeper marketing problem.

Once the research objectives are specified, the **method for collecting the information** is designed. The overall research design is the master plan for conducting the research study. It details the procedures that will be used for collecting, processing, and analyzing the data. A researcher (or, more likely, a research team) must be flexible when approaching each study, because each study has unique objectives. Different types of information can be obtained from respondents. Demographic and socioeconomic characteristics, brand awareness and knowledge, attitudes, buying intentions, purchase motives, and actual purchase behavior are all types of primary data of interest to marketers and researchers.

Next, the research team manages and implements a **data collection process.** As will be elaborated on later, data can be collected using observational methods, via conducting surveys, or by performing marketing experiments. Regardless of method, data collection typically is costly and time-consuming. To ensure accuracy and avoid a high probability of error, the research team must oversee every phase in the process.

The research team is then responsible for **analyzing the results of the study.** In this step, the collected data are translated into relevant information for decision makers. Data analysis includes editing and structuring the data and coding and preparing it for computer analysis. A variety of statistical tools can be applied to the data. These range from simple computations—for example, 1 out of every 5 respondents disliked the flavor—to more complex analyses that test hypotheses by using the tools of statistical inference covered in courses such as marketing research.

The final research activity is the **communication of the findings and their implications** to decision makers. The research team must be careful to use clear and easily understandable terms in the presentation. Some of the jargon used by marketing researchers is very technical and those not trained in the science may find it difficult to follow. The final report may only state the findings or may include recommendations based on the findings. Usually, the research team provides both written and oral presentations.

Types of Market Research Data

The conduct of marketing research is widespread. Most major manufacturing enterprises and many larger wholesalers and retailers have marketing research staffs. In addition, numerous specialized firms are in the business to conduct research studies and provide their services on a for-hire basis. Marketing research also is conducted by industry trade associations, advertising agencies, and other organizations.

Research data can be classified as primary or secondary, the distinction being made on the basis of the purpose for which the data is collected. **Primary data** is information collected by or for an organization to address that organization's specific research question or needs. **Secondary data,** on the other hand, is previously published data collected by a company itself or by other organizations (e.g., marketing research firms, business periodicals, government agencies) that conduct ongoing or occasional studies.

Types of Research Firms

Two types of marketing research firms specialize in the collection of data: syndicated service firms and full-service research firms.

Syndicated Service Firms.   Syndicated service firms collect and distribute information for *many users.* These firms specialize in providing secondary information and other services at lower costs than a potential user of the information would pay if it conducted the study itself. Some of the leading syndicated service firms are A.C. Nielsen, J.D. Powers, Arbitron, Simmons, and Information Resources Inc. (IRI). J.D. Powers, for example, conducts studies on automobile purchasers' satisfaction with their newly purchased cars and then makes the study results available—at a fee, of course—to automobile companies and others who are interested in the study results.

Syndicated reseach firms are excellent sources of information. For example, a manufacturer of consumer package goods (i.e., inexpensive items that are branded, packaged, and sold via self-service in grocery stores, mass-merchandise outlets, and other retail stores) will subscribe to Nielsen's retail research services to obtain a variety of information about its brands and their performance compared to competitive offerings. The manufacturer receives a wealth of valuable information, including

- industry volume in pounds and dollars
- sales information from the previous year
- sales by package size
- competitors' sales
- sales information by localized area
- inventory figures
- market share information in pounds and dollars
- distribution and out-of-stock figures

Purchasers of syndicated research pay for the information under an annual or multi-year contract. The costs of conducting the research are shared among the entire client base. Syndicated research firms collect and disseminate many types of data, but two especially widespread forms of syndicated data are reports of sales and advertising and media exposure.

Sales Data. Until Universal Product Code (UPC) symbols began appearing on products in the 1970s, syndicated service firms, such as the well-known Nielsen company, relied on store audits to gather information on sales. Nielsen employed auditors who literally went from store to store and inventoried merchandise in every product category. Two problems existed with this system of data collection: (1) the accuracy of the information was dependent on the accuracy of the hundreds of auditors who hand-counted the merchandise, and (2) generating and summarizing the data was time-consuming; it took many weeks after the audits were conducted before final reports were available to clients.

By the late 1980s, a majority of supermarkets were using scanners to read the UPC codes and generate sales data. Companies such as Information Resources, Inc. (IRI) began providing scanner data to clients. Manufacturers soon had an abundance of accurate information at their disposal including sales by size and the condition under which sales were generated, for example, on-deal or at regular prices. And the information was provided in a more timely fashion than that generated by store audits.

Advertising and Media Exposure. Other research firms provide information on consumers' exposure to print and TV advertising. Some firms will even tell manufacturers whether users of a specific product are more likely to read newspapers or magazines. For instance, EDK Forecast, a marketing research firm, recently conducted a study to find out how persuasive television advertisements are on children. The results are good news for advertisers and bad news for parents: 74% of the parents surveyed said they bought a toy because their children saw it on TV and wanted it, and 29% said they bought sneakers for the same reason.[3] A number of other syndicated research firms provide advertising and media exposure reports. A sampling of well-known suppliers include Nielsen (TV ratings), Arbitron (radio audience measurement), Simmons Market Research Bureau (magazine audience measurement), and Starch (magazine readership).

Full-Service Research Firms.

If all available secondary data proves unsatisfactory for a firm's purpose, a full-service research firm may be needed to collect primary information. Full-service research firms collect data pertaining to individual clients' specialized research needs. The research is usually conducted on a project-by-project basis with the client bearing the entire cost of the project.

The full-service firm will study specific issues that are affecting a marketer's business. In some cases, the full-service research firm will assume the entire marketing research function for its client. However, many companies have their own in-house marketing research departments, and only occasionally employ the services of full-service research firms or specialists in an aspect of marketing research such as performing data analyses or conducting focus groups.

◆ The Marketing Research Process

Marketing research is an organized *process* for obtaining information for decision-making purposes. Although it is somewhat of a simplication to break any process into specific steps and feign that the steps occur in an orderly step-by-step fashion, it will be useful to examine the various activities that are involved in marketing research studies and to treat these, albeit simplistically, as specific steps in the process. These steps are interdependent, with each step influenced by the preceding step and influencing the subsequent steps. Within each step, the researcher may choose from several alternative methods in determining which will be most effective in getting the desired results. Exhibit 3.1 identifies the steps in the research process, each of which is discussed in the following sections.

Defining the Problem

The research process begins with the definition of the problem at hand. This sounds easy enough, but often it is not. A marketer may recognize a problem exists, but the nature or root of the problem is unclear. The first step in the research process is to carefully define the problem that requires systematic investigation. For example, is the recent decline in market share due to a price problem, insufficient advertising, poor product quality, or something else? If a marketer is able to clearly define the problem, then the problem already is half solved. Defining the problem clearly also helps to set the research objectives and determine the most appropriate data-collection methodology.

Some form of exploratory research often is needed to both define the problem and set research objectives. The marketer can conduct an informal investigation, or exploratory research, into the situation to uncover as much relevant information as possible.

Exhibit 3.1   Steps in the Marketing Research Process

- Define the problem
- Design the research
- Collect data
- Analyze and interpret results
- Report research findings

Exploratory research is the collection of data to gain a greater understanding of the research question. Sources for the investigation might include employees (e.g., salespeople) who are directly involved in the situation, customers who are directly affected by the problem, suppliers who have a stake in the problem, and records or reports that pertain to the situation. After this exploratory research, the marketer should have a good understanding of the actual problem and the questions to be asked in the study.

Consider the case of an electronics manufacturer who introduced a video telephone product that allows the caller to see the person on the other end. Introductory sales of the product were disappointingly slow. The manufacturer's marketing research director decided to interview sales representatives who were selling to retail outlets. The sales reps report some complaints they have received: the image on the screen is blurry, motions are jerky, and the voice and picture are not in sync. Next, the marketing researcher and a sales rep met with a manager of a large retail account that decided to discontinue the item. This manager reported she had received complaints that interference or noise on the line disrupts the picture and becomes annoying. In checking with the public relations department, the marketing researcher found several complaint letters about the quality of the product. And finally, the researcher asked other employees to try the product at home and respond to a short questionnaire. After reviewing all available information, the researcher determined that sales are declining due to mediocre product quality. Thus, the objectives for subsequent and more formal research will be to determine what consumers dislike about the product. A usage test will be a necessary part of the research study.

In this example, the marketing researcher's informal investigation clarified the problem and helped to set the objectives of the study. If the researcher had only defined the problem as slow

Exhibit 3.2   Methods of Primary Data Collection

- Observation
- Surveys
- Experimentation

acceptance or lack of knowledge about the product, a lot of time and money would have been wasted on irrelevant data. The informal investigation proved to be well-worth the time and effort.

Designing the Research

Once the problem is defined, the next step is to develop a research design. The **research design** is the master plan for the study in which the procedures for gathering and analyzing data are detailed. In this stage, the who, what, where, when, and how of the study are determined.

The first decision that needs to be made regards the type of data that will be needed. Is there any published information, that is, secondary data, already available that may be relevant to the problem? Or will a customized study be required to address the specific needs of the problem?

If a customized study is required, a company's own marketing research department may collect primary data or an independent research firm can be employed for this purpose. Primary data are collected through any of the methods identified in Exhibit 3.2: observation, surveys, or experimentation.

Observation.   As the name suggests, observation is used when researchers collect data by recording some aspect of behavior or the unfolding of events. Observation is used to obtain information when respondents are unwilling or unable to communicate their actions or recall their past behavior. Imagine, for example, that a retail executive is interested in knowing the average amount of time consumers spend shopping in the chain's stores. Surveying consumers and asking this question is unlikely to yield accurate, or valid, data because people typically have no reason to record how long it takes to complete their shopping. Hence, in a situation such as this, an accurate response could be acquired by observing when a sample of shoppers entered and departed a store and the length of time that intervened.

In general, humans or electronic monitoring devices are used to observe and record specific marketplace behaviors that are of interest to researchers. Observation is an objective method of collecting data since only actual behavior is recorded; the participants in the study are not asked any questions and, indeed, generally are unaware that their behavior has been recorded.

Human observers or surveillance cameras observe how shoppers inspect merchandise. Eye-tracking cameras capture the flow of eye movement when shoppers peruse package information. Human observers record how shoppers traverse a store so as to identify how best to determine merchandise arrangements. The A.C. Nielsen Company uses electronic devices hooked up to televisions to record what television shows are actually watched in determining rating points for television shows.

One popular form of observation used in research studies today is mystery shopping. Companies such as Feedback Plus of Texas are hired by retailers (fast food chains, department stores) to judge the level of customer service their employees provide. Mystery shoppers are sent into retail stores or restaurants to conduct a specific activity such as to buy or return a sweater, gather product information, or order a meal. After the shopping assignment is completed, the mystery shopper fills out a questionnaire and returns it to his or her employee with relevant observations. This information then is used to provide a report to the retail client.

Although the observation method has a valuable role to play in marketing research, it is noteworthy that observations are limited in that they are unable to provide answers to questions regarding the reasons underlying the behavior in question.

Surveys.   Collecting data with surveys is the most commonly used method for gathering primary data. A **survey** is any research that *asks questions* to understand brand awareness, product knowledge, attitudes, purchase motivations, buying intentions, and so forth. The survey can be very detailed and structured where the interviewer asks the same questions of each respondent in the same manner. A survey also can be flexible and unstructured where the

Exhibit 3.3   Types of Surveys

- Telephone interviews
- Mail surveys
- Personal interviews
- Focus group interviews

interviewer is allowed to ask a variety of questions depending on the respondent's answers. The survey research methods listed in Exhibit 3.3 are commonly used.

Telephone Interviews.   Telephone interviewing can be an effective means of gathering information when time is limited and the budget is slim. Such technological advances as WATS lines make the method most affordable. Interviewers are trained to ask pointed questions from a prepared questionnaire. In fact, in more sophisticated telephone interviewing, questions appear on the interviewer's computer screen and he or she records the respondent's answers directly into computer memory. The response rate for telephone interviews generally is higher than for mail surveys.

In the past, telephone directories were used to obtain potential respondents; however, households with unlisted numbers were not included in surveys. Today, random-digit dialing is used so as to enable contacts with households with unlisted as well as listed telephone numbers.

Mail Surveys.   Mail surveys are used to gather information when the geographical area to be surveyed is large (thereby excluding personal interviewing) and the budget is relatively small (precluding telephone surveying). The response rate for this method is lower than with telephone surveying, because many recipients neglect or refuse to respond to the questionnaire. To enhance the response rate and to ensure accuracy, questions in mail surveys must be direct and clear. And time cannot be a critical factor inasmuch as mail surveys are relatively slow in obtaining completed questionnaires.

Personal Interviews.   Personal interviews are the most direct method of collecting primary data since the interviewer and respondent are face-to-face. This method allows an interviewer to develop a rapport with the respondent, which may result in a longer and more in-depth interview. If the information needed for the study cannot be gathered by mail or telephone, personal interviews are required. The downside of personal interviewing is that it is expensive and time-consuming, and many people refuse to be interviewed.

A **focus group interview** is a specialized form of interviewing whereby a moderator leads a small informal group (typically from six to ten participants) in a discussion on a topic of interest to the client. The moderator begins with some general questions and then focuses on specific details once the discussion develops. Mattel Toys uses focus group interviews in determining children's interests in various toys. Sometimes the children in a focus group are given actual toys to play with and then are asked questions about the toys. At other times, short animated videos illustrate a new toy and the respondents are asked why they would want or not want the toy in the video. The focus group interview is a flexible method of collecting data that often is followed with a more structured survey or other research design.

Experimentation. **Experimental research** is a method of gathering primary data where the researcher manipulates one or more marketing-mix variables (e.g., price, product quality, advertising expenditures) in an experimental group and then compares the results against a control group that was not exposed to the experimental manipulation. By manipulating only select variables and holding all others constant, the effect of those variables can be estimated. Assume, for example, that Taco Bell wants to test a new chicken burrito and that their lab has developed three different potential sauces for the burrito. By using experimental research, each of the three sauces can be tested while all other factors—tortilla, amount of chicken, onions, cheese—remain the same. The research will show which of the three sauces is best liked.

Newspapers are also a useful source of experimental research in the field of advertising. A company may want to test different coupon values for its brand. Ads appearing in various newspapers are all the same except for the coupon value which varies, say, at three face values: 50¢, 75¢, and $1.00. The newspaper coupons are coded by city to determine the various redemption rates. Through this experimental research, the company will determine which value is the most cost-effective for this particular brand and in view of the present competitive situation.

MARKETING HIGHLIGHTS

Buick Goes Golfing with Car Shoppers

Buick would like to treat all of its prospective customers to a round of golf at renowned Warwick Hills Country Club in Grand Blanc, Michigan, home of the Buick Open.

The General Motors Corporation division can't do that, obviously, but it's offering consumers the next best thing: a chance to play the course on their own personal computer and, along the way, learn more about Buick products.

Buick has given away more than a million computer discs to consumers since 1986. The 1994 software, featuring the Warwick Hills Country Club, will go out to an estimated 150,000 people.

"The software gives consumers information to use in a non-threatening environment and is designed to raise consideration of Buick," said Nancy Newell, director of sales-automotive division for the Flint, Michigan, office of Inmar Group, a software company. Ms. Newell started Buick's software program as assistant manager for Buick systems before joining Inmar late this year.

The disc, available for IBM and Macintosh computers, contains two sections. One is a product information section where consumers can learn more about Buick cars. The other is a golf video game that makes extensive use of the Buick logo.

The product information section provides color photos and data for all Buick models, including price, fuel economy and vehicle features. Consumers who aren't aware of Buick products can select features of the vehicle they want. The computer can then choose three to four models for the consumer to study.

Or, a consumer can choose to look at only certain features, such as two-door models or specific price ranges.

The disc also uses animation to offer the user a chance to "watch" a car being built. In one instance, the user sees a Buick LeSabre move across the assembly line as a robotic arm paints it red. Next, the seats are installed.

"Unlike a video where you are forced to watch it from beginning to end, with the software the consumer can interact," Ms. Newell said.

Buick started the software program to reach consumers who use PCs. The purpose was to create a high-tech sales brochure. But along the way, Buick has gained valuable insights into targeting specific audiences.

Advantages and Disadvantages of Primary and Secondary Data.

In summarizing the various primary research techniques—that is, observation methods, surveys, and experimental research—it is worth noting that these techniques share some common advantages and disadvantages. In general, the *advantages* of primary data collection follow:

- primary data are collected to fit the specific purpose of the marketing issue at hand

"The software program resulted in increased sales, test drives, and visits to the dealerships," said Bob Burnside, Buick's national advertising manager. He attributes part of the product's success to its highly targeted audience of computer users.

In addition, Buick's studies show that the interactive nature of the disc makes recall higher than with other media, Ms. Newell said.

Each year, Buick sends a letter asking previous software users if they want a new disc. More than 60% respond, Ms. Newell said.

To reach new prospects, Buick is advertising the disc in the December issues of *PC World* and *PC Computing*, the first time Buick has used media advertising for the project. Buick last year advertised the software in a Sharper Image catalog but has depended mainly on direct mail to previous users.

The 1994 software is designed to mirror Buick's advertising image and quality theme for this year. The disc and its packaging display Buick's ad theme line "The new symbol for quality in America." In addition, when a computer user starts the program, he hears part of Buick's jingle.

The golf game also provides a logical link to Buick's golf sponsorship.

"Golf makes great sense for Buick when it comes to our target buyers," said Mike O'Malley, Buick's general marketing manager. "More of our target customers are interested in golf than any other leisure activity."

Altogether, Buick sponsors four Professional Golfers Association tour events, and is the official car of the PGA tour.

Inmar calls the golf game "advertainment."

"This means we allow advertising to become part of the entertainment process," said Dennis Snyder, Inmar president. During the golf game, the Buick logo pops up in various boxes.

Ninety percent of the users still have their disc a year later, Ms. Newell said. A note on the disc packaging encourages consumers to copy it and pass it along to their friends. Consumers give it to as many as four of their friends, Ms. Newell said.

Source: Leah Rickard, "Buick Goes Golfing with Car Shoppers," *Advertising Age*, December 6, 1993, 18. Reprinted by permission from the December 6, 1993, issue of *Advertising Age*. Copyright, Crain Communications Inc., 1993.

- primary data are current (rather than dated)
- the marketer knows the methodology used in the study and has complete control over the specific questions asked, the characteristics of respondents who are surveyed, and how the data are coded and analyzed

The *disadvantages* of acquiring primary data are that data collection often is expensive and time-consuming. It is for this reason that the first step, prior to conducting an original study, is to investigate presently available data—that is, **secondary data**—that may provide the information a company needs to address its particular information needs. Sources of secondary data include data internal to a company's own database, government data, and a variety of other data.

Most companies have a wealth of information at their fingertips in the form of internal data. Reports made available on a daily, weekly, monthly, or yearly basis may provide answers to a marketer's questions. Revenue and sales analysis, financial performance, cost, profit and loss, and sales by area are all types of internal reports that may enable a marketer to make well-informed decisions without conducting an original study to collect primary data.

The government conducts and publishes numerous studies that are invaluable to marketers. These publications include the *Census of Population*, the *Census of Business*, the *Census of Manufacturing*, and the *Statistical Abstracts of the United States*, to name a few. These publications are available at most local libraries.

Many organizations such as trade associations and advertising agencies publish research findings that are also an excellent source of secondary data. For example, the National Infomercial Marketing Association (a trade association for the so-called long—typically 30 minutes—commercial, or infomercial) conducted a recent study of 3,500 infomercial watchers and purchasers. The study revealed, among many other findings, that 92% of consumers who have bought something through an infomercial are satisfied with their purchase and 95% said they would make another purchase. This study is published and available for those advertisers considering the infomercial as a media vehicle.[4]

In general, the *advantages* of secondary data are

- secondary data are inexpensive compared to primary data
- secondary data are available more quickly than primary data
- several sources of secondary data are usually available

The *disadvantages* of secondary data are

- the information provided may be outdated
- the data available may not be suited to the research question at hand

- the methodology used in the gathering of data may be inappropriate for the user's needs. For example, a published report may classify answers for respondents aged 25 and younger, when the company really is interested in responses of people aged 18 to 22.

Collecting Data

In view of the relative advantages and disadvantages of primary and secondary data-collection techniques, a marketing researcher must decide which technique, or techniques, are most useful and feasible for addressing the problem at hand. If the decision is to conduct some form of primary study (whether observation, survey, or experiment), a fundamental determination is the choice of respondents in the study. The total group that the researcher wants to study is the so-called **population,** or *sampling frame*. A population for a particular marketing research undertaking may be defined as all people over the age of 65 who reside in urban population centers, or all chief executive officers (CEOs) of organizations with annual sales exceeding $50,000,000. What precisely constitutes a population depends entirely on the particular research problem. A **census** has been conducted when data are obtained from every member of a particular population.

Typically, however, the population is too large or widely dispersed to collect data from each and every person (or other sampling unit) that has been classified within the population. Accordingly, a **sample,** or portion of the population, must be selected to provide a realistic representation of the whole. For example, a Florida vitamin company wants to test a new vitamin it has developed for senior citizens. To survey every senior citizen over age 55 in the state of Florida would be expensive, time-consuming, and unrealistic. Instead, surveying a select group of Floridian seniors will save time and money while giving the company the information it needs. Two basic types of sampling are probability sampling and nonprobability sampling.

Probability Sampling.
In this form of sampling, respondents from the designated sampling frame have a known, nonzero chance of being chosen in the sample. For example, probability sampling would be used if a researcher chose every tenth person who entered the main doors at the Mall of America in Minneapolis on a given

CAPTAINS OF INDUSTRY

Linda Johnson Rice

President and Chief Operating Officer

Johnson Publishing Company

Date of Birth: 1958

Education: BA, Journalism, University of Southern California, 1980 MBA J. L. Kellogg Graduate School of Management, Northwestern University, 1987

Career Path: Worked for her father during the summers while in high school and college and became assistant to the fashion editor of *Ebony* magazine upon graduation from college. In 1985 she became vice president and executive producer of *Ebony/Jet Showcase*, a nationally syndicated television show. Named President and Chief Operating Officer upon completion of MBA degree in 1987.

Profile: Young, intelligent, outgoing and practical.

Personal: When asked if she had any advice for working mothers, she responded, "I try, when I see my daughter, to just wipe work out of my mind and totally concentrate on what she is doing, what I can do to make her a better person, what I can teach her in the time I spend with her. That's my advice—as hard as it may seem to some people, you've got to drop those problems at work and focus on that child."[a]

Linda Johnson Rice grew up in the publishing business. Her father, John H. Johnson, founded Johnson Publishing Company in 1942 in Chicago, and Linda worked there as a gofer during the summer while in high school and college. She graduated from the University of Southern California with a degree in journalism and moved back to Chicago to work as vice president and assistant to the publisher (i.e., Dad). She managed to work there during the day and attend Northwestern University at night, earning her MBA from one of the most prestigious schools in the nation and becoming president of the company in 1987. Not bad for a 29 year-old.

Much of the credit for this success story must be given to John Johnson, the founder of Johnson Publishing Company (JPC). Back in 1942 Johnson was working at a black-owned life insurance company, and one of his duties was to compile a weekly digest of events in black America for the company president. Johnson recognized the potential market for this kind of information set in a magazine format and tried to find financial backing for his idea. When he was unable to raise the needed money, he took out a $500 loan using his mother's furniture as collateral to pay for postage to mail letters to the 20,000 people on the insurance company's mailing list, asking those interested in such a magazine focusing on black life to send in $2. When 3,000 people responded favorably, he began publishing *Negro Digest*. Johnson writes in his book, *Succeeding Against the Odds*, that he was aided by former First Lady, Eleanor Roosevelt, who wrote an exclusive article for the October 1943 issue, entitled "If I Were a Negro." He asserts that her article helped double the publication's circulation.[b] *Negro Digest* ceased publication in 1975 as sales dwindled, possibly cannibalized by the success of another of JPC's publications, *Ebony. Ebony Magazine* began publication in 1945 and was patterned after Life Magazine. Today it has the largest circulation among magazines catering to African Americans, averaging 1.8 million circulation in 1991.

Getting companies to advertise in *Ebony* wasn't a piece of cake back in the early days. Johnson remembers it taking 6 years to get Procter & Gamble to advertise in the magazine and 10 years to attract Detroit automakers. Why such reluctance? Ronald Sampson, now senior vice president for Burrell Advertising Co., worked in advertising sales for JPC from 1959 to 1963 and identifies the problem as being one of image. Companies were concerned about how they would be perceived by their other customers if they were seen as catering to blacks. But Johnson and his employees worked hard to produce and sell a magazine dealing with issues concerning African Americans and pointing out contributions black people have made to society. As Johnson says, "It has inspired them to be successful by showing examples of blacks who have made it."[c] Johnson Publishing also owns the men's monthly *EM; Jet Magazine;* the Fashion Fair and Eboné lines of cosmetics; a nationally syndicated TV show, *Ebony/Jet Showcase;* a travel agency; and three radio stations.

Linda's mother, Eunice, has also been active in the business and provided the inspiration to launch Fashion Fair cosmetics. As director of the Ebony Fashion Fair shows in the early 1970s, she noticed that the models couldn't find makeup tones suitable to their complexions and had to resort to mixing their own concoctions. She discussed the problem with her husband, and he decided to create a line of cosmetics to meet the needs of ethnic women. He consulted with cosmetics experts who conducted research to come up with a high-quality product. Samples were offered via mail-order in *Ebony* and *Jet,* and within six months, 100,000 Capsule Collection kits had been sold, and Fashion Fair established its niche. Johnson then went on the road and in 1973 convinced Marshall Field department stores to carry the line. Today Fashion Fair is carried in 2,000 stores internationally and its revenues are estimated at $60–100 million annually.[d]

Although Johnson, now 75, is still active as chairman, CEO, and publisher, he has turned over much decision-making responsibility to Rice. She is married with a young daughter and must juggle work and home like so many other contemporary women. She is upbeat, energetic, and practical in her attitude toward life and work. "I just try to do my work and make the best decisions I can during the day, and then I go to bed at night with a good frame of mind and a good conscience." And she is a great spokesperson for JPC. "Every time I make an appearance somewhere, every time I make a speech, I'm selling the image of Johnson Publishing Co. I'm selling the image of *Ebony* magazine, I'm selling the image of Fashion Fair Cosmetics, I'm selling the image of the Ebony Fashion Flair. I am constantly selling."[e] She refers to her father as the "pre-eminent salesman" for whom she has the greatest respect, describing him as "an incredible well of knowledge."[f] From him she has learned the

Continued on next page

CAPTAINS OF INDUSTRY, continued

importance of paying attention to details and of making coworkers feel they are making a significant contribution to the company.

Rice has been instrumental in pushing the company in new directions, such as overseeing the launch of the Ebone line of cosmetics, the E-Style catalog venture with Spiegel, and a joint venture with Conrad Associates called the "Ebony/Jet Guide to Black Excellence" video series. She wants the company to grow and has hired young talent who have new ideas to share. She has also overseen a redesign in packaging for Fashion Fair Cosmetics, updated the look of *Ebony*, and introduced a new fragrance called Zahra, aimed at a wider audience than the company's traditional base of black women.

Johnson Publishing, with revenues of $274 million annually, has a firmly established image, relationship, and database to reach out to the African-American population because of the vision of John Johnson, and Linda Johnson Rice aims to build on that foundation. "For more than 50 years, the company has built its reputation on accurately capturing and conveying the attitudes, aspirations, and interests of African-Americans." Recent retail industry statistics show that American women each spend an average of $700 to $800 a year on clothing, while African-American women each spend an average of a $1,100 a year.[g] This is good news for E-Style, JPC's catalog alliance with Spiegel. Spiegel chose to set up partnership with JPC when it decided to create a catalog geared to the African-American woman because of its position in the black publishing market. "They're the best," states John J. Shea, Spiegel chief executive. "There are other magazines that cater to the African-American audience, but they are the most knowledgeable."[h] Rice believes the catalog venture really fills a need because it offers customized clothing to fit the African-American woman. Spiegel conducted focus groups to determine the correct fit for this specific segment of the population and as a result also uncovered a desire for more colorful clothing, ethnic prints and patterns and hats as well as other accessories.

JPC's plunge into the mass-market ethnic cosmetics market has been led by Rice. Although JPC was a little behind Maybelline, Avon, and Revlon in entering the mass market ethnic cosmetics market in 1992, Ebone has the advantage of being related to

---

day. The benefit to using probability sampling is that scientific rules can be applied to guarantee that the sample truly represents the entire population. The three methods used to select a probability sample are simple random sampling, stratified sampling, and cluster sampling.

Simple random sampling is used when researchers randomly select respondents from a complete list, or enumeration, of all members of the designated population. Selection is by chance. A simple random sample is usually drawn through the use of a table of random numbers. Assume, for example, that the theater depart-

well-known Fashion Fair, which has a very loyal customer base.

"What we decided to do was start a second line of cosmetics for the black woman that deals with her pocketbook," Rice stated. She is convinced that black consumers will associate Ebone with its older sister, Fashion Fair. The tremendous loyalty Fashion Fair customers have traditionally demonstrated is more than the loyalty of an informed consumer to a good product, Rice remarks. "It's the loyalty of an informed black consumer to a good product put out by a black-owned company."[i] She plans to rely on Johnson Publishing's own publications to spread the word about Ebone to the black community. "We have the most direct access to black women via *Ebony* and *Jet* magazines. We reach 50% of the black women in the United States. You can't get any more direct than that without ringing them up on the phone."[j]

Johnson spent his career providing information to the American black population. Rice may change that relationship from one based heavily on the print media to one of providing products for black and other ethnic women. And with the popularity of Fashion Fair cosmetics overseas, she may be moving the company in just the right direction to make it more globally competitive in the 21st century. So far, the transition from father-in-charge to daughter-run company seems to be a smooth one.

[a] "Ebony Interview with Linda Johnson Rice,"*Ebony,* November 1992, 208.
[b] John H. Johnson, with Lerone Bennett, Jr., *Succeeding Against the Odds* (New York: Warner Books, 1989), excerpt appearing in *Ebony,* November 1992, 38–46.
[c] Herbert G. McCann, "Johnson Publishing Turns 50; *Ebony* Magazine Key to Family-Owned Firm's Success,"Associated Press, *Chicago Tribune,* November 22, 1992, final edition, 8.
[d] "The New World of Black Beauty; Fashion Fair Cosmetics," *Ebony,* November 1992, 70.
[e] *Ebony,* November, 1992, 208.
[f] Ibid.
[g] John Schmeltzer, "Ebony Good Fit at Spiegel," *Chicago Tribune,* July 26, 1993, 1.
[h] Ibid.
[i] Caroline V. Clarke, "Redefining Beautiful," *Black Enterprise,* June 1993, 242.
[j] Julie L. Belcove, "Fashion Fair Answers Mass Market Rivals; Ethnic Cosmetic Line," *Women's Wear Daily,* July 31, 1992, 8.

ment at your college or university is interested in obtaining students' opinions about the types of plays students would most enjoy. The theater department can use student enrollment records and draw a random sample of names from that list. All students, therefore, have an equal chance of being selected for the study. For example, if the school has 20,000 students and the the sample size is to be 200, then the probability that any given student's name will be selected is 1/100.

Another form of probability, or random, sampling is stratified random sampling. **Stratified random sampling** is a two-stage probability sampling method where researchers divide the complete list of the population into groups according to a common trait and then apply simple random sampling techniques on each group. The population can be divided into any number of subsets, or strata. Stratified sampling is used when groups of respondents are expected to respond in different ways. For example, assume the theater department believes that the type-of-play preferences will differ for graduate and undergraduate students. The researcher in this case will first group, or stratify, all students in terms of graduate or undergraduate status. Separate simple random samples of graduate and undergraduate students then will be drawn. Stratified sampling produces less sampling error and hence enables more precise estimates of population parameters than does simple random sampling.

A third form of probability sampling is cluster sampling. **Cluster sampling** is a probability sampling method where researchers randomly choose areas or geographic clusters, first, and then randomly sample within each cluster. Cluster sampling, like stratified sampling, first involves delineating the population into groups that are pertinent to the research question at hand. Each subgroup is a small-scale model of the population. However, unlike stratified sampling, cluster sampling takes a random sample of clusters and then surveys *every* member in the subset of sampled clusters. This sampling technique is used when lists of the sample population are non-existent or costs need to be minimized.

For instance, in the play-preference example for the theater department, all non-commuting students at the university could be clustered according to the dormitory where they live. Then a sample of, say, two out of seven dormitories could be selected and *all* residents of these two dormitories would be surveyed. The advantage cluster sampling offers over stratified or simple random sampling is that it is often less expensive on a per-observation basis due to the physical proximity of respondents who are located in the same cluster.

Nonprobability Sampling.

This second general type of sampling involves researcher judgment (rather than the laws of probability) in the selection process. This type of sampling is acceptable when the representativeness of the sample is not a critical consideration. For example, suppose our theater department is not interested in obtaining a representative sample of all 20,000 students at the university, but is instead merely interested in obtaining some immediate feedback. If a researcher asked the first 50 students who walked into the school union to talk with her about plays at the local theater, she would be using nonprobability sampling. The three methods used to select a nonprobability sample are convenience sampling, judgment sampling, and quota sampling.

Convenience sampling is a nonprobability sampling method where researchers choose respondents based on ease of availability of the respondents. People are chosen because they are in the right place at the right time. Those included in the sample, though, may not necessarily be representative of the target population. If the researcher for the theater department interviews the first 25 people who walk by the theater on Monday morning, the researcher is using a convenience sample.

As the name suggests, **judgment sampling** is a nonprobability sampling method where researchers choose respondents based on judgment. Judgment sampling also is called *purposive* sampling. People are chosen because the researcher feels they are representative of the population to which she or he hopes to draw conclusions. Consider again the theater department example. Suppose our researcher hypothesizes that conservative and liberal students may have different preferences in the types of plays they most enjoy. In an attempt to sample both conservative and liberal students, our hypothetical researcher may use clothing patterns and hair styles as surrogates of political ideology and thereby attempt to slect respondents who span the conservative-liberal spectrum. This is unlike convenience sampling where it is possible that predominantly only conservative or liberal students would happen, as a matter of chance, to be selected. Of course, with purposive sampling, sample representativeness is only as good as the researcher's judgment.

Quota sampling is a type of nonprobability sampling where researchers match characteristics in the population against quotas. Quotas are established for relevant groups. For example, the researcher for our theater department might determine that 55 percent of the student body is male and 45 percent female. To accurately reflect this division, the researcher insists that 55 percent of the sample be comprised of males and 45 percent females.

Analysis, Interpretation, and Presentation of Results

Once the data have been collected, the researcher proceeds to the final stage of the research process, that of analyzing, interpreting, and presenting the findings. This step is critical in the research process. A researcher must rely on experience, intuition, and analytical abilities to effectively interpret the data. A variety of analytical tools are available ranging from simple descriptive statistics (means, medians, proportions) to complex multivariate analyses. Coverage of these topics is beyond the scope of this overview. Marketing majors and other students who are interested in marketing research can learn more about data analysis in a marketing research course.

Once the data are analyzed, the researcher must present the findings in a clear, understandable manner. All the care and effort involved in a good marketing research study will be for naught unless the findings are presented in a clear and readable form. A researcher must keep in mind *who* she or he is communicating with and customize the report and findings to that person or persons. A marketing executive who has come up through the financial ranks may appreciate a more statistical presentation. However, an executive with a sales background may require a less statistical approach.

Chapter Summary

A well-designed research study can provide the answers to almost any marketing dilemma. Marketing decision makers need good, reliable information as the basis for marketing strategies. Internal information, information that comes from within the company itself, typically is in the form of company reports. External data is information that has been generated from outside the company. All of this information must be collected, organized, and made available in a usable form for management. Today, companies use marketing information systems and decision support systems to gather data from internal and external sources, synthesize the information, and disseminate it to decision makers.

Syndicated service firms specialize in providing secondary data, or previously published data to organizations. Full-service research firms specialize in providing primary data, or information collected specifically for a purpose. The marketing research process includes problem definition, research design and data collection (via observation, survey, or experimentatal methods), and analysis, interpretation, and presentation of findings. A researcher must keep in mind the company's needs and the study's objectives, analyze the data accordingly, and present the findings in a clear, understandable manner.

Notes ◆

1. Peter Bennett (ed.), *Dictionary of Marketing Terms* (Chicago: American Marketing Association, 1988), 184.
2. Ajay K. Kohli and Bernard Jaworski, "Market Orientation: The Construct, Research Propositions, and Managerial Implications," *Journal of Marketing,* 54 (April 1990), 1–18.
3. Cyndee Miller, "Parents Tend to Buy What Their Children See on TV," *Marketing News,* January 31, 1994, 2.
4. "TV Audiences Are Happy," *Marketing News,* November 22, 1993, 1.

Study Questions ◆

1. Which of the following is the best description of a marketing information system (MIS)?
   a. A MIS is just another name for a marketing research study such as a telephone survey.
   b. A MIS is the name given to information about a company's competitors.
   c. A MIS is a company's marketing-relevant database consisting of internal and external data that are available in computer form and accessible for decision making purposes.
   d. A MIS is just another name for a company's management information system. Both the managagment and marketing information systems are used for identical purposes.

2. _____ data is information collected by or for an organization to address that organization's *specific* research question or needs.
   a. Primary
   b. Secondary
   c. Marketing research
   d. Marketing information system

3. The collection of data to gain a greater understanding of the research question is termed
   a. secondary data collection.
   b. primary data collection.
   c. syndicated research.
   d. exploratory research.

4. Which of the following marketing research techniques would be least acceptable if the research purpose were to determine

buying motives that underlie consumers' product choices?

a. survey research

b. experimental research

c. observation research

d. All of these are equally acceptable.

5. Which of the following survey techniques can generally be expected to yield the highest response rate?

a. telephone interviews

b. mail questionnaires

c. personal interviews

d. There are no notable differences among these techniques with respect to response rates.

6. A specialized form of interviewing where a moderator leads a small informal group discussion is called a

a. miniature interview.

b. focus group.

c. syndication group.

d. None of the above.

7. Which of the following is *not* an advantage of primary data collection?

a. The data are current.

b. The data fit the specific purpose of the marketing issue at hand.

c. The marketer has complete control over the research methodology.

d. The data are assured of being representative of the population and completely valid.

8. Compared to primary data, which of the following is not an advantage of secondary data?

a. Secondary data are less expensive.

b. Secondary are are available more quickly.

c. Secondary data better fit the researcher's exact needs.

d. All of these are relative advantages of secondary data.

9. Another term for "population" as it relates to the sampling aspect of data collection is

a. sampling frame.

b. strata.

c. cluster.

d. None of these terms are interchangeable with population.

10. A researcher has a complete list of all the students who are advertising majors at a certain university. One hundred of these students are randomly sampled by selecting numbers from a random number table. The researcher has employed which sampling method to select these 100 names?
    a. cluster sampling
    b. stratified sampling
    c. purposive sampling
    d. simple random sampling

11. A researcher has a complete list of all the city blocks in a certain town. The researcher randomly samples three blocks and then interviews every homeowner who resides in each of the three blocks. Which sampling method has the researcher used?
    a. cluster sampling
    b. stratified sampling
    c. purposive sampling
    d. simple random sampling

12. A researcher is interested in determining the average salary of major league baseball players. To save time, the researcher decides to select a sample of 60 ball players. Rather than taking a random sample of all players, he decides to delineate the players into three groups of positions—infielders, outfielders, and pitchers—and to take separate random samples of 20 players from each category. What sampling procedure has the researcher used?
    a. cluster sampling
    b. stratified sampling
    c. purposive sampling
    d. simple random sampling

13. A student is conducting a little study to determine how many soft drinks students in her dorm consume on average each day. She stops the first 25 students she sees and asks them to indicate how many soft drinks they consumer per day on average. Her sampling method is
    a. simple random sampling.
    b. complex random sampling.
    c. unpurposive sampling.
    d. convenience sampling.

CHAPTER 4

Consumer Behavior

Chapter Objectives

Environmental Influences

Individual Differences and Psychological Processes

Chapter Summary

The successful conduct of marketing requires the practitioner to have a keen understanding of his or her target markets and the factors that propel customers to action or inhibit their behavior. This is no easy task inasmuch as customer behavior often is complex, dynamic, situationally specific, and, in short, unpredictable. Indeed, understanding marketplace behavior is not unlike attempting to comprehend any complex human behavior. Why do some people commit crimes? Why do some marriages end in divorce while others last a lifetime? Why do some consumers purchase clothing at expensive boutiques, whereas others prefer to shop at TJ Maxx and other deep-discounters? None of these illustrative questions have simple answers. Nonetheless, these questions intrigue scholars and motivate practitioners to seek answers. Of course, our concern is not with human behavior in general, but only with marketing and the buyer behavior that occurs within that domain.

As a foundation for the ensuing discussion, consider the situation confronting Mike and Angie, who are in the market for a new van. Mike and Angie, who are parents of one preschooler and a second-grader, have been considering the purchase of a van for several years. Now that their 1988 Ford Taurus station wagon is approaching the limit of its usability, they realize that a new purchase is imminent. This couple has a family income of nearly $50,000. Both Mike and Angie were raised in middle-class families and live as such in the suburbs.

Mike and Angie are very motivated to buy a new van. Angie is tired of loading two small children in and out of their old wagon. Mike is concerned about his family's safety; he feels the wagon may not be the best protection in case of an accident.

Many of Mike and Angie's friends in their neighborhood already have minivans. These friends always offer to drive Angie and the children since they have more room in their vans. Angie is often embarrassed that she cannot reciprocate since she does not have enough room in her wagon to take additional passengers.

Mike's family, who lives nearby, is also encouraging the couple to buy a new van. His brothers would like to occasionally borrow the van when they need to haul things. And Mike's parents who don't like to drive at night would like to occasionally hitch a ride with the family, something they cannot do with the wagon.

Mike decided he would do the groundwork for the purchase, since it was nearly impossible to shop with two small children. Mike visited many showrooms around the city and spoke to several salespeople. He gathered information such as brochures and fliers describing all of the available features and colors for the various minivans. Mike became very involved in this purchase and tried to learn as much as he could about the available products.

After talking to several minivan owners in the neighborhood and at work, Mike read up on minivans. *Consumer Reports* published an issue recently on minivans that Mike found in the library. He gathered and organized all of his information and presented it to Angie.

Angie didn't care which model was chosen as long as it had built-in car seats, tinted windows, and air conditioning for the children's safety and comfort. Mike wanted a V-6 engine and an automatic transmission. And both were interested in keeping their monthly payments as low as possible.

Mike and Angie decided to purchase a Plymouth Voyager from a dealership across town that offered an attractive financing package in addition to all of the features the couple wanted. They purchased the minivan the next day.

This example illustrates the fact that a great number of factors influence buyer behavior, especially on major purchases. All marketers must attempt to fully understand the factors that influence buyer behavior. In this chapter we examine the underpinnings of consumer behavior. The word *consumer* refers to people who purchase to fulfill their individual or family consumption needs. The following chapter explores consumption behavior from the perspective of businesses and other non-consumer, organizational buyers. Regardless of perspective, a good understanding of customers, their needs, and buying behavior is critical to successful and profitable marketing.

This chapter delineates the various factors that influence consumer behavior into *environmental influences* (e.g. culture, social class) and *individual differences* and *psychological processes* (motivation, attitudes, personality characteristics, and so forth). Following this general introduction into the factors that influence consumer behavior, we then examine a model of consumer decision making. Finally, the chapter classifies and describes different types of consumer behavior based on the complexity and frequency with which the behavior occurs.[1]

Exhibit 4.1   Environmental Influences on Consumer Behavior

1. Culture
2. Social class
3. Personal influences
4. Family
5. Situational influences

Environmental Influences

Individuals do not behave in isolation, but rather are influenced by various external forces, or environmental influences. The environmental factors that influence consumer behavior are culture, social class, personal influences, family, and situational influences (see Exhibit 4.1). Any one or even all of these factors can act together in determining a consumer's buying decision.

Culture

Social scientists conceptualize **culture** as the set of values, beliefs, artifacts, and other meaningful symbols that facilitate communication and enable people to function within their environments. It was previously pointed out in Chapter 2 that various values are important to today's American consumer: self-respect, security, warm relationships with family and friends, a sense of accomplishment, self-fulfillment, respect from others, a sense of belonging, and the importance of having fun and excitement.[2]

Consider, for example, the value placed on security. The rise in the crime rate and attendant media attention has resulted in many consumers feeling insecure and unsafe. Security is a valued commodity; consumers go to great lengths to protect themselves and their property. Sales of locks, firearms, automobile security devices (e.g., The Club), and other products are propelled by the pursuit of safety. The important point to realize is that behavior follows from values. What consumers value directs what they purchase. All of the above-listed values play important roles in influencing consumer

Exhibit 4.2   Changing Values in Western Civilization

Traditional Values	New Values
Self-denial ethic	Self-fulfillment ethic
Higher standard of living	Better quality of life
Traditional sex roles	Blurring of sex roles
Accepted definition of success	Individualized definition of success
Traditional family life	Alternative families
Faith in industry, institutions	Self-reliance
Live to work	Work to live
Hero worship	Love of ideas
Expansionism	Pluralism
Patriotism	Less nationalistic
Unparalleled growth	Growing sense of limits
Industrial growth	Information/service growth
Receptivity to technology	Technology orientation

Source: Joseph T. Plummer, "Changing Values," *The Futurist*, 23 (January–February 1989), 10. Reproduced with permission from *The Futurist*, published by the World Future Society, 7910 Woodmont, Suite 450, Bethesda, MD 20814.

behavior, the products and brands we purchase, and the types of stores from which we purchase.

Changes in values can alter responses to advertising and buying behavior. Joseph Plummer, a noted advertising researcher, identifies a variety of the changes that are occurring in the 1990s throughout the Western world (see Exhibit 4.2).[3] These changing values are responsible for many fundamental alterations in consumer behavior, and, in turn, influence the actions undertaken by advertisers and other marketing practitioners in their efforts to successfully influence consumer behavior.

Marketers must continuously monitor changes in values because any change will affect consumer preferences for product categories (e.g., a four-wheel-drive vehicle versus a sedan), specific brands (e.g., a Ford Bronco versus a Jeep), the price consumers are willing to pay, the kinds of stores where they prefer to shop, and so on.

Social Class

Social class represents another environmental force on individual consumer behavior. A **social class** is a group of individuals who share similar economic status and who, accordingly, exhibit some similarity in their consumer behavior. One's social class influences what one is able to buy and, perhaps more importantly, what one aspires to buy. A consumer in the upper class, for example, might desire to own and can afford to buy a Rolex watch (versus a Timex), a Mercedes sedan (versus a Ford Taurus), or an Armani suit (versus a John Henry). Consumers in both the middle and lower classes may have the desire to own them, but cannot afford these expensive, status-oriented products.

Several variables determine one's social class; however, the single best determinant of class status is *occupation*. A prestigious occupation usually commands honor and respect. Great emphasis is placed on what one does. When meeting new acquaintances at a social gathering, a way of "breaking the ice" and starting a conversation is to inquire about a person's job. One's occupation affects how one lives and what one buys.

In the context of social class, occupation does not equate to income. A person can earn a high income yet be assigned to a lower social class. A factory worker, for example, may earn more income than a college-educated government official. The official, though, is considered to be in a higher social class.

Other variables that are correlated with or determine one's social class include

- wealth—how much a person is worth
- personal prestige—how much respect peers have for that person
- associations—who a person spends time and shares activities with
- power—a person's ability to exercise control.[4]

Over the years, sociologists and other social scientists have developed schemes that classify Americans into various social classes. A particularly insightful scheme is the following attributable to Gilbert and Kahl.[5] The relative size of each class is shown in parentheses, and salient class characteristics are identified.

Upper Americans

The Capitalist Class (1%). With their income coming mostly from assets earned or inherited, the investment decisions of the capitalist class shape the national economy. This class enjoys prestigious university connections. Bill Gates, the CEO of Microsoft, and J. Paul Getty are examples of the capitalist class.

Upper Middle Class (14%). The upper middle class is comprised of upper managers, professionals, and medium businesspeople who are college educated. Their family income ideally runs nearly twice the national average. Tom Hanks portrayed a member of the upper middle class in his Academy Award winning role as a lawyer in the film *Philadelphia*.

Middle Americans

Middle Class (33%). The middle class is comprised of middle-level white-collar and top-level blue-collar workers. Most have a high school or college education. Their income is somewhat above the national average. The Keaton family on the television sitcom *Family Ties* represents the middle class.

Working Class (32%). Middle-level blue-collar and lower-level white-collar workers are considered the working class. Their incomes and education levels run slightly below the national average. The characters in the television show *Roseanne* exemplify the working class.

Marginal and Lower Americans

The Working Poor (11–12%). Though this class is below mainstream America in their standard of living, the working poor exist just above the poverty line. They are low-paid service workers and operatives who have some high school education.

The Underclass (8-9%). The underclass depend primarily on the welfare system for sustenance. Their standard of living is below the poverty line. They lack regular employment and schooling. The hundreds of thousands of homeless people who live on American streets are part of the underclass.

Marketers recognize the differences in buying behavior among the social classes. For example, advertisements often use models whose clothing and demeanor reflect people in social classes whom

MARKETING HIGHLIGHTS

Delphi Technique Can Work

A significant part in the professional life of all marketers is devoted to tackling problems concerning new products.

The high level of risk peculiar to new products has led to adopting step-by-step methods that allow checking consumers' degree of consensus at the various stages of development.

Nevertheless, comparing research projects on new products carried out in 1968 and 1980 (Booz, Allen & Hamilton, ESOMAR seminar 1983) with the 1993 ones (EFO Group, Marketing News, June 21, 1993), the percentage of failures still remains extremely high, although methodological improvements were introduced (for example, working with project teams, a method adopted a few years ago by Colgate and Chrysler).

One of the weakest points in the development process of new products is that consumer needs are measured in a static, not dynamic, way, which is to say that great importance is attached to the analysis of the present without adequately considering that the greatest competitive advantages are achieved by satisfying needs that are still embryonic, which will give birth to real markets, only some years later.

According to the current approach, consumers are forced to judged new products on the basis of their current range of needs, which generally are met well by existing products.

The result of this approach is that new products usually spring from a priority analysis of the present. Products are derived from the analysis of habits rather than from the study of evolving needs.

If we changed the perspective and the focus of the analysis, shifting from current to future needs, we would gain a competitive advantage in the satisfaction of emerging needs rather than in a better satisfaction of consolidated needs. This would ensure the loyalty of the trendsetters and arouse the interest of the trend followers.

The basic problem is to find a method to address the so called market weak signals indicating a current change so that the concept of the new product to be developed then could be based on such signals.

The tool was found in the Delphi Method. Such a method was developed by the Rand Corp. in the 1950s and 1960s and, though it initially was used for military purposes, it subsequently found several other fields of application ranging from territory planning to consumer goods.

It was introduced into Italy in the early 1970s and used for a large number of significant research projects carried out for consumer goods and services.

For one project, Delphi research was used to develop a food product with a long shelf-life that did not require cooking or warming up.

The research took the following steps:
1. Analysis of the Delphi results, mapping out the various

the advertiser is attempting to appeal. Likewise, retailers regularly cater to select social classes. For example, Neiman Marcus appeals to upper Americans, whereas Sears, Kmart, and Wal-Mart are oriented more to middle Americans and lower classes.

evolving consumption opportunities (and their relevant motives) pertaining to the company's business idea. Although food habits are among the slowest to change, the impact caused by the change in working hours and kinds of jobs (less industry and more services), the population's aging, and a greater attention to health-oriented food are causing changes that will not take many years (five to seven) to occur.

2. Definition of possible alternatives of product concepts, in line with the changes expected in the near future.

3. Identification of weak signals coming from present behaviors by analyzing existing research projects on food habits. Socio-demographic research showed that a few behavioral patterns, for which the Delphi method expected a wide spread during a span of 10 years, were already spreading among population classes with less traditional lifestyles.

4. Confirmation of weak signals and identification of products—five product lines were found—that share a few basic elements such as recipes, ingredients, and service level with the new line concept. Sales trends among the five products showed they had small markets, but trends were favorable.

5. Defining the contents of the concept to convert it into a briefing

for R&D. Elements were separated into these categories: basic ingredients to use; their qualitative features; importance of organoleptic elements (smell, color, taste); importance of esthetic aspects; physical elements of packaging; packaging size; product service level; and emotional elements (naturalness, lightness, taste, health, etc.). Priorities were assigned to the elements because some of them caused technical or economic problems not in line with the product budget.

6. Identification of the positioning, which would influence both the recipe and advertising. Delphi research provided help in determining which food style would be dominant in the years to come and identifying the value system it was based on so that a particular nutritional area could be chosen.

The next steps were the usual ones: elaboration of the recipes, prototypes at experimental cooking level, and the product-concept test, which showed an extremely higher level of consensus on the concept with respect to the results of similar research projects.)

Source: Gianni Bolongaro, "Delphi Technique Can Work for New Product Development," *Marketing News*, January 3, 1994, 11. Reprinted with permission from *Marketing News*, published by the American Marketing Association, Gianni Bologaro, January 3, 1994.

Personal Influences

All consumers are influenced by those with whom they associate, either their reference groups or family and friends. A group of people, or even an individual, who either directly or indirectly represents a group is a **reference group.** A reference group has certain values and standards that dictate how its members should act. Members are expected to and usually abide by these standards to remain in good standing within the group. The Bloods, for example, are a powerful gang in Los Angeles. Members are expected to wear red, the gang's color, at all times. A reference group may require members to behave in certain ways, such as hazing pledges by a fraternity. The members perform these acts if it is important to them to be part of the group. Members of a reference group may hold a certain value as important. The Sierra Club is a reference group for people who value environmental issues. An individual who personifies a certain reference group may act as a spokesperson, influencing product selection. Rush Limbaugh, a radio and television personality, embodies the conservative reference group and endorses certain products. Reference groups are powerful influences on individuals in terms of what products and brands we prefer and choose.

Word-of-mouth (WOM) influence from one person to another is prevalent in the marketplace. A consumer is most likely to accept and respond to word-of-mouth influences when one or more of the following conditions exist:

1. The consumer lacks sufficient information to make an adequately informed choice.
2. The product is complex and difficult to evaluate using objective criteria. Hence, the experience of others serves as "vicarious trial."
3. The person lacks ability to evaluate the product or service, no matter how information is disseminated and presented.
4. Other sources of information (e.g., salespeople) are perceived as having low credibility.
5. An influential person is more accessible than other sources and hence can be consulted with a saving of time and effort.
6. Strong social ties are in existence between the consumer and his or her referent.
7. The individual has a high need for social approval.[6]

Many studies support the fact that personal influence rates higher in influencing behavior than advertising and other marketing efforts.[7] Positive word-of-mouth can make or break a product. Firms often attempt to stimulate positive word-of-mouth among consumers. The key to generating good WOM is the use of "cheerleaders," that is, consumers who will get the talk started. In the movie industry, consumers who are most likely to love a new movie are targeted for movie screenings. Cheerleading is stimulated in the book industry by giving free copies of new books to a select group of leaders. For example, *Megatrends*, a leading seller by John Naisbitt, was given to more than 1,000 CEOs of major corporations. The book became a "must read" within weeks of publication by literally thousands of businesspeople.[8]

Family

Understanding the family and how families buy and consume products is very important in the study of consumer behavior. A **family** is a group of two or more individuals related by blood or marriage. Families act together in purchasing many products, especially expensive ones. For example, in buying a new car, inclusion of certain features such as a CD player may be heavily influenced by the teenagers in the family, whereas a parent may be more concerned with gas mileage and safety features.

Family members are also major influencers of individual member's purchases. Although traditionally the mother is the primary grocery shopper, the children and father will influence her decision of what to buy. Each family member has individual wants and needs. But the family, as a whole, operates with limited resources. The wants and needs of the family and the wants and needs of the individuals are prioritized in determining what products and brands to buy.

Who in the family decides what products will be purchased? Different family members act in different roles in buying decisions. Some typical roles are

- *Initiator/Gatekeeper*—the family member who initiates thinking about buying products and the gathering of information to aid the decision.

- *Influencer*—the individual whose opinions are sought concerning criteria the family should use in purchases and which products or brands most likely fit those evaluative criteria.

- *Decider*—the person, or persons, with the financial authority or power to choose how the family's money will be spent and the products or brands that will be chosen.
- *Buyer*—the person who acts as purchasing agent. He or she visits the store, calls the supplier, writes the check, brings the products into the home, and so on.
- *User*—the person or persons who use the product.

One member is not restricted to only a single role. A child can be both the influencer and user of a product while the parent is both the decider and buyer. It is prudent for marketers to direct communications to all parties in the buying process rather than focusing exclusively on buyers or users. Doing so typically requires the use of multiple advertising media.

Who is more influential in family buying decisions, the husband or the wife? This, of course, varies based on the particular family, the type of product being bought, and the circumstances surrounding the purchase. Although a majority of buying decisions are made by either the husband or wife, children and teenagers are exerting much greater influence than ever before. This influence may be due in part to the increase in households headed by a single parent. The single parent may rely more heavily on children's input because another parent is not present in the household. Also, children often know more about certain products than do their parents (e.g., VCRs and other electronic items) and accordingly have a major say in the choice of brands, features, and even prices.

Situational Influences

Situational influences greatly affect consumer behavior. A **situational influence** results from those factors that are specific to the time and place circumstances of a particular buying choice. A consumer may behave one way in one situation, or set of circumstances, and the same consumer may act differently in another situation. Situations directly influence how consumers behave. For instance, a consumer may buy Budweiser as his preferred brand for home consumption; however, in different social surroundings this same consumer may order Heineken's to impress his friends. The general point to appreciate is that much of consumer behavior is situationally determined rather than pre-planned.

Five major forms of situational influences affect consumer behavior:[9]

Physical surroundings. These tangible properties include geographic location, decor, sounds, aromas, lighting, weather, and visible configurations of merchandise. What the consumer chooses to buy (or not buy) is greatly influenced by the physical features of the buying context. For example, one may be willing to pay a relatively high price for a product when merchandised in an elegant boutique located in a tony shopping district, but not be willing to pay even a moderate price for the same item in a mass-merchandise outlet.

Social surroundings. The presence or absence of other people in a shopping situation can influence how a consumer behaves. When shopping with a daring friend, for example, one might purchase an outfit that she would not consider buying on her own.

Time. Temporal properties of the situation—such as the time of day, day of week, month, or season—can greatly affect one's shopping interest, purchase preferences, and actual choices. A person buying a swimsuit in December for a cruise might be willing to pay more for the suit then than in July.

Task. Task factors are the particular goals or objectives consumers have in a situation. For instance, a person shopping to buy a coffee maker as a wedding gift for a friend is in a different situation than when shopping to purchase the identical product for one's own personal use. As such, the criteria that influence brand choice and price paid likely vary across the two situations.

Antecedent states. Antecedent states are the temporary moods (e.g., anxiety, pleasantness, excitement) or conditions (e.g., cash on hand, fatigue) that the consumer brings to the situation. Needless to say, factors such as one's level of shopping excitement or level of fatigue can play a major role in determining what the consumer does in a shopping context.

As further illustration of the role of situational factors, consider how consumers' beverage preferences are affected by time of day. The diagram on the following page illustrates the influence time has on one consumer's beverage preference at different times of the day.

Marketers have limited control over the situational factors that dictate consumer choice behavior. It nonetheless is prudent for

Beer   Wine   Iced Tea   Water   Soft Drinks   Hot Tea   Fruit Juices   Coffee

Least preferred as part of breakfast   *Most preferred*

Fruit Juices   Wine   Beer   Hot Tea   Water   Iced Tea   Coffee   Soft Drinks

Least preferred as part of lunch   *Most preferred*

Fruit Juices   Hot Tea   Coffee   Soft Drinks   Iced Tea   Beer   Wine   Water

Least preferred as part of dinner   *Most preferred*

Fruit Juices   Water   Soft Drinks   Iced Tea   Beer   Wine   Hot Tea   Coffee

Least preferred after dinner   *Most preferred*

marketers to make adaptations to the situational factors. Among
many other possibilities, this may mean that a company should
expand its product offerings to satisfy demand variability across
usage situations. Another form of adaptation is to vary advertising
messages at different times or in different contexts so as to provide
information that is most congruent with the situation.

Individual Differences and Psychological Processes

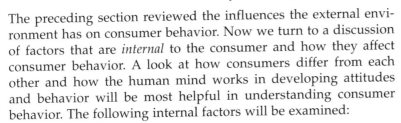

The preceding section reviewed the influences the external environment has on consumer behavior. Now we turn to a discussion of factors that are *internal* to the consumer and how they affect consumer behavior. A look at how consumers differ from each other and how the human mind works in developing attitudes and behavior will be most helpful in understanding consumer behavior. The following internal factors will be examined:

- motivation and involvement
- learning
- information processing
- knowledge and attitudes
- personality and psychographics

Motivation and Involvement

At the core of consumer behavior is the question: What motivates consumers? **Motivation** is the driving force that pushes a consumer to buy a product in an effort to satisfy his or her needs. **Involvement** is a specific form of motivation and represents how important, or personally relevant, a product is to the consumer in a given situation. When a consumer perceives value in a product, motivation is present to take some action and become involved with the product. Involvement is manifest in the form of searching for information, seeking out advice from others, or comparing a brand to competitive offerings. Marketers hope for a highly motivated consumer with a high level of involvement. This consumer will be the most likely to carefully attend marketers' messages and possibly be influenced to purchase the promoted brand.

Understanding and fulfilling consumer needs, or motives, is a basic goal of marketing. The summary in Exhibit 4.3 is a broad classification of needs that underlie consumer behavior.

The physiological and safety needs are the most basic in human beings. People will go to great lengths to be comfortable, secure, and safe. After these needs are satisfied, humans look for love and acceptance by others. Humans then strive to make something of themselves, which encompasses the needs for achievement,

Exhibit 4.3   A Summary Classification of Consumer Needs

1. *Physiological:* the fundamentals of survival, including hunger, thirst, and other bodily needs.
2. *Safety:* concern over physical survival and safety.
3. *Affiliation and belongingness:* a need to be accepted by others, to be an important person to them.
4. *Achievement:* a basic desire for success in meeting personal goals.
5. *Power:* a desire to gain control over one's destiny as well as that of others.
6. *Self-expression:* the need to develop freedom in self-expression and to be perceived by others as significant.
7. *Cognition:* the desire to achieve self-actualization through knowing, understanding, systematizing, and constructing a system of values.
8. *Variety seeking:* maintenance of preferred level of physiological arousal and stimulation often expressed as variety seeking.
9. *Attribution of causality:* estimation or attribution of the causality of events and actions.

Source: James F. Engel, Roger D. Blackwell, and Paul W. Miniard, *Consumer Behavior,* 7th ed. (Ft. Worth, TX: Dryden, 1993), 285.

power, self-expression, and cognition. And finally, the needs to explore and analyze fulfill the person.

Marketers cannot change motivations and needs; marketers can only understand and accept them as part of consumer behavior. Thus, marketers must identify what needs their products satisfy and create an effective marketing mix to convince the consumer of their product's value and, if true, that it has greater need-satisfying potential than do competitive offerings.

Typically every product category includes a variety of brands, and it is common for different brands to appeal to distinct buying motives. Consider the brand appeal of different kinds of wine. Some inexpensive brands appeal to heavy drinkers or alcoholics who want cheap wine because of the amount they consume. Marketers of most wines appeal to consumers' needs to affiliate and belong, claiming their brands are the sociable brand or the "in" drink. On the other hand, some wine connoisseurs seek to satisfy self-expression needs when purchasing a unique wine that is unknown to one's colleagues. In other instances, wine drinkers attempt to fulfill their variety-seeking needs by exploring the vast number of different vintages available in many wine stores.

Learning

Learning takes place in the marketplace just as it does in all aspects of life. In the marketplace, learning occurs when consumers adapt their beliefs, attitudes, and behavior to make sense of new information received from advertisements, packages, sales representatives, or friends and family.[10] It is important to recognize that learning includes the learning of attitudes and other cognitive elements as well as the learning of overt behavioral responses.

General learning theory in psychology and treatments of the subject in consumer literature distinguish two major types of learning: cognitive and associative. The **cognitive orientation** views learning as an active process whereby the consumer forms hypotheses about consumption alternatives, acquires and encodes information, and integrates the new information with preexisting beliefs.[11] The next section, which discusses consumer information processing, typifies the cognitive form of learning.

Associative learning, the second major type of learning, occurs when consumers draw connections between environmental events. One form of associative learning is **classical conditioning.** This form of learning results when consumers develop associations rather effortlessly between a conditioned stimulus (CS) and a biologically salient (e.g., food, fragrance) or symbolically salient (e.g., patriotic symbols such as flags, monuments, and historical persons) unconditioned stimulus (US). In a consumer behavior context, CSs are brands, products, and other consumption objects; USs include celebrities, music, beautiful outdoor scenery, and other salient stimuli. Through their repeated association, the consumer learns to associate the two stimuli, and the brand, or CS, ultimately acquires the ability to evoke a response that is similar to a response elicited by the US itself.[12] For example, if a certain brand of perfume were always advertised in context of a glamorous Hollywood personality, like Elizabeth Taylor, then over time the brand may acquire a sense of glamour itself. The consumer has in a rather automatic manner learned to associate the brand with the famous person who endorses it.

CAPTAINS OF INDUSTRY

Sheryl Leach

President

Lyons Group

Date of Birth: 1953

Career Path: A former teacher and mother decided to produce home videos that would appeal to her two-year-old son. She enlisted the aid of friend and former colleague, Kathy Parker, and together they researched the market, discovered that videos were in demand, and formed their own company, the Lyons Group. They originally had the idea of featuring a teddy bear, but changed to a dinosaur after observing Parker's son's interest in dinosaurs at a local museum exhibit.[a]

Profile: Spunky, creative, with a strong belief in the marketability of her product, and resourceful in her marketing approach. "We didn't have the muscle and money for a traditional marketing campaign. And that turned out to be a good thing, because we had to find untraditional ways."[b]

Personal: She hopes that Barney's success will spawn similar shows and characters whose message is one of love and nurturing aimed at this age group to replace the violence and strife in current children's entertainment.

––––––––––

Sheryl Leach is the creator of Barney the Dinosaur, the pudgy purple and green Tyrannosaurus Rex and star of the PBS children's show, "Barney and Friends." She came up with the idea for Barney while stuck in freeway traffic outside of Dallas, Texas. Leach was frustrated by the lack of appealing videos for her two-year-old son's age group. She linked up with DLM Inc., a small educational and religious publisher that had recently built a commercial video production studio in Allen, Texas, Leach's home town. Armed with her training as a teacher, she enlisted the help of Kathy Parker, also a mother and former educator, now Barney's executive producer, and videographer Dennis DeShazer to make the first Barney videos. Marketing the product proved to be the hardest task for the Barney team.

They first called on Toys 'R' Us, targeting buyers who had children and asking them to play the tape for their children. The retailer agreed to stock the video, but it didn't sell at first. Leach then got the ZIP codes of all the Toys 'R' Us stores that carried the tape and bought mailing lists of preschools and day-care centers in those areas. They sent fliers into the preschools, to the parents, and to the teachers, letting them know where they could purchase the tape if they liked it. The flier included the name and location of the store nearest that particular school. In this way they encouraged foot traffic into the stores, and the tapes began to sell.

Following on this success, Leach and her team gift-wrapped the video in luminescent paper, tied it with a big bow and sent it to buyers at other key retailers. "Even if they didn't watch it, it just made a statement about some creativity that we used in our marketing," Leach recalled.[c]

The Barney team also engaged in some "guerrilla marketing" techniques. Using market research that showed most mothers with preschool children shopped in grocery and drug stores 2 to 3 times a week, they wanted their products to be available there. "Barney's audience was in the shopping cart, and our bet was that they already knew who Barney was from their day-care center or their preschool," Leach explained.[d] They practically had to go store by store to convince each manager to stock their videos, but the effort was worthwhile. In the first two years, about 40% of their sales came from food and drug markets.

Leach secured a national promotion with Blockbuster Entertainment Corp. by stealth. The company headquarters agreed to let Leach try a local promotion with one of their regional managers. She called all six regions and by the end of the day had her national promotion.

The story goes that the four-year-old daughter of Larry Rifkin, a Connecticut Public Television programming executive, saw the videos and fell in love with Barney. Rifkin followed up with the Lyons Group to produce 30 episodes of the show for PBS. "Barney & Friends" has grown to rating second only to "Sesame Street" among PBS kids' shows in the Nielsen ratings. Barney videos have become best sellers in the children's market, and sales of Barney books introduced in 1993 topped one million copies each in the first six months in print. Barney's first record sold more than two million copies in 1993, after being released in August of the same year.

Barney appeals to preschoolers but remains an enigma to many adults. But when PBS considered dropping funding for the show in May of 1992, protests flooded in from station executives across the country as well as cards and phone calls from distraught viewers and their parents, and PBS continued to fund the program.

Not only is Barney popular on TV, his image on a variety of merchandise has brought in millions of dollars. JCPenney signed an exclusive contract to sell Barney-licensed merchandise in 1992 and earned more than $50 million from Barney-licensed goods that year, but other retailers were permitted to sell the products in 1993 and complained that the supply couldn't keep up with the demand. The Lyons Group has made efforts to protect the dinosaur as a classic character and to control the marketing of Barney products. Beth Ryan, manager of communications and public relations at the Lyons Group listed three conditions for making licensing decisions: 1) Is it for the good of the children? 2) Is it good for Barney? 3) Is it a good business decision? The Lyons Group has earned a reputation for closely monitoring where the character appears, limiting selling to the department store tier of retailing, and controlling how he is presented. Even with their tight control, however, knock-offs have popped up everywhere.[e]

Marketing is not "grass roots" for Leach and her team anymore. They are busy producing more Barney episodes for PBS as well as a radio program set to begin in 1994, a prime-time network TV special, and a feature-length movie due for release in 1995. Leach plans to produce foreign language versions of the show for the overseas market and is planning to publish multimedia Barney computer software. This is one dinosaur that doesn't seem headed for extinction any time soon.

[a] "Barney," Newsmakers 1993, *1993 Almanac of Famous People*, October 1993; Issue 4.
[b] Adrienne Ward Fawcett,"The Marketing 100," *Advertising Age,* July 5, 1993, pg. S-20.
[c] Ted Bunker, *Investor's Business Daily,* December 8, 1993, Leader's Success section, pg. 1.
[d] *Investor's Business Daily,* December 8, 1993.
[e] Susan Reda,"The Barney Boom," *STORES,* June 1993, pp. 56-57.

Exhibit 4.4   The Stages of Information Processing

---

1. Exposure

2. Attention

3. Comprehension

4. Acceptance

5. Retention

Source: William J. McGuire, "Some Internal Psychological Factors Influencing Consumer Choice, *Journal of Consumer Research,* 2 (March 1976), 302–319.

Information Processing

Consumers are bombarded with hundreds of stimuli every day of their lives. Everywhere we look, we are exposed to products, advertisements, logos, and other marketing messages. But how one consumer reacts to marketing stimuli will be different from how another consumer reacts. Consumers react differently because they process information differently. **Information processing** is the process by which a person receives, interprets, stores in memory, and later retrieves stored information.[13] Information processing is comprised of five stages (see Exhibit 4.4).

Exposure occurs when relevant marketplace information (e.g., an advertisement) reaches one or more of the consumers' five senses. You are exposed to a television advertisement when you see the action and hear the sound.

Attention involves allocating limited processing capacity to a particular stimulus among the array of stimuli impinging on the consumer's senses. To attend is to focus mental effort on a particular stimulus from all those that are physically present.

Comprehension is the interpretation, or perception, of what the stimulus (e.g., a friend's comments about a product) means, implies, or represents.

Acceptance is the extent to which a consumer agrees with a marketing message that has been attended and comprehended. Often consumers engage in subvocal activity and form *cognitive responses* (e.g., counter arguments) that result in rejecting a communicators' efforts at persuasion.

Retention represents the transfer of marketplace information into long-term memory.

To better understand each stage and the overall process, think about what happens when you are watching a television program that is interrupted by a string of commercials. If you remain in the room during this intermission, you theoretically are *exposed* to all of the commercials that are aired. That is, you hear and see the action taking place in the commercial. You may *attend* to a particular commercial, especially if, as earlier discussed, you are involved in the product category. In attending the commercial, you think about what is being said or portrayed; your mind is focused on the advertised brand and perhaps the music, scenery, and people who are acting out the commercial. Your understanding of what is communicated results in some *comprehension* of what the brand is, what its attributes and benefits are, and how it might fit into your consumption scheme. If the message is presented in a sincere fashion and, say, you trust and respect the celebrity who endorses the brand, then you are likely to *accept* all or at least some of what is said about the brand. To the extent the commercial is memorable, for example, as a result of the enchanting setting in which the commercial is filmed, then chances are you will *retain* the major sales message that has been delivered about the brand. At some late date, you might *retrieve* this information from memory, perhaps facilitated by a point-of-purchase cue, and use it in making a brand choice decision.

In actuality, consumer information processing is considerably more complex than this, but this description provides some inkling of the overall process and the specific stages involved. Successful marketing communications efforts require that all information processing stages be influenced and that the marketing communicator's messages go beyond achieving mere exposure. It is critical that marketing messages grab the consumer's attention, facilitate comprehension of the intended message, and be accepted and incorporated into long-term memory for later use in a brand-selection decision.

Knowledge and Attitudes

Knowledge represents the information consumers have stored in their memories regarding products, prices, brands, and retail outlets. Knowledge for a particular brand ranges from mere awareness of the brand name, to a fundamental understanding of what the brand looks like, to detailed knowledge of how the brand performs and operates. For example, a consumer may have heard of a Dodge Caravan. A more knowledgeable consumer is able to point out the

Exhibit 4.5   A Consumer's Knowledge Structure, or Schema, for L'eggs Pantyhose

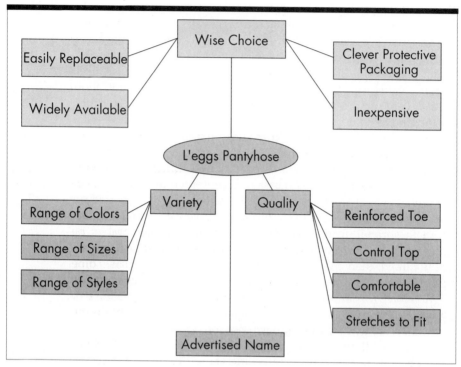

Caravan in traffic. A very knowledgeable consumer can name several features: safety air bags, built-in child safety seats, removable seats, V-6 engine, automatic locking system, and reclining seats.

Memory organizes knowledge in associative networks or knowledge structures referred to as **schemas.** Consumers store schemas for general product categories (e.g., beverages) as well as for particular brands (e.g., Coca-Cola). Exhibit 4.5 illustrates one consumer's schema for L'eggs Pantyhose.

The consumer's knowledge about particular products and brands is the basis on which attitudes toward these consumption objects are both formed and changed. From a marketing perspective, an **attitude** represents a person's positive or negative feeling toward, or evaluative judgment of, a product, brand, or other consumption object. Attitudes are important to the marketer because they influence behavior and also, when measured, provide

Exhibit 4.6   Components of an Attitude

- Cognitive
- Affective
- Conative

diagnostic information that is useful in devising communication strategies to change attitudes.

Once an attitude is developed, it is relatively enduring, particularly if the attitude resulted from a careful consideration of a marketer's message arguments. If the attitude towards a brand is positive, the consumer is likely to make a trial purchase of a brand. If the attitude is negative, however, the consumer will need a strong motivation to change. Perrier, for example, was a market leader in bottled water. However, when the product had to be removed from store shelves due to the discovery that a toxic substance had entered the water during the bottling process, some consumers developed a negative attitude toward the brand. It has taken many months of promotional and informational efforts to change consumers' attitudes back to positive ones and rebuild the brand into a market leader again.

Although the concept of an attitude is most typically thought of in terms of a feeling state or an overall evaluation of some object, event, or idea, psychologists and consumer researchers recognize that attitudes consist of three relatively distinct but related components (see Exhibit 4.6): a cognitive, or "thinking" component; an affective, or "feeling" component; and a conative, or "doing" component.

The **cognitive** component refers to a person's knowledge, or belief, about a consumption object. "Crayola crayons come in great colors"; "Air Jordan shoes are well-made but expensive"; and "Jim Carrey [star of *Ace Ventura: Pet Detective, Mask,* and *Batman Forever*] is a zany actor" all illustrate the cognitive component.

The **affective** component of an attitude is the feeling or emotional evaluation of a consumption object, such as "I like milk"; "I adored the movie *Forrest Gump*; or "I despise Madonna."

The **conative** component refers to how a person is likely to behave or act towards a consumption object. "I'm going to vacation in Colorado as soon as I save enough money" exemplifies the conative component.

These components define how an attitude progresses. Consider the case of a new brand that has just been introduced to the market. First, a consumer becomes aware of the brand. The consumer acquires information about the brand and forms beliefs about how it might satisfy a specific need—the cognitive component. The consumer may then develop a feeling toward, or a like or dislike for the brand—the affective component. And finally, the consumer decides to either purchase or not purchase the brand—the conative component.

This progression (cognition→affection→conation) characterizes those instances of consumer behavior where the consumer is able to acquire useful information prior to making a purchase decision and forms a summary evaluation of the brand (i.e., affect) prior to making a purchase decision. Such an attitude-formation process is typical for expensive, infrequently purchased products such as automobiles and major furniture acquisitions. On the other hand, in the case of many inexpensive nondurable products, consumers are unlikely to form an attitude prior to actually purchasing and trying a new brand. Rather, we merely become aware of new brands and acquire sufficient information (cognition) to encourage a trial purchase (conation). Only after trial do we develop a true sense of liking or disliking for the brand (affect). Hence, the progression in this case can be thought of as extending from initial cognition to conation (i.e., trial) to affect. That is, affect results from purchasing and trying a brand rather than precedes the purchase.

Changing Consumer Attitudes.   If marketing research reveals that most consumers who constitute a brand's target market hold favorable attitudes toward the brand, then no efforts are needed to change consumers' attitudes. Given the dynamic nature of the marketplace, however, consumers' attitudes towards brands *do* change and not always in a positive direction. Hence, because attitudes are not etched in stone, it frequently is necessary to undertake marketing efforts to enhance attitudes. Marketers can attempt to change the consumer's attitude towards their brands by applying one of the following three strategies:

- attempt to change an existing belief on which the attitude is based
- attempt to change the perceived importance of a product attribute

■ encourage consumers to consider a different attribute or benefit of the product that has not been considered before

Changing an existing belief is the most frequently used strategy because consumer expectations, or beliefs, about a brand and its ability to provide desired outcomes are the foundation on which attitudes are formed. Most comparative advertisements such as Shakey's pizza claiming to produce a better pizza than Pizza Hut are attempts to change an existing belief—in this case, about product quality—and thus attitude.

Changing the perceived importance of a particular attribute is a more difficult task. In this strategy, a marketer attempts to convince consumers that a certain product feature is either more or less important than consumers had thought. Tylenol used this strategy when it stressed in advertisements that the product contained no caffeine unlike other pain relievers. Tylenol was encouraging consumers to view caffeine as a negative attribute in its competitors' brands and, thus, to form a more favorable opinion about Tylenol.

Encouraging consumers to consider new product attributes is used when the marketer's product will fare well against its competitors. When high cholesterol levels were linked with heart disease, sales of eggs declined. Egg Beaters were marketed as a cholesterol-free alternative to eggs. The product is targeted to consumers who cut down on their consumption of eggs and possibly felt there were no alternatives.

Personality and Psychographics

Every consumer has a personality that is unique to him or her. **Personality** is those unique characteristics of each individual that predisposes him or her to act in a fairly consistent manner in different types of situations. A person, for instance, who is willing to risk a great deal of money on a promising deal is more apt to bungee-jump or skydive than is a careful, conservative individual. The risk-taker would probably purchase a Mazda Miata sports car rather than a Honda Accord. Personality influences the types of products a person buys, the brands chosen, the stores in which one shops, and most every other consumption decision.

A consumer's lifestyle will also affect his or her behavior. The study of lifestyles, as embodied in a person's activities, interests, and opinions (so-called AIO items), is called **psychographics.**

Psychographics provide quantitative statistics that help define market segments. Psychographic information is more revealing than is demographic information per se. In demographics, census statistics will tell, for example, how many 12 to 18 year olds reside in New York City. In psychographics, statistics will reveal how many of this age group prefer rock 'n' roll, spend their free time skateboarding, or support recycling efforts. The acquisition of psychographic information enables marketers to communicate more effectively with their target markets. Chapter 6 takes up the topic of psychographics in more detail in exploring the topic of market segmentation.

Decision Processes

As illustrated in this chapter, many factors—both external to the consumer and internal—influence a consumer's decision of whether or not to buy a product. Consumers must go through a process of sorting through and evaluating these factors to determine the product's value to them. Sometimes the consumer makes a thoughtful decision based on a detailed analysis of different brands' relative benefits. And sometimes the consumer makes an emotional decision based on, say, a childhood fantasy or current whim.

Consumer behavior certainly is too complicated to be adequately described by any single explanation or process, but consumer researchers have found it useful to conceptualize consumer behavior in terms of a **decision-making process.** At times consumers truly act as decision makers, similar to the decision-making process that one would undergo in deciding which job to take from a set of attractive alternatives, or choosing a political candidate to vote for in an election. In other situations, consumers make purchase decisions with virtually no conscious decision making. The consumer acts on impulse or the choice is so trivial as to require little thought. The following stages describe the mental processes and activities that are involved, to one degree or another, from the time the consumer encounters a need to make a product purchase on to the purchase act and beyond.

Need Recognition.   This stage is activated when the consumer becomes aware of a significant discrepancy between the existing state of affairs and a desired state of affairs. The common causes of need recognition are the routine depletion of an item, an inadequate assortment of products, a dissatisfaction with the present brand or product type, or a change in financial status. An example: John has a tape player but now wants a CD player.

Search for Information.   The consumer then gathers information related to the attainment of a desired state of affairs. An alternative means of problem solution is identified through searching memory for information and, if necessary, engaging in the search for marketplace information—from ads, friends, salespeople, or magazines like *Consumer Reports.* An example: John goes to several stores to look at a variety of CD players. He buys *Consumer Reports* to learn about different makes and models of CD players. He asks his friend who knows a lot about electronic equipment for an opinion.

Evaluation of Alternatives.   The consumer evaluates the positives and negatives associated with each brand that he or she regards as suitable purchase alternatives; these alternatives comprise the consumer's **consideration set.** The criteria used in the evaluation process may change over time. An example: John likes the Kenwood CD player because it can work as a portable player in his car. But he also likes the Sony because its battery is rechargeable. Plus the Sony model is on sale this week.

Purchase Decision and Act.   The consumer narrows the alternatives down to one and decides how to purchase the product—either by telephone, mail order, or making a trip to a retail outlet. John returns to the store where the Sony machine is on sale and buys the product.

Postpurchase Evaluation.   The consumer finds himself satisfied or dissatisfied to some degree with the purchase of the product. The chances of second-guessing his decision, or experiencing **postpurchase dissonance,** increases as the dollar value of the purchase increases; it increases when the decision is a major one; and it increases when the rejected alternatives have desirable features not available in the chosen alternative. An example: Although John likes the Sony player, he cannot take it in his car, and that was an important feature to him. John is not dissatisfied with the choice of the Sony, but he is experiencing some uncertainty about whether this was the best CD player given his needs.

Classifying Consumer Problem-Solving Processes

The time and depth devoted to a decision process varies from consumer to consumer and from situation to situation. The process

utilized by an individual today in buying a new car will differ greatly from the process the same individual will use in buying toothpaste tomorrow. The search for information and alternative
evaluation stages will require much less time and energy for the
toothpaste purchase.

All consumer problem-solving processes can be classified
based on the complexity of the decision as follows:

Routinized Response Behavior.   The process used in routinized
response behavior requires little time and energy. The purchase is
made on the basis of a preferred brand or selection from a limited
group of acceptable brands. The evaluative criteria are set and the
available options identified. The external search for information is
limited. An example: Subhash is out of toothpaste so he goes to the
store and buys the same brand he has been using for years—Crest.

Limited Problem Solving.   The process used in limited problem solving is more complex. The consumer is confronted with a situation
where a product category is in a state of flux and new brands are
being introduced. Although the consumer utilizes the same factors,
called **evaluative criteria** or **choice criteria,** that he or she has previously used in forming judgments and making purchase decisions
from that category, he or she cannot rely on the same routine in
making a brand choice. A moderate amount of time, mental energy,
and even search is required to make a purchase decision. An example: Subhash saw a new brand of toothpaste advertised today.
Rembrandt toothpaste claims to whiten teeth better by using a non-
abrasive special formula. He reads the labels of this new brand at
the store.

Extended Problem Solving.   This process of problem solving is the
most complex. The brand is difficult to categorize or evaluate. The
consumer first needs to identify appropriate evaluative criteria on
which to appraise brand alternatives in the product category. The
process can be lengthy and involve considerable deliberation and
external search. An example: Subhash is buying his first new car.
This is a major decision and he must devote a lot of time to researching available makes and models in his price range.

In sum, routinized response behavior is typified by a repeat
purchase of an inexpensive item. The purchase requires little time or
thought. If the consumer is happy with his current product's performance, he likely will purchase it again when the need arises. Or at 2
A.M., a consumer who needs disposable diapers may have to settle

for whatever brand the nearby 7-Eleven offers. Once again, little time or thought is required for this purchase. At the other extreme, extended problem-solving behavior occurs with only major purchases, ones requiring substantial money, or ones purchased infrequently. Cars, homes, and appliances are typical purchases made using extended problem solving. Limited problem solving falls in the middle of these two extremes. The consumer already knows what evaluative criteria to use in making a purchase decision, but information must be acquired regarding how well alternative brands in the consumer's consideration set perform with respect to each of the salient criteria.

Chapter Summary ◆

Successful marketers must have a good understanding of why customers buy or do not buy their products. This is a difficult task since consumer behavior is complex, dynamic, and unpredictable. Many influences directly affect consumer buying behavior.

Environmental influences that influence consumer behavior include culture (consumer's set of values), social class (group sharing economic status and similar consumer behavior), personal influences (a consumer's reference group), family (group related by blood or marriage), and situational influences (factors specific to a particular buying choice). One or several of these factors can act together in determining a consumer's buying decision.

Individual differences and psychological processes, factors that are internal to the consumer, also affect consumer behavior. These factors include motivation and involvement, learning, information processing, knowledge, attitudes, and personality. Understanding consumer needs, or motives, is a basic premise of marketing. Marketers must identify what needs their products satisfy and create an effective marketing mix to convince the consumer of their products' value.

A consumer's decision process is the third factor that affects consumer behavior. A typical decision process includes the recognition of a need, the search for information, an evaluation of alternatives, a purchase decision, and a postpurchase evaluation. The time and depth devoted to a decision process varies by situation and consumer. Decision processes can be classified in the following

categories based on the complexity of the decision: routinized
response behavior (requires little time and energy), limited problem
solving (moderate amount of time and search), or extended problem solving (lengthy process with considerable external search).

◆ Notes

1. The chapter organization follows the manner in which a leading consumer behavior text treats the topic. See James F. Engel,
Roger D. Blackwell, and Paul W. Miniard, *Consumer Behavior,*
8th ed. (Ft. Worth, TX: Dryden, 1995).

2. Lynn Kahle, Basil Porilos, and Ajay Sukdial, "Changes in Social
Values in the United States during the Past Decade," *Journal of
Advertising Research* , 29 (February/March 1989), 35–41.

3. For more information on these trends, see Joseph T. Plummer,
"Changing Values," *The Futurist,* 23 (January–February 1989),
10.

4. Engel, Blackwell, and Miniard, *Consumer Behavior,* 682.

5. Dennis Gilbert and Joseph A. Kahl, *The American Class Structure:
A New Synthesis* (Homewood, IL: Dorsey, 1982).

6. Engel, Blackwell, and Miniard, *Consumer Behavior,* 725–726.

7. Engel, Blackwell, and Miniard, *Consumer Behavior,* 731.

8. Eileen Prescott, "Word-of-Mouth: Playing on the Prestige
Factor," *The Wall Street Journal,* February 7, 1984, 1.

9. Russell W. Belk, "Situational Variables and Consumer
Behavior," *Journal of Consumer Research,* 2 (December 1975), 157-
164.

10. Stephen J. Hoch and John Deighton, "Managing What
Consumers Learn," *Journal of Marketing,* 53 (April 1989), 1–20.

11. Joseph W. Alba and J. Wesley Hutchinson, "Dimensions of
Consumer Expertise," *Journal of Consumer Research,* 13 (March
1987), 411–454; Hoch and Deighton, "Managing What
Consumers Learn."

12. Terence A. Shimp, "New-Pavlovian Conditioning and Its Implications for Consumer Theory and Research," in T. S. Robertson and H. H. Kassarjian, eds., *Handbook of Consumer Behavior* (Englewood Cliffs, NJ: Prentice-Hall, 1991), 165–187.
13. Engel, Blackwell, and Miniard, *Consumer Behavior*, 472.

Study Questions

1. Which of the following is *not* an external force, or environmental influence, on individual consumer behavior?
   a. culture
   b. social class
   c. psychographics
   d. All of the above are environmental influences.

2. Which of the following statements best captures the essence of culture's influence on consumer behavior?
   a. Cultural values, when internalized, influence individual actions, including consumer behavior.
   b. Cultured individuals have higher social class, which is the means by which culture influences consumer behavior.
   c. Cultural values create knowledge structures, or schemas, that guide an individual's consumer behavior.
   d. All of the above are equally correct.

3. Social class
   a. no longer exists in the United States.
   b. is the term sociologists use to refer to one's occupation.
   c. is a group of individuals who share similar economic status and prestige.
   d. is unaffected by one's occupation.

4. The single best determinant of social class status is one's
   a. personal wealth.
   b. occupation.
   c. level of education.
   d. where one lives.

5. The "capitalist class" in Gilbert and Kahl's framework for delineating social classes represents approximately _____ % of the American population.
   a. 1
   b. 5
   c. 10
   d. 25

6. Pedro Cuello is an upper manager in a large American corporation. His family income runs nearly twice the national average. According to the Gilbert and Kahl social class system, Pedro would be classified as falling in the
   a. capitalist class.
   b. upper middle class.
   c. middle middle class.
   d. middle class.

7. A reference group
   a. dictates how its members should act.
   b. can be an individual or a group.
   c. has a powerful influence on its members.
   d. all of the above.

8. A consumer is most likely to accept and respond to word of mouth influences when
   a. the consumer lacks sufficient information to make an informed choice.
   b. the product is easy to evaluate using objective criteria.
   c. the decision process involved is simple.
   d. it comes from a salesperson.

9. In terms of buying decisions, who is the main decision maker in a family?
   a. father
   b. mother
   c. different family members depending on the purchase
   d. the user

10. In the decision-making process, the person who initiates thinking about buying products and the gathering of information to aid the decision is the
    a. influencer.
    b. gatekeeper.
    c. decider.
    d. buyer.

11. Which of the following is *not* a situational influence that affects consumer behavior?
    a. physical surroundings
    b. social surroundings
    c. time
    d. cultural values

12. In the decision-making process, the person whose opinions are sought concerning criteria the family should use in purchases and which products or brands most likely fit those evaluative criteria is termed a(n)
    a. influencer.
    b. gatekeeper.
    c. decider.
    d. buyer.

13. Associative learning occurs when
    a. a consumer follows his reference group's advice.
    b. a consumer forms hypotheses about consumption alternatives.
    c. a consumer draws connections between environmental events.
    d. a consumer integrates new information with preexisting beliefs.

14. Retention is the information processing stage when
    a. a consumer agrees with a marketing message.
    b. marketplace information is taken into long-term memory.
    c. relevant marketplace information reaches one or more of the five senses.
    d. marketing stimuli are interpreted.

15. Once an attitude is developed
    a. it becomes affective.
    b. it becomes cognitive.
    c. it can easily be changed.
    d. it is relatively enduring.

16. Which of the following sequences best represents the stages of information processing?
    a. attention, comprehension, exposure, acceptance, retention.
    b. comprehension, exposure, attention, acceptance, retention.
    c. acceptance, comprehension, exposure, attention, retention.
    d. exposure, attention, comprehension, acceptance, retention.

17. Cognitive response activity such as counter argumentation occurs at which information processing stage?
    a. exposure
    b. retention
    c. acceptance
    d. attention

18. Three of the following terms represent related concepts. Which of the terms does not belong?
    a. associative network
    b. knowledge structure
    c. comprehension
    d. schema

19. Given an expensive, infrequently purchased product, the attitude formation process is best characterized according to which of the following sequences of attitude components?
    a. conative→cognitive→affective
    b. conative→affective→cognitive
    c. cognitive→conative→affective
    d. cognitive→affective→conative

20. Given an inexpensive, frequently purchased product, the attitude formation process is best characterized according to which of the following sequences of attitude components?
    a. conative→cognitive→affective
    b. conative→affective→cognitive
    c. cognitive→conative→affective
    d. cognitive→affective→conative

21. Which of the following attitude change strategies is most frequently used?
    *a. Changing an existing belief on which the attitude is based.
    b. Changing the perceived importance of a product attribute.
    c. Encouraging consumers to consider a different attribute or product benefit that has not been considered before.
    d. All of these are used with equal frequency.

22. Using the language of classical conditioning, an advertised brand is equivalent to a(n)
    a. unconditioned response (UR).
    b. conditioned response (CR).
    c. conditioned stimulus (CS).
    d. unconditioned stimulus (US).

23. The brands that a consumer devotes serious thought to buying
    constitute his or her
    a. consideration set.
    b. evaluative criteria.
    c. schema.
    d. psychographic profile.

CHAPTER  5

Organizational
Buying Behavior

Chapter Objectives

The Nature of Business-to-Business and Organizational
Customers

Distinguishing Characteristics of Organizational Markets

Organizational Buying Decisions and the Buying Process

SIC Codes: A Valuable Tool for Identifying Business-to-
Business Customers

Chapter Summary

For many people, chicken noodle soup is a favored food, at least on occasion. Campbell's chicken noodle soup dominates the category and is available in virtually every store in America that sells food. It seems like such a simple product—probably one that you never give much thought to. But how does this product find its way to the grocer's shelf and ultimately into your shopping cart? Let's work the product back through the channel of distribution (i.e., from consumer to the manufacturer) to better appreciate the marketing and buying that are involved.

If you look on the label of a can of Campbell's chicken noodle soup, you will see that the ingredients include chicken stock, enriched egg noodles, salt, cornstarch, onion powder, dehydrated garlic, and other items known only to food scientists. Campbell's buys all of these inputs from other companies, including chicken producers, flour millers, salt processors, makers of products like cornstarch, onion powder, and so on. When chicken noodle soup is processed and finally packed in cans, it is shipped to the distribution centers of major supermarkets, to the warehouses of wholesalers—who supply smaller food stores that are unable to purchase directly from Campbell's—to hospitals, to the U.S. Army and Navy, to food service companies (such as the one responsible for the food at your college or university), and to countless other businesses and nonbusiness organizations. The marketing of a simple product involves a lot of transactions and exchanges.

Consider now a more complex product: the Ford Mustang. This product is annually sold to tens of thousands of consumers. Hundreds also are sold to state and local governments that purchase Mustangs for use in law enforcement. Ford Motor Company, the manufacturer, depends on literally dozens of other companies for component parts and raw materials that go into the production of Mustang automobiles: steel companies, tire producers, glass manufacturers, carpet producers, leather companies, and so on.

Both of these products, like the thousands of other products that are available in retail stores, involve a lot of marketing and buying that goes on behind the scenes. The topic of this chapter is organizational buying behavior, the behind-the-scenes aspect of marketing. The objective is to familiarize you with this facet of marketing, one which probably is relatively foreign compared to your more experiential-based understanding of consumer behavior. The chapter first describes the nature of business-to-business and organizational markets. It then discusses the defining characteristics of organizational markets and features of the organizational buying process.

The Nature of Business-to-Business Organizational Customers

Business-to-business marketing refers to the buying and selling and other marketing activities that take place between businesses. Business-to-business marketing occurs both when the Campbell's Soup Company buys flour from General Mills and sells the finished product—the can of soup—to Kroger's. Business-to-business marketing is also occurring between Ford and Corning Glass and between Ford and its dealers. However, when Ford sells Mustangs to the state of South Carolina, or when the U.S. Army purchases thousands of cases of soup from Campbell's, these are not business-to-business relations per se; rather these relations are between business and nonbusiness organizations. Hence, business-to-business marketing is just a subset of organizational marketing, albeit the dominant form of organizational marketing. Whether business-to-business marketing per se or organizational marketing, the important distinction is that these marketing activities are between companies or other organizations and not with consumers. As further point of contrast, the term **customers** can be used to refer to business and other organizational buyers, whereas **consumers** is reserved for relations with individuals buying for their personal or family consumption needs.

There are four major categories of customers who utilize organizational marketing: producers, resellers, governments, and other nonbusiness institutions.

Producers

Organizations that purchase goods and services used in the production of other products for the purpose of making a profit are classified as **producers.** Ford, for example, buys a raw material (steel) and shapes it into a desired product (the Mustang's hood) in its parts factory. Ford buys carburetors for use in the production of the Mustang's engine. And Ford buys computers to run its day-to-day operations. In all of these cases, Ford is operating as a producer, because the products it is purchasing (steel, batteries, and computers) are used to produce other products (Mustangs) or are used in the organization's daily operations. As of 1990, over one million enterprises in the United States were involved in agricultural, mining, construction, and manufacturing operations with over 25 million employees.[1]

MARKETING HIGHLIGHTS

Dry Storage, But Lively Marketing

Warehouses excite her. Trucks positively thrill her. And it's Ann Neumann's job to convey that enthusiasm to her company's customers.

Neumann is assistant marketing analyst for Dry Storage Corporation, which warehouses grocery products and distributes them to retailers. Her customers include some of the hottest names on the check-out line: Philip Morris, M&M-Mars, Lever Brothers, Kellogg's. But while the service her company provides is critical to getting goods on the grocery shelves, marketing warehousing and distribution is no small feat. Let's face it, this isn't a sexy service.

"Warehousing has long been a necessary evil," Neumann says. "Manufacturers often see it as an expense, a liability, and nothing else. But we're starting to change that. We're telling people that efficient distribution can get products to retailers quicker and less expensively."

Dry Storage, which is based in Des Plaines, Illinois, and has warehouses in 11 states, gets the word out by blitzing prospects with direct mail. It also advertises frequently in distribution and warehousing trade journals. "Our direct-mail pieces feature testimonials from manufacturers," Neumann says. "For us, reputation is everything."

Its mail pieces and trade ads cite the company's key capabilities. "We tell people about our advanced computer technologies—we have computers on every truck!" Neumann says. "This gives us great tracking capabilities."

The trucks themselves have become a marketing tool. They feature an icon that highway drivers have come to know as the "Dry Guy": a red, abstract figure of a man holding up two packages. "I've had people come up to me at parties, and when I tell them where I work, they say, 'Oh yeah, you're the people with the Dry Guy,'" Neumann says. "See, there's really nothing dry about what we do."

Geoffrey Brewer, "Dry Storage, but Lively Marketing," *Sales & Marketing Management,* February 1994, 16. Reprinted by permission.

Resellers

Resellers are intermediaries such as wholesalers, industrial distributors, brokers/agents, and retailers who buy finished products to resell for a profit. All consumer products—except for those products that are sold directly to the consumer via a manufacturer's direct-marketing efforts—are first sold to resellers. The Safeway supermarket chain buys Campbell's chicken noodle soup to resell to consumers from their store shelves. Car dealers across the country buy Ford Mustangs from Ford Motor Company to resell to consumers through their local dealerships. Wholesalers purchase products from manufacturers, typically for resell to retailers. There are approximately 500,000 wholesalers in the United States.[2] Wholesalers usually carry hundreds of products for resale.

Retailers purchase products to resell to consumers. As of 1990, over four million retailers were offering products and services in the United States.[3] Retailers vary greatly in terms of their size, function, and types of business. Chapter 11 discusses both wholesale and retail operations in some detail.

Governments

A third category of the organizational market is governments. One federal, 50 state, and 86,692 local governments make up the **government** market.[4] Governments spend billions of dollars each year on goods and services that are needed to fulfill their duties and responsibilities to citizens. Governments buy a wide variety of products including airplanes, munitions, cars, food, clothing, buildings, traffic lights, computers, and office supplies.

The federal government relies on centralized buying for a majority of its purchases. Some agencies within the government, though, buy their own goods and services. Since the government is spending public funds, it is accountable to the public. The government, therefore, creates and follows a very strict and complex set of buying procedures to ensure competitive bidding and an equal chance for all potential businesses. These procedures can be frustrating for companies attempting to sell their products to government entities—there is a lot of red tape involved in selling to federal, state, and municipal governments.

Nonbusiness Institutions

Nonbusiness institutions are organizations that provide services without the motivation of profit. Churches, hospitals, and charitable organizations are all nonbusiness institutions. These organizations purchase a variety of products that are used in their services rather than in the production of other products. For example, the Red Cross may purchase Campbell's chicken noodle soup for their earthquake, flood, and hurricane relief efforts as well as vans and automobiles to meet their transportation needs.

Exhibit 5.1   Characteristics of Organizational Markets

Market Characteristics

- Geographic concentration
- Relatively few customers

Demand Characteristics

- Derived demand
- Joint demand
- Inelastic demand
- Fluctuating demand

Buying Characteristics

- Multiple buying influences
- Close supplier-customer relations
- Negotiations common

Distinguishing Characteristics of Organizational Markets

Organizational buyer behavior shares similarities with consumer buying behavior. Whether a consumer is buying a Ford Mustang for his personal use or a government agency is buying the same car to equip the state law enforcement agency, considerations such as price, quality, service, and dependability are important in varying degrees to all buyers. However, some characteristics distinguish organizational from consumer buying behavior. These are summarized in Exhibit 5.1.

Market Characteristics

Organizational and business-to-business markets tend to be more geographically concentrated than consumer markets. Over half of the business buyers in this country are located in New York, Pennsylvania, Ohio, Illinois, New Jersey, California, and Michigan.

Many industries are also concentrated in certain geographic areas. For example, headquarters for automobile manufacturers are in Detroit, and California's Silicon Valley is home to manufacturers of advanced electronics systems.

The number of customers within the organizational market is far fewer than is the situation in the consumer market. Consider, for example, the carpeting business. A textile mill selling carpeting in the consumer market has a potential market of 96,000,000 households throughout the United States. The same mill, however, has a market of less than 15 if it is selling its products to automobile manufacturers in the organizational market.

Demand Characteristics

The nature of demand in the organizational market differs from consumer demand in several respects. Specifically, it tends to be (1) *derived* from the demand for consumer goods, (2) more price *inelastic* than is the case with consumer goods, (3) more interdependent, or *joint*, with respect to the demand for other products, and (4) more *fluctuating*.

Derived Demand.   Manufacturers buy products to be used in the production of business-to-business and consumer goods. Therefore, the demand for goods at one level of production ultimately is derived from the demand for goods at a lower level of consumption. For example, a furniture manufacturer would not produce couches unless it was fairly certain these items would be purchased by organizational customers or by retailers for resale to consumers. Hence, the furniture manufacturer's demand for materials—steel, wood, and other products that enter into the production of couches—is derived from organization buyers' and consumers' demands for couches.

Organizational marketers, therefore, must closely monitor the consumer market to track changes in demand and preferences. Forecasting future sales in the consumer market is a very tricky and complex procedure for any organizational marketer. Many unexpected and hard-to-predict factors can greatly affect demand at any time. For example, the harsh winter of 1994 created record-setting snowstorms in the Midwest and Northeast. Marketers of snow shovels could not possibly have forecasted or prepared for the resulting boom in sales of snow shovels. The 7,000 True Value hardware stores alone sold 500,000 shovels during this time—up 75 percent from the same period a year earlier. The chain even sold large numbers of gardening shovels after it had sold out of snow shovels.[5]

The producers of aluminum, wood, and plastic used in manufacturing snow shovels face a difficult task. If the demand for shovels and, therefore, the demand for their products is forecasted based on weather predictions months before the season, they face a big risk. If the winter is mild, demand for shovels will be low, which will result in increased inventories in warehouses. However, if the winter is harsh, demand will be high. This situation will result in lost sales due to lack of inventory. The organizational marketer must find a happy medium between the two situations.

Joint Demand.   Joint demand occurs when two or more products are used in the production of a final product. For example, snow shovels are produced from aluminum, wood, and plastic. Every completed snow shovel requires a handle and a shovel. If, for some reason, there is a shortage of aluminum, then the demand for wood also declines. It is in this sense that the demand for these two items is nonindependent, or joint.

Inelastic Demand.   The demand for business-to-business products is relatively inelastic. This means that any increase or decrease in the price of the product will not significantly affect the demand for the product in the *short run*. There are two reasons for inelastic demand. First, the price for one particular component is only a fraction of the total price of the final product of which it is part: when the price of the component product goes up, its price increase has relatively little effect on the total price of the finished product. Second, it is a difficult task for manufacturers to make major changes in their production operations in the short run. For example, if a shortage of rubber causes the price of tires to increase, Ford Motors will continue manufacturing vehicles and possibly pass the price increase onto the consumer. The shortage of rubber and ensuing higher prices will not stop production at Ford.

Fluctuating Demand.   The demand for business-to-business products tends to fluctuate more than the demand for consumer products. This is particularly true of the demand for major purchases such as new plants and manufacturing equipment. A small increase or decrease in consumer demand will produce a much larger change in the demand for manufacturing operations needed to produce the additional output. For example, air travel by businesspeople and consumers increases when the economy is in an upswing. When air travel increases, the airlines order more airplanes to replace the older planes and to provide for the additional demand. This results in increased orders for airplane manufacturers such as Boeing and McDonnell-Douglas. Conversely, when demand for air travel declines, the sales of new airplanes falls precipitously.

Buying Characteristics

The buying characteristics of the organizational market differ from those of the consumer market. Consumer purchase decisions are sometimes made by a single person (e.g., a man buying a new suit for himself), but for other decisions, multiple people (wife, husband, children, or any combination) are involved in the decision (e.g., a family buying new furniture). In the case of organizational buying, sometimes a single individual—a purchasing agent—has the power to make the decision, as typically is the case when a relatively inexpensive product is purchased. But when major capital outlays are involved, it is typical for multiple parties to be involved.

Multiple Buying Influences Typical.
Many organizations rely on buying centers for major capital outlays. A **buying center** is a group of key employees who provide different expertise needed to make major purchases. For example, a buying center may consist of a purchasing agent, an engineer, and a representative from manufacturing. The size and the chosen members of the center vary from company to company—smaller companies may have as few as two members whereas large companies may have as many as ten. The membership may also change within the center depending on the product being purchased. For example, a packaging engineer will be a buying center member if the purchase is new packaging equipment, but an electrical engineer will be involved if the purchase is a new electrical system for the factory. With buying centers, no one individual is saddled with the tremendous responsibility of spending millions of dollars on behalf of the organization. The responsibility is shared among the members of the buying center.[6]

Different members of the buying center have different roles in the decision process. Five key roles prevail in organizational buying behavior: users, influencers, buyers, deciders, and gatekeepers.

Users are the members of the organization who will actually use the product or service. The employee who runs the bottling equipment for a Coca-Cola bottler may use the equipment, but he or she will have little influence in the actual purchasing of the bottling equipment.

Influencers affect the buying decision by providing advice and information for the various alternatives. An influencer may be an outside consultant with expertise in the area or an employee who has had previous experience in a past job with the prospective product. It is typical for technical personnel to be important influencers.

The **buyer** is the employee who actually purchases the product. In the case of a minor purchase such as computer paper, a purchasing agent fulfills this role. In the case of a major purchase such as real estate for a new production facility site, the president of the company and the manager of site location may fulfill this role.

The **decider** is the member who decides which product to buy. As is the case with the buyer, the size and importance of the purchase will dictate the decider.

Gatekeepers control the flow of the information regarding a purchase within the organization. A purchasing agent may be instructed to gather information regarding a purchase even though she may not be the decider.

An employee in an organization can play more than one role in the buying process. For example, a secretary who needs a new word processor may act as the user, influencer, and gatekeeper in the decision-making process. However, he or she may not be the decider nor the buyer. All parties in the decision-making process do not necessarily have equal influence.[7] The roles and the importance of the roles will differ depending on the situation, the size of the purchase, and the product under consideration.

Close Supplier-Customer Relations Desirable.
Many organizational marketers and manufacturers today are recognizing the importance of working closely with each other. A combined effort will produce better products and processes which will, in turn, improve the manufacturing and marketing process. The more talent and expertise that is involved in a new product or process— whether from inside the company or out—the better the product will be. It is a win-win situation for all involved: the manufacturer gets a superior product while the supplier gets more orders. Developing a close supplier-customer relationship is a long-term process, one that may not pay off for years. A supplier must be willing to forego small orders in the short run for the sake of the development of the relationship in the long run.

Close customer-supplier relationships can lead to **reciprocity,** or the practice of purchasing products from a company's own customers. For example, Chrysler may buy computers from IBM, which in turn may buy a fleet of cars from Chrysler. On one hand, it seems reasonable to reward those organizations that help you realize your sales objectives. But on the other hand, choosing a vendor under these circumstances may not ensure the highest efficiency or best prices for the products purchased.

Negotiation Common.   Whether an organizational buyer is dealing with a new supplier or one that has been around for years, a certain amount of negotiation must take place, especially on large purchases. A purchasing agent typically draws up a list of product specifications describing in detail what is needed. The specs are submitted to two or more suppliers for bids. The purchasing agent selects the most attractive bid and then negotiates with the supplier. The negotiations usually pertain to pricing, timing, delivery, and selling terms. Negotiated contracts such as this typically cover one-time purchases, or purchases of large amounts of goods that will be delivered on an on-going basis.

Types of Organizational Buying Decisions and the Buying Process

Types of Organizational Buying Decisions

Organizational buying decisions are highly variable, ranging from purely routine decisions, which require little time and effort, to complex decisions entailing in-depth negotiations between buyer and seller. Exhibit 5.2 illustrates the range of organizational buying decisions: straight rebuy, modified rebuy, and new buy.[8]

Straight Rebuy.   A straight rebuy decision is a purchase that can be handled on a purely routine basis. Straight rebuys recur periodically with little selling effort on the part of the supplier. The products ordered are usually standard products that are always kept in stock. When an organization's inventory of a certain product is low, a straight rebuy order is placed. Terms and conditions of sale have been established in earlier transactions. Straight rebuys are similar to many simple consumer buying decisions insofar as a

Exhibit 5.2   Types of Organizational Buying Decisions

Routine Decisions (little time and effort)		Complete Negotiations (considerable time and effort)
Straight Rebuy	**Modified Rebuy**	**New Buys**
Basic telephone service	Office furniture for new VP	New factory site
Coffee for office	New carpeting for offices	New R&D laboratory
Utilities	Additional word processors	Major equipment acquisition

Source: Patrick J. Robinson, Charles W. Faris, and Yoram Wind, *Industrial Buying and Creative Marketing* (Boston: Allyn & Bacon, 1967).

single (rather than multiple) buying influence is involved and little if any negotiation occurs between buyer and seller.

Modified Rebuy.   In a modified rebuy, the purchaser requires some additional information or a minor change to the original product. The change may be as minor as a change in the color of a plastic bottle cap from yellow to red for a liquid detergent manufacturer. Or, an organization may be unhappy with a current vendor and seek out a new vendor for a product whose specifications are already in place. In either case, slight modifications are required before a purchase order is placed.

New Buys.   A new buy is the purchase of a product or service for the first time. A new buy requires selling on the part of the supplier and an extensive information search on the part of the buying organization. Multiple suppliers are contacted in the information search. Once the new buy is negotiated, the future purchases of the product tend to be rebuys. For example, when McDonald's introduced the McRib sandwich, the organization needed suppliers of pork who would mold the meat into a miniature "slab" shape. The initial purchase was a new buy for McDonald's. However, when the fast-food maker annually reintroduces McRib sandwiches to its menu for a short period, these subsequent purchases are straight rebuys.

Organizational buying decisions can be made by individuals or groups. Individuals typically make straight rebuy decisions, groups new buys, and either individuals or groups the modified

Exhibit 5.3   The Industrial Buying Stream

1 →	2 →	3 →	4 →	5 →	6 →	7 →
Unidentifed Problem	Spotting Problem	Investigate Problem	Identify Problem	Investigate Solutions	Select & Buy	Solve Problem
	■ Sufferers			|		|
	■ Owners			Inquiry		Solution
	■ Beneficiaries			|		
				Inquiry		
				Qualification		

Source: Herbert E. Brown and Roger W. Brucker, "Charting the Industrial Buying Stream," *Industrial Marketing Management*, 19 (February 1990), 55–61.

rebuy decisions. The number of people involved in the decision and their level in the organization depends on the complexity of the decision and the dollar amount of the purchase.

The Organizational Buying Process

As discussed above, the procedures used in buying business-to-business goods and services differ by company and buying situation, whether straight rebuy, modified rebuy, or new buy. Regardless of the situation, however, all organizational purchases can be conceptualized as following the same basic process. Exhibit 5.3 illustrates the process in terms of a seven-step buying stream: unidentified problem, spotting problem, investigate problem, identify problem, investigate solutions, select and buy, and solve problem.[9] The buying stream is based on the premise that all industrial buying stems from the need to solve a problem. A problem may arise unexpectedly, such as a work stoppage due to a machinery breakdown. Or, the problem can be a continuing one, such as the need for quality improvement. Regardless of the reason for the problem, a purchase decision must be made to solve the problem. It is useful to think of the buying process in terms of the following steps in the buying stream.

Unidentified Problem.
Businesses often have problems that are as yet unidentified. No one in the organization may be aware of the problem at this point.

Spotting Problem.
Eventually, however, the problem is spotted by someone in the organization. Three types of employees are likely candidates for spotting problems:

- **The Sufferer.** The sufferer is an employee who is suffering from the problem. A marketing manager is a sufferer when product quality problems result in decreased sales. Even though the marketing manager is not directly responsible for product quality, he or she suffers from the quality problem. Sufferers can raise awareness for the problem and bring it to the attention of decision makers who can do something about it.

- **The Owner.** The owner is the employee who actually "owns" the problem. In this example, the production manager or quality control manager is the owner of the quality problem. These employees typically are responsible for handling the problem.

- **The Beneficiaries.** The beneficiaries are those employees who suffer the consequences of the problem and would benefit from a solution to the problem. In the quality example, the sales department, marketing manager, and production department are all beneficiaries.

Investigate Problem.
Once a sufferer or owner realizes the problem and brings the problem to management's attention, the problem is investigated. Typically technical problem solvers are called upon to investigate the problem and gather facts.

Identify Problem.
Once the situation is fully investigated, the problem is officially identified. The technical problem solver who investigated the problem usually identifies the problem also.

Investigate Solutions.
The next step in the buying stream is to investigate potential solutions to the problem. The responsibility for investigation may fall on a purchasing agent, an engineer, or production department employee who is familiar with the problem and product. Inquiries are made to potential suppliers regarding solutions to the problem.

CAPTAINS OF INDUSTRY

William F. O'Dell

Retired Founder and Former Chief Executive Officer

Market Facts Inc.

Date of Birth: 1909

Career Path: Vice president for Ross Federal Research Corp. based in Chicago until 1946, when he left, taking three employees with him, to begin his own firm. Served as Chairman of the Board of Market Facts until 1963 when he retired. Became a lecturer at McIntire School of Commerce, University of Virginia, until 1975.

Profile: Hard-working, perceptive, with a wry sense of humor and energetic personality who understood the necessity of recruiting and keeping talented executives. O'Dell has also written three books, including one for teenagers, titled *How to Get Along with Parents* since he retired.

Personal: "Creativity is the one most important ingredient in decision making, bar none," O'Dell said. "My advice to people getting into the industry today is to view market research from a management view. In other words, look at the need for the information and how it is to be used. Let technology be the last thing you worry about. Understanding people is as important as the decision-making process itself."[a]

William F. O'Dell founded Market Facts Inc. in 1946 in Chicago. He began business with three employees he brought with him from his former employer, Ross Federal Research Corporation, New York. The group had total assets of one typewriter, a name, and the desire to start their own business. His first contract was with Stran-Steel, a division of National Steel, Detroit. O'Dell had to quickly learn whether farmers would buy the company's Quonset huts, left over from World War II, as outdoor storage. O'Dell had to borrow money and go without pay for two months to pay for the field work needed to get this information, and he and his assistants were just getting survey forms ready when United Mine Workers chief John L. Lewis called a strike. Power companies ran out of coal, electric power failed, and communications were disrupted, so O'Dell's two assistants moved their typewriters next to an outside window in his small office to keep working. They had to work without electricity to power fans or the elevator, but Stran-Steel's survey was ready on time and new business began to roll in. "I never thought of it as a high-risk business because it just had to succeed," O'Dell said.[b]

Another account that Market Facts secured in those early days was the Ford division of Ford Motor Company. Ford quickly became Market Facts' biggest client, representing up to 50% of its revenues and much of its growth well into the 1960s. Apparently the biggest problem in the early days was educating executives at Ford about certain market research fundamentals, such as the fact that a sample survey could reflect the views of a larger population on such factors as auto body styling, pricing, and new products. "A former chairman at Ford found it almost impossible to grasp the concept of a sample survey, which made it extremely difficult to sell the idea that you could

Continued on next page

infer [things] from a small sample," said O'Dell. "The fact is that we tried to work with prospective users because there were so few people who knew anything about marketing research."[c]

Market Facts developed a reputation for challenging clients' assumptions about the need for research, the optimum size of a project and the potential benefits to be derived from it. O'Dell remembers what Arthur Simon, formerly of Chicago-based Tatham-Laird & Kudner, had to say about Market Facts Inc. when he was looking into hiring a marketing research company years ago. "If you want an argument, call on Market Facts."[d]

O'Dell feels that the growth of Market Facts in those days was the result of helping clients optimize allocation of their research dollars. This strategy is typified by its early creation of consumer mail panels, which provide accurate data at a lower cost than that of personal interviews. By 1986, Market Facts' Consumer Mail Panel

had grown to be among the nation's largest, with 250,000 households, compared with its forerunner, the National panel, with 1,000 households. But it took 10 years for it to gain acceptance, O'Dell remembers.

When asked the key to Market Facts' success, O'Dell replied that the secret lies in the company's ability to hire and keep talented executives. "It's the people who make the business run." O'Dell kept talented employees by giving them ownership in the company. "The goal on my part was to get stock into their hands as quickly as possible so they'd be inclined to stay," stated O'Dell.[e] And stay they have. Current Chairman and CEO Verne Churchill began with the company in the late 1950s, and former chairman, Dave Hardin, now deceased, started in 1950.

O'Dell stepped down from the chairmanship in 1963. "I was losing my contact with clients, and that's the fun part of the business. So that's when I gave thought to pulling out. Marketing

Select and Buy.   After all bids and information are received from qualified suppliers, a solution to the problem is selected and purchased.

Solve Problem.   The purchase of the product (goods or services) brings an end to the buying stream as the problem has been solved.

SIC Codes: A Valuable Tool for Identifying Business-to-Business Customers

As noted, organizational buyers are fewer in number and more concentrated than is the case with consumers. This notwithstanding, it still can be a difficult task to determine the number of potential customers for the marketer's product, where they are located, the size of their purchasing needs, and so on. Acquiring this information is

research is a young man's business," he stated. O'Dell became a lecturer at the McIntire School of Commerce at the University of Virginia in Charlottesville, Virginia, until 1975, when he ostensibly retired to Fort Myers, Florida. He has continued to study and write, however, publishing several books.

Today, Market Facts Inc., based in Arlington Heights, Illinois, continues to thrive, with revenues in 1991 at $40.7 million, up 1.2% over 1990, and employing 500 full-time and 600 part-time employees. Most of its work is customer survey, but it provides two shared-cost, omnibus services: Data Gage and TELE-NATION, a regularly scheduled survey.[f] The company is well-known for providing research for the popular *U.S. News & World Report* annual guide to America's best graduate schools.

Market Facts instituted Marketest 2000 in 1991, a sales volume estimation model for new product concept applications, and The Conversion Model, a strategic segmentation procedure that

focuses on commitment of brand users. In 1992 it began a new advertising tracking service.

Market Facts owes much of it current success to its founder William F. O'Dell, who had the vision to see the growth of the market research industry and the courage to start out with little more than that vision and lead his company to become a major player in the U.S. market research arena today.

[a] Richard Edel, "O'Dell's Luck, Good Sense Lead to Market Facts," *Advertising Age*, May 19, 1986, S-64.
[b] *Advertising Age*, May 19, 1986, S-64.
[c] Ibid.
[d] Ibid.
[e] Ibid.
[f] "Top 50 U.S. Marketing/Ad/Opinon Research Firms Profiled: Elrick & Lavidge Inc., Market Facts Inc., MRB Group Ltd., Walker Group, MAI U.S. Information Group," *Marketing News*, June 8, 1992, 10–12."

greatly facilitated by the fact that the United States Department of Commerce has developed a useful scheme for classifying businesses. The Standard Industrial Classification (SIC) system consists of a detailed set of codes for identifying organizations and subdividing the industrial marketplace into groups of firms in similar lines of business.[10] Every class of business in the United States is assigned a two-digit identification code. The major categories of industries and their corresponding SIC codes are shown in Exhibit 5.4.

Industries are further subdivided into smaller segments with three- and four-digit numbers. Let's look at compact disk manufacturers as an example. Compact disk manufacturers are in the manufacturing industry, or Division D. As seen in Exhibit 5.4, the SIC code for manufacturing is 20–39. Exhibit 5.5 illustrates the Standard Industrial Classification System for manufacturers of compact disks. The two-digit code for electronics and other electrical equipment or components is 36. The three-digit industry group for household and

Exhibit 5.4   Standard Industrial Classification Codes by Industry
                Grouping

Division A:	Agriculture	01–09
Division B:	Mining	10–14
Division C:	Construction	15–17
Division D:	Manufacturing	20–39
Division E:	Transportation	40–49
Division F:	Wholesale Trade	50–51
Division G:	Retail Trade	52–59
Division H:	Finance/insurance/real estate	60–67
Division I:	Services	70–89
Division J:	Public Administration	91–97
Division K:	Nonclassifiable establishments	99

Source: *Standard Industrial Classification Manual* (Washington, D.C.: U.S. Government Printing Office, 1987).

audio/video equipment is 365. Finally, the specific identification of compact disks is to be found in the four-digit group, 3652, for phonograph records and prerecorded audio tapes and disks.

The SIC code system is an important tool for organizational marketers. The Federal government publishes volumes of information such as the *Census of Manufacturing* and the *Census of Retailing,* all of which use the SIC code system as a guide to the information. A business-to-business marketer can identify the SIC codes of its existing customers and use this knowledge to obtain SIC-coded lists of prospective customers. With an understanding of the composition of the various SIC groupings from which a supplier draws its customers, it then is possible to observe developments in the SIC-code listings to determine where the growth is occurring and which categories offer the best future potential.

◆ Chapter Summary

Organizational marketing is the marketing of products and services to organizations, both business and nonbusiness, rather than consumers. There are four types of organizational customers: Producers are individuals and organizations that purchase goods and services

Exhibit 5.5   Standard Industrial Classification System for Compact Disks

Division	Major Group (2 digits)	Industry Group (3 digits)	Specific Product (4 digits)
D. Manufacturing	36. Electronic and other electrical equipment	365. Household audio and video equipment	3651. Phono-graph records and prerecorded audio tapes and disks

Source: *Standard Industrial Classification Manual* (Washington, DC: U.S. Government Printing Office, 1987).

used in the production of other products for the purpose of making a profit. Resellers are intermediaries such as wholesalers, brokers/agents, and retailers who buy finished products to resell for a profit. The government sector is comprised of the federal, state, and local governmental units. Finally, nonbusiness institutions are organizations that provide services without the motivation of profit.

Organizational buying behavior is similar to consumer buying behavior in that price, quality, service, and dependability are all considered important factors to varying degrees. However, differences exist between the two markets also. Most industries are geographically concentrated with a limited number of customers. Demand in the organizational market also differs from consumer demand in that it is derived (dependent on the demand of consumer goods), inelastic (not significantly affected by short-term changes in price), joint (two or more products are used in the production of one product), and fluctuating (more unsteady). In the organizational market, multiple parties are involved in the process more so than in the consumer market. Often buying centers are called upon to make major purchases for the organization.

Not all organizational buying decisions are the same. The straight rebuy, which requires little time and effort, is a purchase that can be handled on a purely routine basis. In a modified rebuy, the purchaser requires some additional information or a minor change to the original product. A new buy is the purchase of a product or service for the first time. Each situation requires different amounts of time, research, and negotiations.

Organizational customers are classified by their area of specialization, size, location, and goods purchased. The Standard

Industrial Classification System (SIC) as developed by the federal government provides information on organizational customers. This information is valuable to organizational marketers in identifying prospective customers.

◼ Notes

1. U.S. Department of Commerce, Bureau of the Census, *Statistical Abstract of the United States,* (Washington, DC: U.S. Government Printing Office, 1993), 538.

2. Ibid.

3. Ibid.

4. Ibid.

5. "We Suffered, They Sold," *Newsweek,* March 28, 1994, 44.

6. Frederick E. Webster, Jr., and Yoram Wind, *Organization Buying Behavior* (Englewood Cliffs, NJ: Prentice-Hall, 1972), and Erin Anderson, Wujin Chu, and Barton Weitz, "Industrial Purchasing: An Empirical Exploration of the Buyclass Framework," *Journal of Marketing,* 51 (July 1987), 71–86.

7. Donald W. Jackson, Jr., Janet E. Keith, and Richard K. Burdick, "Purchasing Agents' Perceptions of Industrial Buying Center Influence: A Situational Approach," *Journal of Marketing,* 48 (Fall 1984), 75–83.

8. Patrick J. Robinson, Charles W. Faris, and Yoram Wind, *Industrial Buying and Creative Marketing* (Boston: Allyn & Bacon, 1967).

9. Herbert E. Brown and Roger W. Brucker, "Charting the Industrial Buying Stream," *Industrial Marketing Management,* 19 (February 1990), 55–61.

10. *Standard Industrial Classification Manual* (Washington, DC: U.S. Government Printing Office, 1987).

◼ Study Questions

1. How do business-to-business markets differ from consumer markets?
   a. They sell more products.
   b. Consumer demand is derived from organizational demand.
   c. They tend to be more geographically concentrated.
   d. Organizational markets have more customers.

2. Joint demand occurs when
   a. increases or decreases in product prices do not significantly affect demand.
   b. demand fluctuates.
   c. the level of demand for organizational products is dependent on the demand for consumer products.
   d. two or more products are used in the production of a final product.

3. Which of following explanations best explains why the demand for business-to-business products is relatively inelastic?
   a. The price for one component in a finished product is only a fraction of the total price of the final product for which it is part.
   b. A decline in the availability of one product causes a decline in the production of the final product.
   c. A small change in consumer demand results in a large change in manufacturing operations.
   d. These products are rarely advertised.

4. A buying center
   a. is a group of key employees with different expertise joined together to make major purchases.
   b. is made up of a group of purchasing agents who have different backgrounds and experience; however, all are employed in the purchasing department.
   c. must have a minimum of five members.
   d. is used for all company purchases.

5. The primary determinant of who the "decider" is in the decision process is
   a. the budget.
   b. the individual who has the most information regarding the purchase.
   c. the size and importance of the purchase.
   d. the level of need for the product.

6. Which type of organizational purchase requires complete negotiations?
   a. straight rebuy
   b. new task
   c. modified rebuy
   d. buying center purchases

7. The concept of a buying stream is based on the premise that
   a. all industrial buying stems from the need to solve a problem.
   b. all companies need to buy products for business use.
   c. all purchases must go through a buying process within the company.
   d. technical problem solvers are needed to investigate and solve problems.

8. SIC codes are
   a. government codes covering buying procedures.
   b. a detailed system that classifies companies according to their lines of business.
   c. codes for classifying manufacturers of industrial products.
   d. codes for planning organizational activities.

9. Which of the following is *not* a characteristic of organizational markets?
   a. Derived demand
   b. Inelastic demand
   c. Elastic demand
   d. Joint demand

10. Which of the following best captures the concept of derived demand?
    a. The demand for cereal is influenced by the supply for wheat and other grains.
    b. The demand for wheat is dependent on the supply of competitive foodstuffs (rice, corn, etc.).
    c. The demand for cereal depends both on the demand for good-eating habits among consumers and the availability of other breakfast foods.
    d. The demand for wheat, corn, and rice is determined in part by the demand for cereal.

11. Product X is made of components A and B. The availability of component B has dramatically declined; hence, the demand for component A is substantially reduced. This description characterizes which form of demand condition?
    a. fluctuating
    b. derived
    c. elastic
    d. joint

12. Product X is made of components A, B, C, D, and E. The price of component D increases, but the manufacturer of Product X does not reduce its demand for this component. This description characterizes which form of demand condition?
   a. fluctuating
   b. derived
   c. inelastic
   d. joint

13. In organizational buying, the individuals who control the flow of information regarding a purchase are termed
   a. gatekeepers.
   b. influencers.
   c. peacemakers.
   d. none of the above.

14. A manufacturer of lawn products (lawnmowers, riding mowers, etc.) has spent months investigating the best possible supplier from which to purchase tires. Individuals from production, engineering, purchasing, and the finance department were involved in the decision. These individuals constituted a
   a. purchase squad.
   b. buying center.
   c. purchasing task force.
   d. buying conglomerate.

15. A manufacturer of lawn products (lawnmowers, riding mowers, etc.) has spent months investigating potential suppliers from which to purchase special batteries so that the lawn-products manufacturer can convert from gas engines to battery-powered electrical engines. This purchasing decision in this case would be classified as a
   a. new task.
   b. modified rebuy.
   c. straight rebuy.
   d. crucial rebuy.

CHAPTER ⑥

Market Segmentation

Chapter Objectives

The success of a company, its products, and specific brands depends in large part on selecting the right target markets and marketing mixes to reach these markets.[1] In identifying the target market, a firm recognizes the fact that their product will not meet the needs of all consumers in the market. Consumers' needs and wants are different. It is critical for a firm to determine which consumers' needs and wants will be fulfilled by its product. The firm will focus its marketing efforts on this group of consumers with similar needs, or **target market.**

This chapter introduces the concept of a market, discusses different strategies for successfully serving markets, and then describes in detail the criteria and bases on which markets are segmented into more profitable and actionable submarkets, or segments. The chapter concludes with a description of the process for planning and implementing a segmentation strategy.

◆ What Is a Market?

A **market** is a group of customers who have the need or desire, the ability, and the authority to purchase a specific product (see Exhibit 6.1). All three criteria must be met for a purchase to take place. For example, a new car buyer may really want a Mercedes but her budget limits her to a Hyundai. This buyer is in Hyundai's market, but not Mercedes' since she does not have the ability to buy the higher-priced car.

Different types of markets exist and can be classified by how the purchased product will be used. If a product is purchased by a consumer for her or her household's own use, the product is classified as a **consumer product.** If a product is purchased by an organization to be used in producing other products or in operating its business, the product is classified as a **business-to-business product.**

One product can be classified as both a consumer and business-to-business product. If a buyer purchases Log Cabin Syrup to

Exhibit 6.1   Market Characteristics

A market is a group of consumers who have
1. Product-related need or desire
2. Purchasing ability
3. Purchasing authority

use for his breakfast in his home, the syrup is a consumer product. If International House of Pancakes purchases Log Cabin Syrup to use as part of their menu offering, the syrup is a business-to-business product. A product's classification is based on who purchases the product and how it will be used. In a later chapter, we will look at the subclassification of these types of products.

Marketing Strategies

Any organization must have a thorough understanding of its potential markets. The number of consumers in a specific market will dictate the sales of many goods such as milk, shoes, or refrigerators. Most marketers, though, prefer to concentrate their efforts on those consumers within the market who are *most likely* to purchase their products. In identifying their potential customers, marketers may choose to follow one of two basic marketing strategies:

1. mass-marketing strategy, or undifferentiated marketing
2. market segmentation strategy with either concentrated or differentiated segmentation

Mass-Marketing Strategy

Until the early 1900s, most goods were produced to meet the needs of a specific customer. Carpenters custom-built wagons to accommodate transporting the crops of particular farmers in the area. And seamstresses created clothing based on each individual's specific measurements. As the population grew and became more urbanized, though, this system of production proved to be inefficient.

In the early 1900s, Henry Ford, the founder of the Ford Motor Company, recognized that he could appeal to a wider audience by lowering the price of his automobiles. This was achieved by standardizing his company's operations and scheduling longer production runs. Inventory, distribution, and marketing costs were held to a minimum. This **mass market strategy** limited Ford's product offering, though. Ford offered one product (the Model T) in one color (black) at one price ($360) to the entire market.

In approaching a market, a marketer must first decide whether or not to segment. When Henry Ford was producing the Model T, he chose to sell one product to all customers within the entire market. A marketer who chooses not to segment is employing mass or **undifferentiated marketing.** Ticonderoga pencils are an example of mass marketing. The pencils are mass-produced, inexpensive, and available in most retail outlets in every market. Few changes have been made to the product over the years because it serves a basic need of all consumers.

Undifferentiated marketing has advantages. A firm will minimize production costs and thus be able to offer competitive prices to the consumer. A firm is also able to build and maintain a specific image with consumers. In general, in at least three instances a mass, or undifferentiated, marketing strategy is most appropriate:

1. The market is so small that it is unprofitable to market to just a portion of it.
2. Heavy users are the only relevant target because they make up a large proportion of the market.
3. The brand dominates the market and draws its appeal from all segments of the market, thus making segmentation unnecessary and unprofitable.[2]

Undifferentiated marketing has disadvantages, too. Although this strategy may result in lower costs and retail prices, it is very difficult to attempt to satisfy all customers with one marketing mix. An organization using undifferentiated marketing may also be providing an excellent opportunity for its competition to capture a portion of its sales by appealing to the desires of specific segments.

Market Segmentation Strategy

In some cases it is necessary to appeal to different segments of a market. In the example of cars, automobile manufacturers recognized that subgroups within the market had different needs and desires. The well-to-do consumers in the market were willing to pay a higher price to have more features and a better automobile. This differed greatly from the consumer in the market with limited income who only needed a basic means of transportation for the smallest price.

Ford and General Motors began manufacturing a line of several models to appeal to the different groups within the automobile market. For the next several decades, automobile manufacturers produced cars for low, medium, and high income households to meet the variability of demand within the market.

Most marketers today recognize that demand varies greatly within a market.[3] Different customers seek out products with specific features, benefits, and images to meet their own individual needs. The benefits derived from a product are valued differently by different consumers. Thus, the price customers are willing to spend on products to meet their needs can vary dramatically within the market. A consumer who is rarely at home may be satisfied with spending $139 for a black and white television set for occasional viewing. A consumer who spends most of his free time watching television derives greater satisfaction from viewing and may be willing to spend $1,000 on a 27" color set with many extra features.

An organization deals with this variability in demand by implementing a **market segmentation strategy.** Market segmentation is the process of dividing a large market into smaller markets, or customer groups, with similar needs or desires. Market segmentation allows a marketer the flexibility to create one marketing mix for each specific market segment. If an organization has more than one target market, which typically is the case for large, modern corporations, a customized marketing mix can be developed for each group.

Once an organization or subunit in an organization chooses to segment, two basic approaches are available: (1) concentrated segmentation strategy and (2) differentiated segmentation strategy.

Concentrated Segmentation.

When an organization concentrates its marketing efforts on a smaller segment of a larger market, it is using a **concentrated segmentation** strategy. Starbucks, a retail coffee chain, focuses its marketing efforts and resources on the gourmet coffee drinking segment of the entire coffee market. An organization can successfully carve out a niche for itself and generate a large sales volume by focusing all its resources on satisfying one segment's needs.

Concentrated marketing has its advantages. Smaller local firms with fewer resources can successfully compete with national companies in a market by using a concentrated segmentation strategy. Concentrated marketing also allows a company to specialize and gain an expertise within the market. A firm can become quite efficient by appealing to a particular segment at lower costs.

Concentrated marketing also has disadvantages. If demand within the segment suddenly declines due to a natural disaster or change in consumer preference, the company's overall sales and profitability decline. For example, the Volkswagen Beetle was wildly successful through the 1960s and 1970s, but sales plummeted when consumer preferences shifted toward larger and more luxurious offerings. By limiting its efforts to only one segment, a firm's overall profits also may not be maximized.

A marketer also runs the risk of becoming synonymous with its niche thus making it nearly impossible to expand into new areas. Since McDonald's built its reputation on high caloric, low nutrition fast food, the company has been unsuccessful in its attempts to create a satisfying low-fat hamburger for the health-conscious segment. Also, it would be virtually impossible for McDonald's to expand into the upscale restaurant business using the name, McDonald's, and the golden arches symbol.

Differentiated Segmentation.
An organization may also choose differentiated marketing as a segmentation strategy. When a firm targets multiple market segments and develops specific marketing mixes for each segment, it is employing **differentiated segmentation.** Many companies that enter a market and experience success using concentrated marketing expand their efforts into additional segments. Procter & Gamble has dominated the laundry detergent market by marketing several brands—Tide, Oxydol, Ivory Snow, Bold, Cheer, and Gain—to different segments. Toyota markets the Corolla, Camry, Celica, Paseo, Lexus, and other models to unique market segments. Differentiated marketing, if planned properly, will result in increased company sales and profitability. A company's risks are also minimized since all of their eggs are not in one basket.

Most consumer products companies today practice differentiated marketing. Line extensions, new flavors or scents, multiple sizes, and new product offerings are all examples of differentiated marketing. Differentiated marketing allows marketers the ability to service more customers within the market. Coca-Cola increased its market by offering Diet Coke for those customers who were concerned about calories and desired a lower sugar content. Then it offered Diet Coke and Coke without caffeine to further differentiate its market.

But if an organization attempts to reach too many segments, it may spread its resources too thinly to reach any of its targeted segments effectively. Firms must target only those segments that they realistically can handle using available resources. Marketers may over segment a market. Some consumerist organizations consider the soft drink market, for example, to be "oversegmented" with its extensive offerings of regular, diet, caffeine-free regular, and caffeine-free diet. This abundance of line extensions drives up

Exhibit 6.2   Criteria for Successful Segmentation

1. Segmentation variable must be *identifiable and measurable.*

2. Potential segment must be *substantial* enough to yield a suitable profit.

3. Segment must be reachable, that is *economically accessible.*

4. Consumers in the proposed segment must show a positive and relatively *homogeneous response* to the marketing mix.

production, inventory, distribution, and marketing costs. In some cases, it may cause retail prices to increase. Obviously business must evaluate how much they need to differentiate.

Market Segmentation Criteria and Bases

Discussion to this point has presented an overview of the fundamentals of market segmentation. Now we turn to the practical issue of how markets are actually segmented. To formulate an effective segmentation program, a firm must identify which market segments present the best opportunities for generating revenues. Then, an analysis of the firm's resources—mainly costs—will tell whether or not the organization can effectively service their selected targeted segments. In principle, firms have a variety of ways to segment their markets. Markets can be segmented on the basis of variables such as customers' economic status, age, geographic location, ethnicity, and so on. These variables are referred to as segmentation bases, a detailed description of which will follow. First, however, it is necessary to explore the criteria that any segmentation basis must satisfy if it is to be an effective segmentation basis.

Segmentation Criteria

Exhibit 6.2 identifies four criteria that a segmentation effort must satisfy to be considered successful:

1. An organization must be able to **identify and measure** the segmentation variable, or variables, on which segmentation is to be accomplished. In order to forecast sales and anticipate demand, reliable statistics are needed. If a firm has developed a new dental floss that is easy for children to use,

MARKETING HIGHLIGHTS

Environmentally Conscious Consumers Seek Smaller Packages

Maintaining space on retail shelves is becoming increasingly competitive with the proliferation of brands and private labels. Manufacturers are constantly looking for ways to maximize dollar sales per square foot on the shelf, and the latest trend toward that end is in smaller packaging. In addition, consumers who are environmentally conscious are seeking products that cause less environmental waste. The result has been to target those products that can be reduced in size to fit in smaller packages that take up less space on grocery shelves and storage space at home, use recycled materials in packaging, and cost less. Super-concentrated detergents that offer to get clothes cleaner with half the amount of detergent used formerly, thinner disposable diapers, and concentrated refills of fruit juices are a few examples. Who profits? Do consumers pay more for less? Let's take a closer look at a few of these newly packaged products.

In the spring of 1993, The Lever Brothers Company followed the path taken by Procter & Gamble six months earlier when it introduced super-concentrated versions of its three liquid detergents, Wisk, Surf and All. The company spent three years of R&D to develop a patented technology called "structured liquids," resulting in a liquid detergent that the company promotes as cleaning better than before, using half the amount of liquid per wash load. Although Lever has lagged behind Procter & Gamble in its powdered detergent sales, it leads in the tradition-

al liquid category and is hoping to catch up and overtake P&G in the new super-concentrated liquid segment. While P&G's Ultra varieties are about 22% more concentrated than its non-concentrated formulas, Lever's Double Power Wisk, for example, comes in a 32-oz. bottle that equals the previous 64-oz. size in wash loads per bottle, making the savings 50%. The company has since introduced Double Power Wisk refill, a 26-oz. box, to compete against P&G's Ultra Tide 40-oz. refill. Lever has emphasized the environmental pluses of their packaging of the double power bottles: using at least 30% less packaging than before, made with at least 25% post-consumer recycled plastic, and refills coming in a natural high-density polyethylene, 26-oz. pack made from at least 50% post-consumer recycled plastic.

In the category of disposable diapers, manufacturers are facing an uphill battle for market share. Besides the growing importance of private labels, companies are competing to capture sales from a declining number of consumers as the baby-boomer generation ages. Innovation seems to be the key to generating sales, as in the example of new superabsorbent diapers. In 1992 Kimberly-Clark Corporation introduced Huggies UltraTrim, a very thin superabsorbent diaper which pleased consumers because it took up less storage space and wasn't so bulky on the baby. Huggies UltraTrims were 50% thinner than regular disposable diapers, used 20% less material without sacrificing absorbency, and 25% less plastic while selling at about the same cost as before. P&G introduced Ultra Dry diapers in 1993 to compete with Kimberly-Clark.

Ultra Dry Thins were 50% thinner than regular Pampers Phases and cost about the same, per diaper, as regular Pampers.

Early in 1993 Ocean Spray introduced a 300-ml. aseptic carton refill for its 48-oz. glass bottles. Ocean Spray had been the first to introduce aseptic packaging to the U.S. market in the form of juice boxes to accommodate the consumer's desire for single-servings of juices. Ocean Spray combined the benefits of cost (save up to 30% versus the price of the bottled juice), reusability (pour the refill and water back into the glass bottle previously purchased), and less trash (refill uses 97% less packaging than glass bottles and there is less mass to throw away) to promote the new refill. This is not really a new idea—consumers have been buying frozen concentrated juices for years and diluting them at home—but the aseptic packaging allows them to mix the juice without remembering to thaw the concentrate beforehand and to store it at room temperature until ready to mix.

Late in 1993 Procter & Gamble introduced a 100% recycled bottle for Downy fabric softener that is made mostly from used milk jugs, thus combining factors that consumers evaluate when making a purchasing decision: cost, value, environmental concerns, and convenience. Zeke Swift, manager of environmental marketing at Procter & Gamble, feels that consumers are willing to accept a little inconvenience for the sake of lower cost. For example, upon purchasing P&G's Downy fabric softener refill the consumer must pour it into the original bottle previously purchased. The Downy refill costs less and cuts down on packaging waste, thus providing benefit to the environmentally

conscious consumer. Curiously, a Downy stand-up refill pouch is available in Canada but not in the United States because P&G's market research showed that Americans didn't want to be bothered with pouches. Testing revealed that consumers may have been concerned that the packaging was too flimsy and might not hold up in storage.

What these examples reveal is that consumers in the 1990s are willing to accept packaging changes, even if it means a little inconvenience, if the packaging benefits not only the environment but themselves in the form of value at the same or lower cost.

Source: Pat Baldwin, "Advertisers Beginning to See Green," *The Dallas Morning News,* April 25, 1993, 1J, Home Final Edition. Jack Mans and Bob Swientek, "Electrifying Progress in Aseptic Technology," *Prepared Foods,* August, 1993, 151. "First Technologically Advanced Concentrated Liquid Laundry Detergents Introduced," *PR Newswire,* May 25, 1993. Gabriella Stern, "Good Profits Come in Small Packages," *The Wall Street Journal,* November 1, 1993, B1. Jennifer Lawrence, "It's Diaper D-Day with P&G Rollout; Ultra Dry Thins Seeks to Revive Pampers," *Advertising Age,* September 20, 1993, 1. Bill Deener, "K-C Stock Falls in Diaper Battle," *The Dallas Morning News,* April 15, 1993, 1D, State Edition. David Wellman, "Life after the Juice Box; Packaging Includes Related Articles," *Food and Beverage Marketing,* May 1993, Vol. 12; No. 5; 68. Stuart Elliott, "New! Improved! $100 Million Soap!," *The New York Times,* May 25, 1993, Late Edition-Final, D1. *New Product News,* August 10, 1992, 43. Patricia Gallaher, "P&G Ships New Pampers," *Cincinnati Enquirer,* July 29, 1993, B9.

knowing the number of children age 5–13 by metropolitan area will be critical to the planning process.

2. The segment must be large enough to generate a level of sales that will cover costs and, in the long run, provide a profit. This is the criterion of **substantiability.** A firm's top priority is to make a profit. If a segment is not profitable, the firm would be better off allocating its resources to another segment that will be profitable.

3. The segment must be reachable both from a distribution and promotional standpoint. This is referred to as the **economic accessibility** criterion. It means that a potential market segment is a useful segment only if customers can be accessed through promotional means (e.g., advertising) and distribution outlets at a cost that can be justified by the revenue to be generated from the segmentation effort.

   Distribution and competitive pricing do not guarantee sales success. A firm must be able to inform consumers about its product to encourage trial use and repeat purchase. Thus, affordable media or promotional vehicles—local radio, newspaper, regional magazines, or network television—must exist to reach the segment. Otherwise, consumers may never be aware of the product or develop an interest in it.

4. Customers in the segment must exhibit similarity in their response to and preference for the marketing mix that is designed for them. This is referred to as **homogeneous response.** Consumers within a segment will respond positively to a firm's marketing mix if it is attractive to them. If the pricing is reasonable, the advertising appealing, and the product readily available, consumers will respond by purchasing the product. But if the price is perceived as too high for the benefits received, consumers will respond by not purchasing the product. In summary, the consumers in a proposed market segment must react in similar fashion to all of the variables contained in a brand's marketing mix—they must exhibit homogeneous response—if the segment is to be profitable.

Bases for Segmentation

Markets can be segmented on a variety of marketplace variables. Selecting segmentation variables is crucial to the success of a

Amount Outstanding : £

* Marketing an interactive learning system John H. L.	5004638475	27/02/2013 23:5
* Integrated marketing communications in advertisin	7000442969	20/03/2013 23:5
* Marketing communications : engagements, strateg	7000434559	20/03/2013 23:5
* Marketing : an introduction	7000528671	20/03/2013 23:5
* Essentials of marketing communications	7000533984	27/02/2013 23:5
Item Title		Du

XXXX0803

UWE Library Services
Frenchay Campus
Tel: 0117 32 82277

Exhibit 6.3   Bases for Segmentation

1. Geographic
2. Demographic
3. Psychographic
4. Benefit
5. Usage

marketing program. These segmentation variables are the identifying characteristics of individuals or groups. For example, age, level of income, and climate differences are some potentially useful variables for purposes of segmenting a market. Bases for segmenting a market can be grouped into five categories, as shown in Exhibit 6.3.

An organization formulating a segmentation strategy must decide which basis, or bases, are the most relevant for each of its brands. It is important to realize that actual segmentation efforts by companies are accomplished most typically with multiple variables taken together rather than using single variables. However, for simplicity of discussion we will discuss each category of variables separately.

Geographic Segmentation.   Geographic differences are an important basis for segmenting a market. Geographic segmentation bases include neighborhoods, towns, cities, counties, states, or countries. Consumers living within these various boundaries may share common income levels, cultures, climates, or values, all of which affect the usage of various products. Manufacturers of rock salt segment the market by geographic features, since a majority of rock salt is used by consumers in colder climates to melt ice. Automobile manufacturers also use geographic segmentation when targeting consumers. Cars produced for residents in California have different emission control standards than the balance of the country and therefore require different anti-pollution equipment.

Many of the boundaries that dictate cities, counties, and towns are merely political boundaries. Most marketers are more concerned with population boundaries, or where the people actually live. The U.S. Bureau of the Census recognizes this and designates one or more cities *plus* the surrounding areas tied to the main city socially and economically. These designations provide a more effective means of segmenting by geographic boundaries. Metropolitan areas are identified as one of the following:

1. Metropolitan Statistical Area (MSA)—An independent urban area with a city of 50,000 or an urbanized area of 50,000 and a total metropolitan area population of at least 100,000. Example: Syracuse, New York.

2. Primary Metropolitan Statistical Area (PMSA)—A large urbanized county or cluster of countries tied together either socially or economically with a population of more than 1 million. Example: Gary/Hammond, Indiana.

3. Consolidated Metropolitan Statistical Area (CMSA)—A metropolitan area that includes at least two PMSAs. Examples: Baltimore, Maryland, and Washington, DC.

These broad groupings provide marketing practitioners with a general framework for approaching markets geographically. However, product and brand managers must make a variety of decisions that require more specific information. A growing trend among many corporations, particularly those that market consumer packaged goods to supermarkets, is the practice of **regional marketing,** which also is referred to as **micromarketing.** This practice is one in which firms localize their marketing efforts—including advertising, product formulation, and sales promotions—to accommodate the unique needs of specific geographic regions. Rather than introducing identical products throughout the United States and applying the same advertising and promotions, brand managers are increasingly customizing products and marketing communications to smaller geographic units—regions (e.g., the Northeast), cities (e.g., New York city), and even areas within cities (e.g., Brooklyn). Campbell Soup, for example, markets different soup products to accommodate the regional taste preferences around the U.S.—spicier soups in the Southwest and blander soups elsewhere.

Many companies have reorganized so that decisions can be made at the local level rather than centralized, as in the past, at national headquarters. Regional marketing, or micromarketing, is aided by the availability of data (called *geodemographic* data) from research suppliers who specialize in geographical differences among consumers. These suppliers identify groups, or clusters, of consumers who reside in specific geographical areas and who have similar lifestyles and demographic characteristics. Aided with this information, which is available in CD-ROM or other computerized form, companies can then pinpoint their communications via direct-mail marketing efforts to residents in these areas. This information also informs companies regarding the most appropriate areas to locate their stores, or, from the manufacturer's perspective, where best to obtain retail distribution for its products.

Demographic Segmentation.

Demographic information is basic identifiable characteristics of a given population (age, income, or gender). Population groups with similar characteristics often have similar wants and needs that differentiate the group from others with a variety of backgrounds. These characteristics are easily understood and used and are easy to access through public information available in local libraries or in computerized data files. Examples of demographic information used in segmenting markets are:

1. *Age*   Different age groups have different product needs. Pampers and Huggies disposable diapers are targeted to the 0 to 3 year olds who are yet to be toilet-trained. Other demographic information—income, religion, gender—has little bearing on the product usage; a six-month-old baby *needs* diapers. In a similar sense, senior citizens have unique needs for certain services and products that are not demanded by other age groups.

2. *Income Level*   A consumer's income level will dictate most product purchases, especially major buys. Porsche targets those consumers with a high level of disposable income; Hyundais are targeted to those consumers more likely to be on a budget. Both consumers need transportation, but their levels of income dictate which automobile they can afford.

3. *Family Size*   A family with several children requires different products than a bachelor living alone. The Dodge Caravan and Plymouth Voyager are both minivans targeted to families with children. The Mazda Miata, a two-seat convertible, however, would appeal more to the bachelor than to the family with children or would be purchased as the second or third car by a well-to-do family with children.

4. *Education*   A consumer's level of education greatly influences product selection. A person with a college degree who is well-read on current issues is a good candidate to buy Egg Beaters, the cholesterol-free egg substitute. A person with little education who does not keep up on current issues may not be aware of the dangers of high cholesterol, and therefore is less willing to pay extra for the cholesterol-free product. This consumer is more likely to continue using real eggs.

5. *Ethnicity*   Consumers from different races sometimes need or prefer different products. African Americans require special products for their hair-care needs. Johnson Products' Ultra-Sheen and Pro-Line's product lines are both targeted to this segment of the population.

To summarize this discussion on demographic segmentation, it is important to note that sophisticated marketers typically do *not* segment markets on the basis of a single demographic variable. Indeed, there is no reason to think that all consumers who share a single commonality (such as the same age or race category) have identical needs or preferences. Effective segmentation typically requires that *multiple variables* be applied so as to satisfy the four segmentation criteria previously specified.

Psychographic Segmentation.

When marketers first began to segment markets, they relied on the various demographic variables described above. More sophisticated marketers came to realize, however, that demographics generally provide an insufficient basis for identifying and catering to differences in consumer demand. Starting in the 1970s, marketers turned to consumer lifestyle characteristics as a means of obtaining a richer understanding of marketplace dynamics and differences in consumer behavior.[4] Marketing researchers and advertisers eventually referred to consumer lifestyles with the term psychographics—no doubt to parallel usage of the term demographics that was an everyday word in marketers' vocabularies. In general, the term **psychographics** represents a combination of consumers' activities, interests, and opinions. Marketing researchers customize measures of these AIO items to suit the needs of their particular product categories and brands. For example, a maker of snow skis might design a study to determine the particular *activities, interests,* and *opinions*— collectively, lifestyles—that best characterize the users of its brand and competitive brands. This information would be useful in designing advertising messages and selecting appropriate media vehicles.

VALS (values and lifestyles) is one well-known psychographic classification model developed by the marketing research firm, SRI. In the most recent model, known as *VALS*™ *2*, eight categories are identified based on a combination of demographic and lifestyle factors such as age, income, education, level of self-confidence, health, and interest in consumer issues. Exhibit 6.4 portrays the eight VALS 2 categories in a two-dimensional format. The horizontal

Exhibit 6.4   The VALS 2 Model

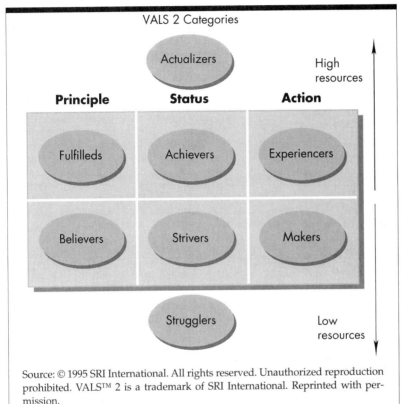

VALS 2 Categories

Actualizers

High resources

Principle   **Status**   **Action**

Fulfilleds   Achievers   Experiencers

Believers   Strivers   Makers

Strugglers

Low resources

dimension represents three self-orientations: (1) *principle-oriented* consumers who are guided by their views of how the world should be; (2) *status-oriented* consumers who are guided by the actions and opinions of others; and (3) *action-oriented* consumers who are guided by a desire for social or physical activity, variety, and risk-taking. The vertical dimension is based on consumers' resources (income, education, intelligence, or health), and ranges from minimal resources at the bottom to abundant resources at the top. The eight VALS 2 categories can be summarized as follows: [5]

Principle-oriented consumers who are guided by their views of how the world should be:

1. *Fulfilleds* are mature, responsible, well-educated professionals who are well-informed about worldly affairs. They have high incomes but are practical, value-oriented consumers. Their

CAPTAINS OF INDUSTRY

Linda J. Wachner

The Warnaco Group, Inc.

President and Chief Executive Officer

Date of Birth: February 3, 1946

Education: B.S., University of Buffalo, 1966, business major.

Career Path: Began as assistant buyer for Associated Merchandising Corp. in 1966. Held buyer positions at Federated Department Stores and Macy's until 1974 when she was named Vice President of the Warner's division of Warnaco. In 1977 became Vice President of Caron International until 1979 when she joined Max Factor & Company as CEO. Led to a buyout of Warnaco in 1985.

Profile: Only woman to head a public company that she neither inherited nor founded but acquired in a takeover.

Personal: Spent two years as an adolescent in a body cast due to severe curvature of the spine that left several fused disks in her back.

By 1985, Linda J. Wachner had been president and CEO of Max Factor & Co. for five years. She had achieved what few other women had: a place at the top of the business world. But she wasn't content to just manage a corporation—she wanted a major stake in one. She and Andrew G. Galef, a California investor who specializes in apparel companies, made a bid in 1985 for Warnaco Group after its then management announced a leveraged-buyout (LBO). Wachner's bid was successful, and by April 1986, her group won the company and took it private in a $486 million LBO. In 1991, following a massive restructuring, she took it public again. Today, Warnaco is a highly successful manufacturer of men's apparel under the Hathaway, Chaps by Ralph Lauren, Catalina and Calvin Klein underwear labels, and a leading producer of intimate apparel that is sold under the Warner's, Valentino, Bob Mackie, Fruit of the Loom, and Olga brand names. The company also manufactures lingerie for Victoria's Secret.

When Wachner took over Warnaco, the company needed help. She adopted

leisure activities center on their home. Fulfilleds are a potential target market for manufacturers of health-conscious products that are low-cholesterol, low salt, less sugar, or nonfat.

2. *Believers* are conservative and predictable consumers who favor established brands and American-made products. They have more modest incomes than Fulfilleds, and their lives are centered around their family, church, community, and the nation. They represent a target market for "buy American" manufacturers like Chrysler-Plymouth and Wal-Mart.

Status-oriented consumers are guided by the actions and opinions of others:

a philosophy she calls "do it now" to get the company back on track. "If we didn't make our people understand that the consumers are our bosses and make them look where the consumers are going and what they will want to buy in five years and ten years, we would not have been able to set the new direction."[a] She had worked in the company 22 years earlier in a much lower capacity, and many of the same people were still there. She realized that she needed to change radically the way business was conducted. How did she proceed? First, she pared down the corporate office from 200 to 7. Then, she invited 100 people in management to buy equity in the new Warnaco and helped them finance their investment. Third, she got her employees to focus on cash flow since Warnaco was a leveraged buyout and she wanted to pare down the company's debt. She also focused on EBIT (earnings before interest and taxes), innovative ideas, and distribution. Each level of management had to make objectives geared to those goals. In six years, they had repaid over $700 million in interest and debt amortization. Fourth, she directed

management toward the goals she set, rather than managing by consensus. She has enormous energy and worked to keep her team focused on these goals. For example, she emphasizes the company's successes, bringing people together to point out what had been accomplished to build energy and momentum. Her "do it now" philosophy is carried out every Friday night when each of eight division presidents prepares a report on critical issues. These are reviewed by Monday, and if there is a problem, "we fix it," she states.[b] The result: sales have increased 30% from 1986 to 1992; EBIT has risen 140%; and market share in all core businesses has grown.

Last, and perhaps most importantly, she has demonstrated exceptional leadership. "When people have a good leader who instills team spirit, and they live in an environment that demands excellence, energy, and the keeping up of momentum in order to achieve a goal, then they want to stay or, if they leave, they want to come back. While I'm pleased to say that we are building a first-rate company, it's

Continued on next page

3. *Achievers* are successful, work-oriented people who mainly get their satisfaction from jobs and family. A politically conservative group who respect authority and the status quo, Achievers favor established products and services that reflect their level of success to their peers. Achievers are a target market for high-end automobile manufacturers, high-end clothing manufacturers, and expensive specialty shops like The Sharper Image.

4. *Strivers* are similar to Achievers but with fewer economic, social, and psychological resources. Style is important to them as they strive to emulate the people they wish they could be. Manufacturers who copy expensive products like cubic zirconium stones may find Strivers to be a receptive target market.

CAPTAINS OF INDUSTRY, continued

even more exciting that we've built a world-class team."[c]

Wachner is also concentrating her attention on Authentic Fitness Corp., of which she is Chairman of the Board and Chief Executive Officer. Authentic Fitness, which manufactures Speedo, Cole of California, Catalina, Anne Cole, and Oscar de la Renta swimwear and White Stag, Edelweiss, Mountain Goat, and Skiing Passport ski wear, had been a division of Warnaco, but was sold to Wachner and other investors for $85 million. In June, 1993, Authentic Fitness completed an initial public offering at $14 per share, netting $39 million to help repay debt. Wachner quickly moved to expand the company's product lines from swimwear and skiwear to a broader market of fitness apparel such as T-shirts and aerobic outfits, all marketed under the Speedo Authentic Fitness brand name. The company also expanded its distribution channels from its traditional sporting goods stores and swim team dealers to include Wal-Mart and others. At year-end 1993, the Company had opened 8 Speedo Authentic Fitness stores with a total of 50 to be opened by the end of 1994.

Today, Wachner continues to have the distinction of being the only female head of a *Fortune* 500 company, and devotes all her energy to making her companies profitable. She has a reputation as being aggressive and demanding but fair. Her "do it now" philosophy means that she wants action from her own management. All indications are that her managers seem to like her straight-ahead approach, however. Her bottom-line focus and knowledge of the business make priorities very clear, and she treats her managers like adults.

She has also earned the respect of retailers and financial analysts alike because of her success in turning around Warnaco and Max Factor. She seems to have boundless energy and focuses it on her business. She arrives at work around 7:30 A.M. and sometimes begins meetings at 5 P.M. that run until midnight or 1 A.M.[d] She is described as tough and a hard-driving manager, but she is given great credit for knowing her businesses inside and out. She is a very determined individual, which, interestingly, goes back to a period in her childhood when she spent two years in a body cast as the result of an injury to her spinal cord. "I was alone," she remembers, "with nothing to do except focus on tomorrow and not know when it would come. Sometimes, when I'm very tired, I still dream about that silver traction triangle hanging over my head." That ability to focus on tomorrow and the determination to move forward remains with her today. "I have an unrelenting need to do the right thing—to be as close to a goal as possible," she remarks. And her goals are not timid, either. "I want to make Warner's the Coca-Cola of the bra business."[e]

[a] Stanley Gault, Linda J. Wachner, Mike H. Walsh, and David W. Johnson with reporter associate Jacqueline M. Graves, "Leaders of Corporate Change," *Fortune*, December 14, 1992, Domestic Edition, 104.

[b] Ibid., 104.

[c] Ibid.

[d] Brian Dumaine, "America's Toughest Bosses," *Fortune*, October 18, 1993, 39.

[e] Laura Zinn, "She Had to Be an Owner," *Business Week*, June 8, 1992, 81."

Action-oriented consumers are guided by a desire for social or physical activity, variety, and risk-taking:

5. **Experiencers** exhibit high energy levels, which they devote to physical exercise and social activities. The youngest of the segments, Experiencers are adventurous and spend heavily on clothing, fast-food, music, and other youthful activities. Experiencers are a promising target market for fast-food restaurants, clothing manufacturers, and health clubs.

6. **Makers** are practical, self-sufficient consumers who focus on family, work, and physical recreation. Makers have little interest in the broader world and are only interested in those material possessions that have a practical or functional purpose. Sporting goods manufacturers and companies offering family-oriented activities and products might find in Makers an attractive target market.

Consumers with resources levels either above or below the other categories:

7. **Strugglers** have the lowest incomes and too few resources to be included in any consumer self-orientation. They do tend to be brand-loyal consumers within their limited means. They represent a market for manufacturers of products emphasizing value within the household products and food categories.

8. **Actualizers** enjoy the highest incomes, highest self-esteem, and abundant resources. Image is important as they buy the finer things in life. They represent a potential market for manufacturers of high end products like luxury automobiles, yachts, and Concorde airline travel, to name just a few products.

Marketers use the detailed information from VALS 2 to position products, select media vehicles, and determine the sizes of the various potential market segments and their corresponding product needs.

Although pyschographic variables provide useful marketing information for segmentation purposes, these characteristics, compared to demographic variables, are more difficult to identify and measure. Secondary research of published data will tell a marketer how many male consumers aged 25 to 34 live in a particular market; however, secondary research cannot tell a marketer how many male Achievers aged 25 to 34 live in a particular market. Often, marketers use psychographic variables *along with* other variables when segmenting markets.

Benefit Segmentation.   Markets can be segmented based on the benefits consumers desire from using a specific product.[6] This approach attempts to identify the needs and wants of a group of consumers and then to satisfy these needs and wants by providing a product that delivers the desired benefits. Different segments may seek different benefits from the same product. For example, toothpaste manufacturers target many consumer concerns, and offer benefits in their various brands such as the following:

Brand	Benefit
Colgate	Cavity fighting toothpaste
Aquafresh	Helps remove plaque
Topol	Smoker's toothpaste—fights tough stains
Pearl Drops	Whitening toothpolish
Crest	Tartar control and cavity fighting toothpaste
Sensodyne	Toothpaste for sensitive teeth

It is interesting to contrast the underlying philosophy of benefit segmentation with that of the previously described bases—that is, geographics, demographics, and psychographics. Whereas the various "graphic" approaches to segmentation start with a particular group in mind and then develop a specific product and related marketing mix for that group, benefit segmentation has no specified group in mind at the outset. Rather, benefit segmentation presents the market with a product possessing distinct benefits vis-à-vis the competition and then allows the target market to self-select itself to that product. Of course, it often is the case that consumers who share common characteristics (e.g., the same age category) also seek similar benefits in products. All consumers who desire a particular product benefit hence become that brand's target market, regardless of whether they share common demographic or other identifying characteristics.

It is worth repeating an earlier point: A meaningful market segment is one where people share **similar purchase needs** and are accessible via promotional and distribution vehicles. This does not mean that everyone must share common background characteristics. Demographic and other "graphic" segmentation bases are useful only to the extent that consumers who share these common characteristics also have the same or similar purchasing needs. The important point to appreciate, then, is that market segmentation is not as simple in practice as the discussion to this point might have implied. All potential bases for segmentation are just that—*potential* bases. The actual value of a segmentation basis is an empirical question that resides in the particulars of a specific product-market situation. In short, only time (and good marketing research) can tell whether a potential segmentation basis is a truly valuable foundation for marketing action.

Usage Segmentation.   Markets also can be segmented by how often or how heavily consumers use a specific product or product category. Consumers' patterns of consumption can be divided into heavy use, moderate use, light use, or no use. The 80/20 principle maintains that 80% of sales are usually generated by only 20% of users. Although the choice of 80 and 20 are arbitrary (for some products the ratios might be 70/30, 75/25, or 85/15), it generally is the case that relatively few people constitute the majority of sales volume for many products. For example, beer marketers gain the majority of their sales from consumers aged 18–35.

Segmenting by usage enables marketers to focus their marketing efforts on heavy and moderate users, those consumers who purchase and use the product the most. Of course, marketers also sometimes aim their efforts at consumers who are light users in the category or even nonusers. While competitors are fighting for the loyalties of heavy and moderate product users (e.g., beer drinkers aged 18–35), a niche marketer may find success in directing its efforts at serving the segment of relatively light users.

Segmenting Business Markets

Business-to-business marketers also use segmentation strategies to meet the needs of different customer groups. Three primary factors used in segmenting business markets are geographic considerations, customer characteristics, and end-use applications.

Geographic Segmentation

Customers can be divided into groups based on their location. Customers within a specific geographic location may need the same product. For example, a manufacturer of heating systems may target the Midwest or Northeast for its products because weather dictates the need for heating systems. Or a firm may designate all customers within a 500-mile radius of its distribution center as a

geographic segment since these customers are those most efficiently serviced by the center.

Customer-Based Segmentation

Customers can be divided into groups based on product specifications and their specialized needs. For example, a cash register manufacturer produces different registers for different customer groups.
Purchasers of registers for grocery stores will require more features
than purchasers of registers for dry cleaners. Registers used in
restaurants will have different specifications than registers used in
flower shops. The manufacturer will offer a customized register for
each customer group.

End-Use Application Segmentation

Business customers also can be divided into groups based on how
the purchasers will use the product. A tire manufacturer sells the
same product to different groups for different uses. Toyota buys tires
from the manufacturer to use in producing automobiles. The tire is
only a part of the overall product Toyota is selling. A Goodyear
retailer, however, buys the same tires from the manufacturer to resell
to consumers. The automobile manufacturers and retail tire stores
are segmented based on the end-use of the same product.

   Historically, business-to-business marketers have not been as
sophisticated in segmenting their potential markets as are consumer
marketers. Many industrial firms have emphasized engineering
and production efficiencies rather than satisfying customer needs.
Other industrial marketers have been involved in customizing
products for each individual customer thus removing the need for
segmenting by groups. But business-to-business marketers are recognizing more and more the need for effective segmentation.

■ Planning and Implementing a Segmentation Strategy

Once market segments with suitable sales and profit potential are
identified, a marketer next develops an appropriate segmentation
strategy to reach these segments. The first step in this planning

process requires a *thorough analysis of the competition* within the segment. How many product entries are being marketed? What are the images of these products? What product benefits are emphasized in each marketing campaign? This analysis will enable a marketer to determine which product benefits best represent its brand and are desirable to the market segment. In this way, a firm differentiates its offering from the competition's. A firm may choose to emphasize a certain product characteristic such as Listerine's medicinal quality and germ-fighting. A product can also be positioned by its price such as McDonald's "Value Menu." Other positioning strategies include how the product will be used and who will use the product

A look at the soap market demonstrates competitive differences. Each brand emphasizes a different product benefit in an effort to appeal to specific consumer wants and desires.

Brand	Benefit Highlighted on Package
Safeguard	Antibacterial deodorant soap
Caress	Body bar with bath oil
Dove	$^1/_4$ Moisturizing cream
Lever 2000	It's better for your skin
Irish Spring	Deodorant soap now with antibacterial protection
Zest	Rinses cleaner than soap
Dial	America's #1 antibacterial deodorant soap
Ivory	$99^{44}/_{100}$% Pure®. It floats.
Tone	With cocoa butter

A marketer then *forecasts the total market potential* for each segment. A sales forecast is generated by segment or market. The forecast will be the yardstick upon which the success of the product is measured. If the costs incurred in reaching a segment outweigh the potential sales, the firm may decide not to apply its resources to that particular segment. If a segment appears profitable, the firm will decide to pursue it.

The next step in the planning process is to *develop an appropriate marketing mix* for each targeted segment. The marketing mix includes the product, price, distribution, and promotion for each market segment. Each of these elements must be analyzed for every target market. Many decisions need to be made regarding each element.

- Product: Is the current product formula appropriate for the segment or are some refinements necessary? Are the current product sizes (e.g., gallon, half-gallon, quart) appropriate or is the addition of a new size necessary (e.g., single-serve)?

- Price: Is the product sensitive to price? Is the same price appropriate for each market segment? Will a value-strategy—pricing below the competition—sell more product? Will setting a price higher than the competition create a better quality image and sell more product?

- Distribution: Will the product be available in all retail outlets within the market? Is the product better suited for some retail outlets (e.g., mass merchandisers and drug outlets) than others (e.g., grocery)?

- Promotion: How can each target market most effectively be reached? Will national, regional, or local media be most effective? What type of media will reach the segment—television, radio, print, or direct mail? Will point-of-sale materials and special trade deals sell enough product without utilizing media?

The final step in the process is to *implement the segmentation strategy*. This will be a critical yet enormous task depending on the number of segments targeted. A marketer who is thorough and detail-oriented establishes a product timetable for all company personnel involved to direct efforts towards achieving goals. The marketer must coordinate the efforts of various personnel both internally—the company's package engineering, production, and shipping departments—and externally—the advertising agency, printers—to ensure that all pertinent dates are met and steps are completed. Communication and follow-through are key to successfully implementing a marketing strategy.

◆ Chapter Summary

A market is a group of customers who have the need or desire, the ability, and the authority to purchase a specific product. Different markets are classified based on who purchases a product and how the product will be used. A product purchased by a consumer for his own use is a consumer product whereas a product purchased by an organization for use in its business operations is a business-to-business product.

Firms focus their marketing efforts for products on target markets, or groups of consumers with similar needs, rather than on the entire market. These consumers are the most likely to purchase a firm's products.

In developing a strategy to identify its potential customers, marketers may choose to segment or not segment a market. A mass-market strategy is used by a marketer who chooses not to segment—the same product and other marketing mix elements are offered to all customers throughout the market. A market segmentation strategy is used by a marketer who realizes that different groups within the market have different needs and divides the market as such. Firms that concentrate their efforts on a smaller segment of the market use a concentrated market strategy. Firms that target multiple segments with different strategies for each segment use a differentiated market strategy. A firm must target only those segments that its resources realistically permit it to pursue.

Markets can be segmented based on identifiable characteristics of individuals or groups. The five most commonly used categories of segmentation bases include geographic, demographic, psychographic, benefits, and usage characteristics. Business-to-business markets also use segmentation strategies to identify customer groups. These include geographic, customer-based, and end-use application segmentations.

For a segmentation strategy to be successful, the chosen segment must be identifiable and measurable, profitable, economically accessible, and exhibit a relatively homogeneous response function to the marketing mix that is designed for it.

Notes

1. Ronald E. Frank, William F. Massy, and Yoram Wind, *Market Segmentation* (Englewood Cliffs, NJ: Prentice-Hall, 1972).

2. Shirley Young, Leland Ott, and Barbara Feigin, "Some Practical Considerations in Market Segmentation," *Journal of Marketing Research*, 15 (August 1978), 405.

3. Peter R. Dickson, "Toward a General Theory of Competitive Rationality," *Journal of Marketing*, 56 (January 1992), 69–83.

4. Joseph T. Plummer, "The Concept and Application of Lifestyles Segmentation," *Journal of Marketing*, 38 (January 1974), 33–37.

5. Martha Farnsworth Riche, "Psychographics for the 1990s," *American Demographics* (July 1989), 24–31, 53.

6. Russell I. Haley, "Benefit Segmentation: A Decision-Oriented Research Tool," *Journal of Marketing*, 32 (July 1968), 30–35.

■ Study Questions

1. What is a market?
   a. A group of consumers who have similar needs or desires.
   b. A group of consumers with purchasing ability.
   c. A group of consumers with purchasing authority.
   d. All of the above.

2. What are the advantages of undifferentiated marketing?
   a. Production costs will be minimized.
   b. Lower, competitive prices can be offered to consumers.
   c. A specific image can be built and maintained with consumers.
   d. All of the above are advantages.

3. Why do organizations implement a market segmentation strategy?
   *a. To deal with the variability in demand.
   b. To achieve lower production costs and retail prices.
   c. To standardize operations.
   d. To appeal to a wide range of consumers within a market.

4. When an organization concentrates its marketing efforts on a smaller segment of a larger market, it is using
   a. an undifferentiated marketing strategy.
   b. a differentiated marketing strategy.
   c. a concentrated marketing strategy.
   d. a mass market strategy.

5. Which of the following is *not* a criterion for successful segmentation?
   a. The segmentation variable must be identifiable and measurable.
   b. The potential segment must break even.
   c. The segment must be economically accessible.
   d. The segment must show a relatively homogeneous response to the marketing mix.

6. Which of the following is *not* a potential basis for segmenting markets?
    a. age
    b. geographic locale
    c. lifestyle
    d. economic accessibility

7. A Primary Metropolitan Statistical Area (PMSA) is
    a. a city.
    b. an area with a population of over 50,000.
    c. a large urbanized county or cluster of counties with a population of 1 million or more.
    d. a metropolitan area that includes at least 2 MSAs.

8. According to VALS 2, which group of consumers are status-oriented?
    a. experiencers
    b. achievers
    c. fulfilleds
    d. believers

9. Industrial markets can be segmented based on all except
    a. geographic location.
    b. product specifications.
    c. psychographic characteristics.
    d. end-use application.

10. Which of the following VALS 2 groups is considered principle-oriented?
    a. achievers
    b. strivers
    c. believers
    d. makers

11. A certain company was considering segmenting its market by directing its efforts at senior citizens. Its marketing research revealed, however, that all senior citizens were not equally responsive to the marketing mix designed for them. In this particular case, age as a potential segmentation variable fails to satisfy which of the following criteria?
    a. homogeneous response
    b. measurability
    c. identifiability
    d. all of these criteria

CHAPTER (7)

Planning and Forecasting for Marketing Decisions

Chapter Objectives

The Nature and Importance of Planning

Fundamentals of Strategic Planning

Marketing Planning

Sales Forecasting

Chapter Summary

The previous chapter discussed the role and importance of marketing segmentation. Subsequent chapters deal in turn with the various marketing mix elements—product, distribution, promotion, and pricing decisions—and their role in developing successful marketing programs. The purpose of this present, linking chapter is to explain how planning and forecasting are key activities that influence and direct the development of specific marketing strategies. Effective implementation of marketing strategy requires careful forethought and analysis. Managers must develop strategic (long-range) and tactical (short-range) plans and prepare accurate forecasts of sales potential. These forecasts enable managers to know how much to invest in particular marketing programs and how to budget for advertising, new product development, and so on.

◼ The Nature and Importance of Planning

Planning is the basis for sound decision making in any situation in life. Whether you are planning a wedding, a vacation, or a multimillion dollar sponsorship program, numerous efforts pertaining to the particular activity must be coordinated and planned well in advance. Without planning, the activity may have disastrous results.

Consider, for example, a wedding. John and Susan get engaged and announce in March they wish to marry in June because they simply can't wait any longer. The bride, groom, and their parents meet to discuss the wedding. In making a list of things to do, the top priorities are to secure the church and reception site for the desired date. Once those details are set, invitations, flowers, bride's and bridesmaid dresses, and tuxedos must be ordered. Next, the music, menus, cake, and invitation list must be decided on. And finally, table seating, rehearsal dinner, and the honeymoon must be planned.

If any of these elements are overlooked or not followed up on, John's and Susan's wedding day will be ruined in their eyes. For example, if the responsibility of ordering the flowers is not assigned to a particular person, there is a risk that no flowers are displayed at the church or on tables at the reception. If the responsibility of ordering and mailing invitations is not assigned to someone, there is a risk that no guests will attend the wedding. John and Susan want everything perfect for that day, so tasks are assigned to the bride, groom, and parents and the group decides to meet in two days to discuss their progress.

When they next meet, John and Susan are very upset. The church and the reception sites are both booked on their desired date. John and Susan learn that most engaged couples have secured these details many months in advance. Susan also discovered that the dress she wanted will take six months to order. And Susan's parents found that the cost of the reception with the desired number of guests far exceeds their budget. The group is forced to rethink their original plan and make the necessary modifications allowing for these environmental factors.

This example demonstrates several elements that are key to any planning activity:

- *Timing.* Planning must occur well in advance of the activity. Planning put off until the last minute will only have negative results.

- *Tasks.* Every activity is comprised of a number of specific tasks. All details about each task must be planned for the entire activity to be successful.

- *Responsibility.* Every task needs a specific coordinator. If one person is not held accountable, the task may not get done.

- *Follow-up.* Even if responsibility for each task has been delegated, one individual must follow up on and coordinate the progress of the overall activity. Even the most responsible person may slip up and forget something.

- *Budgeting.* Budgeting is essential in planning. Plans that are too expensive for an individual or organization can have serious financial consequences. Through planning, costs are estimated and deemed acceptable or unacceptable.

These elements are critical in business planning. However, business planning has more far-reaching consequences than a wedding. Thousands of jobs and millions of dollars rely on solid planning efforts by management.

There are several levels of planning in any organization. The most important level is **strategic planning,** or the organization's overall game plan. This plan typically encompasses the firm's long-range goals and dictates direction for all departments in the firm. The means of achieving the company goals and the resources needed are detailed in full. The plan establishes goals and strategies, delineates activities, and assigns responsibility for every facet of the organization.

Strategic planning differs from marketing planning, another level of organizational planning. **Marketing planning** is the game plan for a particular product or product line. The marketing plan is the detailed scheme of the marketing strategies and activities associated with each product's marketing mix. The strategic plan is the company's overall plan; the marketing plan details the marketing efforts and strategies as outlined in the strategic plan.

Tactical planning is another level of organizational planning. **Tactical planning** involves specifying details that pertain to the organization's activities for a certain time period. For example, the scheduled dates for a radio or television campaign for the third quarter would be included in a tactical plan. So, too would the details regarding the fourth-quarter price deal offered to dealers. The production department's tactical plan may include the testing of a new quality control program on a packaging line. The tactical plan is a detailed account of the firm's short-term activities as outlined in the strategic plan.

Strategic planning is an effective means for an organization to coordinate efforts among various departments, analyze its competitive position within its environment, and allocate its resources. The strategic planning process causes all employees involved in the process to thoroughly think through the strategies that will prove most effective in achieving company goals. We will now turn to a discussion of the fundamental elements involved in strategic planning.

◼ Fundamentals of Strategic Planning

Strategic planning is comprised of four fundamental elements as shown in Exhibit 7.1.

Organization Mission

An organization's mission is the most important element in strategic planning. An organization must define its business, or what makes it different from competition. The entire strategic plan is built around this element. By focusing on its mission, management can concentrate their energies on making sound decisions, allocating resources, and generating profits in the long run. A mission statement is a guideline for the organization's decision making for both

Exhibit 7.1   Elements of Strategic Planning

- Organization mission
- Strategic business units
- Objectives
- Strategic planning tools

the short and long run. The mission provides direction to the strategic planning and marketing planning processes as is illustrated in the following mission statement:

> All of us in the Coca-Cola family wake up each morning knowing that every single one of the world's 5.6 billion people will get thirsty that day . . . and that we are the ones with the best opportunity to refresh them. Our task is simple: make Coca-Cola and our other products available, affordable, and acceptable to them, quenching their thirst and providing them a perfect moment of relaxation. If we do this . . . if we make it impossible for these 5.6 billion people to escape Coca-Cola . . . then we assure our future success for many years to come. Doing anything else is not an option.[1]

Coca-Cola's mission statement has three characteristics that are typical of corporate mission statements. First, the statement is a *vision:* the chairman of the board views the entire world as a potential target market with his company satisfying the needs of the entire target. Second, the statement is *motivational* both for employees and for stockholders. And third, the statement refers to certain *philosophies* or guidelines that will be followed: In the case of Coca-Cola, to make company products available, affordable, and acceptable to the target market. Marketing plans can be developed supporting these elements.

Strategic Business Units

Large companies offering diverse product lines or operating in several countries create **strategic business units (SBUs),** or smaller divisions, to facilitate planning and general operations. Smaller companies also use SBUs as a means of organizing operations. An SBU can be one specific product, one product line, or a particular business. Each SBU establishes its own mission statement, objectives, and strategic and marketing plans independent of other SBUs in the organization. The SBU operates as a separate entity. Typically, the individual SBUs have their own management team and operational facilities, although many organizations realize greater economies by maintaining common management and production facilities.

Digital Equipment Corporation (DEC), for example, recently restructured its business units, organizing them around product groups rather than on vertical markets. The corporation has five business units: client/server software unit; the OpenUMS client/server systems and software unit; the Unix and Microsoft Windows NT client/server software unit; the networking products unit; and the memory and peripheral upgrades unit. The presidents of the five units report to DEC's sales and marketing chief.[2]

Objectives

An organization's mission statement directs the organization's objectives. All strategic and marketing plans are based on these objectives. Every department and SBU can have its own objectives, but these objectives must be guided by the organization's overall objectives.

Any objective must be clear, concise, and realistic. Objectives are typically based on profit, market share, growth, or diversity. For example, an objective for the marketing department may be "to obtain a 15% market share and maintain a profit margin of 20% by the end of the fiscal year" for a specific product or product line. An objective for the production department may be to "reduce the level of rework from the packaging line from 5% to 3% by the end of the fiscal year." An important part of any objective is the time frame assigned for achievement. A time frame is necessary to determine whether or not the objective was met by the department or SBU. Many organizations base management bonuses on the achievement of objectives.

Strategic Planning Tools

Tools are available to help managers in their strategic and marketing planning efforts. Careful planning efforts are acutely important to most large organizations that are structured into multiple SBUs with many product offerings. The fundamental issue is one of resource allocation and prioritization. Which products/SBUs are most and least deserving of additional investments? The situation faced by business planners can be compared to that which confronts medical personnel in times of war and medical crises. These personnel are faced with the wrenching task of determining which of many injured people should receive immediate aid. *Triage* is the medical practice that is used in times of medical crisis. Patients are prioritized in terms of how badly they require immediate medical care and how likely their lives can be saved. Those patients who badly need care and are likely to survive are the top priority for assistance, whereas those who either are unlikely to survive or are not in desperate condition are lower in the priority scheme.

The following sections examine two frameworks that are broadly analogous to the practice of triage. These models are the Boston Consulting Group's Product-Portfolio Analysis and General Electric's Market Attractiveness-Business Position Model.

BCG's Product-Portfolio Analysis.

An organization's products can be viewed as a portfolio with each having a different growth rate and market share. Product-portfolio analysis offers suggestions for appropriate marketing strategies to best utilize an organization's scarce cash and other limited resources.[3]

The BCG model (see Exhibit 7.2) classifies products from the perspective of a single company and its particular products or SBUs. Classification is based on two dimensions. The horizontal axis represents the *relative market share* that a particular product realizes vis-à-vis the dominant brand in the category. Consider, for example, a product category with four brands and the following market shares:

Brand	Market Share	Relative Market Share
Brand A	50%	2.0
Brand B	25%	0.5
Brand C	20%	0.4
Brand D	5%	0.1

Brand A, the industry leader, enjoys a relative market share that is twice as large as its nearest rival, Brand B. Comparatively, Brands B, C, and D realize relative shares of 0.5 (i.e., 25/50), 0.4 (20/50), and 0.1 (5/50), respectively. As can be seen in Exhibit 7.2,

Exhibit 7.2   The BCG Product-Portfolio Model

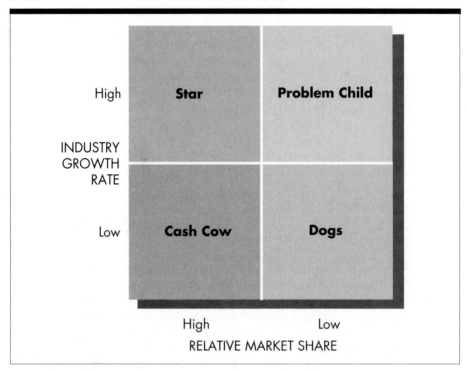

the horizontal axis delineates relative share into "high" and "low" categories. The point of division is at a relative share of 1.0. Hence, in this situation, Brand A has a relatively high market share, whereas Brands B, C, and D are all relatively low.

The vertical axis in the BCG matrix is based on the *product-market*, or *industry, growth rate*. Here, the dividing point, albeit arbitrary, is at 10%. Any growth rate above 10% is relatively high, and below 10% is relatively low. Realizing that the population growth rate in the United States is around 2% per annum, many staple products (milk, bread, industrial commodities) generally grow at a rate commensurate with the population, and, as such, are relatively low. It is in the area of new technologies and fads that growth rates are high. Innovative new products experience growth rates of 50 percent or higher in early years and then eventually decrease over time.

With these distinctions in mind, Exhibit 7.2 categorizes four general types of products and gives each a metaphoric name to suggest the implications each holds for a firm's marketing strategy:

cash cows (to be milked), stars (to sustain their ascendancy), problem children (to treat with caution), and dogs (to avoid).

- *Cash Cows:* **Cash cows** are products that enjoy high market shares but show low levels of market growth. These are generally very profitable products that generate more cash than what is needed to maintain the market share. Strategically, corporate-wide efforts should manage cash cows by investing in improvements to maintain superiority, attempting to maintain price leadership, and using excess cash to support development of new products and growth elsewhere in the SBU.

- *Stars:* **Stars** are products with high market growth rates and high market shares. Stars are market leaders with substantial profits. A large investment is required, though, to generate any growth. Strategically, efforts must be made to protect existing share by obtaining a large share of new users and investing in product improvements, better market coverage, and perhaps price reductions.

- *Problem Children:* **Problem children** are products that enjoy rapid growth but low market shares and poor profit margins. Problem children have an enormous demand for cash, and risk becoming dogs, since growth inevitably will slow, if cash is not forthcoming. Strategically, marketers of a problem child must either invest heavily to earn a disproportionate share of new sales or buy existing shares via acquisition of a competitor.

- *Dogs:* **Dogs** are products with low market shares and low market growth rates. Dogs operate at a cost disadvantage and have few opportunities for growth inasmuch as the markets are not growing and there is little new business. Marketers of dog products can pursue several strategies: (1) focus on a particular segment of the market and attempt to outperform competitors in that segment; (2) harvest the product by cutting back to minimum levels all marketing support and other investments; (3) divest the product by selling the business to a competitor; or (4) eliminate the product from the product line.

Ideally, an organization should have a balance of products in its portfolio to be successful. Products that generate cash offset those products that require additional investment for growth. If a firm has too many cash cows or dogs, overall company growth is unlikely. Likewise, if it has disproportionate numbers of stars or problem children, the cash demands may be excessive to provide sufficient support for these products. The logic underlying product portfolios is similar to financial investment logic: Don't place all your eggs in one basket! Having only a single type of security in one's investment portfolio or a single type of product in the product portfolio can lead to disaster if the market for that one offering experiences a sudden decline.

General Electric's Attractiveness/Strength Model.
General Electric has provided another model useful for strategically evaluating how a company's or SBU's products are faring and what changes might be needed. This model (see Exhibit 7.3), like the BCG matrix, is a two-dimensional matrix that portrays the position of a company's products or SBUs. Unlike the BCG, however, which classifies products on the basis of only two considerations (relative market share and industry growth rate), the GE model employs several measurements and observations to classify products. *Market, or industry, attractiveness* is measured on the vertical dimension of the model. An attractiveness index is constructed for each of an organization's products or SBUs based on such factors as market growth rate, market size, seasonality of demand, economies of scale in the production of a product, extent and likelihood of competition, and the overall cost. More attractive products enjoy larger growth rates, less seasonal demand, less competition, and so on. The matrix (Exhibit 7.3) delineates three levels of attractiveness: low, medium, and high.

A product's *business position,* on the horizontal axis, refers to an organization's strength or ability to take advantage of market opportunities. As with attractiveness, a product's or SBU's strength is indexed based on such considerations as product quality, adequacy of distribution channels, the company's relative market share, price competitiveness, sales force quality, and so on. Business position also is divided into three qualitative groupings: strong, medium, or weak.

Crossing the three attractiveness groupings with the three business-strength breakdowns results in a matrix with nine cells. Individual products or SBUs are shown as circles in the matrix, with the circle sizes representing a product's (or SBU's) dollar sales volume in relation to other product's/SBU's in the matrix. The ideal situation is for an organization to have products with high market attractiveness and strong business positions (the upper-left portion

Exhibit 7.3   GE's Attractiveness/Strength Matrix

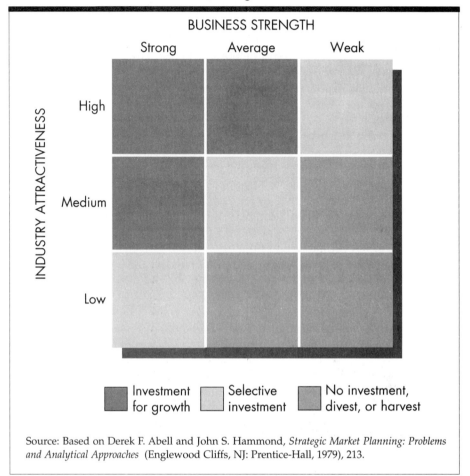

Source: Based on Derek F. Abell and John S. Hammond, *Strategic Market Planning: Problems and Analytical Approaches* (Englewood Cliffs, NJ: Prentice-Hall, 1979), 213.

of the matrix). The worst situation is a product with low market attractiveness and weak business position (the lower-right portion).

The intention is to use the model to chart the status of products or SBUs and determine which products are the best candidates for investment and growth and which are possible candidates for elimination. Resource-allocation decisions, in other words, are based on comparing each product or SBU against other company offerings. Products or SBUs in the upper-left portion of the matrix require investment and management attention; those in the bottom right are candidates for harvesting or divesting.

Marketing Plans

The final fundamental element of strategic planning is the marketing plan. As was outlined earlier in the chapter, the **marketing plan** is the detailed scheme of the marketing strategies and activities associated with each product's marketing mix. The marketing plans emanate from and are inspired by the overall strategic plan. Marketing plays an instrumental role in determining the strategic plan and, in turn, marketing plans are influenced and directed by the strategic plan.

Marketing plans can take many forms depending on the size of the company and the number of products within its portfolio. A marketing plan can be developed for the entire family of products, for each product line, or for each individual product. Most marketing plans are short-term, covering a one-year period. Other marketing plans are much longer, encompassing a period of two to ten years. A combination of the two—a one-year operational plan with a section on long-range goals and plans—is the best of both worlds.

■ Marketing Planning

Once the strategic plan is developed and approved, marketing planning takes place. Marketing plans can be created for an entire product category or for specific brands, depending on the size of each. For example, Procter & Gamble's marketing plan for Pringle's Potato Chips probably includes the entire line—sour cream and onion, original, rippled, barbecue, and so on. There is no need to develop a complete marketing plan for each of these products. On the other hand, even though it is a product within the line, Diet Coke probably has a marketing plan of its own, separate from Coca-Cola.

Marketing plans vary in length. Some companies require only an outline of the overall plan, with details provided on a quarterly basis in a tactical plan. Other companies require a complete product history with a detailed plan covering the upcoming year.

Marketing plans also vary in formality. Some companies do not require a formal marketing plan. A marketing budget is assigned for a product, and the product manager submits proposals as potential promotions arise. In this case, management is taking a Bandaid approach to marketing—competitive "fires" are put out with a quick-and-dirty promotional effort. These companies fail to realize, though, that many of these fires could be avoided if proper planning had taken place well in advance.

Exhibit 7.4   Components of a Marketing Plan

- Executive summary
- Analysis of the marketing situation
- Assessment of opportunities and threats
- Specification of marketing objectives
- Formulation of marketing strategies
- Preparation of action programs and budgets
- Development of control procedures

The most successful marketing efforts are driven by a formal marketing plan, which includes specific objectives, necessary resources, planned activities, and expected results. A detailed plan is critical in creating and coordinating effective marketing activities.

Marketing plans take different forms and follow many formats. The seven major components of a typical marketing plan are listed in Exhibit 7.4 and described hereafter.[4]

In our discussion, a marketing plan will be simulated for the growing consumer product, Rold Gold Pretzels.[5] The discussion includes facts about the product line, but the planned activities are purely conjectural. They are simply included to illustrate the points. Also, keep in mind that the actual plan will be much more detailed and greater in length.

Executive Summary

The executive summary is a recapitulation of the entire marketing plan. Usually included in the summary are a recap of the previous twelve months, objectives of the plan, a list of planned activities, and the resources required to support the plan. The executive summary is useful for those in upper management who need to be aware of these facts and figures but who are not intimately involved with the implementation of the details. In its barest essentials, an executive summary statement for Rold Gold Pretzels would look something like this:

The Rold Gold Pretzel product line increased sales from $122 million in 1992 to $181 million in 1993, a jump of 48% over the prior year. The

MARKETING HIGHLIGHTS

Wal-Mart: The Shape of Success

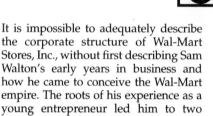

It is impossible to adequately describe the corporate structure of Wal-Mart Stores, Inc., without first describing Sam Walton's early years in business and how he came to conceive the Wal-Mart empire. The roots of his experience as a young entrepreneur led him to two important conclusions: that you did not have to go to the big city to make your fortune and that economies of scale are necessary to maximixe profits.

Walton began his career as a JCPenney managment trainee in Des Moines, Iowa, in 1940. His career was both sidetracked and boosted by World War II. While in the service, he saved his pay and used it to open a Ben Franklin Five & Dime with his brother, Bud. The store was in Rogers, Arkansas, then a very small town (now a rapidly growing retirement community). For the next seventeen years, the Waltons expanded their franchises to a grand total of fifteen stores.

The key to their early success was mastering a small scale hub-and-spoke system. All of their stores were located in a small geographic area, the farming and timber communities of northwest Arkansas and the surrounding three states, Oklahoma, Missouri, and Kansas. By studying how Ben Franklin's supported these stores with efficient distribution and the pooling of advertising monies for specific geographic areas, the Waltons were able to run a very efficient enterprise. Walton put it this way, "We had our buying office, used a Ben Franklin warehouse, and coordinated advertising and marketing. Things were running so smoothly we even had time for our families."[a]

Sam Walton was making money selling to not very wealthy people who lived not too close together. The communities he served were all less than 25,000 people. He made his money by finding the most efficient distribution methods to deliver the goods to his stores. In the 1960s, he combined these two ideas with the growing popularity of "discount" stores on the East Coast and the industrial Midwest.

Sam Walton was not content with just making money. He was a ruthless student of the trade. In the early 1960s, Walton made two important business trips. He went to the East Coast and studied the new discount stores emerging in the urban areas there. He then took these ideas to Ben Franklin's corporate offices near Chicago. He found no backers there for his ideas on starting rural discount stores. While in Chicago, he visited a new suburban store called Kmart. Don Soderquist reports this story of meeting Sam Walton in a newly opened Kmart store during that trip. Walton had his pen in hand, taking notes as he walked through the store. When Walton began to look under a display cabinet, Soderquist asked, "Mr. Walton, what are you doing?" Walton answered, "Just part of the education process, Don."[b]

Not long after this episode, Sam Walton opened the first Wal-Mart

increase was achieved due to the introduction of the brand's first national ad campaign, increased trade support, and line extensions. Sales for the next 12-month period are expected to be $208 million,

Discount City in Rogers, Arkansas. In 1969, he incorporated his 18 Wal-Marts and 14 Ben Franklin franchises. In 1970, he took his company public and opened its first hub-and-spoke distribution center. Still he persisted in targeting towns of 5,000 to 25,000 residents; primarily because his competitors were investing in urban areas.[c] As he expanded he took a very unconventional route. To be successful in his small, out-of-the-way locations, he needed the same low-cost, efficient delivery methods of his big city counterparts. He got them by opening stores in clusters, pooling advertising and distribution overhead. Essentially, he threw up a giant warehouse and then spotted stores around this hub in a 400 mile radius.[d]

When Walton started his journey, he sold to rural customers who had come to town to buy supplies. His store served as a hub and the customers drove in on the spokes. They came because he began to give them the same goods (and better service in many cases) that were available to urban customers, and at a discount of up to 15% off what his mom-and-pop store competitors could offer. In this way he outperformed the local mom-and-pop establishments.[e] Then, to compete with the economies of scale his big city competitors enjoyed by using the existing road and rail infrastructure, Walton set up his exapansion scheme on the hub-and-spoke system.

Finally, in 1982, Walton struck the deal which made his already great fortune skyrocket. He set up a relationship with Procter & Gamble whereby cash register data was fed directly into a computerized reorder system with the giant supplier.[f] This system is specifically designed to speed up the delivery of products along the hub-and-spoke system. According to Wal-Mart President Jack Shewmaker, "After our trucks drop off merchandise at our stores, they frequently pick up new merchandise from manufacturers on the way back to the distribution center. This year [1993] our back-haul rate is running over 60%."[g]

Wal-Mart is a company founded on a personal relationship with customers. Wal-Mart goes where they are. Using this paradigm, the whole company has been shaped to guarantee that low cost goods go to where people buy them, to be responsive to people. It is structured much like our democratic government is supposed to work, and in that way it is the epitome of an American enterprise.

[a] "How Sam Walton Does It," *Forbes*, August 16, 1982, 42.
[b] *Discount Store News*, April 20, 1992.
[c] *Forbes*, August 16, 1982.
[d] Ibid.
[e] "Ecology of Competition," *Harvard Business Review*, May–June 1993, 82.
[f] Ibid, 83.
[g] *Supermarket News*, August 9, 1993, 11.

an increase of 15% over the prior year. One trade promotion will be run in each quarter, supported by a coupon drop in freestanding inserts and a national ad campaign in two of the four quarters. The estimated budget to support these activities is $22 million, an increase of 12% over the prior year.

Analysis of the Marketing Situation

The analysis of the marketing situation is a breakdown of the brand's current status in the marketplace. The prior year's activities are reviewed and analyzed. Actual sales results are compared to the stated objectives in the prior year's plan. Competitive activities that affected the brand are also included. This section acts as the "state of the union" for the brand. An analysis of Rold Gold's situation would be along the following lines:

> Pretzels currently represent a $1 billion industry. It is considered the salty snack industry's fastest-growing category. The Rold Gold brand is the market leader with a market share of 18%. Sales increased 48% over the prior year. In 1992, the brand had no ad support. In 1993, a national ad campaign supported the brand with Jason Alexander, from TV's *Seinfeld,* as the spokesperson. Four trade promotions were run, one per quarter. Coupons were distributed twice during the year. All of these factors contributed to the huge increase in sales and the brand's market dominance. Eagle brand pretzels matched the Rold Gold deal levels to the trade, but ran no supporting media or promotional efforts.

Assessment of Opportunities and Threats

In this section, all opportunities regarding the brand are examined as well as any threats. Threats may come in the form of production or quality control problems within the company, competitive activities that pose problems, or potential problems within the marketing environment. Opportunities may come in the form of increased distribution, new markets, new line extensions, changes in consumer behavior that are conducive to a brand's success, and so on. Rold Gold's assessment, in simplified terms, may look something like the following:

> Rold Gold enjoys an 85 all-commodity volume (ACV) level of distribution according to the latest Nielsen figures.[6] The objective for this coming year is to achieve a 90 ACV distribution level. Sales efforts

will focus on the Southwest, where distribution is the lowest. Also, efforts in the Northeast will focus on cracking a major wholesaler who controls $50 million in sales of salty snack foods. A pretzel nugget is being pursued in R&D. Samples of several types are available and being tested in focus groups. Sales and marketing efforts will also focus on a major chain in the Midwest that has threatened to discontinue the Rold Gold line. Additional support will be given in the form of in-ad coupons. Eagle brand is being highly promoted in the Northwest and taking some Rold Gold share away. The trade allowances will be met by Rold Gold and the situation will be reviewed on a monthly basis.

Inconsistent quality has been found in the pretzels produced at the XYZ site. Production and quality control are aware of the problems and new procedures have been established to prevent further inconsistencies. [This latter statement is hypothetical, not factual.]

Specifications of Marketing Objectives

This section details the objectives upon which the marketing plan is based. As was stated in the Objectives section earlier in the chapter, objectives must be clear, concise, and realistic. Objectives are typically based on profit, market share, growth, or diversity. An important part of any objective is the time frame assigned for achievement. A time frame is necessary to determine whether or not the objective was met by the plan, department, or SBU.

The objective of the Rold Gold marketing plan in the upcoming 12 months is to
1. increase sales of the line by 15% to $208 million
2. increase market share from 18% to 21%
3. achieve a 90 ACV for the line
4. maintain a 19% profit margin on the line

Formulation of Marketing Strategies

The formulation of the marketing strategies details how the marketing objectives will be accomplished. Target markets are outlined as are the marketing mixes that will be used to satisfy the needs of these target markets. All activities that are included in the plan and the budget are detailed in full. This section acts as the blueprint for the building process for the brand that will take place over the next twelve months. Rold Gold's strategy might appear in abbreviated form as follows:

- The national ad campaign introduced in 1993 will continue. Ad flights will be scheduled twice a year, in June and December, the peak selling periods for salty snack foods. The ads will continue to use Jason Alexander as spokesperson, since he is hip and has great appeal. We will continue to stress that the products are low in fat because they are baked; they are a good value; and they appeal to all age groups.

- Trade allowances at the current level of $1.20 per case will be continued once per quarter except in the Northwest where the Eagle's level of $1.80 per case will be met.

- Additional new product slotting allowances will be offered to those accounts who do not currently carry the line in an effort to increase distribution. Two new line extensions will be added in the second quarter. The introduction will be supported by trade allowances only.

Preparation of Action Programs and Budgets

This section of the marketing plan details any programs that are designed to result in some specific action as well as the budget required to support the planned marketing activities and to achieve the marketing objectives. This section is critical in that the entire year's budget is either approved, increased, or decreased based on the plan. If a mistake is made in the budgeting, the manager and the brand may have to live with the mistake for the entire year. All figures must be accurate and precise.

In total, Rold Gold's required budget for the upcoming 12 months is as follows:

	(in millions)
Ad campaign	$ 5.5
Trade allowances	13.0
Special slotting allowances	1.0
Introduction of line extensions	1.5
Regional in-ad coupon support	1.0
Total	$22.0

Special distribution programs as outlined above are scheduled for the first quarter. Heavier allowances in the Northwest are scheduled for the second quarter.

Development of Control Procedures

This final section details how results of the plan will be measured on an ongoing basis. Management may require a monthly or quarterly update of sales versus projections. If sales are far from projections, action can be taken to alleviate the situation. Control procedures keep the marketing plan on course.

> Sales of Rold Gold will be monitored on a monthly basis. Actual case sales for the month and cumulative year will be compared to the prior year same period and to objectives. Achievement of market share and distribution figures will be reviewed semi-annually when Nielsen figures are updated and available. Since Nielsen figures are a few months behind in reporting, final judgment as to the achievement of these goals will be delayed until the Nielsen figures for the entire year are released. Profit margin figures will be judged on the basis of total revenues less total costs for the brand.

Sales Forecasting

A critical element in marketing planning is sales forecasting. A forecast of a product category's or brand's sales is crucial to the development of an intelligent marketing plan. On the other hand, the marketing plan that is developed determines the level of sales that can be accomplished. Thus, marketing planning and sales forecasting are inextricably related. The two do not occur in sequential fashion; planning and forecasting influence one another and occur simultaneously.

Sales forecasts are developed either for the total market or by market segments. In both cases, the market must be able to generate sufficient sales to support the planned marketing activities. If the potential sales are too low, marketing activities must be scaled back in proportion to the sales forecast. The marketer's top priority in developing sales forecasts and marketing plans is always to generate profits for the organization.

CAPTAINS OF INDUSTRY

Eckhard Pfeiffer

Chief Executive Officer

Compaq Computer Corp.

Date of Birth: August 20, 1941

Education: Business degree, 1963, Kaufmaennissche Berufsschule, Nuremberg, West Germany; M.B.A., 1983 Southern Methodist University

Career Path: Worked in marketing in Europe for Texas Instruments in the 1970s and later started up Compaq Computer Corp. in Europe in 1983. Served as Chief Operating Officer until 1991, when he was appointed CEO of Compaq in 1991.

Profile: Born in Lauban, Germany (now Poland). Father was a prisoner of war in World War II. The experience of fleeing his home with his mother and siblings in the wake of advancing Russian troops taught Pfeiffer that bold risk-taking, tempered by careful planning was the way to go, and he has applied that strategy in his responsibilities at Texas Instruments and Compaq.[a]

Personal: His goal is to make Compaq Number 1 in PCs and workstations by 1996.

———

Eckhard Pfeiffer was appointed Chief Executive Officer of Compaq Computer Corp. in 1991. He replaced Ron Canion, Compaq's co-founder, who was dismissed in 1991 in the wake of a disastrous year, with revenues falling 10% and earnings plunging by 70%. Pfeiffer, while working in marketing for Texas Instruments, had watched as calculator prices declined, never to recover. He predicted the same fate for personal computers, and within hours of being appointed Compaq's CEO, established a group to design the

company's first low-cost PC. He enacted sweeping strategic plans, from slashing costs to reorganizing distribution and manufacturing operations.[b] His astonishing turnaround of Compaq earned him a 1994 CEO of the Year Silver Award given by *Financial World*. His changes to the sales organization at Compaq are chronicled in the following article, from *Forbes* magazine.[c]

David Hall used to work at Compaq Computer Corp.'s Houston headquarters. He'd spend an hour in bumper-to-bumper traffic on Interstate 10 getting there from his house on the city's western fringe. But the 32 year-old salesman doesn't commute anymore. In April 1993 Compaq shifted its U.S. sales force into home offices. Even though his territory is Compaq's hometown, Hall stops by headquarters maybe once a week. "The only traffic I have to avoid is my 4 year-old," he says.

That and the customers beating down his door. Since Chief Executive Eckhard Pfeiffer took over in 1991, Compaq has doubled revenues, to $7.2 billion, while cutting its sales force by a third, to 224, saving $10 million annually in salary and rent. Some of the revenue growth has come from expanding into discount department stores like Wal-Mart, but only some. Sales to dealers and businesses still account for 80% of Compaq's revenues, and that's where the productivity gains have been dramatic. Since 1992 Compaq's U.S. sales force has tripled its revenue per person, to $16 million. "We decided to automate instead of populate," explains North American division head Ross Cooley.

When Cooley was helping to set up a sales force for Compaq a decade ago, the upstart company had its hands full just establishing itself as a credible manufacturer. So it replicated IBM's infrastructure of large branch offices in big cities. By 1991, though, the sales force wasn't getting the job done. That year revenues fell 10%; earnings plunged by 70%.

Compaq asked its customers what was wrong. They said they couldn't get a hold of sales representatives. Yet some reps reported getting more than 40 voice-mail messages a day.

Were there too few salespeople? Or were there too many who were organizing their time badly?

Pfeiffer decided it was the latter. He shrank the sales force from 359 to 224 in the U.S. and shut down three of eight regional offices. He moved the survivors into home offices. To eliminate the information bottleneck, Pfeiffer set up a toll-free number to answer routine inquiries about products, pricing and availability, freeing salesmen to focus on developing new business and servicing accounts.

This reduced overhead and, more important, enabled Compaq to use computer and communications technologies to boost the surviving salespeople's productivity. The leaner sales force could keep up only by automating. Hall's office, in the third bedroom of his one-story suburban home, is equipped with a portable Compaq LTE Lite notebook computer with a 486 processor and a 200-megabyte hard disk. The notebook plugs into a docking bay, which gives Hall access to a 15-inch color monitor, wide keyboard, 120-megabyte tape backup drive and laser printer. The office is also outfitted with fax/copier, cellular phone, two phone lines, desk, bookshelf and

credenza. Total cost: about $8,000, reflecting the fact that Compaq makes some of the equipment itself. Ordinary folk might pay $10,000.

Every morning Hall logs onto Compaq's client/server network, whose hub is a Compaq server with 38 gigabytes (billions of bytes) of on-line storage. The database includes a centralized account listing, where Compaq staffers from different departments record their contact with each prospect and client. The system also contains marketing material, technical reports, press releases and electronic mail.

Pre-Pfeiffer, these databases resided on independent networks within each department. That made it tough for the various departments and sales regions to keep abreast of one another's activities. "It was a network of who do you know to ask," recalls Michael Raab, who runs the new system. Now, rather than playing phone tag, sales, management, engineering, and customer service staffers scan the network for updates, using a point-and-click Windows interface.

After checking the network for E-mail and activity affecting his accounts, Hall downloads the material he will need for the day's meetings—what he calls his "bag of tricks"—into his notebook computer. On this slim gadget Hall keeps appointments, telephone numbers, charts, illustrations, and graphics. "We don't have to carry around overhead projectors and transparencies," says Hall. If he wants to leave a brochure with a client, he produces one on the laser printer.

On the road, Hall can plug into Compaq's database from any phone

Continued on next page

CAPTAINS OF INDUSTRY, continued

jack, or in a pinch from a cellular modem. After three or four sales calls, Hall returns home, writes and prints letters, responds to E-mail and updates the common database with the latest news about his accounts. "If I meet a new contact and need a system engineer to follow up with some information, I input that contact's name," Hall explains. "When the engineer looks at his accounts in the database, he'll call the contact.

After supper Hall spends part of his evening faxing clients technical papers or press releases. "It's neat to be able to get immediate information to your accounts," says Hall. "We weren't able to do that in the past."

Corporate users and dealers appreciate the extra attention. Michael St. John of Business Products, a Denver computer dealer that sells Compaq machines to small businesses, says that before the reorganization Compaq salesmen didn't have time to go with him on joint sales calls, but now they're available. His Compaq sales have climbed 30% in dollars during the past year—and this when computer prices were falling by 50%.

The home offices are a great way to sell to customers who themselves have employees working from home. Farmland Foods, the $830 million (revenues) Kansas City meatpacker, recently hooked 50 sales reps who work from home into a database network using Compaq notebooks. "You can see their eyes light up when we access the database right from their office," says Ann Bacon, 36, who works out of her two-bedroom town house in Menlo Park, Calif.

Sales force automation helped reduce Compaq's sales, general and administrative expenses to 12% of revenues in 1993 from 22% in 1991. As a result, even though Compaq's gross margin fell six points last year, to 23%, net income climbed a point, to 6% of revenues. Alex Brown analyst Steven Eskenazi predicts Compaq will soon get SG&A down to 10%, making it possible for the company to live well off a gross margin that will probably skid to 20% amid further price cuts.

Look at how far the world has come in a short time: IBM used to boast of an 80% gross margin, four times as fat, on its mainframes.

The downside? Hall misses the buzz, the camaraderie of colleagues who now exist solely as electronic blips. "Sometimes you feel like you're on the frontier," he reflects. Then there's the danger of putting in too many hours. "You can't leave it behind, because it's always there," says saleswoman Ann Bacon. She says her husband usually wanders in around suppertime and announces, "The office is closed!" But it's a small price to pay for not having to commute.

[a] Peter H. Lewis, "Sound Bytes; He Who Fielded Compaq's 'SWAT Team'," *The New York Times,* October 25, 1992, 9.

[b] "1994 CEO of the Year Silver Award Winners," *Financial World,* March 29, 1994, 60."

[c] R. Lee Sullivan, "The Office that Never Closes," *Forbes,* May 23, 1994, 212–213. Reprinted by permission of *Forbes* Magazine © Forbes Inc., 1994.

Exhibit 7.5   Popular Forecasting Methods

- Survey of executive opinion
- Sales force estimates
- Buyer intention surveys
- Exponential smoothing
- Multiple-factor index method

The Forecasting Process

Before a marketing manager develops the forecast for a particular brand, several other factors must be considered. In fact, a brand-level forecast of sales potential is influenced by preceding forecasts of more general economic, industry-wide, and company conditions. What are the national and international economic trends that might influence demand for the product category? What developments and trends within the industry will affect sales of the product? What trends and situations within the company itself are likely to affect sales? After these factors have been analyzed and forecasted, then specific product categories and individual brands can be addressed. The process is lengthy and complex as a great deal of information must be gathered and analyzed *before* any numbers are put on paper.

Forecasting Methods

A number of forecasting methods are available to marketing managers. These vary in terms of complexity and data requirements. Some techniques use statistical estimation procedures, whereas others are based on surveys. Exhibit 7.5 lists five forecasting methods that are in wide use. Although the following discussion looks at each technique in isolation, in actuality firms use multiple forecasting methods in conjunction with one another. As in all aspects of life, forecasting the future of a product is precarious, and it is advantageous to use multiple methods in hopes of achieving some degree of convergence if not perfect consensus.

Survey of Executive Opinion.   Many companies rely on their own executives to generate sales forecasts. These executives typically have a great amount of experience within the industry and a good feel for where the industry is going. Their expertise and instincts sometimes provide as good if not better forecasts than more analytical forecasting approaches. Executive opinion is an inexpensive and effective method of forecasting sales for existing products with proven track records.

Sales Force Estimates.   Another method of forecasting relies on those who are most familiar with the products—the sales force. Familiarity with their accounts, competitive activity in their specific area, and regional and local trends are factors that make every salesperson an "expert" in his or her own area. Marketing management must be careful, though, in relying completely on estimates from the sales force. Salespeople, whose objectives and quotas may be based on these figures, may generate low figures to help in achieving the goals. Marketers must be prepared to adjust the figures accordingly.

Buyer Intention Surveys.   Companies can also query their customers as an additional input into the sales forecast. A group of present or potential users are contacted through telephone or personal interviews or via mail-in questionnaires to determine what products and product categories they intend to buy during a specified time period. Although this method has a role to play in sales forecasting, it is noteworthy that its usefulness is predicated on two potentially dangerous assumptions: (1) that buyers in fact have specific buying intentions and will admit to these intentions, and (2) that customers will carry through with their buying intentions. In view of these assumptions, buyer intention surveys are most useful for firms who deal with relatively few customers and in situations where market conditions are sufficiently stable that customers have reasonably good ideas of their buying needs in the forseeable future. For example, a manufacturer of bottle-filling packaging lines that has less than 30 customers is likely to be enlightened by a buyer intention survey. But companies such as Lever Brothers and Quaker Oats have too many products and too many customers to effectively use this method.

Exponential Smoothing.   Exponential smoothing is a *quantitative* method of sales forecasting in comparison to the previously described *qualitative* methods. In using exponential smoothing, a company employs historical sales data to generate future sales fore-casts. Sales are listed for a specific period of time, for example, the last five years.

Exponential smoothing is used to forecast sales for only a sin-gle future period. The weighting factor, or *smoothing constant*, which we will label α (alpha), ranges from zero to less than 1.0, but typi-cally is between 0.1 and 0.5. The larger the value of α, the more sen-sitive the forecast will be to recent changes in sales. The forecasting equation in exponential smoothing is

$$\text{Sales next year} = \alpha \text{ (Present year's sales)}$$
$$+ (1 - \alpha) \text{ (Present year's forecast)}$$

Consider a situation where (1) a manufacturer of small trucks has sales in 1995 of 200,000 trucks, (2) the 1995 forecast was for sales of 210,000 trucks, and (3) the firm uses a weighting factor, α, of 0.4. Hence, the forecast of truck sales for 1996 would be calculated as follows:

$$0.4 \text{ (200,000)} + 0.6 \text{ (210,000)} = 206,000$$

Simple exponential smoothing is particularly effective when sales data have little seasonal pattern or trend. If sales change rather dramatically from period to period, the weighting factor should be small to capture the effect of earlier sales rather than basing the fore-cast predominantly on the most recent sales estimate. In practice, forecasters experiment with different values of α and use the value that history has shown does the best job in forecasting future sales.

Multiple-Factor Index.   The methods described to this point are used in forecasting sales for particular products and brands. Another forecasting issue of importance to marketers is the sales potential in particular geographical markets, such as regions, states, counties, or metropolitan areas. The following description of the multiple-factor index describes sales forecasting for this more nar-row, geographically based purpose.

There are situations where a single factor, such as the popula-tion level, provides a good indication of sales potential in the total market or a particular area. For example, the best indicator of how many disposable diapers will be sold in any year is the number of babies of diaper-wearing age. However, in most situations a single factor is not quite up to the task. Companies can design their own multiple-factor indexes based on knowledge of the factors that are most instrumental in determining the sales of their products. Alternatively, firms can utilize "off-the-shelf" indexes that have been developed for more general use. A multiple-factor index published by *Sales and Marketing Management* in its "Annual Survey of Buying Power" is widely known and broadly used by sales departments and other marketing units interested in forecasting sales in particular areas. The index reflects the relative consumer buying power in different regions, states, and metropolitan areas. The index of the relative buying power of a specific area is given by the formula:

$$BPI_i = 0.5(EBI_i) + 0.3(RS_i) + 0.2(P_i)$$

where

BPI_i = Buying Power Index: the percent of total national buying power in area i

EBI_i = Effective Buying Income: the percentage of national disposable (after-tax) income in area i

RS_i = Retail Sales: percentage of national retail sales in area i

P_i = Population: percentage of national population located in area i

This formula places the most importance, or weight, on an area's disposable income relative to the remainder of the United States (0.5); the next most importance is placed on the area's relative retail sales (0.3); and the least weight is assigned to an area's relative population size (0.2). The index, or BPI, for each area is directly comparable to the index for the entire United States, which of course is 100.00.

Consider the situation faced by a Swedish manufacturer and marketer of a line of kitchen appliances that has been very successful throughout much of Europe. This company is just entering the U.S. market and intends to distribute its appliances through specialty appliance stores and department stores. A major decision it must make is how many salespeople to allocate to various markets in the United States and what sales goals to establish for each salesperson. For various reasons, the company decides to initially introduce its kitchen appliances in the New England area, which includes six states: Connecticut, Maine, Massachusetts, New Hampshire, Rhode Island, and Vermont.

The company's review of *Sales and Marketing Management's Annual Survey of Buying Power* identifies the following facts: New England represents 5.11 percent of the total U.S. population (P), but its effective buying income (EBI) and retail sales (RS) represent disproportionately larger percentages at 5.91 and 5.52, respectively.[7] With this information, the buying power index (BPI) for New England is

$$0.5 (5.91) + 0.3 (5.52) + 0.2 (5.11) = 5.63$$

Thus, based on this formula, the Swedish company might anticipate receiving 5.63 percent of its sales volume from the New England area. It accordingly would use this information in determining the number of salespeople to assign to this area and to establish sales goals for the salespeople.

Section Summary

All of the sales forecasting methods play potentially important roles in forecasting sales. It would be misleading, however, to suggest that forecasting is simply a matter of plugging numbers into a formula and the outcome is *the* answer. If it were as simple as this, the task of forecasting could be assigned to a low-level clerical employee. However, because most industries are somewhat dynamic—with technological innovations, new competitors, and changing economic conditions—forecasting requires more than merely extrapolating the past into the future. Executive judgment is critical in guesstimating how the future situation might deviate from the past and whether sales volume for a product or product line can be expected to change and by what magnitude. The best combination is the use of good methods alongside careful managerial judgment.

Chapter Summary ■

Planning is the basis for sound decision making in any situation in life. Strategic planning and forecasting are key activities that influence and direct the development of specific marketing strategies.

The most important level of planning is **strategic planning,** or the organization's overall game plan. This plan typically encompasses the firm's long-range goals and dictates direction for all departments in the firm. Strategic planning differs from marketing planning, or the game plan for a particular product or product line. The marketing plan is the detailed scheme of the marketing strategies and activities associated with each product's marketing mix—product, pricing, distribution, and promotional decisions. **Tactical planning** is another level of organizational planning which involves specifying details that pertain to the organization's activities during the current period.

Strategic planning is comprised of four fundamental elements: organization missions (how an organization defines its business, or what makes it different from competition), strategic business units (smaller divisions, to facilitate planning and general operations), objectives (clear, realistic goals based on measurable achievements such as sales or market share), and strategic planning tools (tools to help managers in their strategic and marketing planning efforts).

Marketing plans emanate from and are inspired by the overall strategic plan. Marketing plans vary in length and formality. A marketing plan can cover a specific product or an entire product line or category. A typical marketing plan includes an executive summary, an analysis of the marketing situation, an assessment of opportunities and threats, specification of marketing objectives, a formulation of marketing strategies, the preparation of action programs and budgets, and the development of control procedures.

A critical element in marketing planning is sales forecasting. Sales forecasts are developed either for the total market or by market segments. In both cases, the market must be able to generate sufficient sales to support the planned marketing activities. Several methods are available that vary in development time and complexity. The method chosen depends on the products being forecasted. Some popular methods of forecasting include executive opinion, composite of sales force estimates, buyer intention surveys, exponential smoothing, and multiple-factor index method.

◆ Notes

1. The Coca-Cola Company's 1993 Annual Report, 8.
2. Susan E. Fisher and Kimberly Patch, "DEC Reorganizes Amid Transition; Moving Back toward Product-Based Units," *PC Week*, January 31, 1994, 103.
3. This discussion is adapted from George S. Day, "Diagnosing the Product Portfolio," *Journal of Marketing*, 41 (April 1977), 29–38.

4. For further reading on marketing planning, see William A. Cohen, *The Marketing Plan* (New York: John Wiley & Sons, Inc., 1995), and Donald R. Lehmann and Russel S. Winer, *Analysis for Marketing Planning*, 2nd. ed. (Homewood, IL: Irwin, 1991).

5. Jennifer Lawrence, "The Marketing 100," *Advertising Age*, July 4, 1994, S8.

6. All-commodity volume (ACV) is a term used by marketing and advertising practitioners to refer to the total sales of a product. An 85 ACV level simply means that Rold Gold brand has obtained distribution in retail outlets that account for 85 percent of the total pretzel volume in the United States.

7. These statistics are from *Sales and Marketing Management*, August 30, 1994, B2–B4.

Study Questions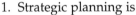

1. Strategic planning is
   a. a game plan for a particular product.
   b. a plan specifying details for, say, the next three months.
   c. a company's overall game plan.
   d. a detailed scheme of marketing activities.

2. An organizational mission is
   a. what makes a company different from competition.
   b. a clear, concise goal.
   c. a means of organizing operations.
   d. a quantifiable objective.

3. SBU stands for
   a. small business undertaking.
   b. smart business undertaking.
   c. strategic business unit.
   d. none of the above.

4. A product that is classified as a "cash cow" by the BCG procedure
   a. enjoys high market share but low levels of market growth.
   b. has high market growth rate and high market share.
   c. enjoys rapid growth but poor profit margins.
   d. has both low market share and market growth.

5. The Boston Consulting Group's portfolio matrix classifies products based on two dimensions:
   a. profit last fiscal period and stock return.
   b. competitive status and earnings potential.
   c. relative market share and earnings potential.
   d. None of the above.

6. A product that is a "problem child"
   a. enjoys high market share but low levels of market growth.
   b. has high market growth rate and high market share.
   c. enjoys rapid growth but poor profit margins.
   d. has a low market share but high market growth.

7. Three brands—X, Y, and Z—constitute an industry for one product category. Their market shares are 50, 30, and 20, respectively. Brand Z's relative market share is
   a. 1.0.
   b. 0.67.
   c. 0.4.
   d. None of the above.

8. One of the products in your portfolio is a "star." Which of the following is *not* an appropriate action for this product?
   a. Protect existing share by going after potential new product users.
   b. Use excess cash to support development of new products.
   c. Invest in product improvements.
   d. All of the above are appropriate strategic actions.

9. Which of the following is *not* a component of a marketing plan?
   a. Executive summary
   b. Creation of strategic plan objectives
   c. Assessment of opportunities and threats
   d. Preparation of action programs and budgets

10. Which of the following is true regarding General Electric's Attractiveness/Strength portfolio model?
    a. It classifies products or SBUs along three underlying dimensions.
    b. It uses more information to classify products than does the Boston Consulting Group.
    c. It is used exclusively for classifying financial investment products: stocks, bonds, mutual funds, etc.
    d. All of the above are true.

11. It is particularly appropriate to use a Survey of Executive Opinion for forecasting sales of
    a. technologically innovative products.
    b. products that competitive under highly dynamic circumstances.
    c. existing products with proven track records.
    d. All of the above.

12. Exponential smoothing gets it name from
    a. the fact that this technique is used for forecasting products that have a past history of non-rollercoaster, or smooth, sales.
    b. the use of a weighting factor, or smoothing constant, that is applied to past sales to forecast future sales.
    c. the use of executive judgment in forecasting sales.
    d. None of the above are correct.

13. A product's revenue this year was $10,000,000, whereas it was forecasted to have enjoyed sales of $11,000,000. Using exponential smoothing with an α of .3, what level of sales would be forecast for next year?
    a. $10,300,000
    b. $10,700,000
    c. $10,500,000
    d. $11,500,000

14. Which is correct regarding the value of the smoothing constant, α, in exponential smoothing?
    a. It typically is set between 0.1 and 0.5.
    b. The higher the value of α, the greater the impact that past (versus recent) sales have on the present forecast.
    c. The value of α and the impact of past and recent sales are unrelated.
    d. An α value of 0.3 is always the best, because this value is midway between the limits of 0.1 and 0.5.

15. With reference to *Sales and Marketing Management's* multiple-factor index for estimating sales potential in a given market, which of the following factors is *not* included in this index?
    a. population
    b. disposable income
    c. retail sales
    d. number of competitive brands

CHAPTER 8

Product Concepts and Strategies

Chapter Objectives

What Is a Product?

Classification of Consumer Products and Business-to-Business Products

Product Line, Mix, and Extension Decisions

Strategic Decisions for Individual Products: Creating the Actual Product

Strategic Decisions for Individual Products: Creating the Augmented Product

Chapter Summary

Product strategy is a critical element in planning both marketing and company strategies. A successful product strategy depends on a thorough understanding of products and the impact such decisions as branding, packaging, and quality have on a firm's success. This chapter discusses the nature of products and the product related decisions a brand owner encounters in developing strategies.

◼ What Is a Product?

At the core of every organization, business or otherwise, is a product. Whether it be a good, service, or idea, an organization needs a product to offer. In general, a **product** is a bundle of attributes that is received when entering into an exchange and which has the ability to meet the need or needs that occasioned the exchange. The Lean Cuisine frozen dinner we buy at the grocery store is a product. Dry cleaning service is a product. Education is a product. A medical exam is a product. Anything we buy, lease, or barter for is considered a product.

But when products are purchased, consumers demand more than simply a bundle of physical attributes. For instance, the consumer who purchases the Lean Cuisine lasagna is not just buying noodles, tomato sauce, mozzarella, and ricotta cheese. The consumer is buying a meal that tastes good, is low in fat, has under 300 calories, is easy to prepare, and will help the person maintain or lose weight.

A consumer buying a Hoover Legacy vacuum is not just buying the screws, nuts, bolts, filter, casing, bags, and accessories. The consumer is actually buying a machine that will clean carpet and floors, clean those hard-to-reach areas, is easy to operate and store, and can be returned for repairs or replacement if something goes wrong during the warranty period. Over and above these physical attributes, the consumer is buying symbolic features such as a dependable name, a 12-month warranty, and the after-sale service the company provides.

In both cases, the consumer is buying the **total product concept.** This total product concept includes everything that adds value to a seller's offering—the product itself, its package and brand name, the service that backs up product performance, on-time delivery, courteous and effective customer relations, an adequate warranty, and so on.

A product can be viewed in terms of three different levels with each level building on its predecessor. The three levels, as shown in

Exhibit 8.1　　Total Product Concept

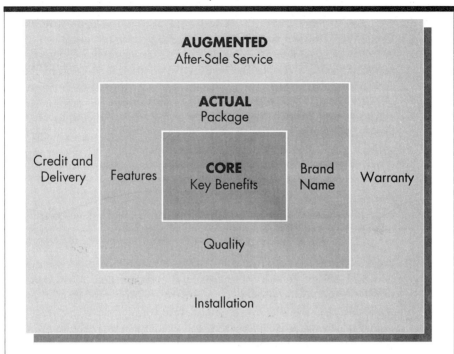

Source: Adapted from Theodore Levitt, "Marketing Success through Differentiation—on Anything,"*Harvard Business Review* (January–February 1980), 83–91, and Philip Kotler and Gary Armstrong, *Principles of Marketing* (Englewood Cliffs, NJ: Prentice-Hall, 1994), 277.

Exhibit 8.1, are the *core* product, the *actual* product, and the *augmented* product.[1]

The Core Product

The core product is comprised of the *key benefits* the product provides to the consumer. These benefits are those features a consumer views as fulfilling his or her needs and the basic reason(s) for buying the product. For instance, a hardworking, bricklaying single man might buy the Swanson Hungry Man frozen dinner because the core product—good food, large portions, and easy preparation—meet his needs. Although Swanson's satisfies his needs, the needs of the weight-conscious single woman are not met by this core product. She may opt for Lean Cuisine instead.

Consumers and business-to-business buyers seek more in products, however, than simply key benefits. If people merely wanted the thirst-quenching benefit of water, for example, there likely never would have evolved a category known as bottled water and the bevy of so-called new age beverages. People want more in their products than just key benefits. This leads to discussions of the extra benefits from products that people seek—the *actual* and *augmented* products.

The Actual Product

Products people desire consist of much more than tangible, physical, or chemical properties. The core product, or key benefit, is merely the starting point from the marketer's perspective. In economies of abundance, people demand more in their products than the provision of key benefits. The **actual product** people desire is a fleshed-out version of the skeletal core product. The marketer adds a brand name, package, extra features, and some level of quality to suit the needs of particular market segments.

For example, all perfumes and colognes possess a fragrance. This is the key benefit of these products—the core product. Yet consumers are buying more than fragrance when they make a brand-selection decision from the perfume and cologne categories. The actual product that consumers purchase includes, in this instance, a fragrance *plus* a brand name, a package, a desired quality level, symbolic features, and so on. Consider also a mother who wants a quality fruit juice to pack in her child's lunch box. She will probably buy Mott's, Tree Top, or HiC juices in individual aseptic packages rather than a bottle of generic juice. The aseptic packaging offers ease of packing, single-serve sizing, and ease of opening and drinking for the child. And the brand names denote quality. The sum total of the product features make the actual product desirable to the consumer.

The Augmented Product

The actual product is itself augmented with additional benefits to the customer. These are added as further means of differentiating a particular marketer's product from competitors' offerings. An **augmented product** is one that includes *post-purchase services* such as credit, service, delivery, installation, and warranties. A Dodge Caravan with a 36-month/36,000 mile warranty, an extended warranty, and the ability to purchase on credit is an augmented product.

This level of product is especially important in business-to-business marketing. For example, a company buying a new computer system may choose an IBM system over an IBM-compatible system for the delivery, training, installation, and postpurchase servicing IBM offers. Although an IBM-clone may be little different than the IBM itself, the marketer of the clone does not offer the same post-sale service that is provided by the IBM Corporation.

Classification of Consumer Products and Business-to-Business Products

Rather than continuing to refer to products in general, as if all are the same, it is useful to consider categories of products that share common elements. In general, products can be classified as either consumer or business-to-business depending on who the buyer is and for what purpose the product is being bought. If a product is purchased by a consumer for her or her household's own use, the product is classified as a **consumer product.** If a product is purchased by an organization to be used in producing other products or in operating its business, the product is classified as a **business-to-business product,** which also are referred to as industrial (or non-consumer) products.

It is possible, of course, that the same product is both a consumer and a business-to-business product. The Macintosh personal computer a student purchases to use in his home is considered a consumer product. The same Macintosh computer purchased by a business for use in its accounting department is a business-to-business product. The Heinz ketchup a father buys for his family's meals is a consumer product. But the same ketchup purchased by McDonald's as one of the garnishes on their hamburgers is a business-to-business product. The classification of the product changed with the buyer and the buyer's use.

A product's classification is important because consumer products and business-to-business products, even if they are the same identical products, are marketed differently. Different pricing, promotional, packaging, and distribution strategies are used to market the products to their respective target markets. Let's take a closer look at both product classifications.

Consumer Products

Consumer products are classified into categories based on how the consumer views and shops for the product. For some products, consumers go to great efforts in searching out stores that carry different brands and making comparisons both across stores and brands. For other products, consumers shop very little, if at all, and expect to find the product in most any retail outlet. How extensively consumers are willing to shop has important implications for the intensity of retail distribution. To better appreciate this issue, it is useful to classify consumer products into four categories: convenience, shopping, specialty, or unsought products (see Exhibit 8.2).

Convenience Products.   A **convenience product** is an inexpensive item that consumers purchase with little effort. Products such as milk, butter, bread, toothpaste, shampoo, gasoline, and soap are all classified as convenience products. A consumer spends little time researching the purchase. Since many consumers purchase convenience products and purchase them often, convenience products must be widely distributed. For example, candy bars are sold in grocery stores, convenience shops, mass merchandise stores such as K-mart, gasoline service stations, in ubiquitous vending machines, and elsewhere. Consumers are not inclined to engage in effortful search for a particular brand in such product categories. Hence, from the manufacturer's perspective, success requires that these products be widely available at a variety of retail outlets.

Shopping Products.   Products that consumers are willing to spend time shopping for and comparing alternative brands are classified as **shopping products.** The consumer searches for more information before selecting a particular brand and compares prices and benefits among brands offering similar characteristics and features. Shopping products are more expensive than convenience products, and the decision is more important. Examples of shopping products are stereo equipment, refrigerators, perfumes, furniture, and clothing. These products need not be intensively distributed, because their relative importance inclines consumers to seek out retail outlets and mail-order houses that carry these products.

Specialty Products.   Sometimes consumers desire a particular brand in a product category. Consumers are willing to spend a great deal of time and effort to acquire *that brand*—they are not willing to

Exhibit 8.2   Classification of Consumer Products

1. Convenience
2. Shopping
3. Specialty
4. Unsought

accept a substitute. The consumer becomes highly involved with a brand that reflects his or her personality or self-image. Inasmuch as consumers are willing to search for favored brands, distribution of specialty products is appropriately limited.

In a sense, what is called a specialty product really should be thought of as a specialty brand. For example, some consumers may go to great lengths to locate and purchase a particular Rolex watch priced at $5,000, and in this sense Rolex is a specialty brand. However, not all watches are specialty brands; in fact, for most consumers, mass-volume brands such as Timex and other low- to medium-priced watches can be thought of as shopping products—consumers shop to compare different brands in the watch category but generally do not insist on any single brand.

Unsought Products.   A product that is unknown to the buyer or a known product that is not actively sought is an **unsought product.** Consumers do not seek out unsought products until they are made aware of or need the products. New products entering the market-place are unsought products. But this status will probably change once the product is advertised and sampled. Other examples of unsought products are cemetery plots, some medical services, and insurance. Personal selling is needed to move these products.

It is important to recognize that the foregoing classification scheme is rather crude and that there are some "fuzzy boundaries" between categories. For example, life insurance is an unsought good for most college students. Who needs it when one still feels immortal? For a young couple just married, life insurance becomes a shopping good from which different policies are evaluated in terms of quality of coverage and price. For an older person who has purchased several insurance policies in earlier years, life insurance may have become a specialty good; only John Hancock, for example, may be acceptable. And for the airline traveler, life insurance becomes a convenience good when at the airport the traveler spontaneously senses that she should purchase flight insurance for this particular business trip.

Exhibit 8.3   Classification of Business-to-Business Products

1. Installations
2. Accessories
3. Raw materials
4. Component parts materials
5. Supplies
6. Business-to-business services

Business-to-Business Products

Business-to-business products are classified into categories based on how the products will be used. Different businesses purchase products for a variety of reasons. Some purchase products for use in conducting their own business activities. Some purchase products for use in manufacturing other products. Wholesalers and retailers purchase products for resale purposes. Consider the case of the General Motors Corporation. It purchases computers, supplies, and office equipment to support its business activities. GM purchases steel sheeting, nuts, bolts, screws, batteries, mufflers, tires, gas tanks, filters, belts, etc. to be used in manufacturing their automobiles. And GM dealers purchase tires for resale purposes.

A university is a service operation that also requires business-to-business products. The product the university sells is education. The university, like General Motors, purchases computers, supplies, and office equipment to support its activities. Professors' talents and abilities are purchased by the university as part of their educational product offering.

Business-to-business products can be classified into the six categories indicated in Exhibit 8.3: installations, accessories, raw materials, component parts/materials, supplies, and business-to-business services. Let's examine each category.

Installations.   Products categorized as **installations** are major capital goods. This means that such products are depreciated for accounting purposes over several years rather than treated as expense items in the current fiscal period. Usually, installations are expensive and purchased infrequently. In most cases, installations are customized to meet the needs of the specific business. Products such as custom made manufacturing lines, buildings, laboratories, and major computer systems are all considered installations.

Because installations are expensive and critical to the success of the firm that purchases them, it is typical for multiple parties to become involved in the decision to purchase an installation. This means that the selling process is typically longer, more complex, and more challenging than for all other types of business-to-business products.

Accessories.   Products that are less expensive and shorter-lived than installations are classified as **accessories.** Since accessories are purchased more frequently than installations, they are expensed in the current year rather than depreciated. Accessories are usually standard products with little customization required. Examples of accessories are Panasonic fax machines, Brother printers, and Master Craft power drills.

Raw Materials.   **Raw materials** are unprocessed products that become part of a company's finished products. For example, farm products such as milk, eggs, corn, wheat, and processed sugar are some of the raw materials Nabisco purchases for its line of cookies and other baked goods. The decision to purchase raw materials typically resides with a single individual, who most often holds the title of purchasing agent.

Component Parts/Materials.   Products already processed and those which need little processing and are ready for assembly within the finished product are **component parts/materials.** Hamburger patties, buns, ketchup, chopped onions, and pickles are all component parts/materials for both McDonald's and Burger King. Automobile tires, carpeting, and many other products are component parts in the manufacturer of new automobiles.

In some instances, the component parts retain their identity even though they are only a part of a finished product. Burger King promotes the fact that it uses Paul Newman salad dressings on its salads. Betty Crocker Supreme Dessert Bar Mixes features Sunkist Lemons in their lemon bars, M&Ms in their cookie bars, Reese's Peanut Butter in their peanut butter bars, and Kraft Caramels in their caramel bars. Betty Crocker prominently features each of these logos on the individual packages.

Supplies.   Products that are used in support of the business operations but are not part of the finished product are considered

Exhibit 8.4   Purex Corporation Product Mix, Lines, and Items

	▪ Width of the Product Mix ▪			
	Detergents	**Fabric Softeners**	**Cleansers**	**Scour Pads**
Depth of Product Lines	Purex Powdered	StaPuf Liquid	Old Dutch	Brillo
	Purex Liquid	StaPuf Sheets	BabO	Dobie
	Purex Liquid with Fabric Softener	Toss'n Soft		Brillo Line
	Trend Powdered			
	Trend Liquid			
	Dutch Liquid			

supplies. These products are purchased often and are inexpensive compared to installations and accessories. Supplies are standard products with little customization. Wearever pens, Ticonderoga pencils, Sparklett's water, and Melita coffee filters are all classified as supplies for a law firm and other businesses that use such products.

Business-to-business services.   Specialized services that support the business operation but are not part of the finished product are **business-to-business services.** A company retains the services of an outside supplier when it proves less expensive than hiring a full-time employee to do the job or when a special expertise is needed. For example, many corporations acquire the business-to-business services of specialists such as marketing research firms, advertising agencies, and specialized consultants.

◆ Product Line, Mix, and Extension Decisions

Few companies are successful by relying on a single product. Most companies manufacture and market a variety of products. All of the products a company markets can be thought of as its **product mix.** The mixture of products typically includes various items that are related in terms of the raw materials used to create them or the

| | | ■ Width of the Product Mix ■ | | | |
	Bleach	Dish Liquids	Soaps	Ammonia	Bowl Cleaners
Depth of Product Lines	Purex	Sweetheart Trend Lemon Trend	Sweetheart	Bo-Peep	SnoBol

product end-uses. A group of related items in a company's product portfolio constitutes a **product line.**

The Purex Corporation had a relatively small product mix when it opened its doors. The company primarily manufactured bleach and a few powdered laundry detergents. Over the years, through new product development and acquisitions, Purex extended its product line by offering fabric softeners (StaPuf), fabric softening sheets (Toss'n Soft), Brillo Soap Pads, Sweetheart Soaps, Sweetheart Dish Liquids, Mildew Stain Removers, and sponge products (Dobie Pads and the Brillo line). These products all relate to household cleaning. Purex also enjoyed qualifying for some price breaks when purchasing ingredients for these products since many share common raw materials. Exhibit 8.4 illustrates the depth and width of Purex's product lines and product mix.

The product mix **width** is the number of different product lines a company offers. Purex's product mix includes detergents, fabric softeners, cleansers, scour pads, bleach, dish liquids, soaps, ammonia, and bowl cleaners. The **depth** of the product lines includes the number of brands within each line. The depth of Purex's detergent product line includes Purex Powdered, Purex Liquid, Purex Liquid with Fabric Softener, Trend Powdered, Trend Liquid, Dutch Powdered, and Dutch Liquid.

Exhibit 8.5   Advantages to Offering Multiple Product Lines

1. Protect against heavy competition in any one product line
2. Increase market growth and company profits
3. Offset fluctuations in sales
4. Achieve greater market impact
5. Enable the economic use of resources
6. Avoid obsolescence

Multiple Product Lines

Any company limits its growth potential if it chooses to concentrate on a single product. A company offers multiple product lines for the reasons identified in Exhibit 8.5.

1. *Protection against competition.* If a company relies on one product for success, a competitor can enter the market, undercut the price, and steal market share. A company with more than one product line will not be devastated by the effects of a competitor's actions in any one particular area.

2. *Increase growth and profits.* Companies offer more than one product line to boost market growth and company profits. If a product category is mature with little to no growth, a company may find it difficult to increase its share and profits unless it is willing to spend more to take market share away from a competitor. By offering multiple product lines, a company has an opportunity to grow within a market and increase profits.

3. *Offset sales fluctuations.* Companies that offer products with seasonal variations find that multiple product lines help to offset these fluctuations in sales. Whitman's, for example, sells Valentine heart box assortments of chocolates from Christmas through Valentine's Day. Throughout the remainder of the year, Whitman's offers a variety of chocolate and non-chocolate products in plain packages. Although the Valentine business represents a good percentage of the

company's business, the other products provide sales in the March though December time period.

4. *Achieve greater impact.* Multiple product lines allow a company to achieve greater market impact. A company with a line of products often is more important to both consumers and marketing intermediaries than is a firm with only one product. Wholesalers and retailers typically prefer to purchase several products from one source for shipping and administrative purposes rather than order single products from many sources.

5. *Enable economic resource usage.* Multiple product lines enable the economic use of resources. Spreading operational costs over a series of products enables a manufacturing enterprise to reduce the average production and marketing costs for all its products; this results in lower prices to customers. Production facilities and personnel expertise can be used more economically in producing a line of products than for a single product.

6. *Avoid obsolescence.* Companies offering more than one product line avoid becoming obsolescent when that product reaches the end of its life cycle. All products eventually lose sales because of consumer disfavor, technologically superior replacements, or natural maturity. Firms must continually add new products to prosper. If one particular product loses sales, it will not be felt as much within the company if other products are bringing in sales.

Expanding and Contracting Product Lines

Marketers must periodically review the performance of all products. A periodic review will help a marketer to see whether each product is acceptable as is or whether improvements or modifications are needed. As each product is reviewed, the marketer will be reviewing the overall market as well. Potential opportunities for expanding a line may surface in a review. If a marketer decides to increase the product line beyond its current range, the product line is being expanded. The simplest way to expand a line is by means of a **brand extension strategy,** which involves using a successful current brand name on a new product. A successful brand name

MARKETING HIGHLIGHTS

The Gap

The first Gap store opened in 1969 in San Francisco with "four tons of Levi's," store ads declared. The owner, Donald G. Fisher, was a real estate developer who got the idea for a store selling jeans in an extremely wide variety of sizes and styles when he couldn't return a pair of jeans that were an inch too short. His idea proved a success and Gap stores opened across the country selling jeans at a 50% markup. An FTC ruling in 1976, however, put an end to the ability of wholesalers to impose prices on retailers, thus allowing retailers to sell jeans at discounted prices. The Gap's profits declined, and the chain was unable to come up with successful new designs or advertising. Fisher liked what Millard S. (Mickey) Drexler had done to turn around Ann Taylor Stores Corp. and in 1983 approached him about heading a new retail chain in an attempt to diversify. Drexler chose instead to overhaul The Gap and, together with Fisher, redirected the course of the chain that has become the retail trendsetter of the late 1980s and early 1990s.

Drexler grew up in the Bronx and graduated with a business degree from what is now the State University of New York at Buffalo and earned an MBA from Boston University. But it took several retailing jobs for him to realize he had the merchant's knack for spotting trends and creating styles. At The Gap, he began a one-man program to communicate his idea of what The Gap could be. Drexler handed out signs to confused employees with a single word in white letters on gray background: Simplify. His notion was not only to simplify the clothes but the entire way The Gap did business. He put new emphasis on The Gap's basic jeans and sweats, brought in all-cotton goods in a seasonally changing array of colors, made space in the aisles, and laid out the goods folded on tables and shelves where customers could easily handle them.

While Fisher has given Drexler free rein about merchandising, he still

gives a new product a better chance for acceptance. The brand extender hopes that the success and equity contained in the current brand will have a positive rub-off effect on the new product. Bayer Aspirin recently extended its product line by introducing the Bayer Select line of pain relievers. Each product within the line carries the Bayer brand name and is marketed to relieve specific problems ranging from arthritis to sinus pain. All of these products were brand extensions for the company.

Expanding the product line offers several advantages:

- Overall company sales and market share can increase with product line expansion.

handles the details of site selection, store construction, and manufacturing. They have made a successful team, focusing on the quality of their goods by establishing ties with manufacturers and by hiring quality-control inspectors working in factories in 40 countries to insure specifications are met. By designing its own clothes, choosing its own materials, and monitoring manufacturing so closely, The Gap has been able to keep quality high and costs low. Rapid turnover of slow-moving merchandise has kept design mistakes from dying on the shelves. By creating a uniformity of store layout and merchandise, they have developed in their customer's eyes a vision of a Gap store as a clean, well-lighted place where harried consumers can shop easily and quickly.

Drexler and Fisher embarked on another successful venture when, perceiving another market potentially receptive to Gap goods, Drexler opened GapKids in 1986 and BabyGap in 1990, adding to the profits and aiding expansion. The chain has grown to over 1,300 stores (including Banana Republic stores bought by Fisher in 1983) in the United States in 1993 and is planning to expand overseas. The company has also announced a new women's gym clothing line called "Gap Workout."

But just as the old Gap in the 1970s had to battle against discounted jeans, The Gap in 1993 is looking for new ways of guarding its share of profits against an increasingly competitive retail market. Discounters like Kmart and Target are now selling Gap-like merchandise using The Gap style of presentation but at a lower price, and the company's net income has declined. In August of 1993 the company introduced the Gap Warehouse concept. They have identified 48 underperforming Gap stores and modified them into low price-point, low margin stores for today's penny-pinching consumer. The collection consists of a broad selection of basic jeans and T-shirts as well as more fashion-oriented items that maintains the Gap's style but costs less. Whereas Gap sweatshirts

Continued on next page

- A company with an expanded product line can become a single source of supply for its customers.

- More products mean more production to a facility that may be underutilizing its capacity.

- Customers will enjoy lower transportation and administrative costs by purchasing several products from one supplier.

- New users may be attracted by products within the expanded product line resulting in increased sales in the current products as well.

- Advertising costs can be spread over several products.

MARKETING HIGHLIGHTS, continued

The Gap, Inc. and Subsidiaries
Results of Operations

| | Thirteen Weeks Ended | |
	May 1, 1993	May 2, 1992
Net sales ($000)	$643,580	$588,864
Total net sales growth	9%	20%
Comparable store sales (decline)/growth	(1%)	5%

| | Fifty-two Weeks Ended | |
	May 1, 1993	May 2, 1992
Stores:		
New	104	125
Expanded	102	74
Closed	21	19

contain 15% polyester/85% cotton, Gap Warehouse sweats contain 59% polyester. Jeans are double-stitched instead of triple-stitched and are 15 oz. denim rather than 16 oz. Many customers might have trouble distinguishing the difference in quality, but the price difference of $22 for Warehouse jeans versus $34 is obvious. As Gap VP-Finance, Warren R. Hashagen, stated, "there are three main factors: style, quality, and price" that attract Gap customers. "Having those three together is value, and that's why Gap has been successful. But there is always a segment of the population for whom price is more significant, and this is the way for us to better serve that market in our lower volume stores."[a] The question now is whether Gap Warehouse stores can successfully attract this price-sensitive customer while continuing to attract its traditional Gap customers and turn a profit.

[a] "Gap knocks off Gap; Copies Discount House Pricing Policies," *Discount Store News*, September 6, 1993, 4–5.
Source: Jeffrey Arlen, "It's a Trend; Retail Industry Piracy of Intellectual Property," *Discount Store News*, September 6, 1993, 2. Kathleen M. Berry, *Investor's Business Daily*, August 20, 1993, 3. Russell Mitchell, "A Humbler Neighborhood for the Gap," *Business Week*, August 16, 1993, 29. Russell Mitchell, "The Gap (cover story)," *Business Week*, March 9, 1992, 58–64. 1993 SEC ONLINE, INC., 1, *8

Expanding product lines has a downside, too. Line or brand extensions may cannibalize the existing brands' sales. For example, users of Arrid Extra Dry deodorant may have switched to Arrid Double-X when it was introduced. Marketers must be careful not to contribute to a current brand's decline by extending a product line.

Sometimes a product line must be decreased, or contracted if the line has become overextended. The product review mentioned above will illustrate the need for contracting a product line. Products need to be eliminated if

- a product is not a positive contributor to company profits
- the product is no longer popular with consumers and sales are low
- newer products make a current product obsolete
- too many company resources are being allocated to a product with mediocre or poor performance

A company's profitability and productivity can be greatly enhanced when products are eliminated from the mix. Eliminating poor performers can free up resources that can be used in pursuing new opportunities.

Strategic Decisions for Individual Products: Creating the Actual Product

As was noted in the chapter's introduction, products consist of more than just a core benefit or service. The actual product includes features such as brand name, package, and quality considerations that serve to differentiate the product from its competitors.

Branding Decisions

A **brand** is a name, term, sign, symbol, or some combination of these used to identify the individual offerings of one firm and to differentiate it from competitive offerings. Branding consists of several factors.

The *brand name* is that part of the brand consisting of words or letters that comprise a name used to identify and distinguish the

Exhibit 8.6   Types of Brands

1. Family brand
2. Individual brand
3. Manufacturer's, or national, brand
4. Private brand

firm's offerings from those of competitors. Xerox, Tide, Coca-Cola, and Levi's are all well-known brand names.

A *brand mark* is the unspoken characteristics of a brand such as a brand logo. The golden arches of McDonald's, the red bow tie representing Budweiser Beer, and the Pillsbury doughboy are all examples of brand marks.

A *trademark* is a brand that has been given legally protected status exclusive to its owner. The protection includes the brand name, the brand mark, and any slogan or product name abbreviation. Budweiser, "The King of Beers," and the red bow tie are all trademarks of Anheuser-Busch.

A *generic name* is a brand name that has become a generally descriptive term for a product category. Kleenex is now the generic name for facial tissues, Bandaid for adhesive bandages, Xerox for copying machines, and Thermos for beverage insulators. A brand name becomes generic through popular usage and after a judicial ruling that the name is now part of the public domain. When a brand becomes generic, this, in a sense, is because the brand owner has done too good a job in marketing the brand. A marketer wants its brand to be well known, but it does not wish to lose its proprietary right to the use of the brand name. Although a consumer may refer to the generic name when thinking about or discussing a product, she may buy another brand when purchasing the product. For example, she may write Kleenex on her list, but she may actually buy Scott's or Puffs instead.

Strategic Branding Decisions.   Manufacturers are confronted with two general branding options (see Exhibit 8.6): (1) either to use a family or individual branding strategy, and (2) to brand under the manufacturer's own name or to produce a brand that becomes the private brand of a particular retailer.

The first decision a manufacturer must make regarding branding is whether or not to brand a particular product. To brand a product is to assume responsibility for both (1) maintaining consistent quality and (2) promoting the brand. Some manufacturers do not want to or are unable to perform these responsibilities. Alternatively, a manufacturer may choose to produce unbranded products (e.g., the plain-wrap, no frills generic brands found in white boxes in supermarkets) or to produce private brands for retailers. This latter type of branding strategy is described in more detail shortly.

If the manufacturer decides to brand a product, either a family branding strategy or individual branding strategy can be followed. **Family branding** is the use of the same name for several related products. An example of a family brand is Lay's potato chips. Lays offers Lay's Sour Cream and Onion, Lay's Cheddar, and Lay's Salt and Vinegar as part of their family of products. Hunt-Wesson offers Hunt's Tomato Sauce, Hunt's Tomato Paste, Hunt's Spaghetti Sauce, and Hunt's Ready Tomato Sauce as part of their family of products. Comparatively, **individual branding** involves the use of a distinct brand name for each product within a company's product line. Tide, Cheer, and Ivory Flakes are all individual brands within Procter & Gamble's detergent line. Returning to Exhibit 8.4, you can see that Purex uses both family branding in the detergent category and individual branding for all of its remaining products.

The choice of a family versus an individual branding strategy rests largely on two considerations. First, family branding is advantageous insofar as it provides a company with a specific identity that can be leveraged across several brands. This is not unlike the case where the actions of various family members influence outsiders' perceptions of other family members. A sibling's achievements, for example, may carry over to other brothers and sisters, who thereafter enjoy some of the celebrity of their more accomplished or successful sibling. But there is a downside to family branding. When a family brand is used, a problem with one brand can contaminate retailer and consumer attitudes toward other similarly named brands in the product line. Many firms eschew family branding, because they do not want to run the risk that one bad brand can have negative effects on other brands. They prefer to market each brand on its unique strengths and weaknesses. Individual branding may be more costly, because each brand must bear the cost of separate brand-building promotions, but is less risky than family branding for the "contamination" reasons noted.

A marketer must also choose between a manufacturer brand strategy versus a private brand strategy. **Manufacturer's branded products,** also known as **national brands,** are sold in a variety of

CAPTAINS OF INDUSTRY

Andrew S. Grove
President and Chief Executive Officer
Intel Corporation

Date of Birth: September 2, 1935

Education: B.S., City College of New York, 1960 Ph.D., University of California, Berkeley, 1963

Career Path: Held title of Assistant Director of Research and Development at Fairchild Semiconductor Research Lab from 1967 to 1968. He participated in the founding of Intel in 1968 and served as Vice President and Director of Operations until 1975, when he was promoted to Executive Vice President. In 1979 he was elected to President, and in 1987 became Chief Executive Officer at Intel.

Profile: A native of Budapest, Hungary, Grove holds several patents on semiconductor devices and technology. He is a prolific author and has written articles for such publications as *Fortune, The Wall Street Journal,* and *The New York Times.* His books include *One-on-One with Andy Grove, High Output Management,* and *Physics and Technology of Semiconductor Devices.*[a] He is described as intense but personable, continually probing every aspect of Intel's business, challenging employees to think through problems with the same dedication and intellectual rigor that he brings to his job.[b]

Personal: Says Grove, "You can't ever get comfortable with your own pace in this business." Then he adds his favorite refrain: "In this business only the paranoid survive."

The following article from *Hemispheres* profiles Andrew Grove.[c]

Almost anyone who uses an IBM-compatible computer is an Intel customer. The Santa Clara, California, company, developer of the world's first microprocessor, has racked up one of the strongest financial records in American industry while manufacturing the chips that provide the brain power for most personal computers.

Last year, with PC sales rising, Intel earned $1 billion on revenues of $5.8 billion. It rose to number 93 among the top *Fortune* 500 companies in sales. Only Wal-Mart and AT&T enjoyed a larger rise in market value (now about $24 billion), according to Business Week's annual survey of 1,000 companies. Only halfway through this year, Intel has already earned more than it did in all of 1992—$1.12 billion on sales of $4.15 billion.

Intel has thrived by remaining nimble on its feet, even while growing to employ 26,000 workers. Intel's management always seems to be a step ahead of the market. The company has cultivated a culture over the years that seems unusually adaptive to change.

Intel CEO Andrew S. Grove personifies that culture. Combative and high strung, he's quick to lash out at rivals or anyone he feels isn't playing fair. He pushes his company, and employees, hard. Not everyone likes the pressure, but those who do, thrive. "Sure, we expect a lot from people," he says. "But if you're a competitor, a tough race will turn you on; an easy race is boring. And by any measure, we're in a tough race."

Grove knows that smaller, fleet-footed rivals are always going to be right behind. His answer: Accelerate the massive development process, and churn out new chips more quickly. Even as the company's new Pentium processor was being announced in March, teams of engineers were already working on two future generations of chips. Grove believes Intel can now introduce new chips every two years, rather than every four, keeping rivals struggling to catch up. "In the end," he says, "speed is our best weapon."

Grove's biggest challenge may be transforming this engineering company's marketing methods. About two years ago he launched a new marketing program to bring Intel's message to the masses of PC users. Glitzy TV commercials carried viewers soaring through the inside of a PC, finally arriving at an Intel chip. PC vendors agreed to put "Intel Inside" stickers on their PCs and use the logo in their advertising.

No PC component company had ever reached out beyond its core customer base like this. But Grove argues that Intel has to move into a new role. "We have to realize that we're a different company, with different customers," he says. "Our customer base is now millions of PC users." The program appears to be working. With Intel slashing prices on its top-of-the-line Intel 486 microprocessor, it sold about 10.7 million i486 chips last year vs. 9.5 million i386 chips, according to Merrill Lynch analyst Thomas Kurlak. These processors have considerably higher margins than the less powerful 386 chips, and demand continues to soar: Kurlak predicts Intel will sell well over 30 million i486 chips this year. Says Kurlak, "No one thought the 486 market would grow so fast. They've done a great job driving it and moving people off the i386 CPU."

Keeping a big company nimble isn't easy. Grove and a small cadre of executive managers are always reorganizing and shifting resources. When a new market opens up, the company will often create new teams to attack it. These teams operate like small business start-ups, with workers making their own marketing decisions. Grove and his executive committee provide guidance and funds, while helping cut through red tape.

Once a target market is chosen, the entire company gets behind the effort to penetrate it. Intel will invest more than $5 billion on the Pentium processor by the time the total tally is made. This year alone, the company will spend more on research and capital equipment than any rival, including larger Japanese companies. For example, Intel recently announced it would invest $1 billion to expand its microchip factory in Rio Rancho, New Mexico, which will make Pentium processors.

To churn out these incredibly complex products (the Pentium processor has 3 million transistors), Intel must be positioned to react when demand rises for new chips. "You have to place all of your bets," Grove says. "You can't hedge on R&D or plant and equipment resources if you're going to build these kind of products and be able to supply the market."

Grove's combative streak runs through Intel's culture. Employees are expected to be forceful in attacking problems, even if that means taking on a superior. This so-called constructive confrontation means that even mundane meetings can turn into lively debates. Sparks were constantly flying during the Pentium processor project, as engineers wrestled with each other over complex problems. Rather than call an official meeting—there wasn't time—one would frequently barge into a colleague's office to discuss a problem. Tempers sometimes flared. But engineers say the open communications helped them solve problems quickly and move the project along faster.

Continued on next page

CAPTAINS OF INDUSTRY, continued

Intel is unusual in other ways. Top managers are not pampered with perks: There are no reserved parking places, executive dining rooms, or oak-paneled offices, just Spartan cubicles. All Intel employees (including Grove) have cubicles. This allows Intel to easily move employees around, which it does frequently. Intel will often shift employees from other divisions rather than hire new ones to handle new products. And people are constantly moving around to new assignments.

This constant upheaval and pressure can be disturbing to some employees. But, says Grove, "You can't ever get comfortable with your own pace in this business." Then he adds his favorite refrain: "In this business only the paranoid survive."

Nowadays, Intel is spending a lot on new technology to make the PC as easy to operate as other home and office appliances—what Grove calls "plug and play."

The most obvious answer is to produce ever-more powerful chips that can handle new versions of software and operating systems that are easier for the user to operate. With Microsoft's Windows, for instance, users can click on an icon to execute a command, rather than type in a DOS command. Intel is also working on new applications that will integrate the PC and the telephone and make motion video a standard feature on PCs. Grove is betting that corporate PC users will buy a product that will allow them to communicate better

from their offices. If he's right about the appeal of new "electronic meetings" capabilities emerging on the PC, it could give another boost to PC sales—and Intel chips.

Even critics admit the future looks pretty bright for Intel. Its Pentium processor is off to a strong start, and market trends are positive. New software will require new, more powerful chips. And while competitors are inching into Intel's market, none have the momentum or market clout to derail the company—at least in the short term.

Still, Grove knows how fleeting success can be in this business. He frets that Intel will become too big or stodgy to change quickly enough to adapt to a new market or new technology. "The more successful we are in one thing, the harder it is to become something else," he says emphatically. "I have to make sure we don't get blinded by our own success."

For now, though, the limelight feels pretty good.

[a] *Business Wire,* September 10, 1993.
[b] Jonathan Weber, "Grove Calculates Intel's Course with Confidence—and Caution," *Los Angeles Times,* February 10, 1991, 1.
[c] Mark Ivey, "Inside Intel," *Hemispheres,* September 1993, 33–36. Reprinted by permission of *Hemispheres,* the inflight magazine of United Airlines, Pace Communications Inc., Greensboro, North Carolina.

retail outlets under the name of a manufacturer. Many of these products are household names such as Hostess Twinkies, Kellogg's Corn Flakes, and Sony televisions. By maintaining consistent quality and undertaking frequent promotional efforts, these brands (along with the many other well-known national brands) have achieved a high degree of brand equity, have earned permanent space on the shelves and floors of thousands of stores, and are able, sometimes, to command premium prices.

However, individual retailers and wholesalers often have exclusive rights to a brand that is manufactured exclusively for them. For example, Ann Page is the private brand of the A&P Supermarket chain. Osco is the private brand of the Osco Drug chain. Craftsman tools, Kenmore appliances, and Canyon River jeans are Sears' private brands. These brands are called **private brands** because they are not available in other stores. In a sense, they are the personal, or private, brand of a particular retailer or wholesaler. The sales of private brands have recently experienced considerable growth due in large part to recessionary pressures and declining consumer incomes during the early 1990s. Many consumers consider private brands to be of comparable quality to national brands and a better value for their money. However, the recent rapid growth of private-brands sales has probably peaked out in many product categories.[2]

Brand Equity.   Brands can be ranked according to their acceptance level with consumers in the marketplace. Some brands in the marketplace are virtually unknown to consumers because of lack of exposure or advertising. Most brands, however, enjoy some degree of brand awareness where the consumer has heard about the brand through advertising or other means.

Other brands have achieved a high level of brand preference. Consumers prefer these brands over competitive offerings. But if the preferred brand is out-of-stock, consumers would buy a substitute brand rather than leave the store empty-handed. A consumer who has NutriGrain frozen waffles on her shopping list may buy Aunt Jemima if her first choice is unavailable.

Then there are those brands that have a high level of brand loyalty among a core of consumers. If the specific brand is out-of-stock, a consumer will leave the store without buying an alternative. Many do-it-yourselfers will only buy Craftsman tools from Sears. To them, no other brand is viewed as an acceptable substitute.

A brand with a high level of sales and brand loyalty, due in large part to a high-quality reputation, is said to have high **brand equity.** The brand equity is higher when the brand has high brand loyalty, name awareness, perceived quality, strong brand associations, and other assets such as patents, trademarks, and strong channel relationships.[3] Coca-Cola, Craftsman, Microsoft, Motorola, Frito-Lay, Toyota, Sony, and Levi's are just a few of the many brands that enjoy high degrees of brand equity. Companies with products enjoying a high level of brand equity have several advantages over competition:

- Consumer demand for the product forces retailers and wholesalers to carry the product.
- The product can carry a higher price than its competitors because of the perceived quality.
- Less sales promotion activity—coupons, cents-off—are required to move the product off the shelves.
- Brand extensions are a real possibility due to the equity contained in the "parent" brand.

Even though a brand has a high level of brand equity, it still must be monitored and managed the same as any other brand. Care must be taken to protect this valuable market position.

Packaging Decisions

Packaging is another strategically critical marketing decision. Although the core product plays an important role in the consumer's buying decisions, other factors, certainly including the package, influence the decision. Some companies who have little to no advertising budget rely totally on the product's packaging to sell the product at retail. Most companies, though, use packaging as part of their overall marketing communications program.

Packaging can make or break a product. If the package fails to clearly communicate the product's benefits and features, consumers are unlikely to purchase it. In the past, it was more likely that manufacturers used packaging merely to contain and protect a product. Today, packaging is a powerful tool that serves to

- attract the consumer's attention
- break through the competitive clutter at the point of purchase
- justify price/value to the consumer

- indicate brand features and benefits
- motivate consumer's brand choices

The basic purpose of a package is to protect products against damage and spoilage. After all, the typical product is handled several times from the time it is produced until the time it reaches the consumer's home. Packaging also serves as a deterrent to product tampering. Many products (e.g., cosmetics, over-the-counter drug items, and CDs) use packaging with oversize cardboard backing to discourage shoplifters from pocketing products.

The package has more functions than mere product protection, however. A good package facilitates marketing communications. Through the use of color, size, shape, and graphics, marketers design packages to establish distinct identities that set their products apart from competitive items. The package, if designed effectively, can also act as a useful promotional tool for the marketer—the package can carry coupons or promotional offerings as a value-added feature to the product.

Packaging also affords a marketer the opportunity to address consumer concerns such as those about the environment. Many companies have chosen to use recyclable or biodegradable packing materials to address the consumer concerns and to reduce the amount of garbage for our landfills. This is referred to as **green marketing.** McDonald's opted for paper and paperboard packages in place of Styrofoam containers for their sandwiches. Many detergent manufacturers such as Colgate's Fab prominently display "The Paperboard in This Box Is Made From 100% Post-Consumer Recycled Paperboard" on their packages. And Procter & Gamble now offers refills of many of their popular brands such as Tide and Downy to reduce the use of packaging materials. Although many companies are making an honest effort to improve the environment, others make claims that their products are "good for the environment" when they actually are not. One observer estimates that only 15 percent of all green claims are true, 15 percent are outright false, and the remainder fall into a gray area.[4]

Besides facilitating marketing communications, a package can also offer the buyer convenience. Scotch Tape in its tear-off dispenser makes the product ready-to-use and convenient. Lunch Buckets, microwavable lunches for the office or school, comes in a microwavable container that is ready to use. Consumers can even eat out of the

Exhibit 8.7   Evaluation of Packaging with the VIEW Model

---

1. Visibility

2. Information

3. Emotional appeal

4. Workability

Source: Dik Warren Twedt, "How Much Value Can Be Added through Packaging," *Journal of Marketing*, 32 (January 1968), 61–65.

---

same container once the product is heated. And pump dispensers are offered as convenient alternatives for messy toothpaste tubes.

It has been established that packaging is an important part of the product. But what constitutes a good package? Although different consumers may like or dislike the same package for a variety of reasons, a package's effectiveness can be evaluated based on four general features as described in the **VIEW** model,[5] which is an acronym for the four components listed in Exhibit 8.7.

Visibility.   Visibility refers to the ability of a package to attract attention on the shelf. Does the product stand out from its competitors? Packaging featuring bright colors, different shapes and graphics, and technological innovations all enhance a package's visibility. L'eggs pantyhose packed in an egg-shaped container is a unique and highly visible product whose package sets it apart from competition. Oscar Mayer Lunchables are also featured in unique packages where the consumer can view each component of the lunch he or she is buying.

Information.   Any printed matter that deals with product usage instructions, claimed benefits, slogans, and supplementary information such as recipes or promotional offers that is presented on or in the package is considered information. Package information can stimulate trial use, encourage repeat purchases, and provide correct product usage instructions. A marketer must be careful not to clutter the package, though, with too much information that may interfere with the primary information or cheapen the look of the package.

Emotional Appeal.   Many packages evoke a desired feeling or mood, which is the package's emotional appeal. Colors, shapes, and packaging materials are all means of evoking emotional appeal.

Through effective application of these packaging materials, a package is capable of connoting a masculine or feminine image; the package design might also evince feelings of wholesomeness, tradition, sex appeal, excitement, and a host of other emotional sensations. Featuring a baby's face on its packages has successfully evoked maternal emotions from consumers who purchase Gerber products.

Workability. Workability refers to the package's ability to function. Workability is based on how well the package protects the product, how well it facilitates easy storage for both the retailer and consumer, how well it simplifies the consumer's task in accessing and using the product, and how environmentally friendly the package is. Ziplock packaging, aseptic cartons, and squeeze bottles are all innovations that have improved the workability of packaging.

Product Quality Decisions

In a highly competitive marketing environment, quality is a competitive advantage for a product. Determining product quality is one of the most basic yet strategic of all business decisions. Companies now emphasize quality to a greater extent than perhaps ever before. It seems intuitive that business success is related to the level of product quality, but only in recent years have marketing scholars devoted much formal attention to the topic. A particularly fascinating study determined that consumer perceptions of brand quality (based on ratings of 100 major brands) are positively related to corporate stock return, a measure based on an index of stock dividends and changes in a stock's market value.[6] This important study suggests that efforts to enhance product quality not only will enhance current sales performance but ultimately might also enhance a corporation's worth in the eyes of the financial community.

A brand owner can choose to offer an inexpensive product with a lower level of quality, an expensive product with a high level of quality, or a product with a quality level and price somewhere in the middle. A generic brand of detergent will utilize fewer active ingredients—expensive ingredients which effectively clean the clothes—in order to charge a lower price at retail. This product will not perform as well as its branded counterparts. Branded detergents require a higher level of quality and therefore more active ingredients to justify the higher retail price. Products such as Wisk and Tide are high quality, effective cleaners. But consumers are pay-

the detergent market for the quality. In the middle
ch as Fab and Surf which offer an average quality
age price.

r level of product quality is chosen, the brand owner
maintain consistency of quality. This can be a tough
ly competitive environment. Pressure is always on to
cut co... make a product more profitable. Ingredients or materials that differentiate a product's quality from competitors are scrutinized by the financial department. Instead of using real sugar in a cereal, for example, a less expensive, sugar-substitute may be recommended as an alternative to save money. This change, though, may prove fatal. If consumers like the taste of the product with real sugar, they may stop buying the product if it no longer tastes the same. And several minor changes in product quality over the years can totally destroy the basic product. The brand owner must always protect the efficacy of the product no matter how tempting it may be to save the company money.

A popular strategy in today's marketplace is to actually *improve* the quality of the product. Improvements can come in the area of durability, reliability, or performance. Raisin Bran added more, plumper raisins to every box. Kleenex touts its tissues as the "softest, thickest *ever!*" And Kraft Grated Parmesan Cheese improved the usage of its product by changing to a new snap tight lid. All of these changes improved the quality of the products while maintaining the same retail price. These improvements were also a source of promotion for the companies. The improved features were promoted on the packages themselves as well as in advertisements.

In the past two decades, Japanese products have made major inroads into the American market. Products such as Honda and Toyota cars have developed reputations for offering a high level of quality. The Japanese reputation for quality stems from their commitment to **total quality management (TQM).** TQM is the commitment by all departments to the strategic goal of achieving quality. TQM does *not*, however, equate to comparing an end-product to an approved standard; quality management is *not* the same as quality control. Rather, departments are encouraged and rewarded for improving the quality of their own operations with the goal of improving the quality of the overall product. If employee turnover is a problem, the personnel department may institute better training, flex hours, or job-sharing to solve the problem and improve the quality of the work force and thus the product. If rework is a problem, perhaps an employee on the line or an outside consultant can

Exhibit 8.8   Augmented Product Features

1. Delivery
2. Installation
3. After-sale service
4. Warranties

offer a means of reducing or correcting the problem, which will result in improving the manufacturing process and thus the product. If all departments are focused on producing a quality product that will satisfy the needs of the consumer, the company will enjoy lower overall costs, more satisfied customers, and, in the long run, higher profitability.

Many American companies such as Ford have emulated the Japanese quality system. Ford stresses Quality Is Job 1 both in their operations and in their advertising. The company has regained lost market share since emphasizing quality.

Strategic Decisions for Individual Products: Creating the Augmented Product

As the preceding section has noted, the actual product consists of features such as the brand name, package, and quality level. In addition, consumers and business-to-business customers often demand post-sale support features that augment products and sometimes differentiate them from competitive offerings. The post-sale support features may actually be of greater importance to the buyer than is the basic product. The means for augmenting a product include product delivery, installation, after-sale service, and warranty provisions (see Exhibit 8.8).

Delivery

Delivery encompasses the condition of a delivered product and how quickly it arrives at its final destination. Most customers require fast and dependable service. For example, a consumer who is purchasing a new refrigerator may find the same product in five different stores at five different retail prices within a $25 range. The consumer decides to buy the one from the company offering free next-day delivery. Such delivery benefits often decide the sale.

Delivery is particularly important in business-to-business marketing. Many companies are interested in reducing inventory and material storage costs. The **just-in-time (JIT)** system, another Japanese innovation, attempts to deliver only *what* is needed by the customer and *when* the customer needs it. The supplier must work very closely with the buyer to coordinate the movement of goods.

Installation

Installation is the process by which a company makes its product usable for the customer. Installation is especially important in business-to-business marketing when major production lines and equipment need to be operational before a company can use it. In the consumer market, installation is important as well. A buyer of a new dishwasher expects the product to be installed and workable by the time the installer leaves the premises. No consumer would consider purchasing a dishwasher without installation unless he or she were a plumber or a home improvement buff. Any buyer, whether in the business-to-business or consumer market, wants fast, effective, and trustworthy installation of the products he or she buys. It is the responsibility of the marketer to ensure these features.

After-Sale Service

The services offered by a company after the product is in its final destination are referred to as after-sale services. These services can include repairs, follow-up calls, mailings of special product related offers, inspections, training services for correct product usage, and reward programs. Most automobile manufacturers send periodic mailers to purchasers reminding them to get a 6-month or 12-month tune-up and servicing. Airlines award frequent flyer miles to customers once the travel has been completed. And consumers who purchase automobiles and electronic equipment want fast, dependable, and inexpensive servicing if something goes wrong with the products.

The importance of after-sale service is greater now than ever. Several factors account for this change. First, because many competitors offer products and prices that are very similar, after-sale service remains a valuable means for differentiating a company's product from its competitors' offerings. Second, consumers are more demanding than ever due to their growing sophistication and heightened expectations. Third, the trend toward direct marketing and the growth of mail-order operations necessitates that direct marketers stand behind their products if something goes wrong. Companies like L. L. Bean, the venerable direct marketer in Freeport, Maine, are legendary for backing their merchandise. If something goes wrong, even years later, L. L. Bean will offer a refund or replacement.

Warranties

Warranties are the written statements and implied promises a manufacturer provides to back up its product performance. Products with warranties can be returned to the manufacturer or its representative for replacement or repair.

Warranties are unwritten or implied as well as expressed. If a consumer purchases a new pair of hiking shoes that fall apart after brief and proper usage, the consumer can return the shoes for a replacement pair or a refund. Even though the consumer did not receive a written warranty for the shoes, an implied warranty covers normal use of the product for a reasonable amount of time.

Companies offer both full and limited warranties. A *full warranty* usually covers the product for its entire life. A *limited warranty*, which is more typical, states what services are covered and not covered for a specified period of time. Roto-Rooter, a plumbing service, offers a 90-day warranty on its parts and services. This warranty is part of the receipt a customer receives upon payment for services rendered. Most car manufacturers provide a limited warranty of 12-months or 12,000 miles on a limited number of parts. Limited warranties are provided with products at no additional charge. Most manufacturers, though, also offer extended warranties, or post-service contracts, for additional coverage but at an additional cost to the customer.

A good warranty assuredly adds value to the overall perception of a product.[7] Consider the warranty offered by Oldsmobile and promoted as the "Oldsmobile Edge." This value-adding warranty augmented the core product by (1) giving the consumer a trial period of 30 days or 1,500 miles to test an Oldsmobile and return it if not completely satisfied, (2) providing a warranty that extends for 3 years or 50,000 miles, and (3) offering a 24-hour roadside assistance service that takes care of road breakdowns (such as flat tires) without cost to the owner. In general, the success of an augmented product depends on the availability and quality of its after-sale services.

■ Chapter Summary

A product is everything a buyer receives in an exchange with a seller. Products can be viewed at three different levels: the core product (consists of the key benefits that satisfy a consumer's need), the actual product (the core product plus the brand name, package, extra features, and quality level), and the augmented product (the actual product plus postpurchase services). When a consumer buys a product, he or she is purchasing the total product concept including everything that adds value to the seller's offering.

Products are classified as either consumer products (products purchased by a consumer for his or her own use) or business-to-business products (products purchased by an organization for use in business operations). Some products can be classified as both a consumer and business-to-business product, since the classification is dependent on who buys the product and how it will be used.

Consumer products are further classified into categories based on how the consumer views and shops for the product. Consumer products are either convenience products, shopping products, specialty products, or unsought products. The product's price and purchase importance determine the level of involvement a consumer will devote to purchasing the product and, in turn, the amount, or intensity, of distribution a product must receive in order to be successful.

Business-to-business products are further classified into categories based on how the product will be used. Categories of business-to-business products include installations, accessories, raw materials, component parts/materials, supplies, and business-to-business services.

All of the products a company offers constitute its product mix. A group of related items is a product line. Multiple product lines enable a company to boost market growth and company profits. The product lines must be periodically reviewed to determine whether the lines should be expanded or contracted.

In creating the actual product, a manager must make many decisions regarding the branding, packaging, and quality of the product. All of these features help to differentiate the product from its competitors. In creating an augmented product, the post-sale support features of delivery, installation, after-sale service, and warranties are features that differentiate the product from its competitors.

Notes

1. This scheme is broadly inspired by Theodore Levitt, "Marketing Success through Differentiation—on Anything," *Harvard Business Review* (January–February 1980), 83–91. The scheme is more directly adapted from Philip Kotler and Gary Armstrong, *Principles of Marketing* (Englewood Cliffs, NJ: Prentice-Hall, 1994), 277.

2. Emily De Nitto, "Back into Focus," *Businessweek*, May 29, 1995, 22–26.

3. David A. Aaker, *Managing Brand Equity* (New York: The Free Press, 1991). See also Kevin Lane Keller, "Conceptualizing, Measuring, and Managing Customer-Based Brand Equity," *Journal of Marketing*, 57 (January 1993), 1–22.

4. Penelope Wang, "Going for the Green," *Money*, September, 1991, 98.

5. Dik Warren Twedt, "How Much Value Can Be Added through Packaging," *Journal of Marketing*, 32 (January 1968), 61–65.

6. David A. Aaker and Robert Jacobson, "The Financial Information Content of Perceived Quality," *Journal of Marketing Research*, 31 (May 1994), 191–201.

7. Terence A. Shimp and William O. Bearden, "Warranty and Other Extrinsic Cue Effects on Consumers' Risk Perceptions," *Journal of Consumer Research*, 9 (June 1982), 38–46.

Study Questions

1. A(n)_____ encompasses the key benefits consumers seek when making a purchase in the product category.
   a. actual product
   b. core product
   c. augmented product
   d. total product

2. An actual product
   a. contains the core product plus a brand name, a package, a desired quality level, symbolic features, and so on.
   b. includes postpurchase services.
   c. is comprised of the key benefits the product provides to the consumer.
   d. is called an actual product in contrast to a service.

3. Which of the following is not one of the various types of business-to-business products?
   a. accessories
   b. component parts/materials
   c. installations
   d. specialty items

4. A specialty product
   a. is an inexpensive item that consumers purchase with little effort.
   b. is a particular brand in a product category that a consumer essentially insists on.
   c. is a known product that is not actually sought by consumers.
   d. is one that consumers find special due to nostalgia or other sentimental reasons for purchasing.

5. Business-to-business products are classified by
   a. how a product will be used.
   b. when a product will be used.
   c. in what department a product will be used.
   d. the type of business that purchases the product.

6. Which of the following is *not* a type of consumer product?
   a. convenience products
   b. shopping products
   c. installment products
   d. unsought products

7. A _____ constitutes all of the products an organization markets.
   a. product mix
   b. product line
   c. product extension
   d. product assortment

8. What is the simplest means of expanding a product line?
   a. By introducing an entirely new product.
   b. By offering a new size or feature to an existing product.
   c. By using a brand extension strategy.
   d. By acquiring a new brand from another company.

9. Which of the following is *not* an advantage of expanding a product line?
   a. Overall company sales and market share can increase.
   b. A company can become a single source of supply for its customers.
   c. Underutilized production capacity may by used.
   d. All of the above are advantages.

10. A product that is unknown to the consumer or one that the consumer does not actively seek is called a(n) _____ product.
    a. unsought
    b avoidance
    c. nonshopping
    d. None of the above.

11. A brand mark is
    a. the unspoken characteristics of a brand such as a brand logo.
    b. that part of a brand consisting of words or letters that comprise a name used to identify the product.
    c. a brand that has been given legally protected status exclusive to its owner.
    d. the form of branding most often used in lesser developed countries where the illiteracy rate is high.

12. A private brand is one that is
    a. one customized for a specific group of wealthy consumers.
    b. marketed exclusively to small grocery stores.
    c. a brand that is manufactured exclusively for a particular retailer and is not available to other retailers.
    d. typically premium priced in comparison to national brands.

13. A brand that has achieved a high level of brand loyalty due to its ability to satisfy consumers is said to possess
    a. a total product concept.
    b. brand equity.
    c. core benefits.
    d. augmentation.

14. Which of the following is not a component of the VIEW model of packaging?
    a. visibility
    b. information
    c. effectiveness
    d. workability

15. An example of an augmented product feature is
    a. the package.
    b. the brand name.
    c. the quality level.
    d. the warranty.

16. A university builds a new indoor practice facility for the soccer team. This product would be classified as a(an)
    a. installation.
    b. accessory.
    c. component part.
    d. business-to-business service.

17. There are various advantages to a firm's offering multiple products (rather than a single product). Which of the following is *not* one of these advantages?
    a. To offset fluctuations in sales.
    b. To achieve greater market impact.
    c. To avoid obsolescence.
    d. All of these are advantages.

18. Expanding a product line offers several advantages to a company. Which of the following is *not* one of these advantages?
    a. A company can become a single source of supply for its customers with an expanded product line.
    b. Advertising costs can be spread over several products.
    c. Maintaining product quality is less important when a company has multiple products in its product line.
    d. More products mean more production to a facility that may be underutilizing its capacity.

19. Although Jockey is the specific brand of a company that markets underwear, many people use the term jockey shorts to refer to a certain style of underwear rather than to the brand per se. Hence, for these consumers the name Jockey has become
    a. preemptive.
    b. exemptive.

   c. restrictive.

   d. generic.

20. Because brands sometimes have problems and even catastrophes, many companies avoid using the same family name for all brands in a particular product category. Thus, instead of using family branding, they prefer to use _____ branding.

   a. private

   b. national

   c. individual

   d. protective

21. Which of the following descriptions best describes the practice of total quality management (TQM)?

   a. The total product concept is more important than the sum of its parts.

   b. All components of a business enterprise should aim to produce the highest quality product in the industry.

   c. All departments in the organization need to be committed to the strategic goal of achieving quality.

   d. The production and engineering departments should determine the level of product quality a firm should offer.

22. Which of the following is *not* an augmented product feature?

   a. Delivery

   b. Installation

   c. After-sale service

   d. Packaging

CHAPTER 9

Product Development and Management

Chapter Objectives

As the last chapter illustrated, numerous decisions must be made regarding a product. When a consumer sees the thousands of products on store displays and shelves, he or she would be surprised to know the great amount of time and effort that went into planning these products. Whether a product is new or established, managers must manage and nurture products and maintain their integrity. Developing new products is especially time-consuming as great care must be taken to ensure that the best decisions are made *before* the product reaches channel intermediaries and final consumers. This chapter takes a closer look at the process and management of product development.

■ Strategies for New Products and New Markets

Established products are the lifeblood for most companies. But a company that depends solely on its current stable of products may be headed for trouble. Aggressive competitive activity or a major change in technology can cause a rapid decline in sales for even the most successful product. Growth is fundamental to the long-term success of any organization. But growth can only come in a limited number of ways:

- by increasing the market share of existing products in existing markets
- by expanding existing products into new markets
- by developing new products

Opportunities for growth are dependent on a firm's ability to expand its operations in existing or untapped markets or to introduce innovative new products into existing or new markets. As shown in Exhibit 9.1, firms can avail themselves of four general options for increasing sales volume.[1]

Market Penetration

Market Penetration is a strategy that is used to increase sales and market share with *existing products* in their *existing markets*. This strategy is used most often for mature products in mature markets.

Exhibit 9.1   Market and Product Development Strategies

- Market penetration
- Market development
- Product development
- Product diversification

Firms attempt to penetrate markets either by improving quality, dropping prices, increasing distribution, or engaging in aggressive advertising and other promotional activities. McDonald's Corporation increased market share in the early 1990s by expanding use of what corporate executives call "association marketing." McDonald's linked itself to a number of major events—the blockbuster movie, *Jurassic Park,* the World Cup soccer tournament held in the United States in 1994, and the "Nothing But Net" advertising campaign featuring NBA greats Michael Jordan and Larry Bird.[2]

Market Development

A **market development** strategy involves *finding new markets* and new users for *existing products*. This strategy is undertaken when (1) new uses are discovered for mature products, (2) new users are found due to a change in consumer behavior or demographics, or (3) new markets are entered with an existing product. In the 1980s Rogaine, a hair-restoration product, was originally targeted to men. Later Upjohn, the maker of Rogaine, began running ads in women's magazines to reach women with thinning hair. Another illustration of a market development strategy is Samuel Adams microbrewery beer, which initially was available only in Boston, but which since has moved both southward and westward in increasing its share of microbrewery sales.

Product Development

A **product development** strategy introduces *new products* into *established markets*. The new product, sometimes, is the firm's first entry in a particular marketplace. Honda in 1994, for example, rather belatedly introduced a four-wheel drive vehicle to compete against

Jeep and the other competitors vying for that market. Computer manufacturers continually introduce faster and smaller personal computers to the established market comprised of computer technocrats who demand the newest and best technology.

Product Diversification

A **product diversification** strategy focuses on developing *new products* for *new markets.* The Chrysler Corporation's introduction of the Neon in 1994 represented a diversification move to appeal to the large and relatively unserved group of Generation Xers. Product diversification enables a company to be less dependent on any one product or product line.

■ From Birth to Death: Product Life Cycles

The significance of the four product and market strategies is better appreciated when recognizing that all products, just like all living things, go through cycles. The **product life cycle** is a conceptual framework that characterizes the typical process products go through from inception until they are withdrawn from the market. In a manner similar to how people advance through age groups (childhood, teenage years, young adults, middle age, retirement), products also can be delineated into relatively distinct stages in their evolutionary process. These stages are introduction, growth, maturity, and decline. Although every product will go through these stages, the length of each stage and of the product life cycle will vary from product to product. Some products experience very short life cycles. For example, cassette tapes and cassette players are rapidly declining in sales with the concomitant growth of compact discs and CD players. Other products last for generations before they are supplanted by technological advances or suffer the fate of falling customer interest. For example, scouring products (such as Brillo pads) have been on the market since the early 1900s with relatively few changes. Only recently, with the introduction of a no-rust scouring item from 3M, has a new product come along to push the traditional scouring pad toward its inevitable demise.

Changing conditions in the marketplace such as new technologies, consumer dissatisfaction, or competitive activities dictate the length of a product's life. Exhibit 9.2 depicts the stages in the

Exhibit 9.2   The Product Life Cycle

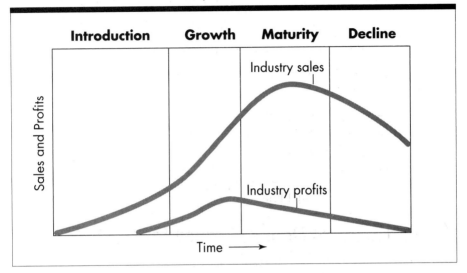

product life cycle and the sales and profit curves that characterize the product category over time.

Before proceeding, it is important to recognize that the product life cycle characterizes the sales and profit pattern for an *entire product category* (e.g., all models of minivans) and *not* the performance of a single brand (e.g., Chrysler or Toyota minivans) in that product category. Before reading on, you should carefully study Exhibit 9.2 and attempt to explain to yourself at this point why the category sales and profit curves differ in their amplitude and the times when each peaks.

Introduction

In the **introduction** stage, a company pioneers a new product and introduces it to distribution intermediaries (wholesalers, distributors, retailers) and if it is a consumer good to consumers. The firm's top priorities are to obtain distribution for the product and to inform channel intermediaries and consumers about the product and the company's particular brand. Sales are relatively slow in this stage as most consumers are still unaware that the product exists and retail distribution is slowly developing. The marketer is investing a great

MARKETING HIGHLIGHTS

Generation X

Call them baby busters, post baby boomers, 20-somethings, or Generation X, they represent a population of approximately 46 million Americans between the ages of 18 and 29, and marketers are seeking ways to appeal to this latest generation of young adults. They have been unable to identify unifying characteristics for this group, however, with the ease with which their parents were identified. These now-grown children of the baby boomer generation lack a common thread and have thus been labeled "Generation X." Those who have sought to understand this group better have noticed more similarities than differences between the baby boomer generation and that of the succeeding baby buster generation, noting that "Every generation is a product of the times in which it comes of age."[a]

Generation X has experienced limited economic horizons because of a sluggish job market, stagnant wages, and the high costs of real estate, higher education, and health insurance even before the recession beginning in 1990. "The ethos of the 1980s was an expectation of prosperity at little cost to government, business, or individuals. As a result, the expectations of those who make up Generation X grew dramatically—much faster, in fact, than their ability to realize their dreams. This led to a huge letdown in the 1990s."[b]

This gap between aspirations and achievements is what characterizes the X Generation. "In 1978, the overwhelming majority of 18- to 29-year-olds said they had at least a fairly good chance of personally achieving the 'good life,' including 41% who said they had a 'very good' chance. [In 1992], just 21% in this age group [felt] they have a very good chance—a huge shift in 14 years.[c] These statistics are from the "Roper Reports," an organization which has measured the aspirations of young people since the 1970s by asking them for their own definition of "the good life." Their findings show that this generation is more materialistic than those surveyed in the late 1970s and aspires to a more traditional lifestyle—one that includes children.

Frustration over wanting more than they feel is possible to attain colors the way Generation X looks at the world. "Living for today is an unquestioned way of life when long-term goals appear to be out of reach.[d] The grunge look associated with this generation exemplifies this "I don't care" attitude that comes from disillusionment. Why bother to "dress for success" when success, at least financially, seems unattainable? And yet this generation represents a large consumer market that marketers can hardly avoid to target.

Marketers have scratched their heads over Generation X—how to appeal to them specifically. What do we know about this demographic group? For starters, they spend a lot of money eating out. "Xers spent almost $30 billion dining out in 1991—compared to $17 billion on household items and $8 billion on videos, tapes, and CDs.[e] According to the Roper Organization, Xers spend 24% of discretionary income on dining out, and they seem to favor inexpensive restaurants: "The typical post-boomer eats at a quick-service restaurant 15 to 16 times a month.[f] Marketers have had trouble marketing to this group because it is diverse in its tastes and doesn't respond well to obvious appeals to them. This is a generation of smart consumers, too, consumers who have been making purchasing decisions for years because both mom and dad have been away from home working. They don't want to be talked down to or given the hard sell in advertising. What they do respond to are messages that are humorous in an off-beat way. Burger King found success in attracting Xers with its BK TeeVee campaign starring MTV personality Dan Cortese. Its irreverent tone appealed to this group without offending everybody else, they found.

The Coca-Cola Company introduced a new soda in the spring of 1994 aimed at rising Generation Xers. "OK Soda" targets 12- to 25-year-olds with marketing heaving on Generation X-style irony, from cans plastered with existential phrases and images to its slogan "Things are going to be OK."[g] OK is packaged in silver cans with cartoon-like drawings and a label that's supposed to look slapped on. Sergio Zyman, Coke's marketing chief, justified the anti-marketing marketing approach for OK because these teens and young 20-somethings don't believe in people who lie to them.[h] Coke views these teenagers as skeptical yet optimistic, willing to buy OK without being wowed with advertising full of hype. OK soda seeks to position itself as a product that understands its potential consumers. It even offers a little advice in it's motto: "Don't be fooled into thinking there has to be a reason for everything."[i]

When Chrysler Corporation put together advertising for its new Neon subcompact car in 1993, it sought to target 20-somethings. Dick Johnson, Vice Chairman and Chief Creative Officer at BBDO advertising agency,

decided not to "pander to the stereotype of grungelike young people dressed in clunky boots and wrinkled dirndl skirts."[j] When competing for the Chrysler Neon account, he decided, instead, to let the car inspire him in creating the advertising. BBDO directed research using nearly 30 focus groups to determine how different age groups view small cars. They found that baby boomers viewed a car more like an appliance and had low expectations of small cars because of past experiences and were mainly concerned with quality, fuel economy and price. The research showed that 20-somethings were more passionate and demanding about a car's appearance and performance and viewed owning an automobile as a right of passage. BBDO realized that if they targeted Generation X, with their long list of demands for the car, they wouldn't need to target any other group because the same advertising would communicate everything boomers needed to know about the car.

The next step for BBDO was to communicate information buyers needed to know about the car while creating a personality for Neon. "Our research said consumers viewed the car as huggable, lovable, a UFO, a Beetle for the '90s, a car for the Jetsons," Johnson said. But, he added, "If we simply created advertising with a personality, it wouldn't be relevant" to Generation X.[k] When BBDO presented its first group of storyboards to Chrysler executives, they weren't impressed. The agency then recruited 12 recognized Generation X experts, most of whom worked for young adult media, to participate in discussions on

Continued on next page

the campaign. The panel met with BBDO's research staff to discuss who Generation X really is. They viewed the proposed Neon ad campaign as well as other automotive and campaigns for other products aimed at Generation X. The panelists pointed out that many campaigns didn't take the generation seriously, and that the proposed Neon spots contained too much hype. The panel members felt strongly that Chrysler should advertise the price of the car fairly loaded, not stripped down.

The agency then decided not to pick a musical theme but to use music as an extension of the mood of the commercial, because of the inability to find music that was universally appealing. BBDO chose a female actress to read the voice-overs, breaking with the tradition of using male voices in car commercials.

When BBDO and Chrysler executives assembled in Highland Park, Michigan, to pitch the advertising, Tom Clark, Chairman and CEO of BBDO North America, opened by calling Generation X the most racially and ethnically diverse generation ever. He dif-

ferentiated baby busters from baby boomers as less interested in show and materialism and more interested in being pragmatic and realistic. BBDO then revealed TV ads featuring a white Neon, because they wanted the essence of the car to be as clean as possible, and surrounded by bright, primary colors to create the feeling that Neon lives in a colorful, happy world. As the audience views the front-end of the Neon, the word "Hi" appears above the car to establish a light-hearted, friendly tone. BBDO proposed a TV and print ad campaign that obviously worked, because Chrysler chose to go with the agency's proposals and planned to commit $15 million toward advertising for Neon. As Robert Lutz, president of Chrysler, put it, "Neon's advertising is like the car: lean, uncomplicated, no b.s., great fun. When you have that synergy, the personality of the product being in tune with its target market, and the advertising in tune with the product and its target market, then the whole becomes greater than the sum of its parts."[1]

deal of money in its marketing efforts to achieve distribution and create awareness for the product. The product is unprofitable in the introduction stage due to heavy research and development expenditures that must be recouped and intensive marketing and selling efforts to gain distribution and create customer awareness.

The company that introduces a new product, the *pioneer,* must build demand for the product category, called *primary demand.* Creating this demand is accomplished through personal selling, advertising, and other promotional efforts. The product may be introduced at either a relatively low ("penetration" price) or high ("skimming" price). The advantage of the former is that more people can afford the new product and hence demand is built more rapidly, whereas the advantage of the latter pricing strategy is that greater per-unit profit is earned. If the introduction is successful, the

Those seeking to successfully define Generation X and differentiate it from the baby boomer group have discovered more similarities than differences in the two groups. Xers are not so different than their parents were when they were in their 20s—rebellious perhaps, materialistic, traditional in some respects. "The interests of young adults and mid-lifers have always been different, so there is no major marketing breakthrough in recognizing such differences. The key is to identify those differences which are generational. In this respect, there is remarkable similarity between the values and aspirations of today's 18–29 and 30–44 cohorts. Although it may simply be a function of mass culture, their music, their heroes, and their pastimes are probably more alike than was the case between the baby boomers and their parents."[m]

[a] W. Bradford Fay, "Understanding 'Generation X'," *Marketing Research: A Magazine of Management & Applications,* Spring 1993, 54.

[b] Fay, "Understanding 'Generation X'."

[c] Fay, "Understanding 'Generation X'."

[d] Fay, "Understanding 'Generation X'."

[e] Alexa Bell, "Searching for Generation X; Catering for the People Aged 18 to 29," *Restaurant Business Magazine,* October 10, 1993, 50.

[f] Bell, "Searching for Generation X."

[g] Keith H. Hammonds, "Coke's New Soda: Just O.K. Won't Do," *Business Week,* May 2, 1994, 38.

[h] Martha T. Moore, "Coke Gives Pop-Culture Drink OK a Flat Debut," *USA Today,* April 21, 1994, 1B.

[i] Cynthia Mitchell, "Don't Be Fooled—OK Soda Is Not Just a Coke," *The Atlanta Journal and Constitution,* April 21, 1994, 1.

[j] Raymond Serafin and Leah Rickard, "How BBDO Turned Chrysler on with New Approach to Generation X," *Advertising Age,* February 7, 1994, 16.

[k] Serafin and Rickard, "How BBDO Turned Chrysler On," 16.

[l] Serafin and Rickard, "How BBDO Turned Chrysler On," 16.

[m] Fay, "Understanding 'Generation X'," 54."

product pioneer may enjoy an advantage over followers (a "pioneer advantage") for a sustained period.[3]

Growth

In the **growth** stage, the product begins to gain consumer acceptance. As a matter of convention, the growth stage is defined as beginning when the product category starts earning a profit (see Exhibit 9.2). The rapid increase in sales volume forces down per-unit costs and enables sales revenue to outpace expenses, thus yielding a profit. Marketing efforts are aimed at encouraging repeat purchases from early users and attracting additional new users. Sales increase quickly during this stage, but so, too, do competitive pressures. Competitors are introducing similar offerings to cash in on these new industry sales. During this stage, improvements in product quality and increased product alternatives (e.g., new flavors) are possible strategies to maintain and gain distribution and reinforce the brand at retail.

Emphasis in the growth stage is on each brand promoting its unique characteristics and benefits in an attempt to build demand for itself, that is, *secondary demand*. Competitors fight for distribution and promote their brands aggressively. Prices tend to be somewhat stable at this relatively early juncture in the product category's life cycle.

Maturity

In the **maturity** stage, sales volume continues to increase but eventually levels off. Most consumers are aware of and have tried the product. Marketers are relying on repeat purchases to keep the brand alive. The increased competition encourages lower prices, greater promotional activity, and lower profits for all firms involved. In fact, as you see in Exhibit 9.2, category profits are declining by this point in the life cycle. Marketing efforts focus on promotion to maintain a competitive edge. Also, firms are introducing product variations and slight product improvements to enhance their competitive positions.

During this stage, many companies with limited promotional budgets and higher requirements for profits find they can no longer compete and withdraw their products from the market. For example, the personal computer industry, which experienced rapid growth in the 1980s, has reached maturity. New models with larger memories, greater speed, and added features (e.g., CD-ROM drives) are continuously introduced to enable companies to maintain competitive positions. And prices continue to fall.

Decline

When a product reaches its **decline** stage, its profitability continues to deteriorate and sales begin to plummet. New products are entering the marketplace, taking sales away from the older established categories and brands. Marketers can continue selling the brand to the loyal users who are left, reposition the brand in hopes of reviving sales, or withdraw it from the marketplace. It is typical at this time for firms to cut back on distribution and to eliminate the slowest selling and least profitable items in their product lines. Advertising and other promotional efforts are also reduced in hopes that the remaining sales can earn a profit.

In sum, all products eventually decline and must be harvested from companies' product lines. Therefore, it is critically important to the long-run success and profitability of a firm to understand and recognize each stage in a product's life cycle and to plan for and manage the development of both established and new products.

Brand-Concept Management

Although the product life cycle as discussed above deals with the sales, profit, and marketing behavior of an entire product category, a company's particular offering, or brand, in a product category also experiences its own life cycle. Whether a brand is new or established, the brand's meaning, or concept, must be successfully managed throughout its life cycle. **Brand-concept management** is the strategic planning, implementation, and control of a brand's concept throughout the brand's life.[4] This process involves creating and managing a *meaning* for the brand and communicating that meaning to the target market. A brand concept, or brand meaning, is accomplished by promoting a brand as appealing to any of three categories of basic consumer needs: functional, symbolic, and experiential.[5]

Functional needs are those involving the customer's current consumption-related problems or potential problems related to the product category. Brand-concept management identifies product attributes or benefits that will solve the problem and then communicates this to customers. In industrial selling, for example, salespeople typically appeal to their customers' functional needs—needs for higher-quality products, faster delivery time, or better service. In the consumer market, NordicTrack appeals to consumers' functional needs by marketing a line of exercise products—treadmills, indoor ski machines, and cross-training devices—to people who are unable or unwilling to exercise outside their homes.

Symbolic needs are those involving psychological needs such as the desire for self-enhancement, role position, or group membership. A brand can be managed symbolically by being associated with people, places, or other symbolically rich objects. In other words, a brand managed in this fashion may eventually acquire a portion of the meanings possessed by the objects or people with which it is associated. Gatorade, for example, was once marketed primarily in terms of its ability to satisfy the functional needs that accompany liquid and mineral depletion during strenuous exercise. But later in its life cycle, Gatorade has been managed as the sports drink that Michael (Jordan) prefers. In a sense, the marketers of Gatorade hope to create an image for their brand that captures the persona of the famous athlete that the brand has associated itself with.

Experiential needs are those involving the desire for products that provide sensory pleasure, stimulation, and variety. A brand managed in terms of its ability to satisfy experiential needs is marketed by emphasizing its uniqueness and sensory value (tasting good, feeling wonderful, smelling great, or sounding divine). Ben & Jerry's Ice Cream personifies the appeal to experiential needs by offering delicious-tasting desserts with unique brand names and a corporate image of hipness and environmental concern.

Keep in mind that a brand is a company's *single offering* in a product category. The individual brands added together are the lifeblood of organizations. Each brand requires its own brand concept, and this concept, or meaning, must be carefully managed throughout the brand's life cycle. Effective marketers and brand managers know when to alter a brand's meaning in light of changing marketplace conditions. For example, Kentucky Fried Chicken was managed for a generation by appealing to experiential needs— a great-tasting, specially seasoned, *fried* product. However, with growing health consciousness, the company changed its corporate name to KFC so as to minimize the direct association with fried products. A brand concept must continually be monitored, managed, and, if necessary, adapted to ensure success and consistency throughout the brand's life cycle.

Organizing for New-Product Development: A Company-wide Undertaking

Although established brands are the foundation for an organization's business, changes in customer preferences, increased competition, and technological advances require a firm to continually develop new products. Without new products, a firm is risking long-term failure. New product development is a necessity for any firm that hopes to be successful in today's and tomorrow's marketplace.

Exhibit 9.3   Structures for New-Product Development

- New-product committees
- New-product departments
- Venture teams
- Product managers

Developing successful new products is a complicated and time-consuming process involving many departments and resources within the organization. Since the efforts of so many are needed to successfully develop a new product, a coordinated, systematic approach is required throughout the process. Several organizational structures are used by companies in their efforts to develop successful new products. Exhibit 9.3 portrays the various structures used by organizations in their new product development efforts.

New-Product Committees

A new-product committee is the most common organizational structure for new product development. The committee—which, by definition of all committees, is a rather loose coalition of members rather than a permanent organizational unit—is typically comprised of members representing the various departments involved in the process: research and development, engineering, finance, accounting, sales, production, and marketing. Usually, executives from the various departments are the chosen representatives for the committee to ensure the commitment and support that will be needed for success. Some new-product committees screen new product ideas as well as review and approve new-product plans. But these committees tend to be slow in decision-making and sometimes members are biased by the parochial interests of their respective departments (e.g., production or finance) rather than viewing matters from the best long-run interests of the enterprise.

New-Product Departments

Companies often create separate, formally organized new-product departments to oversee the planning and development of new

CAPTAINS OF INDUSTRY

R. David Thomas

Founder and Senior Chairman

Wendy's International, Inc.

Date of Birth: 1932

Education: Dropped out of high school at 15.

Career Path: Has spent his entire career beginning at the age of 13 working in restaurants.

Profile: Hard-working, affable, humble but very successful businessman.

Personal: At eight years dreamed of owning his own restaurant—the best restaurant in the world. "All the customers would love my food, and all of my employees would do everything they were supposed to do. But, most important, everyone would think I was a good boss, and every day when I walked into the restaurant, people would be glad to see me."[a]

Dave Thomas founded Wendy's Old-Fashioned Hamburgers with one location in Columbus, Ohio, in 1969. Within 5 years, net income exceeded $1 million and restaurant sales were nearly $25 million.[b] By 1993 sales for Wendy's International, Inc., were $3.8 billion, its fourth consecutive year with over 20% earnings growth. Its 5-year average earnings-per-share growth was 58%, over 4 times that of McDonald's.[c] How did he do it?

Dave Thomas was adopted at birth. At 8 years old he recalls that he wanted to own the best restaurant in the world. When he was 12 he began delivering groceries and at 13 he worked 12-hour shifts at a Knoxville, Tennessee, restaurant. That same year, 1947, he moved with his family to Fort Wayne, Indiana, where he took a job as a busboy at the Hobby House restaurant. He dropped out of school after the tenth grade, a move that he later regretted making. Thomas joined the U.S. Army at 18 where he went to cook and baker's school, then returned to the Hobby House in 1953 to work as a short order cook. There he met a waitress named Lorraine Buskirk whom, after a short courtship, he married in 1954.[d] In his autobiography, *Dave's Way*, he writes that he started out his career in business by getting fired from his first two jobs. "After I lost my second job, my father told me that I would never keep a job and that he might have to support me for the rest of my life. He might have been kidding, but I took him seriously. At that moment, I vowed I would learn what it takes to be a successful and valuable employee."[e] Not only did he learn his lesson but he became a millionaire by the age of 35. He left a secure restaurant job where he was assistant manager to take a job with Kentucky Fried Chicken, trying to resurrect four failing KFC franchises in Columbus. He sold his interests back to the company for $1 million. He later moved on to help found Arthur Treacher's Fish & Chips before founding his own hamburger restaurant in 1969.

What was unique about Wendy's Old-Fashioned Hamburger restaurant? Why was the chain able to grow to over 4,000 locations with operations in more than 29 countries? Thomas's philosophy is very simple: "People want a clean place to eat. They want good service, variety, and quality products."[f] And Dave Thomas certainly knew how to make a fresh hamburger. His entire working life had been spent working in restaurants, and he built on that experience. "When I started Wendy's I really did have a product. I couldn't understand how you could make a hamburger then wrap it and put it under a heat lamp. They put it under that heat lamp and it, the flavor, deteriorates. But I could understand that they sold a lot of 'em." Thomas made his hamburgers from fresh beef, a practice that was scoffed at when he started, and let customers pick their toppings. "When we first started out, we had a hard time convincing people they could have a hamburger prepared the way they wanted. They had been so brainwashed that there was only one way they could get the food they ordered."[g]

What elaborate marketing strategy has the company employed to sustain such growth? Says Thomas, "It's simple. We give customers good food. We have clean restaurants, staffed by clean, polite people. And we offer the food at a good price. That's it. That our marketing strategy." Thomas feels that many marketing people put too much faith in the power of advertising and not enough into learning the operations end of the business. Marketing departments don't make money but operations—the restaurants—do, and he tries to remain focused on them. But television viewers will remember Wendy's advertising campaigns, especially "Where's the beef." Curiously, however, Thomas feels that that campaign caused Wendy's to lose its identity. People remembered the tag line, "Where's the beef," but not necessarily Wendy's. Wendy's has been successful with later campaigns that feature Thomas himself. During the 1994 Winter Olympics, viewers saw Thomas attempting Olympian feats only to end up back at Wendy's eating a hamburger. Viewers could identify with him.

In 1982 Thomas left the daily running of the company and turned it over to a professional management team. That decision proved to be a mistake, Thomas admits. In 1985, Wendy's earned $76 million, a total not equaled since, riding the crest of the "Where's the beef?" TV campaign. However, beneath the surface, standards were slipping in the stores. Self-satisfaction and management miscues made conditions worse. Trouble mounted among franchise owners. A number of original Wendy's franchisees had sold their stores to new owners unconcerned with Wendy's standards. Some of the larger franchisees lost focus by branching into new concepts or going public. Other franchisees became absentee managers, leaving the operations to the local employees. The success of the "Where's the beef" campaign had gone to management's head. A huge investment in a breakfast program in 1987 failed miserably. A year later Wendy's reported a $5 million loss.[h]

Thomas returned to daily management in 1986 to get the company back on track. He drafted James Near, one of Wendy's most successful franchisees and a board member since 1981, to be president and COO. Near, like Thomas, had been born and raised in the business and understood operations. Near accepted the position with the condition that Thomas maintain an active role in the company as spokesperson and ambassador. Near then concentrated on mending operations and customer service and cutting overhead.[i] He cut hundreds of administrative positions, reorganized operations in

Continued on next page

CAPTAINS OF INDUSTRY, continued

the field, and instituted a stock ownership program for all full-time management and administrative employees who had been at the company over a year. Over a six-year period, management turnover fell from over 55% to under 20%.[j]

Thomas now holds the title of senior chairman and Near is chairman and CEO, having assumed that position in 1989. And Wendy's continues to grow. In 1993 about 330 units were opened, bringing the total number of restaurants to 4,200 and adding 15,000 jobs. About two-thirds of the chain's stores are franchise outlets, the balance company-owned.

Thomas now has time to devote to some of his favorite causes—like adoption. Although he was reluctant to admit he had been adopted early in his career, he has become a national spokesperson for the cause. Thomas donates his share of profits from the sale of his autobiography to adoption causes.[k] He founded the Dave Thomas Foundation for Adoption, which focuses on developing public awareness and education. He also urges young people to stay in high school and not drop out like he did—he says its the dumbest thing he ever did—and received his high school equivalency diploma in 1993. Thomas spends his free time golfing and boating, and travels around the country meeting people and promoting Wendy's. He's become quite a celebrity, too. People recognize him from the Wendy's commercials, and fans want to get near him everywhere he goes. Has success changed Dave Thomas? "You can't let recognition go to your head," he was quoted as saying. 'If you're in the public eye, you have to be nice."[l] His low-key, friendly demeanor comes across the TV airwaves, and the company intends to stick with Thomas as their spokesperson. When asked if the person portrayed in the television commercials is the real Dave Thomas, he replied, "What you see is what you get . . . I'm not a celebrity, I'm a hamburger cook."[m]

[a] R. David Thomas, *Dave's Way,* (New York: G. P. Putnam's Sons, 1991), 17.

[b] T. S. Peric, "'Just Call Me Dave': Wendy's Founder Speaks Up," *Morning Journal-Lorain* [Ohio], November 7, 1993, BUS section.

[c] T. L. G., "Dave's World," *Forbes,* January 3, 1994, 149.

[d] Peric, "'Just Call Me Dave.'"

[e] "Wendy's Founder Offers Business Managers and Owners a Yardstick for Measuring People," *PR Newswire,* July 27, 1993, Financial News section.

[f] "Dave Thomas: Building a Better Burger; Founder of Wendy's Old Fashioned Hamburgers; Interview; Cover Story," *Sales & Marketing Management,* May, 1993, 52.

[g] Peric, "'Just Call Me Dave.'"

[h] James Scarpa, "Combo Deluxe; Profile of R. David Thomas and James W. Near, Founders of Ohio-based Wendy's International Inc; Interview," *Restaurant Business Magazine,* May 1, 1992, 114.

[i] Scarpa, "Combo Deluxe."

[j] T. L. G., "Dave's World."

[k] Scarpa, "Combo Deluxe."

[l] Linda Creesy, "Wendy's Founder Gives Kids' Park a Boost," *The Orlando Sentinel,* December 9, 1993, 13.

[m] Paul Dodson, "Thomas Serves More than Food," *South Bend Tribune,* April 30, 1993, BUS section.

products. New-product development is the *full-time responsibility* of this department, rather than the part-time efforts of a new-product committee. The department is responsible for all phases of the product's development. The head of the department, who reports to top management, typically has the authority and responsibility to move the process along within the company.

The downside of a new-product department is the expense entailed in forming and running a permanent department; the upside is a corporate commitment to new products and a formal, systematic unit dedicated to that objective. Many companies today have effectively combined the virtues of new-product committees and new-product departments by creating **cross-functional teams.** As with product committees, these teams are staffed with representatives from engineering, finance, marketing, and operations, and other units. However, unlike a committee, a cross-functional team remains intact after product introduction to run the new product as a fledgling business.[6]

Venture Teams

A venture team, like a new-product committee, is a group within the organization comprised of a small number of specialists from key departments such as research and development, finance, and marketing who typically report to the president or CEO. However, venture teams differ from new-product committees insofar as the team remains intact during the course of a new-product venture rather than returning to their respective departments after every meeting. This group devotes its full-time efforts to an assigned project through the project's completion. The team possesses the authority for both planning and implementing courses of action to bring new products to fruition.

Product Managers

Many companies rely on product managers, or brand managers as they are titled in some companies, for their new-product development work. A product manager is an individual within the marketing department assigned a brand or product line who has the responsibility to determine objectives and establish marketing strategies. The production department may be experts in how a product is manufactured. The finance department may be experts in the costs and profit and loss figures for a product. Research and development may be experts in the ingredients used in the product. And the sales department may be experts in how to get the product on the retail shelf. However, the product manager is the expert on *all facets* of the product as a whole.

The product manager manages a specific brand or product line on a daily basis. The product manager is responsible for setting prices, developing sales promotion and advertising programs, and working with the sales representatives in the field. The manager can utilize the services of various company personnel to implement any approved plan. Some companies assign new-product projects to product managers who have experience with a related product. Other companies assign all new product responsibilities to a new products manager. In either case, the manager is responsible for new-product development, the creation of new-product ideas, and the recommendations for improving existing products.

In recent years, increased fragmentation of the mass market into smaller segments has resulted in more regional marketing efforts. This has forced firms to rethink the product management approach. Some companies are finding success with regional marketing managers who handle a variety of products within one region of the country. They are regional specialists versus product specialists.

■ The New-Product Development Process

A new product is a product that is new in any way to an organization. The product can be an improved version on an established brand, or it can represent an entry into a product category that is totally new for the organization. In either case, the new product represents a major investment of time and resources for an organization, so an organized, effective approach is needed to guarantee as high a success rate as possible. This is particularly crucial in view of the fact that over 80% of new products that reach the market do not live up to their stated objectives.[7]

As stated before, the process of new product development is complex. It often does not conform to a logical, textbook progression of events. However, for purposes of discussion, the process can be viewed as progressing through the six stages identified in Exhibit 9.4.

Exhibit 9.4   Stages in the Product-Development Process

- Idea generation
- Screening
- Business analysis
- Development
- Testing
- Commercialization

Idea Generation

The first step in the product-development process is idea generation. The objective of the idea-generation stage is to create a large number of good ideas, some of which ultimately will culminate in new-product introductions. For example, in 1990 Sharon Rothstein, a product manager in Nabisco's new-business group, began working on the idea for a healthy cookie and cracker line. The result was SnackWell's, which debuted on supermarket shelves in 1992 and achieved over $100 million in sales its first year.[8]

Ideas are constantly generated and must be evaluated based on their potential profitability and ability to satisfy customer needs and to meet corporate marketing and financial objectives. Ideas come from many sources: the sales force, customers, competitors, suppliers, company personnel, retailers, and outside inventors. Ideas sometimes come from consumer letters and telephone calls. And many large companies also monitor overseas markets for new product ideas. Japanese marketers have been particularly successful in borrowing ideas from the United States and elsewhere.

Screening

Once ideas have been generated, the second step in the development process is screening the various ideas. Most companies have limited resources and cannot afford to develop every idea on its list or even to devote resources to further study all ideas. A process is needed to separate ideas with potential from those incapable of meeting company objectives. In this process, marketers attempt to determine what problems may be encountered with each idea and whether or not these problems can be overcome. If the problems are deemed too many or too serious, the idea is rejected at the screening stage, thus saving the company time and money. However, if the problems could possibly be overcome, the idea is subjected to further consideration. Often, new product ideas are screened by representatives of various functional areas, and certainly by cross-functional team members when such arrangements prevail in a company.

When screening new product ideas, those ideas that fit with a company's existing production capability and marketing expertise typically receive the most serious appraisal. However, truly unique and innovative ideas deserve careful scrutiny even if they deviate from a firm's present capability. The issue then becomes one of how much risk is involved relative to the potential payoff. SnackWell's clearly fit Nabisco's production capability and marketing expertise and was not excessively risky when conceived at a time when growing numbers of consumers were more health and weight conscious.

Business Analysis

New-product ideas that survive the screening process proceed to the business analysis stage. At this time, an assessment is made on the new product's potential market, growth rate, compatibility with existing company promotional budgets, financial funding, production and distribution needs, and competitive strengths. Studies may be required to analyze the market, competition, costs, and technical requirements versus the current production capabilities. Preliminary cost and revenue estimates are generated at this stage.

Some companies utilize concept testing during this stage to test the market viability of the idea. **Concept testing** involves querying consumers' thoughts and feelings about the proposed product. Nabisco conducted small-group interviews (focus groups) and asked people to share their thoughts about non-fat and low-fat cookies and crackers. Consumers obviously liked the idea, but some expressed doubts that such products could possibly taste as good as the real thing.

Development

In the development stage, the product idea is converted into an actual product. Research and development personnel develop a *prototype* of the product, and production personnel analyze the feasibility of manufacturing the product. This stage typically is costly and time-consuming. Several variations of the product can be developed before any decisions are made on the final product. No doubt at Nabisco hundreds of batches of SnackWell's cookies were tested before finding the best recipes. After progressing through a series of tests, revisions, and refinements, a product with a high likelihood of success culminates. In this stage, preliminary marketing strategies—especially brand naming and packaging design— are developed. As with the new product development process in general, the development stage is most effective when all departments within the organization work together.

Procter & Gamble has learned firsthand just how costly the product development process can be. In 1968, P&G developed Olestra, a product that provides the cooking benefits and taste of fat but with zero calories. This new product, which was expected to revolutionize the industry, represented a potential $1 billion business for P&G. Over a quarter of a century later, the company is still trying to get approval from the Food and Drug Administration, which is questioning the product's safety. To date, P&G has spent an estimated $300 million in development costs with no end in sight.[9]

Testing

In the fifth stage of the new product development process, testing is conducted to determine consumer reactions to a product under normal marketplace conditions. Testing enables a manager to determine what works and what does not work in the marketing mix that is being tested. Several alternative strategies can be tested depending on the size of the test area.

Test marketing is the first stage at which the product must perform in a real life situation. Because a high percentage of all new product introductions fail, many companies choose to test a new product's entire marketing strategy prior to introducing the product to the full market. This is called **test marketing.** The fundamental purpose of such testing is to provide an in-market opportunity to assess a product's performance against competitive offerings using the same mix of price, promotion, and distribution features that are intended to be employed when introducing the product to the full market. Three forms of test marketing are used:

- A *traditional test market* selects one or two representative cities, and then the product is distributed in the selected area(s) via the company's own sales force—just the way it would be done when the product is distributed to the full market.

- A *controlled test market* involves turning over the product to a market research company that tests the product in smaller markets than typically is the case with traditional test marketing; moreover, the research firm, and not the manufacturer of the new product, secures retail distribution and controls all other aspects of the test marketing effort.

- Finally, *simulated test marketing* does not distribute the new product in the standard sense through retail outlets, but simply makes the product available to small samples of consumers in a simulated buying situation. Trial-purchase and repeat-purchase rates are obtained from these consumers, and with this information a forecast is made of how well the product can expect to do in terms of market share and sales volume if introduced to the full market.[10]

Although success in a test market does not guarantee nationwide success, a test market can increase the odds of success. However, companies sometimes find that acting quickly on a new idea may be more profitable than test marketing where competitors may seize the opportunity of entering the market with a similar offering. Some companies are bypassing test marketing completely. R. J. Reynolds, for instance, went national with its new Camel Wides brand without any testing at all.[11] Any organization must consider its budgetary, time, and investment constraints before planning test marketing.

Commercialization

The sixth and final stage in the new product development process is commercialization. The few product ideas that survive all the previous steps are now ready for full-scale production and marketing. In this stage, a company prepares to rollout a new product, which now has the "green light," into select regional markets or to obtain national distribution as quickly as possible. Based on feedback from test marketing, or in light of a marketing executive's gut feeling, a marketing program is formulated and implemented. Materials are ordered, production facilities are readied, and advertising and sales promotions are prepared. The sales force contacts wholesale and retail accounts and distribution is established. If product quality is suitable, the price competitive, and the advertising capable of exciting consumer interest, then the new product may become a commercial success. Ultimately, this will depend on how consumers respond, which is the topic next addressed.

New Products: A Consumer Perspective

New products enter the marketplace every day. Some of these products enjoy great success early; others take some time before they are accepted and realize success. The process by which new ideas, including new products, spreads throughout a social system or marketplace is termed the **diffusion process.** As the diffusion process progresses, a new product is adopted by more and more customers.

Who Adopts New Products?

Customers within the marketplace will behave differently when a new product is introduced. Some will immediately try new products. They tend to adopt new products early. Others are less adventurous and more cautious, slow to try something new. They tend to adopt the new product late. Five categories of customers are typically identified in the diffusion process: innovators, early adopters, early majority, late majority, and laggards. As a matter of convention, these five categories are presumed to follow a normal (bell-shaped) statistical distribution with respect to each group's average (mean) time of adoption following the introduction of a product innovation. We now discuss the distinguishing characteristics of each of the five groups that are identified in Exhibit 9.5.

It is important to note that these conclusions are generalizations based on literally hundreds of empirical efforts that have studied the adoption of new products and ideas in a variety of settings. The proportionate sizes of each group, which are shown in parentheses alongside each group, do not apply to every product, but rather are merely conventions that approximate the size of each group across the many products that have been studied.

Exhibit 9.5   The Product Diffusion Process

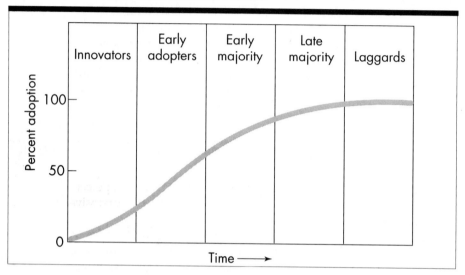

Innovators (2.5%).   The first purchasers of a new product, **innovators** represent 2.5 percent of all potential adopters. Innovators tend to be younger, higher in social status, more cosmopolitan, and better educated than later adopter groups. They rely on objective information sources (e.g., specialized magazines) rather than salespeople or other consumers for their information. Innovators are venturesome individuals who are willing to take risks. And trying new products can be risky—the product may not work as well as expected or it may not be worth the price paid. Consider, for example, the risk of being one of the first customers in the marketplace to own a battery powered car such as General Motor's Impact. Until the product is established, the customer may have a difficult time finding shops to service the car. Plus, the initial investment of over $20,000 may be too steep for an unproven performer.

Early Adopters (13.5%).   **Early adopters** are the second group to adopt a new product. They represent 13.5 percent of all potential adopters. Unlike innovators, the early adopters are more concerned with group norms and values and are reluctant to do anything that violates accepted standards. Early adopters tend to be *opinion leaders,* influencing others within their community to try the new product or new idea. They enjoy the prestige and respect that comes with their leadership role. Early adopters rely on personal salespeople and mass media for their information. This group adopts new ideas and new products with discretion.

Early Majority (34%).   Thirty four percent of potential adopters are categorized as the **early majority.** The early majority will spend more time deciding whether or not to try the new product or idea than any other group in the diffusion process. They are more likely to seek out information regarding the innovation and competitively shop the brand. The early majority relies on opinion leaders within the community and the mass media for their information.

Late Majority (34%).   The **late majority,** or the next 34 percent to adopt a new product or idea, is less cosmopolitan and responsive to change than any of the previous groups. The late majority are skeptics who tend to be older and below average in education, income, and social status. This group tries the new product or new idea because they feel pressure from their social groups to conform. Word-of-mouth tends to influence this group more than the mass media.

Laggards (16%).   The final group to adopt a new product or new idea is the **laggards,** the bottom 16 percent of all potential adopters. Laggards prefer to do things the way they have done them in the past. This conservative group is comprised of older adopters who have low income and social status. These price-conscious individuals are suspicious of change. The new product or idea has usually been outdated by the time the laggards adopt it. Marketers find it difficult to market to this group, because they seem unresponsive to media efforts.

How Rapidly Are New Products Adopted?

The speed, or rate with which a new product or idea is diffused through a market is influenced by five product characteristics that underlie consumers' attitudes toward the innovation. These characteristics are relative advantage, compatibility, complexity, trialability, and observability (see Exhibit 9.6).

Relative Advantage.   **Relative advantage** is the degree to which an innovation is perceived by customers as being superior to existing ideas or products. The greater the relative advantage—

Exhibit 9.6   Rate of Adoption Determinants

- Relative advantage
- Compatibility
- Complexity
- Trialability
- Observability

lower price, ease of use, savings in time and effort, immediacy of reward—the faster a new product will be adopted. For example, the compact disc player has a clear relative advantage over tape players. The Gillette electric razor, called Sensor for women, was an instant success because its shape and design were more esthetically appealing and comfortable to the touch than competitive brands.

Compatibility.   **Compatibility** is the degree to which an innovation is consistent with the values, needs, and experiences of potential adopters. Compatible products diffuse more quickly than incompatible ones, because they are perceived as fitting into the consumer's present way of doing things. Generally speaking, consumers are resistant to radical changes. Battery-powered cars have distinct relative advantages (less noise pollution and friendlier to the environment), but many consumers will resist the extreme change from conventional, combustible engines.

Complexity.   **Complexity** refers to the difficulty of understanding and, therefore, using a new product. In most cases, the more difficult a new product is to understand or use, the longer it will take to gain general marketplace acceptance. Many consumers are wary of personal computers, because they don't understand how to use them. In fact, many older people refrain from purchasing and using electronic gadgetry in general (e.g., VCRs) that younger consumers are comfortable with. Complexity, as with all other perceived phenomena, is in the eyes (and experiences) of the beholder.

Trialability.   **Trialability** is the degree to which an innovation can be used on a limited basis. Products that can be used on a trial basis are usually adopted or accepted more quickly. If the risk of trying the product is reduced—if, say, the consumer can buy a single-use sample size for 49¢ versus a 42-use box at $8.99—then consumers will be more willing to try the product. Once the product is tried, the chance of acceptance increases. This is why marketers encourage test drives of automobiles and trial usage of products such as golf clubs in hopes that the consumer will later commit to purchasing the item.

Observability.
Observability is the degree to which the results of using a product are observable to others. If the product's superiority is visible, the adoption rate will increase. For example, undergarments are less observable than a new style of shoes. A new car is also more observable than a new engine placed in an old car. Products whose benefits lack observability are generally slower in adoptability. This is because the power of word-of-mouth communication is mitigated when the advantages of a new product are not readily seen (or heard or smelled).

In summary, the rate of new product adoption depends on whether a product is perceived as having distinct advantages over entrenched offerings and whether these advantages can be readily communicated to the market, and whether the market is not overwhelmed by the complexity of the product or finds it too expensive or risky to try.

Product Failure and Elimination

While developing new products is extremely critical to a firm, eliminating products that are no longer successful or profitable is an important function, too. As the product life cycle shows us, every product will decline at some point and become unprofitable for the firm. When a product is approaching the end of its life cycle, marketers must plan for its elimination and develop a strategy for withdrawal.

The above discussion identified reasons why products succeed (relative advantages or compatibility). There are also many reasons why products fail. Some of the typical reasons include the following:

- *Bad timing.* An axiom for success in real estate is "location, location, location." With new products, the maxim can be changed to "timing, timing, timing." Many products have failed not because they are inherently bad, but because the time of introduction was in apropos due to deteriorating economic conditions or simply being too avant-garde.

IBM's introduction of the PCjr with its late launch (along with a slow microprocessor, awkward keyboard, and unattractive price) cost the company close to $40 million in marketing costs alone.[12]

■ *Insignificant point of difference.* If the product is a "me too" item, perhaps it provides no distinct relative advantage over existing alternatives. Many personal computer models are doomed to eventual failure, because the points of difference often are trivial. Indeed, as of 1994, more than 300 PC makers have on the market over 1,000 brand names in approximately 11,000 configurations. Many of these products are distinguishable only by price.[13]

■ *Poor quality.* Poor quality will almost invariably eventually doom a product to a fate of failure. General Motors introduced the Cadillac Allante in an attempt to attract younger buyers who were interested in Mercedes and BMWs. However, with a price tag of $54,700, the car was underpowered compared to its foreign rivals and such nuisances as leaky roofs, squeaks, and wind noise contradicted the image of a luxury, sexy Euro-styled automobile. The company admitted the car was brought out too hastily and the quality was poor. The car was discontinued after five years of production.[14]

■ *Poor marketing execution.* Perhaps one or more of the marketing mix variables were inappropriate or inadequate. Was the product priced too high? Were consumers informed of the product and its benefits in effective advertising? Was the product available in key distribution points? Hunt-Wesson learned firsthand that poor marketing execution can kill a product line. The company introduced the Fresh and Lite line of low-fat frozen Chinese entrees by LaChoy. After distribution was secured and advertising begun, consumers who tried the products were dissatisfied. The egg rolls, which turned soggy if microwaved, required a long 30 minutes to cook. Also, the name "Fresh and Lite" did not accurately reflect the fact that the products were frozen. Hunt-Wesson pulled the plug on the line a short time later.[15]

■ *Markets too small or inaccessible.* Perhaps the market is not large enough or is too inaccessible via current distribution channels or promotional efforts to justify the expense.

Many marketers have been disappointed with their abort-
ed efforts in developing products for Generation Xers.
What some of these companies failed to realize is that this
group is a rather amorphous lot rather than a distinct market segment. Certainly, Generation Xers do not satisfy the
segmentation criteria specified in Chapter 6.

■ *Lack of top-management commitment.* A recent survey of new
product managers reveals that these managers attribute
some product failures to the fact that their senior managers
often are too distracted or disinterested in new products.[16]
Senior managers often are more interested in obtaining
growth via investments in established brands or in down-
sizing to control costs rather than committing resources
behind innovative, but risky, new product concepts.

Eliminating a product is an important decision. Many companies rely on a product review committee for recommendations on
the elimination of products. A committee of this nature usually consists of representatives from various key departments who can
speak to the specific problems a particular product may be causing.
For example, a production manager can point out the problems
associated with short production runs of slow-moving products.
The sales manager can speak to the retail problems a product is
experiencing such as declining distribution or increased competitive activity. The committee as a whole is in a position to evaluate
the performance of all products on a periodic basis and recommend
the elimination of weaker ones.

Products are eliminated for any of the following reasons:

1. Poor sales or profits
2. Incompatibility with the organization's business strategies
3. Poor market outlook[17]

Some organizations allow declining products to linger in the
product line too long. Decisions need to be made, though, because
these products may be using too many resources such as a manager's time and budget. These resources may be better spent on a new
product or a more successful existing product.

Once a firm decides to eliminate a product from its line, an
elimination plan must be developed. This plan includes when to

eliminate the product such as immediately or a phase-out over time, which depends on inventory levels of raw materials as well as finished goods. The sales department needs adequate warning so their accounts can be prepared for the elimination in advance. A well-thought-out plan will avoid alienating employees and current customers.

◆ Chapter Summary

Growth is fundamental to a firm's success. Growth can only come by increasing sales of existing products in existing markets, entering new markets, or developing new products. A firm can choose from four basic market and product development strategies all designed to promote growth: market penetration, market development, product development, or product diversification.

All products go through a product life cycle, or a series of stages—market introduction, market growth, market maturity, sales decline—from inception until they are withdrawn from the market. The length of each stage and the entire life of the product will vary from product to product depending on new technologies, consumer dissatisfaction, or competitive activities.

The concept of the brand, or the specific meaning that is created for the brand and communicated to consumers, must be successfully managed throughout the brand's life cycle. A brand concept is created by promoting a brand as appealing predominantly to consumers' functional, symbolic, or experiential needs.

New-product development is a necessity for any firm that hopes to realize long-term success. Developing new products is a difficult, complex process involving many departments and resources within the organization. Since the efforts of so many are needed to successfully develop a new product, a coordinated, systematic approach is required throughout the process. Firms rely on new-product committees, new-product departments, venture teams, product managers, and cross-functional teams to coordinate new product activity. New products typically progress through six developmental stages: idea generation, screening, business analysis, development, testing, and commercialization.

Product diffusion is the process by which a new product spreads through the marketplace. Different consumers will behave differently when a new product is introduced. The five categories of consumer behavior in the diffusion process are innovators, early adopters, early majority, late majority, and laggards. The rate at which a new product is adopted depends on the relative advantage, compatibility, complexity, trialability, and observability of the product.

All products must be periodically reviewed for their contribution to company objectives. Products that are not profitable must be eliminated from the product line so that the resources can be better applied to another product or marketing activity.

Notes

1. These options were introduced by H. Igor Ansoff, "Strategies for Diversification," *Harvard Business Review*, (September–October 1957), 113–124.

2. Matthew Grimm, "The Marketers of the Year," *Brandweek* (November 8, 1993), 52.

3. Peter N. Golder and Gerard J. Tellis, "Pioneer Advantage: Marketing Logic or Marketing Legend?" *Journal of Marketing Research*, 30 (May 1993), 158–170.

4. C. Whan Park, Bernard J. Jaworski, and Deborah J. MacInnis, "Strategic Brand Concept-Image Management," *Journal of Marketing*, 50 (October, 1986), 136.

5. This discussion is based on Park et al., ibid.

6. Peter R. Dickson, *Marketing Management* (Ft. Worth, TX: Dryden Press, 1994), 301–302.

7. Jon Berry and Edward F. Ogiba, "Why Do So Many New Products Fail?" *Brandweek* (October 19, 1992), 17–28.

8. Julie Liesse, "Special Report: The Marketing 100," *Advertising Age* (July 5, 1993), 5–8.

9. Jennifer Lawrence, "Whatever Happened to Olestra?" *Advertising Age* (May 2, 1994), 16.

10. For further information on test marketing, see N. D. Cadbury, "When, Where and How to Test Market," *Harvard Business Review*, (May–June, 1985), 97-98.

11. Mike Pantuso, "Will It Sell in Podunk? Hard to Say," *Business Week* (August 10, 1992), 46.

12. Christopher Power, "Flops," *Business Week* (August 16, 1993), 76.

13. Too Many Computer Names Confuse Too Many Buyers," *The Wall Street Journal* (June 29, 1994), B4.

14. Power, "Flops."

15. Ibid.

16. Berry and Ogiba, "Why Do So Many Products Fail?"

17. Douglas M. Lambert and Jay U. Sterling, "Identifying and Eliminating Weak Products," *Business* (July–September, 1988), 3–10.

◼ Study Questions

1. Market penetration is a strategy that
   a. is used to increase market share with existing products in existing markets.
   b. involves finding new markets and new users for existing products.
   c. introduces new products into established markets.
   d. focuses on developing new products for new markets.

2. Product development is a strategy that
   a. is used to increase market share with existing products in existing markets.
   b. involves finding new markets and new users for existing products.
   c. introduces new products into established markets.
   d. focuses on developing new products for new markets.

3. A market development strategy
   a. is used to increase market share with existing products in existing markets.
   b. involves finding new markets and new users for existing products.
   c. introduces new products into established markets.
   d. focuses on developing new products for new markets.

4. What dictates the length of a product's life cycle?
   a. new technologies
   b. consumer dissatisfaction
   c. competitive activities
   d. All of the above.

5. In the introduction stage of the product life cycle, the pioneering firm's top priority is to
   a. ensure the best possible level of quality.
   b. obtain distribution at retail and to inform consumers about the product.

    c. iron out any problems in production and distribution.

    d. achieve maximum profits.

6. During what stage in the product life cycle is the product the most *un*profitable?

    a. introduction

    b. growth

    c. maturity

    d. decline

7. Sales revenues are maximized at what stage in the product life cycle?

    a. introduction

    b. growth

    c. maturity

    d. decline

8. When a product pioneer introduces a new product with a relatively high price, it is adopting a _____ strategy.

    a. penetration

    b. exploitation

    c. faulty

    d. skimming

9. Primary demand creation is emphasized at which stage in a product's life cycle?

    a. introduction

    b. growth

    c. maturity

    d. decline

10. Brand-concept management is

    a. the process of developing a new product idea.

    b. the process of assigning a brand name to a product.

    c. the marketing activities used during the introduction stage of a product's life cycle.

    d. the planning, implementation, and control of a brand's meaning throughout its life.

11. Appeals to consumers' symbolic needs are those involving

    a. current consumption-related problems.

    b. psychological needs.

    c. the desire for products that provide sensory pleasure, stimulation, and variety.

    d. imaginary needs.

12. A manufacturer of bed sheeting advertises its product as the softest and most comfortable sheet in the industry. This company is appealing to consumers' _____ needs.
    a. symbolic
    b. experiential
    c. functional
    d. All of the above needs are being appealed to.

13. What is the most common organizational structure for new product development?
    a. new-product committees
    b. venture teams
    c. new-product departments
    d. a cross-functional team

14. The screening stage in the new-product development process is involved in
    a. viewing the package for the new product.
    b. identifying the most promising ideas and eliminating the rest.
    c. testing a prototype of a product that will be introduced to the market.
    d. analyzing the cost, revenue, and profit potential of product ideas.

15. In which stage of new product development are preliminary marketing strategies developed?
    a. business analysis
    b. idea generation
    c. commercialization
    d. development

16. In which stage of new product development are assessments made about a new product's market potential, growth rate, and financial funding?
    a. business analysis
    b. idea generation
    c. commercialization
    d. development

17. What is the diffusion process?
    a. The process by which a consumer retains information about a product.
    b. The process by which new ideas spread through a social system or marketplace.

   c. The time it takes for a new product to be developed and introduced to the market.

   d. The process by which new products are eliminated from the marketplace.

18. What group will spend more time deciding whether or not to try a new product than any other group in the diffusion process?

   a. early majority

   b. innovators

   c. early adopters

   d. late majority

19. Which group of adopters are particularly important in their role as opinion leaders?

   a. innovators

   b. early adopters

   c. early majority

   d. late majority

20. A manufacturer of golf clubs touted its product as having a unique metal alloy unlike any other club on the market, stating that this feature would promote greater distance. Consumers, however, could not see the alloy when inspecting the clubs in the store, and hence they were not eager to purchase this new product. In terms of factors that facilitate more rapid product adoption, this product could be said to lack

   a. a relative advantage.

   b. trialability.

   c. observability.

   d. important symbolism.

CHAPTER **10**

The Distribution Component of Marketing: Channels and Physical Distribution

Distribution is a critical component of any product's marketing mix. An organization may have a top-quality product priced below competition with an effective promotional program, but all is for naught unless the product is available to consumers when and where they want it. **Distribution** is the marketing activity that makes products available to marketing intermediaries (wholesalers, distributors, retailers) and to final consumers.

This chapter is the first of two chapters centering on distribution. The present chapter covers the general aspects of channels of distribution and physical distribution. The following chapter focuses on channel intermediaries, primarily wholesalers and retailers.

■ Overview

There are two facets of distribution. One involves the strategic arrangement of institutions (such as wholesalers and retailers) that take title to products and perform a variety of functions needed to effect the transfer of ownership and possession of products. This strategic arrangement is referred to as a *channel of distribution*. The other distribution component is responsible for the physical movement and storage of products; this is known as *physical distribution, or the logistical aspect of marketing.* Following sections explore each distribution component in some detail. First, however, it will be useful to consider a very unconventional (by American standards) business situation to fully appreciate the significance of both of these distribution activities.

This illustration takes us to the homes and offices of Bombay, India. Unlike businesspeople in the United States, Europe, and elsewhere who bring their lunches to work or go out to restaurants, many Indian office workers like to have hot lunches delivered from their homes each workday! How in a city such as Bombay could hot meals emanating from thousands of homes be delivered each day at lunch time to offices separated by as much as 65 kilometers (40 miles) from their homes? The answer is the *dabbawalla* system that has evolved over the years in Bombay.[1] Each morning starting around 10 A.M. mostly illiterate peasants, called dabbawallas, pick up home-cooked meals in lunchpail-like metal containers from more than 100,000 Bombay homes.

After collecting 35 to 40 *tiffins,* the name for the hot lunches, the first dabbawalla then transfers them to another dabbawalla who transports a large wooden tray of tiffins by bicycle to one of Bombay's two main railroad terminals. At this point tiffins are sorted according to their destination markings and transfered to yet another dabbawalla, who runs each tiffin to its designated office location. Later in the day the process is reversed when dabbawallas pick up the emptied tiffins and return them to their owners' homes after the lunch hour.

This incredible system of pickup and delivery costs an office worker less than $5 a month and pays a hardworking dabbawalla less than $50 a month. If a tiffin is lost or stolen, the owner is paid half the price of a new lunch pail, but losses rarely occur because the dabbawallas take great pride in the dependability of their service.

We see in this description the efficient workings of both distribution components. Distribution starts at the home when prepared meals are picked up and transported many miles to their delivery sites. The thousands of wives and servants who produce the meals are equivalent to manufacturers and the office worker recipients are tantamount to customers. Multiple levels of dabbawallas who pick up and return tiffins are the intermediaries who make this intricate system possible.

Discussion turns now to more conventional business situations, but as will be seen, the issues are fundamentally the same: How can products and services be effectively and efficiently exchanged between producers and users? between service providers and consumers? or between parties to any form of exchange?

Channels of Distribution

Consider the marketing of carpeting by a firm located in Georgia, one of the world's major carpet-producing centers. This manufacturer produces a variety of carpets for residential homes, apartments, office buildings, new automobiles, hotels, and a variety of other end uses. In principle, the manufacturer could make direct contact with millions of homeowners and thousands of businesses across the country, but this would be expensive and potentially inefficient and ineffective. Rather than attempting to perform all of the functions (described in Chapter 1) that are needed to create exchanges, the carpet manufacturer most likely will utilize the services of other businesses (agents, wholesalers, and retailers) to assist in carrying the distribution load and performing the functions necessary in order for exchanges to occur (i.e., buying, selling, transporting, storing, risk-taking, financing, providing information, and grading).

This hypothetical manufacturer produces carpets for use by homeowners, and in this capacity is engaged in the marketing of consumer goods. It also markets products to businesses such as architects, building contractors, automobile companies, and hotels, and when so doing is conducting business-to-business marketing. Both as a consumer-goods marketer and as a business-to-business marketer, the carpet manufacturer might attempt to market carpets directly to end users and employ a so-called direct channel of distribution. But the manufacturer has a variety of other arrangements available for getting its products to end users. In general, a **channel of distribution** is the arrangement businesses use when involved in performing marketing functions and transferring goods and services and their ownership from manufacturers to end-users. Later sections describe the various arrangements, or channel structures, that typically are used in marketing both consumer and business-to-business goods.

Now consider the marketing of a compact disc or cassette tape that is easily purchased from a music store. The recording contains the work of a group, symphony, or individual artist whose music was produced in a sound studio or on location, saved in the form of a CD or tape, and then marketed by the company that produced the music—companies such as RCA Corporation, CBS Records, Narada Productions, Inc., and Windham Hill Recordings. These production companies market CDs and tapes directly to large music chains and to other types of retailers (e.g., mass merchandisers such as Kmart and specialty electronic stores such as Circuit City). The record company also distributes its music to mail-order firms such as Columbia Records; and in other instances it markets CDs and tapes to large distributors, who in turn supply smaller music retailers. As with the carpet manufacturer, a variety of channel arrangements are involved in getting music to the millions of consumers who purchase CDs and tapes and to the many businesses (e.g., restaurants or department stores) that purchase music for their daily operations.

Physical Distribution

Physical distribution is the aspect of marketing that physically moves and stores products as they flow through the channel of distribution. The objective of physical distribution is to get the right product to the right place at the right time at a reasonable expense. When effectively accomplished, sales increase, costs are reduced, and customers are more satisfied. The physical distribution function in many firms also includes activities such as order taking, inventory control, and customer service. The final section of this chapter details the nature and role of physical distribution activities.

The Role of Channel Intermediaries

What comes to mind when you hear the term "middleman"? Increased costs? Higher prices? Unnecessary duplication of efforts? Many laypeople hold these negative stereotypes of the middleman. But to the contrary, middlemen play crucial roles in effecting exchanges in the marketplace. The following discussion will clarify the invaluable economic role performed by channel intermediaries.

What Are Marketing Intermediaries?

Marketing intermediaries are the business institutions (wholesalers, retailers, agents and brokers, and industrial distributors) that facilitate the exchange process between the original creators of products (e.g., manufacturers, farmers, miners, and service providers) and the end users of these goods and services. Intermediaries perform a variety of functions that make possible the exchange of products. Consider again the Georgian carpeting manufacturer. When this company sells its products to specialty carpeting stores and department stores, it acquires for a fee (which is the retailer's profit margin) the retailer's efforts in (1) storing carpet at locations convenient to consumers, (2) promoting the brand to consumers, (3) taking risk that the product will not sell, and (4) probably financing consumers' purchases. Without employing the services of retailers, and perhaps also wholesalers, the carpet manufacturer would be solely responsible for making contact with individual households, selling to individuals on a one-on-one basis, and arranging for product delivery and carpet installation. Although the activities would not be beyond the realm of possibility in this era of computer databases and direct marketing, many manufacturers would be unable, or at least unwilling, to assume these responsibilities. Herein rests the justification and economic rationale for marketing intermediaries such as wholesalers and retailers.

In general, intermediaries, also called middlemen, can be classified as either merchant or functional intermediaries. **Merchant middlemen** take title to products and resell them. Most wholesalers that purchase products from manufacturers, warehouse the products, and transport them to retailers are merchant middlemen. So are retailers. By comparison, **functional middlemen** do not take title to products; they simply facilitate the exchange process by performing buying or selling functions. *Agents* and *brokers* are functional middlemen.

Why Are Intermediaries Needed?

Imagine a world without intermediaries. The thousands of manufacturers and other creators of products and services would need to contact the million-plus retail outlets individually to sell their products. (Imagine, for example, the incredible waste of time, money, and other resources that would be neccesitated if over 100,000 housewives or their servants, rather than only 2,000 dabbawallas, hand delivered lunches each day in Bombay.) This would be a horrendous prospect for manufacturers. Endless numbers of salespeople would have to be hired and trained to cover all of their customers. New warehouse facilities would have to be opened to accommodate the increased number of customers. And the amount of paperwork—from orders to billings—would be overwhelming due to the increased number of transactions. This would result in higher prices, because manufacturers would not be as efficient in performing all exchange and other marketing functions as would the middlemen they would be forced to replace.

In general, marketing intermediaries perform invaluable economic roles for the following three reasons:

- *Intermediaries greatly reduce the number of transactions needed in the exchange process.* Consider a situation where a candy manufacturer distributes its products to 100 retailers in a single market. To reach all 100 retailers would require, of course, 100 separate transactions—each involving some form of salesperson contact, product shipment, and customer billing and payment. However, by employing the services of a single wholesaler in this hypothetical market, the manufacturer is able to reduce the multiple transactions with retailers to a single, recurrent transaction. In just one transaction—manufacturer to one wholesaler intermediary—the manufacturer is in reality contacting 100 customers. Thus, the manufacturer's costs are reduced by utilizing intermediaries, and due to the greater efficiencies provided by the wholesaler, costs to retailers and final consumers may also be reduced.

■ *Intermediaries provide a solution to the discrepancies of quantity and assortment that exist between manufacturers and end-users.* A **discrepancy of quantity** is the difference between the quantity of products a manufacturer produces versus the quantity of products the consumer needs and wishes to buy. For example, General Mills produces millions of cereal boxes each week, but the typical consumer wishes to purchase only a single box every week or so. General Mills is hardly in a position to service the individual cereal needs of the millions of households that consume its various brands. The use of wholesaler and retailer intermediaries makes it possible for consumers to conveniently purchase the amounts they wish to buy. A **discrepancy of assortment** is the difference between the number of products a manufacturer produces versus the assortment the consumer needs or wishes to buy. For example, when a consumer goes to a retail outlet to purchase a personal computer, she or he also may want to acquire a mouse pad, a computer dust cover, a printer, diskettes, and software at the same time so the computer will be up and running the same day. Computer manufacturers do not manufacture all of these items. Thus, the retail intermediary overcomes this discrepancy of assortment by ordering a variety of product lines from different vendors and merchandising these to satisfy end users' diverse consumption needs.

■ *Intermediaries share functions with manufacturers.* All or most of the following basic marketing functions must be performed in every exchange transaction: buying, selling, transporting, storing, financing, risk taking, and providing information. No one function can be ignored or eliminated from the process. Someone must perform these functions whether it is the producer, wholesaler, retailer, or another intermediary. Responsibility for some of these functions, though, can be *shifted and shared* among manufacturers, intermediaries, and end users. For example, the responsibility for order taking is shared with wholesalers and distributors. The responsibility for delivering the product is shared with wholesalers who order the product and transportation companies who are hired to deliver the product. This suggests a general axiom about the distribution function in marketing: *Functions can be shifted and shared among producers and intermediaries, but they cannot be eliminated!*[2]

Channel Structures for Marketing Business-to-Business and Consumer Goods and Services

Various channels of distribution exist to perform the marketing functions needed to distribute the vast number of products in the marketplace. For example, the channel structure required by R. J. Reynolds to distribute a convenience good like cigarettes differs greatly from the structure used by Lockheed in selling new airplanes. A number of channel structures have evolved for the marketing of both business-to-business and consumer products. These structures, or arrangements, have an economic function and also sometimes exist as a matter of tradition in some industries. We first focus discussion on business-to-business channels and then turn to the arrangements for consumer goods.

Business-to-Business Channel Structures

Exhibit 10.1 depicts the various channel arrangements that are used in distributing goods from one business to another. Business-to-business marketers typically use any of four channel structures in marketing products to their final customers, or end users: (1) direct to the business customers who are the end users in business-to-business marketing; (2) indirect via agents or brokers; (3) indirect via distributors; and (4) indirect via agents/brokers and distributors. The first, or direct, channel arrangement can be thought of as a *short* channel of distribution in comparison to the *long* channel in the last arrangement.

Producer Direct to Business Customers.   Since most business-to-business marketers have a limited number of customers, the producer often is able to use a *direct channel of distribution*. The producer performs all of the necessary exchange functions or shares them with the business customer without the involvement of intermediaries. The Georgia-based carpet manufacturer, for example,

Exhibit 10.1   Traditional Channel Arrangements for Business-to-Business
                 Products

Producer $\longrightarrow$ Business Customers
Producer $\longrightarrow$ Agents/Brokers $\longrightarrow$ Business Customers
Producer $\longrightarrow$ Distributors $\longrightarrow$ Business Customers
Producer $\longrightarrow$ Agents/Brokers $\longrightarrow$ Distributors $\longrightarrow$ Business Customers

sells its carpeting directly to General Motors and other automobile manufacturers in Detroit as one of several channel arrangements for marketing carpeting. For large, complex products that require a great deal of service on an ongoing basis, it often is more economical for the producer to deal directly with its customers rather than utilizing the services of middlemen.

There has been a tremendous increase in applications of direct marketing for businesses that market to other businesses. Nearly one-third of all money invested in business-to-business marketing goes to direct marketing, especially telemarketing.[3] A major reason for this trend is the cost of an industrial sales call, which is estimated to exceed $250 per call. Direct marketing through telemarketing and direct mail actually replaces the sales force in some companies, whereas in other cases it is used to supplement the sales force's efforts by building goodwill, generating leads, and opening doors for salespeople. Over 90 percent of the respondents to a recent survey indicated that direct marketing is an important tool in their business-to-business marketing efforts.[4]

Mail-order selling, telemarketing, and other forms of direct marketing provide attractive options for firms who either prefer to avoid the tremendous expense of a traveling sales force or desire to supplement sales-force effort with supportive marketing communications. Business-to-business direct marketing can reduce marketing costs substantially and provide firms with larger potential markets.

Producer to Agents/Brokers to Business Customers.

The fundamental distinction between this channel arrangement and the previous, direct channel, is the use of agents or brokers intead of the manufacturer's own sales force, or, in some instances, in lieu of the manufacturer's marketing department. That is, agents and brokers are independent businesses that sell the products of other businesses.

MARKETING HIGLIGHTS

Gillette's Return to Founding Principles Brings Success

The Gillette Company fought off four takeover attempts in the late 1980s. Outsiders viewed the company as having reached middle age and ripe for takeover. Internally, however, the company was healthy. Former CEO Colman Mockler had cut costs and sold off businesses in the 1970s and 1980s and reduced the overall number of employees while improving productivity. At the same time the company returned to the business principle stated by founder King C. Gillette around the turn of the century—"The greatest feature of the business is the almost endless chain of blade consumption, each razor sold paying tribute to the company as long as the user lives."[a]

The key to Gillette's revival was the Sensor razor, a new razor protected by 17 patents, with replaceable blade cartridges. Sensor was conceived in 1979 and developed in top secrecy at a cost of approximately $200 million but not introduced in the United States, Europe, and Japan until January of 1990. The company sold 24 million Sensor razors in that first year, topping their estimate of 18 million. More than 350 million blade cartridges were shipped, compared with the 200 mil-

lion that Gillette had estimated.

In the early 1980s Gillette executives were divided. One group within the company apparently felt that razors were becoming a commodity business, pointing to the trend toward disposable razors, low-profit commodity items sold by the bagful. Another group argued that Gillette should stick to the founder's principles and use its vast resources to concentrate on products with a technological edge that could command a premium price.

The person generally credited with resolving this internal debate was John Symons, an Englishman who became head of Gillette's European operations in the early 1980s and retired in December of 1990. In 1983 Symons told his European management team to study the European market to find out whether men wanted disposables or refillables. They found that shavers over 45 thought of Gillette as a maker of quality shaving products while shavers under 45 were often confirmed users of disposables and had no particular regard for Gillette.

Symons argued that Gillette's success in selling disposables was a result of expensive marketing, not of superior technology, as in shaving systems. He felt that the company was coming close to giving up on what Gillette had formerly stood for. His solution was to

---

A manufacturing enterprise can employ its own sales force and conduct all selling exclusively through that sales force. Alternatively, it may depend entirely on the hired (i.e., commissionable) services of independent agents/brokers; a third possibility is to use a combination of its own sales force supplemented with agents/brokers.

Brokers are in the business of connecting sellers and buyers. Brokers typically are present in industries with many buyers and

stop advertising disposables entirely and to pour marketing money into promoting shaving systems.

Gillette's Trac II and Atra shaving systems began to gain share in Europe and the growth rate of all disposables began to slow. Symons' strategy was risky because it meant the company had to convince consumers to pay more for its shaving systems instead of buying cheap disposables.

But the risk paid off. As sales of Gillette's disposables dropped, sales of its higher-priced systems and their replacement cartridges more than made up for the losses. The result was low-margin business being replaced by high-margin business in Europe.

Symons was then given the added job of managing the shaving business in North America as well as in Europe. He had to fight the disposables versus refillables battle all over again in the U.S. market. This time, however, he had the advantage of selling the Sensor razor, Gillette's newest technologically advanced product.

Symons saw at once that the Sensor could do for Gillette everywhere what shaving systems had already done for it in Europe: move it up from selling 40¢ disposable products to selling $3.30 razors, which in turn created an endless demand for 70¢ blade cartridges.

Although the Sensor cannibalized Gillette's Trac II and Atra razors, as was expected with the introduction of the new product, what was unexpected was that the cannibalization of older Gillette systems was far less than Gillette had expected. The company found that 14% of Sensor sales came from users of competitors' disposable razors, about double what they had expected. The growth rate of disposables, which had been 5% annually in the United States until 1988, flattened, and the big losers in Sensor's surge were Schick in systems, and Schick and Bic in disposables.

Gillette found that it succeeds best when it can use its marketing and product development resources to carve out profitable niches where it has an edge. Sensor was able to successfully compete against disposable razors because it gives a great shave, and it is difficult for competitors to knock off. By producing technologically superior, innovative products that provide benefit to the consumer while holding fast to its founding principles, Gillette has been able to successfully compete in the shaving products market.

[a] This article is adapted from Subrata N. Chakravarty, "We Had to Change the Playing Field," *Forbes*, February 4, 1991, 82.

sellers, such as real-estate brokers, stockbrokers, and food brokers. Brokers are knowledgeable about their products and industries and hence are capable of representing many buyers or sellers. Brokers offer a certain expertise by specializing in a particular market. For example, numerous companies use brokers when marketing to the military. These brokers are expert in the paperwork requirements of the government and the procedures needed to obtain distribution for products.

Agents perform a similar "connecting" function. There are two general types of agents: **Manufacturer's agents** primarily perform a *selling* function for the producers they represent. Manufacturer's agents, also called manufacturer's representatives, or reps, work on a commission basis and typically represent the complimentary products of noncompeting producers. **Selling agents,** like manufacturer's reps, are independent businesses who do not take title to the products they represent or handle inventory. Unlike the more limited role of manufacturer's agents, selling agents perform a *variety of other marketing functions* beyond selling for the producers they represent. In fact, the term "selling agent" is somewhat of a misnomer insofar as selling agents are more like an *independent marketing department* for the producers they represent than merely a selling arm. Manufacturer's agents are much more prevalent, however, than are selling agents. Many producers find that they can more economically and successfully sell their products by contracting with agents on a commission basis compared to employing their own full-time sales forces. In effect, an agent becomes the sales force for the producer it represents. The use of agents is most common when a market is large or geographically scattered and when buyers purchase in relatively small quantities from many vendors.

Producer to Distributors to Business Customers.

In comparison to the direct-to-business customer arrangement, on many occasions a producer would prefer to shift exchange functions to a wholesaler, or industrial distributor, rather than taking full responsibility for these functions. **Distributors** (also called industrial wholesalers) are independent businesses that purchase products from producers (i.e., take title), maintain physical inventories of products, employ salespeople to contact business customers, and typically finance their customers' purchases.

Manufacturers who produce standard and relatively inexpensive business-to-business products used by a large number of customers frequently utilize distributors in their marketing efforts. These distributors take title to the products they carry and store inventories of products in their own warehouses. For example, a major manufacturer of various steel products used in the building trades (e.g., roof decking, culvert pipe) would market some of its products through distributors who would maintain inventories for purchasers whose typical orders are too small to justify direct ordering from the manufacturer.

Exhibit 10.2   Traditional Channel Arrangements for Consumer Goods

Producer → Consumers
Producer → Retailers → Consumers
Producer → Wholesalers → Retailers → Consumers
Producer → Agents/Brokers → Wholesalers → Retailers → Consumers

Producer to Agents/Brokers to Distributors to Business Customers.   The final channel arrangement for business-to-business products is one in which a producer uses both agents/brokers and distributors in selling its products. This arrangement is most common when the market consists of a large number of small customers. A producer could not afford the number of salespeople needed to service these customers, so it relies on channel intermediaries to perform storing, risk-taking, and selling functions. Many industrial supplies such as paper hand towels, protective masks, plastic gloves, and industrial cleaning products are sold under this arrangement.

Consumer Channel Structures

Exhibit 10.2 illustrates the five most frequent channel arrangements that are used in marketing consumer goods. These range from the short, direct-to-consumer arrangement to the long, producer-to-agents/brokers-to-wholesalers-to-retailers-to-consumer channel. The similarities between these channel structures and those used in business-to-business marketing should be obvious. The major differences are (1) the presence of retailers in consumer channel structures, which, of course, are absent in business-to-business marketing, and (2) the change in title from industrial distributor (or simply distributor) to wholesaler.

Producer Direct to Consumer Channel.   The first channel illustrated in Exhibit 10.2 is the direct channel where a producer markets products directly to consumers. Historically, direct marketing represented a relatively small part of most companies' marketing efforts. However, U.S. consumers now spend well over $200 billion annually through mail- and telephone-order sales. Direct marketing is accomplished using direct-response advertising, direct mail (including catalogs), telemarketing, and direct selling.

The growth rate in the volume of sales from direct marketing is far out-pacing sales through indirect marketing channels. In fact, mail order is the fastest growing form of product distribution in the United States. Another important, though relatively minor aspect of direct marketing is direct selling. **Direct selling** involves the personal explanation and demonstration of products and services to consumers in their homes or at their jobs. Amway, Avon, Mary Kay Cosmetics, and Tupperware are just a few of the hundreds of companies that market directly to consumers. Interestingly, America is a distant second to Japan in annual direct sales. Nearly everything is sold direct in Japan—including products ranging from condoms to automobiles. Indeed, over 75% of all automobile sales in Japan are sold by direct salespeople! Compare this with the United States and other western countries, where it is difficult to imagine cars being sold by any means other than retail dealerships.

A variety of factors help to explain direct marketing's growth. Fundamental societal changes (including more women in the work force, greater time pressures, increased use of credit cards, and more discretionary income) have created a need and opportunity for the convenience of direct-marketed products and services. Direct marketing provides shoppers with an easy, convenient, and relatively hassle-free way to buy.

Although database marketing and direct marketing are not equivalent, the increased sophistication of database marketing has been largely responsible for the growing use and effectiveness of direct marketing.[5] Major advances in computer technology and database management have made it possible for companies to maintain huge databases containing millions of prospects and customers. *Niche marketing* can be fully realized by targeting promotional efforts to a company's best prospects (based on past product-category purchasing behavior) and who can be identified in terms of specific geographic, demographic, and psychographic characteristics. Companies have become so proficient with databases that many consumers are concerned about their privacy being invaded.

Producer to Retailers to Consumers.   Many consumer goods are marketed from producer to retailers who, in turn, sell to consumers. Manufacturers' salespeople, or their agents, call on retailers, who stock the manufacturer's products and assume ownership (i.e., take title) to the merchandise. Expensive consumer durables (e.g., automobiles, furniture, or appliances) are generally marketed in this fashion. Many convenience goods, such as supermarket products, also employ this channel arrangement when the retailer purchases in large volume from the manufacturer. (Comparatively, smaller food retailers place orders through food wholesalers.) In using retailers, manufacturers shift functions to retailers whose role is to acquire ownership of the products, maintain inventories, merchandise products, and facilitate their exchange to consumers.

Producer to Wholesalers to Retailers to Consumers.

A third channel arrangement in the consumer market is one in which wholesalers intervene between manufacturers and retailers. Wholesalers perform an essential economic role in those instances where manufacturers do not have the size or financial wherewithal to serve the many retailers the manufacturer needs to merchandise and sell its products.

The use of wholesalers is especially critical in those situations where a large number of retail outlets carry a particular product (e.g., tobacco, candy) or in instances where the producer is relatively small. Producers in certain industries simply cannot support the sales force needed to call on every retail outlet that carries products. Several wholesalers in a geographic area are better able to call on and service these smaller accounts. In these instances, the functions that need to be performed to ultimately facilitate exchanges between producers and consumers are shifted and shared among the producers themselves along with wholesalers and retailers. In addition to maintaining inventories of products purchased from producers, wholesalers also peform selling and risk-taking functions when the wholesaler's salespeople call on retail accounts and provide credit to facilitate retailers' purchases.

From Producer to Agents/Brokers to Wholesalers to Retailers to Consumers.

The final channel arrangement is one in which a producer uses agents or brokers in lieu of its own sale force or to augment its sales force. These agents/brokers sell to wholesalers, who, in turn, sell to retailers from whom consumers fulfill their consumption needs. This channel arrangement is typically used in the situation where a small manufacturer cannot afford or cannot justify maintaining its own sales force and/or when the market is comprised of a number of small retail outlets. Many food manufacturers, for example, use this long channel arrangement to reach all of the mom-and-pop corner grocery stores, convenience stores, supermarkets, mass merchandisers, and even gas stations that carry their products.

Channels for Services

The distribution arrangements for services differ from those used for products since services are typically delivered to the business customer or final consumer at the time when they are used. That is, most services are delivered via direct distribution. Consumers getting haircuts, having their carpets cleaned, or taking their clothes for dry cleaning all deal directly with the service-provider. Arenas offering events such as circuses and concerts utilize direct distribution by selling tickets for the events directly to consumers at the box office.

However, not all services are marketed directly to consumers or business customers. Some service providers use agents, or brokers, to sell their services. A consumer who does not wish to make the trip to the box office may still purchase tickets to an event through a ticket broker such as Ticketmaster or from ticket agents. Airline tickets typically are purchased via travel agencies. Service agents, as is the case with agents of physical products, do not assume ownership (take title) to the services they represent; rather, their role is simply one of facilitating exchanges between service providers and customers via performing a selling function.

Multiple Channels

It would be erroneous to think that products—whether business-to-business items, consumer goods, or services—are marketed via a single channel of distribution. Many producers—especially large enterprises—typically utilize more than one channel for distributing their products. This is true in both the consumer and business-to-business markets. The arena hosting a sporting event uses direct distribution and agents and brokers to sell the available tickets to consumers. The Georgian carpet manufacturer employs multiple channel arrangements in marketing its many products: (1) it sells directly to automobile and van manufacturers, to boat manufacturers, to municipal, state, and federal government accounts such as military installations, and to major building contractors who install carpeting in structures such as office buildings; (2) it also has a direct sales division for marketing carpeting to home contractors; (3) it markets residential carpet to consumers via retailers such as department stores and specialty carpeting outlets; (4) it uses distributors to reach small manufacturers and building contractors; and (5) it uses wholesalers to market its residential carpet to small retailers whose purchases are not sufficiently large to justify contact from the manufacturer's sales force.

Consider also the case of the food manufacturer in marketing its line of snack foods. Just a few of the possibilities: (1) the company's sales force calls on large, national supermarket chains; (2) it supplies smaller food retailers by using agents, brokers, and wholesalers (food distributors); (3) it services the military by selling to commissaries; (4) it distributes products through vending machine companies; and (5) it uses distributors to market its products to high school and college sporting events. In general, manufacturers use various channel arrangements to best meet their customers' needs and to serve the company's own marketing and financial interests.

Distribution Intensity

How many retail outlets in a particular market should a manufacturer use? This question addresses the issue of distribution intensity. The number of retail outlets used in marketing a manufacturer's offerings is determined by several considerations: (1) product price (whether it is relatively low- or high-priced), (2) consumer purchase frequency (frequent or only occasional), (3) the amount of prepurchase search consumers are willing to engage in (little to considerable), and (4) the level of service desired or demanded by consumers (none to extensive). Distribution intensity can be conceptualized as extending from *intensive* distribution at one end of an intensity continuum to *exclusive* distribution at the other end of the continuum, with *selective* distribution at an intermediate point. As is the nature with all continuous concepts, it is important that you recognize that the differences among these three levels of distribution intensity is more a matter of degree than substance.

Intensive distribution is used when a product is sold through virtually every available retail outlet in a particular market. Convenience products such as candy bars, soft drinks, and cigarettes are found in numerous retail outlets—supermarkets, gasoline stations, convenience stores, and ubiquitous vending machines. Intensive distribution is critical for products such as these because

CAPTAINS OF INDUSTRY

Wolfgang Schmitt

Chairman and Chief Executive Officer

Rubbermaid Incorporated

Date of Birth: March 12, 1944

Education: Otterbein College

Career Path: Began as management trainee at Rubbermaid in 1966, shortly after graduating from college. Worked his way through the ranks at Rubbermaid serving as product manager, director of research and development for the home products division, becoming the division's vice president of marketing in 1981. Elected a director and executive vice president of the corporation in 1987 and became Rubbermaid's president and chief operating officer in 1991. Elected co-chairman of the board of directors and chief executive officer in November of 1992 until the third quarter of 1993 when he was elected chairman of the board.

Profile: Born in Germany but raised in Smithville, Ohio, immigrating with his family at the age of 10.

Personal: Set a record for the 180-yard low hurdles in high school, a record that still stands.

Rubbermaid, guided by CEO Wolfgang Schmitt, introduces roughly one new product a day. The company produces rubber and plastic containers for use in the kitchen, bathroom, backyard, office, or to take along anywhere, and the company's success has been founded on product innovation, constantly improving its products. Rubbermaid was voted "most admired company" in *Fortune* magazine's 1994 survey, citing Rubbermaid's record of innovation in the manufacture of such everyday goods as dustpans, dish drainers and plastic storage crates. Schmitt has set goals for the company, including entering a new product category every 12 to 18 months, getting 33% of sales from products introduced in the past five years, and by the year 2000 getting 25% of total revenues from markets outside the United States (18% currently).[a]

Schmitt began his career with Rubbermaid in 1966 in the management training program. He was named director for research and development of the Home Products Division in 1976, Rubbermaid's largest operating business. In that capacity, he was responsible for new product development that involved consumer research, design, engineering and mold technology, as well as applied research. Schmitt was promoted to vice president of R&D in 1978. He became vice president of marketing for that division in 1981 with overall responsibility for strategic planning, new product introduction, acquisition analysis, market research, consumer advertising, merchandising and public relations. In 1984, Schmitt was elected president and general manager of the Home Products Division. Under his management, the division initiated business teams, entered new markets, and upgraded the technology base of the business. Schmitt also implemented the partnership philosophy with customers, suppliers, communities and internal associates. In 1987, he was elected a director and executive vice president of the corporation and became Rubbermaid's president and chief operating officer in 1991. He was elected co-chairman of the board of directors and chief executive officer of Rubbermaid Incorporated in November of 1992.[b] He shared the chairmanship with Stanley C. Gault, retired Rubbermaid chairman and CEO until the third quarter of 1993, when he was elected chairman of the board.

What drives Wolfgang Schmitt? Schmitt is known around Rubbermaid by company nicknames like Submarine Commander.[c] Schmitt expects the most from himself and no less from others, say people who work closely with him. His management style is described as "quiet and intense." He is also known as a tough negotiator, but once you've won him over, he remains loyal to your cause. Don Noble, former CEO of Rubbermaid who hired Schmitt as a management trainee in 1966, remembers how thoroughly Schmitt prepared his presentations. Noble explains, "This [thoroughness] is particularly important to Rubbermaid because we never test-market a product. This requires an exhaustive thoroughness in investigation because the company commits to molds, inventory, distribution and marketing before it ever sees the market's reaction." Schmitt applies that same exhaustive thoroughness to investigating and deciding about new business ideas brought by business associates. He uses a quick grasp of details and a strong work ethic to feed an almost insatiable appetite for new technology and information which can improve business operations or profitability.[d]

Schmitt was born in Germany during World War II and came to the United States at the age of 10. He found acceptance in his new country through athletic accomplishment. His track coach at Otterbein College, Dr. Elmer Yoest, remembers Schmitt as a very competitive and outstanding athlete. When he lost a race he never let his emotions show, but one knew that he really hated losing. And it is that same competitive spirit that Schmitt carried into his professional life, and associates say that he still doesn't take defeat easily.[e]

Employees note that he gets to work before most others, arriving at 7:00 A.M. and leaving well after 6 at night. He doesn't like going out for lunch, unless its a pre-arranged business meeting, and is very conscious of his diet. He stays fit by jogging and playing tennis regularly, but he hates golf. "If a sport doesn't have a lot of excitement or physical activity, if it's the least bit sedentary or lacks intensity, Wolf wants nothing to do with it."[f]

Rubbermaid has been an extremely successful company over the last decade. Since 1982 the company's sales and per-share earnings have grown at compound annual rates of 14.6% and 18%, respectively. On Wall Street, Rubbermaid's common stock has risen 837% since 1982, making it the 25th best performer on the big board during the 1980s. The company has battled stiff competition and a weak economy in the 1990s. Schmitt was forced to lower prices in 1993 for the third year in a row, but still managed to generate 15% earnings growth in the third quarter of 1993. He achieved that by boosting Rubbermaid's operating margin. Some of this improvement has come by way of higher productivity, but most of the increase has come as a result of lower raw material prices and from trimming sales, general, and administrative expenses.

In order to achieve continued growth Schmitt is increasing productivity, acquiring other companies and

Continued on next page

CAPTAINS OF INDUSTRY, continued

expanding internationally. In 1992 Rubbermaid spent $134.5 million, or 7.5% of sales, on capital expenditures. That's the largest amount of sales the company has spent on plant and equipment since 1987. The company has streamlined its factories to make them more productive.

The big challenge for Schmitt is boosting Rubbermaid's international sales. The company currently gets about 18% of its consolidated revenues from outside the United States, almost all from Canada. Schmitt would like to see revenues increase to 25% by 2000. Schmitt hopes to globalize the business by building the company's brands.

In 1990 Rubbermaid entered into a joint venture with DSM, a Netherlands-based conglomerate, to manufacture housewares under the name of Curver Rubbermaid Group. To allow consumers outside North America to get used to the Rubbermaid name, Schmitt kept the Curver brand name on the products but displays it in the red Rubbermaid logo. In 1992 Rubbermaid acquired Cipsa, now called Rubbermaid de Mexico, a plastic and rubber housewares maker with $815 million in estimated sales. Rubbermaid is also increasing its brand exposure overseas by piggybacking on some of its customers. For example, the company has followed the expansion of Toys 'R' Us overseas by building a facility in

Ireland for Rubbermaid's toymaking subsidiary, Little Tykes.[g]

Rubbermaid is recognized for being a socially responsible company. The company has built a drug and alcohol abuse center, repaired deteriorating buildings in its hometown of Wooster, has been an innovator in recycling technology, and supports education through its own Rubbermaid Foundation. "We really come from the notion that things which are for the societal good have to have a sound economic basis before they can succeed," Schmitt says. Social responsibility is a part of Rubbermaid's culture as well as its moneymaking strategy. "When you're ethical, people know it. We happen to think good ethics is good business."[h]

Rubbermaid has also been recognized for its environmentally friendly products, actually helping people to reduce, reuse, and recycle through its own products, such as a stylish, user-friendly composter. The Sidekick, an insulated lunch box, is another example: with plastic containers inside for a sandwich, a drink and something extra, plastic wrappings are eliminated.[i]

Schmitt also fosters a "partnership attitude" with Rubbermaid's own employees, or "associates," as they are called at Rubbermaid. Workers are grouped in "new product teams" of 12 to 15 staff members, including marketing experts, engineers, package

they are purchased frequently and consumers will switch brands if their first choice is unavailable. Also, because little service is required, it is possible for manufacturers to make their brands widely available without concerns that consumers' problems will be unattended. In sum, consumer purchasing behavior dictates the need for manufacturers to intensively distribute inexpensive and frequently purchased products. This intensive distribution requires

designers, even accounting staff. These teams conceptualize new products and see their creations through the production, testing, and sales phases. If the new product is a water jug for joggers, someone on the team tests it in his or her own exercise routines. Interdepartmental rivalry is minimized and team members are entrepreneurs with a common stake.

Creativity is a hallmark of all of Rubbermaid's enterprises. Its own product development is a creative problem-solving process; one of its successes is a ergonomic laundry basket that fits the body's curves as the basket is carried up and down stairs. A new shower caddy dispenses shampoo with the bottle upside down, so that the last half-inch isn't wasted.[j] The War Room in the Customer Center at Rubbermaid houses samples of competing products that are analyzed for their deficiencies. The company does no test marketing, relying on focus groups, instead, for product testing. Schmitt's reasoning is that Rubbermaid doesn't want to be copied. "It's not that much riskier to just roll it out. Plus, it puts pressure on us to do it right the first time."[k]

Schmitt and Rubbermaid have proven to be a winning combination. His drive to succeed is strong, and the company has a proven track record in spinning out innovative products in a hurry. Watching it reach its goal of getting 25% of total revenues from mar-kets outside the United States by 2000 will be a race worth watching. And Wolfgang Schmitt loves a good race.

[a] Alan Farnham, "America's Most Admired Company," Fortune, February 7, 1994, 50–51.
[b] Rubbermaid 1992 Annual Report, 2.
[c] Farnham, "America's Most Admired Company," 51.
[d] Terry Troy, "The Man Rubbermaid Made; How Wolfgang Schmitt Worked His Way to the Top of the Industry's Leading Company," HFD-The Weekly Home Furnishings Newsletter, January 18, 1993, 51.
[e] Troy, "The Man Rubbermaid Made," 51.
[f] Ibid.
[g] Michael K. Ozanian and Alexandra Ourusoff, "Never Let Them See You Sweat," Financial World, February 1, 1994, 34.
[h] Mary Mihaly, "Doing Well by Doing Good: Can a Company Be Socially Responsible and Still Make Money? At Rubbermaid, They've Proven Good Guys Finish First," Repository, October 22, 1993, BUS section.
[i] Mihaly, "Doing Well."
[j] Ibid.
[k] Farnham, "America's Most Admired Company," 54.

the use of agents/brokers and wholesalers to share the selling, transporting, storing, financing, and information functions that have to be performed in gaining distribution with large numbers of retail outlets.

At the other extreme, **exclusive distribution** is practiced when a manufacturer restricts product distribution to a single retailer in a particular market or just a relatively few retailers. Products that are expensive, infrequently purchased, are sought after by consumers (i.e., specialty goods), and which often require considerable after-sale servicing are the most likely candidates for exclusive distribution. Expensive brands of apparel (e.g., Armani suits), prestige brands of jewelry (e.g., Piaget watches), and luxury automobiles (e.g., Lamborghini) are exclusively distributed. Such exclusion supports the prestige image possessed by these brands and reduces manufacturer selling costs.

Selective distribution is an intermediate degree of distribution intensity. That is, selectively distributed brands are available in multiple retail outlets in a particular market but not, as in the case of intensively distributed brands, in virtually every store that could carry the brand. Shopping products, or those that consumers seek out, are sold through selective distribution. Most well-known brands of appliances, apparel, and electronic items are selectively distributed. For example, in most larger markets Timberland shoes are available in a subset of clothing and shoe stores whose image matches the image that Timberland projects.

Conventional Channels versus Vertical Marketing Systems

As previously discussed, marketing channels consist of arrangements of manufacturers, wholesalers, retailers, and various facilitative agencies such as agents and brokers. In an earlier era of marketing, two notable features characterized the operations of the various channel members. First, each type of organization typically engaged in a narrow line of business: manufacturers produced products and sold them to wholesalers and retailers; wholesalers purchased from manufacturers, maintained inventories, and supplied retailers. Retailers purchased from wholesalers (or directly from manufacturers), merchandised their stores, and served their consumers. Second, the various channel members operated virtually as autonomous entities, each linked in a loose and independent fashion and each concerned with maximizing its own sales performance and profitability. Producers, wholesalers, and retailers often dealt with each other in a rather distrustful manner and cooperated with each other only as a matter of necessity in an effort to maintain relations and conduct business. What we have just described can be thought of as the operation of **conventional marketing channels.**

Exhibit 10.3   Three Types of Vertical Marketing Systems

1. Administered Systems **2.** Corporate Systems **3.** Contractual Systems

In the era of modern marketing, the trend has been toward a blurring of the separations among the various channel members and increasing cooperation. Manufacturers, wholesalers, and retailers increasingly have integrated and coordinated their activities to the benefit of all. The term **vertical marketing system** (VMS) describes a marketing channel whereby channel members unify their efforts and cooperate in order to best serve their own needs as well as those of their direct customers and the ultimate consumers. Three types of vertical marketing systems are recognized: administered, corporate, and contractual VMSs (Exhibit 10.3).

Administered VMSs

An **administered VMS** represents the least controlled type of vertical marketing system and, as such, provides a useful point of departure from the loose-jointed conventional marketing channel. An administered VMS is like a conventional channel with the major exception that one channel member (a manufacturer, wholesaler, or retailer) informally acts in the capacity of channel leader. Consider by analogy the operation of the United States government and its executive, legislative, and judicial branches. These branches are constitutionally separate, but the effective functioning of government requires some degree of cooperation and unity among them, particularly the executive and legislative arms. If each branch operated without regard to the interests of the others, government would quickly grind to a near halt and gridlock would set in. There are times when the president "leads" government and other times when Congress is the more influential branch.

Now consider the functioning of marketing channels with economically and legally independent sets of manufacturers, wholesalers, and retailers. In an administered VMS, effective channel functioning and cooperation is achieved when a dominant channel member exercises its economic clout. This channel member, sometimes referred to as the "channel captain" or "channel leader," acts as the coordinator or manager. This leader, by virtue of its economic dominance and influence, can establish policies and coordinate efforts. For example, Procter & Gamble—a world-renowned manufacturer of cleaning products, food items, paper goods, and other categories—exercised its tremendous power in the early 1990s when it fundamentally changed the way it and some of its competitors price products to supermarket accounts. P&G implemented an everyday low pricing policy, or "value pricing," which effectively amounts to selling items to retail accounts at the same price for an extended period until price changes are necessitated (due, for example, to increased production costs). This bold pricing practice deviated from the conventional practice in the grocery industry whereby manufacturers sold their products at a relatively high price, then placed the items on deal for a short period, followed by a return to high pricing, followed by another deal, and so on. Only a company with Procter & Gamble's reputation and power could possibly have introduced such a dramatic change to the grocery industry.

Wholesalers and retailers also play the role of channel leader in some industries. In the pharmaceutical industry, for example, wholesalers play an influential role in determining prices and setting other policies. Wal-Mart at the retail level has assumed channel dominance over many manufacturers who depend on Wal-Mart for large proportions of their sales volume. Wal-Mart works closely with manufacturers in establishing inventory policies that benefit both parties. By coordinating its inventory needs with the production and shipping practices of its suppliers (ever-increasingly via automatic computer-based reordering), Wal-Mart is able to avoid stockouts while simultaneously minimizing the amount of inventory it must carry and finance.

Corporate VMSs

At the other extreme of channel control is the corporate vertical marketing system. A **corporate VMS** combines all levels of the marketing channel under one company's ownership. Carrying through with the government analogy, a corporate system can be compared to a totalitarian form of government where all the power is controlled by a single governmental arm. Oil companies such as Texaco and BP extract oil from the ground or oceans, refine it, store and ship it, and ultimately sell it to consumers in their own company-owned retail outlets. The Tandy Corporation manufactures various electronic products and markets them in its own Radio Shack stores. John Deere produces tractors and lawn equipment and sells these products in company-owned John Deere retail outlets. Sherwin-Williams manufactures paint and related products and distributes these items via its own retail stores. Shoe and apparel manufacturers are beginning to do the same. There now are, for example, Timberland shoe stores, and a few Levi's outlets.

Forward integration occurs when a company that traditionally has been only a producer of products decides to also become a retailer, as the case with companies such as John Deere and Timberland noted above. **Backward integration** results when a retailer acquires a wholesaler or even a producer. Supermarket chains, for example, sometimes purchase manufacturing facilities to produce private label products under the chain's name.

Contractual VMSs

In a **contractual VMS,** channel members are interconnected via contractual agreement. In other words, they are not loosely knit (as with administered VMSs) or fully owned by a single company (as with corporate VMSs) but rather are bound together contractually in some alliance or coalition. **Franchising** represents a major form of contractual VMS. Franchisees make approximately one-third of all retail sales in the United States.[6] McDonald's, Wendy's, KFC, and Dunkin' Donuts are just a few of the many franchises in the retail food industry. Other well-known franchise operations include Pearle Vision, Blockbuster Video, Budget Rent A Car, and Jiffy Lube. For the rights to operate an outlet in a specfied location, franchisees pay the franchisor an initial lump-sum fee (from a few thousand dollars to over $500,000 in the case of McDonald's) and then royalties on all the sales that are generated at that location (typically from 3 to 10 percent of sales[7]). In turn, they receive from the franchisor advertising support, management training, and the goodwill in the name that has been created by the franchisor's past marketing and advertising efforts.

Two other forms of contractual VMSs are wholesaler-sponsored voluntary chains and retailer-sponsored cooperatives. A wholesaler-sponsored **voluntary chain** is an assemblage of independent retailers brought together by a wholesaler to compete against major corporate-owned chains. IGA stores, which stands for

Independent Grocers' Alliance, typifies a voluntary chain. IGA and other such chains embrace features of both family-owned, corner grocery stores and nationally owned chain stores. The independent stores maintain their sole ownership, but by forming an alliance they obtain professional management skills and enjoy the economies of large-scale purchasing and advertising that individual stores cannot achieve. Retailer-sponsored **cooperatives** achieve the same objectives as do wholesaler-sponsored voluntary chains, but the difference is that a consortium of independent retailers ban together to form a collective wholesaling operation. In other words, a voluntary chain is wholesaler driven, whereas a retailer cooperative is retailer driven. Once in operation, both types of contractual chains operate in similar fashion, that is, independent retail stores having the appearance of a chain and enjoying the advantages of large-scale purchasing and merchandising.

Channel Dynamics: Power, Conflict, and Cooperation

The participants in channels of distribution are involved in a complex dynamic in which their economic interests and business preferences are not always in harmony. The channel arrangement is based on a series of business relationships. In the producer-wholesaler relationship, the wholesaler assumes that the producer will provide the products that are needed when they are needed at the prices stated. The producer assumes that the wholesaler is making best efforts to sell its products to all potential customers in the market and to provide service to their clients. In all business relationships, as with other human relations, power struggles occur and conflicts arise especially when one of the channel members fails to perform as expected.

Power and Conflict

Channel power is the ability of one channel member to exert influence over and dictate the behavior of other channel members. Power in channel relationships, as with all human relationships, results from one member controlling valuable resources that are demanded by other members. For example, Procter & Gamble, as noted earlier, is recognized as a manufacturer with channel power.

P&G, especially during the period from the 1950s to 1970s in the United States, used extensive television advertising and sales promotions to get consumers to demand P&G's brands, request grocers to handle them, and effectively "pull" the products through at retail. Because of the high consumer demand, buyers at retail outlets were forced to accept many conditions that they would not otherwise accept, such as stocking brands and sizes they would preferred not to have stocked or paying higher prices than desired. Now that many supermarket chains are larger and more powerful, the P&G tactics are no longer as acceptable as they were in the past. In short, some of P&G's power has been eroded.

Wholesalers can also exert power over other channel members. If the wholesaler is more powerful than a small manufacturer it represents, the wholesaler can dictate policies to the manufacturer. The wholesaler can also exert power over a small retailer by insisting that the retailer stock several slow-moving products if it wants to carry a market leader that the wholesaler represents. This situation is power by coercion.

When channel members disagree on the methods used to perform their channel functions, **conflict** arises. The exercise of power or power disputes typically underlie conflicts.[8] For example, a food manufacturer may want an end-aisle display at the front of supermarkets for a new brand it is promoting. The supermarket chain decides, however, to feature another manufacturer's brand in that space because the resulting sales will generate higher profits. This is channel conflict.

A manufacturer with a new product wants wholesalers to take on a new product line. Some wholesalers are less than enthusiastic, however, since the available profit margin is less than other products they carry. Wholesalers refuse to handle the new line or insist on higher margins. This is a channel conflict.

A Taco Bell franchisee does not want to carry the 39¢ value menu items that the franchisor is prepared to advertise, since the profit margins are low. But Taco Bell headquarters has a major television and newspaper ad campaign scheduled to aggressively promote the line. This is a channel conflict.

Conflict can be very unproductive to channel members. Time spent in conflict is time *not* spent in selling and generating profits. A channel member must step in and attempt to resolve the conflict before too much damage is done. Conflicts can be resolved through open communications, negotiations, role and goal clarification, and channel coordination on an ongoing basis.

Cooperation and Relationship Building

Channel leadership is needed to ensure the efficient operation of the entire channel. A channel member who exerts **channel leadership** is one who uses authority to direct or guide the channel's activities. Typically, a channel member who emerges as a channel leader already has channel power. The channel leader creates marketing strategies for guiding the overall selling effort. Coordination and follow-up are necessary functions of the channel leader. And finally, the channel leader is needed to step in and resolve any conflicts that arise within the channel. If the channel leader is able to get all channel members to focus on their roles and goals, a smooth, efficient operation will result, one in which goals are achieved and profits are realized.

Ultimately, effective channel functioning depends on the willingness of channel members to cooperate and work toward achieving their customer's and/or supplier's goals as well as their own goals. It is a matter of focusing on customer satisfaction and building strong and enduring relations with customers rather than engaging in exploitative behavior. Many businesses have come to the realization that *relationship building* is a key to success. This mind set is very pragmatic: It simply is less expensive to serve existing customers than to constantly search for new customers.[9]

Legal Considerations in Channels of Distribution

Chapter 2 discussed at some length the legal environment and its effect on marketing. It is clear that marketers must be aware of the laws and regulations that affect every aspect of their business. Distribution decisions are under closer legal scrutiny than all marketing decisions other than pricing. Distribution practices receive so much scrutiny because the exercise of channel power sometimes leads companies to limit the supply of their products or impose conditions on what a customer must do to be allowed to carry a supplier's product.

To best understand the laws that shortly will be discussed, it will be helpful to describe a hypothetical situation involving a full-line manufacturer of sporting goods (balls, golf equipment, tennis rackets, etc.) and its marketing practices. This hypothetical company has achieved much success and its various products and brands are in high demand among retailers and consumers. The manufacturer is concerned about its image, however, and is interested in ensuring that its products are merchandised only by retailers whose reputations and practices are compatible with the manufacturer's image. Moreover, the manufacturer would prefer that its retail accounts purchase all sporting goods products from it and not just a subset of items (say, tennis rackets) and that they not purchase lines of sporting goods from the manufacturer's competitors.

Are these policies and practices illegal? There is no simple answer inasmuch as all legal determinations are based on an analysis of all the pertinent facts. In general, it is *not* illegal for a manufacturer to protect its reputation and supply its products on a selective basis. Absent of any intent to create a monopoly, and thus be in violation of the Sherman Antitrust Act and Clayton Act (see Chapter 2), sellers may deal with whomever they wish. There are three problematic situations where sellers may be engaging in unlawful behavior when exerting their market power: exclusive dealing, tying agreements, and closed sales territories.

Exclusive Dealing

Exclusive dealing is practiced when a marketer attempts to prohibit a wholesaler or retailer from handling competitive product lines. Marketers such as our hypothetical sporting goods company would of course want to restrict their retailers in this fashion so that the retailers focus exclusively on the manufacturer's brands. This practice is *not* illegal per se. It is illegal only in those instances where the agreement would lessen competition and thus violate the Clayton Act. That is, if a manufacturer's sales volume represents a substantial percent of the market share in a market where the manufacturer is attempting to impose an exclusive dealing arrangement on a retailer, then the practice could be considered anticompetitive and in violation of the Clayton Act.

Tying Agreement

As the name suggests, a tying agreement is one where a seller requires a buyer to carry other products in addition to just those the buyer would prefer to carry. Our hypothetical sportings goods firm wants to tie retailers to purchasing the entire product line and not just a select few items that the retailer wants most.

Again, just like exclusive dealing, tying agreements are not illegal per se. They are prohibited, however, when the effect is to reduce competition in a particular market. The courts have been inclined to accept tying agreements in situations where only the supplier can provide a certain type or quality of product and when the supplier is new to a particular market. The first qualification simply recognizes that a tying agreement in this situation could not possibly reduce competition (since there are no direct competitors), while the latter exception has been made to promote greater competition by allowing a new supplier to a market the opportunity to establish a meaningful presence.

Closed, or Restricted, Sales Territories

This practice is one where producers grant an exclusive sales territory to a wholesaler, agent/broker, or retailer. An example of this practice is when a beer producer restricts a distributor's geographic market. This restriction can be of benefit to the distributor, because it prevents competition from another distributor selling the same brands. The practice also provides the beer producer with greater control over the distribution and marketing of its products. Because restricted territories can increase competition between distributors that handle competitive brands (e.g., Budweiser versus Coors), the practice of restricted territories is, once again, not illegal per se. Such restrictions are considered illegal only when the effect is to impair competition.

◼ The Physical Distribution Facet of Marketing

Physical distribution involves all activities responsible for the movement of products and their storage along with related activities such as order processing and customer servicing. The physical distribution functions are critical to an organization's success. A manufacturer can produce a warehouse full of products, but those products are worth nothing if they are not where consumers want them and when they are needed. There are two ways in which physical distribution service can favorably impact a firm's bottom line. First, a firm whose physical distribution efforts are particularly effective and efficient can earn a differential advantage over competitors and thereby increase sales volume and revenues. More directly, reductions in the cost of physical distribution activities have a one-to-one impact on profit; that is, every dollar reduction in physical distribution cost increases pretax profit by an equivalent amount.

In the past, organizations considered physical distribution activities such as storing and transporting as separate, unrelated activities. Today, firms are realizing that the physical distribution functions are interrelated and must be viewed as a whole rather than in fragmented parts. If a firm concentrates on minimizing the costs in one physical distribution function—transportation, for example—costs for the other functions may actually increase. If the system is viewed as a whole, then the costs for all of the functions, or the entire system, can be minimized. An organization's objective should be to offer the best possible service to its customers at the lowest possible costs.

Physical distribution activities include receiving and processing orders, storing and controlling inventory, and transporting.

Receiving and Processing Orders

The first step in developing an effective distribution system is to establish an efficient order processing system. **Order processing** is the system through which orders are received and processed. Customer satisfaction depends on this activity being done fast and accurately. Mistakes made in order processing are costly and time-consuming, and ultimately result in customer dissatisfaction.

The order processing system can be conducted either manually or by computer. Most organizations use a computerized system. Although establishing a computerized system may be costly, it will save an organization money in the long run. The system will be more efficient and accurate, resulting in more customers' being satisfied.

Communication is key in this process. All departments involved in order processing must have the necessary information to do their job within the system. The first step in order processing is *order entry*. When a salesperson or customer places an order either via mail, telephone, or direct computer entry, the order officially enters the company's system. The order is printed out on a standard company order form. A standard order includes the following information: (1) customer purchase order number, (2) ship-to address, (3) bill-to address, (4) date of order, (5) requested delivery date, (6) quantities and products desired, (7) sales terms, (8) per-unit price and discounts, (9) preferred transportation method, and (10) any special instructions.

Once the order is entered in the system, the next step is *order handling*. The order is sent to the appropriate warehouse where order quantities are checked against inventory on hand. If inventory is available, the order is filled. If some of the items ordered are not available, the order is referred to either a customer service or sales service representative who contacts the customer to determine whether the unavailable items should be back ordered and shipped when available, substituted for, or cut entirely and ordered on the customer's next order.

The final step in order processing is *order delivery*. When the order is ready for shipment, the shipping department arranges for transportation. If the order is a full truckload (or carload in the case of rail shipments), a truck is ordered. If the order is less than a truckload, several orders from the same geographic area are consolidated for delivery. Once the truck leaves the warehouse dock, the customer is invoiced for the shipment.

Storing and Controlling Inventory

Storing, the physical distribution function of holding products, provides *time utility* to both the buyer and seller. Products may be stored one or more times in the marketing channel. For example, the Georgian carpet manufacturer described earlier sometimes ships finished carpet to customers as soon as it is produced and also stores roles of carpet in warehouses in anticipation of forthcoming orders. If a wholesaler orders the carpet, the wholesaler in turn may store the product until orders are received from its retail customers.

Storing is necessary since manufacturers do not produce goods at the exact time and in the exact quantities that customers need them. Instead, manufacturers produce goods to have on hand to meet customer needs as they arise. Storing coordinates supply with demand.

Products are typically stored in private warehouses, public warehouses, or distribution centers. The number of facilities an organization engages depends on the quantities of products produced, demand for the products by geographical location, and the costs incurred. Storing products can be very costly. Management must analyze the storing function to minimize costs while optimizing service.

Inventories must not only be stored, but they also must be controlled. Inventories that are not effectively managed will be very

Exhibit 10.4   Modes for Transporting Products

1. Railroads
2. Trucks
3. Waterways
4. Pipelines
5. Air Carriers

costly to a firm. The longer a product is stored, the more it costs a company and the more likely the product will be damaged. The carpet manufacturer, for example, may have blue #096 on its production schedule for the upcoming week. If the manager checks inventory, however, he may find that 15 rolls produced two months ago are still sitting in a warehouse. These rolls are costing the company on a daily basis. Instead of producing more, efforts should be made to sell the existing rolls. A warehouse, distribution, or inventory control manager is responsible for tracking these figures to avoid over- as well as under-production of products.

A company must have an accurate and effective inventory control system. This function is critical as an out-of-stock, or lack of inventory, results in lost sales, lost profits, and dissatisfied customers. An inventory control manager must be familiar with all facets of inventory including the point at which a product needs to be reordered, the order lead time or how long it takes to produce the order, and how much of the product is used during a specified period of time. An experienced inventory control manager knows this information and uses it on a daily basis to help control inventories and schedule production.

Transporting

Transporting orders can be the costliest function in physical distribution. **Transporting** involves the physical movement of products from an organization to its customers. A number of transporting alternatives are available to an organization. The challenge is to secure a means of transportation that is fast, efficient, dependable, inexpensive, and most acceptable to the customer. The desired mode of transportation must fit into the firm's overall marketing strategy. Exhibit 10.4 lists the five major modes of transportation available for shipping goods.

Railroads.

Railroads are mainly used for large heavy loads that need to travel a long distance. Railroads have extensive established routes that allow firms to reach thousands of small, medium, and large markets. Rail is a very efficient mode of transportation when a customer orders a full carload.

Railroad service, however, is very slow. Railroads are also inflexible since most organizations must deliver products to the rail yard for shipment. This is more costly since the company is handling the product twice in the process. On the other end, arrangements must be made for pickup as well. Finally, shipments must be coordinated with established rail schedules that may not coincide with required delivery times.

Trucks.

Most product deliveries are made by truck. Trucks offer many advantages over other modes of transportation. Trucks are fast and direct. Trucks offer flexibility—they can pick up and deliver when the product is needed. Trucks can travel to any market as long as it is accessible by road. And with over 25,000 independent trucking firms in operation in this country alone, trucks provide service when and where it is needed.

Trucks have disadvantages, too. Trucks are a costly mode of transportation. Trucks are also limited as to the size of the load they are able to carry. And trucks are greatly affected by weather—a major snowstorm can delay delivery for days.

Waterways.

Shipping by barge or ship is an efficient means of transporting large heavy loads of bulky products such as coal. Costs are held to a minimum on waterways.

Transporting via waterways is slow. Limited routes exist, which don't always service popular markets. And waterways offer little flexibility since delivery is dependent on established schedules.

Pipeline.

Pipelines are typically used to ship liquid products over long distances. Many oil companies such as Exxon and Chevron own and operate pipelines for shipping their petroleum products to processing plants and distribution facilities. Pipelines are reliable and inexpensive but slow, limited by established routes, and inflexible as to the types of products that can be handled.

Air Carriers.

Although air transportation is fast, it is also the costliest mode of shipping products. It is typically used for perishable or fragile products, or orders that must be delivered quickly.

With the number of available air carriers, frequency and flexibility are major advantages. There is also less risk of damage to products that are shipped by air rather than truck or rail. And with companies such as Federal Express and UPS, even the smallest shipments can realize the benefits of shipping by air.

Air carriers are limited, though, in the types of products and amount of weight that can be transported. Shipments also depend on weather and flight schedules that may include delays or cancellations. In most cases, additional transportation is needed to get the products to and from the airports. This results in additional time, planning, and costs.

A firm must analyze all available modes of transportation and select the one or ones that best fit their needs. Factors that enter into the decision are costs, transporting time, dependability, accessibility, flexibility, and follow-through. All of these factors must be closely examined before any decision is made. The firm must consider its own needs as well as its customers' needs in the process.

Servicing Customers

The main objective for all firms should be to satisfy the needs of its customers. **Customer service** are those activities involved in satisfying those needs.

Customers expect to order and receive products when and where they want them. They expect cooperation and a high level of service. If they call the company to check on their order, they expect to deal with a courteous, knowledgeable employee. They expect to hear when the order will ship and when they can expect it. If they need to change their order, they expect the company to make the changes if at all possible. In their minds, they are buying products as well as service from the company.

Companies must be aware of these expectations and needs. Many companies respond by creating customer service departments with representatives who are responsible for geographic territories. The representatives are knowledgeable in their specific area and with their specific customers. The CS reps attempt to establish a rapport with both the salespeople and the customers within their territory. This helps to ensure personal and courteous service.

The importance of customer service cannot be overstated. If a customer is dissatisfied with a company's service, there are always competitors who are willing to service the disgruntled customer and increase their sales base. Firms that establish customer service as a top priority offer training programs, a set of established procedures, and a monitoring system to ensure the highest level of servicing for their customers.

◆ Chapter Summary

Distribution, the function that makes products available to consumers, is a critical component of any product's marketing mix. A channel of distribution is the arrangement of businesses that are involved in performing marketing functions and physically transferring goods and services and their ownership from manufacturers to end-users. Physical distribution is the aspect of marketing that physically moves and stores products as they flow through the channel of distribution. The objective of physical distribution is getting the right product to the right place at the right time.

Marketing intermediaries, all of the business institutions that facilitate the exchange process between buyers and seller, play a crucial role in effecting exchanges in the marketplace. Various types of intermediaries in the marketplace include wholesalers, retailers, brokers, and distributors. Intermediaries are needed to reduce the number of contacts between manufacturers and end-users, provide a solution to the discrepancies of quantity and assortment, and share marketing functions with the manufacturer and other channel members.

Various channels of distribution exist to perform the marketing functions needed to distribute the vast number of products in the marketplace. Business-to-business channel structures differ from consumer channels. Business-to-business channel structures use agents/brokers or distributors to reach the end-user. Consumer channel structures either deal directly with retailers or utilize wholesalers or brokers to reach the wholesaler and retailers. Many companies utilize more than one channel for distributing their products. The number of channels used depends on whether the company wishes to achieve intensive, selective, or exclusive distribution.

In the era of modern marketing, the trend has been toward unified channel arrangements, also called vertical marketing systems (VMSs). In VMSs, channel members cooperate with each other and join forces to effectively and efficiently reach the entire channel's target market. Channel members attempt to share, control, or combine channel functions. The three basic types of VMSs are corporate, contractual, and administered systems.

Marketers must be aware of the issues of power, conflict, and leadership within the channel so every effort can be made to ensure that the highest level of cooperation is maintained. Channel management must be aware of the laws and regulations that affect every aspect of their business.

Channel members perform exchange functions and also the physical distribution functions of buying and selling. Physical distribution includes those activities that get the right products to the right places at the right times to satisfy consumer needs such as receiving and processing orders, storing and controlling inventories, transporting products, and servicing customers. Physical distribution functions are interrelated and must be viewed as a whole rather than in fragmented parts to minimize the firm's costs. An organization's objective should be to offer the best possible service to its customers at a reasonable cost.

Notes

1. This discussion is based on William Claiborne, "Bombay's 'Dabbawallas': Out to Lunch," *International Herald Tribune,* October 23, 1984, 16.

2. Wroe Alderson, *Dynamic Marketing Behavior* (Homewood, IL: Richard D. Irwin, Inc., 1965).

3. Kevin Brown, "Mail, Phone Sell Business-to-Business," *Advertising Age,* May 18, 1987, S–1.

4. *1990/91 Statistical Fact Book* (New York: Direct Marketing Association), 211.

5. See "Database Marketing: A Potent New Tool for Selling," *Business Week,* September 5, 1994, 56–62.

6. Louis Stern and Adel El-Ansary, *Marketing Channels,* 5th. ed. (Englewood Cliffs, NJ: Prentice-Hall, 1993), 332.

7. Michael Levy and Barton A. Weitz, 2nd. ed., *Retail Management* (Chicago: Irwin, 1995), 56.

8. Steven J. Skinner, Jule B. Gassenheimer, and Scott W. Kelley, "Cooperation in Supplier-Dealer Networks," *Journal of Retailing* (Summer 1992), 174–193.

9. For further reading on relationship marketing, see F. Robert Dwyer, Paul H. Schurr, and Sejo Oh, "Developing Buyer-Seller Relationships," *Journal of Marketing,* 51 (April 1987), 11–27, and

Terry G. Vavra, *Aftermarketing* (Homewood, IL: Business One Irwin, 1992).

■ Study Questions

1. What are marketing intermediaries?
   a. All business institutions that facilitate the exchange process between buyers and sellers.
   b. All business institutions that facilitate the exchange process between manufacturers and consumers.
   c. All business institutions that support the marketing function.
   d. Any supporting service business that handles the marketing function for the manufacturer.

2. What function would a marketing intermediary *not* perform?
   a. personal selling
   b. arranging for transportation and warehousing of products
   c. setting wholesale prices
   d. setting objectives

3. Merchant intermediaries
   a. take title to products.
   b. resell products.
   c. warehouse products.
   d. All of the above.

4. A distributor
   a. typically buys several manufacturers' products for resell to retailers.
   b. is typically a wholesaler who sells products in the industrial market.
   c. takes order for products on behalf of the manufacturer who is then responsible for delivering the product to the customers.
   d. sells goods and services to consumers.

5. Which of the following marketing functions can be eliminated from the exchange transaction?
   a. research
   b. negotiating
   c. physical distribution
   d. None of the above.

6. Why would a manufacturer hire a broker to handle the sales function?
   a. It cannot afford a direct sales force of its own.
   b. The market is geographically scattered.
   c. The broker offers a certain expertise by specializing in a particular market.
   d. Any of the above.

7. Intensive distribution is
   a. selling a product through a limited number of channel intermediaries and retail outlets within a market.
   b. selling a product through all potential channel intermediaries and retail outlets within a market.
   c. selling a product through only one channel intermediary or retail outlet within the market.
   d. the amount of product in distribution at any given moment.

8. Which is not a vertical marketing system?
   a. intermediary system
   b. corporate system
   c. contractual system
   d. administered system

9. What is channel power?
   a. the ability of one channel member to exert influence over and dictate the behavior of other channel members
   b. the size of the channel intermediary
   c. the number of dominating brands a channel intermediary handles
   d. the number of manufacturers a channel intermediary represents

10. What type of utility does the storing function provide?
    a. convenience
    b. form
    c. time
    d. information

11. What is the best mode of transportation for customer orders?
    a. truck
    b. train
    c. the least expensive mode available
    d. whatever mode best fits the needs of the company as well as its customer

CHAPTER

Wholesaling and Retailing

Chapter Objectives

Wholesaling

Retailing

Chapter Summary

When we as potential consumers see a new brand advertised on television or in print, we become aware of the brand. If the benefits offered by the brand appear to satisfy our needs, we go to a store that we assume will carry it and we buy it. We take the product home, use it, and may buy it again based on our usage experience.

Do we ever wonder, though, how the brand got into the store? Was it coincidental that the brand was in the store when the advertising was running? How can manufacturers make so many products available to consumers in so many different locations almost at the same time?

The answer to the above questions is simple: Channel intermediaries make it all possible for the manufacturer. Manufacturers cannot do it all alone. Wholesalers and retailers help manufacturers market consumer products to consumers. And industrial distributors and agents help manufacturers market business-to-business products to customers. Manufacturers *need* these intermediaries. Without intermediaries, the right products would not be available at the right time and right place.

Wholesalers and retailers are important cogs in the marketing wheel. Manufacturers depend on them for their market knowledge, expertise, and client contacts. This chapter builds on the previous one by taking a closer look at wholesalers and retailers and how they assist manufacturers in the marketing of products.

Wholesaling

In discussing wholesaling, an initial distinction must be made between wholesaling and wholesalers. **Wholesaling** is the exchange of goods and services between producers and channel intermediaries, but not to the actual consumer. **Wholesalers** are business organizations that perform wholesaling functions among the channel intermediaries. Manufacturers and retailers alike depend on wholesalers who help in providing time, place, and possession utility to all end-users.

Wholesalers are an integral part of marketing. Even though wholesalers are one-third in number to retailers, sales generated by wholesalers exceed by approximately 30% the sales of retailers. Wholesalers generate such volume because they sell in both the business-to-business and the consumer markets, while retailers sell only in the consumer market. In the United States approximately

470,000 wholesalers generate more than $2,525 billion (i.e., over $2.5 trillion) in sales alone.[1]

As was discussed in Chapter 10, some or all of eight basic marketing functions must be performed in marketing exchanges: buying, selling, transporting, storing, risk-taking, providing information, financing, and grading. These functions can be shared or shifted among producers and intermediaries, but they cannot be eliminated. Consider, again, the Georgian carpet manufacturer described in Chapter 10. As noted previously, this carpet manufacturer uses various channel of distribution arrangements in marketing its products. One of its channels is to distribute carpeting to floor-covering wholesalers that carry carpeting in inventory along with other floor-covering products such as vinyl, linoleum, and hardwood flooring. In purchasing carpeting, the wholesaler takes title and assumes the financial and other risks that go along with ownership. The wholesaler stores the carpeting, which reduces both the manufacturer's cost of holding the carpeting in inventory and the retailer's cost of maintaining extra storage space. The wholesaler finances its customers' purchases by extending credit for up to 30 days, and through its sales force provides important information to its retail accounts about carpeting and other floor-covering products. Because the wholesaler inventories different producers' carpeting and carries various qualities and grades, it also performs a grading function. Finally, the wholesaler may have its own trucks for transporting carpeting and other floor-covering products to its retail accounts or arrange shipping via a commercial trucking company.

This wholesaler performs all of the exchange functions and in this sense is a full-service wholesaler. As we will see, not every wholesaler provides all of these services. There are, in fact, a variety of types of wholesaling intermediaries.

The Diversity of Wholesaling Intermediaries

Wholesaling functions are performed by a variety of intermediaries. Different types of wholesalers exist to meet the unique needs of the diverse group of retailers and producers in operation in today's marketplace. Three general forms of wholesaling intermediaries can be distinguished by their specialized activities: (1) a manufacturer's own sales offices and branches, (2) independent merchant

Exhibit 11.1   Types of Wholesalers

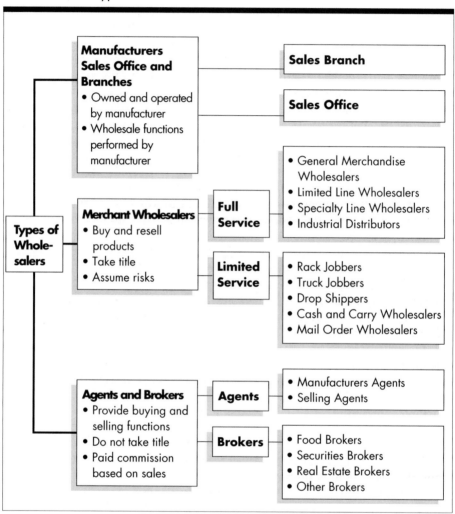

wholesalers, and (3) independent agents and brokers. Exhibit 11.1 identifies the various types of wholesalers. The following sections describe each.

Manufacturers Sales Branches and Offices.   Manufacturers' sales branches and offices are owned and operated by manufacturers. These wholesaling operations generate approximately 31% of all wholesale sales.[2]

A manufacturer's **sales branch** sells products and provides support services for the manufacturer's sales force. Sales branches are typically established in areas away from a manufacturer's production facilities near customers that generate a large percentage of company sales. Among other services, sales branches maintain inventories, offer credit, deliver products, and provide promotional support. A sales branch sells directly to the largest customers in the area and also supplies products to smaller customers through independent wholesalers.

A manufacturer's **sales office** operates like an independent agent. The sales office performs most of the same functions as the sales branch except that it does *not* carry inventory. Sales offices are usually established away from the manufacturer's production facilities. A sales office sometimes sells additional products acquired from other companies that supplement or enhance the manufacturer's lines of products.

By operating its own branch or sales offices, a manufacturer is able to better control its marketing efforts while providing a higher level of service to its customers in the immediate area. A manufacturer may choose this route if no wholesaler is currently offering the same services in the area or if the wholesalers in operation do not provide an acceptable level of service.

Merchant Wholesalers.

A **merchant wholesaler** is an intermediary that purchases products from manufacturers and assumes all risks associated with ownership. Merchant wholesalers, which account for 59% of all wholesale sales,[3] buy products that they resell to business-to-business or retail customers. Merchant wholesalers often specialize based on specific product lines or customers: food products, office supplies, automobile parts, floor-covering products, industrial tools, and so forth. Manufacturers rely on merchant wholesalers when it is uneconomical to operate a sales force in particular geographical areas or when wholesalers have established and strong customer networks. There are two general categories of merchant wholesalers: *full-service* and *limited-service.*

Full-service wholesalers, such as the carpet wholesaler described earlier, perform a wide range of channel activities including order processing, extending credit, storing, delivering, and providing promotional support. Full-service merchant wholesalers provide all of the services that a manufacturer's sales office and sales force normally perform. There are four types of full-service merchant wholesalers:

1. **General merchandise wholesalers** are intermediaries that carry a *wide range of different product lines but with little depth to each line.* The product lines carried are generally nonperishable items such as hardware, clothing, drugs, some foods, cosmetics, and tobacco products. General merchandise wholesalers have the ability to service many different types of retail outlets.

2. **Limited line wholesalers** are intermediaries that carry a *narrow range of product lines but with a great assortment of products within each line.* For example, a kitchen accessories limited-line wholesaler will offer a wide variety of products such as scrubbing brushes, drain protectors, bottle caps, storage racks, storage bowls, silverware, kitchen linens, and kitchen tools.

3. **Specialty line wholesalers** are intermediaries that specialize in *only one or two product lines.* Within these lines, usually only a few products are featured. Specialty line wholesalers are very knowledgeable of the needs of their customers. They are invaluable to retailers in providing useful information, displaying products, and offering specialized promotional and sales support. For example, a specialty line wholesaler of exotic fruits and vegetables will offer products and a certain level of product expertise that is greatly beneficial to retail accounts whose expertise is less than the wholesaler's.

4. **Industrial distributors** are intermediaries that stock inventory *for resale to manufacturers.* The products offered by industrial distributors are those used in the daily operations of a manufacturer but which individually are relatively trivial in relation to the manufacturer's total purchasing requirements. A steel manufacturer, for example, might find it beneficial to purchase products such as hand tools, screws, nuts, bolts, paint, and industrial supplies from one industrial distributor rather than from numerous separate manufacturers or wholesalers.

The second class of merchant wholesalers, **limited-service merchant wholesalers,** *take title to goods* they stock and resell but *offer a narrower range of support services.* Limited-service merchant wholesalers typically do not offer credit, delivery, or merchandise handling. They often offer lower prices to their customers because of the reduced level of services, but their profit margins are lower as well. There are five types of limited-service merchant wholesalers:

1. **Rack jobbers** are intermediaries that supply products and the display units on which the products are displayed. These products are sold to retail outlets such as supermarkets and mass merchandise outlets (e.g., Wal-Mart, Kmart, or Target) and are often seen at the point of checkout. Rack jobbers stock the units, take orders, and control the retailer's inventory. Rack jobbers typically sell products on *consignment* whereby the retailer is not obliged to pay for the product *unless or until it is sold*. If the product is not sold after a specific period of time, the rack jobber takes the product back. Candy, magazines, and cosmetics—products that are sold on a self-service basis—are generally sold by rack jobbers.

2. **Truck jobbers** are small wholesalers that sell directly from their trucks or vans to retailers for cash. Truck jobbers typically have established sales routes but offer limited services. Products such as fruits, vegetables, dairy products, and snack foods often are distributed by truck jobbers.

3. **Drop shippers,** also called *desk jobbers,* are wholesalers that sell products, take orders, and arrange for delivery of products directly to customers. Drop shippers do not store, handle, or deliver any of the products they sell. Little or no promotional assistance or merchandising support is provided. Products that have high shipping costs and thus require direct shipment from the producer (e.g., lumber, coal, and building materials) often are handled by drop shippers.

4. **Cash-and-carry wholesalers** provide products in a warehouse setting for resale. These wholesalers perform most wholesaling functions except delivery, extending credit, and providing promotional support. Cash-and-carry wholesalers usually accept only cash, and their customer base consists primarily of small retailers. Office supplies, groceries, auto supplies, and hardware products are carried by cash-and-carry wholesalers.

5. **Mail-order wholesalers** sell from catalogs rather than via a sales force to their customers, who are usually located in outlying areas. Servicing these customers in person would be too costly for the wholesaler. Although these wholesalers

do store and deliver products, they do not extend credit or provide promotional support to customers. Jewelry, specialty foods, and automotive parts are the types of products handled by mail-order wholesalers.

Agents and Brokers.   As briefly discussed in Chapter 10, agents and brokers provide buying and selling functions, but *do not take title to the products they sell.* Agents and brokers generate about 10% of the total wholesale sales volume.[4] Agents and brokers are paid a fixed percentage of sales, or commission, by the companies they represent, called *principals.* Manufacturers can expand their selling efforts despite limited resources, benefit from a trained sales force, and hold down personal selling costs with the services of agents and brokers.

Agents represent manufacturers on a permanent basis. As noted in the previous chapter, agents are either *manufacturer* or *selling* agents. **Manufacturers agents** represent two or more manufacturers with noncompeting product lines. They work under contract within protected sales territories. Prices, delivery, service, warranties, and order handling are spelled out within the contract. Manufacturers agents are typically highly skilled, knowledgeable salespeople with excellent customer contacts. **Selling agents** represent all of the products manufactured by their principal. Selling agents perform all marketing functions for their principals except for taking title to the merchandise. Selling agents assume control over pricing, selling, and advertising. Smaller companies with limited resources hire selling agents, thus avoiding the costs of a maintaining a marketing department and sales force. In industries such as textiles, selling agents provide small manufacturers with the marketing expertise lacked by the manufacturer.

Brokers bring buyers and sellers together. Brokers either represent the buyer or seller in finding another party to complete an exchange. Brokers do not handle or store merchandise, nor do they extend credit to customers. The broker is paid on a commission, usually a percentage of sales.

Brokers tend to specialize in particular product categories. For example, *food brokers* specialize in selling food and general merchandise to retailers, wholesalers, institutions, and food processors. Indeed, nearly half of all food products are sold in the United States through food brokers. Food brokers do not take title to the merchandise they sell and work within a protected sales territory. *Securities brokers* specialize in selling securities—stocks, bonds, or options—to companies or private investors. They simply arrange for the sale and are paid on a commission basis. Finally, *real estate brokers* specialize in selling property to companies or individuals.

Developments in Wholesaling

Successful wholesalers have been forced to change with the times. In the past, wholesalers were viewed as middlemen who took orders and broke down cases into smaller quantities for smaller retailers. As producers have become more marketing-oriented, so, too, have wholesalers. Today's wholesalers are attempting to satisfy the needs of both their producers and customers. Many wholesalers are providing more services and cooperating more closely with other channel members. A marketing orientation (as discussed in Chapter 1) is becoming a top priority in the wholesaling industry.

Some trends in the wholesaling industry are mirroring general trends in business. Many wholesalers are growing in size through mergers and acquisitions. By merging with or acquiring other channel intermediaries, wholesalers can enter new markets, achieve greater buying and selling efficiencies, increase profit margins, and diversify their operations either into retailing or manufacturing.

Another trend in business is the recent growth of warehouse clubs, or superstores. These retail establishments are a major source of goods for many small- and medium-sized businesses as well as consumers. These businesses such as Price Club, Office Depot, and Home Depot offer a wide variety of product lines. Many wholesalers are adapting to this trend by increasing their product lines and pursuing these new market segments.

Businesses in general are realizing the importance of service within their industry. Wholesalers are no exception. Retailers, especially smaller ones, are depending on wholesalers for their market expertise. Wholesalers are responding by offering a variety of services designed to support the retailer's activities. Some of these expanded services include promotional planning, shelf planning, inventory replacement, and general administrative support.

Retailing ◈

Retailing encompasses those activities involved in the exchange process of goods and services to the final consumer. In the United States in excess of 1.5 million retailers generate nearly $1.9 trillion in sales.[5] The retail segment ranges from the "mom and pop" corner stores to the huge mass merchandisers. Approximately 20 million Americans are employed in retailing positions.[6] Changes in society, business operations, and consumer needs have contributed to the growth of a variety of retail operations. Retailing is a dynamic enterprise that is constantly changing in advanced economies.

Variability in Strategic Emphasis

Retailers differ greatly in terms of how they choose to operate and where they place their strategic emphasis. Their survival depends on creating effective and profitable strategies to service consumers. A variety of marketing options are available to retailers in creating successful strategies. Some of the most important strategic options are width and depth of product offerings, service quality, atmospherics, and prices and margins. These important topics are discussed in the following sections.

Product Lines and Assortments.

One of the most fundamental differences among retailers is the choice of product lines to carry and the *width* (or variety) and *depth* (or intensity) of product-line assortments. Some retailers offer a wide variety of merchandise but with limited offerings in each product category; other retailers provide deep offerings in only a few product categories; while still others offer both variety and depth. For example, a store such as Mrs. Field's Cookies specializes primarily in cookies and offers considerable depth to the line (e.g., chocolate chip cookies, chocolate chip with walnuts, chocolate chip with macadamia nuts, double chocolate chip, oatmeal, or oatmeal raisin). Department stores such as I Magnin, Neiman Marcus, and Macy's offer a wide variety of product assortments but with different levels of product line depth. Mass merchandisers such as Kmart offer a variety of product assortments with limited depth in each category.

Service Quality.

One of the most important factors that distinguishes competitive retailers is the quality of service offered. Consider Nordstrom, which is a leading retailer based in Seattle, that has developed a legendary reputation for its high-quality service. In the Nordstrom stores, beverages are offered to customers in some departments and live musicians serenade shoppers.

Nordstrom stores offer a liberal exchange and return policy. The well-paid employees work after hours, write thank you notes, and even deliver purchases if it means making a sale. Nordstrom truly represents a retail establishment committed to delivering high-quality service.

Retailing has become increasingly competitive, and successful retailers have learned that service quality is critical to achieving and maintaining success. Some of the key features of service quality are the following:[7]

- *Reliability*—providing consistent and dependable service.
- *Responsiveness*—offering timely service.
- *Competence*—furnishing knowledgeable and skillful service.
- *Accessibility*—providing convenient hours and location of service and preventing delays when customers attempt to reach the service provider.
- *Courtesy*—offering polite, respectful, and friendly service.
- *Communication*—presenting clear explanations regarding the nature of the service and its cost.
- *Credibility*—having the customer's best interests at heart in all relations with the company and its service personnel.
- *Security*—protecting the customer's health, safety, financial, and privacy interests in all service encounters.
- *Understanding the customer*—learning the customer's specific requirements and providing individualized attention.

Mobil Corporation, after operating in the red while trying to sell gasoline at low prices, recently introduced a nationwide marketing program, termed Friendly Serve, that applies these service quality features. Mobil's research showed that many gasoline shoppers want better snacks from the food operation, quicker service, and cleaner stations and restrooms. Mobil, accordingly, has cleaned up its stations, increased safety with better lighting, provided better food service, and increased its prices. It anticipates that this enhanced quality of service will appeal to all gasoline shoppers except perhaps 20% of buyers who are estimated to be strictly price shoppers.[8]

Leonard Berry, a leading proponent of service quality, offers the following principles that retailers must adopt to achieve high-quality service:[9]

MARKETING HIGHLIGHTS

Hershey's Hugs

Hershey Chocolate U.S.A., a division of Hershey Foods Corporation, introduced a new variation on its old Kiss theme in August 1993, called the Hug, of course. Although not an earth-shaking event for the rest of the world, for Hershey Chocolate this new product was only the second change to the Hershey Kiss since 1907. The Hershey Kiss with almonds had been launched three years before.

While Hugs retain the distinctive bell shape of a Kiss narrowed to a point at the top, it has thin strips of white chocolate wrapped around it—a Kiss with a Hug. And the white chocolate makes it a little sweeter than a Kiss.

This seemingly small change to an existing product actually took over 15 years of testing and planning. Wrapping those little white chocolate strips around the Kiss required new manufacturing technology, a change in new product development, and millions of dollars to bring Hugs to the public.

Hershey had bought the trademark for the Hugs name in the late 1970s but had not been able to come up with a candy to fit the name until 1982 when Dennis Eshleman, a new member of Hershey's product development team, proposed the idea of putting an almond inside the Kiss. In order to do that, the company had to develop a new method of manufacturing, and this technology remains a closely guarded secret of Hershey's.

When the product team began to design packaging for the product, a brand manager remarked that the candy didn't "feel" like a Hug, but like a Kiss with almonds, and that product became the first change to the Kiss since 1907, but without the Hug name.

The search continued to discover a shape or flavor that would feel like a Hug, and as the emphasis moved from shape to flavor, the team chose to add white chocolate to the Kiss. After experimenting with ways to mix the two ingredients together, R&D came up with the idea of "stripes" made of white chocolate, and finally, in 1991, Hugs was ready for consumer testing.

1. *Allow service quality to be defined by customers.* Conformance to the customer's specifications is what service quality is all about. Retailers achieve a strong quality reputation when they deliver the level of service expected and demanded by consumers. This means providing high-quality service on the service factors that are most important to consumers, such as timely, courteous, and helpful service.

2. *Realize that service quality is a continuous journey and not a trip with a finite endpoint.* Quality service is something that the retailer must continuously work on and redefine. Consumers change, competition changes, and thus service provision must also change.

A year of market testing showed Hugs to be popular with both adults and children and that sales of Hugs did not cannibalize those of Kisses, but rather helped sales. Hershey Foods started construction on a new 350,000-square-foot plant in Hershey, Pennsylvania, to manufacture Hugs, and 18 months before the product was to hit the market, was still in the process of being built.

Hershey had in the past employed a hands-off approach to marketing, but in the case of Hugs, they tried the team concept in order to meet their target of August 1993, to introduce the product. The team agreed to a common mission statement, with specific sales targets, deadlines, and manufacturing goals. They also agreed to have their performance evaluated by senior management as a group instead of as individuals. Nine members met regularly to work out problems and to discuss strategy, while the whole team met quarterly and was kept informed of the smaller group's progress.

It was a race to the finish line to bring it all together. One engineer remembers putting in Hugs machinery before the roof was installed on the new factory.

Since May of 1993, the Hugs line has been running around the clock to meet demand. Third quarter 1993 sales results were strong, and Chairman and Chief Executive Officer Richard A. Zimmerman linked Hershey Chocolate U.S.A.'s volume growth to the national introduction of Hershey's Hugs chocolates along with the Hershey Pasta Group. Will Hugs have the product life of Kisses? Hershey Foods is hoping that Hugs as well as Kisses will be popular for a long time.

Source: Joel Glenn Brenner, "The Sweet, By and By; For Hershey, the 15-Year Effort to Launch the 'Hug' Was No Piece of Cake," *The Washington Post*, September 5, 1993, H1. "Hershey Foods Reports Record Third Quarter Financial Results," *PR Newswire*, October 20, 1993, Financial News Section. "For Your Information," *Star Tribune*, August 11, 1993, Metro Edition, 8D. "

3. *Appreciate the fact that service quality is everyone's job.* Salespeople, merchandisers, credit personnel, cashiers, custodians, repair technicians and many others are responsible for delivering high-quality service. Service excellence in an organization is greatest when all employees truly believe that satisfying customers' service desires is their most important responsibility. Nordstrom typifies this principle.

4. *Recognize that quality, leadership, and communication are inseparable.* To achieve high-quality service, an organization must have a leader who continuously communicates the importance of service quality. "Leadership is the

cornerstone of service quality, and communication is the cornerstone of leadership."[10] The late Sam Walton, founder of Wal-Mart, typified this form of leadership. He was famous for his Saturday morning meetings with key personnel in which he talked about the importance of dependable, courteous service.

5. *Assure the inseparability of service quality and integrity.* An organization must have "fairness" as a core value in order to provide first-rate service quality. The fast buck approach (exploit the consumer) is not the stuff of which integrity is made.

6. *Recognize that service quality is a design issue.* Quality service is achieved only when it is built into every step and plan of a retail organization. Service quality does not happen automatically; it has to be engineered into the day-to-day activities and operations of a retail organization.

7. *Appreciate the fact that service quality is a matter of keeping the service promise.* Consumers expect retailers to do what they promise. The aphorism "The road to hell is paved with good intentions" applies equally well to service quality: It doesn't matter that a retailer intends to offer good service; the only thing that counts to customers is that they actually receive good service.

Offering a high-level of service quality and pleasing customers may be even more important to small retailers than the larger chain operations against which they often compete. Indeed, a recent large-scale study conducted in Illinois determined that 20% of small retailers lose money and 25% earn annual pre-tax income of less than $10,000.[11] To survive and profit, small retailers must differentiate themselves from competitors and offer high levels of service quality. This same study offered the following suggestions to small retailers to enable them to learn more about their customers and competitors and thus enhance service quality:[12]

- Regularly interview customers to get their candid comments on the store's service, prices, merchandise offerings, and hours.
- Provide comment cards for customers to fill out.

- Conduct periodic surveys and focus groups with customers and noncustomers.
- Teach employees to handle customer complaints and train them to respond to complaints on the spot.

Atmospherics.   A retail store in its most limited sense is little more than a venue for economic exchanges in which customers satisfy their needs for acquiring goods and services. In actuality, however, a retail store is much more than this. Shopping and buying in retail outlets and malls also serve to fulfill consumers' entertainment, social, emotional, and other noneconomic needs. Atmospherics represent a crucial aspect of retailing success. By definition, **atmospherics** is "the design of buying environments to produce specific emotional effects in the buyer that enhance his purchase probability."[13] Color, shapes, noise, scents, and temperature are just some of the atmospheric elements that influence shoppers' behaviors. Atmosphere characteristics influence consumers in at least three ways: (1) by *attracting attention,* (2) by *providing information* about the retailer (e.g., neon lights might suggest a youthful image), and (3) by *triggering sensations* in shoppers such as pleasant emotional reactions (fun, joy, or excitement).[14] For example, the live music in Nordstrom stores creates a relaxed and soothing atmosphere in which to shop. But the rock music blasting in a small specialty clothing store for teens conveys an entirely different image, one that is apparently conducive to teen shopping.

The makers of Godiva chocolates, which sell for as much as $45 a pound, realized the importance of atmospherics when they recently redesigned their retail outlets. Godiva's owner, the Campbell Soup Company, engineered a redesign of Godiva's 110 stores after sales of the famous chocolate began to decline. The multi-million dollar renovation involved redesigning Godiva stores into the Art Nouveau style characteristic of architecture in the early 1900s in Brussels where Godiva chocolates first appeared. The objective was to maintain the upscale image of Godiva stores but to make the stores more hospitable to shoppers. Hence, marble floors were replaced with bleached wood, and creamy white walls replaced black lacquer. These changes have had a healthy impact on Godiva profits.[15]

The application of atmospherics can be seen in most any major shopping mall where efforts are increasingly being made to entertain customers. The trend in this direction is due to the fact that adult Americans are shopping less: four hours per month on average in 1992 compared to 12 hours in 1984. Because the amount spent is influenced by how long people spend in the mall, malls are doing everything they can to enhance entertainment value and shopping enjoyment. Mall owners now offer amusement-park rides, miniature golf courses, virtual reality games, play areas for kids, theme museums, and other attractions. For example, owners of the Galleria mall in Cambridge, Massachusetts, included a 17,000 square foot sports museum. The Pier 39 shopping center in San Francisco constructed a $38 million aquarium called Underwater World.[16]

Price and Margins.   Pricing is critical to retailers. Prices offered must be competitive and fair if an exchange is to take place. If products are not priced right, a sale will not occur. A retailer's prices reflect its image. Referring back to the Nordstrom example, this retailer offers high-end merchandise at high prices. But included in the high prices is a high level of service and quality. Thus, their pricing strategy is justified.

To preserve its image and avoid confusion, Nordstrom opened a chain of close-out stores called Nordstrom Rack. Unsold merchandise from Nordstrom's regular stores are sent to these stores where prices, margins, and service quality are all lower than in the regular Nordstrom stores. Recently, Nordstrom announced the opening of two off-price stores where lower-end merchandise will be offered at rock-bottom prices. The level of service in these stores will be the bare minimum, or self-service. This one retailer has created different marketing strategies to appeal to the various target markets. The new Nordstrom off-price stores will offer rock-bottom prices and margins with little to no service. Customers of the Nordstrom Rack and the off-price stores are willing to compromise some of the service and quality for lower prices.

A retailer must create a pricing strategy that will best convey the desired image while generating a sufficient level of profits to support the retail operation. As always is the case in business, there is no single way of succeeding. Different pricing strategies are effective as a function of competitive conditions, economic considerations, and customer characteristics. A discount jewelry store and a high-priced, upscale jewelry store may both prosper in the same marketplace because they cater to different market segments.

Exhibit 11.2   Conventional Forms of Retail Stores

1. Specialty stores
2. Outlet malls
3. Department stores
4. General merchandise outlets
    a. Discount stores
    b. Membership clubs
    c. Hypermarkets
    d. Warehouse and catalog showrooms
    e. Home improvement centers

Diversity of Retail Institutions

The foregoing section has characterized some of the major strategic differences among retail operations. It should come as no surprise to the reader, who has spent a lifetime both casually observing retail stores and actively shopping in a variety of retail outlets, to be informed that retailer operations are highly diverse. It nonetheless will be useful to formally identify the different types of retail outlets and describe how they differ from one another. This discussion is based on the framework presented in Exhibit 11.2. Whereas the present section focuses on conventional forms of in-store retailing, a subsequent section examines the growth of nonstore retailing.

Specialty Stores.   This type of retail store is typified by the limited product lines that are handled. Although only limited lines are offered, specialty stores feature a deep assortment of products within the lines. Specialty stores typically offer relatively high prices and full service. Examples of specialty stores are Lady Footlocker, Naturalizer Shoes, Hallmark Card Shops, and collectible sports card shops. Stores such as Loehmann's and T. J. Maxx are classified as *off-price specialty stores*. These stores offer lower prices and less service than conventional specialty stores.

Supermarkets are also classified as specialty stores. Supermarkets are generally self-service establishments offering wide assortments of food and nonfood products. These low-cost, high-volume stores carry upwards of 20,000 different products, brands, and brand sizes, each of which for inventory purposes is termed a stock-keeping unit, or SKU. The focus of most supermarkets is on products that offer relatively low profit margins but high turnover. Safeway and Kroger are well-known supermarket chains.

One type of specialty store that is gaining in popularity is the **category killer.** These stores offer a large assortment of products at discount prices within a limited number of product lines. Chains such as Toys R Us, Kids R Us, and Office Depot are examples of category killers that have gained market share at the expense of general merchandise outlets and department stores that cannot compete in either price or selection.

Outlet Malls.   Outlet malls are the product of a recent trend in retailing whereby numerous independent and off-price specialty retailers assemble into a single unified location. Regular and irregular products are offered at discount prices in these malls with limited service levels. Outlet malls, which are typically located approximately 30 miles from major metropolitan areas, represent approximately 2% of total non-automobile retail sales, or nearly $10 billion in sales a year. Consumers who shop outlet malls are after the highest possible quality at the lowest possible prices. High prices no longer equate to value in their minds. Outlet mall consumers are very satisfied with their savings even though they travel a further distance. In a recent survey of nearly 9,000 outlet shoppers at 88 centers in 39 states, 87% said the savings they received were worth the travel time and 93% planned to shop there again.[17] Some of the retailers who participate in outlet malls are Hanes, Liz Claiborne, Oshkosh, and Bass.

Department Stores.   Department stores are retail outlets that offer a wide range of product lines in some depth. Department stores are divided into separate departments each offering related products. Typical department stores include sections featuring men's, women's, and children's clothing, housewares, linens, shoes, furniture, and electronics. Most department stores are located in either suburban malls or downtown shopping areas. Macy's, Dayton Hudson, Marshall Field's, Dillards, and Broadway are some better known department stores.

The American department store prospered with the central cities but has faded as the population has moved ever-increasingly to the suburbs.[18] Further contributing to the erosion of department stores' preeminent position in American retailing are the following developments:[19]

1. The mall is now the primary shopping destination.
2. Department stores have been forced into off-price promotion to maintain sales growth, which has resulted in reduced profit margins.
3. Department stores simply no longer are the only game in town. Their business has been challenged by specialty retailers (e.g., Benetton, The Limited), high-fashion specialty retailers (e.g., Neiman-Marcus), and price-value retailers (e.g., Kmart, Wal-Mart, Marshalls).

General Merchandise Outlets.

General merchandise outlets offer a broad range of products. There are five types of general merchandise outlets:

1. **Discount stores** offer brand-name merchandise at low prices and self-service. Discount stores depend on high sales volume to offset the lower margins they receive. Discount stores, like department stores, are divided into separate departments each offering related products. Unlike department stores, discounters offer more product lines including toys, garden supplies, and automotive products but fewer products within each line. Kmart, Wal-Mart, and Target are examples of general merchandise discount stores.

2. **Membership clubs** are discount retailers that are open for shopping only to members, who pay membership fees typically in the range of $25–$35 per year. Membership clubs generally offer the same products as discount operations but feature only multiple bundles of small packages or large sizes. For example, Kmart may carry 5 or 6 different laundry detergents in 2 or 3 sizes. A membership club, by comparison, will only offer 2 detergents in 10 or 20 pound packages. Fewer products are carried, but a broader range of product lines are featured. Membership clubs carry

anything from food products to nonperishables, from appliances to major electronics, and from automobile tires to liquors and office furniture. These are no-frill self-service sales operations. Products are displayed in their original shipping cases on the warehouse floor. Although the prices and profit margins are low, membership clubs enjoy high sales volumes. Sam's Club and Price CostCo are examples of membership clubs.

3. **Hypermarkets** are mass merchandisers and food stores combined. Hypermarkets carry the same products as a supermarket but with a large variety of nonfood items similar to mass merchandisers. Most hypermarkets feature departments like automotive, gardening, and hardware with some even offering specialty departments such as beauty salons and banks. Because of the thousands of products carried, hypermarkets require huge warehouse facilities of 200,000 to 300,000 square feet. Hypermarkets were first introduced in the United States in the early 1970s but failed. In the late 1980s, hypermarkets made a comeback. Carrefour, a European-based hypermarket, and Hypermart USA are examples of hypermarkets.

4. **Warehouse and catalog showrooms** combine wholesale and retail functions as warehouse retailers. These showrooms are mass merchandisers that display available products in their warehouse showrooms. Products such as furniture, electronics, appliances, toys, and jewelry are featured in these retail outlets. Inventory is stored on the showroom floor or in the warehouse facility behind the showroom. These retailers offer a minimum level of service but discount pricing. Levitz and Wickes are well-known furniture warehouse showrooms while Service Merchandise and Best are catalog showrooms.

5. **Home improvement centers** such as HomeBase and Home Depot are warehouse operations that feature all products used in building and maintaining homes. Products such as tools, windows, wallpaper, paint, nuts, bolts, lumber, bricks, cement, and gardening supplies are offered at discount prices. These products are displayed in their original shipping cases on the warehouse floor. Home improvement centers offer more services than membership

clubs or warehouse stores, such as advice on various products and how-to seminars.

Growth of Nonstore Retailing

Nonstore retailing, or selling products and services outside of conventional retail outlets, is a major growth area in retailing. There are five distinct forms of nonstore retailing:

- catalog marketing
- telemedia
- direct selling
- automatic merchandising
- electronic retailing

Catalog Marketing.   In catalog marketing, retailers sell products by sending catalogs to consumers' homes. There are four types of catalogs marketed today: retail catalogs designed by retailer to increase store traffic; full-line merchandise catalogs such as that offered by JCPenney; consumer specialty catalogs such as L.L. Bean and Lands' End; and industrial specialty catalogs used by business-to-business marketers to reach smaller customers. Consumer specialty catalogs represent the greatest growth in catalog marketing.

Catalog marketing is popular with consumers for several reasons. Catalogs save people time inasmuch as consumers do not have to deal with traveling to and from a store, parking, and dealing with crowds. Catalogs offer flexibility to shoppers who can browse through the catalogs during their leisure time and order products during off-hours. Purchases can be made easily and conveniently with credit cards and toll-free numbers. Finally, consumers are satisfied with the level of quality and service offered by catalog marketers.

Telemedia.   Telemedia uses inbound telephone marketing such as toll-free (800) number options and the Dial-it (900) number service to sell products. Television and print advertising, direct mail pieces, and catalogs all feature toll-free numbers for the purpose of selling products, obtaining information, customer service, dealer

CAPTAINS OF INDUSTRY

Howard Schultz

Chairman of the Board and Chief Executive Officer

Starbucks Coffee Co.

Date of Birth: 1954

Education: BBA, Northern Michigan University, 1975

Career Path: Worked for Xerox and Hammarplast after graduating from college. In 1982 Schultz became manager of retail sales and marketing for Starbucks Coffee Company. Schultz left Starbucks in 1984 because of his desire to set up a national chain of cafes based on the Italian coffee bar. He opened his first coffee bar in 1986, called "Il Giornale," serving Starbucks coffee. He soon opened two other cafes and the following year bought out his old bosses at Starbucks. In August of 1987, Schultz dropped the name "Il Giornale" and merged his stores with Starbuck's. By 1993 the company had grown to more than 185 retail outlets nationally.

Profile: Schultz grew up in the housing projects in Brooklyn, New York. He is described as tall, handsome, energetic, compassionate, and driven to make his dream for Starbucks a reality.

Personal: Schultz believes that the quality of Starbucks coffee will one day "alter how everyday Americans conduct their lives." If Schultz has his way, a cup of Starbucks will become as much a part of American culture as a pair of Levi's.[a] His philosophy—if you build a solid infrastructure, hire an all-star management team, and serve the finest product, the customers will come.

The following article, which appeared in *Advertising Age,* March 7, 1994, profiles Howard Schultz and the success of Starbucks.[b]

It hit like a jolt of double espresso of Gold Coast coffee brewed in a French press pot.

Howard Schultz, street-wise from his days in Brooklyn's Canarsie housing projects, was wandering through the piazzas of Italy more than a decade ago. Then director of marketing and retail sales for a small Seattle coffee roaster, Schultz saw the proliferation of coffeehouses, 1,700 alone in Milan, a city of the size of Philadelphia. These were not the smoke-, poetry- and politics-filled hangouts of the Kafka crowd but places where neighbors started the day and gathered later to chat.

"As soon as I saw it, I knew we should be doing this," Schultz says.

His epiphany has changed the way millions of Americans start their day. Instead of grabbing a cup of instant each morning, they queue up at espresso machines ordering designer concoctions with foreign names like caffe latte and macchiato. Not coincidentally since that 1983 trip, industry estimates say sales of gourmet coffee beans and drinks have been hot stuff, increasing fivefold to $1 billion in 1992. On the other hand, sales of regular grinds have dissolved for the big three coffee purveyors, Procter & Gamble Co., Kraft General Foods and Nestlé Beverage Co.

Schultz's coffee-into-gold vision wasn't an easy sell, but he turned a small chain into a national brand while spending a relatively tiny amount on advertising. Today, Starbucks Coffee Co. wants to grow dramatically, to 6,000 outlets in the U.S. And it has put EvansGroup, Seattle, on notice it must grow, too, or Starbucks will put its account up for review.

Schultz got his start with Starbucks Coffee & Tea, which doled out popular free samples of coffee brewed and sold at a shop in Seattle's touristy Pikes Place Market. It took him a year to convince the owners to charge for the samples.

Starbucks was founded in 1971 by three academics, English teacher Jerry Baldwin, history teacher Zev Siegel and writer Gordon Bowker, who had become enamored of the Berkeley, Calif., food scene. There, they met an old Dutchman, Alfred Peet, who ran a coffee shop that was a focal point for the emerging cuisine.

The Academics—armed with beans from Peet—moved into Seattle, opened a shop named Starbucks after the coffee-loving first mate in Herman Melville's "Moby Dick."

"We didn't set out to build a business," says Baldwin, who now owns Peet's. "We were enthusiastic and energetic, but not very focused." Schultz more than made up for that lack of focus when he joined in 1982. In building the company that has become to coffee what Häagen-Dazs was to ice cream, he brought the concept of integrated marketing to Starbucks.

"Marketing, in my view, is the ability to deliver, over and over, a strong level of trust and confidence that the customer comes to expect," Schultz says.

Customers "must recognize you do stand for something." What Starbucks was going to stand for was a good cup of fresh coffee, an affordable luxury that put America's usual cup of morning swill to shame.

In August 1987, Schultz and investors bought the whole of Starbucks, 11 stores with fewer than 100 employees, from the three founders for $4 million. The operation lost money for three straight years.

But Starbucks stuck to its low-key approach, and Schultz refused to franchise or go into artificially flavored beans. Step by step, he set out to hook the nation on his brew.

Starbucks chose the Roberts Group, Portland, Ore., in 1988, for the company's early advertising. That included the "Familiarity breeds contentment" campaign, which began with transit and outdoor boards and consisted of pictures of drinks with architectural drawing lines to illustrate ingredients, later developed into brochures and point-of-purchase displays.

Roberts also did catalogs, packaging, coupons, direct mail and POP advertising. (The agency later merged with EvansGroup, which moved the business to its Seattle office.)

Starbucks' Specialty Sales & Marketing Group began cultivating a taste for the stronger, dark coffee blends by distributing beans and equipment to restaurants and cafeterias. The mail-order business, advertised through *The New Yorker*, also began waking up the national taste buds.

The company saturated Washington state with stores, then moved through California and set up beachheads in Washington, Denver and Chicago. In the next 24 months, Starbucks will add 260 new stores to its base of 280.

Today, Starbucks serves 13 million customers a week, with 1993 sales of $163.5 million, making it North America's leading retailer and roaster of specialty coffee.

Continued on next page

CAPTAINS OF INDUSTRY, continued

So far, marketing the perfect cup has been accomplished with minuscule media spending, for example $6.5 million in 1993.

"The marketing of Starbucks is not only what people see on the outside," Schultz says, adding, "The cost of internal marketing is quite high, but it is the key to our success." He notes that sales total nearly $800 per square foot.

With a target of 35 to 49 year-olds, with higher income and more educated than average and a slightly female skew, Starbucks tried to ease customers into the stronger concoctions and have them graduate to making coffee at home.

"We're trying to appeal to the top and have the market move to us," say former Marketing Director George Reynolds.

But getting consumers to become connoisseurs of the sophisticated alternative was a major task. The typical drill, when the account was handled through EvansGroup's Portland office, was to start with a poster design and extend it to every other medium.

Later work used artistic photographs with a sophisticated, humorous tagline. An illustration of a peacock is labeled "How the tastebuds see Starbucks coffee."

Public relations and promotional efforts were heaped on more traditional advertising. Howard Schultz, offer-

ing a cup of coffee to the world, was featured on the cover of Fortune's "100 Fastest Growing Companies" issue. A Newsweek story on the New Age workplace touted the role played by Starbucks' generous employee benefits in keeping sales percolating.

A public stock offering in June 1991 made the company the darling of Wall Street, with Christopher Vroom of Alex Brown & Sons, Baltimore, putting the company among just a handful of retail businesses with the potential to grow 10 times current size.

But all that was going on while Starbucks was a regional coffee chain. Now, Schultz's ambitious dream of paving the nation with 6,000 outlets by the turn of the century has made Starbucks consider moving into the marketing big leagues.

Reynolds, who left in late February, was soft-spoken but with a "barracuda" reputation among agencies. He told EvansGroup it must grow to Starbucks' national ambitions.

Starbucks is looking at TV commercials later this year but Schultz is concerned the educational message doesn't translate well into traditional 30-second spots. EvansGroup has suggested an infomercial, which the company is considering. Schultz is fascinated with emerging media and expects to see a foray into the world of interactive as well.

location, or promotional inquiries. A call to an 800 number is toll-free to the user. These numbers are popular with marketers today since responses can be measured immediately. For example, within a few days of a 30-minute infomercial on television, the promoters of a new exercise machine will already have substantial orders to ship as a result of the commercial airing. On the other hand, if a product receives few orders after airing, the company may decide to

Mike Mogelgaard, executive creative director on Starbucks at EvansGroup, is "concerned about not getting in the way of the mystique. Look what happened to Coors."

Advertising may not be the only trouble brewing. The move into the East Coast markets may prove more expensive and difficult than conquering the Pacific Northwest, where sophisticated coffee drinkers show off their Starbucks cup like a badge of honor.

Even Schultz's former boss, Baldwin, has regrouped with Starbucks' original partners and is opening more than a half-dozen shops in the Washington area under the Quartermaine Coffee Roasters name, attacking Starbucks' freshness claim.

Starbucks' legacy is also in the proliferation of espresso machines at fast-food chains.

"There's no secret sauce here," Schultz says. "Anyone can do it." That explains Starbucks' sense of urgency about expansion.

"The window's closing," cautions Matthew Patsky, VP at Robertson, Stephens & Co., a San Francisco investment company.

Schultz calls the challenge "the momentum you have in a wind tunnel and you're going the wrong way. The jury is still out on whether we can sustain it."

At the same time, bullish Wall Streeters say Starbucks should move onto supermarket shelves under a dual-brand strategy, but Schultz says that won't happen because the brand might suffer.

In any event, the national push presents ad challenges, and even Starbucks expects same-store sales, which showed 20% increases in the past five years, to fall.

All that said, the mocha mavens are still hooked on Starbucks.

"They don't market," Patsky says. "They've established a major presence all through word-of-mouth. They are not a traditional consumer products company. Starbucks could be one of the nation's leading brands of coffee. They can take on P&G.

The proof will be in the cup.

[a] Ingrid Abramovitch, "Miracles of Marketing: How to Reinvent Your Product; Starbucks Coffee; Includes Related Article on Motivational Books; Company Profile," *Success*, April, 1993, 22.

[b] Alice Z. Cunea, "Starbucks' Word-of-Mouth Wonder," *Advertising Age*, March 7, 1994, 12. Reprinted with permission from the November 8, 1993 issue of *Advertising Age*. Copyright Crain Communications Inc., 1993.

cancel the remaining advertising schedule while improvements are made to the product or the advertisement.

The Dial-it (900) numbers allow callers who pay a fee to call a central number and register an opinion or obtain information about a specific topic. Although 900 numbers often are associated with telephone sex and contest scams, the numbers are legitimate sources for information such as sports scores and travel information.

Direct Selling.   Direct selling involves the selling of products to consumers in their homes or at their place of business. Amway, Mary Kay Cosmetics, Tupperware, and Avon are examples of successful direct sellers, or in-home retailers. Direct salespeople typically work part-time as independent contractors and not employees of the companies they represent. Homemakers and students get into direct selling as a means of supplementing their income. In direct selling, products that benefit from display and demonstration sell well. Products are ordered and the salesperson delivers the products a week or two later. Since direct selling is labor intensive, commissions are high for salespeople. But the rate of salesperson turnover is also high.

Automatic   Merchandising.   Automatic merchandising includes sales of products through vending machines and video merchandising centers. Vending machines can be found everywhere. In the past, only soft drinks, cigarettes, and candy were sold through vending machines. Today, vending machines dispense insurance policies, blood pressure levels, pulse rates, and airline tickets. The majority of products featured in vending machines, though, are low-priced convenience products such as candy and cigarettes. Many companies distribute their products through vending machines as a second or third distribution channel. Recently, for example, Nabisco began vending the highly successful SnackWell's line of cookies and crackers to carve out a wellness niche in the $22.8 billion vending industry. SnackWell's products are sold through distributors who stock and maintain vending machines.[20]

Video merchandising centers (VMCs) represent another form of automatic retailing. VMCs are free-standing units located in retail outlets that both display and sell entire product lines through audio and video presentations. VMCs both inform and educate consumers about product features and order delivery. Procter & Gamble successfully used VMCs in supermarkets and mass-merchandise outlets to increase sales of its Pantene haircare product line. In recent years, Sears has installed Florsheim shoe kiosks in many of its stores to provide shoppers with access to styles and sizes not carried in Sears' stores. Shoppers can scan the computerized kiosk to locate styles and sizes and place orders. Sears sales of Florsheim shoes increased 30% since installing kiosks.[21]

Electronic Retailing.   Electronic retailing is another form of nonstore retailing offering consumers the opportunity to shop from their homes. Two forms of electronic retailing are *shop-at-home tele-vision networks* and *interactive computer shopping.*

The rise in cable television has contributed to the increase in popularity of television home shopping. Some shows like the Home Shopping Network continuously display, demonstrate, and sell a variety of products. Interested callers phone-in to ask questions about products and make purchases using credit cards. Shoppers also are responsive to 30-minute commercial programs called *infomercials.*   Consumers can purchase anything from Kenny Rogers–endorsed golf products to Cher-endorsed haircare products to jewelry, kitchen appliances, and clothing. Home shopping represents a multibillion dollar industry.

Interactive computer shopping is also gaining in popularity. Computer operations such as Prodigy, CompuServe, and America Online feature catalog shopping to their subscribers. Consumers scroll through a catalog of products. Orders are placed electronically directly through the system using a credit card. Consumers can buy a variety of products such as computer accessories and airline tickets.

The Evolution of Retailing Institutions

Retail institutions are not static but rather are constantly changing. This evolution occurs due to societal developments (e.g., increasing time pressures on shoppers), technological innovations (e.g., cable television and electronic shopping), and competitive dynamics. There is no formal theory that fully explains why retail institutions change or accounts for when additional changes might occur, but one of the first and most widely accepted explanations is the wheel of retailing hypothesis.[22]

The Wheel of Retailing.   The **wheel of retailing hypothesis** describes how retail institutions change during their evolutionary life cycles. New retailing institutions, according to this explanation, typically enter the market as low-status, low-margin, low-price operations. As these retailers achieve success, attempts are made to increase their customer base and sales. Products are upgraded, facilities are improved, and new services are added. Prices and margins are increased to support these higher costs. As these retailers enjoy their higher prices and status, new retailers enter the market to fill the low-status, low-margin, low-price niche. The cycle begins again.

For example, supermarkets entered the market in the 1920s as low-priced, limited-service operations. Over time services and specialty departments were added to attract new customers. This resulted in higher prices. Now, hypermarkets and membership clubs have filled the low-price void supermarkets left.

Scrambled Merchandising.

Another evolution in retailing is the practice of scrambled merchandising. **Scrambled merchandising** occurs when a retail establishment veers away from its original marketing strategy and adds product lines that are unrelated to the retailer's original product offering. By engaging in scrambled merchandising, the retailer attempts to

- offer a one-stop shopping institution
- generate more traffic by attracting new customers
- achieve higher profit margins
- increase impulse purchases

Supermarkets, for example, are much different institutions than they were at the time of their inception. Initially supermarkets sold only food products. Modern supermarkets have added to their facilities dry cleaning, video rental, flower departments, and even insurance and banking services. Gasoline stations now sell convenience food products and even some clothing items.

Scrambled merchandising can have a negative effect on a retailer. By expanding into unrelated product lines, the retailer's buying, selling, and servicing expertise may be reduced. The image of the store may be confused in consumers' minds. Finally, scrambled merchandising increases competition between retailers who normally do not compete with each other.

The Growth of Franchising.

A final noteworthy development in retailing is the growth of franchising. **Franchising** is a contractual arrangement between a supplier—either a manufacturer, wholesaler, or service sponsor—and a retail franchisee who buys the rights to sell products under an established name while following a specific set of guidelines. The franchisor lends experience, buying capabilities, and marketing support for an already-established product. In return, the franchisor agrees to some form of compensation such as a percentage of total sales, royalties, or franchise fees. The franchisee is typically guaranteed an exclusive selling territory.

Franchising exists at different levels. In the lowest level, a manufacturer authorizes a network of retailers to sell a specific product. Pella windows are sold only through authorized dealers. The second level of franchising is when a manufacturer authorizes, or licenses, distributors to sell a specific product to retailers. Local bottlers who franchise soft drinks from producers buy the concentrated syrups from the producer. In turn, they bottle, promote, and distribute the products to retailers and consumers. In the third level of franchising, the franchisor provides the operational and marketing know-how to the franchisee who provides the labor and capital. McDonald's, Burger King, Taco Bell, Subway, KFC, and most other fast-food outlets are franchised operations of this nature.

Franchising first emerged in the early 1900s in a few selected industries such as auto parts and service stations. Since the 1960s, franchising has experienced tremendous growth. As the fast-food industry boomed, so too did franchising. Other industries have jumped on the franchising bandwagon. Exhibit 11.3 lists different industries utilizing franchising and their sales.

Future Prospects

Predicting the future of retailing is a nearly impossible task. But several trends are expected to continue and further develop during the next few decades.

Shopping that offers convenience will continue to grow. Although sales have recently declined, catalogs will continue to be popular with consumers who have little time to shop. Shop-at-home networks and shopping by computer will also offer the convenience and savings in time consumers seek. It is virtually certain that nonstore marketing will increase throughout the 1990s and into the next millennium.[23]

The retailing industry will experience greater vertical integration both on the part of retailers moving vertically backward and manufacturers moving vertically forward. More retailers will develop and sell their own brands in an effort to increase sales and profit margins. And more producers will open their own retail outlets to sell their products rather than relying on third-party retailers. Hanes, Levis, and VanHeusen are manufacturers that are experiencing success with this strategy.

Exhibit 11.3   Franchising—Number of Establishments and Sales

Kind of Franchised Business	Number of Establishments (in thousands)	Sales (in billions)
Auto and truck dealers	26.5	$354.5
Restaurants	103.3	85.5
Gasoline service stations	107.0	143.2
Retailing (nonfood)	57.0	31.4
Auto and truck rental services	11.1	8.0
Automotive products and services	42.2	15.5
Business aids and services	69.5	20.8
Construction, home improvement, maintenance, and cleaning	30.6	7.1
Convenience stores	17.3	15.0
Educational products and services	13.9	2.3
Equipment rental services	2.9	0.8
Food retailing	25.4	12.2
Hotels and motels	11.4	26.0
Laudry, dry cleaning services	3.5	0.5
Recreation, entertainment, travel	11.6	4.8
Soft drink bottlers	0.8	28.0
Miscellaneous	8.6	2.6
Total all franchising	542.5	$757.8

Source: U.S. Department of Commerce, Bureau of the Census, *1994 Statistical Abstract of the United States*, (Washington, DC: U.S. Government Printing Office, 1994), 790.

As with other industries, retailing will become more global. Agreements such as NAFTA and GATT and the emergence of a more competitive environment in Europe represent excellent opportunities to international retailers. Those retailers who are quick to act and adapt will realize success in a very competitive marketplace.

Chapter Summary ◼

Manufacturers cannot perform all of the necessary channel functions to get the right product to the right place at the right time. These functions can be shared among channel intermediaries, but they cannot be eliminated. Wholesalers and retailers help manufacturers market consumer products to consumers. Industrial distributors and agents help manufacturers market business-to-business products to customers.

Wholesalers are an integral part of all marketing systems. Wholesalers are individuals or organizations that help in providing time, place, and possession utilities to business-to-business customers and retailers. Many different types of wholesalers exist to meet the unique needs of the diverse group of retailers and producers in operation in today's marketplace. There are three general forms of wholesaling intermediaries each distinguished by their specialized activities. The manufacturers' sales offices and branches are owned and operated by manufacturers. A merchant wholesaler is an intermediary that purchases, takes title to goods, and assumes all risks associated with ownership. Merchant wholesalers can be either full-service—including general merchandise, limited line, specialty line, or industrial distributors—or limited service—including rack jobbers, truck jobbers, drop shippers, cash and carry wholesalers, or mail-order wholesalers. Agents and brokers provide the buying and selling channel functions but do not take title to the products they sell. As producers become more marketing-oriented, so, too, have wholesalers. Today's wholesalers are attempting to satisfy the needs of both the producers they represent and the customers they serve.

Retailing encompasses those activities involved in the exchange process of goods and services to the final consumer. Retailing is a dynamic enterprise that is constantly changing in advanced economies. Retailers differ greatly in terms of how they choose to operate and where they place their strategic emphasis. Product lines and assortments, service quality, atmospherics, and price levels and margins are just some of the strategic tools that enable retailers to differentiate themselves from competitors and meet consumers' needs.

The retailing industry is highly diverse, consisting of the following retail types: specialty stores, outlet malls, department stores, and general merchandise outlets, including membership clubs, hypermarkets, warehouse and catalog showrooms, and home improvement centers.

Many marketers today, though, are finding a niche by selling to consumers through nonstore retailing, or selling products and services outside of conventional retail outlets. Several trends such as catalog marketing, telemedia, direct selling, automatic merchandising, and electronic retailing in the marketplace are seeing more out-of-store and in-home buying. Retailing practices are continuously changing because of competitive pressures, technological developments, and societal changes.

◆ Notes

1. U.S. Department of Commerce, Bureau of the Census, *1994 Statistical Abstract of the United States* (Washington, DC: U.S. Government Printing Office, 1994), 794.

2. U.S. Department of Commerce, Bureau of the Census, *1987 Census of Wholesale Trade* (Washington, DC: U.S. Government Printing Office, 1987), Table 1, US–9.

3. U.S. Department of Commerce, *1987 Census of Wholesale Trade.*

4. U.S. Department of Commerce, *1987 Census of Wholesale Trade.*

5. U.S. Department of Commerce, Bureau of the Census, *1992 Census of Retail Trade* (Washington, DC: U.S. Government Printing Office, 1992), Table 1, US–11.

6. *1994 Statistical Abstract of the United States,* 784.

7. Based on Table 1, p. 47 in A. Parasuraman, Valarie A. Zeithaml, and Leonard L. Berry, "A Conceptual Model of Service Quality and Its Implications for Future Research," *Journal of Marketing,* 49 (Fall 1985), 41–50. For further reading on service quality, see also R. Kenneth Teas, "Expectations, Performance Evaluation, and Consumers' Perceptions of Quality," *Journal of Marketing,* 57 (October 1993), 18–34.

8. Allanna Sullivan, "Mobil Bets Drivers Pick Cappuccino over Low Prices," *The Wall Street Journal,* January 30, 1995, B1, B8.

9. Leonard J. Berry, "Delivering Excellent Service in Retailing," *Retailing Issues Letter* (Center for Retailing Studies, Texas A&M University), 1988 (Vol. 1, No. 4).

10. Berry, "Delivering Excellent Service in Retailing," 2.

11. Stanley N. Logan, "The Small Store—A Struggle to Survive," *Retailing Issues Letter* (Center for Retailing Studies, Texas A&M University), 1995 (Vol. 7, No. 1).

12. Logan, "The Small Store," 3.

13. Philip Kotler, "Atmospherics as a Marketing Tool," *Journal of Retailing* (Winter 1973–74), 50. For further reading on atmospherics, see also Frederick W. Langrehr, "Retail Shopping Mall Semiotics and Hedonic Consumption," *Advances in Consumer Research*, 18, Rebecca H. Holman and Michael R. Solomon, eds. (Provo, UT: Association for Consumer Research, 1991), 428–433; Mary Jo Bitner, "Servicescapes: The Impact of Physical Surroundings on Customers and Employees," *Journal of Marketing* (April 1992), 57–71; and Robert Donovan and John Rossiter, "Store Atmosphere: An Environmental Psychology Approach," *Journal of Retailing*, 58 (Spring 1982), 34–57.

14. Kotler, "Atmospherics," 54.

15. Fara Warner, "Upscale Chocolate's Not Hot, So Godiva Does a Makeover," *Brandweek*, July 4, 1994, 21.

16. Gregory A. Patterson, "Malls Draw Shoppers with Ferris Wheels and Carousels," *The Wall Street Journal*, June 22, 1994, B1.

17. Caity Olson, "Outlet Stores Win Satisfied Consumers," *Advertising Age*, July 11, 1994, 33.

18. George Sternlieb and James W. Hughes, "The Demise of the Department Store," *American Demographics*, August 1987, 31–33, 59.

19. Walter K. Levy, "Department Stores the Next Generation: Form and Rationale," *Retailing Issues Letter* (Center for Retailing Studies, Texas A&M University), 1987 (Vol. 1, No. 1).

20. Betsy Spethmann, "Nabisco's SnackWell's Go Vending," *Brandweek*, November 14, 1994, 4.

21. Wendy Marx, "Shopping 2000," *Brandweek*, January 9, 1995, 20–21.

22. For review of other explanations, see Michael Levy and Barton A. Weitz, *Retailing Management*, 2nd ed. (Chicago: Irwin, 1995), 88–92.

23. Robert A. Peterson (ed.), *The Future of U.S. Retailing: An Agenda for the 21st Century* (New York: Quorum, 1992).

◆ Study Questions

1. As a form of wholesaling, a manufacturer's sales office
   a. is always located at the production facility.
   b. operates like an independent agent.
   c. carries inventory.
   d. All of the above are correct.

2. Which is not a full-service wholesaler?
   a. rack jobber
   b. specialty line wholesaler
   c. general merchandise wholesaler
   d. limited line wholesaler

3. How do limited-service merchant wholesalers differ from full-service merchant wholesalers?
   a. Limited-service wholesalers do not take title to the goods.
   b. Limited service wholesalers do not store products.
   c. Limited-service wholesalers offer a narrower range of support services.
   d. Limited-service wholesalers offer higher prices than full-service wholesalers.

4. Drop shippers
   a. are wholesaling intermediaries that sell products, take orders, and arrange for delivery of products.
   b. do not store, handle, or deliver any of the products they sell.
   c. offer little or no promotional assistance to their retail customers.
   d. All of the above are accurate descriptions of drop shippers.

5. Agents and brokers
   a. do not take title to the products they sell.
   b. always represent buyers instead of sellers.

   c. are virtually useless as marketing intermediaries because they do not maintain inventories.

   d. take title to the products they sell.

6. Wholesaling entities that supply products to retailers and the display units on which the products are displayed are called
   a. full-service merchant wholesalers.
   b. drop shippers.
   c. truck jobbers.
   d. rack jobbers.

7. Which of the following statements is false regarding drop shippers?
   a. They also are called desk jobbers.
   b. They take orders and arrange for delivery of products directly to customers.
   c. They are typically used in high-tech industries such as computers and communications equipment.
   d. They are typically involved in the marketing of products that have high shipping costs.

8. Which type of agent effectively represents the marketing department for the manufacturer it represents?
   a. selling agents
   b. marketing agents
   c. manufacturers agents
   d. merchandise agents

9. Which of the following is not a key feature of service quality?
   a. reliability
   b. suitability
   c. responsiveness
   d. accessibility

10. The practice of designing retailing environments that have emotional effects on shoppers and enhance their purchase probability is termed
   a. emotion engineering.
   b. retail entertronics.
   c. atmospherics.
   d. All of the above.

11. Hypermarkets
    a. are mass merchandisers and food stores combined.
    b. are full-service wholesalers.
    c. are warehouse operations featuring all products used in the home.
    d. are discount retailers that offer brand-name electronic and telecommunications merchandise at low prices.

12. Which is not a form of nonstore retailing?
    a. catalog marketing
    b. telemedia
    c. direct merchandising
    d. outlet malls

13. The wheel of retailing hypothesis
    a. describes how retail institutions evolve from low-priced, low-service operations to higher-priced and higher-service operations.
    b. explains why nonstore retailing will eventually eliminate all conventional forms of store retailing.
    c. describes the flow of products through channel intermediaries.
    d. occurs when a retailer adds product lines that are unrelated to its traditional product offerings.

14. A form of specialty store that offers a large assortment of products within a limited number of product lines at discount prices is called a
    a. category killer.
    b. hypermarket.
    c. scrambled merchandiser.
    d. department store.

15. Which of the following is false regarding department stores?
    a. They offer a wide range of product lines with some depth in each line.
    b. They are divided into separate departments each offering related products.
    c. They are experiencing a more rapid rate of sales growth than any other form of retail institution in the United States.
    d. They have been hurt by the movement of the population to the suburbs.

16. _____ occurs when a retail establishment veers away from its original marketing strategy and adds product lines that are unrelated to the retailer's original product offering.
    a. Mass merchandising
    b. Scrambled merchandising
    c. Wheel-of-retailing merchandising
    d. Hyper merchandising

CHAPTER **12**

Pricing Concepts and Price Determination

Chapter Objectives

The Nature and Importance of Price

An Outside-In Look at Price: The Customer's Perspective

An Inside-Out Look at Price: The Price-Setter's Perspective

Demand-Based Determinants of Price

Cost-Based Determinants of Price

Chapter Summary

◼ The Nature and Importance of Price

Of all the marketing mix variables, the pricing element is the *most dynamic* because it is the most subject to external forces such as competitive pressures, economic developments, and demand fluctuations. Consider the frequently changing prices of food products such as poultry, seafood, beef, and cereal. Adverse weather conditions in the mid-1990s, for example, caused the lowest level in nearly two decades of wheat and corn production in the United States. The effect was a consumer-price increase of about 5% on pasta, breads, cereals, and other wheat-based products. Meat prices fell in the short-run, as producers harvested their cattle and pig stocks rather than paying higher corn-feed prices, but Agriculture Department forecasters predicted price increases in about two years of approximately 10–15% due to reduced animal stocks.

Beyond being the dynamic element in the marketing mix, pricing in many respects is the *most unique* variable. This uniqueness vis-à-vis other marketing mix variables arises because price is the only mix element that *does not involve an actual expenditure.* This enables more frequent and quicker changes in price than in any other mix variables.[1] Whereas management commitments to advertising, sales promotions, packaging, product development, and distribution all involve costs, pricing changes do not necessitate increased expenditures. In fact, rather than increasing costs, price is the only marketing mix variable that directly increases income.[2]

Price unquestionably is one of the *most important* marketplace cues by virtue of its pervasiveness in all exchange relationships.[3] Needless to say, a product's price is a key determinant of whether customers will purchase the product, how much they will purchase, and whether they will be satisfied with their purchases. From the marketer's perspective, it can be argued that the most effective way for a firm to realize maximum profits is by getting its pricing "right."[4]

Precisely What Is Price?

To this point we have referred only obliquely to price, recognizing that all students have at least a fundamental understanding of this concept. We need now to formalize the treatment so as to avoid a too-narrow interpretation of this important marketing mix variable. A well-known pricing expert offers this definition: "Price is the amount of money and services (or goods) the buyer exchanges for an assortment of products and services provided by the seller."[5] This definition suggests that a product's price represents a *quid pro quo* between buyer and seller: Each gives up something to receive something.

The definition also recognizes that a price is not always quoted or charged in monetary terms, but rather may involve services or goods as well as or in lieu of money. In **bartering,** for example, goods and services, rather than money, are exchanged by both parties. Bartering is big business in North America and elsewhere. Companies offer their goods and services for barter through an intermediary, called a bartering exchange, that serves as a clearing-house to link businesses who want to trade goods and services. A company that barters goods or services receives barter credits to spend with any other company in the exchange.[6] There are about 500 bartering exchanges throughout the United States, in which over $7 billion in goods and services were bartered in 1993 alone.

Countertrade is a form of bartering undertaken in international trade. When one or both trading parties have undesirable currencies or no foreign exchange reserves, countertrading products presents a means whereby companies in these countries can trade their products for the products of companies in other countries. These acquired products can then be sold in the domestic economy. For example, U.S.-made Pepsi was countertraded for Russian-made Stolichnaya, a brand of vodka.

Price as an Exchange Rate.   The term *exchange rate* typically is used in connection with monetary valuations. Countries' currencies are traded in international finance circles just as any other commodity is traded. One country's currency has a value vis-à-vis other countries' currencies. This is the monetary exchange rate. For example, on June 23, 1995, the U.S. dollar was worth (i.e., valued at) approximately 1.38 Canadian dollars ($), 0.63 British pound sterling (£), 1.40 German Deutsche marks (DM), and 84.55 Japanese yen (¥). Considering just the Canadian-American interface, this means that a U.S. dollar in Canada would enable one to purchase approximately $1.38 of Canadian goods, whereas a Canadian dollar in the U.S. allows the purchaser to acquire about 73¢ of American goods.

The concept of a monetary exchange rate applies more generally to all forms of pricing. The exchange rate (price) to procure a new textbook is about $50–$60, whereas to resell that same, but now-used, textbook would bring the student one-half the original price paid. **Price,** then, can be thought of as the amount that buyer and seller agree on to exchange a product or service for money or another product/service. Price *is* an exchange rate.

Alternative Terms.   Various other terms are used in unique exchange situations to represent the exchange rate, or price, in those situations. If you live in an apartment, you pay *rent*, or if your residence is a dormitory, you call it a *dorm fee*. Students who are purchasing houses have a *mortgage* payment. The term *rent* also applies when one selects a movie from a video-rental store. An employer pays *salary* to managerial-level employees and *wages* to employees who work on an hourly basis—both payments are the amount the employer pays (the exchange rate, or price) to acquire human resources. A *fare* is the amount a passenger pays to enjoy (not enjoy?) public transportation. To acquire public utilities (water, electric, and gas) one pays a certain *rate*. We pay doctors and lawyers *fees*. And when we are ready to settle our charges at a restaurant we ask for the *bill* or, in some locales, the *ticket*. One can purchase a new automobile outright or rent it at a *lease* rate. Recording artists and book authors charge studios and producers a *royalty* for making their creative works available. Marketing intermediaries such as advertising agencies, manufacturing and selling agents, and the bartering exchange noted above get paid a *commission* for the services they render.

Although the specific term varies from situation to situation, all of these italicized terms refer to the price that one party pays another to receive something in exchange. Price by any term is an exchange rate!

When Are Pricing Decisions Necessary?

The pricing decision is complicated by the fact that it is not just a one-time decision involving a single price, but, rather, is a recurring decision involving multiple aspects of a product's or service's price. Consider the pricing decisions faced by a basic steel producer that manufactures products for sale to other businesses (e.g., automobile and appliance manufacturers) whose finished products contain steel sheeting. The steel company faces a pricing decision in each of the following situations:

- When it introduces a new product and must establish a price for the first time.

- When a Japanese, German, or domestic competitor changes the price it charges on a similar product.

- When costs increase following the negotiation of a new labor contract with the members of the United Steel Workers' union.

- When a major customer (e.g., Ford Motor Co. or General Electric) presents a compelling argument that the volume it purchases from the steel manufacturer warrants its receiving a quantity discount.

What Types of Pricing Decisions Are Made?

One might think that the pricing decision simply involves setting a base, or list, price for a product. This, of course, is an important aspect of pricing but certainly does not exhaust the types of decisions that must be made. Consider the pricing decisions made by a manufacturer such as General Electric. GE markets its products using multiple channels of distribution—to large building contractors, to government purchasers, and to retail outlets. GE establishes a list price for each of the products sold to each general type of customer and additionally makes pricing decisions regarding the following aspects of the final price a customer actually pays:

- Cash discount—the discount a customer receives for paying an invoice within a specified period such as 10 days.

- Quantity discount—a discount received for purchasing an amount during a designated period that exceeds a specified quantity.

- Functional discount—a discount extended to wholesalers or retailers for the functions performed on behalf of the manufacturer.

- Shipping terms—an issue of who pays freight costs (the seller, the buyer, or both) and how these charges are allocated.

- Promotional allowances—customers often receive discounts, or allowances, for performing special advertising or display services in behalf of the manufacturer's products they merchandise.

As can be seen, the price setter makes a variety of pricing decisions. The next chapter discusses these specific practices, while this
chapter concentrates on more general considerations that determine
how basic, or list, prices are set. Major sections in this chapter
examine cost- and demand-based determinants of price. First, however, it will be useful to examine the meaning and role of price from
the customer's perspective.

An Outside-In Look at Price: The Customer's Perspective

From the customer's perspective, price plays both negative and positive roles.[7] The *negative role* results from the fact that price represents an outlay of economic resources: $40 to attend a concert, $100
to get a tooth filled, $450 for an airline ticket to travel home at
Thanksgiving, $225 for new books this semester, $14 for a CD, and
so on. This negative aspect of a product's price serves as an imped-
iment to purchase if the customer perceives the price as too high and
if alternative solutions to a purchase problem are available. Perhaps
more interesting is the fact that price also performs a *positive role*—
higher prices often suggest higher quality and better products.

The Price-Quality Relationship

Have you ever paid a higher price to buy one brand rather than
another because you assumed that the higher-priced brand probably also was of higher quality? Maybe you have not done this, but
millions of consumers have many times. Why do consumers use
price as a *signal* of product quality? If consumers are able to objectively judge product quality (via physical inspection or tasting),
why do they need to rely on price (or on other cues such as brand
name) to form impressions of product quality?

The fact is that in some situations consumers *can* objectively
judge product quality reasonably well and need not use brand
name, price, physical appearance, or other cues to signal product
quality. People who are experts are particularly adept at judging
quality and, hence, are least likely to use nonobjective cues to gauge
product quality. But what about the bulk of consumer situations in
which most of us are not experts? How, for example, does the

typical consumer know in some objective sense whether a specific brand of paint, or a brand of motor oil, or a brand of automobile tire is objectively superior to other brands in the category? The fact is that we often do not know in any technical sense how good brands actually are, especially by merely inspecting them at the point of purchase. Herein exists the role for price and other cues to signal product quality.

The literature of marketing and economics shows that price (as well as brand name and other cues) are most likely to be used by consumers as indicators, or *signals*, of product quality under the following conditions:[8]

1. When purchase risk is high, quality is especially important to consumers because they want to minimize the odds of making an unwise decision.

2. When objective quality is difficult to assess or consumers have not the time or desire to attempt to appraise product quality, they turn to readily available and easily understood cues such as price to suggest the level of product quality.

3. When consumers lack expertise, and thus the ability to assess objective quality, they turn to price.

4. When consumers are relatively uninvolved in the purchase situation, they rely on cues of quality like price rather than engage in the effort to make an objective determination of quality.

In these circumstances, which represent the bulk of purchase situations for most consumers, quality is an important purchase consideration, and price (and other cues) are useful signals to quality. Precisely to what extent consumers rely on price as an indicator of quality remains a matter of some dispute.[9]

A recent cross-cultural study provides important new evidence on the price-quality relationship.[10] This study administered questionnaires to over 600 MBA students from 38 mostly industrialized Western countries. Respondents were asked about their use of four signals of product quality—brand name, price, physical appearance, and retailer reputation—when making purchase decisions for several consumer electronic products. A variety of statistical analyses converged on the general conclusion that these signals are universally used across cultures. Moreover, brand name was uniformly revealed to be the most important indicator of product quality followed by price.

Reference Price Information

Is the price for a particular brand too high, too low, or just about right? Is the price reasonable, fair? Implicit in these questions is the idea that consumers have some benchmark, standard, or reference point against which to judge the relative level and reasonableness of a particular price. And, in fact, considerable research shows that consumers do have reference prices as comparison points. Simply, a **reference price** is "any price to which other prices are related."[11] Two kinds of reference prices have been shown to influence consumers' perceptions: internal and external reference prices.[12] **Internal reference prices** are stored in the consumer's memory and are based on past experience and knowledge about prices in a particular product category. For example, if a particular consumer *expects* to pay around $14 when purchasing compact discs (CDs), $14 is her internal reference price. **External reference prices** are those that are found in contexts such as advertisements that state "typical" prices (e.g., "Was $100") or are available on price tags at the point of purchase.[13] When Best Buy, a retail chain that specializes in consumer electronic products, advertises that its most expensive CD is priced at $12.95, some consumers will use this external reference price to judge CD prices at other stores.

Because people have internal reference prices and marketers supply external reference prices, it stands to reason that consumers in most purchase situations would refer to reference prices in identifying brands that are acceptably priced. Research reveals, in fact, that consumers have a range, or latitude, of price acceptance around their internal reference price for a particular product. Consumers who are more frequent purchasers in the product category have a narrower range of price acceptability, whereas those with higher reference prices have wider latitudes of price acceptability.[14]

These facts hold several important implications for marketing decision makers: First, it is important that price increases not exceed the latitude of acceptance; hence, small increases are less hazardous than large increases—"nibble" but do not "bite."[15] Second, it is imprudent to place a brand on deal too frequently, because this has the effect of lowering the reference price and thus making it difficult to increase price in the immediate future. Finally, because consumer brand loyalty leads to greater tolerance of price variability for their favored brands, anything a marketer can do to enhance consumer loyalty will result in greater pricing flexibility among the loyal segment.

An Inside-Out Look at Price: The Price-Setter's Perspective

The above discussion identified some relevant aspects of consumers' use of pricing information. The important point is that consumers' use of price information to make brand judgments and purchase decisions imposes limits on the price setter's discretion. Focus now turns to pricing from the price-setter's perspective and the identification of factors, in addition to consumer perceptions, that affect price determination.

Let us first consider some interesting prices. At a recent Thanksgiving, a 15-pound Honeysuckle brand turkey was priced at 36¢ per pound for a total price of $5.40. Comparatively, the McCormick brand rubbed sage that went into the turkey's stuffing cost $3.29 for a 0.5-ounce container. On a per-pound basis, the price of sage was $10.53. The turkey at this same per-pound price would have cost $157.95! Probably not many turkeys would have been sold at this price. Why is turkey so inexpensive on a per-pound basis while sage is so costly? A lot of considerations go into pricing, not the least of which is how much consumers are willing to pay as well as how much the marketer much charge to earn a reasonable profit. Certainly, McCormick would not make a profit if it priced sage at 18¢ per can, the same per-pound price of turkey. Competition also has a major impact in determining prices. Their are numerous poultry farms, all producing a physically similar turkey product, but there are not many companies that manufacture rubbed sage to be sold in 0.5 ounce cans.

In general, there are five sets of factors that need to be weighed when setting prices:

- *demand,* which sets a ceiling on the price that can be charged

- *costs,* which set a floor below which a product's price cannot go without suffering a financial loss
- *competitive factors,* which act to reduce the price ceiling
- *corporate profit and market objectives,* which translate into financial requirements to cover costs and achieve profit goals
- *regulatory constraints and ethical considerations,* which limit a price setter's discretion[16]

A product's cost and the prices of competitive products provide the lower and upper bounds, respectively, on the price setter's "range of discretionary pricing."[17] This statement translates into the following equation:

$$\text{Seller's cost} \leq \text{Seller's price} \leq \text{Competitor's price}$$

This equation represents the most extreme pricing case inasmuch as it suggests that a price setter cannot price below a product's cost nor above competitors' prices. In actuality, prices sometimes are set below full costs and losses are incurred. This, nonetheless, may be preferable to not being able to sell a product at a price equal to or above its full cost. Retailers, for example, often unload unfashionable and out-of-season merchandise at prices substantially below full cost.

Prices also are often set above competitors' prices, especially when the price setter is the market leader. From our previous discussion of reference prices, it should be apparent that a company is able to charge higher prices than competitors if its brand is perceived as superior, either due to better quality, a more prestigious image, or both. In other words, the upper bound of the consumer's latitude of price acceptability for their preferred brand exceeds the price of competitive products.

Pricing Objectives

As with all business decisions, objectives provide the starting point for making decisions about price. In response to the question, "What should be Brand X's price?" the resounding reply is "What objective do you hope to accomplish?"

Exhibit 12.1   Pricing Objectives

- Cash flow and survival
- Profit maximization
- Target return on investment
- Sales and market share
- Status quo
- Brand positioning and image

At one extreme, prices can be set (or changed) to enable a firm to generate sufficient cash flow to survive a short-run challenge. At the other extreme, the price setter may establish prices with the intent of maximizing long-term profits. In between these extremes are objectives such as achieving sales and market share goals, obtaining a desired return on investment, maintaining the status quo, or projecting a desired image via pricing. Exhibit 12.1 lists various objectives that direct pricing decisions.

Cash Flow and Survival.   In the summer of 1995, the Clinton Administration and the Japanese government averted a trade war in which the United States had threatened to impose a 100% tariff on Japanese luxury cars imported into the United States. Had this quota gone into effect, import costs of these automobiles to dealers in the United States would have doubled. For argument sake, let us assume that the 100% tariff actually went into effect. Further assume that you are owner of a dealership that sells Japanese-made Lexus automobiles. You cannot possibly increase retail prices by the amount necessary to cover the added cost burden imposed by the tariff. You have sold almost all of the pre-tariff autos you had in stock. What do you do, sit idly by while BMW and Mercedes dealers take all your business? Certainly, a $70,000 or $80,000 Lexus falls outside most consumers' latitude of acceptable price.

At a time like this, the dealership's decision might be to continue to purchase new cars at the tariff cost and to sell them at a price just slightly above that cost. This would enable the dealership to weather the storm and stay in business. In general, a survival objective is necessitated when short-term events or competitive actions imperil a product or company, forcing it to price products

MARKETING HIGHLIGHTS

A Car or a Club? Lexus Wants Both

Lexus would like consumers to feel that ownership of an exclusive car entitles them to membership in an exclusive club: The Lexus Club.

The luxury car division of Toyota Motor Sales USA takes pains to include existing customers in all of its integrated marketing plans. When the division introduces a new model, it makes sure current Lexus owners, as well as prospective buyers, know about it.

Lexus keeps in steady contact with current owners and prospective buyers through a variety of techniques: database marketing, special events, sports sponsorships, and media advertising under the "relentless pursuit of perfection" theme.

The thinking behind this strategy is two-fold: Lexus owners report higher satisfaction than owners of any other marque, so they also become the best promoters of the brand through another proven tool, word-of-mouth. That's why Lexus strives to keep its customer base excited about what the automaker is doing.

At the same time, Lexus has built a dossier on its buyers. The four-year-old division has logged every new Lexus owner into a database now totaling more than 300,000 names.

"We like to think that by going into the database and analyzing the characteristics of the existing Lexus owners, we can extend those characteristics to a broader market," says Fred Arnow, Lexus national marketing development manager.

Lexus faces a problem common to all luxury car marketers: The buyer group is small. Only about 9% of all cars sold are luxury vehicles, with near-luxury cars representing an additional 3.8%, according to Automotive News.

This makes mass media, such as network TV or general magazines, inherently wasteful.

Mr. Arnow sees database marketing as "relationship marketing" that, when done correctly, can keep a customer in the fold while at the same time further identifying common denominators among customers.

As Lexus better identifies bona fide prospects from its owner base, it can justify spending more on higher-quality marketing materials.

Even before the first pre-launch ads for its new GS 300 mid-luxury model appeared in February, all Lexus owners received a letter alerting them to "the news Lexus," the same positioning line used later in traditional media ads.

at a lower-than-desired level but one which enables survival until circumstances change.

Profit Maximization.

Business people sometimes claim that they set prices to maximize profits, and classical economic theory upholds profit maximization as the theoretical ideal for business decisions. Technically, profit maximization is achieved when the price set for a product assures a theoretically optimal profit; no other price will generate greater total profit than the chosen price. As explained more fully in a later section, this theoretical ideal is accomplished when the

But the letter included an offer for a free videotape on the new car.

Lexus also mailed the letters and videotapes to key prospects, primarily owners of competitive models such as the Infiniti J30, the BMW 535i, and the Mercedes-Benz 300E.

Because Lexus sees its owner-base as a significant source of word-of-mouth endorsements, it attempts to keep them excited about the marque.

Lexus' ad agency, Team One Advertising in El Segundo, California, maintains extensive resources to handle the integrated communications. For direct marketing alone, the shop has dedicated an account supervisor, account executive, and two creative teams.

Apart from the direct-mail efforts, Lexus associates its cars with activities important to its customers and prospective owners.

"Similar to all our programs, we try to put the car right in their backyards," says Cathy Shepherd, Team One senior VP-promotion director. Team One also staffs an 11-person promotion department for Lexus, headed by Shepherd.

Lexus has identified both sporting and cultural events as prime activities for its owners. As such, it sponsors more than 100 events annually, where it can place a car among its prime targets and owners.

For example, Lexus used its sponsorship of the Lipton Tennis Tournament, held last march in Key Biscayne, Florida, to highlight the GS 300 sedan. In addition to having a car on display at the event, Lexus was an advertiser on the telecast.

Golf, another sport that attracts upscale car buyers, figures heavily in Lexus' promotional efforts. Working with its 150 dealers, the division sponsors individual golf tournaments around the country.

On the cultural side, Lexus was part of a fund-raiser for a musicians' pension fund held prior to the Grammy Awards in February. Lexus follows up such events with thank you letters to participants.

"I don't think Lexus even questions 'is there value here,'" says Shepherd.

Mr. Arnow agrees. "We believe absolutely that we are identifying the correct prospects."

Source: Cleveland Horton, "A Car or a Club? Lexus Wants Both," *Advertising Age*, November 8, 1993, S-11–12. Reprinted by permission from the December 8, 1993, issue of *Advertisng Age*. Copyright, Crain Communications Inc., 1993.

marginal revenue from a particular price and quantity combination equals the *marginal cost* associated with that quantity.

Profit maximization represents a normative ideal, but in practicality it is nonoperational because (1) firms often do not maintain precise cost data to adequately calculate marginal costs, and (2) price setters are unable to accurately estimate the demand schedules that are needed to calculate marginal revenues. Nonetheless, the concept of profit-maximizing pricing is a worthy ideal even if it is unachievable. It is important to recognize that profit-maximizing pricing does not mean setting unfair or excessively high prices. In all but monopolistic markets, the competitive marketplace of price-conscious customers and aggressive competitors simply will not permit one firm to charge outrageously high prices.

Target Return on Investment.   This pricing objective also focuses on profit, but it focuses on setting prices to achieve a desired profit goal rather than an optimal profit. Assume, for example, that Microsoft determines that its total investment in the software package, Windows 95, is $900 million and that its profit goal is to earn a return on investment (ROI) equaling 35%, or $315 million. This ROI goal is greater than most firms strive for (15–30% is more typical), but Microsoft's more lofty goal is justified because this entrepreneurial company is more clever, daring, and innovative than most firms.

With knowledge of per unit cost and an accurate forecast of how many Windows 95 units will be sold, Microsoft has the necessary data to set a price that will recover cost and yield the desired 35% return on investment. Let us assume that Microsoft will sell 20,000,000 Windows 95 units in 1996, the first full year of product availability. This implies a $15.75 return per unit ($315 million ROI ÷ 20 million units). Hence, determining the selling price under this scenario would be straightforward: set the selling price equal to the total cost per unit plus the desired ROI in pretax dollars. A later section in the chapter discusses target-return price setting in greater detail.

Sales and Market Share.   Firms also set prices to realize desired sales and market share goals. **Market share** represents a particular brand's revenue as a proportion of the total revenue generated in the product category. The soap pad business, for example, is a relatively small product category (annual sales of approximately $120 million), which, until recently, had only two major competitors, S.O.S and Brillo pads. Then Minnesota Mining and Manufacturing (3M) introduced its Scotch-Brite Never Rust soap pad and quickly earned a 15.4% market share, while S.O.S's share dropped to 36.2% and Brillo fell to a 15.2% share.[18]

3M priced Scotch Brite at a level low enough to quickly steal market share from the two entrenched brands and to establish a presence in the market. Managers at 3M could have priced Scotch Brite at a higher price in view of the major no-rust product innovation—the first major product innovation in the category since Brillo introduced soap pads in 1917!—but it was important to gain a large sales volume and market share quickly; a relatively low price made this possible. Many firms, in fact, will not enter a product category unless they project being able to obtain no lower than the second or third highest market share in a product category. Their rationale is that it is impossible to earn sufficient profits when placed in a low-market share position.[19] Earning a relatively large market share typically requires establishing a competitive price.

Status Quo.   At times a price setter is primarily interested in maintaining a currently acceptable position rather than attempting, via pricing, to improve that position. Although market power might permit a company to increase or decrease its price, it is deemed preferable to preserve the present price so as not to force retaliation from competitors, complaints from consumerists, or threats from government officials. Drug companies that hold patents on innovative brands often choose not to increase prices beyond the present profitable level because they know consumerist groups will be highly critical of what they perceive is exploitative pricing.

Brand Positioning and Image.   A final pricing objective is to set the price for a brand to achieve a desired positioning and image. Some brands attempt to maintain upscale, prestige images and are priced accordingly. The price is part and parcel of the brand's positioning. Any lowering of price would likely hurt the brand's image. Rolex watches are high-quality and high-priced items. The market for the Rolex brand could be expanded, at least in the short run, by lowering prices, but this famous brand's image likely would suffer. Wal-Mart, on the other hand, maintains relatively low prices that are compatible with its value positioning. As developed earlier, price is an important signal of product quality (as well as of other ascriptions such as value or fairness), and firms must set prices to maintain consistency with the position they hope to achieve in consumers' minds.

Competitive Considerations

We already have alluded to the fact that competitors' prices impose a ceiling of sorts above which a brand's price can not go. This extreme statement was qualified by recognizing that superior product quality or an upscale image enable a brand to carry a premium price. Nonetheless, competitive prices represent an important constraint (or, from the consumer's perspective, a reference point) on a price setter's discretion. The magnitude of constraint depends on the nature of the competitive situation. It may be recalled from an economics course or from our discussion back in Chapter 2 that firms compete in four basic forms of competitive structures: pure competition, monopolistic competition, oligopolies, and monopolies. The pricing implications associated with these competitive structures will be discussed, but first it is necessary to introduce the concept of price elasticity.

Price elasticity, or, more technically, price elasticity of demand, is a measure of customer responsiveness to price changes. The issue is this: If a product's price is increased or decreased by a certain percent, what percentage increase or decrease will be registered in the quantity purchased? In equation form,[20]

$$\text{Price elasticity of demand } (E_d)$$
$$= \% \text{ change in Quantity} \div \% \text{ change in Price}$$

or, equivalently

$$E_d = \frac{\Delta Q/Q_1}{\Delta P/P_1} = \frac{(Q_1 - Q_2)/Q_1}{(P_1 - P_2)/P_1}$$

where,
   Δ (delta) stands for "change in"
   E_d = Coefficient of price elasticity
   Q_1 = Quantity demanded at the original price, P_1
   Q_2 = Quantity demanded at the changed price, P_2
   P_1 = The original price
   P_2 = The changed price

Consider the following simplistic situation. A large supermarket chain has its own private brand of breakfast cereal that competes against General Mills' Cheerios. The supermarket has been selling its private brand for $3 per box ($P_1$), and has recorded weekly average sales of 500,000 boxes (Q_1). The store decides to reduce the price to $2.75 ($P_2$) and shortly thereafter average sales increase to 550,000 boxes (Q_2). Price elasticity in this situation is as follows:

$$\text{Price elasticity } (E_d) = (Q_1 - Q_2)/\ Q_1 \div (P_1 - P_2)/P_1$$
$$= (500{,}000 - 550{,}00)/500{,}000$$
$$\div (3.00 - 2.75)/3.00$$
$$= -10\% \div 8.33\%$$
$$= -1.2$$

This elasticity coefficient's negative sign simply reflects the typical *inverse relation* between price and quantity demanded; that is, quantity demanded typically decreases with increases in price, and vice versa. However, it is more convenient to express elasticity coefficients in absolute terms, that is, sign free. In absolute terms, –1.2 equals 1.2. Elasticity coefficients in excess of 1 are referred to as **elastic,** which indicates market responsiveness to price changes; that is, the percent change in price is offset by a *greater* percent change in quantity purchased, as in the above illustration. Elasticity coefficients less than 1 are termed **inelastic,** which indicates that the percentage increase or decrease in quantity demanded is *less* than the percentage decrease or increase in price. For completeness, elasticity coefficients equal to 1 are called **unitary elastic.**

With **total revenue (TR)** defined as the product of price times quantity ($P \times Q$), the following very important conclusions directly follow from the above definitions:

If price elasticity is *elastic*

- *decreases* in price will result in increases in total revenue
- *increases* in price will result in decreases in total revenue

If price elasticity is *inelastic*

- *decreases* in price will result in decreases in total revenue
- *increases* in price will result in increases in total revenue

In the above cereal illustration, where price elasticity was elastic, the total revenue associated with the original price is $1,500,000 (500,000 boxes sold at $3 each). However, with a price decrease of 8.33%, quantity sold increased by 10%, which yields total revenue of $1,512,500 (550,000 boxes sold at $2.75 each).

With these fundamentals established, we now return to brief discussions of each of the four market structures and the pricing implications associated with each structure.

Pure Competition.   Pure competition exists when many firms are selling the same basic product such as an agricultural commodity. No one competitor has the power to affect supply or price. All buyers and sellers have full knowledge of the market. And competitors can freely enter or exit the market at their own discretion.

Exhibit 12.2   Pure Competitive Market Situation

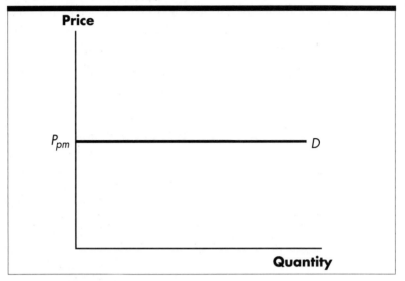

In a situation such as this, price is dictated by the amount in supply and demand. The demand curve (Exhibit 12.2) is perfectly flat (i.e., perfectly *elastic*) at the prevailing market price (P_{pm}). At this price each supplier can sell any quantity it brings to market. However, it cannot sell any quantity above P_{pm}, and it would make no sense to sell at a lower price. A pure competitive situation obviously is a situation a marketer would hope to avoid insofar as the price level is dictated by the market rather than the marketer.

This is why suppliers of commodity-type products engage in product differentiation efforts such as branding and advertising so as to effectively extricate themselves from a pure competitive situation. Chiquita bananas, Foxy lettuce, and Intel computer chips are some of the more notable efforts to brand and advertise products that consumers would otherwise regard as mere commodities. These brands command premium prices due to their effective marketing efforts. In fact, some would claim that there is no such thing as a commodity because creative marketing efforts can differentiate an otherwise homogeneous product.

Oligopoly.   An oligopoly exists when a few firms control the majority of an industry's sales.[21] Each firm has a powerful influence on the market price. Oligopolies range from relatively *pure oligopolies*, where competitors offer essentially undifferentiated

Exhibit 12.3   Pure Oligopolistic Market Situation

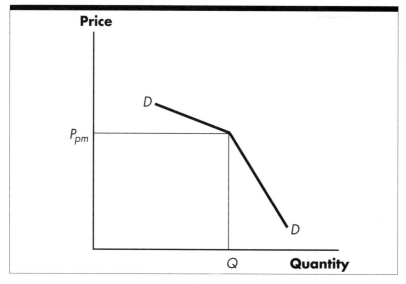

products (e.g., steel sheeting, industrial-grade petroleum), to *differentiated oligopolies*, where competitive offerings are somewhat differentiated through styling, image, or product features (e.g., automobiles and breakfast cereal). The demand curve in a pure oligopoly is "kinked" at the prevailing market price (Exhibit 12.3). A **kinked** demand curve is one that is relatively flat (*elastic*) above the prevailing market price (P_{pm}) and relatively steeply sloped (*inelastic*) below P_{pm}.

What this suggests is that a firm will suffer reduced total revenue if it changes its price, either increasing or decreasing, from P_{pm}. Prices above P_{pm} will fall in the elastic zone, and, as established previously, result in decreases in total revenue. In practical terms, if only one firm increases its prices, customers will refuse to purchase from that firm and will switch to its competitors, whom, it is assumed, will not increase their prices. Similarly, prices below P_{pm} will fall in the inelastic zone, and also result in decreases in total revenue—competitors' will be forced to also lower their prices, and, thereafter, all firms will be selling essentially the same quantities as before the price reduction but, of course, at a lower price. In other words, in a pure oligopolistic market situation a price setter faces a "no win" situation when contemplating price changes and effectively has little more pricing discretion than do suppliers in a pure competitive situation.[22]

Exhibit 12.4   Pure Monopolistic Market Situation

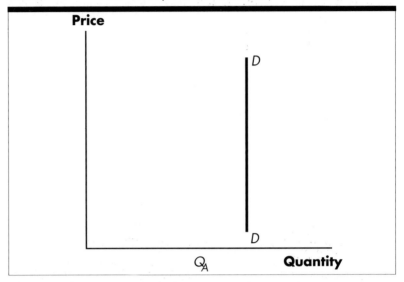

Monopoly.   A pure monopoly exists when there is only one firm producing and selling a product to an entire market. Because there are no substitutes for the product, the demand curve is perfectly inelastic (Exhibit 12.4). This is to say that buyers will pay whatever price (within reason) that a supplier charges for the available quantity it can supply. Assume, for example, that a community is totally isolated from the rest of humanity and in that community resides only one physician who is capable of performing cardiac surgery. This physician could charge virtually any price (within reasonable bounds) she or he wants to patients whose lives depend on the physician's services. The price actually charged would be limited only by the physician's personal sense of ethics and by governmental restraint or community pressure—topics that are discussed in a subsequent section.

Monopolistic Competition.   Monopolistic competition is the most frequent market structure. This form of competition exists when a large number of sellers produce and sell similar products that are differentiated by minor characteristics such as formula variations, packaging innovations, or flavors. Competition is intense due to the large number of companies making essentially the same, undifferentiated product. Pricing is based primarily on image factors: Consumers may be willing to pay higher prices than the

Exhibit 12.5   Monopolistic Competitive Market Situation

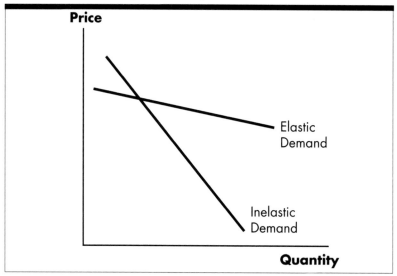

market average if they perceive a brand to be somewhat superior to competitive offerings.

The demand curve facing monopolistic competitors may be relatively elastic or inelastic, depending on a firm's ability to differentiate its offering (Exhibit 12.5). The flashlight market, for example, has historically included many producers selling basically undifferentiated brands at an average price of $5. The demand historically has been highly elastic for flashlights. Then, in 1995, Black & Decker introduced the Snakelight (a flexible flashlight that, among other features, can be wrapped around a drain pipe) at a price of $30! Over one million Snakelights were sold in less than one year after introduction.[23] This brand clearly faces a relatively inelastic demand curve in comparison to the elastic curves confronted by its undifferentiated competitors.

Regulatory Constraints

Regardless of the market structure, price setters do not have complete discretion in setting prices. Because pricing is so important to the free flow of products in market-driven economies, governments have intervened to prevent certain pricing practices and to protect consumers and facilitate competition.

To better appreciate the material to follow, consider how you might go about setting prices if you operated in a business world that was fully *unregulated* and you had no regard for anything or anyone other than your company's short-term financial welfare. That is, there is no "big brother" peering over your shoulders and your only ethic is to maximize your company's profits. Here are some of the things you might consider doing:

1. Collude with competitors to fix prices at a level higher than what any of you would sell the product at in the absence of collusion.
2. Charge very low prices in the short run; force competitors out of business and then substantially increase prices after you dominate the market.
3. Charge different prices to different customers based on whatever serves your purposes without regard for whether your pricing behavior might upset the competitive scheme at your customers' level of competition.
4. Market your product at relatively high prices in your domestic market but then ship the product to customers overseas at very low prices.

As you may have surmised, the "hypothetical" practices in points one through four are not all that hypothetical. These pricing activities have, in fact, been practiced since at least early industrial times. Because these practices harm competitors and injure consumers, legislation has been enacted and imposed to prevent all four illustrative practices. The practices in points 1–4 above represent, respectively (1) price fixing, (2) predatory pricing, (3) price discrimination, and (4) dumping.

Price Fixing.   The practice of **price fixing** occurs when managers from two or more companies *collude* in some fashion to artificially maintain or set prices or at least make an attempt to do so.[24] For example, a former president of American Airlines phoned the president of Braniff Airlines and suggested that American would raise its fares on flights in and out of the Dallas–Fort Worth airline hub if Braniff would also raise its fares. In another case, representatives from the Texas-based Quality Trailer Products, a manufacturer of axles, made contact with a competitor, American Marine Industries (AMI), and lobbied to have both firms increase their prices.[25]

At the time of this writing, there is some possibility that legal action might be brought against companies in the $8 billion U.S. cereal industry. The staffs of Congressmen Charles Schumer (D-N.Y.) and Sam Gejdenson (D-Conn.) studied pricing in the cereal industry and learned that the prices of some well-known brands increased by nearly 90% during the 1980s and early 1990s, which is twice the increase for other food products during this period. In a March 1995 letter to the Justice Department, Representatives Schumer and Gejdenson requested the Justice Department investigate whether the four major cereal manufacturers are colluding to control the market and keep prices and profit margins high.[26]

In another unsettled case, the American Society of Travel Agents Inc. (ASTA) has brought an antitrust lawsuit against the nation's major airlines with charges that the airlines have colluded to reduce commissions paid to travel agents on sales of domestic airline tickets. Commissions paid by airlines in 1994 exceeded $6 billion. To reduce these massive expenditures, airlines reduced commissions from 10% per ticket, regardless of face amount, to a maximum of $25 per one-way ticket or $50 for a round-trip ticket.

Price fixing via collusive efforts are illegal under the **Sherman Act (1890),** which specifically prohibits any contract, combination, or conspiracy in *interstate* commerce that restrains trade or attempts to monopolize a specific market or industry. The Federal Trade Commission and the Justice Department have statutory authority to regulate collusive practices.

Predatory Pricing.   When, for the purpose of putting competitors out of business, a firm sets a price in the short-term that is below its cost only later to raise its price to a very high level and earn exorbitant profits, it is practicing **predatory pricing.**[27] Predatory pricing is unlawful under the Sherman Act and also the **Federal Trade Commission Act (1914),** which was passed by Congress to strengthen the Sherman Act and which empowered the FTC to deal with antitrust matters and investigate deceptive and unfair marketing practices.

Price Discrimination.   Businesses at times charge different prices to different customers. Sometimes this practice is economically justified and legally permissible; at other times regulatory agencies initiate legal action against the price discriminator on grounds that such practice is anti-competitive and injurious to customers. As an initial point of clarification, it is important to note that when a seller, such as a manufacturer, charges unequal prices to different customers for an identical product, the seller has, by definition, discriminated on the basis of price. However, price discrimination is not illegal per se. We will identify when it is legally acceptable to discriminate in price and when it is not.

From an economic perspective, price discrimination is unhealthy if its effect is to place a customer who pays a higher price in an uncompetitive position versus a customer who has the good fortune of receiving a lower price. Because price discrimination practices were widespread in American business early in the twentieth century, the **Clayton Act (1914)** was passed by Congress to make it unlawful for firms to discriminate in price where the effect of such discrimination lessens competition.

However, weaknesses in the wording of the Clayton Act and problems in its interpretation by judicial bodies led to the passage of the very important **Robinson-Patman Act (1936),** which amended the Clayton Act. The Robinson-Patman Act was a product of post-depression thinking and the corresponding belief that big business is bad. In fact, the act was largely directed at preventing the incipient growth of big chain stores, and is sometimes referred to as the "Anti A&P Act" (where A&P stands for the supermarket chain originally known as the Atlantic and Pacific Tea Company).

The Robinson-Patman Act declares: "it shall be unlawful for any person engaged in commerce . . . to discriminate in price between different purchasers of commodities of like grade and quality . . . where the effect of such discrimination may be substantially to lessen competition, or tend to create a monopoly."[28] This act does not make all price discrimination illegal. **Price discrimination** is illegal only if identical products (i.e., "commodities of like grade and quality") are sold to competitive customers and the result is to create substantial economic injury to one or more competitors.

There are various situations when charging different prices to competitive customers is legally permissible:

1. There is *no harm to competition* resulting from the price discrimination.

2. The *cost differences* in the manufacturing process, selling, or delivery of products justify price differences being charged to different customers. A manufacturer of clothing items such as socks, for example, would be fully justified in pricing its product at a lower price when selling to Wal-Mart

than to a small clothing store that purchases only a fraction as many socks as does Wal-Mart. In selling massive quantities to Wal-Mart, the sock manufacturer incurs less handling, packaging, selling, and perhaps production expenses than when servicing a customer's small-quantity orders.

3. The reason for charging lower prices is to *match a competitor's lower prices.* In the "good-faith clause" provision of the Robinson-Patman Act, a seller is economically justified and legally permitted to charge a lower price to one customer, say customer A, than to another, customer B, if this price reduction is occasioned by the need to match a competitor who is charging a lower price to customer A.

4. *Changes in interim market conditions* justify price differences. If, say, a manufacturer's production costs have risen due to a re-negotiated labor contract, it would be permissible for the manufacturer to charge a higher price to a customer that places an order after higher labor costs are in force than a customer who ordered prior to the higher costs.

It should be apparent that the Robinson-Patman Act applies to many pricing situations. Price setters have to be vigilant when contemplating unequal prices to different customers. The burden of proof is on the price discriminator to justify its differential pricing activities.

As a final point, it is important to note that the Robinson-Patman Act deals only with pricing from a seller to a business customer. Retail prices to consumers are not within the scope of price-discrimination legislation. How otherwise would automobile salespeople be able to sell cars at differential prices, largely as a function of the customer's ability to haggle? Retailers can charge different prices to different consumers with legal impunity. Of course, price discrimination at the retail level *is* illegal under civil statute if it is undertaken on the basis of racial, religious, or another form of class discrimination.

Dumping.   **Dumping** is a form of import price discrimination that occurs when a U.S. firm sells goods in a foreign market for less than their fair value or when a foreign firm prices products to be sold in the United States substantially below what they are sold in that firm's domestic market. The U.S. Commerce Department's

CAPTAINS OF INDUSTRY

Frederick W. Smith

Chairman, President, and Chief Executive Officer

Federal Express Corporation

Date of Birth: April 11, 1944

Education: B.S., Economics, Yale University, 1966

Career Path: Marine Corps pilot from 1966 to 1973; founded Federal Express in 1973 with money from a family trust.

Profile: Competitive, charismatic, inspirational leader who is the ultimate risk-taker.

The story of Federal Express' conception is legendary. When Fred Smith was in college, he handed in the idea for an overnight package delivery service as a term paper assignment in an economics class at Yale. The professor gave the paper a "C," noting that the idea did not take into consideration federal airline regulations, the vast amounts of capital required, and competition from the large airlines, who already had package deliveries on their passenger routes. But this professor didn't take into account the determination of Fred Smith.

Smith learned to fly an airplane at the age of 15 and took up crop-dusting as a part-time hobby. Upon graduation from Yale in 1966 he enlisted in the Marine Corps and spent two tours of duty first as a platoon leader and then as a reconnaissance pilot, flying 200 combat missions in Vietnam. After this experience he took the $4 million (some

say $8.5 million) from his family trust in 1972 to establish an overnight package delivery system based on the hub and spoke strategy of distribution—establishing a tightly controlled single hub in Memphis in 1973 and owning his own jets so that he would neither be tied to commercial schedules nor limited to what could be carried on passenger planes. Initially, the service was limited to small parcels, those weighing 70 pounds and under. Each night parcels from all over the United States were picked up and flown to a sorting center in Memphis, and then rerouted to their final desintations before dawn. The company was not an overnight success, however. It managed to lose $29 million during the first 26 months of operation, but an infusion of $72 million from a venture-capital package, the United Parcel Service, Inc. strike in 1974, and the demise of REA Express helped improve business conditions. By 1976 the company began showing a profit with earnings multiplying at an annual rate of 76% by 1981. Total revenues in 1993 grew to $7.8 billion, on the company's 20th anniversary.

Federal Express has continued to innovate in order to maintain its superior status in the overnight parcel delivery service business. In 1979 when the U.S. Postal Service changed regulations to allow private delivery of "extremely urgent" mail, Federal Express immediately began planning an overnight letter. The company was well-positioned to lead the industry in the delivery of the overnight letter since it had its hub and spoke distribution well in place plus the long-term investment of capital expenditures, allowing it to keep its cost to the consumer attractively low. But Federal Express has built its reputation on its reliability, and consumers are willing to pay a little more for that peace of mind. The 1993 Federal Express annual report states the three fundamental strategies that have guided the company since its inception:

1. A global network of aviation, ground and information links, providing express transportation between the world's great trading centers.
2. An unyielding commitment to industry leadership in technology and innovation.
3. The relentless pursuit, through people and processes, of 100% customer satisfaction after every contact with Federal Express.

Smith went out on a limb in 1989 to purchase Tiger International's Flying Tiger cargo line for $880 million. Many felt he had overpaid for an aging fleet of planes, and the acquisition proved costly to integrate with Federal Express. The company's overseas operating losses totaled $629 million for the first three years it owned Flying Tiger, dropping the company's net income from $185 million in fiscal 1989 to $6 million in fiscal 1991. But Fred Smith was determined to turn Federal Express into a global overnight delivery system, and he was willing to endure financial pains to achieve his goal. The company earned its first quarterly profit on overseas operations in November of 1993. He used his fleet of 467 airplanes and 30,000 trucks as a worldwide network of mobile warehouses, allowing customers to use a just-in-time inventory system for parts and goods sourced globally and delivered overnight or second day. And in keeping with the company's goal of industry leadership in technology and innovation, Smith has developed a computerized customs clearing system to speed the flow overseas goods to its U.S. customers, thereby saving them time and money. The system alerts U.S. customs agents to pinpoint which shipments to hold for inspection, while allowing the bulk of the deliveries to move quickly.

Fred Smith's story is not exactly that of Horatio Alger. His father died when Smith was four years old, but Smith was educated in private schools and knew he would inherit several million when he came of age. He overcame a hip disorder as a child and was able to become a U.S. marine after graduation from Yale University. Smith is described as a fantastic motivator of people who inspires great loyalty from the people who have worked for him. His vision for a company that could deliver goods "when it absolutely, positively has to be there overnight" has changed the way the world does business. Federal Express was awarded the Malcolm Baldrige National Quality Award in 1991 and continues to excel and innovate with new service-driven technologies such as the Command and Control vehicle coordination system FedEx On-Line and Powership. What lies ahead for Federal Express? Maybe Fred Smith could tell us.

International Trade Administration is responsible for determining whether a product is being dumped.[29]

Ethical Considerations

Beyond the legal implications of one's pricing actions, a price setter must confront ethical considerations. For example, is it ethical (moral) for a professional such as a lawyer to charge higher prices to some clients simply because these clients are less sophisticated, less able to know what lawyers' fees should be, and hence more willing to pay inflated fees? Is it ethical for a supermarket chain to charge higher prices in its inner-city stores than at its suburban outlets? Reversing the situation, would it be unethical for this same retailer to charge relatively higher prices at suburban than at inner-city stores? Is it ethical for a marketing research firm to charge customers for unrendered services? Is it ethical for computer manufacturers to charge initially very high prices for new technology and then to sharply reduce prices after the most price-insensitive customers have made purchases at the high (inflated?) prices? Is it unethical for a retailer to price dresses at 400% above their cost? Is it ethical for a consultant to price her services at $3,000 per day?

These are just a few of the ethical dilemmas that confront price setters. Of the above situations, the only one most people would agree is unethical is the charging of higher fees for undelivered market-research services. However, for every reader who answers in the affirmative to any of the remaining ethical-or-unethical questions, there likely is another reader who disagrees. This lack of consensus simply demonstrates the difficulty of determining what is unethical behavior. Each individual has his or her own set of ethical beliefs; moreover, many pricing situations (as well as other business decisions) are not black or white in terms of what is appropriate behavior. When, for example, is a price too high? If product innovators are willing to pay very high prices to be among the first to own, say, a new electronic innovation, have they been overcharged? If a supermarket chain charges higher prices in its inner-city stores because the cost of doing business is higher in the inner city (due to higher real-estate expenses or higher storage costs), has the chain been unethical in passing on its higher costs in the form of higher retail prices? If this chain charges higher prices in its suburban stores because customers in these locales are more able and/or willing to pay higher prices, has it engaged in unethical pricing behavior?

If, indeed, it is more expensive to serve customers in one locale than another, it would seem fully merited for a price setter to expect customers in the more-expensive locale to absorb the higher costs. And when is a price too high? In all but monopolistic market structures, customers have the option of not paying prices they regard as inflated. Is it unethical for the makers of Princess Marcella Borghese's Superiore State-of-the-Art lipstick to charge $20 for a 0.15 ounce tube (equivalent of $133 per ounce) when one can buy the same amount of Wet 'n' Wild lipstick for basically $7 an ounce?[30] On the other hand, if a pharmaceutical manufacturer charges an extremely high price on a patent-protected drug that is in high demand due to its efficacy, one may assert that the firm is reaping abnormally high profits at the expense of consumer welfare. A ready counter to this position is that the pharmaceutical manufacturer is in business to serve its stockholders' interests, not to provide inexpensive products for consumers. Resolving ethical dilemmas is not easy!

In concluding this section, we would simply add that businesses can foster ethical or unethical cultures by establishing *ethical core values* to guide pricing and other marketing behaviors. One core value that would go a long way in enhancing ethical behavior is this: Treat customers with respect, concern, and honesty, the way you would want to be treated or the way you would want your family treated.[31] Firms can facilitate ethical marketing behavior from their employees by suggesting that employees apply each of the following tests when faced with an ethical predicament: (1) act in a way that you would want others to act toward you (*the Golden Rule*); (2) take only actions which would be viewed as proper by an objective panel of your professional colleagues (*the professional ethic*); and (3) always ask, would I feel comfortable explaining this action on TV to the general public? (*the TV test*).[32]

Demand-Based Determinants of Price

The determination, or setting, of prices depends on various factors, of which cost and demand are preeminent. Whereas demand sets a ceiling on prices, costs set a floor. This section describes the role of demand factors in price determination. The following section then discusses the function of costs.

To say that demand imposes a ceiling on prices is equivalent to saying that a seller cannot charge a price higher than what customers are willing to pay. We need to more formally develop the

Exhibit 12.6   Demand Schedule and Corresponding Demand Curve for a Concert

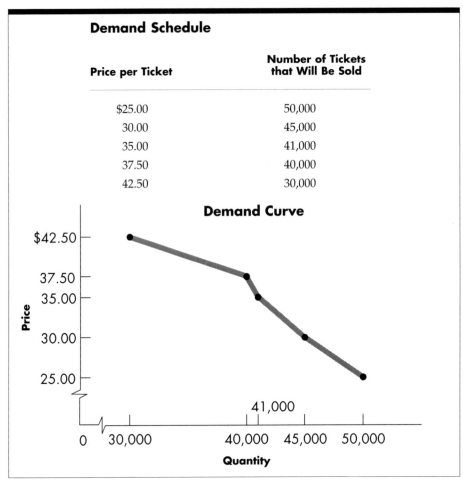

Demand Schedule

Price per Ticket	Number of Tickets that Will Be Sold
$25.00	50,000
30.00	45,000
35.00	41,000
37.50	40,000
42.50	30,000

Demand Curve

concept of demand and the role it plays in determining prices. For starters, we define **demand** as the quantity of a product that will be sold during a period of time, say a year, at different prices. Note carefully in this definition that demand is not tantamount to a forecast. A **forecast** estimates the amount that will be sold during a specified period at a *particular price*—for example, we expect to sell 78,000 exercise machines this year at a price of $299. By comparison, demand is best thought of in terms of a **demand schedule,** which is the mapping of specific quantities onto specific prices: At a price of

Exhibit 12.7   Total Revenue for Concert

Price per Ticket	Number of Tickets	Total Revenue (TR)
$25.00	50,000	$1,250,000
30.00	45,000	1,350,000
35.00	41,000	1,435,000
37.50	40,000	1,500,000
42.50	30,000	1,275,000

P_1, Q_1 units will be sold; Q_2 will be sold at P_2; Q_3 at P_3 . . .; and Q_n at P_n. Typically, the relation between price and quantity demanded is inverse: The higher the price, the less the quantity demanded and vice versa.

A demand schedule when graphed, as in Exhibit 12.6, on page 404, becomes a demand curve. The hypothetical demand schedule and demand curve in Exhibit 12.6 assume that marketing research has been conducted to determine how many concert tickets will be sold by Ticketmaster for a Neal Young and Pearl Jam concert with a seating/standing capacity of 50,000.

As previously discussed, the shape of the demand curve depends on the market structure, whether pure competition, pure oligopoly, monopolistic competition, or pure monopoly. In pure competition, the curve is flat at the prevailing market price, or highly elastic; in pure oligopoly it is kinked at the prevailing market price—elastic above the price and inelastic below it; in pure monopoly the curve is vertical, or highly inelastic; and in monopolistic competition the curve typically is elastic due to the availability of acceptable alternatives.

Revenue and Cost Concepts

The price and quantity information contained in a demand schedule permits a price setter to calculate the revenue associated with each price under consideration. **Total revenue (TR)** simply equals the product of price times quantity, or $P \times Q$. Exhibit 12.7 presents revenue information for the hypothetical Neil Young and Pearl Jam concert.

Another very useful concept is that of marginal revenue. **Marginal revenue (MR)** is the change in total revenue associated

Exhibit 12.8   Revenue and Cost Figures Associated with John's Ticket Pricing

Price (P)	Quantity Sold (Q)	Total Revenue (TR)	Marginal Revenue (MR)	Total Cost (TC)	Marginal Cost (MC)	Total Profit (TR – TC)
$100	0	$0	—	$200	—	$–200
75	1	75	$75	205	$5	–135
70	2	140	65	210	5	–80
65	3	195	55	215	5	–20
60	4	240	45	220	5	20
55	5	275	35	225	5	50
50	6	300	25	230	5	70
45	7	315	15	235	5	80
40	8	320	5	240	5	80
35	9	315	–5	245	5	70
30	10	300	–15	250	5	50

with selling one additional unit. This can be stated in equation form as $\Delta TR / \Delta Q$, where ΔTR stands for change in total revenue and ΔQ represents a unit increase in quantity sold. We can best illustrate this concept with a simple illustration. Assume that John, an avid concert goer and ticket scalper,[33] purchased 10 tickets each at $20 to the Neil Young and Pearl Jam concert to resell at scalped prices. Based on his past experience in selling tickets at comparable concerts, John's best estimate of the quantities of tickets he can sell at various prices along with revenue and cost figures are as presented in Exhibit 12.8.

John's cost for all 20 tickets is $200. At a price of $100 he is unable to sell any tickets, thus suggesting he would suffer a loss of $200 if he were to stubbornly attempt to sell concert tickets at this price. In general, total cost (TC) consists of fixed costs plus variable costs; that is, TC = Fixed Costs + Variable Costs. By definition, **fixed costs (FC)** are costs that are fixed in total and invariant to the number of units sold. In this case, John has made an investment of $200 in purchasing 10 concert tickets. Whether he sells zero tickets or all 10, he still has incurred an expenditure of $200—his fixed cost. In addition to fixed costs, sellers also incur variable costs. **Variable costs (VC)** are cost items that vary in total depending on the number of units sold but are constant per unit. For example, in a box of Cheerios priced at $3.29 in a grocery store, there is an average labor cost of 19¢ per box and an average materials cost of 83¢ per box. These costs are basically fixed per unit but vary in total—the more boxes of Cheerios produced the higher the total variable costs.[34]

Returning to the concert illustration, let's assume that John pays a $5 FedEx mailing expense for each ticket he sells. This amount, $5, is John's variable cost associated with selling each additional ticket. Marginal cost is conceptually equivalent to the concept of marginal revenue. Specifically, **marginal cost (MC)** is the change in total cost associated with selling an additional item, or, in equation form, $MC = \Delta TC/\Delta Q$. In this illustration, marginal cost is a constant $5 per unit, because it is assumed that John's variable costs remain constant at $5. It is essential that you work carefully through Exhibit 12.8 to obtain a clear understanding of each revenue and cost component.

Profit Maximization and Marginal Analysis

In economic theory, the price setter's objective is to establish a price that will yield maximum profits. Although in reality other pricing goals (such as maintaining the status quo or maximizing sales and market share) predominate over profit maximization, it nonetheless is useful to explore this theoretical ideal before moving on to more practical matters. By definition, a profit maximizing price is one that yields higher profits than any other price. With profit defined as total revenue minus total cost ($TR - TC$), profit maximization occurs, of course, when the spread between TR and TC is the greatest, or, in graphical form, at the apex of the total profit curve.

Economists have provided a simple yet elegant rule for profit maximization. This rule states that the profit-maximizing price occurs at that price where the marginal revenue (MR) associated with that price is equal to the marginal cost (MC). In Exhibit 12.8, this occurs at a price of $40 per ticket (see the shaded area). At a price of $40 John will sell 8 tickets and earn a profit of $80. No other price will yield a higher profit, although it will be noted that an equal profit of $80 could also be earned by pricing the concert tickets at $45 each. Had John attempted to sell all 10 tickets at $100 (and had he stubbornly refused to budge off that price), he would have suffered a loss equal to the amount of his investment, $200. Had he sold tickets at the lowest conceivable price of $30, he would have earned only $50 in profit. But by pricing tickets at an intermediate level, $40, John will sell only 8 of the 10 tickets, but his profits are greatest at this price.

The logic and mathematics of marginal analysis establish that profits will be maximized at that price where $MR = MC$. Hence, if profit maximization is the pricing goal and if the price setter knows *a priori* (before the fact of setting prices and selling products) the exact demand schedule, then marginal analysis will assure the selection of a profit-maximizing price. The difficulty of knowing the exact demand schedule makes profit-maximizing pricing a theoretical ideal but a practical impossibility. (How, for example, would John in our concert-ticket example, know exactly how many tickets he could sell at each possible price before he actually attempts to sell the tickets at each of the prices under consideration?) It is for this reason that price setting in practice establishes prices with costs as the basis for price determination rather than profits. This is not to suggest that profits are a nonconsideration; the point, rather, is that it simply is more feasible to set prices that recover costs and yield a desired profit margin than it is to think in terms of maximizing profits.

◆ Cost-Based Determinants of Price

If price setters do not, as a matter of impracticality, set prices that maximize profits, then how is price setting accomplished? Before reading on, stop and imagine that you are a purchasing agent for an industrial firm or a buyer for a retailer. In this capacity you purchase a large quantity of a certain item that costs, say, $100 per unit. Your job is to price the item for resale to your customers. How would you set price?

Your instincts and/or prior business experience probably tell you that you would establish a price by adding a markup to your $100 cost. This markup would have to be sufficiently large to provide you with an adequate profit margin, but it could not be so large as to place you at a competitive disadvantage or prevent customers from wanting to purchase the item. And which costs would your markup have to cover: just the direct purchase cost, $100, or your total cost including some portion of the overhead associated with conducting your business? Price setting is simple to do—anyone can add a markup to a product's cost—but it is not simple to do well! The following sections will discuss tools that facilitate price setting and some of the procedures that are used.

What Price Is Needed to Just Break Even?

Businesses are interested in doing better than just breaking even, but a useful way to initiate the pricing task is to evaluate the breakeven point. Definitionally, breakeven occurs when total revenue equals total cost ($TR = TC$)—there is no profit but no loss either.

Mechanics of Breakeven Analysis   As earlier established, total cost (TC) equals the sum of fixed costs (F) plus variable costs (V). Variable costs equal the per unit variable cost (V) times the number of units sold (Q). Total revenue equals the product of price times quantity, $P \times Q$. Hence, $TR = TC$ is equivalent to the following equation:

$$PQ = F + V \times Q$$

Performing the simple algebra and solving for Q yields the breakeven point:

$$BEP_Q = F \div (P - V)$$

In other words, the selling quantity (Q) at which a firm breaks even (BEP_Q) is obtained simply by dividing fixed costs by the expected selling price (P) minus the per unit variable cost (V). The denominator in this equation ($P - V$) is called the **contribution margin,** or, in other words, the *per unit contribution* to the recovery of fixed costs.

Exhibit 12.9 graphically portrays the breakeven concept. It shows that the breakeven point occurs at the intersection of the total revenue (TR) and total cost curves (TC). At any quantity below the breakeven point a *loss* occurs, whereas at any quantity above that point a *profit* is experienced. Of course, the TR curve is based on the assumption of a fixed price, and the TC curve consists of total fixed costs and a constant per unit variable cost.

Consider the case of a regional manufacturer of deluxe, propane-gas barbecue grills. This manufacturer's cost accounting department has determined that the annual fixed costs to produce and market the product is $5,000,000. Included as fixed costs are elements such as executive salaries, plant and equipment overhead, costs to maintain a sales force, and advertising expenditures. The variable cost to produce and market each unit are estimated at $70. The firm is considering a selling price of $135 to retailers. The breakeven quantity is calculated as follows:

Exhibit 12.9   Graphical Portrayal of Breakeven Analysis

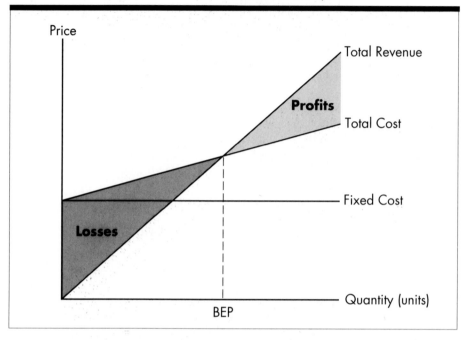

$$BEP_Q = F \div (P - V)$$
$$= \$5,000,000 \div (\$135 - \$70)$$
$$= 76,923 \text{ units}$$

At this quantity, the barbecue manufacturer would realize total revenue of $10,384,605 ($135 × 76,923) and identical total costs [$5,000,000 + ($70 × 76,923)], hence neither earning a profit nor incurring a loss. It should be noted that the breakeven point was calculated in units (BEP_Q = 76,923). When that quantity is multiplied by the selling price, it can be expressed as the breakeven point in dollars (i.e., $BEP_\$$ = $135 × 76,923 = $10,384,605).

Usefulness of Breakeven Analysis.   The usefulness of conducting a breakeven analysis is that it provides a reference point, or benchmark, against which the price setter can make some intelligent judgments, such as the following:

■ Let us assume that the grill manufacturer's sales and marketing personnel feel confident that substantially more than 76,923 grills—say 100,000 grills—will be sold at the contemplated price of $135. It thus directly follows that the company will earn a substantial profit—specifically, $3,115,395—inasmuch as every grill sold beyond 76,923 will contribute $135 to pretax profits.

- On the other hand, assume the company's sales and marketing personnel have serious doubts that 76,923 grills can be sold at a price of $135, because competitor's prices are somewhat lower. However, their experience and wisdom lead them to think that a price of $125 would be competitive. At this price, the breakeven quantity (BEP_Q) is 90,909 units [$5,000,000 ÷ ($125 − $70)]. If the decision makers believe the company can sell, say, 100,000 units at a price of $125, then the total pretax profit at this price would equal $1,136,375 (9091 units sold above the breakeven quantity each priced at $125).

It is important to recognize that breakeven analysis is not a technique for setting prices. It rather is an approach that enables a price setter to evaluate the profit consequences of different prices. As the above examples indicate, breakeven analysis provides a useful framework for initiating a series of what-if judgments: What are the profit consequences if we establish a particular price and sell a given quantity given knowledge of our fixed and variable costs?

Using Breakeven Analysis to Estimate Profitable Quantity.
A natural extension of the above comments is that breakeven analysis can be used to evaluate the pricing and quantity prospects of earning a desired profit. Suppose, for example, our barbecue grill manufacturer desired to earn a profit of $2,000,000 in the coming fiscal year and was considering a wholesale selling price of $135. Our breakeven equation would now be slightly altered to reflect the profit objective. With the symbol π (pi) representing a profit objective, our revised breakeven equation is

$$BEP_\pi = (F + \text{Profit Objective}) \div (P - V)$$
$$= (\$5,000,000 + \$2,000,000) \div (\$135 - \$70)$$
$$= 107,692 \text{ units}$$

Whereas it was necessary to sell 76,923 barbecue grills at a price of $135 just to recover fixed costs, the manufacturer will have to sell 107,692 units at $135 in order to recover fixed costs *and* earn a profit of $2,000,000. Only managerial experience and judgment can determine whether this is realistic. Nonetheless, the logic and method of breakeven analysis provides us with a useful framework for initiating price determination. Marketing managers should *always* conduct breakeven analyses as an initial pass at making a pricing decision. Moreover, rather than limiting the analysis to a single price, it is wise to consider different prices and different quantities that might be sold at these prices.

Cost-Plus and Markup Pricing

Despite the fact that price determination should be based on strategic considerations such as consumers' willingness to pay certain prices (consumer demand) and competitive price pressures, the most common approach used both by manufacturers and middlemen is some form of *cost-plus pricing*. The prevalence of this pricing approach is most likely due to the fact that (1) cost data are relatively easy to obtain compared to acquiring price-volume, or demand, data and (2) basing prices on cost has historically been considered "just" or "fair" to both buyer and seller.[35]

Pricing by Manufacturers.   The predominant form of cost-plus pricing used by manufacturers is known as target-return pricing. **Target-return pricing** is designed to provide the producer with a predetermined return on the *capital* that is invested in the production and marketing of products.[36] To illustrate this pricing method, consider the case of a manufacturer of golfing equipment. Our hypothetical manufacturer is especially well-known for its "Big Bomber" driver. The company has $80,000,000 invested in operating capital, and its objective is to earn a 30% target return on each product it produces.

Price determination when using target return pricing is based on the following equation:

$$\text{Price} = \text{Per unit cost} + \frac{(\text{Target return} \times \text{Capital})}{\text{Projected volume}}$$

where,

$\text{Price} = $ The manufacturer's selling price based on target-return pricing

Per unit cost = The sum of unit variable costs (labor and materials primarily) and fixed costs per unit (i.e., total fixed costs ÷ projected volume)

Target return = The desired profit rate expressed as a percent, which for the "Big Bomber" is 30%

Capital = Total assets involved in a product's production and marketing

Projected volume = Amount of product expected to be produced and sold over a number of years

Returning to the Big Bomber example, assume that the per unit cost equals $100 and that the projected volume of production and sales is 1,500,000 units. Applying the above equation, the selling price necessary to return 30% profit on the capital investment would be determined as follows:

$$\text{Price} = \text{Per unit cost} + \frac{(\text{Target return} \times \text{Capital})}{\text{Projected volume}}$$

$$= \$100 + (.3 \times \$80,000,000)/1,500,000$$
$$= \$116$$

The manufacturer's selling price to retailers (called the **wholesale selling price**) would thus be $116. This price would yield a return of 30% profit on invested capital provided that (1) the projected volume of 1,500,000 units is indeed realized and (2) per unit costs do not change.

Pricing by Retailers.

Retailers also typically price products based on adding a markup, or profit provision, to a product's cost. The amount of markup varies as a function of retailer cost, consumer demand, and intensity of competition, and, generally speaking, higher markups are taken when consumer demand is perceived as more inelastic and competition is less intense. Retailers of high-fashion merchandise, for example, often take very large markups, whereas supermarkets operate on very small markups.

To illustrate the role of markups in retail pricing, imagine that Nevada Bob's, a national chain of stores that resells golfing merchandise, purchases "Big Bomber" drivers at $116 each. How might Nevada Bob's establish a price (called a **retail selling price**) for these drivers? Based on extensive experience in understanding consumer behavior and with knowledge of how competitors would price "Big Bombers," Nevada Bob's would simply add a standard markup to its $116 invoice price to determine the selling price.

Markups, which are stated in percentage terms, are based either on a retailer's cost or on the selling price. Suppose, for example, that Nevada Bob's decides to sell the Big Bomber at $225. The dollar markup in this case is $109 ($225 – $116). With cost as the basis for the calculation, the percent markup is approximately 94% ($109 ÷ $116). However, with the selling price as the basis for the markup calculation, the percent markup is approximately 48% ($109 ÷ $225).

In general, **markup on cost** is calculated as

$$\text{Markup on cost} = \frac{\text{Selling price} - \text{Cost}}{\text{Cost}}$$

and, **markup on selling price** is

$$\text{Markup on selling price} = \frac{\text{Selling price} - \text{Cost}}{\text{Selling price}}$$

Either markup can be converted to the other by performing these simple calculations:

$$\text{Markup on cost} = \frac{\text{Markup on selling price}}{100\% - \text{Markup on selling price}}$$

$$\text{Markup on selling price} = \frac{\text{Markup on cost}}{100\% + \text{Markup on cost}}$$

When discussing markups, retailers typically refer to *markup on selling price* rather than markup on cost. A 50% markup (on selling price) is thus equivalent to a 100% markup on cost [.50/(1.00-.50) = 1, or, equivalently, 100%]. Similarly, a 25% markup on selling price is equal to a $33^1/_3\%$ markup on cost, and a $33^1/_3\%$ markup is equal to a 50% cost markup.

Retailers often use standard markups for related lines of merchandise. Assume, for example, that Nevada Bob's takes a 40%

markup on all golf clubs. It would determine the selling price for the "Big Bomber" using this straightforward calculation:

$$\begin{aligned} \text{Selling price} &= \text{Cost} \div (1 - \text{Markup}) \\ &= \$116 \div (1 - .4) \\ &= \$193.33 \end{aligned}$$

This price would probably be adjusted to a round number, $193, or perhaps expressed as an odd-numbered price such as $193.99. At markups of 50%, $33^{1}/3\%$, and 25%, the selling prices (rounded) for the "Big Bomber" would be $232, $174, and $155, respectively. (You should perform the calculations and convince yourself that these values are correct.)

Chapter Summary

Of all the marketing mix variables, price is the most dynamic, unique, and perhaps the most important. Price can be thought of as the amount that buyer and seller agree on to exchange a product or service for money or another product or service. There are a variety of terms for price, but by any name price represents an exchange rate.

From the consumer's perspective, price plays both negative and positive roles—negative in the sense that price represents an outlay of economic resources, but positive in the sense that consumers sometimes infer quality from prices: higher prices often suggest higher quality and better products. Research shows that consumers use price as a signal of product quality when risk reduction is important in making purchases, when objective quality is difficult to assess, when consumers lack expertise, and when they are relatively uninvolved in the purchase situation. Consumers use reference prices to judge product offerings. Products priced at levels that exceed the consumer's latitude of acceptance are subject to rejection.

Five sets of factors are considered by marketing managers when setting prices: demand, which sets a ceiling on the price that can be charged; costs, which set a floor; competitive factors, which act to reduce the price ceiling; marketing objectives, which establish financial requirements for product prices; and regulatory constraints and ethical considerations, which limit a price setter's discretion.

The type of market structure—whether pure competition, pure monopoly, oligopolistic, or monopolistic competitive—plays an important role in determining price elasticity and thus the price setter's pricing freedom. Price elasticity, which measures customer responsiveness to price changes, is highly elastic in pure competition, highly inelastic in pure monopoly, and varies from elastic to inelastic in monopolistically competitive and oligopolistic market structures. In the latter situation, the demand curve is presumed to be kinked at the prevailing market price such that price elasticity above the prevailing price is elastic and inelastic below the price. In either event, the price setter faces potential loss in total revenues when unilaterally increasing or decreasing prices.

Pricing legislation has been enacted to prevent four untoward pricing practices: (1) price fixing, (2) predatory pricing, (3) price discrimination, and (4) dumping. Some of the more notable legislative acts that prevent these practices are the Sherman Act, the Federal Trade Commission Act, the Clayton Act, and the Robinson-Patman Act. The latter act is particularly important in its efforts to prevent price discrimination. Charging unequal prices to competitive sellers is evidence of price discrimination, but the Robinson-Patman Act specifies situations when price discrimination is and is not unlawful.

In theory, prices should be set so that profits are maximized. Marginal analysis from economics provides a simple yet eloquent procedure for setting profit-maximizing prices. To use this approach, the price setter must determine marginal costs and marginal revenues associated with different price and quantity combinations. Then, a profit maximizing price is determined by identifying that price-quantity combination where marginal revenue equals marginal cost. In practice it is virtually impossible to construct demand schedules, and it is for this reason that profit-maximizing pricing is more a theoretical ideal than practical reality.

Price setting in practice depends more on cost estimation than on demand estimation. Prices typically are set by both manufacturers and retailers using some form of cost-plus pricing method. In the case of manufacturers, target return pricing is especially prevalent. This method requires the price setter to add a desired rate of return on invested capital to the full cost of producing and marketing a product. Retailers typically set prices by simply adding a markup to product cost or to the selling price. The markup represents an amount that is sufficient for recovering costs and returning an adequate profit. Breakeven analysis is an especially valuable tool for initiating the price-determination process. The breakeven point is achieved when the contemplated price yields no profit or loss.

Price setters can "play" with different prices and sales forecasts to identify a relevant range of pricing options.

Notes ◆

1. Vithala R. Rao and Joel H. Steckel, "A Cross-Cultural Analysis of Price Responses to Environmental Changes," *Marketing Letters,* 6, 1 (1995), 5–14.

2. Kent B. Monroe, *Pricing: Making Profitable Decisions,* 2nd ed. (New York: McGraw-Hill, 1990), 8.

3. Donald R. Lichtenstein, Nancy M. Ridgway, and Richard G. Netemeyer, "Price Perceptions and Consumer Shopping Behavior: A Field Study," *Journal of Marketing Research,* 30 (May 1993), 234.

4. Michael V. Marn and Robert L. Rosiello, "Managing Price, Gaining Profit," *Harvard Business Review,* 70 (September/October 1992), 84.

5. Monroe, *Pricing,* 7.

6. Bruce Smith, "High-Tech Bartering Is Growing Industry," *The State,* September 10, 1994, B8.

7. Lichtenstein, Ridgway, and Netemeyer, "Price Perceptions and Consumer Shopping Behavior."

8. This summary is provided by Niraj Dawar and Philip Parker, "Marketing Universals: Consumers' Use of Brand Name, Price, Physical Appearance, and Retailer Reputation as Signals of Product Quality," *Journal of Marketing,* 58 (April 1994), 81–95. For further discussion, see also Valarie A. Zeithaml, "Consumer Perceptions of Price, Quality, and Value: A Means-End Model and Synthesis of Evidence," *Journal of Marketing,* 52 (July 1988), 2–22; William B. Dodds, Kent B. Monroe, and Dhruv Grewal, "Effects of Price, Brand, and Store Information on Buyers' Product Evaluations," *Journal of Marketing Research,* 28 (August 1991), 307–319.

9. Compare, for example, Zeithaml, "Consumer Perceptions of Price, Quality, and Value" and Dodds et al. "Effects of Price, Brand, and Store Information on Buyers' Product Evaluations."

10. Dawar and Parker, "Marketing Universals: Consumers' Use of Brand Name, Price, Physical Appearance, and Retailer Reputation as Signals of Product Quality."

11. Robert Jacobson and Carl Obermiller, "The Formation of Expected Future Price: A Reference Price for Forward-Looking Consumers," *Journal of Consumer Research*, 16 (March 1990), 421.

12. Glenn E. Mayhew and Russell S. Winer, "An Empirical Analysis of Internal and External Reference Prices Using Scanner Data," *Journal of Consumer Research*, 19 (June 1992), 62–70.

13. For example, Donald R. Lichtenstein and William O. Bearden, "Contextual Influences on Perceptions of Merchant-Supplied Reference Prices," *Journal of Consumer Research*, 16 (June 1989), 55–66; K. N. Rajendran and Gerard J. Tellis, "Contextual and Temporal Components of Reference Price," *Journal of Marketing*, 58 (January 1994), 22–34; Joel E. Urbany, William O. Bearden, and Dan C. Weilbaker, "The Effect of Plausible and Exaggerated Reference Prices on Consumer Perceptions and Price Search," *Journal of Consumer Research*, 13 (September 1986), 250–256.

14. Gurumurthy Kalyanaram and John D. C. Little, "An Empirical Analysis of Latitude of Price Acceptance in Consumer Packaged Goods," *Journal of Consumer Research*, 21 (December 1994), 408–418. It must be emphasized that these conclusions are based on findings from only two product categories, sweetened and unsweetened drinks. It is likely that the findings are generalizable to a broader range of, at least, consumer packaged goods, but this remains an empirical question.

15. This point and the following recommendation are from Kalyanaram and Little, 416.

16. Adapted from Monroe, *Pricing*, 12–13.

17. Rao and Steckel, "A Cross-Cultural Analysis of Price Responses to Environmental Changes."

18. Eben Shapiro, "Minnesota Mining's Wool Pads Grab Sizable Chunk of Business," *The Wall Street Journal*, January 13, 1994, B6.

19. The assumption that market share is a powerful determinant of firm profitability has been challenged. See in particular Robert Jacobson and David A. Aaker, "Is Market Share All That It's Cracked Up To Be?" *Journal of Marketing*, 49 (Fall 1985), 11–22.

20. Monroe, *Pricing*.

21. The strange word, oligopoly, emanates from Greek oligo, meaning few or little.

22. This discussion presents the classic argument regarding oligopolistic pricing, but the explanation's ability to predict actual price behavior is not undisputed. For an interesting discussion and study on this matter, see Peter R. Dickson and Joel E. Urbany, "Retailer Reactions to Competitive Price Changes," *Journal of Retailing*, 70, 1 (1994), 1–21.

23. Leah Rickard, "Snakelike," *Advertising Age*, June 26, 1995, S–2.

24. Price fixing takes various forms. For discussion, see Dorothy Cohen, *Legal Issues in Marketing Decision Making* (Cincinnati, OH: South-Western, 1995), 221–222.

25. The first case is described in "Legal Developments in Marketing," *Journal of Marketing*, 49 (Fall 1985), 117; the second case appears in "Legal Developments in Marketing," *Journal of Marketing*, 57 (April 1993), 109.

26. "Beating the High Cost of Cereal," *Consumer Reports*, July 1995, 446; Brigid Schulte, "Lawmakers Put Crunch on Pricing of Cereals," *The State*, March 8, 1995, B1.

27. Mary Jane Sheffet, "The Supreme Court and Predatory Pricing," *Journal of Public Policy and Marketing*, 13 (Spring 1994), 163–167.

28. Cohen, *Legal Issues in Marketing*, 238–239.

29. Cohen, 252.

30. "What Price Beauty?" *Consumer Reports*, July 1995, 455.

31. Donald P. Robin and R. Eric Reidenbach, "Social Responsibility, Ethics, and Marketing Strategy: Closing the Gap between Concept and Application," *Journal of Marketing*, 51 (January 1987), 44–58.

32. Based on Gene R. Laczniak and Patrick E. Murphy, "Fostering Ethical Marketing Decisions," *Journal of Business Ethics*, 10 (1991), 264.

33. Scalping occurs when a person sells tickets at a price above the face-value of the ticket. In some states scalping is illegal but nonetheless widely practiced.

34. The labor and material costs for Cheerios are based on "Beating the High Cost of Cereal," *Consumer Reports*, July 1995, 446.

35. Monroe, *Pricing*, 143.

36. Monroe, 239.

◼ Study Questions

1. Which of the following statements is false regarding price?
   a. Price represents an exchange rate.
   b. A product's price represents a *quid pro quo* between buyer and seller.
   c. Prices always are quoted and charged in monetary terms.
   d. None of the above are false.

2. Price is likely to be used by consumers as an indicator, or signal, of product quality in all of the following situations except statement _____.
   a. The consumer feels a need to reduce perceived purchase risk by selecting a brand that is of sufficient quality.
   b. Objective product quality is easy for consumers to assess.
   c. Consumers lack the ability to assess objective quality.
   d. Consumers are relatively uninvolved in the purchase situation.

3. Which of the following is true regarding reference prices?
   a. Internal reference prices are stored in the consumer's memory and are based on knowledge about prices in a particular product category.
   b. Internal reference prices refer to price information possessed by and protected by retailers and other marketing intermediaries.
   c. External reference prices are stored in the consumer's memory and are based on knowledge about prices in a particular product category.
   d. Consumers who are frequent purchasers in a product category possess an especially wide range of price acceptability.

4. Which of the following is *not* a recognized pricing objective?
   a. Cash flow and survival.
   b. Profit maximization.
   c. Target return on investment.
   d. Breakeven analysis.

5. At an initial price (P_1) of $10, a firm sold 1,000 units (Q_1) of Product X. At an increased price (P_2) of $12, the firm sold 900 units (Q_2) of Product X. Price elasticity in this situation is _____.

a. elastic
b. inelastic
c. unitary
d. both elastic and inelastic

6. At an initial price (P_1) of \$10, a firm sold 1,000 units (Q_1) of Product X. At an increased price (P_2) of \$12, the firm sold 700 units (Q_2) of Product X. Price elasticity in this situation is

_____.

a. elastic
b. inelastic
c. unitary
d. both elastic and inelastic

7. The kinked demand curve represents which market structure?
a. pure competition
b. pure monopoly
c. monopolistic competition
d. oligopoly

8. Which of the following statements is false regarding elasticity of demand?
a. The demand curve in pure competition is perfectly elastic.
b. The demand curve in a pure monopoly is perfectly inelastic.
c. When price elasticity is elastic, an increase in price will result in an increase in total revenue.
d. When price elasticity is inelastic, an increase in price will result in an increase in total revenue.

9. When two or more companies collude in some fashion to artificially maintain or set prices, this is called _____.
a. dumping
b. predatory pricing
c. price fixing
d. monopolistic activity

10. When a firm sets a price in the short-term that is below its cost only later to raise its price to a very high level and earn exorbitant profits, this is called _____.
a. dumping
b. predatory pricing
c. price fixing
d. monopolistic activity

11. The _____ Act is the primary legislation that is applied in cases of price discrimination.
    a. Sherman
    b. Robinson-Patman
    c. Miller-Tydings
    d. Federal Trade Commission

12. There are various situations where charging different prices to competitive customers is legally permissible and not in violation of price-discrimination legislation. Which is not one of these?
    a. There is no harm to competition.
    b. The price setter needs to charge differential prices in order to maximize its profits.
    c. Differential prices are charged to match a competitor's lower prices.
    d. Changes in interim market conditions justify charging differential prices.

13. Which of the following statements is incorrect regarding cost concepts?
    a. Variable costs are fixed in total but variable per unit.
    b. Fixed costs are fixed in total but variable per unit.
    c. Marginal revenue is the change in total revenue associated with selling an additional item.
    d. Marginal cost is the change in total cost associated with selling an additional item.

14. The rule for profit maximization is
    a. increase prices until costs go down.
    b. set prices at the particular price-quantity combination where total revenue equals total cost.
    c. set prices at the particular price-quantity combination where total revenue is just slightly less than total cost.
    d. set prices at the particular price-quantity combination where marginal revenue is equal to marginal cost.

15. A firm's fixed cost for a particular product is $5,000,000. Its unit variable cost is $10. With a contemplated price of $15, how many units must be sold for the firm to break even?
    a. 100,000
    b. 20,000,000
    c. 1,000,000
    d. Not enough information is provided to perform a breakeven calculation.

16. The breakeven amount expressed in dollars in the previous question is
    a. $1,500,000.
    b. $35,000,000.
    c. $15,000,000.
    d. It cannot be determined due to insufficient information.

17. A retailer purchases an umbrella for $7 and sells it for $12. The markup on selling price in this case is
    a. approximately 71%.
    b. 140%.
    c. approximately 42%.
    d. 240%.

18. If a retailer's markup on selling price is 35%, the equivalent markup on cost is
    a. approximately 25%.
    b. approximately 54%.
    c. approximately 75%.
    d. approximately 46%.

CHAPTER **13**

Pricing Strategies
and Approaches

Chapter Objectives

Overview

New-Product Pricing Strategy

Price-Flexibility Strategy

Discount and Allowance Strategies

Product-Line Pricing Strategies

Psychological Pricing Strategies

Geographic Pricing Strategies

Bid-Pricing Strategies

Chapter Summary

◼ Overview

The previous chapter explored fundamental pricing concepts and general aspects of price determination. Primary focus was on the issue of how price setters establish an overall, or *base*, price for their products and services. The present chapter demonstrates that a number of additional pricing decisions are required in response to anticipated events and changing marketplace conditions. In this chapter we categorize these decisions under seven sets of pricing strategies. Each is labeled a pricing *strategy* to capture the idea that the price setter has (or should have) a specific plan or method in mind when setting prices so as to achieve a desired goal or result. The following strategies are discussed:

- New-product pricing strategy
- Price-flexibility strategy
- Discount and allowance strategies
- Product-line pricing strategies
- Psychological pricing strategies
- Geographic pricing strategies
- Bid-pricing strategies

◼ New-Product Pricing Strategy

Situation: A company is prepared to introduce a new product. The new product may be nothing more than another brand in an established product category or it may represent, at the extreme, a new-to-the-world product—something heretofore unavailable to business-to-business users or ultimate consumers. *Question*: How should the product be priced?

In the case of the new brand, or *imitative product*, the price setter is largely constrained by competitive prices. It would be difficult to charge higher prices than those charged by competitors unless the new brand is demonstrably superior. Lower prices can be charged if the firm chooses to compete on the basis of value. More often than not, a middle-of-the-road strategy is used whereby the price setter prices the new brand at parity with established brands and competes by attempting to establish a desirable positioning or image for the new brand.

Pricing strategies for truly *innovative, or pioneering, products* are particularly interesting. In this situation the price setter has greater pricing latitude inasmuch as the new product has, at the time of introduction, no direct competition. Over time, the "seller's zone of pricing discretion narrows as his distinctive 'specialty' fades into a pedestrian 'commodity' which is so little differentiated from other products that the seller has limited independence in pricing, even if rivals are few."[1] Two general pricing strategies are available to the product pioneer: skimming or penetration prices.

The Strategy of Price Skimming

A **skimming price** is a strategic option for innovative products that couple relatively *high prices* with heavy promotional expenditures. Several reasons for price skimming follow:[2] (1) price elasticity is relatively *inelastic* in the early stages of a truly innovative product; (2) a relatively high price enables the product pioneer to *skim the cream* of the early-purchase segment—that is, "product innovators" and "early adopters" (see Chapter 9)—who are particularly price insensitive; (3) high initial prices enable the innovator to recoup quickly the heavy investment in the new product.

As you know from personal experience, innovative products that are introduced with skimming prices invariably fall in price over the course of their life cycles. VCRs, compact disc players, cellular phones, and multimedia computers are just a few of the products that are much less expensive now than when they were introduced.

The Strategy of Price Penetration

Comparatively, a **penetration price** involves the use of relatively *low prices* as the means for rapidly penetrating the mass market. A penetration price is most warranted when (1) the price setter senses a strong threat of *imminent competition*, (2) there is a *substantial reduction in production costs* to be realized by virtue of greater volume, and (3) price elasticity is relatively *elastic*.[3] Easily imitated products most justify penetration pricing. The product innovator can, by introducing a product at a relatively low price, dissuade competitors from rapidly entering the market or entering at all. Potential competitors know that they will have to price their brands at low prices and also have to engage in aggressive promotion in order to compete against the entrenched innovator.

◆ Price-Flexibility Strategy

Should a business—whether it be a manufacturer, service provider, or retailer—charge all customers the identical price or should prices be flexed, or adjusted, to accommodate the specifics of the situation? As typically is the case, there are no simple or pat answers. Circumstances (economic factors, competitive conditions, legal boundaries, and ethical considerations) influence, if not dictate, what should and can be done.

To intelligently discuss this issue, we first need to understand what charging one price to all customers means versus charging flexible prices to different customers. At the level of retail pricing, this is a straightforward matter: a one-price strategy is in effect if all consumers pay the same amount to acquire the identical item; on the other hand, a flexible-price strategy is operative if different consumers obtain different prices. This issue is discussed subsequently in context of price haggling.

Manufacturers' Price Flexing

From the manufacturer's perspective, the issue of one-price versus flexible-price strategy is more complicated because in addition to the base, or list, price, manufacturers also employ a variety of discounts and allowances in pricing their products. Whereas a manufacturer may charge the same list price to all customers, different discounts and allowances are provided in recognition of differential circumstances across buying situations. In other words, manufacturers often adopt a **flexible-price strategy** by varying the discounts and allowances on a transactional basis. The list price charged by a manufacturer does not reflect the true *transaction amount* (that is, the actual out-of-pocket price paid by a customer) because a host of pricing discounts and allowances are necessitated by the economics and pragmatics of the transaction.[4] These include prompt-payment discounts, quantity discounts, advertising allowances, and transportation discounts.

Manufacturers typically flex the transaction amount as dictated by circumstances. The makers of Wrangler jeans offer a quantity discount to Wal-Mart due to this retail giant's buying power. A small retailer pays the same list price as Wal-Mart when purchasing the identical pair of Wrangler jeans, but the economics in this instance do not justify its receiving the quantity discount extended to Wal-Mart. Procter & Gamble, Lever Brothers, Johnson & Johnson, Pillsbury, and hundreds of other consumer-goods manufacturers flex their prices by extending advertising and display allowances to some retailers, but not others, so as to increase retailer promotional and display support for the manufacturer's brands.

The point should be clear: Manufacturers routinely flex prices to accommodate the circumstances of the particular purchase transaction. However, manufacturers do not have complete pricing discretion. The Robinson-Patman Act, as discussed in the previous chapter, places limits on when manufacturers can charge differential prices. Aside from legality considerations, manufacturers should carefully study their pricing practices to assure that the effect of offering discounts and allowances is not one of diluting profits.[5]

Retailer Price Flexing

Price flexing takes on a slightly different form at the level of retail pricing. As noted in the previous chapter, retailers are not subject to Robinson-Patman violations when charging variable prices to different customers. The retailer's price flexing is limited only by ethical and pragmatic considerations. In many lines of retail business, the identical price is charged to all customers. Price flexing is a non-consideration. Can you imagine, for example, a supermarket charging different prices to different customers?

Many other retailers do charge uneven prices. A bank may charge some customers a fee for certain services but extend a no-charge privilege to large-account customers—a practice somewhat akin to a manufacturer's providing quantity discounts. A carpet dealer will negotiate prices, charging some customers lower per-yard prices than other customers receive. Automobile dealers are particularly well-known for flexing prices: the "sticker" price sets the price ceiling; the retailer's cost sets the price floor; and the price the consumer actually pays is determined by his or her negotiating (haggling) ability and the dealer's desire or need at the moment to sell a particular automobile.

Haggling is commonplace practice throughout most of the world. Haggling is most likely under these circumstances:[6]

1. Consumers' prior purchasing experiences have provided them with a reference point of what the fair price should be.
2. The asking price is perceived as unreasonable.
3. Prices are known to differ among sellers, thus providing the consumer with haggling leverage.
4. Quality differs or is perceived as differing among the goods offered by competitive merchants.

These conditions largely prevail in the automotive industry where haggling has become a tradition. The Saturn Corporation introduced a dramatic shift, however, when it introduced a no-haggle, one-price policy. The director of consumer marketing for Saturn claims that this policy is merely the last step of an entire selling philosophy that treats the customer with respect.[7] According to a study by an automotive industry research firm, J.D. Power and Associates, about 10% of the 15,000 U.S. auto dealers use some form of no-haggle pricing. A survey of consumers revealed that slightly over one-half actually enjoy negotiating price, whereas about one-third like to avoid haggling.[8]

In sum, price setters (manufacturers as well as retailers) generally would prefer, as a matter of administrative convenience, to charge all customers the same price. But competitive factors and economic circumstances often dictate charging flexible prices.

◆ Discount and Allowance Strategies

The previous section emphasized that the net, or "pocket," prices that customers pay are frequently lower than the seller's base, or list, price. This is because a variety of discount and allowance strategies have evolved in commerce to induce desired actions from buyers and/or to reward them for having taken certain actions. A **discount** is a percentage reduction from the seller's list price, whereas an **allowance** is a payment to the buyer for providing a service to the seller or for trading in a product.

Discounts and allowances are offered for exchanges at different points throughout the channel of distribution; however, our discussion focuses primarily on two levels of channel exchanges: (1) from manufacturers to the trade (wholesalers and retailers) and (2) from retailers to consumers. Following sections are devoted to the discounts and allowances listed in Exhibit 13.1.

Exhibit 13.1   Common Types of Discounts and Allowances

From Manufacturers to the Trade

1. Functional, or trade, discounts
2. Quantity discounts
3. Seasonal discounts
4. Cash discounts
5. Sales promotion allowances

From Retailers to Consumers

1. Trade-in allowances
2. Cash discounts
3. Rebates

Functional (Trade) Discounts

Wholesalers and retailers (the trade) perform functions for the manufacturers whose products they handle. Wholesalers play a particularly important role in stocking products, sometimes financing retailer purchases, promoting products to retailers, and incurring risks attendant to performing the other functions (e.g., being unable to sell some products). Retailers also perform valuable functions such as stocking merchandise, advertising that fact, and financing consumers. **Functional discounts** compensate the trade for functions performed. You may recall a discussion back in Chapter 10 on the topic of channels of distribution where it was claimed that "marketing functions can be shifted or shared but they cannot be eliminated." At this time we can expand that assertion by stating that when manufacturers shift functions, it is necessary to compensate the trade for the services they render.

Functional discounts for retailers and wholesalers typically are quoted in conjunction with one another. For example, a manufacturer of hardware products offers a 25% discount to retailers and then an additional 10% discount to wholesalers. Hence, on direct sales to retailers, this manufacturer's price on a $10 item is $7.50

($10 less 25% discount). When selling through wholesalers, however, the price is $6.75 because, for the extra functions performed, the wholesaler receives a 10 percent discount on top of the 25% discount offered to retailers. Hence, the net price of $6.75 results from the wholesaler receiving a 25% discount from the $10 list price and an additional 10% discount ($10 – $2.50 = $7.50 – $0.75 = $6.75). The 75¢ differential between the price retailers pay ($7.50) and the price wholesalers pay ($6.75) is the gross profit margin available to wholesalers when reselling to retailers.

Quantity Discounts

Manufacturers offer quantity discounts to induce larger-quantity purchases and to reward customers for making fewer purchases but purchasing in larger quantities. When customers purchase in larger quantities, manufacturers generally incur lower total handling, shipping, and clerical expenses. Moreover, by encouraging larger-quantity purchasing, a manufacturer effectively prevents competitors from getting the customer's business during that period when the customer has sufficient stock in inventory. **Quantity discounts**, which are percent discounts from the list price for purchases in excess of specified quantities, are economically justified due to the cost savings obtained. There are two forms of quantity discounts: noncumulative and cumulative discounts.

Noncumulative Quantity Discounts.   A **noncumulative quantity discount** bases the discount on *individual orders*. Customers receive a quantity discount only if their order quantity or dollar amount meets or exceeds a specified minimal level. The hardware manufacturer in the above illustration gives quantity discounts of 5% for all orders exceeding $1,000. Hence, if a customer placed an order for $1,500 of hardware, it would deduct $75 from the invoice amount and remit payment of $1,425.

Cumulative Quantity Discounts.   A **cumulative quantity discount** bases the discount *not* on individual orders but on the cumulative quantity purchased during a specified period, which usually is a year. For example, this same hardware manufacturer would offer a 5% discount if orders during the next year exceed $10,000. A customer purchasing, say, $12,000 of hardware would receive a rebate of $600 from the hardware manufacturer.

Cumulative quantity discounts encourage customer loyalty and relationship building between seller and buyer.

Seasonal Discounts

The **seasonal discount** is a pricing mechanism that permits manufacturers of seasonal merchandise to maintain steady production and seasonal service providers (e.g., resort hotels) to sustain operations during out-of-season lulls. In offering seasonal discounts, the seller wishes to acquire liquid assets (cash and accounts receivable) and to shift the function of inventory maintenance and its associated risk to buyers. Buyers can be induced to purchase seasonal merchandise only if the discount adequately compensates them for the risk assumed and the added expenses incurred. Hardware wholesalers and retailers would be willing to purchase snow-removal products in May only if manufacturers of these products offer substantial price reductions from the normal list prices. Producers of fashion products such as clothing must offer especially attractive seasonal discounts because retailers cannot be sure that clothing items will remain popular next season.

Cash Discounts

Cash discounts are used to encourage prompt payment from customers. Invoices include payment terms regarding the period of time in which the buyer must pay the seller for the invoiced amount. A standard term of payment is "2% 10, net 30." Assume, for example, that a retailer places an order from "our" hardware manufacturer totaling $2,250 and that the invoice date is July 10. The above payment terms signify that the buyer has until August 9 (i.e., within 30 days) to remit the full amount of $2,250 to the hardware manufacturer, but that if the retailer makes payment by July 20 (within 10 days of July 10) a 2% discount, or $45, can be deducted from the invoice.

Sales Promotion Allowances

The topic of sales promotions is covered in detail in Chapters 14 and 15 with the latter chapter devoting considerable discussion to various

MARKETING HIGHLIGHTS

The Price Is Right

Ask consumers if they want multimedia electronic gear, and many will say yes. But then ask the tough question: How much will they pay for it?

That's the question that confronts the makers of multimedia equipment: computers that combine audio, video, graphics, and text; and high-definition televisions, which will offer sharper resolution and a gateway to interactive services.

If history is any guide, household media appliances that merely entertain don't command big-ticket prices, no matter how dazzling the technology. For instance, compact-disk players and videocassette recorders didn't start to sell fast until prices averaged below $400. And one video-game player is wildly popular at $150, but another model that offers richer graphics flops at $650.

Personal computers for home use became a mass-market item at a higher price—about $2,000—but they promised to do many new things. Owners could, at least in theory, catch up on their office work, broaden their kids' educational horizons, and balance their checkbooks. Many consumers ended up using them just to play games and process words, but the perceived utility of the machines was, and is, immense.

Multimedia equipment seems to be following a similar pattern. PCs equipped with CD-ROM drives, sound boards, and speakers have already become well established. As with regular PCs, the $2,000 price has proved a powerful lure. When the multimedia machines were introduced at an average price of $4,500 in 1988, sales were anemic. They barely picked up, to 87,000 units, when prices fell to $2,500 in 1992. But last year, as prices fell to $2,000, multimedia PC sales erupted to 1.7 million units, according to Dataquest Inc., a San Jose, California, market-research firm.

The systems are being snapped up mostly by home, rather than business, users. "In the consumer market, you have to hit certain price bands to be successful," say Bruce Ryon, Dataquest's multi-media analyst. "Price has to come first, and features are next. In the business market, it's the other way around."

Multimedia computers have invaded homes for the same reason they have stayed out of offices: entertainment value. The soft side of the technology—the elements of movement, sound, and color—doesn't translate into obvious productivity gains in the workplace. Now that price isn't as much of a deterrent for consumers, shipments are expected to more than double by 1996, to 3.8 million units.

WILL PEOPLE PAY?

High-definition televisions, which won't reach the market until 1996, face a much higher hurdle. Despite all the talk of 500 channels, movies-on-demand and electronic shopping, the question remains: Will consumers plunk down $3,500 to $5,000 for a television, at least initially, when they're used to paying only several hundred dollars?

"Companies are spending a lot of money on [HDTV development] that is very speculative," says Byron Reeves, a professor in the communications department at Stanford University.

"How long will [consumer acceptance] take and how much will prices come down is the No. 1 question in terms of who wins and who loses."

Robert Rast, vice president of HDTV business development at General Instrument Inc. in Chicago, adds, "The challenge of the business is, can we get down to $2,000 by the year 2000?"

Companies are counting on consumers being willing to shell out a lot more money for HDTV than current TV sets because they believe people will consider televisions even more important in the interactive era. HDTV sets are being designed from the outset to be information as well as entertainment appliances, gateways that will be capable of downloading custom services, such as electronic messages, databases and movies-on-demand. And they will permit two-way communications, such as selecting merchandise and even trying on clothes through a surrogate persona, or "agent."

"The TV set will be a communicator out into the world, an electronic marketplace," says Marc Porat, chairman and chief executive of General Magic Inc., a software consortium in Mountain View, California.

There's one problem: Television and computer companies are developing set-top boxes that will allow conventional TVs to do most of those same things. And history says consumers won't pay $2,000 for an appliance that doesn't offer added functionality.

'TV ON STEROIDS'

But HDTV fans say that as consumers get hooked on all the new activities, and as they see the much-higher quality of HDTV, they will consider the new sets a necessity, even at $2,000.

"This is a TV picture on steroids," says John Taylor, a spokesman for Zenith Electronics Corp., Glenview, Illinois. "It's like looking through a highly polished window." The screens will be larger than most and horizontal, as in movie theaters. Add a sound system that virtually envelops the viewer, and today's color set soon begins to seem like yesterday's black-and-white.

Undoubtedly, the transition will strain the pocketbooks of most consumers. Moreover, as with cellular phones and on-line data networks, high monthly service charges are apt to discourage use.

But service subsidies may emerge. For example, merchants could help consumers defray the cost of plugging in to the marketplace through electronic coupons and frequent-buyer programs, Mr. Porat says.

"In aggregate, consumers are close to reaching a saturation for their time budget and financial budget," he says. The electronic marketplace "is an expansion of that pie. It gives consumers a method of funding their high-tech TV. They won't be buying it for the better picture or the sound, but as a method of sending an agent into the world of electronic merchants."

Source: Ralph T. King, Jr., "The Price Is Right," *The Wall Street Journal*, March 21, 1994, R19. Reprinted by permission of *The Wall Street Journal*, © 1994 Dow Jones & Company, Inc. All rights reserved worldwide.

forms of allowances. Suffice it to say at the present time that manufacturers offer wholesalers and retailers a variety of promotional inducements, most of which are some form of allowance. **Off-invoice allowances**, the most widely used form of trade-oriented sales promotion, are deals offered periodically that allow the trade to deduct a fixed amount, say 15%, from the full price. These allowances are designed to encourage greater purchasing of the manufacturer's brands. **Bill-back allowances** are offered as payment to retailers for featuring the manufacturer's brands in advertisements or for providing special display space. **Slotting allowances** are paid to retailers to induce their carrying new products offered by the manufacturer. Chapter 15 provides complete descriptions of these practices and also discusses everyday low pricing (EDLP) by grocery manufacturers to overcome problems stemming from the excessive use of these allowances.

Consumer Allowances, Discounts, and Rebates

Just as manufacturers offer discounts to retailers and wholesalers, retailers also offer a variety of allowances, discounts, and rebates to induce desired actions from consumers. **Trade-in allowances** are offered to encourage consumers to upgrade to newer and more expensive products. **Seasonal discounts** are also offered to consumers. For example, hotels located at beach or ski resorts must offer attractive discounts to gain business during off-season times. In pure economic terms, a hotel is financially better off to remain open during the off-season so long as its rates recover variable costs and contribute some return to fixed expenses even if it does not make a profit. **Age-based discounts** are offered to special groups, especially children and senior citizens. Senior citizens, for example, often receive discounts for attending entertainment events and using recreational facilities. **Rebates** are provided when after purchasing a product consumers are invited to submit a proof-of-purchase indicator to the manufacturer, who remits payment at a later date.

◈ Product-Line Pricing Strategies

Manufacturers often produce multiple products in the same product category with each having its own brand name. Clothing manufacturers, for example, produce different qualities of suits. The well-know men's clothing manufacturer, HartMarx, manufactures and markets three suit lines: Its best suits are sold under the Hickey Freeman label; the next line is the Hart, Schaffener, and Marx brand; and the least expensive label is the Austin Reed line.

Furniture manufacturers, appliance makers, carpet producers, sports shoe manufacturers, and hardware producers are just a few of the companies that produce multiple levels of product quality. Retailers naturally merchandise multiple product-quality levels in the same category. Clothiers, for example, typically merchandise multiple suit lines at price points such as $299, $399, $599, and $799. Their ties are sold at price points such as $24.95, $29.95, $39.95, and $49.95. Carpet stores carry different grades of carpeting at price points such as $7.99, $11.99, $15.99, and $18.99 per square yard. This practice of producing or merchandising multiple products at different price points is called **price lining**. In many industries the price points are well-established, and competitors charge similar prices.

The Price-Line Pricing Issue

Because customers are differentially responsive to product quality, price, and value, manufacturers produce multiple versions of the same product and retailers merchandise different quality levels in the same product category. The pricing issue faced both by manufacturers and retailers when practicing price lining is one of whether to price each product in a line *separately* on the basis of its own cost, demand, and competitive characteristics or to *jointly* price the multiple products in recognition of the overall image that the firm wishes to convey and the interrelated demand, or *cross elasticity*, between the products.[9] Because the various products in a line are somewhat *substitutable*—that is, a price change for one product influences the quantity demanded of another product in the line—price setters must take this factor into consideration when pricing their multiple products. It typically is nonoptimal to price each product as if it were a separate, independent entity. Firms that are organized in a manner such that multiple related products are managed as a "team" rather than individually (e.g., a *category management* structure) should realize greater profits as a result of the ability to price products with recognition of their joint costs and interrelated demand.[10]

The Practice of Bundling

A variant of product-line pricing is price bundling. **Bundling** is "the practice of marketing two or more products and/or services in a single 'package' for a special price."[11] For example,

- Fast-food restaurants offer meals where a sandwich, fries, and drink are bundled into an overall price that is less than the combined price of the individual items.

- Vacation packages are offered by hotels and air carriers that unitize, or bundle, the price of the flight, accommodations, and perhaps an entertainment deal such as skiing or golf.

- This text includes a traditional book and two CD-ROM discs, which collectively represent a bundle of learning components priced at a single competitive price.

- Cable TV companies offer packaged deals on basic service plus access to multiple movie and sports stations at bundled prices.

- Banks bundle their services by giving preferred customers free checking and other services if they maintain a certain amount in their savings accounts.

The objective of price bundling is to enable a firm (or a coalition of firms, such as an airline and a resort) to increase overall profits while achieving cost economies. Managers are forced to focus on the entire product line when using price bundling and to carefully evaluate the benefits each product and various combinations of products provide to market segments that vary in terms of quality, price, and value sensitivity.[12] Because consumers perceive distinct savings when purchasing bundled merchandise and marketers increase overall profits when they bundle the right combination of items and set the right price, bundling is a growing practice that has virtually no limits in the marketing of products and services.[13]

◼ Psychological Pricing Strategies

The psychology of pricing was alluded to above when discussing price lining and bundling, but in this section we introduce additional psychological pricing practices. Although many aspects of price decision making involve calculated and systematic appraisals of product costs and demand economies, the successful price setter—in addition to being an applied accountant and an econo-mist—must also have the blood of the psychologist running through his or her veins. The price of a product or service is more than just an economic exchange mechanism; price also conveys notions of product quality, value, and getting a deal or, alternative-ly, being exploited. In the previous chapter we discussed the price-imputed quality relation and also the role of reference prices. Three psychological-based pricing practices—prestige pricing, odd-even pricing, and loss-leader pricing—are now reviewed.

Prestige Pricing

In the previous chapter it was noted that the relationship between price and quantity demanded typically is assumed to be inverse—less quantity is demanded at higher prices. There are exceptions to this general case. Price setters sometimes price their products or ser-vices at relatively high levels so as to convey an image of high qual-ity and perhaps also snobbishness, or exclusivity. Premium-priced brands are found in most every product category including lingerie, perfumes, liquors, and cigars to name just a few. This is the practice of **prestige pricing**. Higher prices are used to signal higher quality when consumers have difficulty in assessing objective quality and when they have a need to reduce the various risks (financial or psy-chological) that accompany faulty purchase decisions.

It should be clear that the mere fact of charging a relatively high price is not tantamount to the practice of prestige pricing. High prices often simply reflect the high costs associated with producing and marketing products. Rather, prestige pricing involves a strate-gic decision by the price setter to exploit customers' tendency to assume that higher prices mean higher quality and greater prestige. Charging higher prices is not inherently unethical on the marketer's part, because in many product categories there is a segment of con-sumers who gain psychological value from acquiring, owning, or giving higher-priced products.

Odd-Even Pricing

Prices end in even numbers such as zero (e.g., $250) or in odd num-bers such as 5 or 9 (e.g., $19.95, $249.99). **Odd pricing** refers to a price that ends in an odd number or just under a round number (e.g., 49, 98, 99).[14] Prices ending in odd numbers clearly predominate, as any perusal of newspaper advertisements or store visits will reveal. Why is this the case? First, there seems to be an historical rationale in that merchants used odd prices to force clerks to make change and reduce the possibility that clerks would simply pocket the customer's payment. But in the modern era of computerized cash registers and other controls, why does odd pricing persist? It may simply be that price setters think that odd prices convey a deal to buyers.

Exhibit 13.2 shows a *jagged-shaped* demand curve that reflects how price setters think odd pricing operates. This hypothetical demand curve shows the quantity of CDs demanded at various prices. The overall relation is downward sloping (to reflect the typical inverted relationship between price and quantity), but the interesting aspect of the demand curve is the change in quantity demanded at odd versus even prices. The vertical axis shows CD prices of $16.00 at the high end down to $11.95 at the low end. Between these prices are even prices ending in zero ($12, $13, $14, and $15) or odd prices ending in .95 ($12.95, $13.95, $14.95, $15.95). Note carefully that the demand curve shows big jumps in the quantity demanded at the odd prices compared to the quantity demanded at the even prices.

Although many retailers believe in the "magical power" of odd prices, there is virtually no empirical evidence that supports the correctness of this assumption.[15] In fact, research has shown that consumers have difficulty recalling odd prices,[16] and that odd pricing may communicate low quality.[17] Even prices, on the other hand, are more likely to convey high quality.

Loss-Leader Pricing

A different form of psychological pricing is practiced when retailers offer products at prices below or near the cost the retailer has paid for the items. These items, called **loss leaders**, are designed to attract consumers who might otherwise shop in a competitor's store. Whereas prestige pricing and odd-even pricing are based on the psychological premise that price conveys to consumers notions of product quality and deals, respectively, loss-leader pricing involves a different psychology. Specifically, the psychology underlying loss-leader pricing is that consumers will visit a store to obtain

Exhibit 13.2   Jagged Demand Curve for Odd Pricing

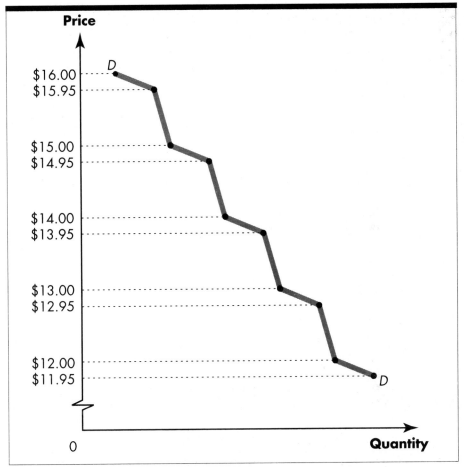

the loss-leader item, but once in the store they will be inspired to purchase other products. Hence, the store will lose money, or perhaps just breakeven, on the loss-leader item, but it will profit on sales of other items that consumers would not otherwise have purchased unless they visited the store.

Does loss-leader pricing work? Many retailers apparently think it does or it would not be practiced so widely. However, it may be that in offering loss leaders retailers are merely giving price reductions to customers who regularly shop the store rather than attracting other stores' customers. There is some research to suggest that retail executives in the grocery industry overestimate the percentage of consumers who are price sensitive.[18] It may be that much loss-leader pricing does not serve the primary purpose for which it is intended. Unfortunately, research evidence is unavailable to settle the issue of whether loss-leader pricing works to attract new shoppers or merely reward already loyal shoppers.

A Caveat

The foregoing discussion has discussed various forms of psychological pricing. You should not assume from this discussion that these various psychological pricing strategies are universally effective. Whether a particular marketing technique works as intended depends entirely on the specifics of the situation—in this case, on the nature of the product, the competition, and the customer segment. Whereas an odd price, for example, may be very effective for one product, it may not be at all effective for another product. A good marketer is careful not to make simplistic generalizations or assume that a particular practice will be universally effective.

◆ Geographic Pricing Strategies

In shipping goods from sellers to buyers, the transportation cost component as an element of the total product price represents a trivial cost component for some products but a substantial cost for others. The cost of transporting products via truck, train, plane, or other mode depends, in general, on two major factors: the amount of *volume* that is transported and the *distance* the freight is shipped. It is this second, distance factor that creates special complications, because all buyers are not equidistant from sellers. Hence, those buyers located greater distances from sellers incur higher prices if they are charged the full cost of transportation, whereas sellers located more proximate to buyers have an advantage over more distal sellers.

There are different ways that sellers deal with freight charges. One way is to simply charge the cost of transportation to customers. This practice is called **FOB origin pricing**, which means that the buyer pays the transportation charges and also chooses the mode of transportation and specific carrier. (FOB stands for *free on board*, and origin represents the point of shipment, which typically is the seller's factory or distribution center.) In one sense, this transportation pricing method is ideal for the seller insofar as the customer pays the shipping bill. However, in product-market situations where (1) freight charges represent a *substantial portion of total product price* and (2) products are *largely undifferentiated* among competitors, sellers would have geographical limits imposed on the size of their markets if they charged buyers the full shipping charges. This is because price-conscious buyers would purchase only from the most proximate sellers to obtain lower shipping charges and, hence, lower overall cost of goods.

Sellers, thus, are faced with the choice of either having geographical restrictions imposed on the size of their markets or incurring the added expense of paying for freight charges in order to expand the geographical size of their markets. A variety of geographic pricing practices have evolved to deal with the complications of freight charges. In the following sections we discuss freight absorption pricing, uniform delivered pricing, zone pricing, and basing-point pricing.

Freight Absorption Pricing

As the name suggests, with **freight absorption pricing** the seller pays for, or absorbs, the transportation charges. Shipping terms are quoted *FOB destination,* which means that the seller pays for the freight charges and is responsible for product safety until the goods are delivered to the buyer. By using freight absorption pricing, the seller removes geographical limits that would otherwise exist. The only limit on the seller's market when using freight absorption pricing is the amount of freight charges the seller is willing to absorb. Companies whose cost structures reflect *high fixed costs and low variable costs* (e.g., basic industries such as aluminum and steel) use freight absorption pricing because it is imperative that they obtain wide product distribution and spread fixed costs among as many customers as possible.

Uniform Delivered Pricing

Uniform delivered pricing means that the seller charges all customers the same transportation cost regardless of where they are located. This same cost is an *average of shipping expenses to all customers.* Thus, customers located closest to the seller's shipping origin effectively subsidize those who are located at distant points. It is for this reason that this pricing practice sometimes is referred to as "postage stamp pricing." The U.S. Postal Service charges 32¢ for each regular letter, regardless of whether the letter is mailed to a recipient living 10 blocks from your home or 3,000 miles away.

Uniform delivered pricing is an appropriate geographic pricing strategy for nationally advertised products that have a suggested retail price imprinted on the package (such as salty snack products, gum, candy, etc.) and are advertised as having a specific retail sales price. Greeting cards, which typically are imprinted with the retail sales price, is another product category that has to be priced FOB destination so that all dealers can earn equivalent profit margins.

Zone Pricing

Zone pricing is simply a special case of uniform delivered pricing. In **zone pricing** the seller divides the geographic market into multiple zones and then charges the same delivered price in each zone. That is, prices are uniform within zones but differ from zone to zone due to differences in average shipping charges. Many companies use zone pricing for the same reason as when discussing uniform delivered pricing. Companies that specialize in shipping letters and packages, such as FedEx and UPS, divide their mailing areas into multiple zones. UPS has four zones for its second-day air service: the 48 continental states, Puerto Rico, Hawaii and urban parts of Alaska, and rural Alaska. Prices are over four times higher in parcels mailed to rural Alaska compared to those mailed anywhere in the 48 states.

Basing-Point Pricing

This geographic pricing practice is a modified form of FOB origin pricing. Basing-point pricing originated in the steel industry and, because Pittsburgh, Pennsylvania, was the original hub of the U.S. steel industry, basing-point pricing was once referred to as "Pittsburgh freight." To better understand why basing-point pricing originated and how it operates, a simplified market situation is portrayed in Exhibit 13.3 in the form of a geometric representation (a parallelogram) consisting of two sellers and two buyers. In this market the two buyers are able to purchase essentially identical products from either of the two sellers, but the transportation charges they have to pay are vastly different depending on which seller they choose.

Exhibit 13.3   An Illustration of Basing-Point Pricing

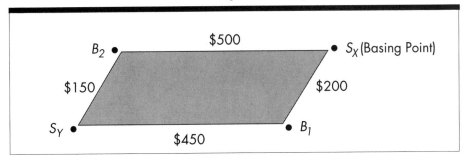

S_X (standing for seller X) in Exhibit 13.3 is the basing point. S_Y (seller Y) is a competitive seller located a considerable distance from S_X's business. B_1 and B_2 are two buyers who compete in this small industry. As represented geometrically by the length of the lines, B_1 is located more closely to S_X, the basing point, than to S_Y. Comparatively, B_2 is considerably closer to S_Y than to S_X. The dollar amounts shown in the exhibit represent the cost to ship a full railroad car of the product produced by sellers X and Y. For example, a shipment from S_X to B_1 costs $200, whereas the same-size shipment from S_Y to B_1 would cost over two-times greater, $450.

Now, if sellers X and Y produced a virtually identical product and charged equivalent prices, who would you buy from if you were B_1 and you had to pay the shipping bill (i.e., FOB origin shipping terms apply)? Who would you buy from if you were B_2? The answer is obvious in both cases: you would buy from the seller to whom you are more closely located and thereby minimize your transportation costs and thus your overall purchase costs. Because of this reality, S_Y could never get the business of B_1 and S_X could never get the business of B_2. Each seller has in effect a geographical monopoly. It is for this reason that basing-point pricing came into being. Sellers wanted to expand their markets rather than remain captive to geographic economics.

As originally practiced, a **single basing point** was used and all freight costs were priced as if they originated from the basing point (S_X in this example) regardless of whether they actually did. In this case, S_Y would compete for B_1's business by charging B_1 the same freight charge, that is, $200, as if the shipment originated from S_X's place of business. By absorbing the $250 differential (i.e., actual charge of $450 – $200 basing point charge) S_Y is able to compete for B_1's business.

CAPTAINS OF INDUSTRY

David Rosen

Founder, Sega Enterprises Ltd.

Co-Chairman of Sega of America

Education: Completed one year of college before joining the Air Force.

Career Path: Began Rosen Enterprises in 1951 and bought Sega Enterprises in 1965. Sold out to Gulf & Western Industries in 1971 but bought the Japanese assets of Sega and went public in 1986. Now co-chairman of Sega of America, Inc. and advisor to Hayao Nakayama, chief executive officer of Sega Enterprises Ltd.

Hayao Nakayama

Chief Executive Officer and President

Sega Enterprises Ltd.

Date of Birth: May 21, 1932

Career Path: Japanese entrepreneur who founded a distribution company that was bought by David Rosen in 1979. Invested in Japanese assets of Sega with Mr. Rosen and became CEO of Sega Enterprises Ltd.

Thomas Kalinske

Chief Executive Officer

Sega of America

Career Path: Joined toy division of Mattel Toys in 1972. Promoted to President in 1985 and cleaned up the mess left by Intellivision, Mattel's venture into videogames. Left Mattel in 1987 to purchase Matchbox Toys Ltd. In 1990 he joined Sega as chief executive of Sega of America Inc.

David Rosen started Rosen Enterprises in Japan in 1951 when he was 20 years old. He hailed from Brooklyn but returned to Tokyo after a tour of duty there with the U.S. Air Force during the Korean War. Rosen began in business importing and exporting and discovered a need in Japan for identification photo booths. He modified U.S. instant photo booths to produce higher quality identification photos and brought them to Japan. The machines were a huge success, and he ended up licensing the machines to Japanese operators before looking for new opportunities in business in Japan. He successfully lobbied the Ministry of International Trade and Industry to let him import $100,000 worth of mechanical coin-operated games in 1956.[a] These games had become popular on U.S. military bases in Japan and Rosen thought they would be marketable to the civilian population in Japan as well. He became dissatisfied with the quality of games then available from his resources in Chicago, so he decided to make his own. In 1965 he bought a Tokyo jukebox and slot-machine maker who stamped "SEGA"—short for "Service Games"—on its products, and Rosen adopted the name for his enterprise. The next year Sega Enterprises produced "Periscope," a game in which players torpedo ships by aiming through a periscope, and the game became an international hit. He learned early on that better technology wins markets, and this strategy still guides Sega. By 1971 he was a millionaire and sold out to Gulf & Western Industries but stayed with the company as CEO.[b]

Sega continued to increase its profits until 1982, with revenue reaching $214 million in the year ended June 30, 1982, when sales to arcades and in the U.S. home market took a nose-dive, mainly due to a rash of mediocre games. Gulf & Western sold off Sega's U.S. operations because of reduced demand for video games in the early 1980s.[c]

Sega managed to survive in Japan, however. Rosen had bought a distribution company in 1979 that was founded by a young Japanese entrepreneur, Hayao Nakayama. Rosen, along with Nakayama and other Japanese investors, bought the Japanese assets of Sega for $38 million. Nakayama became CEO, and Rosen managed the U.S. subsidiary. Sega then entered the U.S. market as a Japanese company and went public in Japan in 1986. Together Rosen and Nakayama decided not to stick with any one product too long in order to avoid future disasters, but to be technology-driven.

Sega's chief rival until 1994 was Nintendo, another Japanese company that had a lock on the industry until 1989, when Sega introduced Genesis, a 16-bit machine that was superior to Nintendo's 8-bit machines. Genesis was not an immediate hit, however. There weren't many usable games on the market and few companies would write games for it. Nintendo used its clout to insist that games written for its 8-bit machines not be licensed to Sega or any other company for two years. Sega needed a brand-new product to captivate video machine players enough to make them want to purchase the Genesis system. A Sega artist in Japan came up with Sonic, the hedgehog, and players liked it. Sonic could only be played on Sega machines, and sales of Genesis hardware took off. Nakayama is credited with realizing the tremendous potential of the hedgehog and decided to turn him blue to differentiate him from competing video game characters.[d]

Thomas Kalinske was hired from Matchbox Toys Ltd. to head up Sega of America in 1990. His strategy to slash prices on the Genesis machine, include Sonic the Hedgehog software in the purchase of Genesis, and aggressively take on the competition in its advertising is heralded as propelling Sega's U.S. division to go head to head with Nintendo in just three years. Nintendo's share dropped from around 90% in 1990 to an estimated 50% in 1993, with Sega climbing from 7% to almost 50%, according to toy retail analysts. Sales of Sega's U.S. division grew from an estimated $280 million in 1990 to more than $1 billion in 1993.[e]

One of Sega's marketing strategies was to position itself to an audience older than that of Nintendo, going after teenagers and adults with sports games and violent arcade games. Even when Congress held hearings in 1993 to try and curb violence in video games, Sega refused to edit its Mortal Kombat games, while Nintendo removed the most violent sequences from its version. Sega of America Vice President Bill White, appearing before a Congressional panel, stated that there was a legitimate market for older people who wanted to buy violent games and Sega was willing to produce games for them. His solution was to set up a rating system to keep the games out of the hands of minors.[f] However, Sega pulled Digital Pictures Inc.'s Night Trap game because of pressure from Congress and children's advocates.[g]

Continued on next page

CAPTAINS OF INDUSTRY, continued

Sega continued to fight hard against Nintendo and succeeded in increasing profits and market share until early 1994 when a fierce price war with Nintendo in Europe caused Sega's profits to plunge. Sega then launched on a 2-pronged strategy to spark earnings. It will introduce Saturn, a compact-disk machine used to play more realistic games than on former CDs or cartridges and hopes to enter the market a year ahead of Nintendo. It also plans to challenge Walt Disney Company with virtual-reality theme parks, to introduce electronic toys, and to enter the information highway with interactive entertainment.

Sega executives consider entertainment as the primary use for interactive communications in the home in the future, and to that end Sega plans to be a player on the information highway. "I see us as a new form of entertainment company," Thomas Kalinske was quoted as saying.[h] Kalinske has sought new opportunities to move Sega along the information highway by establishing a venture with cable operators Time Warner and Tele-Communications to download video games into game machines over a pay-cable channel. A separate venture with AT&T allows customers using a special modem called the Edge 16 to play video games over phone lines. Sega's role in these collaborations is its ability to create interactive software that consumers can use without a manual.

Nakayama is very optimistic about the potential success of virtual reality high-tech theme parks, viewing these parks as a chance to create a whole new market. Sega's virtual reality (VR) theme parks take visitors and place them inside windowless, truck-size capsules and make them feel like they're driving a race car or piloting a spaceship. Sega has already built VirtuaLand, an experimental arcade at the Luxor Hotel in Las Vegas. From Sega's point of view, VR parks present a viable alternative to theme parks like Disneyland because they would operate more cheaply by the substitution of computer graphics for physical structures like castles and roller coasters, occupy less land, and be cheaper to build. Renovation would consist of a change of software. Two parks are set to open in Japan in 1994 and Sega hopes to open 50 by 1997.[i]

Sega is facing new competition as other companies have introduced new games for the video game player who is always seeking new excitement. Atari is making a comeback, as well as Commodore International, Philips, 3DO, and Sony. Sega is banking on the introduction of Saturn, which plays both CDs and cartridges, to help it maintain market share. For Nakayama, the challenge is to constantly come up with new games. Video game customers like what's new, and game software, he feels, has run into a dead end. Sega is turning to software labs in Japan and the United States to create more sophisticated games, turning out about 65 new games in 1993 alone.[j] Artists, programmers, and writers work together to create the games; musicians record game sounds; and Hollywood studios produce interactive games in which many outcomes are filmed and a player's actions determine which one appears on the screen. Sega of America has been successful in obtaining the rights to such Hollywood box office hits as *Jurassic Park* and *Aladdin* to produce CD games that incorporate actual animation from the movie.[k]

In an effort to make the change to 32-bit technology more affordable and to speed up its availability, Sega announced in March of 1994 a hardware upgrade called "Genesis Super 32X" which would attach to either the Sega Genesis or Sega CD machine, priced at $149 retail. This upgrade would make available some of the exciting game play the company has been promising with its upcoming Saturn hardware to current owners of Sega's 16-bit Genesis hardware. Games developed for the Sega CDs and Genesis cartridges can be played on the Genesis Super 32X and 30 titles are under development.[l]

Sega's costs have soared along with its revenues because of its new ventures. But it is seriously adhering to its technology-driven strategy, and new technology isn't cheap. About a third of Sega's employees work in research and development, evidence of its commitment to innovation. Sega needs a steady flow of appealing new games to keep its cash-cow business from running dry.[m] Whether Sega will be a winner on the information highway and with virtual reality parks is yet to be seen. "In the videogame business, if you stop moving, you will fail," observes Shoichiro Irimajiri, ex-head of Honda of America, hired by Nakayama as executive vice president at Sega in 1993.[n] With Sega's clear strategy for the future, it appears poised to continue to be a key player in the entertainment business.

[a] Steve Higgins, "The Founding Father of Japan's Electronic Games Industry Comes from Brooklyn, N.Y.," *Investor's Business Daily,* March 29, 1994, 1.

[b] Richard Brandt, Neil Gross, and Peter Coy, "SEGA!" *Business Week,* February 21, 1994, 66.

[c] Higgins, "The Founding Father," 1.

[d] Dean Calbreath, "Hedgehog Heaven: Sega Plays to Win in Video-Game Arena," *San Francisco Business Times,* August 20, 1993, 9A.

[e] Nikhil Hutheesing, "Games Companies Play," *Forbes,* October 25, 1993, 68.

[f] John Burgess, "Sega's Sonic Boom," *Washington Post,* December 19, 1993, H1, H4.

[g] Brandt, Gross, and Coy, "SEGA!" 66.

[h] Ibid.

[i] Ibid.

[j] Patricia Sellers, "They Understand Your Kids," *Fortune,* Autumn/Winter 1993, 29.

[k] Calbreath, "Hedgehog Heaven," 9A.

[l] "Sega Announces New Product which Will Boost Existing Genesis 16-bit Hardware to 32-bit Power," *Business Wire,* March 14, 1994.

[m] Brandt, Gross, and Coy, "SEGA!" 66.

[n] Gale Eisenstodt, "Virtual Disney," *Forbes,* February 28, 1994, 46."

Single basing-point pricing had one major flaw: it created a practice called "phantom freight." Referring again to Exhibit 13.3, when S_Y ships freight to B_2, the actual freight charge is $150. However, because S_X is the single basing point and all freight costs are billed as if they originated from that basing point, S_Y would charge B_2 $500 for a full shipment rather than the actual amount of $150. The $350 differential in this case ($500 – $150) is the amount of phantom freight for which B_2 is charged and from which S_Y would unfairly profit. Clearly a pricing system that charges customers in excess of the actual costs incurred is detrimental to customer welfare. It is for this reason that steel producers and other users of basing point pricing were forced to adopt **multiple basing-point pricing**. In this system the basing point switches depending on which shipping point charges *lower* freight rates. In our example, the basing point would remain S_X when quoting prices to B_1 but would be S_Y when vying for B_2's business. In a multiple basing point system, phantom freight is eliminated and sellers can compete for customers located anywhere as long as the sellers are willing to quote freight charges from a competitor's basing point and absorb the difference between the actual cost of freight and the basing point cost.

Bid-Pricing Strategies

All of the above strategies involved situations where managers establish prices for marketing multiple quantities of a product at the same price. Bid pricing addresses a different issue, namely the matter of pricing a product, project, or service on a one-time, bid-by-bid basis. **Bid pricing** entails establishing a *specific price for each exchange relationship* in contrast to setting a basic, or list, price that applies to all exchanges. Bid pricing is especially prevalent in doing business with government agencies, on construction projects, and in pricing some services to business customers. Even residential jobs are often bid on. A prospective home owner, for example, presents various housing contractors with architectural specifications and asks each contractor to bid on building the home. Those contractors who provide a price are in effect bidding on the job.

The issues in bid pricing are not unlike those in conventional, non-bid pricing. Price setters in both instances must consider elasticity of demand, costs, competitive prices, and desired profit returns. Bid pricing is complicated, however, by the fact that companies and government agencies that "let" (i.e., put out) bids often make their selection of a contractor or vendor based on who offers the lowest

Exhibit 13.4   Key Elements in FineHome's Bid-Pricing Decision

Bid Price (B)	Cost (C)	Immediate Profit (B − C)	Probability of Getting Job (P)	Expected Profit [P × (B − C)]
$270,000	270,000	$ 0	1.00	$ 0
290,000	270,000	20,000	0.90	18,000
300,000	270,000	30,000	0.80	24,000
320,000	270,000	50,000	0.65	32,500
330,000	270,000	60,000	0.50	30,000
350,000	270,000	80,000	0.33	26,640
360,000	270,000	90,000	0.20	18,000

bid, subject, of course, to the bidder's being able to meet all specifications included in the contract. This considerable emphasis on price
requires that the bidder set a low enough price to get the contract but
not so low that the job is unprofitable. Moreover, gaining contracts
through bid pricing requires the price setter to have a good understanding of competitors' price-bidding practices. In a sense, this
requires the bidder to be able to successfully "guesstimate" the odds,
or probabilities, of getting the job at different bid prices that are
under consideration.

Let us return to the above home-contractor situation to illustrate these issues. Assume that a well-off family has had architectural specifications drawn up for a large house of approximately
4,000 square feet. The FineHomes Contracting Company estimates
that its cost will be $270,000 to build this home. What price should
FineHomes bid on this house? If there were no competitors in this
housing market, FineHomes would have considerable latitude in
setting a price. However, the marketing manager for FineHomes
knows that at least two other home contractors will bid on this
house. The key issues in bid pricing are illustrated in Exhibit 13.4.[19]

This illustration shows that FineHomes is considering prices
ranging from $270,000, which would be the breakeven price, to a
high of $360,000. Regardless of the price, it will cost FineHomes
$270,000 to build the home, which will yield different "immediate"
profits at each possible price. However, the probability that the
prospective homeowners will award the contract to FineHomes
decreases the higher FineHomes' bid price. Hence, FineHomes'

expected profit is the immediate profit adjusted by the probability of receiving the bid. In this illustration, the highest expected profit is $32,500 at a bid price of $320,000. If the marketing manager at FineHomes believes in probabilities, she or he would be wise to bid $320,000 on this home.

It should be apparent that a price bidder has to do a good job in identifying all cost components and accurately estimating total costs. However, the most difficult aspect of competitive bidding is estimating the probabilities of winning the bid at various bid prices.[20] The only way this can be accomplished with accuracy is by carefully studying competitors' past bidding practices.

Sometimes the initial bid is just the beginning of a more involved pricing process. Companies or government agencies that get bids often reduce the number of original bidders to a subset of those offering the most attractive bids, and then go to a subsequent round of negotiations. **Negotiated pricing** occurs when the subset of selected bidders are requested to revise their opening bids. The negotiations include contract terms such as completion dates and penalty terms if, say, in the case of a construction project the job is not completed on time. Bids sometimes are "rigged" in instances of governmental purchasing when companies are allowed to write the bid specifications. This is tantamount to allowing the "fox to guard the henhouse"—companies write the specs such that only they can meet them, thus assuring that they are awarded the bid but not assuring that taxpayers receive the cheapest or best deal!

◼ Chapter Summary

Price setters make a variety of pricing decisions beyond merely establishing the base price for a product. These decisions, or pricing strategies, include new-product pricing, price-flexibility strategies, discount and allowance strategies, product-line pricing, psychological pricing, geographic pricing strategies, and bid pricing.

Product pioneers have two general pricing options: skimming or penetration pricing. Skimming pricing involves charging relatively high prices and supporting this strategy with heavy promotional expenditures. Skimming pricing is most appropriate when price elasticity is inelastic and high initial prices are necessary to recoup quickly the heavy investment in a new product. Penetration prices involve the use of relatively low prices because price elasticity is elastic, strong competition is imminent, and production costs can be substantially reduced if greater volume is achieved.

Manufacturers often adopt a flexible-pricing strategy by varying discounts and allowances on a transactional basis. Manufacturers typically flex the transaction amount as dictated by economic, competitive, and other marketplace circumstances. Pricing flexibility is constrained, however, by pricing restrictions imposed by the Robinson-Patman Act. At the retail level, price flexing occurs when price haggling transpires between retailer and customer. Haggling is commonplace throughout most of the world, but is less prevalent in more economically developed economies.

A variety of discounts and allowances are used in flexing prices and accommodating the specific circumstances surrounding a particular exchange situation. These include (1) functional, or trade, discounts; (2) quantity discounts, both cumulative and noncumulative; (3) seasonal discounts; (4) cash discounts; (5) sales promotion allowances such as price-off, bill-back, and slotting allowances; (6) trade-in allowances; (7) cash discounts; and (8) rebates.

Product-line pricing strategies are necessitated when manufacturers produce multiple brands in the same product category and when retailers merchandise multiple product-quality levels in the same category. The pricing issue faced both by manufacturers and retailers is one of whether to price each product in a line separately on the basis of its own cost, demand, and competitive characteristics or to jointly price the multiple products in recognition of the overall image that the firm wishes to convey and the interrelated demand, or cross elasticity, between the products. A related situation occurs when firms bundle two or more products or services in the same unit at a special price, which typically is below the price of the components priced separately.

Three psychological-based pricing practices—prestige pricing, odd-even pricing, and loss-leader pricing—are prevalent in retailing. Prestige pricing is used when a product is priced at a relatively high price under the assumption that the relation between price and quantity demanded is direct rather than inverse, which means greater quantities will be sold at higher rather than lower prices. Odd-pricing, as contrasted with even-pricing, occurs when the end digits of a price use odd numbers (3, 5, 7, 9) or when the price is just below a whole number (e.g., $9.98 instead of $10.00). Price setters, when using odd-pricing, operate under the assumption that such prices convey a deal to consumers. Even-pricing, on the other hand, can be used to convey a prestige, high-quality image. Loss-leader pricing is practiced by retailers when an item is priced below or near cost to draw people to the store in anticipation that while there they will purchase other items, thus yielding an overall profit to the retailer.

Geographic pricing strategies are used when freight charges play an important role in the overall, or delivered, price of a product. FOB origin pricing charges the cost of transportation to customers. The amount depends on the volume shipped and the distance separating the customer and the seller's shipping point, with longer distances typically entailing higher costs. Uniform delivered pricing, a variant of FOB origin pricing, simply charges all customers the same, average shipping charge. Zone pricing is a special case of uniform delivered pricing where the seller divides the total territory into multiple zones and bills the same average shipping charge in each zone.

However, customers sometimes refuse to purchase from sellers unless the seller is willing to pay all or a portion of the transportation costs. Hence, FOB destination pricing, where the seller absorbs the freight charges, is used in highly competitive situations, especially where industry characteristics are such that sellers have high fixed-cost and relatively low variable-cost structures. Basing-point pricing is a special case of FOB origin pricing. With this practice, freight charges are billed to the customer based on the cost of freight from a basing point (such as a competitor's shipping point) rather than the seller's actual shipping point. Basing-point pricing removes geographical monopolies and allows sellers to extend their markets.

Bid pricing addresses a different issue, namely the matter of pricing a product, project, or service on a one-time, bid-by-bid basis. Effective bid pricing requires that companies accurately estimate all cost components, have a good idea of how competitors might bid on a project, and build in a reasonable profit margin but not one that is too high to lose the bid to a competitive bidder.

◼ Notes

1. Joel Dean, "Pricing Policies for New Products," *Harvard Business Review,* November-December 1976, 141. (This "HBR Classic" was originally published in November 1950.)
2. Dean, "Pricing Policies,"147.
3. Dean, "Pricing Policies," 148.
4. Michael V. Marn and Robert L. Rosiello, "Managing Price, Gaining Profit," *Harvard Business Review,* September-October, 1992.

5. Marn and Rosiello, *ibid.*, provide an excellent discussion of this possibility.

6. W. Wossen Kassaye, "The Role of Haggling in Marketing: An Examination of Buyer Behavior," *The Journal of Consumer Marketing*, 7 (Fall 1990), 54.

7. Mary Connelly, "Philosophy of Car Pricing Is Clear: Cut Out Games," *Advertising Age*, March 28, 1994, S–28, 34.

8. Eric Hollreiser, "To Haggle or Not to Haggle? Dealers, Makers Roll the Dice," *Brandweek*, November 21, 1994, 18–19.

9. Cross elasticity measures the change in quantity demanded for one product to the change in price of another product. In equation form, cross elasticity is $(\Delta Q_A / \Delta P_B) \times (P_B / Q_A)$; where ΔQ_A stands for change in quantity of product A demanded, ΔP_B signifies change in price for product B, P_B is the price for product B, and Q_A is the quantity of product A demanded.

10. See Michael J. Zenor, "The Profit Benefits of Category Management," *Journal of Marketing Research*, 31 (May 1994), 202–213.

11. Joseph P. Guiltinan, "The Price Bundling of Services: A Normative Framework," *Journal of Marketing*, 51 (April 1987), 74.

12. Kent B. Monroe, *Pricing: Making Profitable Decisions*, 2nd ed. (New York: McGraw-Hill, 1990), 320.

13. For discussion of consumer savings from bundling, see Manjit S. Yadav and Kent B. Monroe, "How Buyers Perceive Savings in a Bundle Price: An Examination of a Bundle's Transaction Value," *Journal of Marketing Research*, 30 (August 1993), 350–358.

14. Monroe, *Pricing*, 48.

15. Monroe, *Pricing*.

16. Robert M. Schindler and Alan R. Wiman, "Effects of Odd Pricing on Price Recall," *Journal of Business Research* (November 1989), 165–178.

17. Robert M. Schindler and Thomas Kibrarian, "Image Effects of Odd Pricing," University of Chicago Graduate School of Business, 1987 Working Paper.

18. Joel E. Urbany, Peter R. Dickson, and Rosemary Key, "Actual and Perceived Consumer Vigilance in the Retail Grocery Industry," *Marketing Letters*, 2 (January 1991), 15-26.

19. This illustration is adapted from Monroe, *Pricing*, 412.

20. Monroe, *Pricing*.

◆ Study Questions

1. A skimming price would be justified in all of the following circumstances except the following situation:
   a. A product innovator wants to quickly recoup the heavy investment in a new product.
   b. The innovator realizes that product innovators and early adopters are relatively price insensitive.
   c. Price elasticity is elastic.
   d. All of the above justify a skimming strategy.

2. Price haggling is most likely under all of the following circumstances except the following:
   a. Consumers' prior purchasing experience has provided them with a reference point of what the fair price should be.
   b. The asking price is perceived as unreasonable.
   c. Consumers know that prices for comparable products differ among sellers.
   d. All of the above are circumstances favoring price haggling.

3. A manufacturer's pricing sheet informs purchasers that they will receive a 10% discount from the total invoice price for all orders in excess of 100 units. This discount is a _____ discount.
   a. noncumulative quantity
   b. cumulative quantity
   c. functional
   d. cash

4. A manufacturer's pricing sheet informs purchasers that they will receive a 2% discount from the total invoice price if they pay their bill within 10 days from the invoice date. This discount is a _____ discount.
   a. noncumulative quantity
   b. cumulative quantity
   c. functional
   d. cash

5. The most widely used form of trade-oriented sales promotion is a(n) _____ allowance.
   a. off-invoice
   b. bill-back
   c. slotting
   d. discount

6. The jagged-shaped demand curve is associated with which form of psychological pricing?
   a. prestige pricing
   b. price-lining
   c. loss-leader pricing
   d. odd pricing

7. FOB origin pricing means that
   a. the seller pays the transportation charges.
   b. the seller offers a discount based on the quantity purchased.
   c. the buyer pays the transportation charges.
   d. the buyer receives a discount based on the quantity purchased.

8. Which of the following is *not* an accurate statement about uniform delivered pricing?
   a. The seller charges all customers the same transportation cost.
   b. This form of geographic pricing is most appropriately used when retail prices are highly variable.
   c. Uniform delivered pricing is especially appropriate for nationally advertised products that have a suggested retail price.
   d. Greeting card companies use uniform delivered pricing.

9. What geographic pricing practice is being used when a manufacturer charges the customer transportation costs that are determined from a competitor's shipping point rather than from the manufacturer's shipping point?
   a. uniform delivered pricing
   b. zone pricing
   c. basing-point pricing
   d. FOB origin pricing

10. A company is considering bidding on a government contract to construct a new building. It estimates its cost at $2 million. It thinks it has a .7 probability of being awarded the contract if it bids $3 million for the contract. What is its expected profit?
    a. $700,000
    b. $1,000,000
    c. $1,400,000
    d. $2,100,000

CHAPTER (14)

Promotion Management and Integrated Marketing Communications

◈ Communications

Out of the thousands of products on store shelves today, what is the chance that a consumer will *see* any one particular item, much less buy it? In today's society, consumers are rushed for time. They do not have the time to leisurely walk up and down every aisle, perusing all of the wares. Brands which possess high quality and value and are fairly priced may nonetheless fail to achieve sales and profit objectives if potential customers are unaware of the brands or do not perceive the brands favorably. Effective advertising and other forms of marketing communications are crucial to creating brand awareness, establishing positive brand identities, and moving products from distributors' warehouses and off store shelves.

Marketing communications also are critical to the success of business-to-business marketers in their efforts to achieve market share and profit objectives. Many, if not most, business-to-business products share similarities from one supplier to the next. Product quality often is not that different among competitors, and prices often are near equal. The real distinctions among business-to-business competitors frequently amount to created differences achieved through effective advertising and, more importantly, via superior service and personal selling attention.

Regardless of the nature of the product category or type of business, marketing communications are key to a company's overall marketing mission and represent a major determinant of its success; indeed, it has been claimed that "marketing in the 1990s is communication and communication is marketing. The two are inseparable."[1]

The following section details the nature of marketing communications and the promotion mix. Subsequent sections (1) discuss communications objectives and the communications process, (2) explore the determinants of an appropriate promotions mix, and (3) examine the promotion management process.

◈ Marketing Communications and the Promotion Mix

Marketing communications represent the collection of all elements in an organization's marketing mix that facilitate exchanges by establishing shared meaning with an organization's customers or clients. All marketing mix variables communicate with customers:

the *product* itself communicates through its size, shape, brand name, and package design. *Price* communicates by suggesting savings, a deal, or indicating quality, luxury, and prestige. Retail outlets, and other aspects of *distribution*, also have significant communications value for consumers. Stores, like people, possess personalities that consumers associate with the merchandise located in the stores. Consider, for example, a brand name such as Polo, which is currently available in upscale specialty shops and department stores. These outlets project a high-quality image, something that Ralph Lauren desires for its Polo brand of clothing. How would consumers view Polo if suddenly the shelves at Kmart, Wal-Mart, and Target stores were flooded with garments inscribed with the famous Polo insignia?

Promotion Management and the Promotion Mix

The promotion element of the marketing mix is a subset of overall marketing communications. As noted above, all elements of the marketing mix communicate meaning about a brand. However, it is the promotion component of the mix that is designed specifically for this purpose. In its broadest sense, **promotion** means "to move forward."[2] In marketing, promotion means to motivate—or move in a sense—customers to action. Promotion management employs a variety of tools for this purpose: personal selling, mass-media and direct-to-consumer advertising, publicity, sales promotions, point-of-purchase communications, and sponsorship marketing. These tools collectively can be termed the **promotions mix** (see Exhibit 14.1).

The expression "promotions mix" captures the idea that all forms of promotion are combined and coordinated, or mixed, to achieve corporate goals and brand objectives. **Promotion management** is the practice of coordinating the various promotional mix elements and entails the following activities: (1) *setting objectives* for each of the promotional elements in terms of what they are intended to accomplish (e.g., increase brand awareness by 20%), (2) *establishing budgets* that are sufficient to support the objectives, (3) *designing specific programs* (e.g., advertising campaigns) to accomplish objectives, and (4) *evaluating performance and taking corrective action* when results are not in accordance with objectives.

Brief descriptions of each of the promotion-mix elements are provided shortly, and Chapter 15 then covers all elements—except personal selling, which is covered in Chapter 16—in detail.

Exhibit 14.1   The Promotional Mix

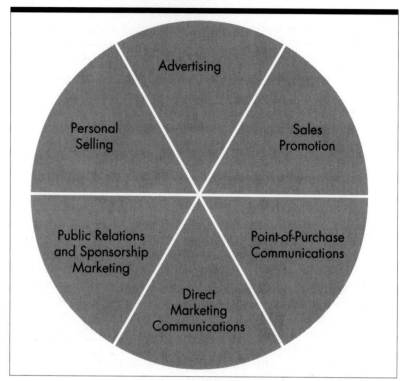

However, prior to describing these elements, it will be useful to draw an analogy between the process of mixing promotion elements and the task of creating a basketball team.

In brief (and simplistically), a basketball team includes five players who differ in the positions they play, the strengths they offer, and the roles expected from them. One player, the point guard, has primary responsibility for bringing the ball up the court, controlling the tempo of the offense, and setting up plays. Another guard, the shooting guard, has a greater scoring responsibility. Both guards also play defense. The center, who typically is the tallest player on the team, has major responsibility for both "inside" scoring (i.e., close to the basket), rebounding, and defending against the opposing center. The other two players, referred to as forwards, score from intermediate range and also have responsibility for rebounding and defending. The quality of a basketball team depends on all players working together and playing as a unit. Offense is important, but so is defense. Players who can score points quickly and in spurts are important, but so are those who are steady and dependable rather than erratic. A basketball team would not be a very good team it if consisted only of five Shaquille O'Neals (contrary to the commercial), or five Michael Jordans, or five Larry Birds, or five of any single player. An outstanding team requires players representing different dimensions—different height, weight, speed, quickness, shooting ability, rebounding ability, shot-blocking ability, and so on.

So it is with the promotion mix and the various elements that comprise the mix. Personal selling, in a sense, is like a basketball team's point guard. It sets the tempo for all other promotion-mix elements. Advertising is more flamboyant—the Michael Jordan of the promotion mix. Public relations (PR) is a great adjunct to advertising, working together, assisting, and augmenting advertising to accomplish mutual goals. PR also is great when the need for defense is especially important—such as when a firm or one of its brands is surrounded with negative publicity. Sales promotion is like the player who scores a lot of points quickly; it can achieve sales results in a shorter period than can other promotion-mix elements. There is no need to strain the analogy any further. The point should be clear: The promotion mix is like a team consisting of players who bring different abilities to the team and perform different but mutually reinforcing roles.

Personal Selling.   **Personal selling** is *person-to-person communication* in which a seller informs and educates prospective customers and attempts to persuade them to purchase the company's products or services. Many marketers rate personal selling as the most critical element of the marketing mix. Business-to-business marketers rely especially heavily on personal selling in marketing their products. In the consumer market, products such as insurance, automobiles, and real estate are sold mainly through personal selling efforts. Historically, personal selling involved face-to-face interactions between salesperson and prospect, but telephone sales and other forms of electronic communications are increasingly being used.

Advertising.   **Advertising** involves either *mass communication* via newspapers, magazines, radio, television, and other media (e.g., billboards, bus stop signage) or *direct-to-consumer communication* via direct mail. Both forms of advertising are paid for by an identified sponsor, the advertiser, but are considered to be *nonpersonal* because the sponsoring firm is simultaneously communicating with multiple receivers, perhaps millions, rather than talking with a specific person or small group. The purpose of advertising is to inform the customer about the advertiser's products and brand benefits and ultimately to influence brand choice. Advertising attempts to keep the brand's name and image in the customer's mind over a long period of time.

Publicity.

Publicity, like advertising, is *nonpersonal* communication to a mass audience, but unlike advertising, publicity is not directly paid for by the company that enjoys the publicity. Publicity usually comes in the form of news items or editorial comments about a company's products or services. These items or comments receive free print space or broadcast time because media representatives consider the information pertinent and newsworthy for their reading or listening audiences. It is the job of a firm's public relations personnel to garner positive publicity for the company and its brands. The PR staff also faces the challenge of overcoming negative publicity when a company is faced with a product disaster (e.g., Perrier bottled water contaminated with benzene) or confronted with claims of untoward business practices (e.g., Denny's restaurants accused of racial discrimination).

Sales Promotion.

Sales promotion consists of all marketing activities that attempt to stimulate quick buyer action, or, in other words, attempt to promote immediate sales of a product (thereby yielding the name *sales promotion*). In comparison, advertising and publicity are designed to accomplish other objectives such as creating brand awareness and favorably influencing customer attitudes. Sales promotions are directed both at the trade (wholesalers and retailers) and at consumers. *Trade-oriented sales promotions* include the use of various types of allowances and merchandise assistance that are used to activate wholesaler and retailer response. *Consumer-oriented sales promotions* include the use of coupons, premiums, free samples, contests or sweepstakes, rebates, and other devices. Although manufacturers hope to stimulate long-term use of their brands, these consumer promotions often result only in short-term brand usage. Consumers who have used a $1.00 off coupon for a can of coffee, for example, generally will switch back to their favorite brand when no coupons are available from competitors.

Point-of-Purchase Communications.   **Point-of-purchase communications** include all signage—displays, posters, signs, shelf cards, and a variety of other visual materials—that are designed to influence buying decisions at the point of sale. Point-of-purchase communications are a final effort by the manufacturer to motivate consumers and encourage purchase of the manufacturer's brands. Research has shown that perhaps as many as two out of three buying decisions are made at the point of purchase.[3]

Sponsorship Marketing.   **Sponsorship marketing** is the practice of promoting the interests of a company and its brands by associating the company with a specific *event* (e.g., a golf tournament) or a charitable *cause* (e.g., the Leukemia Society). An advertisement by the Lincoln National Life Insurance Co. (Exhibit 14.2) shows the appropriate use of a sponsorship relationship that ties in nicely with the company name. In general, sponsorships represent a unique promotional opportunity for a company and its brands to directly target communications toward narrow but highly desirable audiences. The use of sponsorship marketing generally is not expected to substitute for more traditional forms of marketing communications such as advertising, but rather to complement these activities.

In summarizing this section it is important to recognize the similarity and difference between the terms promotion management and marketing communications. The similarity arises because both terms contain the notion of communicating with customers. However, whereas the term "promotion management" is restricted to communications undertaken by the subset of mechanisms catalogued under the promotion variable in the marketing mix, marketing communications is a general concept that encompasses communications via all of the marketing mix variables, promotional as well as nonpromotional tools.

Integrated Marketing Communications

Companies in the past often treated the promotion elements as virtually separate activities, whereas current marketing philosophy holds that integration of all promotional and nonpromotional elements is absolutely imperative for success. One of the significant marketing trends of recent years is a move toward fully integrating all business practices that communicate something about a company's brands to

Exhibit 14.2   Sponsorship Marketing

**Lincoln always believed the word was
mightier than the sword.**

In 1858, Abraham Lincoln debated Stephen Douglas on the social issues of the time. In 1995,
nearly 20,000 high school students will argue significant moral and value issues facing our society in
the Lincoln Life Lincoln-Douglas Debates, sponsored jointly with the National Forensic League.

Our sponsorship underscores our dedication to the preservation of President Lincoln's legacy of
truth, straight talk, and personal conviction. By participating in the debates, students arm themselves
with the power of words—which indeed are mightier than the sword—to resolve differences, tackle
tough issues, and build character.

To learn more about the Lincoln Life Lincoln-Douglas Debates, write the National Forensic League,
P.O. Box 38, Ripon, WI 54971, or call (414) 748-6206.

A Lincoln

LINCOLN LIFE

©1995 Lincoln National Life Insurance Co. Fort Wayne, Indiana 46801

present or prospective customers. This development is known as integrated marketing communications, although it could just as well be called integrated promotion management. The reason companies are increasingly integrating their marketing communications activities is nicely captured in the following quotes:

> The marketer who succeeds in the [1990s and beyond] will be the one who coordinates the communications mix so tightly that you can look from [advertising] medium to medium, from program event to program event, and instantly see that the brand is speaking with one voice.[4]
>
> The basic reason for integrated marketing communications is that marketing communication will be the only sustainable competitive advantage of marketing organizations in the 1990s and into the twenty-first century.[5]

In order to optimize an organization's communications effort, a company must integrate all of its communications to customers. If the various promotional elements and other nonpromotional marketing mix elements are viewed in isolation, these elements may actually work against one another.

Integrated marketing communications, or **IMC**, can be thought of as the coordination of advertising, publicity, sales promotion, point-of-purchase communications, sponsorship marketing, and personal selling with each other and with other elements of a brand's marketing mix. Integrating the various communications elements seems very basic, but many companies traditionally have resisted integrating these elements. Managers of individual promotional elements (e.g., advertising, sales promotions) have feared that change might lead to reduced budgets, authority, and power. Advertising agencies also have been reluctant to change since they were not interested in broadening their responsibilities beyond advertising. However, advertising agencies have recently taken on expanded roles by merging with existing companies or creating new departments that specialize in the growth areas of sales promotions, sponsorship marketing, and direct marketing.[6] Discussion of several key aspects of IMC follow.

Starting with the Customer. A key feature of integrated marketing communications is that the starting point of all marketing communication decisions is the customer or prospect. The IMC process requires careful study of customers' communication usage patterns and information needs, and only then does it determine the best way to communicate with customers. No effort is made to use the same advertising media or other communication tools to reach every target group. Instead, the target group's specialized media consumption patterns are studied and communication decisions are made accordingly. Hence, for example, the back page of a comic magazine may represent the most effective and efficient medium for reaching a difficult-to-reach target group of teenage boys, whereas television advertising on Saturday morning often is unparalleled in effectiveness when attempting to reach preteens. The point is that the choice of communication media, or *contact points*, is dictated by the customer's needs and behavior and not by the communicator's preferences or past successes. IMC involves an outside-in approach to decision making (i.e., from market to company) rather than imposing an inside-out solution on the market.

Achieving Synergy.

Another key aspect of IMC is the need for synergy. All of the communication elements (e.g., advertising or sponsorships) must speak with a *single voice*; coordination is absolutely critical to achieving a strong and unified brand image.[7] The key theme or selling point in a brand's advertising campaign should also be stressed by salespeople, emphasized in sales promotions, featured on the brand's package, emphasized in sponsorships, and made prominent at the point of purchase. In short, all communication elements should convey the same, unified message. Consumers will be confused if disparate messages are delivered by different promotion-mix elements.

Building Relationships.

Another fundamental characteristic of IMC is the belief that successful marketing communications requires *building a relationship* between the brand and the customer. It can be argued, in fact, that relationship building is the key to modern marketing and that IMC is the key to relationship building.[8] A relationship is an enduring linkage between a brand and consumers; it entails repeat purchase and perhaps even loyalty. Companies have learned that it is more profitable to build and maintain relationships than it is to continuously search for new customers. This explains the growth in frequent-flyer programs and many other "frequency" programs that are used to encourage customers to repeatedly purchase the company's products.

The adoption of an IMC mind set necessitates some fundamental changes in the way marketing communications have traditionally been practiced, including the following:[9]

Reduced Faith in Mass-Media Advertising.   Many marketing communicators now realize that communication methods other than mass-media advertising often better serve the needs of their brands. As noted above, the objective is to effectively contact customers and prospects. Media advertising is not always the most effective or financially efficient medium for accomplishing this objective.

Increased Reliance on Highly Targeted Communication Methods.   Direct mail, special-interest magazines, cable TV, sponsorship of events, and alternative media such as videocassettes, CD-ROM, and messages via the Internet are just some of the contact methods that enable pinpointed communications. The use of database marketing is a key aspect of this second feature. Today many business-to-business and consumer-oriented companies maintain large, up-to-date databases of present and prospective customers. These customers and prospects are periodically contacted via direct mail messages and telecommunications.

Greater Demands Imposed on Marketing Communications Suppliers.   Marketing communication suppliers such as advertising agencies, sales promotion firms, and public relations agencies have historically offered a limited range of services. Now it is increasingly important that suppliers offer multiple services. It is for this reason that some major advertising agencies have expanded their offerings beyond just advertising services to include sales promotion assistance and event marketing support.

Increased Efforts to Assess Communications' Return on Investment.   A final key feature of IMC is that it demands that systematic efforts be undertaken to determine whether communication efforts yield a *reasonable return on their investment*. All managers, and marketing communicators are no exception, must ever-increasingly be held financially responsible for their actions. The investment in marketing communications must be assessed in terms of the profit-to-investment ratio so as to determine whether changes are needed and whether other forms of investment might be more profitable.[10]

MARKETING HIGHLIGHTS

UPC and Electronic Scanning Changing Inventory Systems

There's a revolution taking place in the food industry. Consumers may not be aware of it, but every component of the supply chain is furiously working to adapt to the change toward consumer-driven systems. Code words used in the battle are value, name brands, private brands, ECR, EDI, and CRP. What do these terms means and why all the uproar?

Probably the answer is two-fold: economic and technological. The recession-plagued economy of the late 1980s caused manufacturers and retailers alike to rethink the way they were doing business in order to remain competitive. They were forced to analyze the innovative methods adopted by companies like Wal-Mart to improve distribution and lower costs in order to pass the savings on to the customer. In bygone days consumers purchased name-brand products from their neighborhood stores, where clerks rang up sales on old-fashioned cash registers. The implementation of UPC labeling and electronic scanning at the checkout counter armed retailers with data on sales that had never before been available. As the saying goes, "knowledge is power," and the knowledge retailers gained from analysis of their own sales data caused a major shift in the food industry, from one where manufacturers viewed retailers as "provincial bumpkins and conduits for their products" to a new appreciation for retailers as sophisticated marketers who use this scanner data to study their consumers' demographics and psychographics and run focus groups.[a] Many cite Sam Walton's electronic partnership with Procter & Gamble in 1987 as the beginning of the change to new strategies like efficient consumer response (ECR) and its component, the continuous replenishment program (CRP). Wal-Mart linked up technologically with P&G, using computer systems to share data and, thereby, vastly reducing constraints imposed by time and space in acquiring, interpreting, and acting on information.[b] This cross-company distribution system brought about a higher level of manufacturing efficiency and allowed Wal-Mart to keep prices on P&G products low.[c]

ECR stands for efficient consumer response, which is defined as a process for achieving marketing, merchandising, sales, and margin and profit objectives and goals by managing product groups as strategic business units that focus on delivering consumer value.[d] ECR can perhaps be better understood in light of its similarity to supply chain management in which the supply represents the pipeline that delivers products to the customer. Products flow from the manufacturer to the warehouse/broker and on to the retailer while information travels in the opposite direction of the products' pathway. This information is triggered by replenishment orders at the retailer. ECR then is defined as a joint grocery industry strategy between manufacturers and distributors to streamline the grocery chain through an integration of manufacturer, wholesale, and retail information and distribution systems.[e] Under ECR, products are expected to move much more quickly from the packaging line to the checkout counter. ECR provides benefit throughout the supply chain through improved manufacturing efficiencies, lower packaging costs, and streamlined raw materials purchasing.[f]

Campbell Soup Company provides a good example of how ECR has changed the way it does business. Chicken soup represents one of the company's most successful products, sold everyday in every supermarket. Yet, until about 1993, the company offered supermarkets off-invoice deals each January to coincide with its "Soup Month" promotions. Most major retailers would buy large quantities of the soup at this time to last far beyond the promotion period. Campbell Soup would begin running its poultry plants overtime in August, stockpiling deboned frozen chicken meat, and begin running its canning lines overtime in October, stockpiling finished product in outside storage. Then in January, the company would put its shipping crews on overtime, and supermarkets put their receiving crews on overtime while employees in Campbell's boning plants and canning plants were laid off until the next surge in production.

Harry Tetlow, vice president of logistics at Campbell Soup, Camden, New Jersey, admits that implementing the ECR system means a truly cultural change as the industry shifts from a push system that was production and distribution-driven to a pull system that is consumer- and micro-marketing-driven but added that Campbell Soup Company is committed to ECR strategies which make its year-round continuous product replenishment program attractive. The company (in 1993) had about 15% of its sales tied to CPR and hopes to extend that to 100%.[g]

Pepperidge Farm's biscuit/bakery plant in Denver, Pennsylvania, is linked via its IBM AS/400 to corporate headquarters in Norwalk, Connecticut. Distributors equipped with hand-held computers transmit sales orders daily to computers in Norwalk, which digest the data and transmit information to the appropriate plant. The computer system utilizes this information to generate production schedules.

What, then, is CRP and how does it differ from ECR? CRP is an integration of operations and technology between retailers and wholesalers and their suppliers that changes the traditional replenishment process from a distributor generating a purchase order based on economic order quantities to a system of replenishing product on the basis of actual and forecast store demand by suppliers. Information is provided via integrated EDI (electronic data exchange) standards and deliveries are accomplished on a just-in-time basis using reliable carriers to arrive at pre-scheduled times. CRP can be made available either as a retailer/wholesaler-managed or vendor-managed service.[h]

Again we look to Wal-Mart to provide a good example of how CRP works. Wal-Mart has established a partnership with Wrangler whereby the two companies are linked electronically. Each day at close-of-business, Wal-Mart transmits data about the day's sales of Wrangler jeans to Wrangler. The two companies share both the data and a model that interprets the meaning of the data. They also share software applications that act on that interpretation to send specific quantities of specific sizes and colors of jeans to specific stores from specific warehouses. Thus, both companies can know almost instantaneously which styles, sizes, and

Continued on next page

MARKETING HIGHLIGHTS, continued

colors of jeans are selling best and at which locations and can react quickly to move needed merchandise to stores in short supply. In this way, Wal-Mart only reorders from Wrangler the items that are selling best based on point-of-sale data. Wrangler has immediate results on sales and can adjust inventory and manufacturing needs in order to meet demand.[i]

Quaker Oats Company is aligning with several regional grocery chains to set up continuous replenishment systems for its entire product line to provide real-time, demand-based product stocking systems for stores. The appeal of the system to supplier as well as retailer is its ability to remove guesswork by relying on store sales scanner data to trigger shelf-restocking and manufacturer product deliveries. CRP also cuts down on the amount of time a supply of goods needs to be warehoused, cuts down on forward buying, and promotes cost efficiency, fresher products, and ensures availability of goods in stores.[j]

CRP systems are an important part of the ECR strategy because they aim to even the flow of merchandise between a supplier and retailer and remove excess inventory from the pipeline.

Fred Meyer Inc., headquartered in Portland, Oregon, has profited from its partnership with Procter & Gamble for the delivery of laundry detergents. After a two-month trial of a continuous replenishment program with vendor-managed inventory at the warehouse level, Scott Gray, EDI and quick response manager for Fred Meyer Inc., outlined the benefits at an efficient consumer response conference sponsored by the Marketing Institute. He cited:

- Reduction in baseline inventory from 8,000 to 5,700 cases.
- Increase in turns from 16 to 35.
- Increased movement of 700 cases compared to a year ago.
- Increased service level from 96% to 99.7%.

Following the results of the test, the company worked to fully implement the system to encompass the full line of P&G products.

Implementation of these strategies is costly, and some in the industry are skeptical of how beneficial the system will be. Carrying lower inventories means risking running out of a product because of lack of raw materials or breakdowns in delivery along the way. Inventory management, then, must be the effort, with continuous replenish-

■ Communications Objectives and the Communications Process

An organization advertising a product, sponsoring an event, or creating point-of-purchase materials for retailers' use is communicating with its customers. But any communication is wasted if it is not designed effectively. For communications to be effective, a marketer must set objectives for the communications and follow an effective process of communicating the message.

ment the process, and reliable operations and reduced inventories the
result.[k] Abandoning forward buying
may be a struggle as wholesalers question how it will affect their bottom
lines. The cost in purchasing and
installing the computer technology is a
drawback to others.

Doug Warner, president of
Inventory Management Services,
Germantown, Tennessee, believes that
ECR and CRP are here to stay. He
writes that "inventory, which is expensive, has been more available than
information, which is less expensive.
As we move deeper into the
'Information Age,' we will begin taking
advantage of the computer . . . to provide data to people throughout the
supply chain. Timely, accurate data
generates information that allows for
better business decisions, which lead to
managing time rather than cost.
Reliable supply systems made possible
by continuous-replenishment processes will be a prerequisite to the next generation of business management."[l]

[a] Anil Jagtiani and Jon Berry, "Three
Imperatives," *Brandweek*, October 25, 1993,
23–24.

[b] Stephan H. Haeckel and Richard L. Nolan,
"Managing by Wire," *Harvard Business
Review*, September–October 1993, 122.

[c] "The Evolution of Wal-Mart: Savvy
Expansion and Leadership," *Harvard
Business Review*, May–June 1993, 82.

[d] "A User's Guide to Efficient Consumer
Response," *Grocery Marketing*, August,
1993, 14.

[e] Bob Swientek, "Automation Drivers for
World Class Manufacturing," *Prepared
Foods*, October, 1993, 132.

[f] Swientek, "Automation Drivers."

[g] Bruce Fox, "Inefficient Chicken Soup; The
Use of the Efficient Consumer Response
System in the Supermarket Industry,"
*Chain Store Executive with Shopping Center
Age*, July, 1993, 52.

[h] *Grocery Marketing*, 14.

[i] *Harvard Business Review*, September–
October, 1993, 129.

[j] Betsy Spethmann, "Quaker Gets a Lock on
its Stock," *Brandweek*, November 15, 1993,
3.

[k] Doug Warner, "Process of Continuous-
Replenishment Helps Mills Better Manage
Inventories; Focus: Transportation," *Pulp
and Paper*, October, 1993, Vol. 67, No. 10, 75.

[l] Warner, "Process of Continuous-
Replenishment Helps Mills."

Communication Objectives

All marketing mix variables, promotion and otherwise, are directed
at accomplishing the following objectives:

1. Building product category wants
2. Creating brand awareness
3. Enhancing attitudes and influencing purchase intentions
4. Facilitating purchase[11]

The promotion-mix elements (e.g., advertising or sales promotions) are particularly consequential in determining whether these overall objectives are achieved.

Building Product Category Wants.

An organization's main objective is to motivate customers to buy its particular brands rather than a competitor's. But customers must want the general product category before they want a specific brand within that category. Product innovators must first attempt to build product category wants, also known as creating *primary demand*.

Building category wants is *not* an issue for a new brand being introduced into an established product category. Other manufacturers and advertisers have already laid the groundwork for the product category. For example, advertisements for the new pain reliever, Aleve, did not need to build product category wants; consumers already were aware of the need for and benefits of pain relievers. However, marketers who are introducing a new brand into a new product category—one that consumers are unfamiliar with—face a different task. Their first objective must be to build product category wants *then* brand awareness.

Creating Brand Awareness, Enhancing Attitudes, and Influencing Purchase Intentions.

Once category wants are established, marketers compete against one another for the consumers' dollars. Each competitor attempts to create *secondary demand* for its brand. This is done by creating awareness for the brand and favorably influencing attitudes and intentions. Consider again the pain reliever market. For several decades Bayer Aspirin was the cure-all, dominating brand in the category. Then, Tylenol and later Advil, Nuprin, Motrin, and Aleve entered the market aggressively, eroding Bayer's share. Each of these brands is aggressively promoted in an effort to create awareness and influence attitudes and purchase intentions.

Creating awareness involves familiarizing consumers with the company's brand through advertising, sales promotions, and other communications methods. Consumers need to be informed about a brand's special features and benefits and how it differs from competitive brands. The issue from the consumer's viewpoint: Why, for example, should I buy Aleve rather than Tylenol or Bayer? The goal of Procter & Gamble would be to create consumer awareness of Aleve, so that consumers would form favorable *attitudes* toward the brand and possibly develop an *intention* to purchase that brand the next time they need a pain reliever.

Facilitating Purchase.   The odds that consumers ultimately will purchase the marketer's brand depends on whether the promotion and marketing communications variables *facilitate purchasing*. In our pain reliever example, Procter & Gamble may have successfully created awareness and built favorable attitudes for Aleve, but if the product is not available on the store shelf, if the product is only available in one large size, or if the product is priced $1.00 more than Bayer or Tylenol, the likelihood of Aleve being purchased is greatly reduced, unless P&G is able to convince consumers that Aleve's benefits are worth the additional cost. Effective advertising, packaging, and other marketing communications variables serve to facilitate purchasing and possibly overcome obstacles created by the nonpromotional marketing mix variables such as price.

The foregoing discussion has provided a general description of how marketing communications accomplish general objectives. It now will be helpful to consider a more precise account of communication objectives and the promotional efforts that are used to attain them. The **hierarchy-of-effects** is a common framework to illustrate the idea that marketing communications progress the consumer from an initial stage of brand awareness, to interest in the brand, to desire, and, finally, to action. The hierarchy-of-effects metaphor implies that successful marketing communications must move consumers from one goal to the next goal, much in the same way that one climbs a ladder—one step at a time until the top rung is reached.

A variety of hierarchy-of-effects models exist, but all are predicated on the idea that marketing communications attempt to drive people from an initial state of unawareness about a brand to a final stage of purchasing that brand. Intermediate stages in the hierarchy represent progressively closer steps to purchase as seen in Exhibit 14.3.

The different stages in the hierarchy are best understood by examining an actual communications situation. Consider the magazine advertisement in Exhibit 14.4 for Easy Spirit dress shoes manufactured by the U.S. Shoe Corporation. (It will be helpful to peruse the advertisement before proceeding with your reading of the text.) When this brand was introduced to the market, consumers were *unaware* of both the brand name and the particular set of advantages offered by Easy Spirit dress shoes. Hence, the objective of U.S. Shoe's

Exhibit 14.3   The Hierarchy of Effects

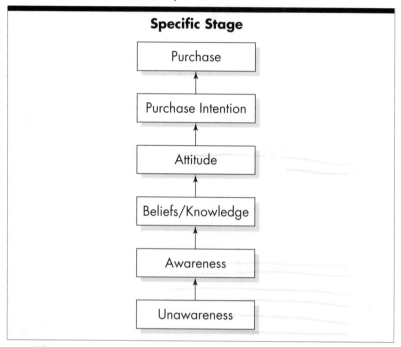

initial advertising efforts was to create consumer *awareness* of the Easy Spirit brand name. However, creating awareness alone would not necessarily motivate consumers to choose this brand over alternative brands. Advertising had to persuade consumers that Easy Spirit shoes possess the dual features of feeling like sneakers but looking like pumps (see the ad copy). The ad in Exhibit 14.4 attempts to accomplish this by describing the various features and benefits provided by this brand—"Only Easy Spirit pumps feature the patented Easy Spirit suspension system: layers of shock-absorbing foam to cushion your feet from even the hardest surfaces"—and visually supporting the claim with the photo of an athletic model (perhaps portrayed as a coach) shown holding a basketball while standing on a hard-surface gym floor. These claimed brand benefits should serve to influence consumers *beliefs/knowledge* as they relate to Easy Spirit shoes and contribute to consumers' forming positive *attitudes* and *purchase intentions* toward this brand of rather hybrid sport and dress shoe. The U.S. Shoe Corporation hopes that the purchase intention will develop into an actual *purchase* the next time the consumer is in need of another pair of dress shoes.

Exhibit 14.4   An Example of Hierarchy Effects in Advertising

After this demonstration,
the floor wasn't in great shape.
But her feet were.

It takes an extremely supportive dress shoe to endure this kind of torture. Only Easy Spirit pumps feature the patented Easy Spirit suspension system: layers of shock-absorbing foam to cushion your feet from even the hardest surfaces. The result is classic, elegant *Easy* SPIRIT. shoes that look like pumps, but feel like sneakers. Quality leathers and scuff-resistant heels keep them looking great. If we can do this with pumps, think how comfortable our casual shoes are. There's one to fit every occasion, and every foot. But maybe not quite every surface.

There really is a sneaker inside every shoe.

©1994 U.S. Shoe Corp.

Exhibit 14.5   Elements in the Communications Process

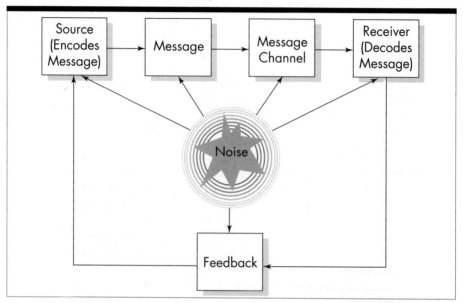

The Communications Process

The achievement of marketing communication objectives depends upon how effective the communication process is. If a breakdown occurs at any stage of the process, the odds of achieving desired objectives are greatly reduced.

Communication can be a very difficult task. Two people can hear one message yet interpret the meaning of the message in different ways. Mass marketers have the added burden of attempting to effectively communicate with large, diverse audiences. These messages are bound to be interpreted differently by some consumers among the thousands or even millions who see or hear the message. Therefore, marketers must make their messages as clear as possible to at least minimize, if not avoid, misinterpretations.

The communication process involves a sender transmitting a message to a receiver. Both sender and receiver must be active participants in the process in order for the message to be successfully transmitted. Communication is an activity one does *with* another person, not something one does *to* another person.

As portrayed in Exhibit 14.5 and in the following list, the communications process involves the following eight elements:

- a source
- encoding
- a message
- a channel
- a receiver
- decoding
- the possibility of noise
- feedback potential

The **source** in the communication process is a person or group of persons (such as U.S. Shoe Corporation) who has thoughts to share with some other person or group of persons. These thoughts can be ideas, product benefits, or competitive comparisons. The source then **encodes** the message, or puts the thought into symbolic form, in an effort to accomplish the communication objectives previously discussed.

The source selects specific *signs* from an infinite variety of words, symbols, phrases, and nonverbal elements to encode the message that will communicate effectively with the selected target audience. The **message** is the symbolic expression of the sender's thoughts. In marketing communications, the message takes the form of advertisements, package designs, point-of-purchase display materials, sales promotions, and so on.

The **message channel** is the path through which the message moves from the source to the receiver. Channels such as television, radio, print media, telephone, direct mail, and the Internet are used by organizations to transmit advertising messages to their customers.

The **receiver** is the person or group of persons for whom the message is intended. Receivers are the current and potential customers of an organization's products or services. **Decoding** is the process by which receivers interpret, or derive meaning from the message. For example, some receivers of the Easy Spirit advertisement in Exhibit 14.4 may accept this dual-concept shoe as absolutely perfect for their comfort and appearance needs. Others may reject the concept on the ground that shoes are either dressy or sporty but cannot simultaneously satisfy both sets of requirements.

At any point in this process, noise can occur and disrupt the process. **Noise** is any interference or distraction that interferes with the preparation, transmission, or reception of a marketing message. The term is borrowed from its original meaning as an electric disturbance, but has a broader meaning when applied to the communications process. For example, noise arises at the encoding stage when, say, a salesperson is unclear of the message he or she wants to present the customer with. Noise at the decoding stage happens when, for example, the receiver leaves during a television advertisement to get something to eat in the kitchen or answer the telephone.

Feedback is the final element in the communication process. **Feedback** is a measure of how well the message is received. Feedback will reflect whether the message hit the target market accurately or whether it needs some alterations to make it stronger and clearer. Positive feedback for a marketer would be reflected as the sale of the product, whereas negative feedback comes in the form of confusion about what the message is conveying and, ultimately, nonpurchase of the promoted product.

Determinants of an Appropriate Promotions Mix

In determining an appropriate mix of promotional elements for a specific brand in a particular product category, a product or brand manager must weight a variety of factors related to the category, the brand, and the market. The marketing manager typically has considerable discretion in determining which promotion elements to use and how much relative emphasis each should receive. Should the entire budget go towards supporting the sales force, or should some be allocated to a network television advertising schedule? Will point-of-purchase materials be needed at retail? Will coupons or bonus packs help move more product? There is no right formula a manager can use to determine the "correct" blend of promotional elements. The manager must thoroughly analyze the product, the competition, the brand's strengths and weaknesses, and the target market to determine the brand's promotional needs and opportunities. The decision is guided by addressing each of the following issues:

- Who is the intended market?
- What objectives does the communicator hope to accomplish?
- What is the nature of the product?
- What is the product life-cycle stage?
- What are competitors doing?
- What is the available budget for promotion?

■ Will a push or pull strategy be more effective in promoting the product?

Who Is the Intended Market?

A marketer's approach will differ considerably depending on the character of the intended market. Is it an organizational buyer in the business-to-business market, or is it the mass market of consumers? Chapter 5 previously established that in the business-to-business market the number of organizational buyers are fewer, decisions are often made in groups, and buyers are more geographically concentrated. The marketing budget would be more effectively used in personal selling to reach this target market. However, in the consumer market—where individual buyers number in the millions, where decisions are made by each consumer individually, and where consumers are widely dispersed throughout the country, and, perhaps, world—the marketing budget would be more effectively spent on personal selling (to reach middlemen) and advertising, sales promotion, and other communication devices to reach consumers. A clear understanding of the product's target market is vital in determining how best to allocate the promotional budget.

What Objectives Does the Communicator Hope to Accomplish?

The objectives of the marketing communications also affect the promotional mix. If the objective is to build product category wants, greater advertising effort will be required. If the objective is to create brand awareness, then a blend of advertising and sales promotions will be needed. If the objective is to gain increased support from retailers for the manufacturer's brands, then trade-oriented sales promotions will be required. If the objective is to encourage repeat purchases from consumers, then consumer-oriented sales promotions will be called for. Different objectives require different emphases on the various promotional elements.

What Is the Nature of the Product?

The nature of the product itself will dictate the promotional mix. For example, an industrial machine that is marketed to a small segment of business-to-business customers will utilize different promotional elements than will a brand of toothpaste, deodorant, snack food, or other convenience good. Although some advertising or sales promotions might be used by the industrial machine marketer, personal selling efforts must be emphasized to make sales. In this case, the marketer's budget may be divided as follows: personal selling—70%; trade-oriented media advertising—20%; and telemarketing and direct-mail advertising—10%.

In promoting consumer goods, especially convenience items, other forms of promotion take on added importance. In this case, the marketer's budget may be divided as follows: personal selling to the trade—20%; trade-oriented sales promotions—30%; advertising to consumers—25%; consumer-oriented sales promotions—20%; and point-of-purchase materials—5%. No one element within the mix will be omitted completely from the budget. The focus on each element will change, though, depending on the product.

What Is the Product Life-Cycle Stage?

Is the brand well-established and in the maturity stage of the product life cycle, or is it a new product in the introduction stage? Which stage a product is in will have a major impact on the promotional mix. In the introduction stage, advertising is especially critical to create awareness and to inform consumers about the brand and its benefits. Trade-oriented sales promotions are essential for gaining wholesaler and retailer support, and consumer sales promotions (such as coupons and cents-off deals) also are important for purposes of creating consumer trial, especially when marketing consumer packaged goods. Later on as the product reaches the maturity stage, advertising and sales promotions both remain crucial but both undergo qualitative changes. Advertising now is needed to maintain a positive brand image and differentiate the brand from competitive offerings, while sales promotions are used to encourage repeat purchase behavior. Regardless of the life cycle stage, personal selling by the manufacturer's sales force is key to gaining trade acceptance and continual support for the product.

What Are Competitors Doing?

Competitive activity cannot be ignored in any market. Competitive action generally dictates what can or must be done. For example, in the deodorant category if Soft 'n' Dri offers a trade allowance that reduces the retail price to $1.99 and then offers a 75¢ coupon, consumers are able to buy this brand for only $1.24. Ban, Lady Speed Stick, and Secret cannot ignore this activity or they may see an erosion of their market shares, even if it's only on a temporary basis. These companies may be forced to take action to offset Soft 'n' Dri's competitive push.

In the disposable diaper market, though, a different situation recently occurred. Pampers, Huggies, and Luvs were routinely distributing $1.00-off coupons in print advertisements. The marketers—Procter & Gamble and Kimberly Clark—in due time realized that consumers who need disposable diapers must buy them whether or not they have a coupon. Diapers are not a purchase that can be put off for very long. One manufacturer first reduced the coupon value, the other followed suit, and eventually both discontinued the mass coupon drops altogether. Consumers continued buying these disposable diaper brands and both companies saved promotional dollars. Following competitive actions in this case saved both companies considerable money.

What Is the Available Budget for Promotion?

The marketer's budget will determine what promotion mix can be emphasized. In the business-to-business market, a marketer may emphasize personal selling and forego advertising if the total promotional budget is limited due to a poor performance the previous year or because the economic forecast for the coming year is unattractive. The sales force is a relatively fixed expense, whereas advertising can be increased or decreased depending on the situation and financial circumstances. In lean times less money is invested in advertising, whereas the sales force budget remains basically constant.

In the consumer market, on the other hand, a nationally distributed brand is forced by the competition to devote some funds to advertising and sales promotions. The actual amount varies depending on the product category and the economic situation, but most brands invest anywhere from 2% to 10% of sales volume on advertising and an equal or greater amount to trade- and consumer-oriented sales promotions collectively. For example, in a product category that generates $5 billion in annual sales, a company with a 10% market share (i.e., $500 million sales volume) that devotes 5% of sales to advertising and 6% to sales promotions would spend $25 million on advertising and $30 million on sales promotions.

CAPTAINS OF INDUSTRY

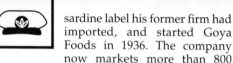

Joseph A. Unanue

President

Goya Foods Inc.

Date of Birth: 1925

Education: College graduate; engineering major

Career Path: Worked in family-owned business. Became president in 1977 when his father, Prudencio Unanue, died.

Profile: Parents immigrated from Spain in 1915 and settled in New Jersey. Goya Foods is the largest privately held Hispanic U.S. company, and Unanue tops the Hispanic Business Rich List of America's 50 richest Hispanic individuals and families for 1993.[a]

Personal: Refers to his daily work schedule as half-days because he only works 12 out of every 24 hours in a day.

Joseph Unanue's parents, Prudencio and Carolina Unanue, started Goya Foods Inc. in 1936. Prudencio had come to the United States via Puerto Rico from his native Spain in 1915 and held various jobs in the food industry for 20 years before working for a Spanish firm that imported olives and canned sardines. The Spanish Civil War caused the company to curtail trade, however, and Prudencio lost his job. Prudencio Unanue used this setback to capitalize on a need he recognized: that of providing foods native to Spain and Puerto Rico to the growing number of Hispanics in the United States and neighboring countries. He and his wife, Carolina, took the name Goya from a sardine label his former firm had imported, and started Goya Foods in 1936. The company now markets more than 800 products and ingredients, ranging in variety from olive oil and sardines to piña colada mix and frozen pound cake.

Goya Foods Inc. has been the market leader in the northeast United States for decades, where it sells 80% of Hispanic foods. It supplies more than 800 of its own products, including 34 varieties of beans alone. But since the elder Unanue died in 1977 and Carolina Unanue in 1984, their sons have been aggressively changing the company's marketing strategy. Joseph Unanue took over as president in 1977, and his brother, Frank, is president of Goya de Puerto Rico. All of their children, as well as those of their brothers Charles (who traded his inheritance for $4 million in 1973) and Anthony (deceased) now work for the company.[b]

Goya's three-pronged marketing strategy aims to expand its market base by adding new products based on analysis of emerging consumer needs, (e.g., Mexican foods); by expanding into new areas such as the Southwest and particularly Texas, and targeting the mid-west for future growth; and by extending its reach beyond traditional core markets (e.g., a new warehousing facility outside Buffalo built to facilitate expansion into upstate New York, Ohio, and part of Pennsylvania).[c]

Immigrants from Mexico and Central America are used to foods and spices that differ from those offered by Goya's traditional Caribbean product mix, and in an effort to win this growing segment of the population, the company has had to greatly expand its product line. The Mexican foods market is already served by major U.S. food companies, and Goya wants a share of the action. In 1990 it introduced its first salsa, directly competing with such salsa giants as Pace Foods and Pet's Old El Paso. Goya realizes that it must protect its market share in Hispanic-owned stores while increasing its presence in the mainstream to stay ahead of its competition. The company has responded by introducing more spices, sauces, and other products aimed at immigrants from Mexico and Central and Latin American countries, and plans to shift its product mix, aiming to quadruple its revenue from Mexican foods from 5% to 20% in five years by seeking to enter new areas such as the West Coast, where the Hispanic population is 70% Mexican descent.[d]

One of Goya's main strengths is its sales force. At least once a week, these sales people visit each bodega, or neighborhood grocery store, to talk to owners and customers. These sales people can, in turn, provide information back to the company about the changing ethnic makeup of these neighborhoods so that Goya can adjust its product mix and the words on its packaging. And wording can be tricky since Cubans, Puerto Ricans, Dominicans, and Argentineans all have different names for the same bean, Conrad Colon, executive vice president and director of marketing, reveals.[e]

Goya's goal, then, is to become nationally known and has hired distributors who know the Mexican market to help them compete against the likes of Campbell Soup Company and Knorr Foods, both aggressively going after the Hispanic population. And Joseph Unanue, who had once considered market research a waste of time, is

now studying the demographics of various zip codes to locate where Hispanics live as well as supermarkets in those predominately Hispanic areas. Judging from the results of a DRI/McGraw-Hill report projecting a 41% increase in the Hispanic population this decade compared with a 5% increase for everyone else, there is money to be made from this growing segment of the U.S. population.[f]

Goya has recently changed its advertising theme from "Goya, oh boya" to "For better meals, turn to Goya," hoping to link its products to health benefits sought by today's consumers while widening its appeal to include third- and fourth-generation Hispanics as well as Anglos. In 1993 Goya introduced frozen bread pudding and cornbread, several Caribbean-style rice mixes, and is planning another salsa and guacamole. And they are constantly working to develop new products to replace items that were declining in sales. For example, Goya has sold canned pasteles, or meat pies, for more than 40 years, but when the product began to decline in sales the company came out with a frozen product, and Colon states that they have now recovered that market. "We are selling now to a different generation, following their trends, habits, and assimilation."[g]

Joseph Unanue is a hard-working man with a quick wit. His company employs nine third-generation family members. They aren't given offices on the management floor, however, but are expected to work their way up the company ladder. He and his brother, Frank, allowed their children to work for the company while they were in

Continued on next page

CAPTAINS OF INDUSTRY, continued

grade school or high school, putting them to work in the warehouse, the packing room, or doing routine office work. After the children graduated from college they were offered the chance to work for the company, starting on the bottom and working themselves up. He considers his father to have been a better businessman than himself because he was a great teacher and a man of humility. "He taught us—it sounds archaic and everything else—that honesty is the best policy and I believe that's right."[h] Unanue believes in hard work, putting in 12-hour days at the age of 68 which he jokingly refers to as "half-days," and has his eye on the goal of making Goya a billion-dollar company by the turn of the century. And the ambition driving the goal is "to show the Hispanic population of this world that it doesn't matter what you are, you can grow a company, you can make it grow, you can make it work. I think it would give most of the Hispanic population or some of them in there the idea that they could do it also, and I hope they do."[i]

GOYA'S GROWTH[j]

Sales of Goya Foods Inc. have grown 166% in the past 10 years, or an average of about 16% a year.

[a] "The Hispanic Business Rich List," by the editors, *Hispanic Business*, March 1993.
[b] "Unanues Make this Business a Family Affair," *USA TODAY*, May 10, 1993, 1E.
[c] "And the New Number 1 Is . . . ," *Hispanic Business*, June 1993, 76.
[d] Rhonda Richards, "From Desperation, an Empire; Goya Foods Born of a Job Lost," *USA Today*, May 10, 1993, 1E.
[e] David C. Walters, "Goya Grows, Seeks New Markets," *The Christian Science Monitor*, May 27, 1993, 8.
[f] Ibid.
[g] Ibid.
[h] Pinnacle, *CNN*, Transcript #185, October 31, 1993. Interview with Joseph Unanue by Beverly Schuch, *CNN Business News*.
[i] Ibid.
[j] "And the New Number 1 Is . . . ," *Hispanic Business*, June 1993, 76."

Will a Push or Pull Strategy Be More Effective in Promoting the Product?

The concepts of push and pull characterize the promotional activities marketers undertake to encourage channel members to handle products. The terms "push" and "pull" are metaphors that characterize the nature of the promotional thrust through the channel of distribution. A manufacturer's **push** strategy involves utilizing aggressive trade allowances and personal selling efforts to obtain distribution for a product through wholesalers and retailers. The product is "pushed" through the channel system in the sense that there is a forward thrust from the manufacturer to the trade.

Personal selling to the trade is the primary push technique. Once the product is on the shelf, advertising and sales promotion are used to encourage the consumer to try the product.

A **pull** strategy involves encouraging consumer demand for the product to obtain distribution. If a product is heavily advertised and supported with major high-value coupon drops or other sales promotions, consumers will request the product from retailers. Retailers, in turn, will order the product from wholesalers or directly from manufacturers. The product has been "pulled" through the system.

Both the push and pull strategies utilize personal selling, advertising, sales promotion, and so on. Each strategy, though, requires a different emphasis on the individual promotional elements. Personal selling is much more important in the push strategy than in the pull strategy. Advertising is much more important in the pull strategy than in the push strategy. Marketers must decide which strategy will be more effective in promoting their specific brands. It is very important to recognize, however, that most manufacturers use a combination of push and pull techniques. These techniques complement one another rather than representing perfect substitutes. The primary determination for most manufacturers is one of how much pull and how much push should be used rather than a matter of whether to depend exclusively on pull- or on push-oriented promotion techniques.

The Promotion Management Process

As the previous sections illustrate, many factors must be considered in creating an effective promotional mix for a product. A marketer must thoroughly examine and analyze every factor that affects the product *before* any plans or strategies are created. The promotion process—like any other business process—must be managed. The following are the various types of decisions involved in the promotion management process.

Promotion Decisions

The promotion management process can be conceptualized in terms of five primary steps: selecting target markets, establishing objectives, setting the budget, implementing message and media strategies, and evaluating program effectiveness.

Selecting Target Markets.   Selection of target markets is the critical first step toward effective and efficient marketing communications. Targeting allows marketing communicators to pinpoint the product's potential audience and to more precisely deliver messages to this group. Targeting attempts to avoid wasting valuable promotional dollars on those consumers outside the target market. Companies identify potential target markets in terms of a combination of characteristics—demographics, lifestyles, product usage patterns, geographical location—that will cause these consumers to act in a similar fashion. For example, the target market for Easy Spirit shoes (Exhibit 14.4) probably consists primarily of women aged 18–49, who are employed full time, and who are on their feet either at work or on their way to and from work. Working women in major urban centers such as New York City would seem to represent a particularly attractive market for this shoe line.

As discussed in Chapter 6, a meaningful market segment, or target market, is one consisting of consumers who (1) can be *identified and measured* in terms of market size, (2) represent *substantial sales and profit potential* to the company who targets them, (3) are *economically accessible* via distribution and media channels, and (4) exhibit *relatively homogeneous response tendencies* to a brand's marketing mix elements. Marketing research efforts to identify appropriate target markets are well worth the expense inasmuch as *marketing communications* are both more effective and efficient when directed at customers who are prime prospects for the marketer's offering.

Establishing Objectives.   As discussed earlier in the chapter, it is important for marketing communicators to establish clear and achievable objectives as a prelude to designing messages and executing communication programs. Marketing communication objectives must fit within the company's overall corporate and marketing objectives. The objectives must also be realistic and stated in quantitative terms with the amount of projected change and the time duration specified. For example, the objective "to increase brand awareness" is too general to be of much value. A much better objective would be "to increase brand awareness by 20% within the next 6 months."

Setting the Budget.   After determining the target market and specifying objectives, the next step in the promotion management process is to develop an accurate budget. An organization's financial resources are budgeted to specific promotion elements in order to accomplish the communications objectives established for its various brands. The amount of resources allocated to specific promotion elements is typically the result of an involved process in most sophisticated corporations. Companies use different budgeting processes in allocating funds to promotion managers. At one extreme is **top-down budgeting (TD)**, in which senior management decides how much each subunit receives. At the other extreme is **bottom-up budgeting (BU)**, in which managers of subunits (such as brand managers) determine how much is needed to achieve their objectives; these amounts are then combined to establish the total marketing budget.

Most budgeting practices involve a combination of top-down and bottom-up budgeting. For example, in the bottom-up/top-down process (BUTD), subunit managers submit budget requests to a chief marketing officer (say, a vice president of marketing), who coordinates the various requests and then submits an overall budget to top management for approval. The top-down/bottom-up process (TDBU) reverses the flow of influence by having top managers first establish the total size of the budget and then divide it among the various subunits. Research has shown that combination budgeting methods (BUTD and TDBU) are used more often than the extreme methods (TD or BU). The BUTD process is by far the most frequently used, especially in more sophisticated firms where marketing-department influence is high compared to finance-department influence.[12]

Each promotional element within the overall plan will have a specific cost. All of the costs must be added together to determine the overall budget. Some companies set their budgets using the **competitive parity method**—they will spend whatever is necessary to meet competitors' actions. Other companies set promotional budgets as a percentage of past or anticipated sales. This, naturally, is called the **percentage of sales method**. For example, a company may allocate 15% of the next fiscal period's anticipated sales for promotion. If sales are estimated to be $100,000,000 for the upcoming year, the promotional budget will be $15,000,000. The most common method for promotional budgeting, called the **objective and task method**, is one where (1) objectives are specified, (2) the promotional elements needed to reach those objectives are identified, and (3) the budget is determined by accumulating anticipated costs among the various promotional elements. Whatever budgeting process is used, marketing communication managers must be sure to include all plans and costs *upfront*—it is very difficult to add promotional elements and new costs once the current budget is being implemented.

Implementing Message and Media Strategies.

Decisions must be made regarding the message to be communicated and the media within which the message will be sent. The message is a critical component of marketing communication effectiveness. Marketers must decide how best to present their ideas to achieve the established objectives. In creating a message, a marketer may choose from a variety of message alternatives including what image to create, how to position the brand, and what types of appeals to employ such as humor, nostalgia, informational, and so on.

A variety of media strategies also must be considered by the marketer. Media typically connotes a mode of advertising such as via television, radio, or magazines. But the term media can be applied to any promotional element. Point-of-purchase display materials, for example, can be a simple message on the shelf, or shelf talker, a take-one pad, or a sophisticated display. A sales promotion can range from a simple coupon distributed via freestanding insert to a more involved sweepstakes offer. Each of these alternatives is a different medium that has a different rate of effectiveness as well as cost. The marketer must determine which message and media will be most effective—from both a communications as well as cost standpoint—in delivering the desired message.

Evaluating Program Effectiveness.

Once the promotional program is in place and being implemented, the program must be evaluated for its effectiveness. This is a necessary and important part of the promotional process. Only through evaluation can marketers learn what works, what does not work, and why. This information will be critical in creating future programs and taking corrective action when necessary.

A program is evaluated by measuring the results of the program against the objectives established in the planning stage. For some promotional elements it is relatively simple to assess effectiveness because the results generated are easily attributable to just that promotional element. Consider a direct-mail campaign where the measure of effectiveness is the *actual response rate*, or the number of orders received as a percentage of the number of mailings, say, a

2% response rate. Effectiveness is evaluated by comparing the actual response rate with the objective established in the form of a *projected response rate*. For a premium offer, the total number of consumers sending in proofs-of-purchase can be compared against the number of submissions contained in the original objective. In either event, corrective action is called for if the actual response rate falls significantly below that which was projected.

Other promotional elements such as advertising are more difficult to evaluate inasmuch as objective outcomes—such as the amount of sales generated in a period—are not directly or exclusively attributable to the ads per se. In other words, sales are the result of *all marketing mix variables* and not just advertising. Moreover, current sales may be due to past marketing efforts and are not solely attributable to current advertising; that is, the advertising and sales relation is typically *lagged*, with advertising in the current period influencing sales at later times as well as in the current period. Due to these complications, advertisers typically assess advertising effectiveness in terms of so-called *communication outcomes* such as changes in consumers' awareness of the advertised brand, knowledge of copy points, or attitudes toward the brand. All of these factors, if measured and known before an advertising campaign begins, can be measured again at the end of the campaign and compared to objectives to determine effectiveness.

This is why the setting of clear and measurable objectives is so very important in marketing. Without these characteristics in a marketer's objectives, the objectives are useless. Evaluation can only occur when there are concrete goals against which to compare results.

Key Participants in Promotion Management

A general marketing manager has overall responsibility for all aspects of a firm's marketing programs. However, most day-to-day, or tactical, marketing decisions occur at the product management or brand management levels. A product manager for a business-to-business company or a brand manager for a consumer-goods company has profit-and-loss responsibility for the particular product or brand that she or he manages. This product or brand manager also is responsible for long-term (strategic) and short-term (tactical) decisions relating to the product or brand he or she manages.

However, the various promotion decisions are not the sole responsibility of the product/brand manager. Instead, in most corporations managers of departments are responsible for the planning and implementation of individual promotion elements. Sales management, for example, is responsible for the personal selling function of the promotion mix. (More on this in Chapter 16.) Advertising managers are responsible for the entire advertising function, much of which is "farmed out" to independent advertising agencies. These agencies, working with their client's product or brand managers, create advertising copy, schedule media, and assess advertising effectiveness. Public relations managers are responsible for providing news media with positive messages about the company and its activities. As with advertising, in many instances public relations is delegated to independent PR agencies. Likewise, sales promotion managers have responsibilities for carrying out the variety of trade- and consumer-oriented promotions, and, again, oftentimes outside vendors that specialize in specific forms of promotions (e.g., premium offers or sweepstakes and contests) are contracted to perform these specialized services. But regardless of the number of managers or independent agencies involved in the promotion management process, product and brand managers must oversee the entire program and monitor its progress throughout the promotional period. One individual needs to have the "big picture" of the program at all times in order to ensure success of the program as well as the product or brand itself.

Advocates of integrated marketing communications recommend that corporations reorganize by setting up an organizational unit headed by someone with the title Marketing Communications director.[13] This MARCOM "czar" would have full responsibility for all promotional elements and could assure that all aspects of marketing communications are indeed integrated. Most companies have not gone to this extreme, but as noted earlier, some outside vendors have integrated their services to form full-service marketing communication operations. Agencies that historically just provided advertising services have expanded their operations to include direct-marketing services, public relations, and sales-promotion services. Product and brand managers turn to these agencies and engage in "one-stop shopping" in much the same way that consumers do when shopping at department stores and other full-service retail outlets.

■ Chapter Summary

The product and its benefits must be communicated to consumers through marketing communications and the promotional element of the marketing mix. In today's highly competitive and dynamic marketing world, effective communications are critical to a company's success. Marketing communications represent the collection of all elements in an organization's marketing mix that facilitate exchanges by establishing shared meaning with the organization's customers or clients.

In marketing, promotion means to motivate—or move in a sense—customers to action. Promotion management employs a variety of tools for this purpose including personal selling, advertising, sales promotions, point-of-purchase communications, direct marketing communications, public relations, and sponsorship marketing. These elements along with the other communication elements in the marketing mix must be treated as a unified whole, rather than as separable and independent activities.

For communications to be effective, a marketer must set objectives for the communications and follow an effective process of communicating the message. The marketer communicates either directly with the consumer or with the overall market. In communicating with a consumer, a marketer attempts to progress the consumer from unawareness to purchase. Regarding the overall market, all marketing communications efforts are aimed at building product category wants, creating brand awareness, enhancing attitudes, influencing intentions, and facilitating purchase. All communication processes involve a source, encoding, a message, a channel, a receiver, decoding, the possibility of noise, and feedback potential. Flawed efforts at any stage in the communication process will greatly reduce the odds of achieving the desired objectives.

Marketing managers have considerable discretion in determining which promotional elements to use and how much relative emphasis each should receive. Various factors such as the target market, product life-cycle stage, objectives, competitive activity, budget, and nature of the product all affect the promotional mix. The promotion management process includes determining the target market, specifying objectives, setting the budget, determining message and media strategies, and evaluating the results of the program.

Where historically many promotion and marketing communication decisions were treated as rather disparate and managed by independent departments that failed to carefully coordinate their activities, the current trend is toward integrated marketing communications, or IMC. Some key elements of IMC are that all marketing communication decisions start with the customer, which reflects the adoption of an outside-in mentality versus an inside-out position that historically has dominated this field. Another fundamental feature is that all communication elements must achieve synergy, or speak with a single voice. The belief that successful marketing communications must build a relationship between the brand and the customer is another key IMC feature.

The adoption of an IMC mind set leads to several changes in the way marketing communications are practiced. Some of the changes include (1) reduced faith in mass-media advertising, (2) increased reliance on highly target communication methods such as direct mail and Internet advertising, (3) increased demands imposed on marketing communications suppliers for full services, and (4) expanded efforts to assess the return on investment yielded by marketing communication activities.

◆ Notes

1. Don E. Schultz, Stanley I. Tannenbaum, Robert F. Lauterborn, *Integrated Marketing Communications* (Lincolnwood, IL: NTC, 1993), 46.

2. *Promotion* is derived from the Latin word *promovere; pro* meaning forward and *movere* meaning to move.

3. *1986 Supermarket Buying Habits Study* (Englewood, NJ: Point-of-Purchase Advertising Institute).

4. Quoting Spencer Plavoukas, chairman of Lintas: New York, and cited in Laurie Petersen, "Pursuing Results in the Age of Accountability," *Adweek's Marketing Week*, November 19, 1990, 21.

5. Schultz, Tannenbaum, and Lauterborn, *Integrated Marketing Communications*.

6. For further discussion of the resistance to integrate, see Scott Hume, "New Ideas, Old Barriers," *Advertising Age*, July 22, 1991, 6.

7. This "one-voice perspective" is widely shared by various writers on the topic of IMC. See Schultz et al., *Integrated Marketing Communications*; Tom Duncan, "Integrated Marketing? It's Synergy," *Advertising Age*, March 8, 1993, 22; and Glen J. Nowak and Joseph Phelps, "Conceptualizing the Integrated Marketing Communications' Phenomenon: An Examination of Its Impact on Advertising Practices and Its Implications for Advertising Research," *Journal of Current Issues and Research in Advertising*, 16 (Spring 1994), 49–66.

8. See Schultz et al., *Integrated Marketing Communications*, 52–53.
9. Nowak and Phelps, "Conceptualizing the Integrated Marketing Communications' Phenomenon."
10. For discussion of how to assess the ROI for marketing communications, see Don E. Schultz, "Trying to Determine ROI for IMC," *Marketing News*, January 3, 1994, 18; Don E. Schultz, "Spreadsheet Approach to Measuring ROI for IMC," *Marketing News*, February 28, 1994, 12.
11. These objectives were delineated by John R. Rossiter and Larry Percey, *Advertising & Promotion Management* (New York: McGraw-Hill, 1987), 131.
12. Nigel F. Piercy, "The Marketing Budgeting Process: Marketing Management Implications," *Journal of Marketing*, 51 (October 1987), 45–59.
13. Schultz et al., *Integrated Marketing Communications*.

Study Questions

1. Which of the following is *not* a promotion-mix element?
   a. Personal selling
   b. Sales promotions
   c. Advertising
   d. Pricing
2. Which of the following statements is *not* true for advertising?
   a. Advertising is a form of personal communications in the sense that most advertisements include pictures of people.
   b. Advertising includes both mass communication and direct-to-consumer communication.
   c. By definition, advertising is a paid for by an identified sponsor.
   d. Advertising is *not* equivalent to publicity.
3. Which statement is most true regarding sales promotions?
   a. Sales promotions represent advertising undertaken by retailers.
   b. Sales promotions are a form of sponsorship marketing.
   c. Sales promotions are directed either at the trade or to ultimate consumers.
   d. Sales promotions are prohibitively expensive for most firms.

4. Which of the following is *not* a key aspect of integrated marketing communications?
   a. It is critical that all marketing communication decisions be integrated with production and engineering capabilities. ✓
   b. All marketing communications decisions should start with the customer.
   c. The promotion-mix elements should all speak with a single voice.
   d. Efforts should be made to build long-term relations with customers.

5. When an IMC mind set is adopted, which of the following changes is *unlikely* to occur?
   a. Mass-media advertising will diminish in importance.
   b. Mass-media advertising will increase in importance. ✓
   c. There is likely to be an increased reliance on highly targeted communication methods.
   d. Greater demands are imposed on marketing communications suppliers to offer a fuller range of services.

6. Which of the following marketing objectives is also known as creating primary demand?
   a. Building product category wants. ✓
   b. Creating brand awareness.
   c. Enhancing attitudes and influencing intentions.
   d. Facilitating purchase.

7. When a communications source puts thoughts into symbolic form, this is called
   a. decoding.
   b. encoding. ✓
   c. recoding.
   d. signing.

8. Which of the following statements is true regarding the communications process?
   a. All communications involve, at minimum, a source and a receiver. ✓
   b. Noise is present only at the decoding stage of the process.
   c. Feedback occurs at all stages of the communications process.
   d. The communications process applies to advertising but not to other promotion-mix elements such as sales promotions.

9. A manufacturer's _push_ strategy involves utilizing aggressive trade allowances and personal selling efforts to obtain distribution for a product through wholesalers and retailers.
   a. IMC
   b. pull
   c. push
   d. encoding
10. A manufacturer's _pull_ strategy involves heavy advertising to encourage consumer demand for the product.
   a. IMC
   b. pull
   c. push
   d. decoding
11. Which of the following is the best marketing communications objective?
   a. Increase brand awareness in 1997.
   b. Increase sales volume in 1997.
   c. Increase consumer attitudes in 1997.
   d. None of the above are good objectives. ✓
12. Which is the most frequently used budgeting approach, especially in firms where marketing-department influence is high?
   a. top-down budgeting (TD)
   b. bottom-up budgeting (BU) ✗
   c. BUTD budgeting ✓
   d. TDBU budgeting
13. In terms of specific methods for promotion budgeting, which is the most popular?
   a. The objective-and-task method ✓
   b. The competitive parity method
   c. The percentage-of-sales method
   d. The spend-what-remains method
14. A firm uses the percentage-of-anticipated-sales method for allocating money to its promotional budget. With last year's sales at $10 million and next year's sales expected to grow by 20%, how much will the company invest in promotion next year if it allocates 5% of sales to promotion?
   a. $2,000,000
   b. $2,400,000
   c. $500,000
   d. $600,000 ✓

CHAPTER  15

Advertising, Sales Promotion, and Other Elements of the Promotion Mix

Chapter Objectives

Advertising

Public Relations

Direct Marketing Communications

Sales Promotion

Point-of-Purchase Communications

Sponsorship Marketing

Chapter Summary

This chapter discusses in some detail six elements of the promotion mix that were alluded to in the previous chapter: advertising, publicity and public relations, direct marketing communications, sales promotions, point-of-purchase communications, and sponsorship marketing. The remaining promotion-mix element, personal selling and sales management, is treated separately in Chapter 16. Although each element of the promotions mix is discussed in isolation, it is important to remember the emphasis in the previous chapter on the importance of treating all elements of the marketing communications mix as integrated and, ideally, speaking with a single, unified voice.

◼ Advertising

In its most basic sense, advertising is an economic investment, an investment regarded very favorably by numerous businesses and not-for-profit organizations throughout the United States and the world. Advertising expenditures in 1994 in the United States were approximately $147 billion, which amounts to over $550 in advertising expenditures for each of the 260 million men, women, and children comprising the U.S. population.[1] The biggest advertising spenders following the United States are Japan, Germany, the United Kingdom, France, and Canada. Exhibit 15.1 identifies the top 10 leading advertisers throughout the world in 1994 and their expenditures. However, advertising expenditures in these countries are small compared to those in the United States, amounting in all countries except Japan to less than 12% of the amount spent on advertising in the United States. Even in Japan advertisers, who invested $34.6 billion in advertising, spend only about half as much per capita (approximately $277) as do U.S. advertisers.[2]

Some U.S. companies invest well over $1 billion a year on domestic advertising. In 1993, for example, Procter & Gamble spent $2.4 billion, Philip Morris $1.8 billion, General Motors $1.5 billion, and Sears, Roebuck & Co. $1.3 billion. Even the U.S. government advertises to the tune of over $300 million.[3] The government's advertising promotes areas such as military recruiting, the Postal Services, Amtrak rail services, the U.S. Mint (e.g., commemorative coins), and AIDS awareness.

A completed advertisement, such as television commercial or a magazine ad, results from the collective efforts of various participants. Four major groups are involved in the total advertising process: (1) companies and other organizations that advertise

Exhibit 15.1   1994 Advertising Expenditures by the Top 10
Advertising Countries

1994 Rank	Country	1994 Spending (in billions)
1	United States	$147.0
2	Japan	34.6
3	Germany	17.3
4	United Kingdom	13.4
5	France	8.1
6	Canada	7.2
7	Italy	5.7
8	Brazil	5.0
9	Spain	5.0
10	South Korea	4.8

Sources: Zenith Media Worldwide; Robert Coen, McCann-Erickson Worldwide; Advertising Age International. Adapted from Todd Pruzan, "Spending '94: Europe Mired But Asia Grows," *Advertising Age*, February 10, 1995, I–9.

(Procter & Gamble, the U.S. Government, and so on), (2) advertising agencies (such as Ogilvy and Mather, J. Walter Thompson, BBDO, and Tokyo-based Dentsu), which are responsible for creating and placing ads for their clients, (3) advertising production companies (i.e., independent businesses that photograph, film, and other kinds of advertisements), and (4) advertising media (e.g., newspapers, television). The following discussion examines advertising only from the perspective of companies and other organizations that purchase advertising to promote their products, brands, and services.

The Value of Advertising

Advertising is a valuable economic activity because it performs a variety of critical communications functions. Specifically, advertising informs, persuades, reminds, adds value, and assists other company efforts.[4]

Informing.   Advertising makes consumers aware of new products, informs them about specific brands, and educates them about particular product features and benefits. Because advertising is an efficient form of communication, capable of reaching mass audiences at a relatively low cost per contact, it facilitates the introduction of new products and increases demand for existing products. Ford Motor Corporation, for example, invested an estimated $110 million to inform consumers of its new Ford Contour and Mercury Mystique vehicles. Strong competition from other auto manufacturers and the need to recoup an investment of $6 billion in these two cars fully justified what might appear to be an outrageously high advertising investment.[5]

Persuading.   Effective advertising persuades customers to try new products, brands, and services. Sometimes the persuasion takes the form of influencing primary demand, that is, creating demand for an entire product category. More frequently, advertising attempts to build secondary demand, that is, demand for a specific company's brand. It is for this reason that AT&T telephone services, Kellogg's cereals, and McDonald's restaurants, to name just a few brands, all spend over $400 million per year to persuade consumers to purchase their brands rather than competitors'.[6]

Reminding.   Advertising also keeps a company's brand fresh in the consumer's memory. When a need arises that is related to the advertised product, past advertising impact makes it possible for the advertiser's brand to come to the consumer's mind as a purchase candidate. For example, quickly think of long-distance telephone carriers. In addition to AT&T, names like MCI and Sprint probably enter your mind, because these telephone services advertise extensively just for this purpose, that is, to achieve top-of-mind awareness, or *TOMA*.

Adding Value.   Companies can add value to their offerings in three basic ways: by innovating, by improving quality, or by altering consumer perceptions. These three value-added components are completely interdependent:

> Innovation without quality is mere novelty. Consumer perception without quality and/or innovation is mere puffery. And—both innovation and quality, if not translated into consumer perceptions, are like the sound of the proverbial tree falling in the empty forest.[7]

Advertising adds value to products and specific brands by influencing consumers' perceptions. Effective advertising causes brands to be viewed as more elegant, more stylish, more prestigious, perhaps superior to competitive offerings, and, in general, of higher perceived quality. Hence, advertising is an important value-adding function, because, when done effectively, brands are perceived as higher quality, which in turn can lead to increased market share and greater profitability. It is little wonder why Procter & Gamble, perhaps the leading consumer-goods firm in the world, fully appreciates advertising's value-adding role. Indeed, a P&G vice president of worldwide advertising has characterized strong advertising as "a deposit in the brand equity bank."[8]

Assisting Other Company Efforts.   Advertising is just one member of the promotion team that facilitates other company efforts in the marketing communications process. For example, advertising may be used as a vehicle for delivering sales promotions. That is, advertisements are the physical vehicles for delivering coupons and sweepstakes and attracting attention to these sales promotion tools. Another crucial role of advertising is to assist sales representatives. Advertising presells a company's products and provides salespeople with valuable introductions prior to their personal contact with prospective customers. Sales effort, time, and costs are reduced because less time is required to inform prospects about product features and benefits. Moreover, advertising legitimizes or makes more credible the sales representative's claims and, reciprocally, personal selling also paves the way for advertising.[9] Advertising also enhances the results of other marketing communications. For example, consumers can identify product packages in the store and recognize the value of a product more easily after seeing it advertised on television or in a magazine.

The Advertising-Management Process

Exhibit 15.2 provides a framework around which we will overview the advertising-management process. The figure shows that *advertising strategy* extends from a company's overall *marketing strategy*. **Marketing strategy** involves the plans, budgets, and controls needed to direct a firm's product, promotion, distribution, and pricing activities. **Advertising strategy** entails four major activities (see Exhibit 15.2). The first two, *objective setting* and *budgeting*, were

Exhibit 15.2   The Advertising-Management Process

```
┌──────────────────────────────────────────┐
│           ┌─────────────────────┐          │
│           │  Marketing Strategy │          │
│           └─────────────────────┘          │
│                      │                      │
│                      ▼                      │
│           ┌─────────────────────┐          │
│           │ Advertising Strategy│          │
│           │  ▪ Objective Setting│          │
│           │  ▪ Budgeting        │          │
│           │  ▪ Message Strategy │          │
│           │  ▪ Media Strategy   │          │
│           └─────────────────────┘          │
│                      │                      │
│                      ▼                      │
│           ┌─────────────────────┐          │
│           │ Strategy Implementation │      │
│           └─────────────────────┘          │
│                      │                      │
│                      ▼                      │
│           ┌─────────────────────┐          │
│           │      Assessing      │          │
│           │ Advertising Effectiveness │    │
│           └─────────────────────┘          │
└──────────────────────────────────────────┘
```

described in Chapter 14 in context of promotion management and are discussed only briefly in the present advertising context. Suffice it to say that the objective-setting and budgeting processes are fundamentally the same regardless of which promotion-mix element is involved. The third and fourth aspects of advertising strategy, *message strategy* and *media strategy,* are discussed in subsequent sections.

Returning to Exhibit 15.2, **strategy implementation** deals with the tactical, day-to-day activities that must be performed to carry out an advertising campaign. For example, whereas the decision to emphasize television over other media is a strategic choice, the selection of specific types of programs and times at which to air a commercial is a tactical implementation matter. Likewise, the decision to emphasize a particular brand benefit is a strategic message consideration, but the method of delivering the message is a matter of creative implementation.

Assessing advertising effectiveness is a final critical aspect of advertising management inasmuch as only by evaluating results is it possible to determine whether objectives are being accomplished. This evaluation often requires that baseline measures be taken before an advertising campaign begins (to determine, for example, what percentage of the target audience is aware of the brand name) and then afterwards to determine whether the objective was achieved. Because research is fundamental to advertising control, a brief section later discusses some of the techniques that are widely used to evaluate advertising effectiveness. We now return to the advertising strategy component of the overall advertising management process.

Setting Advertising Objectives.   Advertising objectives provide the foundation for all remaining advertising decisions. There are three major reasons for setting advertising objectives: (1) the process of setting objectives literally forces top marketing and advertising management to agree upon the course advertising is to take for the following planning period as well as the tasks it is to accomplish for a product category or specific brand; (2) objective setting guides the budgeting, message strategy, and media strategy aspects of advertising strategy; (3) advertising objectives provide standards against which results can be measured.[10]

Advertising may be designed to accomplish several goals: (1) to make the target market aware of a new brand, (2) to facilitate consumer understanding of a brand's attributes and its benefits compared to competitive brands, (3) to enhance attitudes, (4) to influence purchase intentions, and (5) to encourage product trial.

Budgeting for Advertising.   The advertising budgeting decision is, in many respects, the most important decision advertisers make. If too little money is spent on advertising, sales volume will not be as high as it could be, and profits will be lost. If too much money is spent, expenses will be higher than they need to be, and profits will be reduced.

Budgeting is also one of the most difficult advertising decisions. This difficulty arises because it is hard to determine precisely how effective advertising has been or might be in the future. The sales-response function of advertising is influenced by a multitude of factors (quality of advertising execution, intensity of competitive advertising efforts, customer taste, and other considerations), thereby making it difficult if not impossible to know with any certainty what amount of sales advertising will generate.

In theory, advertising budgeting is a simple process, provided one accepts the premise that the best (optimal) level of any investment is the level that maximizes profits. This assumption leads to a simple rule for establishing advertising budgets: continue to invest in advertising as long as the marginal revenue from that investment exceeds the marginal cost. This statement amounts to precisely the same claim as established in Chapter 12 when discussing the profit-maximizing price, specifically, profit maximization occurs at the point where marginal revenue is equal to marginal cost ($MR = MC$). At any quantity level below this point (where $MR > MC$), profits are *not* maximized because at a higher level of output more profit can be earned. Similarly, at any level above this point (where $MC > MR$), there is a marginal loss.

In practical terms, this means that advertisers should continue advertising as long as it is profitable to do so. For example, suppose a company is currently spending $1 million on advertising and is considering the investment of another $200,000. Should the investment be made? The answer is simple: only if the additional advertising generates more than $200,000 revenue. Now say the same company is contemplating an additional advertising expenditure of $300,000. Again, the company should go ahead with the advertising if it can be certain that the investment will yield more than $300,000 in additional revenue.

It is evident from this simple exercise that setting the advertising budget is a matter of answering a series of if-then questions—if $X are invested in advertising, then what amount of revenue will be generated? Because budgets are set before the fact, this requires that the if-then questions have advance answers. In order to employ the profit-maximization rule for budget setting, the advertising decision maker must know the advertising-sales response function for every brand for which a budgeting decision will be made. Because such knowledge is rarely available, theoretical (profit maximization) budget setting is an ideal that is generally nonoperational in the real world of advertising decision making.

Due to the impracticality of profit-maximizing budget setting for advertising, companies ordinarily set budgets by using judgment, applying experience with analogous situations, and using simple rules-of-thumb, or heuristics, as guides to setting budgets.[11] Although criticized because they do not provide a basis for advertising budget setting that is directly related to the profitability of the advertised brand, these heuristics continue to be widely used.[12] The two most pervasive heuristics in use by both industrial advertisers and consumer-goods advertisers are the percentage-of-sales and objective-and-task methods,[13] both of which were discussed in Chapter 14 with reference to promotion budgeting in general, but are applied in an analogous fashion to advertising budgeting.

Creating Advertising Messages.   Advertisers use a vast array of techniques to present their brands in the most favorable light and persuade customers to contemplate purchasing these brands. Frequently employed techniques include

- Informational ads (such as automobile ads in the classified pages of a newspaper)
- Humor (e.g., Little Caesar pizza ads)
- Sex appeals (e.g., Calvin Klein ads)
- Celebrity endorsements (e.g., Michael Jordan, Candice Bergman, or Shaquille O'Neal)
- Various emotional appeals (e.g., nostalgia, romance, or excitement)
- Animation (e.g., Levi commercials)

The techniques used to persuasively advertise products are limited only by advertisers' creativity and ingenuity. It is beyond the scope of this text to go into detail concerning these and other advertising techniques. We pose a more straightforward question: What makes an advertisement good, or effective? Although it is impractical to provide a singular, all-purpose definition of what constitutes effective advertising, it is meaningful to talk about general characteristics.[14] At a minimum, good (or effective) advertising satisfies the following considerations:

1. *Extends from sound marketing strategy.* Advertising can be effective only if it is compatible with other elements of an integrated and well-orchestrated marketing communications strategy.
2. *Must take the consumer's view.* Consumers buy product benefits, not attributes. Therefore, advertising must be stated in a way that relates to the consumer's needs, wants, and values and not strictly in terms of the marketer's needs and wants.
3. *Is persuasive.* Persuasion usually occurs when there is a benefit for the consumer and not just for the marketer.
4. *Must find a unique way to break through the clutter.* Advertisers continuously compete with competitors for the

MARKETING HIGHLIGHTS

Hello in 140 Languages

People who do not speak English as their primary language are an easily segmented market for long distance telephone carriers. The number of immigrants and foreign-born U.S. workers who still have family living abroad is an exciting growth market.   AT&T, MCI, and Sprint, the three largest carriers, are in a race to see who can capture and retain the non-English speaking customer's business by providing new products targeted by language groups.

For the big three, it is a question of growth. Domestic long distance calls grow in an orderly, incremental progression. Calls to Asia from the United States are reported growing at eight times the domestic growth rate. Calls to Spanish-speaking (and Portuguese-speaking) countries in Latin America are growing at a rate seven times that of non-Spanish speaking long distance calling. AT&T, MCI, and Sprint are definitely interested in reaping profit in rapid growth markets.

The big three have implemented a variety of strategies to capitalize on this growth. At the corporate level, AT&T has been particularly agressive in mergers, partnerships, and acquisitions overseas. Sprint acquired La Conexíon, an established Latin American long distance carrier, in February 1994. MCI has been working on global expansion for years. All three companies are committed to the infrastructure to compete worldwide.

But what about at home? In an effort to secure the business of customers who call overseas, all three companies are competing on both price and service. They have also retained the services of advertising firms from key ethnic groups.

The services provided by long-distances carriers boil down to communicating with customers in their native language. For instance, John Kim of Washington, D.C. has lived in the United States for five years. Although he speaks English, he likes to have the option of asking an operator detailed

consumer's attention. This is no small task considering the massive number of print advertisements, broadcast commercials, and other sources of information available daily to consumers. Indeed, the situation in television advertising has been characterized as "audio-visual wallpaper," which implies sarcastically that consumers pay just about as much attention to commercials as they do to the detail in their own wallpaper after it has been on the walls for awhile.[15]

5. *Should never promise more than it can deliver.* This point speaks for itself, both in terms of ethics and in terms of smart business sense. Consumers learn quickly when they have been deceived and resent it.

questions in Korean when making one of his frequent calls to his family. Such services are sold from special language centers. MCI recently opened a new center in Arlington, Virginia, which employs 75 customer service and sales-people. These employees are fluent in most of the major East and Southeast Asian languages. Potential customers are targeted through ethnically orient-ed ads on television. The service and sales representatives explain the pro-gram, sign customer's up, and help customers acclimate to the U.S. phone system (an often difficult transition).

One set of television ads aimed at Asian-Americans shows a pair of grandparents listening to their U.S.-born grandchild cry over the phone. They sing a lullaby in their native tongue. AT&T shot this ad using Korean, Japanese, and Chinese actors speaking in those three languages. Customers then call the special toll-free number associated with the ads. Air time is concentrated where the Asian and Asian-American populations are highest; California and New York.

Sprint has been active in corporate sponsorship programs like the Asian American Association. The association provides acclimation services such as lessons in how to negotiate the U.S. medical system and getting children enrolled in the right programs in school. Sprint uses this altruistic oppor-tunity to introduce their telephone ser-vices. AT&T, in a similar vein, has set up storefronts in low income commu-nities where international long distance calls can be made by people who do not own telephones. These phones are connected directly to foreign language operators. In all, AT&T is able to handle 140 languages at any time of the day or night.

Sources: Sandra Sugawara, "Making Long-Distance Multilingual," *The Washington Post,* May 4, 1994, D1, D3. Laurant Belsie, *The Christian Science Monitor,* June 7, 1993, 6, col. 3. Reese Erlich, "Winning over Spanish Speakers," *The Christian Science Monitor,* March 8, 1994, 8, col. 1.

6. *Prevents the creative idea from overwhelming the strategy.* The purpose of advertising is to persuade and influence; the purpose is not to be cute for cute's sake or humorous for humor's sake. The ineffective use of humor, for example, results in people remembering the humor but forgetting the selling message.

The following quote aptly summarizes the essentials of effec-tive advertising:

[It] is advertising that is created for a specific customer. It is advertis-ing that understands and thinks about the customer's needs. It is advertising that communicates a specific benefit. It is advertising that pinpoints a specific action that the consumer takes. Good advertising understands that people do not buy products—they buy product benefits ... Above all, [effective advertising] gets noticed and remembered, and gets people to act.[16]

Effective advertising is usually creative. That is, it differentiates itself from the mass of mediocre advertisements; it is somehow different and out-of-the-ordinary. Advertising that is the same as most other advertising is unable to break through the competitive clutter and fails to grab the consumer's attention. It is easier to give examples of creative advertising than to define exactly what it is. Here are three examples of what many advertising practitioners would consider effective, creative advertising:

- The long-standing pink bunny campaign for Energizer batteries.
- The "milk mustache" campaign for the National Fluid Milk Processor Promotion Board featuring celebrities such as Christie Brinkley, Naomi Campbell, Joan Lunden, and Mary Lou Retton.
- Little Caesars' humorous "pizza, pizza" campaign.
- The "Yes I *am!*" campaign for Bud Light featuring a comical character who cons himself into various situations where he doesn't belong.

Most readers probably remember all four campaigns. They appealed because they offered solid reasons for wanting to watch them, and they made their selling points in an entertaining, creative fashion. Creative advertising makes a relatively lasting impact on consumers. This means getting past the clutter from other advertisements, activating attention, and giving consumers something to remember about the advertised product.

Selecting Advertising Media.

Outstanding message execution is to no avail, however, unless the messages are delivered to the right customers at the right time and with sufficient frequency. In other words, advertising messages stand a chance of being effective only if the media strategy itself is effective. Good messages and good media go hand in hand; they are inseparable—a true marriage. Improper media selection can doom an otherwise promising advertising campaign.

Creative advertisements are more effective when placed in media whose characteristics enhance the value of the advertising message and reach the advertiser's targeted customers at the right time. In many respects, media strategy is the most complicated of all marketing communications decisions. This is because a variety of decisions must be made when choosing media. In addition to determining which general *media* to use (e.g., television, radio, or magazines), the media planner must also pick specific *vehicles* within each medium (e.g., select specific magazines or TV programs) and decide how to allocate the available budget among the various media and vehicle alternatives. Additional decisions involve determining when to advertise, choosing specific geographical locations, and deciding how to distribute the budget over time and across geographic locations.

Media strategy necessarily evolves from the more general advertising strategy involving budgeting, objective setting, and message considerations. The media strategy itself consists of four sets of interrelated activities:

1. selecting the target audience
2. specifying media objectives
3. selecting media categories and vehicles
4. buying media

Successful media strategy requires first that the *target audience* be clearly pinpointed. Failure to precisely define the audience results in wasted exposures; that is, some nonpurchase candidates are exposed to advertisements while some prime candidates are missed. As noted in Chapter 14, target audiences are usually selected based on geographic factors (e.g., ads are aimed at people residing in urban centers), demographic considerations (e.g., ads are directed to women aged 18–49), product-usage concerns (e.g., ads are focused on heavy product users), and lifestyle/psychographic characteristics (e.g., ads are directed to people with active, outdoor lifestyles).

A second aspect of media strategy is establishing specific *objectives*. Four objectives are fundamental to media planning: reach, frequency, continuity, and cost. Media planners seek answers to the following types of questions: (1) What proportion of the target audience do we want to see (or read, or hear) the advertising message? (a *reach* issue); (2) How often should the target audience be exposed to the advertisement? (a *frequency* issue); (3) When are the best times to reach the target audience? (a *continuity* issue); (4) What is the least expensive way to accomplish the other objectives? (a *cost* issue).

Advertisers work with statistics such as ratings, gross rating points (GRPs), and cost per thousand to compare different vehicles within the same medium and to make intelligent selections. For example, an advertiser might consider advertising its brand on *Seinfeld*, a TV program that appeals to a wide-audience and produces a *rating* of about 20 at a cost of approximately $300,000 per 30-second commercial. The 20 rating means that of the approximately 96 million U.S. households, on average, 20%, or 19.2 million, are tuned in to this program. Theoretically, then, the advertiser would reach 19.2 million households every time it places a commercial on the *Seinfeld* program. If, say, during a 4-week period the advertiser placed a total of 8 commercials on *Seinfeld* (i.e., 2 ads each episode), it would accumulate a total of 160 *gross rating points*. Gross rating points, or GRPs, are simply the accumulation of ratings.

Cost per thousand, or CPM (where the *M* is the Roman numeral for 1,000) is a useful statistic for comparing the cost efficiency of vehicles in the same medium. For example, in 1995 a single 4-color full-page advertisement placed in *Sports Illustrated* cost the advertiser about $140,000 and reached approximately 23 million readers of the magazine. CPM is simply the cost of an ad divided by the number of people, expressed in thousands, who are reached by the ad. In this example CPM = cost of ad placement ($140,000) ÷ size of audience expressed in thousands (23,000) = $6.09.

The advertiser would compare this value with the CPM to advertise in alternative vehicles. For example, a full-page, 4-color ad placed in *Sport* magazine costs nearly $30,000 and reaches approximately 4 million readers. Its CPM is thus $7.50 ($30,000 ÷ 4,000). *Sports Illustrated* is a less expensive vehicle on a per-thousand basis than *Sport*. However, the choice of which magazine to select is based on matters other than mere cost comparisons. Also crucial in the decision are matters such as how closely vehicle's readers/viewers match the brand's target audience and the fit between the image of the vehicle and the brand's desired image.

Advertisers have 4 major mass media from which to choose: television, radio, magazines, and newspapers. Each medium possesses various strengths and weaknesses. Some of the most prominent of these are summarized in Exhibit 15.3.

One additional advertising medium deserving brief mention is the **Internet,** or what is variously called the *information superhigh-*

way, cyberspace, or the *worldwide web.* Many advertisers are turning to the Internet as a supplemental and experimental advertising medium. As of early 1995, there were about 30 million Internet users worldwide, of whom 18 million resided in the United States. Literally thousands of companies have opened so-called home pages containing information about their products, services, and specific brands. Zima (the unique beer from Coors brewing) was the first consumer brand to open a home page. Since then hundreds of brands have developed their own home pages.

Internet advertising offers exciting opportunities for prospective advertisers. First, and most important, the Internet is an *interactive medium* where consumers seek out information and devote their time to a particular home page only if it offers informational, educational, or recreational value. In a sense, the Internet is the 1990s version of the *Yellow Pages*— "Let your mouse do the walking" so to speak. Both media are successful only to the extent that they are easy to access and provide useful or interesting information. Creative advertisements on the Net are potentially capable of drawing and holding consumers' attention and serving to build relations between consumers and advertised brands. Second, Internet advertising provides advertisers with a medium to reach audiences (predominately relatively well-educated and young people) who are difficult to access via other media. Third, it is estimated that in a few years the Internet will offer video quality as good as TV and voice quality as good as telephone. This prospect will greatly expand the advertising value of this medium. Finally, the cost of advertising on the Net is extremely low compared to established media. On the downside, there are not as yet (as of mid-1995) any syndicated services available to measure the effectiveness of advertising on the Internet. Needless to say, various companies are currently developing methods for this purpose.

Assessing Advertising Effectiveness.

Because, as noted at the beginning of the chapter, billions of dollars are invested in advertising, advertisers want to accurately measure the effectiveness of their advertisements. An entire industry of companies are in business to measure advertising effectiveness. Companies have developed services to measure magazine readership—Simmons Market Research Bureau (SMRB) and Mediamark Research, Inc. (MRI). Other companies measure television audience size, most notably Nielsen and Arbitron. Services assess consumer recognition and recall of magazine ads (Starch Readership Service) and of

Exhibit 15.3   Relative Strengths and Weaknesses of Major Advertising Media

Medium	Strengths	Weaknesses
Television	Dramatic presentation and demonstration ability	Relatively downscale audience profile
	High reach potential	Network audience erosion
	Attain rapid awareness	Growing commercial clutter
	Relatively efficient	High out-of-pocket cost
	Intrusive and high impact	High production costs
	Ability to integrate messages with other media such as radio	Long lead-time to purchase network time
		Volatile cost structure
Radio	Target selectivity	Commercial clutter
	High frequency	Some station formats relatively uninvolving for listeners
	Efficient	
	Able to transfer image from TV	Relatively small audiences
	Portable, personal medium	High out-of-pocket cost to attain significant reach
	Low production cost	Audience fractionalization
	Use of local personalities	
	Ability to integrate messages with other media such as TV	

Source: Adapted from *Marketer's Guide to Media Fall/Winter 1994–1995*, 17, 2 (New York: ADWEEK, 19⁻

television commercials (Burke Day-After Recall). Many other companies measure the persuasive and emotional impact of TV commercials.

Perhaps the most notable development in all advertising-effectiveness measurement is the advent of so-called **single-source systems,** which, fundamentally, are concerned with measuring whether advertising leads to increased sales activity. Single-source

Medium	Strengths	Weaknesses
Magazines	Efficient reach of selective audiences	Not intrusive; reader controls ad exposure
	Ability to match advertising with compatible editorial content	Slow audience accumulation
	High-quality graphics	Significant slippage from reader audience to ad-exposure audience
	Reach light TV viewers	Clutter can be high
	Opportunity to repeat ad exposure	Long lead times to purchase magazine space
	Flexibility in target market coverage	Somewhat limited geographic options
	Can deliver complex copy	Uneven market-by-market circulation patterns
	Readership is not seasonal	
Newpapers	Rapid audience accumulation	Limited target selectivity
	Timeliness	High out-of-pocket costs for national buys
	High single day reach attainable	Significant differential between national and local rates
	Short lead times to purchase newspaper space	Not intrusive
	Excellent geographic flexibility	Cluttered ad environment
	Can convey detailed copy	Generally mediocre reproduction quality
	Strong retail trade support	
	Good for merchandising and promotion	
	Low production cost	
	Excellent local market penetration	

Posters + Cinema.

systems, which are named after the fact that all relevant data are available from one research supplier, have become possible with the advent of two electronic-monitoring tools: television meters and optical laser scanning of universal product codes (UPC symbols). Single-source systems gather retail purchase data from panels of households using optical scanning equipment and merge it with household demographic characteristics and, most important, with information about causal marketing variables that influence household purchases (e.g., television commercials, coupons, in-store displays, or trade promotions).

Information Resource Inc.(IRI) pioneered single source data collection in 1979 with its *BehaviorScan* system. BehaviorScan operates panel households in more than 25 markets around the United States with approximately 2,500 panel members in each market. Of the 70,000 total BehaviorScan households, 10,000 are installed with electronic television meters.[17] Panel members provide IRI with information about the size of their families, their income, number of televisions owned, the types of newspapers and magazines they read, and who in the household does most of the shopping.[18] IRI then combines all of these data into a single source and thereby determines which households purchase what products/brands and how responsive they are to advertising and other purchase-causing variables.

BehaviorScan markets are located in relatively small cities, because all grocery stores in these cities have to be equipped with automatic scanning devices that read UPC symbols from grocery packages. Each household receives a coded identification card that must be used every time a shopper visits the supermarket. Panel members are eligible for prize drawings as remuneration for their participation.

To better understand how BehaviorScan's single-source data can be used to show the relationship between advertising and sales activity, consider a situation where a manufacturer of a new snack food is interested in testing the effectiveness of a television commercial promoting this product. BehaviorScan would do the following: (1) stock the manufacturer's product in supermarkets in two or three markets; (2) selectively broadcast the new commercial using special split-cable television so that the commercial is received by only a portion of the panel members in each market; (3) record electronically (via optical scanners) grocery purchases made by all panel members; and (4) compare the purchase behavior of those panel members who were potentially exposed to the new commercial with those who were not exposed.

If the advertising is effective, a greater proportion of the panel members exposed to the test commercial should buy the promoted item in comparison to those members not exposed to any advertising. The percentage of panel members who undertake a trial purchase behavior would thereby indicate the effectiveness of the television commercial and the percentage who repeat purchase the product would indicate how much the product is liked.

This type of research is not restricted to testing the effects of advertising. It can be used to examine other marketing-mix variables such as coupons, cents-off deals, trade allowances, and in-store merchandising activity. The technology also permits forecasts of product success. For example, when G. D. Searle introduced Equal, a low-calorie sweetener, BehaviorScan predicted annual initial sales of $50 million after a national rollout. This prediction proved to be 100% correct.[19]

Public Relations

Public relations, or **PR,** is that aspect of promotion management uniquely suited to fostering *goodwill* between a company and its various publics. When effectively integrated with advertising, personal selling, and sales promotion, public relations is capable of accomplishing objectives other than goodwill. It can also increase brand awareness, build favorable attitudes toward a company and its products, and encourage purchase behavior. PR is similar to advertising inasmuch as both are forms of mass communications; the difference, as noted in the previous chapter, is that the publicity generated by PR receives free news space or air time in comparison to the paid-for space and time in the case of advertising. The public-relations department serves as the prime source of an organization's contact with the news media.

PR efforts are aimed at various publics, primarily the following: consumers, employees, suppliers, stockholders, governments, the general public, labor groups, and citizen action groups. Our concern, however, is only with the more narrow aspect of public relations involving an organization's interactions with customers. This marketing-oriented aspect of public relations is called **marketing PR,** or **MPR** for short. Marketing PR can be further delineated as involving either proactive or reactive public relations.[20]

Proactive MPR

Proactive MPR is dictated by a company's marketing objectives. It is offensively rather than defensively oriented and opportunity-seeking rather than problem-solving. Proactive MPR is another tool in addition to advertising, sales promotion, and personal selling for promoting a company's products and services.

The major role of **proactive MPR** is in the area of *product introductions* or *product revisions.* Proactive MPR is integrated with other promotional devices to give a product additional exposure, newsworthiness, and credibility. This last factor, *credibility,* largely accounts for the effectiveness of proactive MPR. Whereas advertising and personal selling claims are sometimes suspect—because we question salespeople's and advertisers' motives, knowing they have a personal stake in persuading us—product announcements by a newspaper editor or television broadcaster are notably more believable. Consumers are less likely to question the motivation underlying an editorial-type endorsement.

Publicity is the major tool of proactive MPR. Like advertising and personal selling, the fundamental purposes of marketing-oriented publicity are to engender brand awareness, enhance attitudes toward a company and its brands, and possibly influence purchase behavior. Companies obtain publicity using various forms of news releases, press conferences, and other types of information dissemination. *News releases* concerning new products, modifications in old products, and other newsworthy topics are delivered to editors of newspapers, magazines, and other media. *Press conferences* announce major news events of interest to the public. Photographs, tapes, and films are useful for illustrating product improvements, new products, advanced production techniques, and so forth. Of course, all forms of publicity are subject to the control and whims of the media. However, by disseminating a large volume of publicity materials and by preparing materials that fit the media's needs, a company increases its chances of obtaining beneficial publicity.

Reactive MPR

Unanticipated marketplace developments can place an organization in a vulnerable position that demands reactive marketing PR. **Reactive MPR** is undertaken as a result of external pressures and challenges brought by competitive actions, changes in consumer attitudes, changes in government policy, or other external influences. Reactive MPR typically deals with changes that have *negative consequences* for the organization. Reactive MPR attempts to repair a company's reputation, prevent market erosion, and regain lost sales. Product defects and failures are the most dramatic factors underlying the need for reactive MPR.

A number of negative-publicity cases have received widespread media attention in recent years. For example, Audi of America experienced an irreversible loss in sales after news reports were disseminated claiming that the Audi 5000-S sometimes lunged out of control when shifted into drive or reverse gears. Sales plummeted from approximately 74,000 units in 1985 to projected sales of only 12,000 in 1991.[21]

Food Lion, a regional supermarket chain, suffered grave losses and was forced to close some stores after news reports charged that Food Lion stores were unsanitary and that they sold out-of-date meat, fish, and poultry products.

Cans of Pepsi Cola were rumored to be contaminated with hypodermic needles, but adroit public relations quickly dispelled this hoax.[22]

Movie theaters were embarrassed when reports announced that a medium-sized container of popcorn popped with coconut oil contains more saturated fat than would a daily menu of bacon-and-eggs for breakfast, a Big Mac and a large order of fries for lunch, and a steak dinner.[23]

Finally, Intel, the huge computer-chip manufacturer, was embarrassed by reports that its new Pentium chip failed to correctly perform some mathematical calculations. Although corrective technical alterations were made, Intel was slow in reacting to this negative publicity and suffered a credibility gap and lost sales.[24]

Direct Marketing Communications

What Is Direct Marketing?

Direct marketing is one of the major growth areas in business.[25] Experts place the annual growth rate between 10 and 16%.[26] A variety of factors help to explain direct marketing's growth. Fundamental societal changes (including more women in the work force, greater time pressures, increased use of credit cards, and more discretionary income) have created a need and opportunity for the convenience of direct-marketed products and services. Direct marketing provides shoppers with an easy, convenient, relatively hassle-free, and safe way to buy. Many shoppers feel unsafe even in shopping malls. Indeed, a recent survey revealed that only 25% of shoppers consider malls a safe and secure shopping environment.[27]

In addition to the growth of consumer-oriented direct marketing, there has been a tremendous increase in applications of direct marketing by businesses that market to other businesses (business-to-business marketers). Nearly one-third of all money invested in business-to-business marketing goes to direct marketing, especially telemarketing.

But what precisely is direct marketing? The Direct Marketing Association, a trade group whose members practice various forms of direct marketing, offers the following definition:

> Direct marketing is an *interactive system* of marketing which uses *one or more advertising media* to effect a *measurable response* and/or transaction *at any location*.[28]

Note the special features in this definition. First, direct marketing involves *interactive marketing* in that it entails personalized communications between marketer and prospect. Second, direct marketing is not restricted to just direct mail but rather involves *one or more media* (e.g., Nordic Track products are advertised via direct mail combined with magazine and television advertising). Third, marketing via media such as direct mail allows for relatively greater *measurability of response* in comparison to indirect media such as television advertising. Greater measurability is possible because purchase responses to direct marketing (1) typically are more immediate than responses to mass-media advertising and (2) can be tracked to specific customers. Finally, direct marketing takes place at a *variety of locations*—by phone, at a kiosk, by mail, or by personal visits.

With direct marketing the marketer's purpose is to establish a direct relationship with a customer in order to initiate immediate and measurable responses. Direct marketing is accomplished using (1) direct-response advertising, (2) direct mail (including catalogs), (3) telemarketing, and (4) direct selling (e.g., home visits via Tupperware and Avon salespeople). We restrict discussion in this chapter to direct-response advertising and direct mail; telemarketing is discussed further in the next chapter, and direct selling has been alluded to at points throughout the text.

The growth of direct marketing and the increased sophistication of direct-response advertising has been due in large part to the advent of database marketing. **Database marketing,** which is used by indirect as well as direct marketers, involves collecting and electronically storing (in a database) information about present, past, and prospective customers. Typical databases include purchase data and other types of relevant customer information such as demographic details and geographic information. The information is used to profile customers and to develop effective and efficient marketing programs by communicating with individual customers and by establishing long-term communication relationships.[29]

Major advances in computer technology and database management have made it possible for companies to maintain huge databases containing millions of prospects/customers. *Niche marketing* can be fully realized by targeting promotional efforts to a company's best prospects (based on past product-category purchasing behavior), and who can be identified in terms of specific geographic, demographic, and psychographic characteristics. Growing numbers of marketers are making heavy investments in database marketing.[30] For example, in an interesting use of its database, Saab mailed all past owners an invitation to a sneak preview of its totally redesigned Saab 900. Thousands of people attended this unique promotion in 21 cities throughout the United States. Saab also uses its database to maintain relations with its customers by mailing a magazine called *Saab Soundings*.[31]

Database marketing offers companies four distinct "abilities":[32]

- *Addressability*—being able to identify every customer and reach each one on an individual basis. This could also be referred to as targetability.
- *Measurability*—knowing whether or not each customer purchased exactly what he or she purchased and how, where, and when he or she purchased along with his or her purchase history.
- *Flexibility*—having the opportunity to appeal to different customers in different ways at different times.
- *Accountability*—having precise figures on the gross profitability of any marketing event and qualitative data showing the type of customers who participated in each particular event.

Direct-Response Advertising and Direct Mail

Direct-response advertising involves the use of any of several media to transmit messages that encourage buyers to purchase directly from the advertiser rather than through retail outlets or through intermediaries in the case of business-to-business marketers. Direct-response advertising uses television, magazines, direct mail, and other media with the intent of creating immediate action from customers. *Direct mail* is the most important direct-advertising medium.

In general, three distinct features characterize direct-response advertising: (1) it makes a definite offer, (2) it contains all the information necessary to make a decision, and (3) it contains a response device (coupon, phone number, or both) to facilitate immediate action.[33] The direct marketer's objective is to select a medium (or multiple media) that provides maximum ability to segment the market at a reasonable cost. Effective direct-response media selection demands that the marketer have a clearly defined target market in mind.

Exhibit 15.4, an ad for the Killer Bee Long Driver, offers a good example of these features. First, the ad, which was placed in *Senior Golfer* magazine, is aimed at a segment of older golfers who no longer hit the ball as far as they used to and now are looking at new equipment to augment their power. Second, the ad contains rather detailed information that would permit prospective purchasers to at least solicit further information. Third, the ad contains the needed information for interested readers to know whether they can afford this driver. (The ad copy toward the bottom claims "Only $199.95 or three easy payments of $66.65 each . . . .) Finally, a response device in the form of a toll-free number simplifies the interested customer's desire for further information and the ability to place an order that is backed up with a 30-day money-back guarantee.

Although direct-response advertisers use various media (such as the magazine ad just described) direct mail is by far the most important direct-response medium. **Direct mail** advertising is any advertising matter sent through the mail directly to the person whom the marketer wishes to influence; these advertisements can take the form of letters, postcards, programs, calendars, folders, catalogs, blotters, order blanks, price lists, or menus. Direct mail's primary advantages are that it targets specific market segments and measures success immediately by knowing how many customers actually respond.

Additional positive features of direct mail are that it permits greater personalization than does mass media advertising; it can gain the prospect's undivided attention because it is not subject to competing adjacent ads (as is the case with advertising in other printed and broadcast media); it has no constraints in terms of form,

Exhibit 15.4   Direct Response Advertising

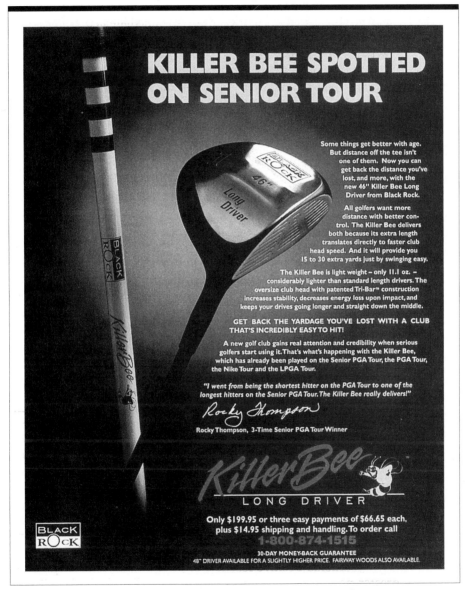

color, or size (other than those imposed by cost and practical considerations); and it is relatively simple and inexpensive to change direct-mail ads.[34]

An alleged disadvantage of direct mail is that it is more expensive than other media. On a cost-per-thousand (CPM) basis, direct mail *is* more expensive. For example, the CPM for a particular direct mailing may be as high as $250, whereas a magazine's CPM might be as low as $4. However, compared with other media, direct mail is much less wasteful and will usually produce the highest percentage of responses. Thus, on a cost per order basis, direct mail is often less expensive and a better bargain.

All types of marketers use direct mail as a strategically important advertising medium. *Business Week* magazine claims, albeit with some hyperbole, that marketers of all types of consumer goods "are turning from the TV box to the mailbox."[35] Some automobile manufacturers, for example, are budgeting as much as 10% of their advertising expenditures to direct mail.

At least four factors account for the trend toward widespread use of direct mail by all types of marketers. First, the rising expense of television advertising along with increased audience fragmentation has led many advertisers to reduce investments in television advertising. Second, direct mail enables unparalleled targeting of messages to desired prospects. Why? Because, according to one expert, it is "a lot better to talk to 20,000 prospects than 2 million suspects."[36] Third, increased emphasis on measurable advertising results has encouraged advertisers to use that medium—namely, mail—which best lends itself to a clear identification of how many prospects purchased the advertised product. Finally, consumers are responsive—surveys indicate that Americans like mail advertisements.

Success with direct mail depends greatly on the quality of mailing lists. Mailing lists of past customers (either of the company's own customers or customers of related products) enable direct marketers to pinpoint the best candidates for future purchases. One observer has aptly dubbed mailing lists "windows to our pocketbooks."[37] The success of direct mail is largely due to the availability of huge computer databases and the huge data lists containing customer and/or prospect names and detailed information for each listing. For example, Blockbuster, the home video chain, has a database consisting of nearly 40 million customers that contains a complete history of their past movie selections and hence their movie preferences. Many businesses would pay dearly to obtain this database, but charges of invasion of privacy prevent Blockbuster from selling their database.

Catalog marketing, a special form of direct mail, deserves a separate section due to its distinctiveness and tremendous growth in recent years. For clarity, it should be noted that there are actually four types of catalogs: (1) retail catalogs designed by retailers to increase store traffic; (2) full-line merchandise catalogs (such as JCPenney); (3) consumer specialty catalogs (like the L. L. Bean sporting goods and ready-to-wear catalog); and (4) industrial specialty catalogs, which are used by business-to-business marketers to reach smaller customers while freeing up the sales force's time to devote to larger, more promising accounts.

The greatest growth in cataloging is consumer specialty catalogs. Name the product, and at least one company is probably marketing that item via catalog—food items (cheese, candy, pastry, steaks), clothing, or furniture; the list goes on and on.

The growth rate for catalog sales in the United States far exceeds the growth rate for retailers, with a current annual growth of about 12% and annual sales in 1994 estimated to exceed $75 billion in the United States alone![38] Various factors account for this growth. From the marketer's perspective, catalog selling provides an efficient and effective way to reach prime prospects. From the consumer's perspective (1) catalogs save time because people do not have to find parking spaces and deal with in-store crowds; (2) catalog buying appeals to consumers who are fearful of shopping due to rising crime rates; (3) catalogs allow people the convenience of making purchase decisions at their leisure and away from the pressure of a retail store; (4) the availability of toll-free numbers and credit-card purchasing has made it easy for people to order from catalogs; and (5) people are confident in purchasing from catalogs because merchandise quality and prices are often comparable to what is available in stores and guarantees are attractive.

Sales Promotion

What Exactly Is Sales Promotion?

The diversity of tools and techniques that are included in sales promotion makes it difficult to provide a simple definition. We define **sales promotion** as the use of any *incentive* by a manufacturer to induce the *trade* (wholesalers and retailers) or *consumers* to buy a brand and to encourage the *sales force* to aggressively sell it. The incentive is *additional to the basic benefits* provided by the brand and *temporarily changes its perceived price or value.*[39] The italicized features require comment. First, by definition, sales promotions involve

CAPTAINS OF INDUSTRY

Lillian Vernon

Chief Executive Officer

Lillian Vernon Corporation

Date of Birth: 1927

Education: Attended New York University for two years. Left college to start business.

Career Path: Started her own mail-order business, called Vernon Specialties, in 1951; began publishing a catalog in 1954 and began manufacturing exclusive products in 1956. Company became Vernon Corporation in 1964, went public in 1987, and trades on the American Stock Exchange. Company's slogan is "Living better for less."

Profile: Started a business in her home because she was pregnant and wanted to earn a little extra income in a time when it was not "fashionable" for women to work outside the home.[a]

Personal: When asked if she viewed herself as a feminist, she responded, "You've got Gloria Steinem . . . and Betty Friedan. They just talked about it. But you know what? I went out and did it."[b]

Just another success story? Not exactly. Vernon (who legally changed her name from Katz to Vernon in 1991) was just a child when she and her family were forced to flee Nazi Germany before the outbreak of World War II. They first went to Holland in 1933 and then came to New York in 1937, where her father ran a small leather factory. Vernon's business acumen didn't come as a result of graduate school business education, but from her astute business sense and natural talent for recognizing her customers' needs and finding the products to fill them.

In 1951 Vernon was in her early 20s staying at home while expecting a baby and trying to make ends meet on her husband's $75-a-week salary. Not being one to just sit at home idly, she considered ways she could supplement their income from her home. And right from the start she seemed to have an uncanny understanding of what women were willing to buy. She hit upon the idea of personalizing an otherwise ordinary product like a woman's handbag by monogramming a customer's initials on it, capitalizing on her ability to provide the monogramming and using her father as the leather goods supplier. She took $2,000 in savings accumulated from wedding gifts and placed a $495 ad in *Seventeen* magazine for a monogrammed leather pocketbook and matching monogrammed belt in black, tan or red for $7.[c] "Be the first to sport that personalized look," the ad read.[d] This one ad generated $32,000 in orders in less than three months, causing Vernon to transform her kitchen table into an assembly line.

In 1954 she published her first catalog, an eight-page, black-and white publication sent out to 125,000 customers. It was a big success, and her business grew to the point that in 1956 she set up a warehouse in Mount Vernon, rented the building next door to handle monogramming, and opened a shipping department across the street. She also began manufacturing custom-designed products for such major companies as Max Factor, Elizabeth Arden, Avon, and Revlon. Nine years later Lillian Vernon Corporation was formed, and, in 1969 when Vernon and her husband, Sam

Hochberg, divorced, he took the manufacturing business and she retained the catalog division. By 1970 it was bringing in $1 million in sales. The company went public in 1987 with annual sales at $112 million. Vernon used the proceeds of the public offering to help finance a $25 million national distribution center built in Virginia Beach, Virginia. The company now has four outlet stores in Virginia as well as two in New York, and moved its headquarters from Mount Vernon to New Rochelle, New York, in 1992.

Vernon relies on her own intuition as well as market research, operating on the principle that she won't sell anything she wouldn't use herself. For example, Vernon is a very organized person and looks for items that will help organize her home. As she says, "I like my house organized with corner racks, pullout dish racks, drawer dividers. I wouldn't sell anything I wouldn't use myself."[e] And Vernon has never forgotten who her customers are: other women. More than 90% of her customers are women, specifically those who have an average household income of $53,000, work outside the home and have children, but have little time or desire to shop in stores. She scours the world along with her merchandising department of 20 professionals, traveling to such markets as Paris, London, Milan, and Hong Kong, looking for new and unusual products. She has buying and quality control offices in Florence, Italy, and Hong Kong.

Leafing through a Lillian Vernon catalog may cause some initial confusion to the catalog shopper since the merchandise is not arranged methodically, but rather mixed up "like an old-fashioned five-and-dime store" in the hopes that the browser will look all the way through the catalog.[f] Vernon draws from her familiarity with browsing catalogs, which were popular when she started her business, and states that she has kept this type of eclectic organization for her catalogs "because it works."[g] She has also maintained her pricing strategy, offering reasonably priced merchandise and to this day will monogram products offered in the catalog free of charge. One of her best-selling items has been a set of 12 snowflake Christmas tree ornaments that sold for $6 in 1992, bringing in over $1 million that year. Her business has profited from current demographic trends such as more women now working outside the home who have little time to shop as well as the fact that consumers are more concerned with value for their money. Lillian Vernon's products shine in this category. And, above all, she states, "We have always featured the product categories we know best. Our products are basics. We have stayed away from apparel, sportswear, and electronics, as they tend to be linked to constantly changing trends and rapid technological obsolescence."[h]

Lillian Vernon catalogs feature gift, household, gardening, decorative, and children's products. In addition to the regular catalog, the company launched a very successful children's "Lilly's Kids" catalog in 1990. With such a large customer base of parents and grandparents for the main catalog, the company was able to target her customers who had bought children's items and initially mailed the Lilly's Kids catalog to them. It also introduced an "At Home" furnishings catalog in 1989 but decided in 1991 to incorporate those

Continued on next page

CAPTAINS OF INDUSTRY, continued

offerings into her core catalogs. It was less successful because it offered high-priced merchandise in a time when consumers were cutting back on non-essential items.[i] At the same time the company adjusted its circulation and began timing its mailings to go out later in each period, recognizing a buying trend toward last-minute purchasing, helped by faster home delivery. Home organization products represent 25% of the company's $176.3 million business. Over 1,100 SKUs are featured in the 140 million catalogs it mails out annually, with prices averaging about $17 per product.[j]

Lillian Vernon uses private labels for over 50% of its total business, allowing the company to produce unique products. "This gives us exclusivity," says David Hochberg, Vernon's son and vice president of public affairs. "Products are designed to our specifications so no one else will have them. This also gives us pricing flexibility since customers can't compare our products with other's."[k] And they just keep adding to their extensive array of innovative but practical organization and storage products.

Competition in the mail-order catalog business has become increasingly stiff, but Lillian Vernon has continued to be a leader. The company constantly updates its mailing lists, deleting those who don't make purchases and targeting new segments of the population. In 1992 the company launched an exclusively Christmas catalog, Christmas Memories, mailing to 3 million of its 12.5 million buyers.[l] In 1993 they began mailing "Welcome," a new catalog targeted toward people who have recently moved, featuring items a new home-dweller might want or need.[m] These specialized catalogs are,

perhaps, a way of organizing the original eclectic catalog offerings into categories so that the customer doesn't get frustrated wading through pages of items in search of, say, a lamp or a coat rack. With the deluge of catalogs being mailed out to homes, catalog companies must constantly look for ways of ensuring that the customer will take the time to browse through their particular catalog. And focusing on specific segments like Christmas-related goods, home products, sale items, and toys for children has been successful for Lillian Vernon in generating sales. And in 1993 the company began testing direct response television on QVC, a cable TV in-home shopping channel, perhaps providing yet another way of targeting new customers.[n, o]

Vernon has also been successful with her growing premiums and incentives wholesale division, offering specialized services to companies that buy corporate gifts or buy large quantities of items. This division focuses on product development, fulfillment of service recognition, incentive and gift certificate programs. They can incorporate a logo, name or message on a variety of Vernon's merchandise. The wholesale division targets other catalog companies; the premium, incentive market; and advertising specialty field, as well as national retailers, and the corporate gift market.[p] And Vernon is always looking for new business. When she lost her passport while traveling overseas, she discovered a new market: embassies and State Department personnel who are far from home and have few shopping outlets.[q]

Vernon cites the company's financial strength as well as its commitment to quality and service as prime reasons why Lillian Vernon Corporation

---

Lillian Vernon Corp. (AMEX)

(unclear if numbers are in thousands or millions—see inside cover of annual report)

Revenue	$172,932	162,397	160,293	154,687	140,647
	1993	1992	1991	1990	1989

should continue to increase its market share while maintaining its low debt status.[r] The company maintains an aggressive posture in the catalog business, and, judging from its financial performance over the years, will remain strong.

Vernon was named one of America's top 25 women business owners by *Working Woman* magazine in its May 1992 issue and was profiled in *Chain Store Age Executive with Shopping Center Age* in December 1992, as a "Retail Entrepreneur of the Year."[s] Vernon's practical, upbeat attitude toward life hasn't changed over the years, and she has some advice for others who want to succeed. "Never let your mistakes defeat or discourage you," she says. "Learn and grow from them and then move on."[t]

[a] Lisa Coleman, "I Went Out and Did It," *Forbes,* August 17, 1992, 102.

[b] Ibid.

[c] Ibid.

[d] "Entrepreneur of the Year: Lillian Vernon," *Fairfield County Business Journal,* June 22, 1992, vol. 31; no. 26; sec. 2; 18.

[e] "Lillian Vernon; Retail Entrepreneurs of the Year Company Profile," *Chain Store Age Executive with Shopping Center Age,* December, 1992, vol. 68; no. 12; 50.

[f] *Forbes,* August 17, 1992, 102.

[g] Ibid.

[h] Caryn A. McBride, "Lillian Vernon's Mail-Order Empire Continues to Expand and Prosper," *The Westchester County Business Journal,* November 18, 1991, vol. 30; no. 48; sec. 1; 10.

[i] Joan Gunin, "Lillian Vernon Cuts Its Catalog Circulation for Fiscal '92; Cites Soft Market and Costs," *DM News,* July 29, 1991, 1.

[j] Debby Garbato Stankevich, "Lilly's Red-Hot Affair; Lillian Vernon Corp.'s Mail-Order Sales of Home Storage Products Secrets of the Stars," *HFD—The Weekly Home Furnishings Newsletter,* June 21, 1993, vol. 67; no. 25; 52.

[k] Ibid.

[l] Larry Jaffee, "Lillian Vernon to Launch Catalog Featuring Only Christmas Products," *DM News,* July 27, 1992, 2.

[m] Larry Jaffee, "Vernon Tests New-Mover Catalog; Reports 13% Net Income Increase," *DM News,* August 2, 1993, 10.

[n] Jim Emerson, "Sharper Image May Join the Parade of Catalogs Testing Shows on QVC," *DM News,* May 24, 1993, 2.

[o] *Westchester County Business Journal,* November 18, 1991, 10.

[p] Ibid.

[q] Marlene Aig, "Unusual, Useful Help Lillian Vernon Prosper," *Associated Press, Chicago Tribune,* May 10, 1992, Final Edition, 9.

[r] "Lillian Vernon Reports Record Third Quarter Results," *Business Wire,* January 5, 1993.

[s] *Working Woman,* May 1992.

[t] Ibid.

incentives—that is, a bonus or reward for purchasing one brand rather than another. Second, these incentives (sweepstakes, coupons, premiums, or display allowances) are additions to, not substitutes for, the basic benefits a purchaser typically acquires when buying a particular product or service. For example, getting 50¢ off the price of a new brand of shampoo would be little consolation if the shampoo failed to work properly. Third, the target of the incentive is the trade, consumers, the sales force, or all three parties. Finally, the incentive changes a brand's perceived price/value, but only temporarily. A sales-promotion incentive for a particular brand applies to a single purchase or perhaps several purchases during a period, but not to every purchase a consumer would make over an extended period.

The Shift from Advertising to Sales Promotion

Historically, at least through the mid-1970s, the promotional emphasis in many consumer-goods firms was on creating promotional *pull*. Manufacturers advertised heavily, especially on network television, and literally forced retailers to handle their products by virtue of the fact that consumers demanded heavily advertised brands. However, over the past two decades, pull-oriented marketing has become less effective. Along with this reduced effectiveness has come an increase in the use of *push-oriented* sales promotion practices.[40]

The result of these developments is that advertising expenditures in mass media (television, radio, magazines)—which practitioners refer to as *above-the-line expenditures*—have declined in most firms as a percentage of their total promotional spending. On the other hand, expenditures on sales promotions, direct marketing, sponsorships, and point-of-purchase items (collectively referred to as *below-the-line expenditures*) have steadily increased. In fact, annual studies have shown that media advertising expenditures as a proportion of companies' total promotional spending have declined steadily for over a decade. Whereas media advertising averaged 42% of companies' promotional budgets in 1977, by 1993 media advertising's portion of the total budget had fallen to just over 25%. Comparatively, consumer promotions (coupons, bonus packs, or premiums) represented approximately 28% of the total promotional budget in 1993, and trade promotions constituted the remaining 47%.[41] These statistics make it clear that the biggest shift in promotional

Exhibit 15.5   Factors Giving Rise to the Growth of Sales
Promotions

1. Balance of power transfer

2. Increased brand parity and price sensitivity

3. Reduced brand loyalty

4. Splintering of the mass market and reduced media effectiveness

5. Short-term orientation and corporate reward structures

6. Trade and consumer responsiveness

expenditures has been away from media advertising toward trade-support expenditures. The major form of trade promotions are deals, or discounts (called *trade allowances*) that encourage wholesalers and retailers to purchase larger quantities of promoted brands during the period when the manufacturer places them on deal.

Increased investment in sales promotions, especially trade-oriented promotions, has gone hand-in-hand with the trend toward greater push-oriented marketing. A variety of factors account for the shift in the allocation of promotion budgets away from advertising toward sales promotion and other forms of below-the-line promotions. These are summarized in Exhibit 15.5.

Balance of Power Transfer.

Until recently, national manufacturers of consumer goods generally were more powerful and influential than the supermarkets, drug stores, and mass merchandisers that carried the manufacturers' brands. However, the balance of power began shifting when *network television* dipped in effectiveness as an advertising medium and, especially, with the advent of *optical scanning equipment*, which gave retailers as much "informational market power" as possessed by manufacturers. The consequence for manufacturers is that for every promotional dollar used to support retailers' advertising or merchandising programs, one less dollar is available for the manufacturer's own advertising.

Increased Brand Parity and Price Sensitivity.

In earlier years when truly new products were being offered to the marketplace, manufacturers could effectively advertise unique advantages over competitive offerings. As product categories have matured, however, most new offerings represent slight changes from existing products, thus resulting in greater similarities between competitive brands than differences. With fewer distinct product differences, consumers have grown more reliant on price and price incentives (coupons, cents-off deals, or refunds) as a way of differentiating alternative parity brands. Because real, concrete advantages are often difficult to obtain, firms have turned increasingly to sales promotion as a means of achieving at least temporary advantages over competitors.

Reduced Brand Loyalty.

Consumers have become less brand loyal than they once were. This change is partly due to the fact that brands have grown increasingly similar, thereby making it easier for consumers to switch among brands. Also, marketers have effectively trained consumers to expect that at least one brand in a product category will always be on deal with a coupon, cents-off offer, or refund; hence, many consumers rarely purchase brands other than those on deal. The upshot of all of this dealing activity is that marketers' extensive use of sales promotions has reduced brand loyalty and increased switching behavior, thereby requiring evermore dealing activity to feed consumers' insatiable desire for deals.

Splintering of the Mass Market and Reduced Media Effectiveness.

Advertising efficiency is directly related to the degree of homogeneity in consumers' consumption needs and media habits. The more homogenous are these needs and habits, the less costly it is for mass advertising to reach target audiences. However, as consumer lifestyles have become more diverse and advertising media have become more narrow in their appeal, mass-media advertising is no longer as efficient as it once was. In addition, advertising effectiveness has declined with simultaneous increases in ad clutter and escalating media costs. These combined forces have influenced many brand managers to devote proportionately larger budgets to sales promotions.

Short-Term Orientation and Corporate Reward Structures.

The brand-management system and sales promotion are perfect partners. The reward structure in firms organized along brand-manager lines emphasizes short-term sales response rather than slow, long-term growth, and sales promotion is incomparable when it comes to generating quick sales response. In fact, for many brands of packaged goods, the majority of their sales are associated with some kind of promotional deal.[42]

Trade and Consumer Responsiveness.   A final force that explains the shift toward sales promotion at the expense of advertising is that retailers/wholesalers (the trade) and consumers respond favorably to money-saving opportunities. Businesspeople and people in everyday life like deals, and this is what sales promotion is all about—"Buy my brand and save money."

What Sales Promotion Can and Cannot Do

Sales promotion has been, and will continue to be, a very important component of many firms' overall promotion budgets, but like every other promotion-mix element, sales promotion is capable of accomplishing certain objectives but not others. First let us examine the tasks that sales promotion is well suited for accomplishing.[43]

Facilitating the Introduction of New Products to the Trade.
In order to achieve sales and profit growth objectives, marketers continuously introduce new products. Sales promotions to wholesalers and retailers are often necessary to encourage the trade to handle new products. In fact, many retailers refuse to carry new products unless they receive extra compensation in the form of trade allowances, display allowances, and other forms of allowances.

Obtaining Trial Purchases from Consumers.   Marketers
depend on free samples, coupons, and other sales promotions to encourage trial purchases of new products. Many consumers would never try new products without these promotional inducements.

Stimulating Sales-Force Enthusiasm for a New, Improved, or Mature Product.   Exciting sales promotions give salespeople extra ammunition to use when interacting with buyers; they revive enthusiasm and make the salesperson's job easier and more enjoyable.

Invigorating Sales of a Mature Product.   Sales promotion
can invigorate sales of a mature product that requires a shot in the arm.

Increasing On- and Off-Shelf Merchandising Space.
Trade-oriented sales promotions enable a manufacturer to obtain extra shelf space for a temporary period. This space may be in the form of extra facings (i.e., rows of shelf space) or off-shelf space in a gondola or end-aisle display.

Neutralizing Competitive Advertising and Sales Promotion.
Sales promotions can be used to offset competitors' advertising and sales-promotion efforts. For example, one company's 50 cents-off coupon loses much of its appeal when a competitor simultaneously comes out with a $1 coupon.

Holding Current Users by Encouraging Repeat Purchases.
Brand switching is a fact of life faced by all brand managers. The strategic use of certain forms of sales promotion can encourage at least short-run repetitive purchasing. Premium programs, refunds, and various other devices are used to encourage repeat purchasing.

Increasing Product Usage by Loading Consumers.
Consumers tend to use more of certain products (e.g., snack foods and soft drinks) when they have more of them available in their homes. Thus, sales-promotion efforts that load consumers generate temporary increases in product usage. Bonus packs and two-for-the-price-of-one deals are particularly effective loading devices.

Preempting Competition by Loading Consumers.
When consumers are loaded with one company's brand, they are temporarily out of the marketplace for competitive brands. Hence, one brand's sales promotion serves to preempt sales of competitive brands.

Reinforcing Advertising.
A final can-do capability of sales promotion is to reinforce advertising. An advertising campaign can be strengthened greatly by a well-coordinated sales promotion effort.

Sales promotions clearly are capable of performing important tasks. There are, however, distinct limitations that are beyond the capability of sales promotion. In particular, sales promotions *cannot* accomplish the following functions.

Compensate for a Poorly Trained Sales Force or for a Lack of Advertising.
When suffering from poor sales performance or inadequate growth, some companies consider sales

promotion to be the solution. However, sales promotion will provide at best a temporary fix if the underlying problem is due to a
poor sales force, a lack of brand awareness, a weak brand image, or
other maladies that only proper sales management and advertising
efforts can overcome.

Give the Trade or Consumers any Compelling Long-Term Reason to Continue Purchasing a Brand.
The trade's deci-
sion to continue stocking a brand and consumers' decision to repeat
purchase are based on continued satisfaction with the brand.
Satisfaction results from the brand's meeting profit objectives (for
the trade) and providing benefits (for consumers). Sales promotion
cannot compensate for a fundamentally flawed or mediocre product.

Permanently Stop an Established Product's Declining Sales Trend or Change the Basic Nonacceptance of an Undesired Product.
Declining sales over an extended period
indicate poor product performance or the availability of a superior
alternative. Sales promotion cannot reverse the basic nonacceptance
of an undesired product. A declining sales trend can be reversed only
through product improvements or perhaps with an advertising campaign that breathes new life into an aging product. Sales promotion
used in combination with advertising effort or product improvements may reverse the trend, but sales promotion by itself is a waste.

The Nature and Objectives of Trade Promotion

As earlier noted, manufacturers use some combination of push and
pull strategies to accomplish both retail distribution and consumer
purchasing. Trade promotions, which are directed at wholesalers,
retailers, and other marketing intermediaries, represent the first
step in any promotional effort. Consumer promotions are likely to
fail unless trade-promotion efforts have succeeded in getting
wholesalers to distribute the product and retailers to stock adequate
quantities. The special incentives offered by manufacturers to their
distribution channel members are then expected to be passed
through to consumers in the form of price discounts offered by
retailers and often stimulated by advertising support and special
displays.[44] As we will see later, this transfer does not always occur.
    A manufacturer has various objectives for using trade-orient-
ed sales promotions: (1) to introduce new or revised products, (2) to

increase distribution of new packages or sizes, (3) to build retail inventories, (4) to maintain or increase the manufacturer's share of shelf space, (5) to obtain displays outside normal shelf locations, (6) to reduce excess inventories and increase turnover, (7) to achieve product features in retailers' advertisements, (8) to counter competitive activity, and, ultimately, (9) to sell as much as possible to final consumers.[45]

Manufacturers employ a variety of trade-oriented promotional inducements, most of which are some form of trade allowance.[46] **Trade allowances,** or trade deals, come in a variety of forms and are offered to retailers simply for purchasing the manufacturer's brand or for performing activities in support of the manufacturer's brand. These allowances and deals are needed to encourage retailers to stock the manufacturer's brand, discount the brand's price to consumers, feature it in advertising, or provide special display or other point-of-purchase support.[47]

The most frequently used allowance is an **off-invoice allowance.** These allowances, as the name suggests, are deals offered periodically to the trade that allow wholesalers and retailers to simply deduct a fixed amount, say 15%, from the full price. By using off-invoice allowances, manufacturers hope to increase retailers' purchasing of the manufacturer's brand and increase consumers' purchasing from retailers. This latter objective is based on the expectation that retailers will in fact pass along to consumers the discounts they receive from manufacturers. This, unfortunately, does not always happen. Some retailers take advantage of allowances without performing the services for which they receive credit.

Another form of allowance are so-called **bill-back allowances.** Retailers receive allowances for featuring the manufacturer's brand in advertisements (*bill-back ad allowances*) or for providing special displays (*bill-back display allowances*). The expression "bill-back" indicates that the allowance is not simply deducted directly from the invoice by virtue of ordering products, as is the case with off-invoice allowances, but rather is earned by the retailer by performing designated advertising or display services. The retailer effectively bills (i.e., charges) the manufacturer for the services rendered, and the manufacturer pays an allowance to the retailer for the services received in behalf of the manufacturer's brand(s).

A final form of trade allowance, which applies specifically to new products, is a **slotting allowance,** which also is called a *stocking allowance* or *street money.* A slotting allowance is the fee a manufacturer is charged by a supermarket chain or other retailer to get that retailer to handle the manufacturer's new product. The allowance is called slotting in reference to the slot, or location, that the retailer must make available in its distribution center to accommodate the manufacturer's product. The retailer who demands slotting allowances denies the manufacturer shelf space unless the manufacturer is willing to pay the upfront fee, the slotting allowance, to acquire that space for its new product. Second, manufacturers tolerate slotting allowances because they are confronted with a classic dilemma: Either they pay the fee and eventually recoup the cost through increased sales volume, or they refuse to pay the fee and in so doing accept a fate of not being able to successfully introduce new products.

In certain respects, slotting allowances are a legitimate cost of doing business. When, for example, a large multi-store supermarket chain takes on a new product, it incurs several added expenses. These expenses arise because the chain must make space for that product in its distribution center, create a new entry in its computerized inventory system, redesign store shelves, and notify individual stores about the new product. In addition to these expenses, the chain takes the risk that the new product will fail. This result is likely in the grocery industry, where at least half of the thousands of new products introduced annually fail. Hence, the slotting allowance serves as an insurance policy for the retailer against product failure.

It is questionable whether the actual expenses incurred by retailers are anywhere near the slotting allowances they charge. Actual charges are highly variable. Some supermarkets charge as little as $5 per store to stock a new item, while others charge as much as $50 or $100 per store. Some grocery chains charge as much as $15,000 to $40,000 for a single new product. Large companies can afford to pay slotting allowances because their volume is sufficient to recoup the expense. However, brands with small consumer franchises are frequently unable to afford these fees.

Forward Buying, Diverting, and EDLP

Off-invoice trade allowances create notable problems for the manufacturers that use them. A particularly major problem is that off-invoice allowances often induce the trade to stockpile products in order to take advantage of the temporary price reduction, which merely shifts business from the future to the present. Two prevalent practices are forward buying and diverting, both of which represent efforts on the part of wholesalers and retailers to earn money from *buying* on deal rather than from selling merchandise at a profit.[48]

Manufacturers' off-invoice allowances typically are available every four weeks of each business quarter (which translates to about 30% of the year). Retailers take advantage of manufacturers' deals by buying larger quantities than needed for normal inventory and warehousing the excess quantity, thereby avoiding purchasing the product at full price. Retailers often purchase enough product on one deal to carry them over until the manufacturer's next regularly scheduled deal. This is the practice of **forward buying,** which, for obvious reasons, is also called *bridge buying.* When a manufacturer marks down a product's price by, say, 10%, wholesalers and retailers commonly stock up with a 10 to 12 week supply. A number of manufacturers sell upward of 80 to 90% of their volume at less than full price. Wholesalers and retailers are rational businesspeople: they take advantage of deals!

It may appear that forward buying benefits all parties to the marketing process, but this is not the case. First, retailers' savings from forward buying often are not passed on to consumers. Second, forward buying leads to increased distribution costs since wholesalers and retailers pay greater carrying charges in inventorying larger quantities. Third, manufacturers experience reduced margins due to the price discounts they offer as well as the increased labor costs and shipping expenses that occur during periods of peak demand. It is estimated that forward buying costs manufacturers between 0.5 to 1.1% of retail prices, which translates into hundreds of millions of dollars annually.[49]

A related buying practice, **diverting,** occurs when a manufacturer restricts a deal to a *limited geographical area* rather than making it available nationally. The manufacturer's intent is that only wholesalers and retailers in that area will benefit from the deal. However, what happens with diverting is that wholesalers and retailers buy abnormally large quantities at the deal price and then *transship* the excess quantities to other geographical areas. It is estimated that the volume of merchandise involved amounts to at least $5 billion a year.[50]

Many retailers blame manufacturers for offering irresistible deals; the retailers argue that they must take advantage of the deals in any way legally possible in order to remain competitive with other retailers. Manufacturers could avoid the problem by placing brands on national deal only. This solution is more ideal than practical, however, since regional marketing efforts are expanding, and local deals and regional marketing go hand in hand.

Manufacturers lose billions of dollars every year due to inefficient and ineffective trade deals stemming from the trade's practice of forward buying and diverting. It is for this reason that the powerful Procter & Gamble Corporation (P&G) under the leadership of CEO Edwin Artzt undertook a bold move in the early 1990s to bust the practice of forward buying and diverting. P&G introduced a new form of pricing called everyday low pricing, or EDLP. Because some retailers also practice everyday low prices, we will distinguish between "backdoor" EDLP as used by P&G and other manufacturers from the "frontdoor" variety of EDLP used by retailers. Our interest is with the backdoor variety of EDLP, which for clarity sake we label EDLP(M) to stand for manufacturer's use of EDLP.

EDLP(M) is a form of pricing whereby a manufacturer charges the same price for a particular brand day in and day out. In other words, rather than charging "high" prices for a period followed by "low" (i.e., off-invoice) prices for a shorter period, EDLP(M) involves charging the same price over an extended period. Because no deal is offered the trade, wholesalers and retailers have no reason to engage in forward buying or diverting. Hence, their profit is made via selling merchandise rather than by buying it. Many retailers and wholesalers initially resisted the move toward EDLP(M), but P&G persisted and other manufacturers followed suit. Today over 80% of P&G's brands are sold via EDLP(M) pricing and the amount of forward buying and diverting have declined.

Consumer-Oriented Sales Promotions

A variety of sales promotion methods are used to encourage consumers to purchase one brand over another, to purchase a particular brand more often, and to purchase in larger quantities. Such activities as sampling, couponing, refunding, rebating, and offering premiums, sweepstakes, and contests are all part of the promotions landscape.

Why do consumers respond to coupons, contests, sweepstakes, and other sales-promotion techniques? What objectives do manufacturers hope to accomplish by using these techniques?

Consumer Rewards.   Consumers would not be responsive to sales promotions unless there was something in it for them—and, in fact, there is. All sales-promotion techniques provide consumers with incentives or inducements that encourage certain forms of behavior desired by marketers. Rewards are typically in the form of cash savings or free gifts. Sometimes rewards are immediate, while other times they are delayed.

An *immediate reward* is one that delivers the savings or gift as soon as the consumer performs a marketer-specified behavior. For example, you receive cash savings at the time you redeem a coupon; pleasure is obtained immediately when you try, say, a free product while shopping in a grocery store. *Delayed rewards* are those that follow the behavior by a period of days, weeks, or even longer. For example, you may have to wait weeks before a free-in-the-mail premium object can be enjoyed. Generally speaking, consumers are more responsive to immediate rather than delayed rewards. Of course, this is in line with the natural human tendency to seek immediate rather than delayed gratification.

Manufacturer Objectives.

Manufacturers use sales promotions to accomplish any of three general categories of objectives: trial impact, franchise holding/loading, and image reinforcement.

Some sales promotions (primarily samples and coupons) are used primarily for *trial impact* purposes. A manufacturer employs these techniques to induce nonusers to try a brand for the first time or to encourage retrial for consumers who have not purchased the brand for an extended period. At other times, manufacturers use sales promotions to hold on to their franchise of current users by rewarding them for continuing to purchase the promoted brand or to load them so they have no need to switch to another brand. This is sales promotions' *franchise holding/loading* objective. The primary tools of franchise holding/loading are cents-off deals, bonus packs, premiums (all of which provide immediate rewards to consumers), and in- or on-pack coupons and refunds/rebates (which provide delayed rewards). Sales promotions also can be used for *image-reinforcement* purposes. For example, the careful selection of the right premium object or appropriate sweepstake prize can serve to reinforce a luxury brand's high-quality image.

Exhibit 15.6 provides a convenient summary of the foregoing discussion by classifying a variety of sales promotion techniques under the specific objective each is primarily responsible for accomplishing and the type of reward, either immediate or delayed, provided consumers.[51] It is important to recognize that most forms of

Exhibit 15.6   Major Consumer-Oriented Forms of Sales Promotions

Consumer Reward	Manufacturer's Objective		
	Trail Impact	Franchise Holding/Loading	Image Reinforcement
Immediate	■ Sampling	■ Price-offs	
	■ Instant coupons	■ Bonus packs	
	■ Shelf-delivered coupons	■ In-, on-, and near-pack premiums	
Delayed	■ Media- and Mail-delivered coupons	■ In- and on-pack coupons	■ Self-liquidating premiums
	■ Free-in-the-mail premiums	■ Refunds and rebates sweepstakes	■ Contests and
	■ Scanner-delivered coupons		

sales promotions perform more than a single objective. For example, refunds and rebates are classified as franchise holding/loading techniques but on some occasions they may also encourage trial purchasing. Note also that two techniques, coupons and premiums, have multiple entries. This is because these techniques achieve different objectives depending on the specific form of delivery vehicle. Coupons delivered through the media (e.g., newspapers) or in the mail offer a form of delayed reward, whereas instant coupons that can be peeled from a package at the point of purchase offer an immediate reward. Similarly, premium objects that are delivered in, on, or near a product's package provide an immediate reward, while those requiring mail delivery yield a reward only after some delay.

In sum, it is important to appreciate the fact that marketing communicators have a variety of sales promotion tools at their disposal. The choice of which to use depends on the specific objectives that must be accomplished for a brand at a particular point in time and an evaluation of the relative expense of using different tools. Coupons, for example, are especially widely used because different forms of couponing are capable of achieving different objectives (see Exhibit 15.6) and the cost typically is not prohibitive.

◆ Point-of-Purchase Communications

Marketers use a variety of items at the point-of-purchase (P-O-P) to draw attention to their brands and activate consumer purchases. These items include various types of signs, mobiles, plaques, banners, shelf tapes, mechanical mannequins, lights, mirrors, plastic product reproductions, checkout units, full-line merchandisers, wall posters, motion displays, and other materials. Many of these materials are *temporary* items, with useful life spans of only weeks or months. Others are relatively *permanent* fixtures that can be used for years. Whereas temporary signs and displays are particularly effective for promoting impulse purchasing, permanent P-O-P units compartmentalize and departmentalize a store area to achieve high product visibility, facilitate customer self-service, prevent stockouts, and help control inventory.

P-O-P's Dramatic Growth

Companies are increasingly investing promotional dollars in point-of-purchase materials. P-O-P expenditures have been growing in the United States by 10% or more each year. Expenditures on in-store promotional materials exceed $15 billion per year in the United States. This impressive growth is due to the fact that point-of-purchase materials provide a useful service for all participants in the marketing process.

For *manufacturers,* P-O-P keeps the company's name and the brand name before the consumer and both reactivates and reinforces brand information the consumer has previously received through advertising. P-O-P calls attention to special offers such as sales promotions and helps stimulate impulse purchasing.

P-O-P serves *retailers* by attracting the consumer's attention, increasing his or her interest in shopping, and extending the amount of time spent in the store—all of which mean increased sales. P-O-P helps retailers utilize available space to the best advantage by displaying several manufacturers' products in the same unit (e.g., many varieties of vitamins and other medicinal items all in one well-organized unit). It enables retailers to better organize shelf space and to improve inventory control, volume, stock turnover, and profitability.

Consumers are served by point-of-purchase units that deliver useful information and simplify the shopping process by setting products apart from similar items.

In addition to benefiting all participants in the marketing process, point-of-purchase plays another important role: It serves as the capstone for an integrated marketing-communications program. P-O-P by itself may have limited impact, but when used in conjunction with advertisements and sales promotions, P-O-P can create a synergistic effect.

Functions Performed by P-O-P Materials

P-O-P materials perform four important marketing functions: informing, reminding, encouraging, and merchandising.

Informing. Informing consumers is P-O-P's most basic communications function. Signs, posters, displays, and other P-O-P materials alert consumers to specific items and provide potentially useful information. Displays that move are especially effective for this purpose. Motion displays, though typically more expensive than static displays, represent a sound business investment because they attract significantly higher levels of shopper attention.

Reminding. A second point-of-purchase function is reminding consumers of brands they have previously learned about via broadcast, print, or other advertising media. This reminder role serves to complement the job already performed by advertising before the consumer enters a store.[52]

Encouraging. Encouraging consumers to buy a specific item or brand is P-O-P's third communication function. Effective P-O-P materials influence product and brand choices at the point of purchase and can encourage impulse buying. Studies of consumer shopping behavior have shown that a high proportion (over 65%) of all purchases in supermarkets, drugstores, and other retail outlets are unplanned.

In a general sense, this statistic indicates that many product- and brand-choice decisions are made while the consumer is in the store rather than before he or she arrives at the store. Point-of-purchase materials play a role, perhaps the major role, in influencing unplanned purchasing. Indeed, the Point-of-Purchase Advertising Institute's "Supermarket Consumer Buying Habits Study," which measured the behavior of 4,000 national shoppers, determined that approximately two-thirds of all grocery purchase decisions are made while the consumer is in the supermarket aisle.

Merchandising.   The merchandising function is served when point-of-purchase displays enable retailers to utilize floor space effectively and boost retail sales by assisting consumers in making product and brand selections. The merchandising role is well-illustrated with the information-center displays developed by Clairol to merchandise women's hair-coloring products and to answer questions concerning these products. Product information appears on large, colorful header signs above Clairol products placed on the display's shelves. The information center makes product selection easy: Color-coded labels identify product subcategories and shelf dividers separate the various products.

One of the major developments of in-store promotions is the interactive display. **Interactive displays** are computerized units that allow consumers to ask and have answered questions pertaining to their product-category needs. Examples of interactive displays abound. For example, L'eggs Products distributed a 14" interactive unit, called the Pantyhose Advisor, in 2,000 food and drug chains and mass merchandisers. Shoppers who visited the unit were asked questions (via liquid crystal displays) about their height, weight, the occasion for which they were buying pantyhose, and the style of shoes they would be wearing. The unit then recommended two styles of pantyhose and the appropriate size from the L'eggs and Just My Size brands of pantyhose. This unit served to reduce the confusion women face when choosing among a wide variety of styles and shades.

A particularly sophisticated version of interactive unit is the **video merchandising center (VMC),** which displays and sells entire product lines through audio and video presentations. VMCs perform both informational and transactional functions. That is, they inform and educate consumers about product features and process orders for delivery.

Sponsorship Marketing

One of the fastest growing aspects of marketing and marketing communications is the practice of corporate sponsorships.

Corporate expenditures on sponsorships exceeded $4 billion in 1994 and are increasing at about 15% per year.[53] Sponsorships range from supporting athletic events (e.g., golf and tennis tournaments or college football bowl games) to underwriting rock concerts and throwing corporate weight behind worthy causes such as efforts to generate funds for cancer research. Sponsorships involve investments in *events* or *causes* for the purpose of achieving various corporate objectives: increasing sales volume, enhancing a company's reputation or a brand's image, increasing brand awareness, and so on.

At least four factors account for the growth in sponsorships.[54] First, by attaching their names to special events and causes, companies are able to *avoid the clutter* inherent in advertising media. Second, sponsorships help companies *respond to consumers' changing media habits*. For example, with the decline in network television viewing, sponsorships offer a potentially effective and cost-efficient way to reach customers. Third, sponsorships help companies *gain the approval of various constituencies*, including stockholders, employees, and society at large. Finally, the sponsorship of special events and causes enables marketers to *target their communication and promotional efforts* to specific geographic regions or to specific lifestyle groups. For example, the marketers of Fleischmann's margarine aligned that brand with health-conscious aging baby-boomers by sponsoring a 22-city Beach Boys concert tour.[55] Philip Morris reached 800,000 bowlers, many of whom smoke, by sponsoring the Merit brand bowling competition.[56]

Event Marketing

Though relatively small compared to the major components of the promotions mix, expenditures on event sponsorship are increasing. Thousands of companies invest in some form of event sponsorship. Defined, **event marketing** is a form of brand promotion that ties a brand to a meaningful cultural, social, athletic, or other type of high-interest public activity. Event marketing is separate from advertising, sales promotion, point-of-purchase merchandising, or public relations, but it generally incorporates elements from all of these promotional tools.

Event marketing is growing rapidly because it provides companies alternatives to the cluttered mass media, an ability to segment on a local or regional basis, and opportunities for reaching narrow lifestyle groups whose consumption behavior can be linked with the local event. Events are effective because they reach people when they are in a relaxed atmosphere and receptive to marketing messages.[57]

As with every other marketing and promotion-management decision, the starting point for effective event sponsorship is to clearly specify the objectives that an event is designed to accomplish. Event marketing has no value unless it accomplishes these objectives. For example, to create a fun and exciting image for Cool Mint Listerine mouthwash, Warner-Lambert literally pitched tents at ski resorts. Product samples and Cool Mint headbands were distributed from the tents. The event was further tied in to retail displays that offered lift-ticket discounts to consumers who appeared at ski resorts with a Cool Mint proof-of-purchase.[58]

Cause-Related Marketing

Cause-related marketing (CRM) is a relatively narrow aspect of overall sponsorship. **CRM** involves an amalgam of public relations, sales promotion, and corporate philanthropy; however, the distinctive feature of CRM is that a company's contribution to a designated cause is linked to customers' engaging in *revenue-producing exchanges* with the firm.[59] Cause-related marketing, in other words, is based on the idea that a company will contribute to a cause every time the customer undertakes some action. The contribution is contingent on the customer performing a behavior (such as buying a product or redeeming a coupon) that benefits the firm.

The following examples illustrate how cause-related marketing operates. For each Heinz baby-food label mailed in by consumers, H. J. Heinz Company contributed 6¢ to a hospital near the consumer's home. Nabisco Brands donated $1 to the Juvenile Diabetes Foundation for each dollar donation certificate that was redeemed with a Ritz brand proof of purchase. Hershey donated 25¢ to local Hospitals for Children for each Hershey coupon redeemed. Dutch Boy paint contributed 25¢ to Healthy Families America for each gallon of paint sold during a designated period.[60]

Cause-related marketing is corporate philanthropy based on profit-motivated giving. But, of course, the primary purpose is to help the corporate cause while simultaneously helping a worthy social cause. In addition to helping worthy causes, corporations satisfy their own tactical and strategic objectives when undertaking cause-related efforts. By supporting a deserving cause, a company can (1) enhance its corporate or brand image, (2) thwart negative publicity, (3) generate incremental sales, (4) increase brand awareness, (5) broaden its customer base, (6) reach new market segments, and (7) increase a brand's level of merchandising activity at the retail level.[61]

Chapter Summary

This chapter discusses six elements of the promotion mix: advertising, publicity and public relations, direct marketing communications, sales promotions, point-of-purchase communications, and sponsorship marketing. Although each are treated in relative isolation, the importance of integrating the various elements—so that they speak with a single, unified voice—is emphasized throughout.

Advertising is a critical aspect of business, especially in the United States, where annual expenditures in 1994 alone were approximately $147 billion. Advertising is a valuable economic activity because it performs a variety of critical communications functions: It informs, persuades, reminds, adds value, and assists other company efforts.

The advertising management process consists primarily of advertising strategy, which extends from a company's overall marketing strategy, strategy implementation, and efforts to assess effectiveness. Advertising strategy, the guts of the process, entails four major activities: setting objectives, budgeting, developing a message strategy, and undertaking a media strategy.

Public relations, or PR, is the aspect of promotion management uniquely suited to fostering *goodwill* between a company and its various publics. Public relations involves interactions with multiple publics (e.g., government, stockholders), but emphasis in this chapter is limited to the more narrow aspect of public relations involving an organization's interactions with customers. This marketing-oriented aspect of public relations is called marketing PR, or MPR for short. Marketing PR can be further delineated as involving either proactive or reactive public relations. Proactive MPR is another tool in addition to advertising, sales promotion, and personal selling for promoting a company's products and services. Its major role is for disseminating information about product introductions or revisions. Reactive MPR is undertaken as a result of external pressures and challenges brought by competitive actions, changes in consumer attitudes, changes in government policy, or other external influences. Reactive MPR typically deals with changes that have negative consequences for the organization, such as instances of product defects or failures.

Direct marketing is a major growth area in marketing and an important form of marketing communications. Direct marketing is accomplished using (1) direct-response advertising, (2) direct mail (including catalogs), (3) telemarketing, and (4) direct selling (e.g., home visits via Tupperware and Avon salespeople), although discussion in this chapter is restricted to direct-response advertising and direct mail. Database marketing, the computer storage and retrieval of huge data files, is the cornerstone of effective direct-response advertising. Database marketing has the virtues of addressability, measurability, flexibility, and accountability.

Sales promotion, the use of any incentive by a manufacturer to induce the trade (wholesalers and retailers) and/or consumers to buy a brand and to encourage the sales force to aggressively sell it, is an important element of the promotion mix for most businesses, especially consumer packaged goods. Consumer promotions (such as coupons, cents-off deals, premiums, and sweepstakes) and trade-oriented promotions (primarily off-invoice allowances to wholesalers and retailers) constituted, on average, 75% of businesses' promotional budgets in 1993, with media advertising receiving only 25% of the budget. Various factors account for the shift in the allocation of promotion budgets away from advertising (an above-the-line promotion) toward sales promotion and other forms of below-the-line promotions: (1) balance of power transfer; (2) increased brand parity and price sensitivity; (3) reduced brand loyalty; (4) splintering of the mass market and reduced media effectiveness; (5) short-term orientation and corporate reward structures; and (6) trade and consumer responsiveness. Sales promotions are particularly useful for purposes of introducing new or revised products to the trade, obtaining trial purchases from consumer, and enhancing repeat purchasing; however, sales promotions cannot makeup for inadequate personal selling or advertising, give the trade or consumers any long-term reason for buying a product, or permanently stop an established product's declining sales trend.

Trade-oriented sales promotions consist primarily of various forms of discounts, or deals, offered to wholesalers and retailers. These include off-invoice and bill-back allowances, and, in the case of new product introductions, slotting allowances to obtain retail distribution. Pernicious aspects of trade promotions from the manufacturer's perspective include forward buying and diverting. The practice of everyday low pricing, EDLP(M), was introduced by Procter & Gamble to offset these practices.

Consumer-oriented promotions have as their objective obtaining consumer trial, holding or loading consumer franchises, and reinforcing brand images. Devices such as coupons, samples, premiums, bonus packs, sweepstakes, and contests, are used to achieve different objectives and accomplish these objectives by offering consumers either immediate or delayed rewards.

Communication at the point of purchase is another major growth area in marketing. Point-of-purchase materials provide a useful service for all participants in the marketing process. P-O-P communications also serve as the capstone for an integrated marketing-communications program. P-O-P materials perform four important marketing functions: informing, reminding, encouraging, and merchandising products.

One of the fastest growing aspects of marketing and marketing communication is the practice of corporate sponsorships. Corporate expenditures on sponsorships exceeded $4 billion in 1994 and are increasing at about 15% per year. Sponsorships take two forms: event sponsorships such as sporting events and recreational events and cause sponsorships. Event marketing is growing rapidly because it provides companies alternatives to the cluttered mass media, an ability to segment on a local or regional basis, and opportunities for reaching narrow lifestyle groups whose consumption behavior can be linked with the local event. Cause-related marketing, a form of corporate philanthropy with benefits accruing to the sponsoring company, is based on the idea that a company will contribute to a cause every time the customer undertakes some action. In addition to helping worthy causes, corporations satisfy their own tactical and strategic objectives when undertaking cause-related efforts. By supporting a deserving cause, a company can enhance its corporate or brand image, generate incremental sales, increase brand awareness, broaden its customer base, and reach new market segments.

Notes

1. Todd Pruzan, "Spending '94: Europe Mired But Asia Grows," *Advertising Age,* February 20, 1995, I–9.
2. Pruzan, "Spending '94."

3. "100 Leading National Advertisers," *Advertising Age*, September 28, 1994, 4.

4. These objectives are similar to those identified by the noted advertising pioneer, James Webb Young, "What Is Advertising, What Does It Do," *Advertising Age*, November 21, 1973, 12.

5. Raymond Serafin, "Ford Contours Ad Blast," *Advertising Age*, July 18, 1994, 1.

6. "Top 200 Mega-Brands by 1994 Ad Spending," *Advertising Age*, May 1, 1995, 34.

7. *The Value Side of Productivity: A Key to Competitive Survival in the 1990s* (New York: American Association of Advertising Agencies, 1989), 12.

8. John Sinisi, "Love: EDLP Equals Ad Investment," *Brandweek*, November 16, 1992, 2.

9. William R. Swinyard and Michael L. Ray, "Advertising-Selling Interactions: An Attribution Theory Experiment," *Journal of Marketing Research*, 14 (November 1977), 509–516.

10. Charles H. Patti and Charles F. Frazer, *Advertising: A Decision-Making Approach* (Chicago: Dryden, 1988), 236.

11. Gary L. Lilien, Alvin J. Silk, Jean-Marie Choffray, and Murlidhar Rao, "Industrial Advertising Effects and Budgeting Practices," *Journal of Marketing*, 40 (January 1976), 21.

12. Fred S. Zufryden, "How Much Should Be Spent for Advertising a Brand?" *Journal of Advertising Research*, April/May 1989, 24–34.

13. Lilien et al., "Industrial Advertising Effects and Budgeting Practices," and Kent M. Lancaster and Judith A. Stern, "Computer-Based Advertising Budgeting Practices of Leading U.S. Consumer Advertisers," *Journal of Advertising*, 12, 4 (1983), 6.

14. For similar views, see A. Jerome Jewler, *Creative Strategy in Advertising* (Belmont, CA: Wadsworth, 1985), 7–8, and Don E. Schultz and Stanley I. Tannenbaum, *Essentials of Advertising Strategy* (Lincolnwood, IL: NTC Business, 1988), 9–10.

15. Stan Freberg, "Irtnog Revisited," *Advertising Age*, August 1, 1988, 32.

16. Schultz and Tannenbaum, *Essentials of Advertising Strategy*, 75.

17. Joe Schwartz, "Back to the Source," *American Demographics* (January 1989), 22–26.

18. "What the Scanner Knows about You," *Fortune,* December 3, 1990, 51–52.

19. Grace Conlon, "Closing in on Consumer Behavior," *Marketing Communications* (November 1986), 56.

20. Jordan Goldman, *Public Relations in the Marketing Mix* (Lincolnwood, IL: NTC Business, 1984).

21. David Kiley, "After Peugeot and Sterling, Who's Next?" *Adweek's Marketing Week,* August 19, 1991, 9.

22. Marcy Magiera, "Pepsi Weathers Tampering Hoax," *Advertising Age,* June 21, 1993, 1, 46; Marcy Magiera, "The Pepsi Crisis: What Went Right," *Advertising Age,* July 19, 1993, 14–15.

23. Mary Agnes Carey, "Popcorn at Movies Gets Thumbs Down for Being Full of Fat," *The Wall Street Journal,* April 26, 1994, B5.

24. Alex Stanton, "Pentium Brouhaha a Marketing Lesson," *Advertising Age,* February 20, 1995, 18.

25. Stan Rapp and Thomas L. Collins, *MaxiMarketing* (New York: McGraw-Hill, 1987).

26. William A. Cohen, "The Future of Direct Marketing," *Retailing Issues Letter,* vol. 1, published by Arthur Andersen & Co. in conjunction with the Center for Retailing Studies, Texas A&M University, November 1987.

27. Elain Underwood, "Mall Busters, Like Crime, A Boon for Home Shopping," *Brandweek,* January 17, 1994, 18, 20.

28. *Fact Book on Direct Response Marketing* (New York: Direct Marketing Association, Inc., 1982), xxiii. Italics not in original.

29. Description adapted from Don E. Schultz, "The Direct/DataBase Marketing Challenge to Fixed-Location Retailers," in Robert A. Peterson (ed.), *The Future of U.S. Retailing: An Agenda for the 21st Century* (New York: Quorum, 1992), 165–184.

30. Good overviews are provided in Jonathan Berry et al., "A Potent New Tool for Selling: Database Marketing," *Business Week,* September 5, 1994, 56–62; Glenn Heitsmith, "Database Promotions: Marketers Move Carefully, But Some Are Still Faking It," *Promo,* October 1994, 37–50.

31. "Car Maker Uses Direct to Drive Loyalty," *Promo,* January 1994, 21.

32. Terry G. Vavra, *Aftermarketing* (Homewood, IL: Business One Irwin, 1992), 32.

33. Bob Stone, "For Effective Direct Results," *Advertising Age,* March 28, 1983, sec. M, 32.

34. Richard Hodgson, *Direct Mail and Mail Order Handbook* (Chicago: Dartnell, 1974).

35. "What Happened to Advertising," *Business Week,* September 23, 1991, 69.

36. Don Schultz as quoted in Gary Levin, "Going Direct Route," *Advertising Age,* November 18, 1991, 37.

37. Robert J. Samuelson, "Computer Communities," *Newsweek,* December 15, 1986, 66.

38. This is based on research by direct-marketing consultant Maxwell Sroge as cited in Elaine Underwood, "Sara Lee Rides Catalog Boom," *Brandweek,* November 28, 1994, 9.

39. Terence A. Shimp, *Promotion Management and Marketing Communications,* 3rd. ed. (Fort Worth, TX: Dryden, 1993), 442.

40. Alvin A. Achenbaum and F. Kent Mitchel, "Pulling Away from Push Marketing," *Harvard Business Review,* 65, May-June 1987, 38–40; Robert J. Kopp and Stephen A. Greyser, "Packaged Goods Marketing—'Pull' Companies Look to Improved 'Push'," *The Journal of Consumer Marketing,* 4 (Spring 1987), 13–22.

41. *The 16th Annual Survey of Promotional Practices* (Donnelley Marketing Inc., 1994).

42. Robert C. Blattberg and Scott A. Neslin, "Sales Promotion: The Long and the Short of It," *Marketing Letters,* 1, 1 (1989), 81–97.

43. This discussion is guided by Charles Fredericks, Jr., "What Ogilvy & Mather Has Learned About Sales Promotion," *The Tools of Promotion* (New York: Association of National Advertisers, 1975), and Don E. Schultz and William A. Robinson, *Sales Promotion Management* (Lincolnwood, IL: NTC Business, 1986), Chap. 3.

44. Robert C. Blattberg and Alan Levin, "Modelling the Effectiveness and Profitablilty of Trade Promotions," *Marketing Science,* 6 (Spring 1987), 125.

45. See Chakravarthi Narasimhan, "Managerial Perspectives on Trade and Consumer Promotions," *Marketing Letters,* 1, 3 (1989), 239–251.

46. Fourth Annual Survey of Manufacturer Trade Promotion Practices (Nielsen Marketing Research), December, 1992, 10.

47. Rajiv Lal, "Manufacturer Trade Deals and Retail Price Promotions," *Journal of Marketing Research,* 27 (November 1990), 428–444; Ronald C. Curhan and Robert J. Kopp, "Obtaining Retailer Support for Trade Deals: Key Success Factors," *Journal of Advertising Research,* 27 (December 1987/January 1988), 51–60.

48. For further reading see Howard Schlossberg, "Exposed: Retailing's Dirty Little Secret," *Promo,* April 1994, 50–55, and Patricia Sellers, "The Dumbest Marketing Ploy," *Fortune,* October 5, 1992, 88–94.

49. Robert D. Buzzell, John A. Quelch, and Walter J. Salmon, "The Costly Bargain of Trade Promotion," *Harvard Business Review,* March-April 1990, 145.

50. Buzzell, Quelch, and Salmon, "The Costly Bargains."

51. For further discussion, see Shimp, *Promotion Management and Marketing Communications,* 3rd ed., 489–526.

52. Kevin Lane Keller, "Cue Compatibility and Framing in Advertising," *Journal of Marketing Research,* 28 (February 1991), 42–57.

53. Glenn Heitsmith, "Event Promotions: Get Them by Their Hearts and Minds," *Promo,* March 1994, 31.

54. Meryl Paula Gardner and Phillip Joel Shuman, "Sponsorship: An Important Component of the Promotions Mix," *Journal of Advertising,* 16, 1 (1987), 11–17.

55. Kerry J. Smith, "Nabisco Sets Sail with Beach Boys," *Promo,* May 1994, 69.

56. Howard Schlossberg, "Weighing in with Events," *Promo,* May 1994, 66–67.

57. Heitsmith, "Event Promotions," 32.

58. Heitsmith, "Event Promotions," 103.

59. P. Rajan Varadarajan and Anil Menon, "Cause-Related Marketing: A Coalignment of Marketing Strategy and Corporate Philanthropy," *Journal of Marketing,* 52 (July 1988), 58–74.

60. Kerry J. Smith, "Promoting with a Cause," *Promo*, February 1995, 68.

61. Howard Schlossberg, "For a Good Cause," *Promo*, February 1994, 38–49.

62. Varadarajan and Menon, "Cause-Related Marketing."

◆ Study Questions

1. Total annual advertising expenditures in 1994 in the United States were approximately
   a. $500 million.
   b. $500 billion.
   c. $147 billion.
   d. $47 billion.

2. Which of the following is *not* a major reason for setting advertising objectives?
   a. To force management to agree upon the course advertising should take.
   b. To prevent advertising from being dominated by sales promotion.
   c. To guide the budgeting, message strategy, and media strategy activities.
   d. To provide standards against which results can be measured.

3. The optimal (i.e., profit maximizing) level of an advertising budget occurs at the point where
   a. $MR = MC$.
   b. $MR > MC$.
   c. $MR < MC$.
   d. $TR > TC$.

4. Assume that 40% of all U.S. households tuned in to the 1995 Superbowl football game. This figure, 40%, in advertising-media language is called a(n)
   a. gross rating point.
   b. rating.
   c. market share.
   d. audience.

5. A certain magazine is read by 10,000,000 people. An advertiser pays $125,000 for a single, four-color page in this magazine. The cost-per-thousand (CPM) is

a. $0.0125.
b. $80.00.
c. $12.50.
d. None of the above.

6. Which of the following is *not* a strength of television advertising?
   a. high reach potential
   b. attain rapid awareness
   c. intrusive
   d. upscale audience profile

7. Which of the following is *not* a weakness of newspaper advertising?
   a. poor geographic flexibility
   b. high out-of-pocket costs for national buys
   c. not intrusive
   d. cluttered ad environment

8. Which of the following terms has absolutely no relation with single-source systems for assessing advertising effectiveness?
   a. split-cable television
   b. optical scanners
   c. Burke day-after recall
   d. BehaviorScan

9. Proactive marketing PR is
   a. a defensively oriented form of publicity aimed at customers.
   b. an offensively oriented form of publicity aimed at customers.
   c. a publicity method directed primarily at communicating with stockholders.
   d. a publicity method directed primarily at communicating with government officials.

10. _____ is undertaken as a result of external pressures and challenges brought by competitive actions, changes in consumer attitudes, changes in government policy, or other external influences.
    a. Proactive MPR
    b. Publicity
    c. Public relations
    d. Reactive MPR

11. Which of the following is *not* one of the distinct abilities of data-base marketing?
    a. factorability
    b. addressability
    c. measurability
    d. accountability

12. Which of the following is a correct statement about direct-mail advertising?
    a. It is less expensive on a cost-per-thousand basis than, say, television advertising.
    b. It is more wasteful than mass media.
    c. Its CPM is more expensive than mass media.
    d. It is inappropriate for use by business-to-business marketers.

13. Four factors account for the trend toward widespread use of direct mail by all types of marketers. Which of the following is *not* one of them?
    a. Increased cost of TV advertising and audience fragmentation.
    b. Direct mail enables unparalleled targeting of messages to desired prospects.
    c. Direct mail enables measurable advertising results.
    d. All of the above factors account for the widespread use of direct mail.

14. Which of the following is considered an above-the-line expenditure?
    a. advertising
    b. sales promotion
    c. event sponsorships
    d. point-of-purchase communications

15. The biggest chunk of the promotional mix for most consumer brands goes to
    a. advertising.
    b. consumer-oriented sales promotions.
    c. sponsorships.
    d. trade-oriented sales promotions.

16. Which of the following is *not* one of the factors giving rise to the growth of sales promotions?
    a. balance of power transfer
    b. reduced brand loyalty

c. corporate reward structures supporting a long-term orientation
d. increased brand parity and price sensitivity

17. Sales promotions can accomplish all of the following tasks except
   a. increase product usage by loading consumers.
   b. compensate for a poorly trained sales force.
   c. encourage repeat purchases.
   d. stimulate sales force enthusiasm.

18. A large retail chain purchases chicken noodle soup from Campbell's Soup only when Campbell's offers an off-invoice allowance. The retail chain is engaging in
   a. forward buying.
   b. diverting.
   c. bridge buying.
   d. More than one of the above are correct.

19. A retailer receives credit in the form of a _____ from a manufacturer after the retailer merchandises the manufacturer's brand on a special display.
   a. off-invoice allowance
   b. slotting allowance
   c. bill-back allowance
   d. trade allowance

20. A form of marketing-based corporate philanthropy is
   a. sponsorship marketing.
   b. event marketing.
   c. corporate gift giving.
   d. cause-oriented marketing.

CHAPTER  16

Personal Selling and Sales Management

Chapter Objectives

Overview

Selling Activities and Types of Personal-Selling Jobs

Salesperson Performance and Effectiveness

The Personal Selling Process

Sales Force Management

Chapter Summary

◆ Overview

Personal selling is a fundamental and critically important aspect of marketing and an exciting career prospect for many students. This chapter will introduce you to the subject, overview the various types of personal selling jobs and selling activities, discuss key characteristics of effective sales performance, describe the nature of modern selling philosophy, and then review some key aspects of sales force management.

By definition, **personal selling** is a form of person-to-person communication in which a salesperson works with prospective buyers and attempts to influence their purchase in the direction of his or her company's products or services. The most important feature of this definition is the idea that personal selling involves *person-to-person interaction*. This aspect contrasts with other forms of marketing communications (advertising, sales promotions, publicity, and event marketing) in which the audience typically consists of many people, as in the case of mass-media advertising where audiences for prime-time TV advertising sometimes exceed 20 million households. Some organizations—mostly in the business-to-business sector—rely almost exclusively on personal selling efforts in marketing their products. Most companies use personal selling as part of their overall marketing communications mix. The degree to which personal selling is used depends on a variety of factors, including selling costs, customers' needs, the locations of customers' businesses, and the nature of the product. For example, personal selling plays a particularly strategic role when a company markets technically sophisticated products to customers who require in-depth product information.

Today, over 14 million people in the United States are employed in sales positions.[1] Approximately 6.3 million people work in retail selling for companies such as The Gap, Sears, and automobile dealers, and approximately 8 million are involved in non-retail positions as sales representatives for manufacturers (working for companies such as IBM, Procter & Gamble, General Electric, and Levi Strauss), as salespeople who are employed by thousands of wholesalers, agents, and brokers, and as salespeople who represent the services of insurance companies, stock brokerages, and other service providers. Many additional people are employed in sales-support jobs that facilitate and assist salespeople and the companies they represent. For example, sales-support technicians at Xerox are responsible for equipment installation and maintenance of that company's photo-reproduction equipment after it has been sold by Xerox's salespeople.

Attractive Features of Personal Selling

The field of sales offers many challenging and exciting job opportunities. Some of the attractive features of a job in personal selling include the following.

Job Freedom.   Field-sales positions—those outside of retail settings—offer a person freedom in planning and setting his or her own daily schedule. The salesperson sets appointments and makes calls at his or her discretion with little direct supervision. Of course, with freedom comes responsibility. The salesperson must be a motivated, responsible individual who conducts business professionally and achieves sales objectives for the company.

Variety and Challenge.   Being a salesperson involves managing one's own time, a challenge many salespeople enjoy. A salesperson who devotes a great amount of time to selling and prospecting will generate greater sales and therefore greater financial rewards than the salesperson who only devotes part of the time or energy to his or her job.

Opportunities for Advancement.   Sales positions are often the stepping-stones for higher-level positions within the company. Since sales positions provide a knowledge of the customer, the trade, the competition, and the company, employees with sales experience are viewed as well-rounded employees who have a good understanding of the business from the ground-level up. More and more companies expect their middle- and upper-level managers to have sales experience.

Attractive Compensation and Nonfinancial Rewards. Personal selling is both lucrative and rewarding. Salespeople are well paid, and the nonfinancial rewards of pride, self-worth for a job well done, and the satisfaction of helping a customer are just as important as the financial rewards.

Misconceptions about Selling

Personal selling historically has been held in low esteem by many people who think of salespeople as con artists and tricksters. This reputation dates back at least to the time of the ancient Greek philosophers. Movie and television directors and playwrights continue to perpetuate the myth. For example, two heralded Broadway plays—Arthur Miller's classic *Death of a Salesman* and David Mamet's more recent *Glengarry Glen Ross*, which later was made into a movie—depicted salesmen as rather pathetic characters who struggle for an existence and earn their living through ingratiation, deceit, and unethical practices. In real life, there indeed are con men and women who rely on deception, false promises, trickery, and misrepresentation to persuade people to buy products and services they do not need or items that do not work. Although this still happens today, it represents a small percentage of the personal-selling business.

Fortunately, the continuing trend among college students is toward more favorable attitudes toward selling. Exhibit 16.1 compares results of two studies separated by a 30-year interval. It shows that student attitudes have improved rather dramatically.[2] Personal selling is a much more attractive career option than many students previously thought.

Personal Selling's Role in the Marketing Communications Mix

Personal selling is a vital element of the marketing communications mix. Previous chapters have pointed out that the elements of the marketing communications mix must be tightly integrated so as to effectively communicate a common message about a company's offerings. The sales function must be carefully coordinated with a brand's advertising and sales promotion efforts so that all tools are working to the accomplishment of common goals.

Each element in a firm's marketing communications mix has its own unique strengths, weaknesses, and capabilities. The primary purposes of personal selling are to educate customers about a firm's offerings, provide product usage and marketing assistance, and provide after-sale service and support to buyers. Personal selling, in comparison to other communication elements, is uniquely capable of performing these functions because of the person-to-

Exhibit 16.1   College Students' Changing Attitudes toward Personal Selling

I associate a job in personal selling with	1958 Study	1988 Study
Insincerity and deceit	Agree	Disagree
Low staus/low prestige	Agree	Disagree
Much traveling	Agree	Agree
Salespeople being money hungry	Agree	Disagree
High pressure forcing people to buy unwanted goods	Agree	Disagree
Low job security	Agree	Disagree
Just a job, not a career	Agree	Disagree
Personality is crucial	Agree	Agree
Too little monetary reward	Disagree	Disagree
I prefer a nonsales position much more than sales	Agree	Disagree

Source: Adapted from Rosemary R. Lagace and Timothy A. Longfellow, "The Impact of Classroom Style on Student Attitudes toward Sales Careers: A Comparative Approach," *Journal of Marketing Education*, 1989 (Fall), 74.

person interaction that is the basis of personal selling. Various advantages accrue to personal selling compared to communication via other marketing communication methods such as advertising:[3]

1. Personal selling contributes to a *relatively high level of customer attention*, since in face-to-face situations it is difficult for a prospective customer to avoid a salesperson's message.

2. It enables the salesperson to *customize the message* to the customer's specific interests and needs.

3. The two-way communication characteristic of personal selling yields *immediate feedback*, so that an alert salesperson can know whether or not his or her sales presentation is working.

4. Personal selling enables a salesperson to *communicate a larger amount of technical and complex information* than could be communicated using other communication methods.

5. In personal selling there is a greater ability to *demonstrate a product's functioning and performance characteristics.*

6. Frequent interactions with a customer permit the opportunity for *developing long-term relations* and effectively merging selling and buying organizations into a coordinated unit where both sets of interests are served.

When considering only the outcomes, or results, accomplished with the personal-selling effort (an effectiveness consideration), personal selling is generally *more effective* than other promotion elements. However, when considering the ratio of inputs to outputs (cost to results), personal selling is typically *less efficient* than other promotion tools. In other words, the primary *disadvantage* of personal selling is that it is more costly than other forms of marketing communications because sales representatives typically interact with only one customer at a time. In practice, allocating resources to personal selling and the other marketing communication elements amounts to an effort at balancing effectiveness and efficiency. It often is desirable, indeed essential, to allocate a large portion of the marketing communications budget to personal selling because other communication functions, such as advertising, are incapable of accomplishing the tasks that personal sales effort can achieve.

Selling Activities and Types of Personal-Selling Jobs

Selling Activities

Salespeople perform a variety of tasks. These vary depending on the type of product being sold, the competitive environment in which their companies operate, and the specific requirements imposed by their companies and sales managers. In some companies, one salesperson may sell only a few of the company's numerous products to key accounts. But in other companies, a salesperson may be required to sell the entire line to all key accounts, wholesalers, and distributors in the area. Regardless of the the job specifics, the following ten activities are common to nearly all selling jobs:[4]

Performing the Sales Function. These activities are those typically associated with a personal selling job. Sales-function activities include planning the sales presentation, making the presentation, overcoming objections, and closing sales.

Working with Orders. A great portion of the salesperson's time is spent writing orders, tracking lost orders, handling shipping problems, expediting orders, and handling back orders.

Servicing the Product. People who sell technical products (e.g., industrial machinery) primarily perform these activities, including testing a newly sold product to ensure it is working properly, training customers on the new equipment, and teaching safety procedures.

Servicing the Account. Salespeople typically service accounts by performing activities such as inventory control, stocking shelves, handling local advertising efforts, and setting up and working with point-of-purchase displays. Such activities are primarily performed by salespeople who call on customers in supermarket, drugstore, and mass-merchandising outlets such as Wal-Mart and Kmart.

Providing Information to Management. Quite often the salesperson is required to provide information to management such as customer feedback about product performance. Much of this information gathering is done in the normal course of a salesperson's day but some information-management work requires the salesperson to serve in the capacity of a field marketing researcher.

Participating in Conferences and Meetings. Nearly all salespeople are called upon at least occasionally to participate in conferences, trade shows, and sales meetings hosted by the division, home office, or trade group.

Training and Recruiting Salespeople. Experienced salespeople are often called upon to train new salespeople, travel with trainees, and perform other such duties.[5]

Entertaining Customers. Some salespeople are required to entertain their customers through activities such as dinners and sporting events. Although the old school of thought was that customers could be bought by wining and dining them, modern selling philosophy includes a role for customer entertainment but recognizes that customers are earned (through loyal, efficient, dependable service) rather than bought.

Traveling.   Although sales jobs involve some travel, the amount of time a salesperson spends on the road varies depending on the size of the sales force, the size of the salesperson's territory, the product, and the company. Out-of-town travel ranges from virtually no travel to journeying thousands of miles each year.

Working with Distributors.   A final category of selling activity is selling to or establishing relations with distributors and collecting past-due accounts.

General Types of Sales Jobs

As described in a subsequent section, there are a variety of specific sales jobs. In general, however, sales jobs can be classified into three categories: order takers, order getters, and sales support.

Order Takers.   Order takers maintain sales rather than generate new sales for a company. This job entails monitoring customers' inventory levels and replenishing or reordering product when levels are low. In some companies, accounts with low sales volumes are serviced by inside order takers, or a telephone sales staff, instead of via face-to-face sales calls. Telephone sales enables a company to maintain accounts that might otherwise be dropped due to the high costs of personally selling the account. Order takers are typically assigned accounts that have been presold at the headquarter level or were previously established.

Order Getters.   On the other end of the selling spectrum are order getters, or those salespeople who must actively search out prospective new customers. The order getter's main objective is to convert a potential customer into an user of his or her company's product. Order getters require a higher level of sales expertise and technical knowledge than required of order takers. An order getter needs a thorough knowledge of the product, the competition, and the potential customer in order to sell the account. Most order getters utilize creative selling skills in selling their accounts. The order getter's main focus is to generate new sales rather than to maintain current sales.

Sales-Support Positions.   The third general type of sales job is a sales support position. Sales support personnel do not sell products to customers. Their focus is on providing pre-sale support to the salesperson as well as after-sale service to the customer. Many companies have a sales assistant assigned to a unit, district, division, or region depending on the size of the sales force and width and depth of product lines. This sales assistant performs a variety of functions. A salesperson who is preparing a major sales presentation for a new account, for example, may call upon the assistant to provide competitive information, special brochures, or company background. The assistant may also be responsible for producing reports representing the unit's activities. If the unit is having a sales meeting, the assistant may perform a good deal of the leg work involved in setting up and conducting a meeting.

Once a salesperson has made the sale, the sales assistant is called upon to service the account. The assistant ensures that the order is shipped as requested and that all special instructions are followed. The name and telephone number is provided to the customer in case the salesperson cannot be reached and the customer needs to speak to someone within the company. The sales assistant and salesperson act as a sales team for the customer.

Specific Types of Sales Jobs

The three general forms of sales jobs can be further classified based on the job's focus and expertise. The following six categories encompass the major types of sales jobs:[6]

Trade Selling.   The primary task of trade salespeople is to build sales volume by providing customers with promotional assistance in the form of advertising and sales promotion. Little prospecting is done in this position. Trade salespeople focus on *servicing accounts*. A sales representative for a packaged goods manufacturer who sells to the grocery and drug industries typifies trade selling. Major packaged goods companies such as Lever Brothers, Hunt Wesson, Johnson & Johnson, and Campbell's Soup typically hire recent college graduates as trade salespeople.

Missionary Selling.

Like trade salespeople, missionary sales-people typically are employees of manufacturers. However, the difference is that trade salespeople sell *to* their direct customers, whereas a missionary sales force sells *for* its direct customers.[7]

The pharmaceutical industry typifies missionary selling. Nearly two-thirds of all pharmaceutical sales to retailers are through wholesalers. In other words, manufacturers of pharmaceuticals typically market their products to wholesalers who in turn market to pharmacies and other retailers. Thus, the wholesaler is the pharmaceutical manufacturer's direct customer. Sales representatives for pharmaceutical manufacturers (called *detail reps*, or *detailers*) nonetheless call on physicians and pharmacies to detail (explain) the advantages of the manufacturer's brands compared to competitive offerings. Detail reps are not selling directly to physicians (i.e., selling in the sense that a physician will place an order with the salesperson's company); rather, they are trying to get physicians to prescribe their brands. In so doing, they benefit both the manufacturer (via increased sales volume) and their direct customers (wholesalers).

Technical Selling.

In some industries such as chemicals, machinery, and sophisticated services, technical salespeople are needed to sell the products. These salespeople, who are typically trained in technical fields such as chemistry, engineering, and computer science, either support the regular sales force by offering expertise and detail often needed to close a sale or sell the products themselves. For example, in the chemical division of DuPont, 95% of the company's salespeople start out in a technical field and then are recruited into sales.[8] Later, many sales technicians attain advanced training in business administration. Good technical salespeople must be thoroughly knowledgeable about the company's products and be able to explain the benefits to potential customers in language they can understand.

New-Business Selling.

All of the previously mentioned salespeople spend a majority of their time servicing current customers with very little time spent on prospecting new accounts. The previously described sales positions are involved primarily in *order taking*. In some industries where sales are infrequent such as data-processing equipment, sophisticated packaging equipment, business forms, and personal insurance, new-business salespeople are hired by the manufacturer to continually prospect and call on new accounts. Terms such as bird-dogging, cold calling, and canvassing are used to describe this type of selling situation. New-business salespeople must constantly develop new leads to generate sales since most sales are either one time occurrences or very infrequent.

Retail Selling.   All of the previously mentioned salespeople call on customers usually at the customers' places of businesses. Retail salespeople differ, however, in that the customer comes to the salesperson. Many retail salespeople require limited sophistication and training, while others—for example, electronics, personal computers, and appliances—require considerable product knowledge, strong communication skills, and an ability to work with a diversity of customers.

Telemarketing.   Telemarketing is a rapidly growing form of selling activity. These salespeople perform most of the same selling activities as salespeople who call on customers directly. Some manufacturers hire their own telemarketing departments while others employ the services of outside telemarketers. In either case, telemarketing allows a manufacturer to maintain and service those customers that are uneconomical to call on with a direct sales force.

Many companies use the telephone to support or even replace their conventional sales forces. Telemarketing uses outbound calls from telephone salespersons for purposes of (1) opening new accounts, (2) qualifying advertising leads, and (3) servicing existing business, including reorders and customer service. Telemarketing is used in conjunction with advertising, direct mail, catalog sales, and face-to-face selling. Telemarketing's versatility applies to both consumer-oriented products and business-to-business marketing. IBM, for example, uses telemarketing to cover its small- to medium-size accounts, generate incremental sales, enhance the productivity of traditional sales representatives via the leads and information that it provides, and ensure customer satisfaction and buying convenience.

Salesperson Performance and Effectiveness

Regardless of the type of sales job, certain aptitudes and skills are needed to perform effectively. Indeed, people in all facets of life are ultimately judged in terms of their performance and effectiveness. These evaluations often are based on quantitative assessments: number of arrests by a police officer, number of indictments by a prosecuting attorney, number of hits by a baseball player, number of units produced by a factory worker, number of articles published by a professor, and so on. Likewise, salespeople are typically judged in terms of the number of units sold or dollar volume.

Academic and business researchers have long been intrigued with explaining and predicting salesperson performance. The fundamental issue is one of identifying the specific factors that determine salesperson effectiveness—the factors that distinguish the outstanding salesperson from the good, the mediocre, and the bad salespeople. (Stop reading for a few moments and think about your own ideas on this issue. Jot down what you think are the most important determinants of salesperson success and later compare your thoughts with the ideas presented.)

Before a specific discussion of the determinants of salesperson performance and effectiveness, two general points require careful attention. The first is that *no single factor is able to adequately explain salesperson performance*. In a very thorough and insightful analysis of sales research conducted over a 40-year span, researchers examined over 1,500 correlations in some 100 separate studies that related salesperson performance with a wide variety of potential predictors. Their analyses revealed that, on average, no single predictor explained more than four percent of the variability in salesperson performance![9] The conclusion to be drawn is clear: Sales performance is based on various considerations; to expect any single factor (or even several factors) to adequately explain a complex behavior is expecting too much.

A second general conclusion is that salesperson performance and effectiveness are contingent on a host of factors; indeed, selling performance and effectiveness depend on the total situation in which sales transactions take place. Specifically, salesperson performance depends on factors such as (1) the salesperson's own resources (e.g., product knowledge, analytical skills), (2) the nature of the customer's buying task (e.g., whether it is a first-time or repeat decision), (3) the customer-salesperson relationship (e.g., relative power, level of conflict), and interactions among all three of these general sets of factors.[10]

Specific Determinants of Salesperson Performance

Researchers have identified six general characteristics that determine salesperson performance: (1) aptitude, (2) skill level, (3) motivational level, (4) role perceptions, (5) personal characteristics, and (6) adapt-ability.[11]

Aptitude.   An individual's *ability* to perform certain tasks depends greatly on his or her aptitude, which includes interests, intelligence, and personality characteristics. Because different sales-people have different tasks and activities to perform, some people are better suited to one type of sales job than another. For example, technical sales positions require individuals with the strong analyt-ical aptitude and technical knowledge needed for explaining com-plex product features to customers, whereas trade selling requires individuals who have good interpersonal skills and are highly adaptive, because they meet with many different types of cus-tomers. Regardless of the specific type of sales position, all profes-sional salespeople must be customer oriented and empathetic.

Skill Level.   Whereas aptitude is a matter of native ability, skill level refers to an individual's *learned proficiency* at performing nec-essary selling tasks. These skills include salesmanship skills (such as knowing how to make a sales presentation), interpersonal skills (such as how to cope with and resolve conflict), and technical skills (such as knowledge about a product's features, performance, and benefits). These skills are partially brought to a sales job as a func-tion of an individual's educational preparation, but are also learned and fostered on the job.

Motivational Level.   Motivational level refers to the *amount of time and energy* a person is willing to expend performing tasks and activities associated with a job (such as filling out reports, calling on new accounts, creating new sales presentations, and following up on sales). Research reveals, perhaps not surprisingly, that salesper-son effort has strong effects both on job performance and job satis-faction: *harder workers are better performers and are more satisfied.*[12] An interesting thing about motivation is that it is reciprocally related to performance. That is, motivation is a determinant of performance and also is determined by performance—we often become even more motivated after we have enjoyed some success. Another important characteristic of salesperson motivation is the distinction between *working hard and working smart.* Motivation is not simply the amount of effort but also how the effort is directed. Salespeople who work smart are typically more effective than those who just work hard.[13]

MARKETING HIGHLIGHTS

Warehouse Club Owners Hope to Sign Up Everybody Eventually

Sharpen your pencils: You'll need them to fill out your warehouse club membership forms.

Sooner or later (probably sooner), social trends and the concept's pervasiveness will have you applying for membership. Traditional grocery stores, though registering roughly 10 times the volume of warehouse clubs, will not be able to hold off the onslaught as the larger-than-life facilities invade your neighborhood and many others, from bustling suburban strip centers to smaller, closer-to-rural communities.

That was the consensus at the recent Institute for International Research conference in Chicago that explored the concept. Industry analysts, club operators, and even some manufacturers testified to the segment's solvency, growth, adherence, and service potential, even if it is experiencing traditional industrial-segment growing pains that include mergers and acquisitions, slow same-store sales rates, and mounting competitive pressures from within and from related retailers, particularly traditional grocers.

If they don't put a gun to their own (greedy) heads, or cut off their noses to spite their faces, the club operators of today should continue to find open-armed consumers ready to welcome their bulk-purchasing opportunities and low, low prices.

The clubs' abilities to operate at half the gross margins of grocery stores are offset by their selling three times as much per unit, selling more than one-third more per square foot, and generating less than half the SG&A (selling, general, and administrative) expenses that groceries do. While club sales pretty much cover all operating expenses, those $25 and $30 membership fees go straight to the bank.

Although the industry currently has some 600-plus stores generating more than $33 billion in volume, according to Dean Witter Reynolds analyst Patrick McCormack, it could grow to support 1,700 stores nationwide, according to Mike Bantuveris, president of InterQuest Inc. Both men have extensively studied or consulted to the industry, although Bantuveris' estimates for number of stores far exceeded the 1,100–1,200 that seemed to be generally espoused by many other conference speakers and attendees.

McCormack wasn't exactly pessimistic, though. He estimates that the industry has a $1 trillion potential in the not-too-distant future, with Wal-Mart's Sam's operation and the newly combined Price/Costco operation dominating to the tune of $30 billion in sales each among a total of 450 stores they currently operate.

Consolidation like that can be expected to continue, he predicted. Only 6 of the 20 major players that started out in the segment a decade ago are still around. More will fall, he predicted, including Pace (114 units) and BJ's (39), to Sam's augmenting the Wal-Mart operation's current 256 units.

The 20% sales growth rate that has characterized the industry in the last nine years will disappear, according to many analysts, including Dan O'Connor, president of Management Ventures. As consolidation among players increases, and growth rates decrease, he sees "complexities" creeping into the industry that could offset some of its competitive advantages against groceries.

Couponing, private-label merchandising, service enhancements, and promoting, merchandising, and advertising are probably on the competitive horizon, all of which will erode profitability to an extent, as they were unheard-of-expenses for clubs in their early, super-growth days.

Although electronic scanning in stores, decision support system technologies, and other modern advances are large expenses upfront, they will drive greater efficiencies for the clubs in the long term and help to build better relationships with mainstream manufacturers.

The manufacturers also like what they see about the stores, especially the numbers: $62 million in sales per store per year; projected same-store sales growth of 3%–4% annually; average shopping trips of $80–$150 per consumer (depending upon whose estimates you listen to); a national 13-mile-drive average to get to a store (and decreasing with store penetration); and overwhelmingly powerful sales per square-foot numbers.

All of that is shrouded by favorable demographic trends for the clubs, according to Doug Tigert, the Babson College professor who closely studies the industry. With the emerging 35-to-44-year-old household predominance of what he called "middle-class poor" who are budget-conscious and value-driven, the clubs will easily maintain and increase their membership rolls.

In addition, with clubs still selling as much as 60% of their memberships to small businesses, they continue to take that business away from supermarkets.

With the whole thing driven by a singularly focused strategy—price-clubs are a runaway hit, he said. His research leads him to believe that up to 85% of club consumers shop there for the prices combined with the bulk-buying opportunities. His math leads him to conclude that all this works for clubs; they've stolen 8% of market share away from grocery stores.

"Clubs are getting significant share in key product lines," he said, adding that marginal supermarket competitors will be driven out of business by a combination of the clubs and the stronger operators in their own segment. He urged supermarket operators to do what they do best rather than gripe about clubs and their direct, cost-saving relationships with manufacturers, or go out of business.

Supermarkets that have responded to clubs with aggressive pricing, club-size packaging, and the flexing of their marketing muscles will find that the same complexities that will hurt clubs upfront will eventually be advantages taken away from supermarkets in the form of scanning technologies, coupons, private-label merchandise, and advertising, according to O'Connor.

No matter how aggressive the supermarkets get in response to clubs, they'll still never match the 25%–30% price savings clubs offer. Even a 5% savings, said Tigert, will attract "customers from hell" in these wallet-sensitive times.

The other thing supermarkets can't do is generate the magic clubs do, said O'Connor. Super-sized clubs make it almost impossible for consumers to stick to a grocery list. It's a treasure hunt, said O'Connor, as clubs continue to give consumers values they don't have on their shopping lists, but can't afford to pass up.

As long as they can do that, they'll "keep the magic happening," he said.

And the performance growing.

Source: Howard Schlossberg, "Warehouse Club Owners Hope to Sign Up Everyone Eventually," *Marketing News*, September 13, 1993, 1, 10. Reprinted with permission from *Marketing News*, published by the American Marketing Association.

Role Perceptions. In order to perform their jobs well, salespeople must know what is expected of them and have accurate perceptions of their role. Their jobs are defined by people both within and outside the organization, including family, sales managers, company executives, and customers. Thus, how well people perform in sales jobs depends on the accuracy of their perceptions of management's stated goals, demands, policies, procedures, and organizational lines of authority and responsibility. In general, accurate role perceptions are a very important determinant of sales performance, effectiveness, and organizational commitment. Research has shown that role ambiguity in the early stage of employment decreases salesperson commitment to their companies and increases turnover.[14] Accurate perceptions are instilled during initial sales training and over time during periodic sales meetings and through interactions with sales supervisors.

Recent research has revealed that organizational citizenship behaviors, or OCBs, represent a very important aspect of salesperson role perceptions and managerial evaluation of salesperson performance. **Organizational citizenship behaviors** are "discretionary behaviors on the part of a salesperson that directly promote the effective functioning of an organization, without necessarily influencing a salesperson's objective sales productivity."[15] OCBs include helping fellow salespeople or other personnel with important tasks (*altruism*), tolerating less-than-ideal working circumstances without complaining (*sportsmanship*), participating in and being concerned with organizational welfare (*civic virtue*), and going beyond the mimimum role requirements of the job—such as working extra hours, never bending the rules, and spending corporate money only when it is in the best interest of the company (*conscientiousness*). Research across a variety of sales situations has determined that these organizational citizenship behaviors have a greater impact than does actual sales success in determining sales managers' overall evaluations of salesperson performance.[16]

Personal Characteristics. Another determinant of salesperson effectiveness is an individual's personal characteristics—his or her age, physical size, appearance, race, and gender are some of the personal characteristics expected to affect sales performance. Research has shown that these personal factors may be even more important than the other factors in determining sales performance.[17] It would be erroneous, however, to conclude that one's personal characteristics ensure sales success or failure. To the contrary, personal characteristics merely may make it more or less difficult to succeed in sales. Performance by any individual depends ultimately on his or her ability, skill, and motivation level. One can either misuse personal advantages or overcome disadvantages. For example, women and African Americans were at one time perceived to be less qualified for sales positions than white males. The number of sales opportunities for both groups have increased significantly in recent years, partly because both groups have overcome what used to be erroneously perceived as sales-related disadvantages.[18] In research with the sales staff of a large national over-the-counter skin care products company, it was determined, contrary to prior anecdotal evidence, that female and male salespeople are more alike than different in terms of job satisfaction, organizational commitment, and self-reported job performance.[19]

Adaptability.   A final determinant of salesperson effectiveness is one's ability to adapt to situational circumstances. This ability is due in part to personal aptitude but also includes learned skills. Researchers have built a compelling case that adaptability is an absolutely essential characteristic for success in selling.[20] Formally, **adaptive selling** is "the altering of sales behaviors during a customer interaction or across customer interactions based on perceived information about the nature of the selling situation."[21] A low level of adaptability is manifest when a salesperson uses the same presentation approach and methods during a single sales encounter or across encounters. Effective salespeople adapt their presentation to fit the situation; they are able to pick up signals and "read" the situation. For example, a brief, matter-of-fact presentation may be called for when meeting with a time-pressured and impatient customer, whereas a longer, more-detailed presentation is appropriate when interacting with a customer who wants all the details before making a decision.

Excellence in Selling

What does it take to be a truly outstanding salesperson, to be a high performer, to excel in sales? As is always the case, there are no simple answers. Moreover, achieving excellence in one type of sales endeavor, say selling personal insurance, undoubtedly requires somewhat different aptitude and skills than achieving excellence when selling sophisticated information systems to corporate buyers.

However, although there are differences from sales job to sales job, there also are similarities.

High-performing salespeople generally differ from other salespeople in terms of some general attitudes they have about the job and the manner in which they conduct their business. High-performing salespeople do the following: [22]

- Represent the interests of their companies and their clients simultaneously to achieve *two-way advocacy.*
- Exemplify *professionalism* in the way they perform the sales job.
- Are *committed to selling and the sales process,* because they believe the sales process is in the customer's best interest.
- Actively *plan and develop strategies* that will lead to programs benefiting the customer.

In addition to these general practices, excellence in selling is associated with a variety of specific characteristics that are reflected in the salesperson's personal features and job behavior.[23] These include possessing depth of knowledge about the products one sells, and about the competition and customers' buying needs; having a breadth of knowledge on a broad spectrum of subjects and therefore being able to interact effectively with a variety of customers; being adaptable, sensitive, and enthusiastic; possessing positive self-esteem; exhibiting an ability to focus efforts into achieving specific goals; having a good sense of humor; being creative and willing to take risks; and, last but certainly not least, possessing a strong sense of honesty and ethics.

Contrary to widespread myths about personal selling, excellence in personal selling requires as high a degree of honesty and ethical behavior as in any of life's lasting relationships. The key word is *relationship.* In some sales jobs only a single transaction between buyer and seller takes place; however, most personal-selling interactions involve long-term relationships with customers. Building relationships is not accomplished with deceit, misrepresentation, or undependable behavior. The excellent salesperson is seen by the customer as trustworthy and dependable. We expect these qualities in our friends, and the same expectations carry over on a professional level to the marketplace.

Modern Selling Philosophy

Successful sales organizations and effective salespeople adhere to and practice what can be termed a "modern selling philosophy." In most prospering firms, modern selling philosophy has supplanted an antiquated, seller-oriented approach in which the seller's interests are paramount, high-pressure selling tactics dominate, little effort is undertaken to understand the customer's business, and little attention is placed on customer satisfaction. Modern selling philosophy is compatible with the practice of *market orientation*, which was discussed in Chapter 1.[24] When salespeople perceive their firms as having a high marketing orientation, they practice greater customer orientation, experience less role stress, and enjoy greater job satisfaction.[25]

A *partner-oriented* selling mind-set today exists in most successful firms. These firms realize that their own success rests with their customers' successes. Hence, modern partner-oriented wisdom makes customer satisfaction its highest priority. Modern selling practice is based on the following principles.[26]

1. *The sales process must be built on a foundation of trust and mutual agreement.* Selling should not be viewed as something someone does to another; rather, it should be looked on as something two parties agree to do for their mutual benefit. In fact, it is easy to argue that modern salespeople do not sell but rather facilitate buying. This difference is not merely semantics—it is at the root of the transformation from the antiquated to modern selling philosophies.

2. *A customer-driven atmosphere is essential to long-term growth.* This is a corollary point to the preceding principle. Modern selling requires that the customer's welfare, interests, and needs be treated as equal to the seller's in the partnership between seller and buyer. A customer-oriented approach means avoiding high-pressure tactics and focusing on customer satisfaction. Salespeople have to be trained to know the customer and to speak in a language that the customer understands. Perhaps the preceding points are best summed up in these terms: "Be product-centered, and you will make a few sales; be prospect-centered, and you will gain many customers."[27]

3. *Sales representatives should act as if they were on the customer's payroll.* The ultimate compliment a salesperson can receive is a comment from a customer to the sales supervisor along these lines: "I'm not sure whether your sales rep works for me or for you."[28] The closer salespeople are to the customer, the better they will be at providing solutions to the customer's problems.

4. *Getting the order is only the first step; after-sale service is what counts.* No problem a customer has should be too small to address. Modern selling philosophy calls for doing whatever is necessary to please the customer in order to ensure a satisfying long-term relationship.

5. *In selling, as in medicine, prescription before diagnosis is malpractice.* This principle holds that no one solution is appropriate for all customers any more than any single diagnosis is appropriate for all patients. Customers' problems have to be analyzed by the modern salesperson and solutions customized to each problem. The days of "one solution fits all" are gone. Moreover, because most people like to make their own decisions or at least be involved in making them, a salesperson should treat the customer as a partner in the solution.

6. *Salesperson professionalism and integrity are essential.* Customers expect high standards of conduct from their salespeople and dislike unprofessional, untrustworthy, and dishonest behavior.

◆ The Personal Selling Process

As the preceding section illustrates, a saleperson's responsibilities vary greatly depending on the company and the product being sold. But whether the salesperson is an order taker or an order getter, the selling situation must be approached in much the same way as solving a problem. An order taker might not need the depth of analysis or detail an order getter needs, but every sale must follow some basic steps in the personal selling process in order to be effective.

Steps in the Selling Process

Exhibit 16.2 lists six steps involved in the selling process. The following sections discuss each of these steps.

Exhibit 16.2   Steps in the Personal Selling Process

---

1. Prospecting
2. Approach
3. Sales Presentation
4. Overcoming Objections
5. Closing the Sale
6. Follow-up

Prospecting.   In the first step of the selling process, a salesperson identifies sales prospects. Although some companies provide leads to the sales force, diligent salespeople are always interested in expanding their customer list by pursuing their own leads. Just as a business relies on new products to increase its business, a salesperson relies on new business to maintain and increase business. Whether the lead has been provided or is self-generated, the salesperson must prospect the lead. **Prospecting** is the process of identifying the best potential customers. Leads can be generated from many sources. Some of the more important are (1) referrals from current customers; (2) articles in newspapers, trade journals, and periodicals; and (3) databases that contain names, addresses, telephone numbers, and job titles of prospective customers.

Once the salesperson identifies leads, he or she then determines which customers are the most likely to buy. This is referred to as *qualifying prospects*. A salesperson qualifies prospects by (1) determining the customer's need for the product, (2) determining their financial condition, (3) estimating their potential sales volume, (4) estimating the amount of time required to maintain the sales volume, and (5) determining who should be contacted at the account. In general, salespeople classify leads as hot (high priority), warm (medium priority), or cold (low priority). The salesperson must be sure to thoroughly investigate every lead to ensure that his or her sales time will be maximized and not wasted.

Approach.   The **approach** entails making contact and establishing a relationship with the customer. Initial contact is made by letter, telephone, or in person, although many buyers require company and product information *before* meeting with a representative.

Since the buyer meets with suppliers all day long, the salesperson's job is to make him or herself and his or her company stand out in the buyer's mind.

The salesperson's appearance, mannerisms, attitude, and professionalism all contribute to the buyer's favorable or unfavorable opinion of him or her. The outcome of a sales call is greatly influenced by the first impression a salesperson makes on the customer. The likelihood that a salesperson's ideas will be accepted depends largely on the initial encounter. Determinants of the first impression include personal looks, dress, body language, eye contact, handshake, punctuality, and courtesy.

Sales Presentation.

The next step in the personal selling process is the **sales presentation** where the salesperson relays information about the product and its benefits to the buyer. In any presentation, the salesperson must first get the buyer's attention. This step is critical since buyers' busy schedules often only allow a salesperson a limited amount of time, perhaps as little as 10 to 20 minutes. A visual demonstration of the product, competitive comparison, or a dramatic remark such as "Let me show you how I can save your company $3,000 a year" are all means of getting the buyer's attention.

Once the buyer's attention is secured, the salesperson's next task is to generate interest in the product he or she is selling. In this part of the presentation, the salesperson explains in detail the product benefits and why the product meets the needs of the particular customer. Once again, visual aids such as charts or slides, product demonstrations, brochures, and competitive comparisons can be used to effectively sell the product.

The purpose in generating interest is to create a desire for the product. A salesperson who is successful in generating interest will find the buyer asking for additional information about the product, shipment and delivery procedures, sales terms, and so on. If successful in creating a desire for the product, the salesperson must obtain some form of action from the buyer such as a follow-up sales call or, in the best circumstance, receipt of an order.

Overcoming Objections.

Rarely will a buyer place an order without some amount of conflict or resistance. Ordering products through a new supplier involves additional paperwork and effort from the buyer, so she or he may resist acting on the new product or company. Resistance comes in the form of objections to price or sales terms, disbelief in product quality or competitive comparisons, or the lack of desire or need to change the status quo, or current supplier situation.

A well-prepared salesperson anticipates all objections and overcomes the objections with thoughtful, positive responses. The number of objections can be a gauge of the level of interest a buyer has in the product. Often, objections represent opportunities for the salesperson to provide additional information, reiterate benefits, and determine which elements are of the greatest importance to the buyer. For example, if the buyer objects to the price, the salesperson can acknowledge the price differential and quickly point out the product features that warrant the higher price. Overcoming objections involves a great deal of listening on the part of the salesperson, who must fully understand the objection *before* formulating a response.

Closing the Sale.   Once the buyer shows a desire in the product, the salesperson must close the sale. This step may be the most difficult one in the personal selling process. Many salespeople are uncomfortable with asking for an order or waiting for the buyer to offer an order on his own. In any case, the salesperson must recognize when it is time to ask for the order. This step usually occurs when the salesperson has completed the presentation, the buyer has no further questions, and all objections have been overcome. This timing may be obvious to the salesperson, but sometimes the point of potential closing may not be so clear. The salesperson can "test the waters" by attempting to pin down the buyer by asking which product or size best fits his or her needs, when will delivery be needed, or applying some time pressure such as saying "Our special promotional program only lasts through the end of this month." In any case, the salesperson is more likely to get an order if she or he asks for one from the buyer.

Follow-up.   Almost as important as getting the order is ensuring that the customer is satisfied. A satisfied customer will reorder, cooperate with special requests, recommend the product to his or her peers, and be an ally of the company and salesperson.

Satisfaction can only be ensured through effective follow-up activities after the sale. These activities include checking on the status of the order, confirming shipping and delivery instructions, keeping the customer informed, and making sure everything goes as planned and promised to the buyer. If the product requires any

CAPTAINS OF INDUSTRY

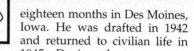

Samuel Moore Walton
Born: March 29, 1918
Died: April 5, 1992
Title: Founder, Wal-Mart

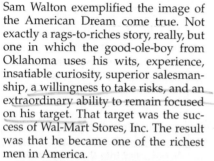

Sam Walton exemplified the image of the American Dream come true. Not exactly a rags-to-riches story, really, but one in which the good-ole-boy from Oklahoma uses his wits, experience, insatiable curiosity, superior salesmanship, a willingness to take risks, and an extraordinary ability to remain focused on his target. That target was the success of Wal-Mart Stores, Inc. The result was that he became one of the richest men in America.

Sam Walton built his discount store empire by challenging the way other retail stores did business. Instead of locating stores in large urban areas, he chose to build in small towns in rural population centers of 5,000 to 25,000 people. He opened his first Wal-Mart Discount City in Rogers, Arkansas, in 1964.

Leading up the first Wal-Mart was a series of successes in retailing. Beginning in 1940, Walton was employed as a JCPenney management trainee for eighteen months in Des Moines, Iowa. He was drafted in 1942 and returned to civilian life in 1945. During the war years, Walton saved his pay and used that capital to purchase a Ben Franklin Five & Dime in Newport, Arkansas. His brother, Bud, was his partner in this store, and soon, fifteen other stores.

Sam and Bud studied their business with ruthless curiosity; namely, they studied the Ben Franklin Company's methods of distribution and how they pooled advertising dollars for specific geographic regions in support of their franchisees. The Waltons warmed to their later task with a chain of Ben Franklin franchises centered on the corners where Oklahoma, Arkansas, Missouri, and Kansas meet. They capitalized on the ability of the group to order for all the stores and to use advertising money efficiently.

Walton's curiosity is best exemplified in two business trips he pursued in the 1960s. On the first trip he went to the East Coast and studied the new "discount" stores appearing in urban centers there. He took the discount store idea to Ben Franklin's headquarters near Chicago and tried to convince the corporation to bankroll a joint venture. Ben Franklin's declined.

special handling or installation, the salesperson should schedule an appointment to be at the facility when the order arrives to oversee or help his or her customer in any way possible. A diligent salesperson will schedule a follow-up meeting or telephone call to check on the customer's satisfaction or dissatisfaction with the product soon after receipt of the goods. If there is a problem with the product, the salesperson still has the opportunity to correct the problem before any lasting damage is done to either the product or the company. Follow-up is especially important in today's competitive

However, on that trip Walton had a chance to take a look at his major future rival, Kmart. He liked what he saw and within a short while, the first Wal-Mart Discount City was launched.

Walton's later innovation, the introduction of hub-and-spoke warehousing to the retail industry, was a natural outgrowth from his early experience with Ben Franklin's. Computerizing the sales and ordering process is another area in which his company lead the way. Partnering with major producers like Procter & Gamble to produce buying economies of scale was his other great innovation.

Until his death, Sam Walton lead the way in modern retailing. But he was always first to note that is was people, customers, who made his success. Despite the gargantuan size of his enterprise, Sam Walton knew the names of employees at his stores, not just managers, but clerks and stockers. His philosophy encouraged those employees to treat their customers with the same courtesy. Every customer is greeted at the door. Store cleanliness and friendliness is still a hallmark of his enterprises even after his death. In some small towns, the boost to the economy of having a Wal-Mart opened is enough to ensure a built-in customer base of the family and friends of the employees. Although his stores have certainly also made an impact on urban centers, there is a pervasive small town friendliness required for success at each and every store.

Ultimately, it was Sam Walton's binding tie with the customers, to go where they needed his services, to treat them well, that lead to his success. A success honored by his peers with the following awards: the 1978 Discounter of the Year Award from the Discount Store News; a 1984 Horatio Alger Award; a 1988 National Retail Merchants Association Gold Award; named Chief Executive Officer of the Decade for the 1980s by *Financial World* magazine; and shortly before his death he was inducted into the National Sales Hall of Fame. The life of this individual is infinitely interesting. His story is colored with amusing anecdotes, anecdotes that show the virtues of having clear goals and a clearer vision.

Sources: "How Sam Walton Does It," *Forbes*, August 16, 1982, 42; *Discount Store News*, April 20, 1992; "Ecology of Competition," *Harvard Business Review*, May–June 1993, 82–83; and *Supermarket News*, August 9, 1993, 11.

environment since numerous other businesses are prepared to claim any account that a competitor is unable to properly service.

Team Selling

The discussion to this point has suggested that the personal selling process entails selling activity by a single salesperson. This typically is how it has been done in the past—one salesperson calling on customers or prospects and attempting to gain an initial sale or repeat business. The trend in recent years is toward the formation of selling teams that combine representatives from marketing, logistics, finance, sales, and other corporate units. Procter & Gamble has established customer account teams that are assigned to specific retailers and wholesalers. One of P&G's first teams was assigned to Wal-Mart stores.[29] Kraft Foods also has an integrated sales team for calling on key retailers.[30] The purpose in both instances is to best represent the customer's interests by capitalizing on the strengths and expertise of various personnel who, in one way or another, play important roles in determining how well the organization fulfills the needs of important customers.

Team selling also is prevalent in business-to-business selling situations. The key aspect of team selling here, as with consumer-goods sales situations, is to include experts drawn from throughout the organization—engineers, product developers, customer service representatives, finance experts, and so on. Usually an account executive coordinates the team's efforts, which are used to produce creative solutions to a customer's purchasing needs.[31]

◆ Sales Force Management

As the preceding section illustrates, salespeople can be a very diverse group of talented professionals each possessing unique strengths and weaknesses. Managing a diverse group is both challenging and difficult. In general, **sales management** involves acquiring, directing, and stimulating competent salespeople to perform tasks that move the organization toward accomplishment of its objectives and mission. Sales management provides a significant link between an organization's corporate and marketing strategies and the salespeople who actuate the marketing transaction. A sales manager translates plans into action, implements sales programs, directs the sales effort, trains salespeople, appraises their performance, determines their compensation, and has a longer-term responsibility for market development and account coverage in his or her area.[32]

Sales management involves the performance of five basic functions: (1) planning, (2) organizing, (3) staffing, (4) directing, and

(5) evaluating and controlling sales-force performance and satisfaction. Each function is discussed in the following sections.

Planning the Sales Function

Planning is the process of establishing a broad set of goals, policies, and procedures for achieving sales and marketing objectives. Three of the most important planning activities undertaken by sales managers are (1) developing sales budgets, (2) designing sales territories, and (3) setting sales-force quotas.

Developing Sales Budgets.   The sales force budget is the amount of money a sales department has assigned to it for an annual period. The budget is based on estimates of expenditures during that period of time, with the amount budgeted depending on the forecasted amount of revenue expected to be generated for the organization during that time period.[33]

The first step in developing a budget is to analyze market opportunity and forecast sales potential. Sales management next must estimate the amount of money required to accomplish the tasks necessary to achieve its forecasted sales. Two basic procedures for allotting funds are (1) the line-item budget and (2) the program-budget method. In **line-item budgeting**, management allocates funds in meticulous detail to each identifiable cost center. For example, the sales department may budget funds for areas such as office supplies, wages, research, and travel. **Program budgeting** avoids many of the problems of line-item budgeting. With this approach, management provides each administrative unit with a lump sum of money that each administrative head can use as he or she sees fit to accomplish the stated objectives. This method provides considerable flexibility by allowing managers to shift funds as deemed necessary.

Designing Sales Territories.   Sales territories are created when present or prospective customers are assigned to a sales unit such as a sales branch or to a specific salesperson or selling team. The ideal situation is to create sales territories of equal sales-generating potential and equal workload. In this way, the sales manager can more easily evaluate and control each salesperson's performance. Also, having equal workloads among the sales representatives leads to greater sales force motivation and morale.

Setting Sales-Force Quotas.   Sales quotas are specific performance goals that management sets for territories, branch offices, and individual sales representatives. The primary functions of quotas are to establish goals and incentives for the sales force and to give management yardsticks by which to evaluate each salesperson's performance on the job, thus providing a basis for job promotion, salary raises, or commissions.

Sales managers most frequently base quotas on (1) sales volume, (2) profit, (3) activities performed, or (4) some combination of the preceding methods.[34] The most typical method for developing quotas is by the use of **sales-volume quotas**. These quotas are based on geographical areas, product lines, individual customers, time periods, or a combination of these factors. For example, a quota for a particular sales representative might be to sell at least 20 units of product X in region Z during the next quarter. The major advantage of basing quotas on sales volume is these quotas are easy to understand and simple to use. A disadvantage, however, is that sales-volume quotas, if used alone, can encourage selling behaviors that disregard expenses and neglect nonselling activities. In other words, in attempting to meet and exceed sales-volume quotas, sales might be made that are unprofitable because expenses are excessive, accounts are not adequately serviced, and so on.

Sales quotas are an extremely important aspect of the sales-management function. If set fairly and realistically, they can encourage highly motivated salesperson performance and reward quota achievers for their efforts. On the downside, quotas set too low may fail to provide sufficient challenge or incentive for the sales force; or quotas set too high may serve as a disincentive because salespeople feel they cannot possibly meet what is expected of them. Setting challenging yet realistic quotas is truly an art that only the most effective sales managers ever accomplish.

Organizing the Sales Function

Most companies organize or specialize their sales departments in one of four ways: (1) geographically, (2) by product types, (3) by market or customer classes, or (4) by function.

Geography-Based Sales Organization.   Specialization by geographical territories is probably the most common form of sales management organization. Exhibit 16.3 provides an illustrative

Exhibit 16.3   Geography-Based Sales Organization

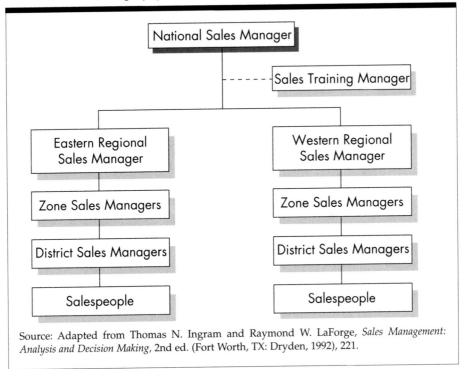

Source: Adapted from Thomas N. Ingram and Raymond W. LaForge, *Sales Management: Analysis and Decision Making*, 2nd ed. (Fort Worth, TX: Dryden, 1992), 221.

organizational chart that is based on geographical specialization. Depending on the size of the business, the manager who runs a geographical sales unit is called a regional, divisional, or district sales manager. In the organizational arrangement in Exhibit 16.3, regional sales managers supervise zone managers, who in turn supervise the district sales managers to whom salespeople report. In many cases the sales manager, regardless of the title he or she is given, is basically running his or her own business within a business. That is, he or she is like the president of his or her own firm.

A trend toward *regional marketing*, which has shifted marketing decision making from the corporate to regional level, has encouraged many firms to reorganize their sales departments along geographical lines. Campbell Soup is one of the many consumer package-good companies that has reorganized geographically. For many years, the sales function at Campbell Soup was organized along product lines. Each of four product lines (canned foods, frozen foods, special products, and fresh foods) had its own vice

Exhibit 16.4   Product-Line Sales Organization

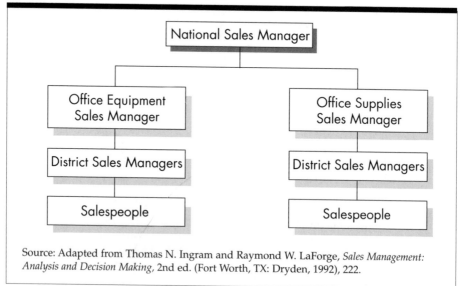

Source: Adapted from Thomas N. Ingram and Raymond W. LaForge, *Sales Management: Analysis and Decision Making,* 2nd ed. (Fort Worth, TX: Dryden, 1992), 222.

president of sales. Reporting to each vice president was a chain of sales managers and sales representatives. This arrangement created a major problem: up to four different Campbell sales representatives, one from each product line, called on a single retail account. Duplicated efforts made the selling costs excessive, and the rigid sales structure was unable to accommodate new product introductions. These factors along with the growing power of supermarket chains and the increased sophistication in their buying practices necessitated sales reorganization. Campbell reorganized along geographical lines. General sales managers head up sales departments in each of four U.S. regions: West, Central, South, and East. Reporting to these four general managers are 22 regional managers. Directors of retail operations report to each regional manager. The director of retail operations is responsible for the field sales force. Sales representatives now sell all Campbell products rather than only a single product line as they did in the past.[35]

Product-Line Sales Organization.   Although a company's sales organization can be very effective for one product line, the same type of organizational structure may not be effective for a company that carries diverse product offerings. A company that offers a set of unrelated or heterogeneous products should consider

Exhibit 16.5   Market-Based Sales Organization

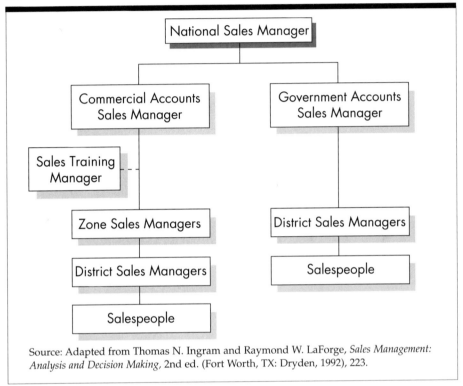

Source: Adapted from Thomas N. Ingram and Raymond W. LaForge, *Sales Management: Analysis and Decision Making,* 2nd ed. (Fort Worth, TX: Dryden, 1992), 223.

organizing or reorganizing by product types or groups. Exhibit 16.4 shows a basic example of a sales organizational structure used in product specialization. In this case, the company has separated sales activity between its office-equipment and office-supply products. Management's idea is that sales representatives should use their particular knowledge about specific products to increase company profits. This organizational structure works well if the customers the sales representatives call on do not overlap, which was the problem with Campbell Soup's former product-based sales structure.

Market- or Customer-Based Sales Organization.   This structure emphasizes specific markets or customer groups rather than products. A market-based sales structure is needed when a company sells to multiple customers whose buying needs and procedures differ greatly. Exhibit 16.5 illustrates an organization based on market-based specialization. In this instance, a company has

Exhibit 16.6   Function-Based Sales Organization

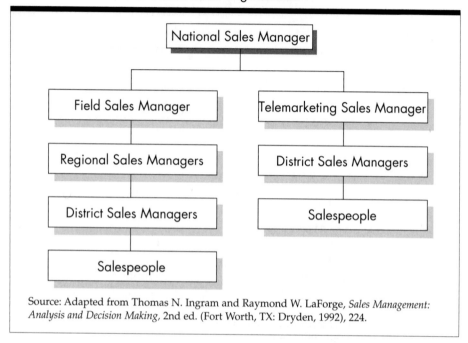

Source: Adapted from Thomas N. Ingram and Raymond W. LaForge, *Sales Management: Analysis and Decision Making,* 2nd ed. (Fort Worth, TX: Dryden, 1992), 224.

separated its sales force into one group calling on commercial accounts and another group that caters to government customers.

Companies may find that specialization by market is to their advantage when the needs of customer groups differ significantly, when the customer groups are geographically concentrated, or when the company uses different channels of distribution and therefore wants to minimize friction among them.[36] An automobile manufacturer, for example, may want to have different sales forces (and in fact, a different marketing plan) when selling to the government market (e.g., post office or military), to the industrial market, and to the ultimate consumer (through dealers). Each market's buying behavior is different and therefore requires a different approach and a different sales organization.

Function-Based Sales Organization.

Exhibit 16.6 illustrates a sales organization that separates its sales force into field sales and telemarketing sales. As previously discussed, increasing numbers of companies—especially in the case of business-to-business marketing—have established telemarketing sales forces. In this particular

Exhibit 16.7   Comparison of Sales Organization Structures

Organization Structure	Advantages	Disadvantages
Geographic	Low cost No geographic duplication No customer duplication Fewer managment levels	Limited specialization Lack of management control over product or customer emphasis
Product	Salespeople become experts in product attributes and applications Management control over selling effort allocated to products	High cost Geographic duplication Customer duplication
Market	Salespeople develop better understanding of unique customer needs Management control over selling effort allocated to different markets	High cost Geographic duplication
Functional	Efficiency in performing selling activities Customer duplication	Geographic duplication Need for coordination

Source: Thomas N. Ingram and Raymond W. LaForge, *Sales Management: Analysis and Decision Making,* 2nd ed. (Fort Worth, TX: Dryden, 1992), 229. Copyright © 1992 The Dryden Press, reproduced by permission of the publisher.

case (Exhibit 16.6) the role of the field sales force is to generate sales and that of the telemarketing sales force is to perform account-servicing activities.

Which Organizational Arrangement Is Best?

There is no simple answer to questions such as this; rather, the answer always is contingent on the circumstances. However, the comparative advantages and disadvantages of each form of organization structure are summarized in Exhibit 16.7.

Staffing the Sales Function

Staffing a sales organization involves both recruiting prospective salespeople and interviewing, testing, and hiring them. A critical step in this process is creating a written job description. The **job description** includes a job title, the specific duties and responsibilities of the sales representative, the authoritative relationships with other immediate members of the organization, and the opportunities for advancement. Good job descriptions include the following: (1) a description of the products or services the sales representative will sell; (2) the types of customers the sales representative must call on, the desired frequency of sales calls, and the specific personnel the sales representative should contact; (3) the specific tasks and responsibilities the sales representative must carry out, including customer service, clerical work, reports, information collection, and promotional activities; and (4) the authoritative relationships between the sales representative and other positions within the company. This statement provides information regarding who the sales representative reports to and under what circumstances he or she interacts with other departmental personnel. In addition to the job description, the sales manager should develop a statement of **job qualifications**. This document describes the personal features, characteristics, and abilities that management believes a salesperson needs in order to perform the job effectively and efficiently. These qualifications may include educational background, business experience, personality, work ethic, ability to get along with others, personal appearance, and so forth.

Recruiting.   Sales recruiting efforts attempt to match people who have the specific and desired qualifications with management's written job descriptions in order to meet sales, marketing, and company objectives. To locate potentially qualified applicants for a sales job, recruiters use advertising, employment agencies, employee referrals, internal training programs, educational institutions, internal transfers, unsolicited applications, competitors' employees, and those people with whom management deals—from suppliers of products or information (such as an account executive from an advertising agency) to customer salespeople (someone in a wholesale or retailing business, for example).

Interviewing, Testing, and Hiring.   In the final stage of the staffing function, the manager must determine whether applicants match the company's job specifications and which applicant(s) will do the best job. Several methods for accomplishing this objective are available to the sales manager, including interviews, reference checks, and various types of intelligence, aptitude, and personality tests. The initial source of information typically available to a sales manager is an applicant's *résumé*. Applicants who pass the initial résumé inspection are personally interviewed. The interview allows sales management to verify the information in the prospect's application form and gives the interviewer the opportunity to evaluate the prospect in person. The recruiter can evaluate the applicant's verbal skills—vocabulary, grammar, and general conversational ability—and can observe the prospect's mannerisms, physical appearance, voice quality, and eye contact to gain insights into the candidate's personal and persuasive skills.

Sales managers often use references as an additional source of information in the evaluation of prospective sales representatives. However, it must be noted that the references suggested by the candidate are often biased in his or her favor. For this reason, sales managers or their staffs often check with sources that are probably more impartial, such as the prospect's present and former employers and professors. The best way for an interviewer to obtain solid references is through face-to-face contact or voice-to-voice contact on the telephone with each referent. More open dialogue occurs in these ways rather than by letter.

Psychological tests are another valuable input to a sales manager's selection decision. The four most common tests are (1) *personality tests* (to measure a person's affability, confidence, poise, aggressiveness, and other job-related attributes); (2) *sales-aptitude tests* (to measure a person's verbal ability, tactfulness, persuasiveness, tenacity, memory, and social extroversion or introversion, among many other traits); (3) *interest tests* (to identify a person's vocational and avocational inclinations); and (4) *intelligence tests* (to measure memory ability, critical-reasoning ability, and ability to draw inferences).

Directing the Sales Force

This sales-management function involves the training of new recruits, the continuing education of existing personnel, and motivational and incentive plans for all sales personnel. This section describes briefly the elements of sales-force direction.

Training the Sales Force.

Training programs vary considerably from company to company, but all successful sales organizations have excellent training programs for new members of the sales force as well as periodic refresher courses for current salespeople. The general objectives of sales training should be to (1) provide new salespeople with product, customer, and competitor knowledge; (2) improve salesperson morale and reduce turnover; (3) establish expected salesperson behavior; (4) improve customer relations; (5) lower selling costs; and (6) show salespeople how to use time efficiently.

These broad sales-management objectives for a sales-training program should then be broken down into specific objectives for the sales representatives. These objectives may include training sales representatives to fill out reports, demonstrating how management uses reports, providing salespeople with methods for keeping records, training salespeople how to allocate their selling time with and among customers, suggesting ways to improve prospecting, and explaining how to handle objections.[37]

The content of the sales training program varies from company to company depending on the level of sophistication among the firm's sales personnel. Also, the content varies according to whether new sales personnel or veteran sales personnel are the audience. However, the content generally focuses on corporate policies, selling techniques, product knowledge, and self-management skills.

Companies vary in their philosophies regarding when training should take place. Some companies feel that extensive training in basic product knowledge, sales techniques, company policies, and so on should be concentrated in the first several weeks after a person is hired. After this period of training, the person is qualified to go out and sell. Other companies prefer to give new hirees a quick, basic course, have the applicants go into the field and gain some practical experience, and then provide them with an intensive period of training. Some companies schedule several one- to two-day training seminars per year, whereas others schedule several intensive one- to two-week annual training programs.

The training techniques a company uses depend on the objectives that sales managers want to accomplish and on the amount of time that the trainer has to achieve these objectives. Lectures, discussion, demonstrations, role playing, and on-the-job training are the basic training techniques. The *lecture method* is the most efficient way to present company policies, procedures, and selling concepts and principles. Lectures provide the new salesperson with an introduction to the company and the subject of selling. The *discussion method* provides salespeople with the opportunity to state their ideas and opinions on a variety of subjects related to personal selling and company policies. By using the discussion method, the group leader can draw out experiences from the new sales representatives that are informative and useful to other members who have had or are having similar problems in the field. *Demonstration* involves showing rather than explaining the best way to sell a product. Sales representatives can see how their job should be performed instead of merely hearing an explanation. *Role playing* places sales trainees closer to the actual sales situation by having them sell a product in a hypothetical situation. If the situation and the prospect are presented realistically, the trainee learns how to translate lectured concepts and principles into real-life presentations. Finally, in *on-the-job training*, the sales trainer accompanies the sales trainee in actual selling situations. Feedback is provided immediately after the fledgling salesperson has performed admirably or made mistakes.

Motivating the Sales Force.

In motivating the sales force, sales management can use both financial and nonfinancial incentives. Financial rewards are extremely important but usually are not enough. Sales managers use three basic compensation plans: salary plan, commission plan, and a combination plan (salary plus commission).

A **straight salary plan** provides sales representatives with a fixed amount of income regardless of sales productivity. This method of compensation gives management maximum control over the sales force's activities because management can dictate the activities salespeople must perform in servicing current customers, creating new merchandise displays, and filling out reports for the home or district office. Thus, this plan is best for companies who have a large amount of work devoted to nonselling activities and routine selling tasks. Such selling jobs are found in the grocery and pharmaceutical industries. Straight salary provides relatively little incentive for sales representatives to increase sales. However, it is a good plan for new salespeople who are still learning the ropes.

A **commission plan** is payment based directly on performance. There are two basic commission plans: straight commission or draw against commission. *Straight commissions* can be based on a fixed percentage of a sales representative's dollar sales or product units sold or can be based on a multiple percentage rate that increases as dollar sales volume or some other performance measure increases. The *draw against commission* method is based on draw accounts, which are accounts from which the sales representative receives (or draws) a fixed sum of money on a regular time basis. The money in a draw account comes from either earned or unearned commissions. A salesperson, for example, may draw $1,000 per pay period but may have earned $800 or $1,200 during the same period. In the case of an underage ($800), the salesperson owes the company money. In the case of an overage ($1,200), the salesperson may take the extra commission, apply it against past underages, or defer the amount to the future.

A **bonus** is usually a lump-sum payment that the company makes to sales representatives who have exceeded a set sales quota. However, management may use bases other than sales, such as number of new accounts opened, reduction in expenses, and divisional profits, to set the requirements for a bonus.

Within the three basic plans, there are many possible combinations involving base earnings and incentive pay. Six of the most common methods of paying the sales force are (1) straight salary, (2) straight commission, (3) draw against commission, (4) salary plus commission, (5) salary plus bonus, and (6) salary plus bonus plus commission. Combination plans (salary plus commission, salary plus bonus, and salary plus bonus plus commission) are most commonly used by sales managers because they provide sales representatives with a broader range of earnings opportunities. Regardless of which specific compensation plan is selected, it is critical that the plan be competitive within the industry, equitable within the company, and fair among members of the sales force.

In addition to financial compensation, salesperson job satisfaction and motivation rest strongly on *nonfinancial rewards*. Achievement or recognition awards are commonly presented to sales representatives at sales meetings and award banquets as a means of giving sales representatives psychological rewards. Companies also frequently use newsletters, publicity in local media, published sales results, personal letters of commendation, and other psychological rewards to encourage sales performance. Sales managers also motivate sales-force members with face-to-face encouragement, telephone calls of commendation, and by providing assistance when the salesperson requires help in closing a sale or performing other job responsibilities. Some companies also award honorary job titles to outstanding sales representatives, induct them into honor societies, and present distinguished sales awards, often in the form of plaques or certificates.

Sales managers frequently conduct annual sales meetings in attractive vacation sites as another incentive to the sales force. A company may take its sales representatives to a beach retreat and schedule sales meetings in the morning and recreation in the afternoon. Sales managers use meetings to generate enthusiasm for new product lines and marketing and selling programs. Generally, the sales representatives remain extremely enthusiastic for weeks following these meetings.

Evaluating and Controlling Sales Force Performance and Satisfaction

This management function requires the sales manager to monitor actual salesperson performance, to reward the performance when it meets expectations, and to take corrective action when performance is below the preestablished standard. The basic objective is to determine how well salespeople have performed so as to make corrective changes if necessary and to maintain salesperson satisfaction. Salesperson performance evaluations are used for at least five reasons:

1. To ensure that rewards given salespeople are consistent with their actual performance.
2. To identify salespeople who deserve promotions.
3. To identify salespeople who should be terminated.
4. To determine specific training and counseling needs of individual salespeople.
5. To identify criteria for the future recruitment and selection of salespeople.[38]

Performance standards include the salespersons' sales volume, percentage of quota met, selling expenses, profit contributions, and customer services rendered. Through sales analysis, cost analysis, and personal evaluations, sales managers can determine whether a salesperson's performance meets preestablished standards. When the actual and planned performances of a salesperson differ significantly, the sales manager must determine the underlying reasons and take appropriate corrective actions if necessary. Sometimes performance is not up to par due to extenuating circumstances. For example, a union strike in a particular territory may have affected sales; a salesperson may have suffered from an extended illness; he or she may be experiencing marital difficulties; or the sales quota may be unattainable.

When attempting to correct inadequate salesperson performance, it is important that the sales manager avoid excess negativity. In fact, research evidence (and common sense) suggest that managers should seek opportunities to provide positive feedback to salespeople rather than accentuating deficiencies.[39] Negative feedback does not motivate salespeople as much as positive feedback does. Moreover, positive feedback serves to clarify what behaviors are expected of salespeople.[40]

◆ Chapter Summary

Personal selling is a form of person-to-person communication in which a salesperson works with prospective buyers and attempts to influence their purchase in the direction of his or her company's products or services. The degree to which personal selling is used by a company in its promotional mix depends on the product, selling costs, customers' needs, and customer locations.

The field of sales offers many exciting job opportunities because of the job freedom, variety and challenge, opportunities for advancement, and the attractive compensation and nonfinancial rewards that go along with sales.

The primary purposes of personal selling are to educate customers, provide product usage and marketing assistance, and provide after-sale service and support to buyers. Most selling jobs, regardless of the product being sold, include the following activities: selling, working with orders, servicing the product, information management, servicing the account, attending conferences and meetings, training and recruiting, entertaining, out-of-town travel, and working with distributors.

The three main types of sales jobs are order takers who monitor inventory levels and reorder product, order getters who actively search out accounts and buyers, and sales support positions who provide pre- and post-sale support to both the salesperson and the customer. More specific types of sales positions are trade selling, missionary selling, technical selling, new-business selling, retail selling, and telemarketing.

In order for the personal selling process to be effective, all salespeople must follow some basic steps which are prospecting, approach, sales presentation, overcoming objections, closing the sale, and follow-up. The focus in personal selling today is on partner-oriented selling since firms now realized that their own success depends on their customers' successes. This modern selling philosophy is based on trust and mutual agreement, a customer-driven atmosphere, getting the order *and* providing service, and maintaining professionalism and integrity.

A salesperson who has achieved excellence in selling makes a good first impression, has a depth and breadth of knowledge, adapts well, is sensitive, enthusiastic, has self-esteem, extended focus and a sense of humor, is creative, takes risks, and possesses a sense of honesty and ethics.

Sales management involves sales planning (the process of establishing a broad set of goals, policies, and procedures for achieving objectives), organizing the sales function (by establishing sales organizations structured geographically, by product types, by market or customer classes, or by function), staffing the sales function (including recruiting salespeople and interviewing, testing, and hiring them), directing the sales force (via training and motivating), and evaluating and controlling sales force performance and satisfaction.

Notes

1. U.S. Department of Commerce, Bureau of the Census, *Statistical Abstract of the United States* (Washington, DC: U.S. Government Printing Office, 1994), 408.

2. The 1958 study was conducted by the *American Salesman* magazine. The 1988 study was performed by Rosemary R. Lagace and Timothy A. Longfellow, "The Impact of Classroom Style on Student Attitudes toward Sales Careers: A Comparative Approach," *Journal of Marketing Education* (Fall 1989), 72–77.

3. Gilbert A. Churchill, Jr., Neil M. Ford, and Orville C. Walker, Jr., *Sales Force Management: Planning, Implementation, and Control* (Homewood, IL: Richard D. Irwin, 1990) 67–68.

4. William C. Moncrief III, "Selling Activity and Sales Position Taxonomies for Industrial Selling," *Journal of Marketing Research*, 23 (August 1986), 261–270.

5. For a discussion of different stages of sales careers, see William L. Cron, Alan J. Dubinsky, and Ronald E. Michaels, "The Influence of Career Stages on Components of Salesperson Motivation," *Journal of Marketing*, 52 (January 1988), 78–92.

6. Ronald B. Marks, *Personal Selling: An Interactive Approach* (Boston: Allyn and Bacon, 1988), 39.

7. Marks, *Personal Selling,* 45.

8. "Du Pont Turns Scientists into Salespeople," *Sales and Marketing Management,* June 1987, 57.

9. Gilbert A. Churchill, Jr., Neil M. Ford, Steven W. Hartley, and Orville C. Walker, Jr., "The Determinants of Salesperson Performance: A Meta Analysis," *Journal of Marketing Research,* 22 (May 1985), 103–118.

10. Barton A. Weitz, "Effectiveness in Sales Interactions: A Contingency Framework," *Journal of Marketing,* 45 (Winter 1981), 85–103.

11. The first five factors and the ensuing discussion are based on Churchill, Jr., Ford, and Walker, Jr., *Sales Force Management: Planning, Implementation, and Control.*

12. Steven P. Brown and Robert A. Peterson, "The Effect of Effort on Sales Performance and Job Satisfaction," *Journal of Marketing,* 58 (April 1994), 70–80.

13. Harish Sujan, "Smarter versus Harder: An Exploratory Attributional Analysis of Salespeople's Motivation," *Journal of Marketing Research,* 23 (February 1986), 41–50. See also, Harish Sujan, Barton A. Weitz, and Nirmalya Kumar, "Learning Orientation, Working Smart, and Effective Selling," *Journal of Marketing,* 58 (July 1994), 39–52.

14. Mark W. Johnston, A. Parasuraman, Charles M. Futrell, and William C. Black, "A Longitudinal Assessment of the Impact of Selected Organizational Influences on Salespeople's Organizational Commitment During Early Employment," *Journal of Marketing Research,* 27 (August 1990), 333–344.

15. Scott B. MacKenzie, Philip M. Podsakoff, and Richard Fetter, "The Impact of Organizational Citizenship Behavior on Evaluations of Salesperson Performance," *Journal of Marketing,* 57 (January 1993), 71.

16. MacKenzie, Podsakoff, and Fetter, "The Impact of Organization Citizenship Behavior."

17. Churchill, Ford, Hartley, and Walker, "The Determinants of Salesperson Performance: A Meta Analysis."

18. See, for example, Michelle Block Morse, "Rich Rewards: For Ambitious Blacks, Selling Can Mean Pride, Power, and High

Pay," *Success*, 35 (March 1988), 50–61. Also, "Women Keep Coming On," *Sales and Marketing Management*, February 1989, 26.

19. Patrick L. Schul and Brent M. Wren, "The Emerging Role of Women in Industrial Selling: A Decade of Change," *Journal of Marketing*, 56 (July 1992), 38–54.

20. See Siew Meng Leong, Paul S. Busch, and Deborah Roedder John, "Knowledge Bases and Salesperson Effectiveness: A Script-Theoretic Analysis," *Journal of Marketing Research*, 26 (May 1989), 164–178; Rosann L. Spiro and Barton A. Weitz, "Adaptive Selling: Conceptualization, Measurement, and Nomological Validity," *Journal of Marketing Research*, 27 (February 1990), 61–69; Weitz, "Effectiveness in Sales Interactions: A Contingency Framework"; Barton A. Weitz, Harish Sujan, and Mita Sujan, "Knowledge, Motivation, and Adaptive Behavior: A Framework for Improving Selling Effectiveness," *Journal of Marketing*, 50 (October 1986), 174–191.

21. Weitz, Sujan, and Sujan, "Knowledge, Motivation, and Adaptive Behavior: A Framework for Improving Selling Effectiveness."

22. Thayer C. Taylor, "Anatomy of a Star Salesperson," *Sales and Marketing Management*, May 1986, 49–51.

23. For more discussion, see Anthony Alessandra, James Cathcart, and Phillip Wexler, *Selling by Objectives* (Englewood Cliffs, NJ: Prentice-Hall, 1988), and Lawrence W. Lamont and William J. Lundstrom, "Identifying Successful Industrial Salesmen by Personality and Personal Characteristics," *Journal of Marketing Research*, 14 (November 1977), 517–529.

24. Ajay K. Kohli and Bernard J. Jaworski, "Market Orientation: The Construct, Research Propositions, and Managerial Implications," *Journal of Marketing*, 54 (April 1990), 1–18; Bernard J. Jaworski and Ajay K. Kohli, "Marketing Orientation: Antecedents and Consequences," *Journal of Marketing*, 57 (July 1993), 53–70.

25. Judy A. Siguaw, Gene Brown, and Robert E. Widing, II, "The Influence of the Market Orientation of the Firm on Sales Force Behavior and Attitudes," *Journal of Marketing Research*, 31 (February 1994), 106–116.

26. Based on Alessandra, Cathcart, and Wexler, *Selling by Objectives;* and Paul Hersey, *Selling: A Behavioral Science Approach* (Englewood Cliffs, NJ: Prentice-Hall, 1988).

27. C. Conrad Elnes, *Inside Secrets of Outstanding Salespeople* (Englewood Cliffs, NJ: Prentice-Hall, 1988), 6.

28. Hersey, *Selling: A Behavioral Science Approach,* xi.

29. Jennifer Lawrence, "P&G Redirects Sales Force," *Advertising Age,* June 28, 1993, 52.

30. Julie Liesse, "Kraft Retires General in Reorganization," *Advertising Age,* January 9, 1995, 4.

31. Frank V. Cespedes, "Industrial Marketing: Managing New Requirements," *Sloan Management Review,* 35 (Spring 1994), 45–60.

32. John P. Steinbrink, "Field Sales Management," in *Marketing Manager's Handbook,* eds. Stuart Henderson Britt and Norman F. Guess (Chicago: Dartnell Corporation, 1983), 984.

33. Charles Futrell, *Sales Management,* 3rd ed. (Chicago: Dryden, 1991), 128–129.

34. Futrell, *Sales Management,* 176–180.

35. Rayna Skolnik, "Campbell Stirs Up Its Salesforce," *Sales and Marketing Management,* April 1986, 56–58.

36. William J. Stanton and Richard H. Buskirk, *Management of the Salesforce* (Homewood, IL: Richard D. Irwin, 1983), 431.

37. Stanton and Buskirk, *Management of the Salesforce,* 186–188.

38. Adapted from Thomas N. Ingram and Raymond W. LaForge, *Sales Management: Analysis and Decision Making,* 2nd ed. (Fort Worth, TX: Dryden, 1991), 543.

39. Bernard J. Jaworski and Ajay K. Kohli, "Supervisory Feedback: Alternative Types and Their Impact on Salespeople's Performance and Satisfaction," *Journal of Marketing Research,* 28 (May 1991), 190–201.

40. For further reading on salesperson job satisfaction, see Steven P. Brown and Robert A. Peterson, "Antecedents and Consequences of Salesperson Job Satisfaction: Meta-Analysis and Assessment of Causal Effects," *Journal of Marketing Research,* 30 (February 1993), 63–77.

◼ Study Questions

1. A salesperson who calls on retail stores and handles inventory control, stocks shelves, or sets up point of purchase displays is
   a. working with orders.

   b. servicing the account.

   c. engaged in missionary selling.

   d. engaged in new business selling.

2. Which of the following is *not* true of personal selling?

   a. It is person-to-person interaction.

   b. It educates customers.

   c. It provides product-usage and marketing assistance.

   d. It usually is a highly structured job.

3. Which one of the following is least true of personal selling?

   a. It enables a relatively high level of customer attention.

   b. It yields more immediate feedback than any other form of marketing communications.

   c. It allows the salesperson to customize the message to the customer's specific interests and needs.

   d. It is more efficient in terms of the ratio of cost to results than any other form of marketing communications.

4. Which item is *not* characteristic of field sales?

   a. job freedom

   b. structured supervision

   c. variety and challenge

   d. advancement opportunity

5. Which of these is *not* a characteristic of modern selling practice?

   a. spirit of trust and mutual agreement

   b. a customer-driven atmosphere

   c. seller-centered marketing

   d. a solution customized to each problem

6. Brad works for Johnson & Johnson. He sells to grocery and drug stores and spends most of his time servicing accounts and providing customers with advertising and sales-promotion assistance. Brad's sales job would be classified as

   a. retail selling.

   b. new business selling.

   c. technical selling.

   d. trade selling.

7. Nearly two-thirds of pharmaceutical sales to retailers are through wholesalers. The wholesaler is the pharmaceutical manufacturer's direct customer. When the manufacturer's sales representative calls on retail pharmacies, he or she is not trying to make a direct sale to the pharmacies but rather to create business for wholesaler customers. This form of selling is called

    a. missionary selling.
    b. retail selling.
    c. new business selling.
    d. technical selling.

8. The sales representatives for pharmaceutical companies are called
    a. preapproach negotiators.
    b. detail reps.
    c. relational communicators.
    d. middlemen.

9. Regarding the various determinants of salesperson performance, which of the following is false?
    a. Salesperson aptitude and skill level are the same thing.
    b. Skill level refers to a salesperson's learned proficiency at performing selling tasks.
    c. Accurate role perceptions are a very important determinant of salesperson performance.
    d. Personal characteristics such as physical size and appearance are important determinants of salesperson performance.

10. The highest priority in modern selling philosophy is
    a. corporate success.
    b. customer satisfaction.
    c. the bottom line.
    d. treating customers the same way you would treat family members.

11. Which of the following is *not* part of modern selling philosophy?
    a. trust between seller and customer
    b integrity
    c. adapting
    d. a customer-driven atmosphere

12. Robert, a smooth-talking salesman of the old-school variety, regularly sells different people the identical insurance policy, regardless of their individual needs. He would rather persuade them to buy the policy he feels comfortable selling rather than spend time to analyze each customer's unique needs. Robert is in violation of which tenet of modern selling philosophy?
    a. He is not a hard worker.
    b. He is uncaring.

c. He prescribes before diagnosing.

d. He doesn't know his product.

13. Which of the following is *not* one of the five basic functions that sales managers must perform?

a. staffing

b. adapting

c. controlling

d. organizing

14. The ideal situation in designing sales territories is to establish

a. sales territories of varying degrees of potential.

b. sales territories of equal potential and equal work load.

c. sales territories of equal potential with levels of work load proportionate to the salesperson's aptitude.

d. sales territories of equal geographic size and work load.

15. Probably the most common form of sales management organization is specialization by

a. geographical territories.

b. product types.

c. customer classes.

d. brand classes.

16. The financial plan that most sales managers use to motivate their sales forces is

a. the straight salary.

b. the commission plan.

c. the combination plan.

d. the monitor plan.

17. The type of sales budgeting that allocates funds in detail to each cost center and requires sales management to forecast and account for each item is

a. program budgeting.

b. itemized budgeting.

c. line-item budgeting.

d. typical budgeting.

18. Sales training of new recruits, continuing education of existing personnel, and motivational and incentive plans for all sales personnel are involved in

a. staffing.

b. controlling.

c. planning.

d. directing.

◆ Answers to Study Questions

Chapter 1
1. c
2. d
3. a
4. c
5. a
6. c
7. a
8. d
9. b
10. a
11. d
12. d

Chapter 2
1. b
2. d
3. c
4. d
5. b
6. d
7. a
8. c
9. b
10. a
11. a
12. b
13. d
14. c
15. a
16. d
17. c
18. d
19. d
20. c
21. c
22. c
23. b
24. d
25. c

Chapter 3
1. c
2. a
3. d
4. c
5. a
6. b
7. d
8. c
9. a
10. d
11. a
12. b
13. d

Chapter 4
1. c
2. a
3. c
4. b
5. a
6. b
7. d
8. a
9. c
10. b
11. d
12. a
13. c
14. b
15. d
16. d
17. c
18. c
19. d
20. c
21. a
22. c
23. a

Chapter 5
1. c.
2. d.
3. a.
4. a.
5. c.
6. b.
7. a.
8. b.
9. c.
10. d.
11. d.
12. c.
13. a.
14. b.
15. a.

Chapter 6
1. d
2. d
3. a
4. c
5. b
6. d
7. c
8. b
9. c
10. c
11. a

Chapter 7
1. c
2. a
3. c
4. a
5. d
6. d
7. c
8. b
9. b

10. b
11. c
12. b
13. b
14. a
15. d

Chapter 8
1. b
2. a
3. d
4. b
5. a
6. c
7. a
8. c
9. d
10. a
11. a
12. c
13. b
14. c
15. d
16. a
17. d
18. c
19. d
20. c
21. c
22. d

Chapter 9
1. a
2. c
3. b
4. d
5. b
6. a
7. c
8. d
9. a
10. d

11. b
12. b
13. a
14. b
15. d
16. a
17. b
18. a
19. b
20. c

Chapter 10
1. a
2. c
3. d
4. b
5. d
6. d
7. b
8. a
9. a
10. c
11. d

Chapter 11
1. b
2. a
3. c
4. d
5. a
6. d
7. c
8. a
9. b
10. c
11. a
12. d
13. a
14. a
15. c
16. b

Chapter 12
1. c
2. b
3. a
4. d
5. b
6. a
7. d
8. c
9. c
10. b
11. b
12. b
13. a
14. d
15. c
16. c
17. c
18. b

Chapter 13
1. c
2. d
3. a
4. d
5. a
6. d
7. c
8. b
9. c
10. a

Chapter 14
1. d
2. a
3. c
4. a
5. b
6. a
7. b
8. a
9. c

10. b
11. d
12. c
13. a
14. d

Chapter 15
1. c
2. b
3. a
4. b
5. c
6. d
7. a
8. c
9. b

10. d
11. a
12. c
13. d
14. a
15. d
16. c
17. b
18. d
19. c
20. d

Chapter 16
1. b
2. d
3. d

4. b
5. c
6. d
7. a
8. b
9. a
10. b
11. c
12. c
13. b
14. b
15. a
16. c
17. c
18. d

A

Acceptance The extent to which a consumer agrees with a marketing message that has been attended and comprehended.

Accessories Products that are less expensive and have a shorter life-span than installations.

Achievers Successful, work-oriented people who mainly get their satisfaction from jobs and family. A politically conservative group who respect authority and the status quo. Achievers favor established products and services that reflect their level of success to their peers.

Actual product Comprised of key benefits under a brand name, package, extra features and some level of quality specific to a market segment.

Actualizers Actualizers have the highest incomes, highest self-esteem, abundant resources. Image is important as they buy the finer things in life.

Adaptive selling The altering of sales behaviors during a customer interaction or across customer interactions based on perceived information about the nature of the selling situation.

Administered vertical marketing system (VMS) Effective channel functioning and cooperation is achieved when a dominant channel member exercises its economic clout.

Advertising Involves either mass communication via newspapers, magazines, radio, television, and other media or direct-to-consumer communication via direct mail.

Advertising strategy Entails four major activities: objective setting, budgeting, message strategy and media strategy.

Affective component Is the feeling or emotional evaluation of a consumption object.

Age-based discounts Offered to special groups, especially children and senior citizens.

Agents Represent manufacturers on a permanent basis.

Allowance Payment to the buyer for providing a service to the seller or for trading in a product.

Approach Entails making contact and establishing a relationship with the customer.

Assessing advertising effectiveness Final critical aspect of advertising management inasmuch as only by evaluating results is it possible to determine whether objectives are being accomplished.

Atmospherics   The design of buying environments to produce specific emotional effects in the buyer that enhance the purchase probability.

Attention   Involves allocating limited processing capacity to a particular stimulus among the array of stimuli impinging on the consumers' senses.

Attitude   Represents a person's positive or negative feeling toward, or evaluative judgment of, a product, brand, or other consumption object.

Associative learning   The second major type of learning, occurs when consumers draw connections between environmental events.

Augmented product   Is the actual product plus post-purchase services such as credit, service, delivery, installation, and extended warranties.

B

Baby boom generation   The more than 75 million Americans born between 1946 and 1964.

Backward integration   Results when a retailer acquires a wholesaler or even a producer.

Bartering   Goods and services, rather than money, are exchanged by both parties.

Believers   Conservative and predictable consumers who favor established brands and American-made products. They have more modest incomes than fulfilleds and their lives are centered around their family, church, community and the nation.

Benefit segmentation   Grouping consumers based on the benefits consumers desire from using a specific product.

Bid pricing   Entails establishing a specific price for each exchange relationship in contrast to setting a basic, or list, price that applies to all exchanges.

Bill-back allowances   Offered as payment to retailers for featuring the manufacturer's brands in advertisements or for providing special display space.

Bonus   A lump-sum payment that the company makes to sales representatives who have exceeded a set sales quota.

Bottom-up budgeting (BU)   Managers of subunits determine how much is needed to achieve their objectives.

Brand   Name, term, sign, symbol, or some combination of these used to identify the individual offerings of one firm and to differentiate it from competitive offerings.

Brand-concept management Strategic planning, implementation, and control of a brand's concept throughout the brand's life.

Brand equity Brand with high level of sales and brand loyalty, due in large part to a high-quality reputation.

Brand extension strategy Simplest way to expand a product line using a successful current brand name on a new product.

Brokers Are in the business of connecting sellers and buyers.

Bundling Practice of marketing two or more products and/or services in a single package for a special price.

Business cycles Recurring fluctuations in the economy that run from prosperity to recessions to eventual recovery.

Business-to-business marketing Refers to the buying and selling and other marketing activities that take place between businesses.

Business-to-business product A product purchased by an organization to be used in producing other products or in operating its business. Also called industrial or non-consumer products.

Business-to-business services Specialized services that support the business operation but are not part of the finished product.

Buyer The employee who actually purchases the product.

Buying center A group of key employees who provide different expertise needed to make major purchases.

Buying function The buying function seeks, evaluates, and pays for a desired good or service.

C

Cash and carry wholesalers Provide products in a warehouse setting for resale.

Cash cows Products that enjoy high market shares but show low levels of market growth.

Cash discounts A discount offered on the price in order to encourage prompt payment from customers.

Catalog marketing Special form of direct mail.

Category killer Type of specialty store that offers a large assortment of products at discount prices within a limited number of product lines.

Cause-related marketing (CRM) Involves an amalgam of public relations, sales promotion, and corporate philanthropy.

Census Process where data is obtained from every member of a particular population.

Channel of distribution The arrangement of businesses that are involved in performing marketing functions and transferring goods and services and their ownership from manufacturers to end-users.

Channel leadership Channel member who uses authority to direct or guide the channel's activities.

Channel power The ability of one channel member to exert influence over and dictate the behavior of other channel members.

Choice criteria Factors used in formulating judgments and making purchase decisions.

Classical conditioning A form of associative learning that results when consumers develop associations rather effortlessly between a conditioned stimulus and a biologically salient unconditioned stimulus.

Clayton Act (1914) Legislation passed in 1914 to strengthen the vaguely written Sherman Antitrust Act. Also intended to make it unlawful for firms to discriminate in price where the effect of such discrimination lessens competition.

Cluster sampling A probability sampling method where researchers randomly choose areas or geographic cluster, first, and then randomly sample within each cluster.

Cognitive component Refers to a person's knowledge, or belief, about a consumption object.

Cognitive orientation View of learning as an active process whereby the consumer forms hypotheses about consumption alternatives, acquires and encodes information, and integrates the new information with pre-existing beliefs.

Commission plan Payment based directly on performance.

Compatibility Degree to which an innovation is consistent with the values, needs, and experiences or potential adopters.

Competitive parity method Spending whatever is necessary to meet competitors' actions.

Complexity Refers to the difficulty of understanding and, therefore, using a new product.

Component parts/materials Already processed products or products that need little processing and are ready for assembly within the finished product.

Comprehension The interpretation, or perception, of what the stimulus means, implies, or represents.

Conative component Refers to how a person is likely to behave or act towards a consumption object.

Concentrated segmentation Concentrating marketing efforts on a smaller segment of a larger market.

Concept testing Involves querying consumers' thoughts and feelings about the proposed product.

Conflict Occurs when channel members disagree on the methods used to perform their channel functions.

Consideration set Purchase alternatives based on an evaluation of the positive and negative characteristics of each brand under consideration.

Consumer An individual buying for his or her personal or family consumption needs.

Consumer product A product purchased by a consumer for his or her household or individual use.

Consumer Product Safety Commission (CPSC) An organization that protects the safety and health interests of consumers in their homes.

Consumerism Ideological movement that seeks to protect and increase the rights of consumers.

Contractual vertical marketing system (VMS) Channel members are interconnected via contractual agreement.

Contribution margin Per unit contribution to the recovery of fixed costs.

Convenience product An inexpensive item that consumers purchase with little effort.

Convenience sampling A nonprobability sampling method where researchers choose respondents based on ease of availability of the respondents.

Conventional marketing channels Arrangement of manufacturers, wholesalers, retailers, and various facilitating agencies such as agents and brokers, where each type of organization is engaged in a narrow line of business and operates autonomously.

Cooperatives Retailer-sponsored cooperatives achieve the same objectives as do wholesaler-sponsored voluntary chains.

Corporate vertical marketing system (VMS) Combines all levels of the marketing channel under one company's ownership.

Countertrade Form of bartering undertaken in international trade.

Cross-functional teams A group of people combining the best features from new-product committees and new-product departments.

Culture Set of values, beliefs, artifacts, and other meaningful symbols that facilitate communication and enable people to function within their environments.

Cumulative quantity discount Discount based on not on individual orders but on the cumulative quantity purchased during a specified period.

Customer-based segmentation Grouping business-to-business customers based on product specifications and the specialized needs of customers.

Customer service Activities that satisfy the needs of an organization's customers.

Customers Business and other organizational buyers.

D

Database marketing Involves collecting and electronically storing information about past, present, and prospective customers.

Decider The member of a household or business who decides which product to buy.

Decision-making process Stages that describe the mental processes and activities that are involved from the time the consumer encounters a need to make a product purchase on to the purchase act and beyond.

Decline Stage in which profitability continues to deteriorate and sales are beginning to plummet.

Decoding Process by which receivers interpret, or derive, meaning from the message.

Demand Quantity of a product that will be sold during a period of time at different prices.

Demand curve Graphed demand schedule.

Demand schedule Mapping of specific quantities onto specific prices.

Demographic segmentation Grouping consumers based on demographic characteristics (such as as age, income, or gender).

Demographic variables Measurable characteristics of populations.

Depth Includes the number of individual products within each line.

Differentiated segmentation Targeting multiple segments and developing specific marketing mixes for each segment.

Diffusion process Process by which new ideas, including new products, spread throughout a social system or marketplace.

Direct mail Any advertising matter sent through the mail directly to the person whom the marketer wishes to influence.

Direct selling Involves the personal explanation and demonstration of products and services to consumers in their homes or at their jobs.

Discount Percentage reduction from the seller's list price.

Discount stores Stores that offer brand-name merchandise at low prices and self-service.

Discrepancy of assortment The difference between the number of products a manufacturer produces versus the assortment the consumer needs or wishes to buy.

Discrepancy of quantity The difference between the quantity of products a manufacturer produces versus the quantity of products the consumers needs and wishes to buy.

Discretionary income Income that remains after consumer has purchased basic necessities such as food, clothing, and housing.

Disposable income After-tax income.

Distribution The marketing activity that makes products available to marketing intermediaries and to final consumers. Involves channel management and physical distribution.

Distribution strategy Getting the right product or service to the right placewhere the consumer wants it.

Distributors Independent businesses who purchase products from producers, maintain physical inventories of products, employ salespeople to contact business customers, and typically finance their customers' purchases (also called industrial wholesalers).

Diverting Occurs when a manufacturer restricts a deal to a limited geographical area rather than making it available nationally.

Dogs Products with low market shares and low market growth rates.

Drop shippers Wholesalers that sell products, take orders, and arrange for delivery of products directly to customers, also called desk jobbers.

Dumping Form of import price discrimination that occurs when a U.S. firm sells goods in a foreign market for less than their fair value or when a foreign firm prices products to be sold in the United States substantially below what they are sold in that firm's domestic market.

E

Early adopters Second group to adopt a new product. Represent 13.5% of all potential adopters.

Early majority Represent 34% of potential adopters who spend more time deciding whether or not to try the new product or idea.

Economic accessibility The segment must be reachable from a distribution and promotional standpoint.

Economic order quantity   Basic tool for controlling inventory levels.

Elastic   Elasticity coefficient in excess of 1, indicating market responsiveness to price changes.

Electronic data interchange (EDI)   Computer systems that are linked electronically between retailers and their suppliers.

Encodes   Puts the thought into symbolic form.

End-use application segmentation   Grouping business-to-business customers based on how the purchasers will use the product.

Environment   All forces outside marketing management's direct control that influence marketing programs and their potential success.

Environmental management   When a firm attempts to influence the external environment in which it operates through the implementation of strategies.

Environmental scanning   Collection and analysis of pertinent information about the company's marketing environment collected through marketing research, trade publications, and government data.

Evaluative criteria   Factors used in formulating judgments and making purchase decisions.

Event marketing   Form of brand promotion that ties a brand to a meaningful cultural, social, athletic, or other type of high-interest public activity.

Everyday low pricing (EDLP)   Form of pricing whereby a manufacturer charges the same price for a particular brand day in and day out.

Exchange   The process by which two or more parties give something of value to each other to satisfy each party's perceived needs.

Exchange functions   Involve the performance of the buying and selling functions.

Exclusive distribution   Is practiced when a manufacturer restricts product distribution to a single retailer in a particular market or just a relatively few retailers.

Experiencers   Exhibit high energy levels, which they devote to physical exercise and social activities. The youngest of the segments, experiencers are adventurous and spend heavily on clothing, fast food, music, and other youthful activities.

Experiential needs   Needs involving the desire for products that provide sensory pleasure, stimulation, and variety.

Experimental research   Method of gathering primary data where the researcher manipulates one or more marketing-mix variables in an experimental group and then compares the results against a control group that was not exposed to the experimental manipulation.

Exploratory research   Collection of data to gain a greater understanding of the research question.

Exposure   Occurs when relevant marketplace information reaches one or more of the consumers' five senses.

External data   Information that has been generated from outside the company, for example, reports generated by the government, trade associations, and advertising agencies.

External reference prices   Those prices that are found in contexts such as advertisements that state typical prices or are available on price tags at the point of purchase.

F

Facilitating functions   Involve the financing, risk-taking, information, and standardizing/grading functions.

Family   A group of two or more individuals related by blood or marriage who live in the same household.

Family branding   Use of the same name for several related products.

Federal Trade Commission (FTC)   Government organization that has the most power to influence and control marketing activities.

Federal Trade Commission Act   Legislation passed in 1914 to regulate untoward business practices. Also intended to strengthen the Sherman Act; empowers the FTC to deal with antitrust matters and investigate deceptive and unfair marketing practices.

Feedback   Measure of how well the message is received.

Financing function   Involves the extension of credit to aid the exchange process.

Fixed costs   Costs that are fixed in total and invariant to the number of units sold.

Flexible-price strategy   Strategy that varies the discounts and allowances on a transactional basis.

FOB origin pricing   Practice of charging the cost of transportation to customers.

Forecast Estimate of the amount that will be sold during a specific period at a particular price.

Form utility Involves the transformation of raw materials and/or labor into a finished good and/or service that the consumer desires.

Forward buying Purchasing enough of the product on one deal to carry over until the next regularly scheduled deal.

Forward integration Occurs when a company that traditionally has been only a producer of products decides also to become a retailer.

Franchising Contractual agreement between a supplier and a retail franchisee who buys the rights to sell products under an established name while following a specific set of guidelines. Form of contractual VMS.

Freight absorption pricing Seller pays for transportation costs.

Fulfilleds Mature, responsible, well-educated professionals who are well-informed about worldly affairs. They have high incomes but are practical, value oriented consumers.

Full-service wholesalers Perform a wide range of channel activities including order processing, extending credit, storing, delivering, and providing promotional support.

Functional discounts Compensate the trade for functions performed.

Functional middlemen Intermediaries who do not take title to products; they simply facilitate the exchange process by performing buying and/or selling functions.

Functional needs Needs involving the customer's current consumption related problems or potential problems related to the product category.

G

Gatekeepers Control the flow of the information regarding a purchase within the organization.

General merchandise wholesaler Intermediaries that carry a wide range of different product lines but with little depth to each line.

Geodemographic data Data identifying groups of consumers who reside in specific geographical areas and who have similar lifestyles and demographic characteristics.

Geographic segmentation Grouping consumers based on geography or location.

Government market Consists of one federal, 50 state, and 86,692 local governments.

Green marketing Use of recyclable or bio-degradable packing materials as part of marketing strategy.

Growth Stage in which the product begins to gain consumer acceptance.

H

Hierarchy-of-effects Common framework to illustrate the idea that marketing communications progress the consumer from an initial stage of brand awareness, to interest in the brand, to desire, and, finally, to action.

Home improvement centers Warehouse operations that feature all products used in building and maintaining homes.

Homogeneous response Customers in the segment must exhibit similarity in their response to end preference for the marketing mix that is designed for them.

Hypermarkets Mass merchandisers and food stores combined.

I

Identify and measure An organization must be able to identify and measure the segmentation variable, or variables, on which segmentation is to be accomplished.

Industrial distributors Intermediaries that stock inventory for resale to manufacturers.

Inelastic Elasticity coefficient less than 1, indicating market responsiveness to price changes.

Individual branding Use of a distinct brand name for each product within a company's product line.

Inflation Rise in price levels.

Influencers Affect the buying decision by providing advice and information for the various alternatives.

Information processing The process by which a person receives, interprets, stores in memory, and later retrieves stored information.

Innovators Represent 2.5% of all potential adopters. They tend to be younger, higher in social status, and better educated than later adopter groups.

Installations   Major capital goods that are depreciated for accounting purposes over several years, rather than being treated as expense items in the current fiscal period.

Integrated marketing communications   Coordination of advertising, publicity, sales promotion, point-of-purchase communications, sponsorship marketing, and personal selling with each other and with other elements of a brand's marketing mix.

Intensive distribution   Used when a product is sold through virtually every available retail outlet in a particular market.

Interactive displays   Computerized units that allow consumers to ask and have answered questions pertaining to their product-category needs.

Internal data   Information that comes from within the company itself, typically in the form of company reports.

Internal reference prices   Stored in consumer's memory and based on past experience and knowledge about prices in a particular product category.

Internet   Information superhighway, cyberspace, or worldwide web.

Introduction   Stage in which a company pioneers a new product and introduces it to distribution intermediaries, and if it is a consumer good, to consumers.

Involvement   A specific form of motivation that represents how important, or personally relevant, a product is to the consumer in a given situation.

J

Job description   Includes job title, the specific duties and responsibilities of the sales representative, the authoritative relationships with other immediate members of the organization, and the opportunities for advancement.

Job qualifications   Document that describes the personal features, characteristics, and abilities that management believes a salesperson needs in order to perform the job effectively and efficiently.

Judgment sampling   A nonprobability sampling method where researchers choose respondents based on judgment.

Just-in-time (JIT)   Japanese innovation that attempts to deliver only what is needed by the customer and when the customer needs it.

Just-in-time inventory (JIT) management Procedure whose fundamental objective is to minimize inventory carrying costs.

K

Knowledge Represents the information consumers have stored in their memories regarding products, prices, brands, and retail outlets.

L

Laggards Last group to adopt a new product or idea.

Late majority Represent 34% of potential adopters who are less responsive to change than the other groups.

Limited line wholesalers Intermediaries that carry a narrow range of product lines but with a great assortment of products within each line.

Limited-service merchant wholesalers Class of merchant wholesalers that take title to goods they stock and resell but offer a narrower range of support services.

Line-item budgeting Management allocates funds in meticulous detail to each identifiable cost center.

Logistic functions Involve the performance of the transportation and storing functions.

Loss leaders Products offered at prices below or near the cost the retailer has paid for them.

M

Mail-order wholesalers Those who sell from catalogs rather than via a sales force to their customers, who are usually located in outlying areas.

Makers Practical, self-sufficient consumers who focus on family, work and physical recreation. Makers have little interest in the broader world and are only interested in those material possessions that have a practical or functional purpose.

Manufacturer branded products Sold in a variety of retail outlets under the name of a manufacturer.

Manufacturer's agents   Agent that performs a selling function for the producers they represent. They represent two or more manufacturers with noncompeting product lines.

Marginal cost   Change in total cost associated with selling an additional item.

Marginal revenue   Change in total revenue associated with selling one additional unit.

Market   A group of customers who have the need or desire, the ability, and the authority to purchase a specific product.

Market development   Strategy that involves finding new markets and new users for existing products.

Market orientation   The organization-wide generation of market intelligence pertaining to current and future customer needs, dissemination of the intelligence across departments, and organization-wide responsiveness to it.

Market penetration   Strategy that is used to increase sales and market share with existing products in their existing markets.

Market segmentation strategy   The process of dividing a large market into smaller markets, or customer groups, with similar needs or desires.

Market share   Represents a particular brand's revenue as a proportion of the total revenue generated in the product category.

Marketing communications   Represent the collection of all elements in an organization's marketing mix that facilitate exchanges by establishing shared meaning with an organization's customers or clients.

Marketing concept   An organization focuses all of its efforts on making products or providing services that satisfy its customers at a profit.

Marketing database   Is composed of combining both internal data and external data.

Marketing decision support system (MDSS)   Provides the mechanisms that make it possible for a manager to obtain answers to key questions.

Marketing era   The marketing era characterizes modern marketing in the United States as well as in other advanced economies. Firms must emphasize customer fulfillment and customer satisfaction.

Marketing information system (MIS)   Deals specifically with the information needs of marketing managers.

Marketing intermediaries   The business institutions that facilitate the exchange process between the original creators of products and the end-users of these goods and services.

Marketing mix A specific combination of four sets of variables: products, distribution elements, prices, and marketing communications or promotions designed to appeal to and satisfy the needs of market segments.

Marketing myopia Defining the organizations purpose too narrowly.

Marketing plan The detailed scheme of the marketing strategies and activities associated with each product's marketing mix.

Marketing planning The game plan for a particular product or product line; the detailed scheme of the marketing strategies and activities associated with each product's marketing mix.

Marketing public relations (MPR) Marketing-oriented aspect of public relations.

Marketing strategy Involves the plans, budgets, and controls needed to direct a firm's product, promotion, distribution, and pricing activities.

Marketing strategy formulation Marketing strategy entails (1) identifying target markets and (2) developing marketing mixes directed at fulfilling the needs of specific market segments.

Marketing research Marketing research is the function that links the consumer, customer, and public to the marketer through information.

Markup on cost (Selling price - Cost)/Cost.

Markup on selling price (Selling price - Cost)/Selling price.

Mass market strategy Process of selling one product to all consumers within the entire market.

Maturity Stage in which sales volume continues to increase but eventually levels off.

Membership clubs Discount retailers that are open for shopping only to members, who pay membership fees typically in the range of $25-$35 per year.

Merchant middlemen Intermediaries who take title to products and resell them.

Merchant wholesaler Intermediary who purchases products from manufacturers and assumes all risks associated with ownership.

Message Symbolic expression of the sender's thoughts.

Message channel Path through which the message moves from the source to the receiver.

Micromarketing Localizing marketing efforts to accommodate the unique needs of specific geographic regions.

Monopolistic competition Most common type of competitive market structure in the United States and other advanced economies. A large number of sellers produce and sell similar products that are differentiated by minor characteristics.

Monopoly   Type of competitive market structure where only one firm is producing and selling a product to an entire market.

Motivation   The driving force that pushes a consumer to buy a product in an effort to satisfy his or her needs.

Multiple basing-point pricing   System where the basing point switches depending on which shipping point charges the lower freight rates.

N

National Advertising Review Board (NARB)   Created by the Council of Better Business Bureaus and three advertising trade organizations, the NARB monitors truth in advertising cases.

National brands   Same as manufacturer's branded products.

Nationalism   Ideological movement where a country's interests become the top priority.

Negotiated pricing   Occurs when the subset of selected bidders are requested to revise their opening bids.

Noise   Any interference or distraction that interferes with the preparation, transmission, or reception of a marketing message.

Nonbusiness institutions   Organizations that provide services without the motivation of profit.

Noncumulative quantity discount   Discount based on individual orders.

Nonstore retailing   Selling products and services outside of conventional retail outlets.

North American Free Trade Agreement (NAFTA)   An agreement passed in 1993, which creates a free flow of products among Canada, Mexico, and the United States.

O

Objective and task method   Promotional budgeting where objectives are specified, promotional elements needed to reach those objectives are identified, and the budget is determined by accumulating anticipated costs among the various promotional elements.

Observability   Degree to which the results of using a product are observable to others.

Odd pricing   Refers to a price that ends in an odd number or just under a round number.

Off-invoice allowances   Most widely used form of trade-oriented sales promotion; periodic deals that allow the trade (wholesalers and retailers) to deduct a fixed amount from the full price.

Oligopoly   Type of competitive market structure where a few firms control the majority of the industry's sales.

Order processing   The system through which orders are received and processed.

Organizational citizenship behavior   Discretionary behaviors on the part of a salesperson that directly promote the effective functioning of an organization, without necessarily influencing a salesperson's objective sales productivity.

Ownership separations   Exist when producers own products that consumers want to hold title to.

Ownership utility Involves the transfer of title for goods and services from the producer to the consumer.

P

Penetration price   Involves the use of relatively low prices as the means for rapidly penetrating the mass market.

Percentage of sales method   Setting promotional budgets as a percentage of past or anticipated sales.

Perceptual separations   Exist when consumers lack information about producers offerings and producers lack information about consumers.

Personal selling   Person-to-person communication in which a seller informs and educates prospective customers and attempts to persuade them to purchase the company's products or services.

Personality   Those unique characteristics of each individual that predisposes him or her to act in a fairly consistent manner in different types of situations.

Physical distribution The aspect of marketing responsible for the movement and storage of products as they flow through the channel of distribution. Involves all activities responsible for the movement of products and their storage along with related activities such as order processing and customer servicing.

Place utility   Involves making goods and services available where consumers want and need them.

Planning   Process of establishing a broad set of goals, policies, and procedures for achieving sales and marketing objectives.

Point-of-purchase communications   Includes all sign displays, posters, signs, shelf cards, and a variety of other visual materialsthat are designed to influence buying decisions at the point of sale.

Population   The total group that the researcher wants to study. Also called the sampling frame.

Post-purchase dissonance   May occur during post-purchase evaluation, where the consumer finds himself satisfied or dissatisfied to some degree with the purchase of the product.

Predatory pricing   When a firm sets a price in the short-term that is below its cost only later to raise its price to a very high level and earn exorbitant profits for the purpose of putting competitors out of business.

Prestige pricing   Higher prices are used to signal higher quality.

Price   The amount that the buyer and seller agree on to exchange a product or service for money or another product/service. Involves setting price objectives and policies, as well as, price determination.

Price discrimination   When businesses charge different prices to different customers.

Price elasticity   A measure of customer responsiveness to price changes.

Price fixing   Occurs when managers from two or more companies collude in some fashion to artificially maintain or set prices or at least make an attempt to do so.

Price lining   Practice of producing or merchandising multiple products at different price points.

Price strategy   Setting the right price to facilitate the exchange between the consumer and the producer.

Primary data   Information collected by or for an organization to address that organization's specific research question or needs.

Private brands   Brand manufactured exclusively for individual retailers and wholesalers.

Proactive MPR   Dictated by a company's marketing objectives. Offensively oriented and opportunity seeking.

Problem children   Products that enjoy rapid growth but low market shares and poor profit margins.

Producers   Refer to organizations that purchase goods and services used in the production of other products for the purpose of making a profit.

Product   A bundle of attributes that is received when entering into an exchange and which has the ability to meet the need or needs that occasioned the exchange. Includes identifying consumer wants and needs, developing new products, designing and re-designing products, branding, and packaging.

Product development   Strategy that introduces new products into established markets.

Product diversification   Strategy that focuses on developing new products for new markets.

Product life cycle   Conceptual framework that characterizes the typical process products go through from inception until they are withdrawn from the market.

Product line   A group of related items in a company's product portfolio.

Product mix   All of the products a company markets.

Product strategy   Developing the right product for the target market.

Production era   The production era coincided with the Industrial Revolution in the United States, a period extending roughly from 1870 to 1930. During the production era businesses emphasized manufacturing efficiency; relatively little consideration was given to consumers and their needs.

Program budgeting   Avoids many of the problems of line-item budgeting. Provides each administrative unit with a lump sum of money that each administrative head can use as he or she sees fit to accomplish the stated objectives.

Promotion   Activities used to motivate customers to action. Involves advertising, personal selling, sales promotion, point of purchase, sponsorships, and public relations.

Promotion management   Practice of coordinating the various promotional mix elements.

Promotion strategy   Involves communication from the producer to the consumer.

Promotions mix   Variety of tools used in promotion: personal selling, mass-media and direct-to-consumer advertising, publicity, sales promotions, point-of-purchase communications and sponsorship marketing.

Prospecting   Process of identifying the best potential customers.

Providing information function   Involves the exchange of information between consumers and producers.

Psychographic segmentation   Grouping consumers based on activities, interests, and opinions (AIO).

Psychographics   The study of lifestyles, as embodied in a person's activities, interests, and opinions.

Public relations (PR)   Aspect of promotion management uniquely suited to fostering goodwill between a company and its various publics.

Publicity   Nonpersonal communication to a mass audience but it is not directly paid for by the company that enjoys the publicity. Major tool of proactive MPR.

Pull   Involves encouraging consumer demand for the product to obtain distribution.

Push   Involves utilizing aggressive trade allowances and personal selling efforts to obtain distribution for a product through wholesalers and retailers.

Pure competition   Type of competitive market structure where many firms are selling the same basic product. No one competitor has the power to affect supply or price. All buyers and sellers have full knowledge of the market, and competitors can freely enter or exit the market.

Q

Quantity discounts   Percent discounts from the list price for purchases in excess of specified quantities.

Quota sampling   A type of nonprobability sampling where researchers match characteristics in the population against quotas.

R

Rack jobbers   Intermediaries that supply products and the display units on which the products are displayed.

Raw materials   Unprocessed products that become part of a company's finished products.

Reactive MPR   Undertaken as a result of external pressures and challenges brought by competitive actions, changes in consumer attitudes, changes in government policy, or other external influences.

Rebates   Provided when, after purchasing a product, consumers are invited to submit a proof-of-purchase indicator to the manufacturer, who remits payment at a later date.

Receiver   Person or group of persons for whom the message is intended.

Reciprocity   The practice of purchasing products from a company's own customers.

Reference group   A group of people, or even an individual, who either directly or indirectly represents a group.

Reference price   Any price to which other prices are related.

Regional marketing   Localizing marketing efforts to accommodate the unique needs of specific geographic regions.

Relative advantage   The degree to which an innovation is perceived by customers as being superior to existing ideas or products.

Research design   The master plan for the study in which the procedures for gathering and analyzing data are detailed.

Resellers   Intermediaries such as wholesalers, industrial distributors, brokers/agents, and retailers who buy finished products to resell for profit.

Retail selling price   Retailer's selling price to consumers.

Retailing   Encompasses those activities involved in the exchange process of goods and services to the final consumer.

Retention   Represents the transfer of marketplace information into long-term memory.

Risk-taking function   Involves the risks associated with holding title to goods and services (such as spoilage or changes in demand).

Robinson-Patman Act   Legislation passed in 1936 to prohibit the practice of price discrimination, whereby sellers offer different prices or price-related deals to different customers. Also intended to prevent incipient growth of big chain stores.

S

Sales branch   Sells products and provides support services for the manufacturer's sales force.

Sales era   During the sales era firms focused on selling existing products. Their philosophy was to sell what the firm produced, which was not exactly what the consumer needed.

Sales office   Operates like an independent agent; performs most of the same functions as the sales branch except that it does not carry inventory.

Sales management   Involves acquiring, directing, and stimulating competent salespeople to perform tasks that move the organization toward accomplishment of its objectives and mission.

Sales presentation   Step in the personal selling process where the salesperson relays information about the product and its benefits to the buyer.

Sales promotion Consists of all marketing activities that attempt to stimulate quick buyer action or to promote immediate sales of a product. Use of any incentive by a manufacturer to induce the trade and/or consumer to buy a brand and to encourage the sales force to aggressively sell it.

Sales-volume quotas Quotas are based on geographical areas, product lines, individual customers, time periods, or a combination of these factors.

Sample A portion of a population.

Schemas Associative networks or knowledge structures in which memory organizes knowledge.

Scrambled merchandising Occurs when a retail establishment veers away from its original marketing strategy and adds product lines that are unrelated to the retailer's original product offering.

Seasonal discount Pricing mechanism that permits manufacturers of seasonal merchandise to maintain steady production and seasonal service providers to sustain operations during out-of-season lulls.

Secondary data Previously published data collected by a company itself or by other organizations that conduct ongoing or occasional studies.

Selective distribution An intermediate degree of distribution intensity; selectively distributed brands are available in multiple retail outlets in a particular market but not, in virtually every store that could carry the brand.

Selling agents Agents that are independent businesses who do not take title to the products they represent or handle inventory. They represent all of the products manufactured by their principal.

Selling function The selling function involves the promotion of products through personal selling, by telephone, via computer, interactive network and by other means.

Sherman Antitrust Act Legislation passed in 1890 to prevent businesses from restraining trade and monopolizing markets. Prohibits any contract, combination, or conspiracy in interstate commerce that retains trade or attempts to monopolize a specific market or industry.

Shopping products Products that consumers are willing to spend time shopping for and to compare alternative brands.

Similar purchase needs A meaningful market segment where people are accessible via promotional and distribution vehicles.

Simple random sampling Used when researchers randomly select respondents from a complete list, or enumeration, of all members of the designated population.

Single basing point Modified form of FOB origin pricing.

Single-source systems Concerned with measuring whether advertising leads to increased sales activity.

Situational influence Results from those factors that are specific to the time and place circumstances of a particular buying choice.

Skimming price Strategic option for innovative products that couple relatively high prices with heavy promotional expenditures.

Slotting allowance Stocking allowance or street money; applies to new products. The fee a manufacturer is charged by a supermarket chain or other retailer to get that retailer to handle the manufacturer's new product.

Social class A group of individuals who share similar economic status and who, accordingly, exhibit some similarity in their consumer behavior.

Societal marketing concept Adopted when firms factor environmental, health, and safety considerations into their decision making.

Source Person or group of persons who has thoughts to share with some other person or group of persons.

Spatial separations Exist when consumers and producers are separated by space and geography.

Specialty line wholesalers Intermediaries that specialize in only one or two product lines.

Sponsorship marketing Practice of promoting the interests of a company and its brands by associating the company with a specific event.

Standardizing/grading function Involves the sorting of goods by size and quality.

Stars Products with high market growth rates and high market shares.

Stocking allowances Paid to retailers to induce their carrying new products offered by the manufacturer.

Storing The physical distribution function of holding products.

Storing function The storing function is the holding of goods and services until the customer needs them.

Straight salary plan Provides sales representatives with a fixed amount of income regardless of sales productivity.

Stratified random sampling Two-stage probability sampling method where researchers divide the complete list of the population into groups according to a common trait and then apply simple random sampling techniques on each group.

Strategic alliances Agreements between organizations who work together toward a common goal.

Strategic business units (SBUs) An division or unit used to facilitate organizational operations. An SBU can be one specific product, one product line, or a particular business.

Strategic planning The most important level of planning that typically encompasses the firm's long-range goals and dictates direction for all departments in the firm.

Strategy implementation Deals with tactical, day-to-day activities that must be performed to carry out an advertising campaign.

Strivers Similar to achievers but with fewer economic, social, and psychological resources. Style is more important to them as they strive to emulate the people they wish they could be.

Strugglers Strugglers have the lowest incomes and too few resources to be included in any consumer self-orientation. They tend to be brand-loyal consumers within their limited means.

Substantiability The segment must be large enough to generate a level of sales that will cover costs and, in the long run provide a profit.

Supplies Products that are used in support of the business operations but are not part of the finished product

Survey Any research that asks questions to understand brand awareness, product knowledge, attitudes, purchase motivations, buying intentions, and so forth.

Symbolic needs Need involving psychological needs such as the desire for self-enhancement, role position, or group membership.

T

Tactical planning Involves specifying details that pertain to the organization's activities for a certain time period.

Target market Group identified as potential users of the product.

Target-return pricing Designed to provide the producer with a predetermined return on the capital that is invested in the production and marketing of products.

Temporal separations Exist when consumers and producers want to consume and produce at different times.

Test marketing   Testing a new product's entire marketing strategy prior to introducing the product to the full market.

Time utility   Involves making goods and services available when consumers want and need them.

Top-down budgeting (TD)   Senior management decides how much each subunit receives.

Total product concept   Includes everything that adds value to a seller's offering the product itself, its package and brand name, service, warranty, etc.

Total quality management (TQM)   Commitment by all departments to the strategic goal of achieving quality.

Total revenue (TR)   The product of price times quantity (P x Q).

Transporting   The physical movement of products from an organization to its customers.

Transporting function   The movement of goods and services from the seller to the buyer.

Trade allowances   Trade deals come in a variety of forms and are offered to retailers simply for purchasing the manufacturer's brand or for performing activities in support of the manufacturer's brand.

Trade-in allowances   Offered to encourage consumers to upgrade to newer and more expensive products.

Trialability   Degree to which an innovation can be used on a limited basis.

Truck jobbers   Small wholesalers that sell directly from their trucks or vans to retailers for cash.

U

Undifferentiated marketing   Marketing that does not segment.

Uniform delivered pricing   Seller charges all customers the same transportation cost regardless of where they are located.

Unitary elastic   Elasticity coefficient equal to 1, indicating market responsiveness to price changes.

Usage segmentation   Grouping consumers based on how often or how much consumers use a product.

Users   Members of the organization who will actually use the product or service.

Unsought product   Product that is unknown to the buyer or a known product that is not actively sought.

V

Value separations Exist when producers value products and services based on costs and competitive prices and when consumers value products and services based on how much they have to pay for them.

Variable costs Cost items that vary in total depending on the number of units sold but are constant per unit.

Vertical marketing system (VMS) Marketing channel whereby channel members unify their efforts and cooperate in order to best serve their own needs as well as those of their direct customers and ultimate consumers.

Video merchandising center (VMC) Sophisticated version of interactive unit that displays and sells entire product lines through audio and video presentations.

VIEW Model for evaluating packaging effectiveness: Visibility, Information, Emotional appeal, Workability.

Voluntary chain An assemblage of independent retailers brought together by a wholesaler to compete against major corporate-owned chains.

W

Warehouse and catalog showrooms Combine wholesale and retail functions as warehouse retailers.

Wheel of retailing hypothesis Describes how retail institutions change during their evolutionary life cycles.

Wheeler-Lea Act Legislation passed in 1938 to strengthen the Federal Trade Commission Act.

Wholesale selling price Manufacturer's selling price to retailers.

Wholesalers Business organizations that perform wholesaling functions among the channel intermediaries.

Wholesaling The exchange of goods and services between producers and channel intermediaries, but not the actual consumer.

Width The number of different product lines a company offers.

Z

Zone pricing Seller divides the geographic market into multiple zones and then charges the same delivered price in each zone.

Index